Sustainable Justice

Reconciling Economic, Social and Environmental Law

SUSTAINABLE JUSTICE

Reconciling Economic, Social and Environmental Law

by

MARIE-CLAIRE CORDONIER SEGGER & C.G. WEERAMANTRY

Editors

with a Preface by

HAROLD KOH

MARTINUS NIJHOFF PUBLISHERS
LEIDEN / BOSTON

A C.I.P. Catalogue record for this book is available from the Library of Congress.

Printed on acid-free paper.

ISBN 90 04 14182 0
© Copyright 2005 by Koninklijke Brill NV, Leiden, The Netherlands

Koninklijke Brill NV incorporates the imprints Brill Academic Publishers, Martinus Nijhoff
Publishers and VSP.

http://www.brill.nl

Printed and bound in The Netherlands.

FOREWORD

Harold. H. Koh[1]

Perhaps the most intriguing development, in today's process of globalization, has been the emergence and growth of a large body of transnational law that is fundamentally public in its character.[2] This volume provides an essential collection of scholarly and judicial insights into one of the most fascinating areas of this emerging transnational law: sustainable development.

Domestic and international legal processes will soon become so integrated that we will no longer know whether to characterize certain concepts as local or global in nature. Is the metric system of standards fundamentally national or international? Is the use of the Internet fundamentally national or international? And is the objective of sustainable development fundamentally national or international? None of these questions are really worth asking any more. In each case, the answer is so obviously 'both.' All have become, over time, genuinely transnational concepts, in which a global concept has become fully recognized, integrated, and internalized into the domestic system of nearly every nation of the world. Transnational public law is neither fully international, nor is it based only on one domestic law or another. It is both. Many domestic actors face similar dilemmas, and seek international guidance, while many international jurists and law-makers seek examples from national jurisprudence and regulations. International rules are shaped by national actors, international courts influence and guide national judicial decisions.

At the areas of overlap between human rights, economic and environmental, at the essence of public law, this reinforcing transnational influence is profound and immediate. The present volume makes a valuable contribution to the analysis and development of a transnational public law, a law that I believe is real and extremely necessary. The principles and legal instruments which can reconcile environment, developmental and economic law must be developed and strengthened through a web of regulations and treaties, jurisprudence and tribunal decisions, between the national, the regional and the global level. No solution stands alone. Each level references the other.

In sustainable development law, transnational legal process is the primary mechanism for the creation and internalization of norms crucial to the survival of our species, and to the urgent, pressing needs of the majority of our worlds' populations. The key will be successful internalization of the norms of

---

[1] Harold Hongju Koh, A.B. (Harvard), B.A. (Oxon, Marshall Scholar), J.D., (Harvard), M.A. (Oxon), Dean, Yale Law School, Gerard C. and Bernice Latrobe Smith Professor of International Law, Yale Law School.
[2] H. H. Koh, "The Globalization of Freedom" (2001) 26 *Yale J. Int'l L.* 305 at 306.

sustainable development law. By what process does this norm-internalization occur? How do we transform occasional or grudging compliance with global norms into habitual obedience? As I have suggested elsewhere,[3] such a process can be viewed as having several phases.

International norms and transnational process can permeate and influence domestic policy. As transnational actors interact, they create patterns of behaviour that ripen into institutions, regimes, and transnational networks. The interactions between these systems generate both general norms of external conduct (such as treaties) and specific interpretation of those norms in particular circumstances, which they in turn internalize into their domestic legal and political structures (executive action, legislation, and judicial decisions). Legal ideologies prevail among domestic decision makers and cause them to be affected by perceptions that their actions are, or will be seen as, unlawful. Domestic decision making becomes 'enmeshed' with international legal norms, as the institutional arrangements for the making and maintenance of an international commitment become entrenched in domestic legal and political processes. Domestic institutions adopt symbolic structures, standard operating procedures, and other internal mechanisms to maintain habitual compliance with the internalized norms. These institutions become 'carriers of history', and evolve in path-dependent routes that avoid conflict with the internalized norms. These institutional habits lead nations into default patterns of compliance. Thus, in Henkin's words, "almost all nations observe almost all principles of international law. . . almost all of the time."[4]

When a nation deviates from that pattern of presumptive compliance, frictions are created. To avoid such frictions in a nation's continuing interactions, national leaders may shift over time from a policy of violation to one of compliance. It is through this transnational legal process, this repeated cycle of interaction, interpretation, and internalization, that international law acquires its 'stickiness', that nation-states acquire their identity, and that nations come to 'obey' international law, out of perceived self-interest. In tracing the move from the external to the internal, from one-time grudging compliance with an external norm to habitual internalized obedience, the key factor is repeated participation in the transnational legal process. That participation helps to reconstitute national interests, to establish the identity of actors as ones who obey the law, and to develop the norms that become part of the fabric of emerging international society.

As I have described it, transnational legal process presents both a theoretical explanation of why nations obey and a plan of strategic action for prodding nations to obey. How, then, to study this process? I have, in several places,

---

[3] H. H. Koh, "Why do Nations obey International Law?" (1997) 106 *Yale L.J.* 2599 at 2646.
[4] See Herbert C. Kelman, "Compliance, Identification, and Internalization: Three Processes of Attitude Change" (1958) 2 *J. Conflict Resol.* 51, 52-53

suggested certain basic inquiries that are needed. I will offer one example, from the area of sustainable development. In both environmental law and human rights, treaty regimes are notoriously weak, and national governments, for reasons of economics or realpolitik, are often hesitant to declare openly that another government engages in abuses. In such an area, where enforcement mechanisms are weak, but core customary norms are clearly defined and often peremptory (*jus cogens*), the best compliance strategies may not be 'horizontal' regime management strategies, but rather, vertical strategies of interaction, interpretation, and internalization.

If transnational actors obey international sustainable development law as a result of repeated interaction with other actors in the transnational legal process, a first step is to empower more actors to participate. It is here that expanding the role of intergovernmental organizations, nongovernmental organizations, private business entities, and 'transnational moral entrepreneurs' deserves careful study. How, for example, do international sustainable development 'issue networks' and epistemic communities form among international and regional intergovernmental organizations, international and domestic NGOs on human rights, and private foundations? How do these networks intersect with the international human rights, environmental or economic 'regimes', namely, the global system of rules and implementation procedures centered in and around the United Nations; regional regimes in Europe, the Americas, Africa, Asia, and the Middle East; single-issue regimes regarding workers' rights, racial discrimination, women's rights, the climate, biodiversity, health, intellectual property rights; and 'global prohibition regimes' against slavery, torture, nuclear waste and the like? Within national governments and intergovernmental organizations, what role do lawyers and legal advisers play in ensuring that the government's policies conform to international legal standards and in prompting governmental agencies to take proactive stances toward abuses?

Second, if the goal of interaction is to produce interpretation of sustainable development norms, what fora are available for norm-enunciation and elaboration, both within and without existing social, environmental or economic development regimes? If dedicated fora do not already exist, how can existing fora be adapted for this purpose or new fora be created? In other words, how can sustainable development best be governed?

Third, what are the best strategies for internalization of sustainable development norms? One might distinguish among social, political, and legal internalization. Social internalization occurs when a norm acquires so much public legitimacy that there is widespread general obedience to it. Political internalization occurs when political elites accept an international norm, and adopt it as a matter of government policy. Legal internalization occurs when an international norm is incorporated into the domestic legal system through executive action, judicial interpretation, legislative action, or some combination of the three. Judicial internalization can occur when domestic litigation provokes judicial incorporation of human rights norms either implicitly, by construing existing statutes consistently with international sustainable development norms, or explicitly, through 'transnational public law litigation.' Legislative internalization occurs when domestic lobbying embeds international law norms into binding domestic legislation or even constitutional law that officials of a noncomplying government must then obey as part of the domestic legal fabric. The relationship among this social, political, and legal internalization can be complex, and deserves study.

Such issues, within the context of transnational legal process, have important implications, not just for international law and international relations theorists, but also for activists and political leaders. For activists, the constructive role of international law in the post-Cold War era will be greatly enhanced if nongovernmental organizations seek self-consciously to participate in, influence, and ultimately enforce transnational legal process by promoting the internalization of international norms into domestic law. Nor can political leaders sensibly make foreign policy in a world bounded by global rules without understanding how legislative, judicial and executive branches can and should incorporate international legal rules into their decision making.

These pressing questions, concepts and issues need to be further researched and debated, by the present and future generations of legal scholars, lawmakers, jurists, activists and policy makers. International cooperation needs to be more than just strategic. There needs to be an internalisation of certain norms and not just lip service. In the area of sustainable development, governments should not be requested politely to protect their peoples from human rights abuses, economic depression or environmental degradation. Rather, an integrated approach must be investigated and activated, at the local, the national and the international levels, simultaneously, to address these problems as each manifests.[5]

The present volume contributes deeply and genuinely to this urgently needed research and debate. It recounts and analyses legal experiences of the process of internalization and activation of the norms of the concept of sustainable development. Drawing on the experience, knowledge and wisdom of renowned judges, the heads of multilateral treaty secretariats, international law professors and scholars, from diverse backgrounds and countries, this volume proposes a constructive, optimistic, future-oriented study of the transnational legal process of sustainable development. It is an essential new addition to the library of any student, professor or practitioner of globalization and sustainable development, and it is with great pleasure that I commend it to you.

---

[5] H. H. Koh, "Jefferson Memorial Lecture - Transnational Legal Process after September 11th" (2004) 22 *Berkeley J. Int'l L.* 337 at 350.

SUSTAINABLE JUSTICE:
RECONCILING ECONOMIC, SOCIAL AND ENVIRONMENTAL LAW

TABLE OF CONTENTS

Part IV: Future Directions for Sustainable Development Law

EDITORS

Marie-Claire Cordonier Segger, MEM (Yale), BCL & LLB (McGill), BA Hons (Carl.) Director, Centre for International Sustainable Development Law (CISDL), Chair, CISDL/ILA/IDLO Partnership on International Law on Sustainable Development, Senior Manager, Americas Research Portfolio, International Institute for Sustainable Development & United Nations Environment Programme ROLAC, British Chevening Scholar & SSHRC Fellow, Exeter College, Oxford University Faculty of Law, Lecturer, International Development Law Organisation (IDLO) & Member, International Law Association (ILA) Committee on International Law on Sustainable Development.

H.E. Mr. Justice Christopher Gregory Weeramantry, BA Hons, LL.B, LL.D (London), LL.D h.c. (Colombo, Monash, N.L.S. India), D.Litt h.c. (London), Founder & Chairman of Board of the Weeramantry International Centre for Peace Education and Research, former Judge and Vice-President of the International Court of Justice, Justice, Supreme Court of Sri Lanka, former Professor of Law, Australia, Chairman of a Commission of Inquiry on phosphate mining in Nauru.

CONTRIBUTORS

Dr. Sumudu Atapattu, LL.M, PhD (Cantab), Adjunct Faculty & Visiting Scholar, University of Wisconsin-Madison Law School, Lead Counsel for Human Rights and Poverty Eradication, Centre for International Sustainable Development Law (CISDL), Consultant, Law & Society Trust, (Colombo, Sri Lanka) & former Senior Lecturer, Faculty of Law, University of Colombo, Sri Lanka.

Hon. Mr. Justice U.C. Banerjee, former Judge, Supreme Court of India, Founder President of NALSAR University of Law, Head of the Indian High-Level Committee to probe into the Godhra incident.

Dr. Solomon R Benatar, MBChB, FFA (SA), FRCP, FRSSAfr., Professor of Medicine, Director Bioethics Centre, University of Cape Town.

Jorge Cabrera Medaglia, B.C.L & LL.M (University of Costa Rica), Lead Counsel for International Sustainable Biodiversity Law, Centre for International Sustainable Development Law (CISDL), Professor, University of Costa Rica Faculty of Law & UNED University, Tutor, WIPO Intellectual Property Law, Legal Advisor, National Biodiversity Institute (INBio) of Costa Rica, former Co-chair, UN Convention on Biological Diversity Expert Panel on ABS & Chair, CBD Sub-Working Group on IPRs.

Hama Arba Diallo, B.A. (Poli Sci), Executive Secretary, United Nations Convention to Combat Desertification and Drought, Particularly in Africa, former Special Representative of the Secretary General of the United Nations Conference on Environment and Development (UNCED), former Minister of Foreign Affairs & Ambassador of Bukina Faso, former Deputy Director of the United Nations Sudano-Sahelian Office (UNSO).

Xabier Ezeizabarrena, M.Sc. (University of Basque Country), Lawyer, Member of the Bar of San Sebastian (Spain) and Staff Lawyer of the International Court of Environmental Arbitration and Conciliation (ICEAC), Assistant Professor, University of the Basque Country Faculty of Law (Administrative and Environmental Law), Member, International Bar Association, Visiting Fellow 2003/04, European Studies Centre, St. Antony´s College, Oxford, Councillor of San Sebastian City Council.

Mary Footer, BA (Hons.), LL.M. (University of London, UCL), Member, International Trade Law Committee of the ILA, Deputy-Director of the Amsterdam Center for International Law, Associate Professor of Law, Universiteit van Amsterdam.

Dr. Duncan French, B.A. (East Anglia), LL.M (Nottingham), Ph.D (Wales, Cardiff), Lecturer in Law, University of Sheffield, United Kingdom, Senior Research Fellow, Centre for International Sustainable Development Law (CISDL), Co-Rapporteur of the International Law Association Committee on International Law on Sustainable Development.

Kathryn Garforth, LL.B. (Osgoode Hall), M.E.S (York), Research Fellow, Centre for International Sustainable Development Law (CISDL).

Markus W. Gehring, LLM (Yale), BCL (Hamburg) i.p., Lead Counsel for Trade, Investment and Competition Law, Centre for International Sustainable Development Law (CISDL), Researcher, Concerted Action on Trade and Environment (funded by the European Commission), Tutor of Public International Law, University College, Oxford Law Faculty.

Hon. Mr. Justice Charles D. Gonthier, B.CL., LL.D. (McGill), Chair, Board of Governors of the Centre for International Sustainable Development Law, Wainwright Senior Research Fellow, McGill Faculty of Law, Of Counsel, McCarthy Tétrault LLP, former Justice, Supreme Court of Canada.

Chris Huggins, M.A.(Strathclyde) M.A. (Glasgow), Research Fellow, African Centre for Technology Studies (ACTS).

Michael Kerr, B.A (Monash), LL.B. (Hons.)(Bond), Legal Research Fellow for Sustainable Corporate Law, Centre for International Sustainable Development Law (CISDL) & Consultant, International Trade and Corporate Social Responsibility.

Ashfaq Khalfan, B.A (Hons.), B.C.L., LL.B. (McGill), Director, Centre for International Sustainable Development Law (CISDL), Programme Director, Water Rights, Center on Housing Rights and Evictions (COHRE).

Harold Hongju Koh, A.B. (Harvard), B.A. (Oxon, Marshall Scholar), J.D., (Harvard), M.A. (Oxon), Dean, Yale Law School, Gerard C. and Bernice Latrobe Smith Professor of International Law, Yale Law School.

Karin Krchnak, A.B. (Duke University), J.D. (University of Maryland School of Law), Director of The Access Initiative (TAI) and the Partnership for Principle 10 (PP10), World Resources Institute (WRI).

Dr. Bronwen Morgan, B.A.Hons., LL.B.Hons. (Sydney), Ph.D. (U.Cal., Berkeley), Harold Woods Research Fellow in Law, Wadham College & Centre for Socio-Legal Studies, University of Oxford, UK.

Hon. Mr. Justice N. J. McNally, former Appellate Judge of the Supreme Court, Zimbabwe, and member of a joint mission to Malaysia for the International Bar Association (IBA), the Centre for the Independence of Judges and Lawyers of the International Commission of Jurists (CIJL), the Commonwealth Lawyers' Association (CLA) and the Union Internationale des Avocats (UIA).

Dr. Emmanuel Owoku Apuku, M.A. Law (Voronezh University, Russia), Ph.D. LLM (University of London, SOAS), MCIArb. (Chartered Institute of Arbitrators, UK), Member, International Trade Law Committee, ILA, Senior Programme Officer, Commonwealth Secretariat, Legal and Constitutional affairs Division.

Romina Picolotti, BCL (Córdoba), LL.M (American University), is President and Founder of the Center for Human Rights and Environment.

Dr. Maya Prabhu, A.B. (Harvard), M.Sc. (LSE), M.D. (Dalhousie), LL.B. (McGill), Lead Counsel for International Sustainable Health Law, Centre for International Sustainable Development Law (CISDL).

Hon. Mr. Justice Albie Sachs, B.A., LL.B. (Cape Town), Ph.D. (Sussex), Justice, Constitutional Court of South Africa, Professor Extraordinary, University of the Western Cape, Honorary Professor, University of Cape Town Law Faculty, Member, Constitutional Committee & National Executive, ANC. Formerly, Director of Research, South African Ministry of Justice, Director, South Africa Constitution Studies Centre (University of London),Professor of Law, Eduardo Mondlane University (Maputo, Mozambique), Nuffield Fellow of Socio-Legal Studies, Bedford College, London & Wolfson College, Cambridge, author of numerous books and articles, including *Soft Vengeance of a Freedom Fighter* (San Francisco: U. Cal. Press, 2000).

Prof. Nico Schrijver, Ph.D. (Groningen), Professor Public International Law, Free University of Amsterdam, Chair of the International Law Association (ILA) Committee on Int'l Law on Sustainable Development, former Rapporteur, the ILA Committee on Legal Aspects of Sustainable Development, Chairperson, Academic Council on the United Nations.

George Michael Sikoyo, MSc. (Ecological Economics), BSc. Forestry (Hons), Dip. (Education), Research Fellow, African Centre for Technology Studies (ACTS).

Matthew Stilwell, B.Ec, LL.B (Hons) (University of Tasmania), LLM (Columbia University), Director, Institute for Governance and Sustainable Development's European Office, Legal Counsel, UN Environment Programme's Economics and Trade Branch. Mr. Stilwell is Bren Scholar, Donald Bren School of Environmental Science and Management, University of California, Santa Barbara, Senior Economic Law Advisor, Secretariat of Basel Convention on Transboundary Movement of Hazardous Wastes and Their Disposal, and a Special Fellow, UN Institute for Training and Research

Jorge Daniel Taillant, B.A. (U. Cal., Berkeley), M.A. (Georgetown), Executive Director of the Center for Human Rights and Environment (CEDHA), Argentina.

Ko-Yung Tung, A.B. Physics magna cum laude, J.D., (Harvard), Fellow, University of Tokyo Faculty of Law, Of counsel, O'Melveny & Myers LLP, former Vice President and General Counsel, The World Bank and Secretary-General, International Centre for the Settlement of Investment Disputes.

Xueman Wang, LL.M. (Wu Han, China), M.A. (Fletcher School, Tufts), Lead Counsel for Climate Change and Vulnerability Law, Centre for International Sustainable Development Law (CISDL), Legal Officer, Secretariat for the Convention on Biological Diversity, former Legal Officer, Climate Change Secretariat.

Jeremy Wates, M.Phil. Hons. (Cantab), Secretary to the Aarhus Convention, United Nations Economic Commission for Europe.

RESEARCHERS

Jessica Adley, B.A. (Concordia), BCL/LLB expected 2007 (McGill), Researcher, Centre for International Sustainable Development Law (CISDL), former conference administrator for Canadian Asbestos: A Global Concern, Sierra Club of Canada. She is indebted to David Adley for his unwavering support, as well as Dr. Peter Stoett, Marc Stamos, Elizabeth May and 1 Nicholas St. for their invaluable insight and commitment to environmental sustainability

Sarita Keirouz, B.Sc. (American University of Beirut), BCL/LLB/MBA expected 2008 (McGill), Researcher, Centre for International Sustainable Development Law (CISDL), formerly with UN-Economic and Social Commission for Western Asia, Beirut Ministry of the Environment, & British Council, Beirut.

Chris Pettit, BA 2 (New College, Florida), JD cum laude (Florida), LLM expected 2005 (Cape Town) Fellow, University of Florida Institute of Human Rights, Peace and Development, Research Associate and Project Coordinator, Weeramantry International Center for Peace Education and Research.

Sidney Thompson, B.A. Specialist International Development (University of Toronto), B.C.L./LL.B expected 2005 (McGill, Montreal), Publications Officer, Centre for International Sustainable Development Law (CISDL).

TABLE OF TREATIES

1982	*Protocol Concerning Regional Co-operation in Combating Pollution by Oil and Other Harmful Substances in Cases of Emergency,* 14 February 1982, UNEP Sales No: GE.83-lX-02934.
1982	*Convention for the Conservation of Salmon in the North Atlantic,* 2 March 1982, 1338 U.N.T.S. 33, T.I.A.S. No. 10789.
1982	*United Nations Convention on the Law of the Sea,* 10 December 1982, 1833 U.N.T.S. 3, 21 I.L.M. 1245 (entered into force 16 November 1994) [*UNCLOS*].
1983	*Convention for the Protection and Development of the Marine Environment in the Wider Caribbean Region (Cartagena Convention),* 24 March 1983, 22 I.L.M. 221 (entered into force 11 October 1986).
1983	*International Tropical Timber Agreement,* 18 November 1983, U.N. Doc. TD/TIMBER/11.
1984	*1.a. Protocol to the 1979 Convention on Long-range Transboundary Air Pollution on Long-term Financing of the Co-operative Programme for Monitoring and Evaluation of the Long-range Transmission of Air Pollutants in Europe (EMEP),* 28 September 1984, 1491 U.N.T.S. 167, UN Doc. EB.AIR/AC.1/4, Annex, and EB.AIR/ CRP.1/Add.4 (entered into force 28 January 1988).
1984	*Convention against Torture and Other Cruel, Inhuman or Degrading Treatment or Punishment,* 10 December 1984, 1465 U.N.T.S. 85 (entered into force 26 June 1987).
1985	*Vienna Convention for the Protection of the Ozone Layer,* 22 March 1985, 1513 U.N.T.S. 293, 26 I.L.M. 1529 (entered into force 22 September 1988).
1985	*Convention for the Protection, Management and Development of the Marine and Coastal Environment of the Eastern African Region,* 21 June 1985, 985 I.E.L.M.T 46.
1985	*1.b. Protocol to the 1979 Convention on Long-Range Transboundary Air Pollution on the Reduction of Sulphur Emissions or their Transboundary Fluxes by at least 30 per cent,* 8 July 1985, 1480 U.N.T.S. 215 (entered into force 2 September 1987).
1985	*Association of South East Asian Nations (ASEAN) Agreement on the Conservation of Nature and Natural Resources,* 9 July 1985, 15 Envtl Pol'y. & L. 64, 68 (1985) (not yet in force).
1985	*Cartagena de Indias Convention,* 5 December 1985, 25 I.L.M. 529 (1986).
1986	*Single European Act,* 17 February 1986, 25 I.L.M. 503 (entered into force 1 July 1987).

1991   *Treaty of Asunción,* 26 March 1991, 30 I.L.M. 1041 (entered into force 1 January 1995).

1991   *Protocol to the Antarctic Treaty on Environmental Protection (with Schedule on Arbitration and four Annexes - Environmental Impact Assessment, Conservation of Antarctic Fauna and Flora, Waste Disposal and Waste Management, and Prevention of Marine Pollution),* 24 April 1991, 30 I.L.M. 1455

1991   *Convention on Biological Diversity,* 5 June 1991, 31 I.L.M. 818 (entered into force 29 December 1993).

1991   *Arctic Environmental Protection Strategy,* 14 June 1991, 30 I.L.M. 1624.

1991   *Agreement between the Government of the United States of America and the European Communities Regarding the Application of Their Competition Laws,* 23 September 1991, 4 *Trade Ref. Rep* (CCH) 13,504.

1991   *1.d. Protocol to the 1979 Convention on Long-Range Transboundary Air Pollution concerning the Control of Emissions of Volatile Organic Compounds or their Transboundary Fluxes,* 18 November 1991, 2001 U.N.T.S. 187, 31 I.L.M. 568 (entered into force 29 September 1997).

1992   *Treaty on European Union (Maastricht Treaty),* 7 February 1992, 1992 O.J. (C 191) 1, 31 I.L.M. 253.

1992   *Convention on the Protection and Use of Transboundary Watercourses and International Laws,* 17 March 1992, UN Doc. ENVWA/R.53 and Add.1, 31 I.L.M. 1312 (entered into force 6 October 1996).

1992   *Agreement on the Conservation of Small Cetaceans of the Baltic & North Seas,* 17 March 1992, 1772 U.N.T.S. 217 (entered into force 29 March 1994) *[ASCOBANS].*

1992   *Convention on the Protection of the Marine Environment of the Baltic Sea Area,* 9 April 1992 (entered into force 17 January 2000).

1992   *United Nations Framework Convention on Climate Change,* 9 May 1992, 1771 U.N.T.S. 107, 31 I.L.M. 849 (entered into force 21 March 1994) *[UNFCCC].*

1992   *United Nations Convention on Biological Diversity,* 5 June 1992, 1760 U.N.T.S. 79, 31 I.L.M. 822 (entered into force 29 December 1993).

1992   *Convention for the Protection of the Marine Environment of the North-East Atlantic,* 22 September 1992, reprinted in (1993) 32 I.L.M. 1069 (entered into force March 25, 1998).

1992   *North American Free Trade Agreement,* 17 December 1992, Can. T.S. 1994 No. 2, 32 I.L.M. 289 (entered into force 1 January 1994) *[NAFTA].*

1992	*Terms of Reference for a Multilateral Fund, Annex IV,* U.N. Doc. UNEP/OzL.Pro.4/15, (1992) YB Int'l L. 824.
1993	*North America Agreement on Environmental Cooperation,* 14 September 1993, 32 I.L.M. 1480 (entered into force 1 January 1994).
1994	*International Tropical Timber Agreement,* 10 January 1994, U.N. Conference on Trade and Development, UN. Doc. TD/TIMBER.2/Misc.7/GE.94-50830 (1994).
1994	*Marrakesh Agreement Establishing the World Trade Organization,* 15 April 1994, 1867 U.N.T.S. 154, (entered into force 1 January 1995).
1994	*Agreement on Trade-Related Aspects of Intellectual Property Rights, Including Trade in Counterfeit Goods,* 15 April 1994, 33 I.L.M. 1125.
1994	*Agreement on Trade-Related Investment Measures,* 15 April 1994, being part of Annex 1A to the *Agreement Establishing the World Trade Organization,* 15 April 1994, 33 I.L.M. 1144.
1994	*Dispute Settlement Understanding, being Annex 2 to the Agreement Establishing The World Trade Organisation,* 15 April 1994, 33 I.L.M. 1125 (entered into force 1 January 1995).
1994	*General Agreement on Tariffs and Trade, being part of Annex IA to the Agreement Establishing the World Trade Organisation,* 15 April 1994, 33 I.L.M. 1144.
1994	*General Agreement on Trade in Services* (GATS), 15 April 1994, 33 I.L.M. 44.
1994	*Convention to Combat Desertification in Those Countries Experiencing Serious Drought and/or Desertification, particularly in Africa,* 17 June 1994, 33 I.L.M. 1328.
1994	*1.e. Protocol to the 1979 Convention on Long-Range Transboundary Air Pollution on Further Reduction of Sulphur Emissions,* 14 June 1994, Doc. EB.AIR/R.84; 33 I.L.M. 1542 (entered into force 5 August 1998).
1994	*United Nations Convention to Combat Desertification in those Countries Experiencing Serious Drought and/or Desertification, Particularly in Africa,* 14 October 1994, 1954 U.N.T.S. 3, (entered into force 26 December 1996) [UNCCD].
1995	*Treaty on Good Neighbourly Relations and Friendly Cooperation between the Republic of Hungary and the Slovak Republic,* 19 March 1995.
1995	*Maseru Protocol on Shared Watercourses in the SADC Region, under the auspices of the South African Development Community (SADC),* 16 May 1995, available online: <http://www.sadcreview.com/>.

1998 *Convention on Access to Information, Public Participation in Decision-Making and Access to Justice in Environmental Matters,* 25 June 1998, 2161 U.N.T.S. 447 (entered into force 30 October 2001).

1998 *Rotterdam Convention on the Prior Informed Consent Procedure for Certain Hazardous Chemicals and Pesticides in International Trade,* 10 September 1998, UN Doc. UNEP/FAO/PIC/CONF/5, (entered into force 24 February 2004).

1999 *International Labour Organisation Convention No. 182 Concerning the Prohibition and Immediate Action for the Elimination of the Worst Forms of Child Labour,* 17 June 1999, 38 I.L.M. 1207 (entered into force 10 November 2000).

1999 *1.h. Protocol to the 1979 Convention on Long-range Transboundary Air Pollution to Abate Acidification, Eutrophication and Ground-level Ozone,* 30 November 1999, UN Doc. EB.AIR/1999/1 (not yet in force).

1999 *Basel Protocol on Liability and Compensation for Damage resulting from Transboundary Movements of Hazardous Wastes and their Disposal,* 10 December 1999, UN Doc. UNEP/CHW/5/29.

2000 *Cartagena Protocol on Biosafety to the Convention on Biological Diversity,* 29 January 2000, 39 I.L.M. 1027, available online: <http://www.biodiv.org> (entered into force 11 September 2003).

2000 *Partnership Agreement between the Members of the African, Caribbean and Pacific Group of States, of the one part, and the European Community and its Member States ("Cotonou Agreement"),* 23 June 2000, 317 O.J.L.3.

2000 *Constitutive Act of the African Union, arts. 3(d) and 3(j),* 11 July 2000, OAU Doc. LOME- TOGO, (entered into force 26 May 2001).

2001 *Convention on the Conservation and Management of Fishery Resources in the South-East Atlantic Ocean,* 20 April 2001, 41 I.L.M. 257.

2001 *Free Trade Agreement between Canada and Costa Rica,* 23 April 2001, published in La Gaceta of Costa Rica, No. 127 (3 July 2002) (entered into force 1 November 2002).

2001 *Environmental Cooperation Agreement between the Government of Canada and the Government of the Republic of Costa Rica (Canada-Costa Rica) (Canada-Costa Rica Agreement on Environmental Cooperation),* 23 April 2001, published in La Gaceta of Costa Rica, No. 127 (3 July 2002) (entered into force 1 November 2002).

2001 *Stockholm Convention on Persistent Organic Pollutants,* 22 May 2001, 40 I.L.M. 531 (entered into force 17 May 2004).

2001   *Acuerdo Marco sobre Medio Ambiente del Mercosur,* 22 June 2001, reprinted in Ley Nacional 25.841 Argentinean Official Bulletin (15 January 2004) (Mercosur Framework Agreement on the Environment).

2002   *Monterrey Consensus on Financing for Development,* 22 March 2002, U.N. Doc. A/AC.257/32.

2002   *Council Regulation (EC) No 1/2003 of 16 December 2002 on the implementation of the rules on competition laid down in Articles 81 and 82 of the Treaty,* available online: <http://europa.eu.int/cgi-bin/eur-lex/udl.pl?REQUEST=Seek-Deliver&COLLECTION=oj&SERVICE=eurlex&LANGUAGE=en&DOCID=2003l001p00010025&ext=.pdf>.

2003   *Framework Convention on Tobacco Control (FCTC),* 21 May 2003, WHO Doc. A56/INF.DOC/7, available online at <http://www.who.int> .

2003   *Free Trade Area of the Americas Draft Agreement, chapter on Competition Policy,* document FTAA.TNC/w/133/Rev.2, available online: FTAA http://www.ftaa-alca.org/.

2004   *Council Regulation (EC) No 139/2004 of 20 January 2004 on the control of concentrations between undertakings (the EC Merger Regulation),* available online: < http://europa.eu.int/cgi-bin/eur-lex/udl.pl?REQUEST=Seek Deliver&COLLECTION=oj&SERVICE=eurlex&LANGUAGE=en&DOCID=2004l024p00010022&ext=.pdf>.

TABLE OF CASES

PERMANENT COURT OF INTERNATIONAL JUSTICE

S.S. Lotus (France v. *Turkey)*, (1924) P.C.I.J. (Ser. A) No. 10.

ICJ CASES

Corfu Channel Case (UK v. *Albania)*, [1949] I.C.J. Rep. 4 at 22.

Anglo-Iranian Oil Co. Case (United Kingdom / Iran), [1952] I.C.J. Rep. 93.

Case Concerning the Barcelona Traction, Light and Power Company Limited (New Application: 1962) (Belgium v. Spain), Second Phase, [1970] I.C. J. Rep. 3.

Case Concerning Nuclear Tests (New Zealand and Australia / France), [1974] I.C.J. Rep. 457.

Case Concerning Military and Paramilitary Activities in and Against Nicaragua (Nicaragua / U.S.A.), [June 27, 1986] I.C.J. Rep. 14 (Judgment on Merits)

Case Concerning Elettronica Sicula S.p.A. (ELSI) (United States / Italy), [1989] I.C.J. Rep. 15

Case Concerning Certain Phosphate Lands in Nauru (Nauru / Austl.), [June 26, 1992] I.C.J. 240 (Preliminary Objections)

Case Concerning Maritime Delimitation in the Area between Greenland and Jan Mayen (Denmark / Norway), [1993] I.C.J. Rep. 38

Legality of the Threat or Use of Nuclear Weapons, [July 8 1996] I.C.J. Rep. 226 (Advisory Opinion)

Case Concerning Kasikili / Sedudu Island (Botswana / Namibia), [December 13 1999] I.C.J. Rep. 14.

Legal Consequences of the Construction of a Wall in the Occupied Palestinian Territory, [July 9 2004] I.C.J. List 131 (Advisory Opinion)

WTO CASES

United States – Standards for Reformulated and Conventional Gasoline (1996) WTO Doc. WT/DS2/AB/R, AB-1996-1 (Appellate Body Report).

European Communities - Measures Concerning Meat and Meat Products (Hormones) (1998) WTO Doc. WT/DS26/AB/R, WT/DS48/AB/R (Appellate Body Report), WT/DS26/R/USA, WT/DS48/R/CAN (Panel Report).

Australia-Salmon Australia – Measures Affecting Importation of Salmon (1998) WTO Doc. WT/DS18/AB/R, AB-1998-5 (Appellate Body Report).

Japan – Measures Affecting Agricultural Products (1999) WTO Doc. WT/DS76/AB/R, AB-1998-8, (Appellate Body Report).

United States - Import Prohibition of Certain Shrimp and Shrimp Products (1999), WTO Doc. WT/DS58/AB/R (Appellate Body Report), WT/DS58/R (Panel Report).

European Communities – Measures Affecting Asbestos and Asbestos-Containing Products (2001), WTO Doc. WT/DS135/AB/R (Appellate Body Report), WT/DS135/R (Panel Report).

United States - Import Prohibition of Certain Shrimp and Shrimp Products: Recourse to Article 21.5 of the DSU by Malaysia (2001), WTO Doc. WT/DS58/AB/RW (Appellate Body Report), WT/DS58/RW (Panel Report).

Japan - Measures Affecting the Importation of Apples (2003), WTO Doc. WT/DS245/AB/R (Appellate Body Report), WT/DS245/R (Panel Report).

CANADIAN CASES

114957 Canada Ltée (Spraytech, société d'arrosage) v. *Hudson (Town)*, [2001] 2 S.C.R. 241 (Supreme Court of Canada).

U.S. CASES

Cape May County Chapter, Inc., Isaak Walton League of America v. *Macchia*, 329 F. Supp. 504 (D.N.J. 1971).

Sierra Club v. *Morton*, 405 U.S. 727, 92 S.Ct. 1361 (1972).

United States v. *18.2 Acres of Land*, 442 F. Supp. 800, 806 (E.D. Cal. 1977).

Crosby v. National Foreign Trade Council, 120 S. Ct. 2288 (2000).

Aguinda v. *Texaco, Inc.*, 142 F. Supp. 2d 534 (S.D.N.Y. 2001).

ASIAN CASES

Zia v. WAPDA, P L D 1994 Supreme Court 693 (Pakistan Supreme Court).

Bulankulama v. The Secretary, Ministry of Industrial Development (2000) Vol. 7, No. 2 South Asian Environmental Law Reporter 1 (Sri Lankan Supreme Court).

COURT OF JUSTICE OF THE EUROPEAN COMMUNITIES

Plaumann v. Commission, C-25/62, [1963] E.C.R. I-95.

Spijker v. Commission, C-231/82, [1983] E.C.R. I-2559.

Procureur de la Republique v. Association de Defense des Bruleurs d'Huiles Usagees, C-240/83, [1985] E.C.R. I-531.

Deutsche Lebensmittelwerke v. Commission, C-97/85, [1987] E.C.R. 2265.

Commission v. Denmark, C-131/88, [1988] E.C.R. 4607.

Commission v. Germany, C-361/88, [1991] E.C.R. I-825 and I-2567.

Matra v. Commission, C-225/92, [1993] E.C.R. I-3203.

Cook v. Commission, C-198/91, [1993] E.C.R. I-2487.

Air France v. *Commission,* T-2/93, [1994] E.C.R. II-323.

Consorzio Gruppo di Azione Locale "Murgia Messapica" v. Commission, T-465/93, [1994] E.C.R. II-361.

United Kingdom v. Commission, C-180/96, [1996] E.C.R. I-3903.

Greenpeace Int'l v. Commission, C-321/95 P, [1998] E.C.R. I-1651.

R. v. *Secretariat of State for the Environment, Transport and the Regions, ex parte First Corporate Shipping Ltd.,* C-371/98, [2000] ECR I-9235.

Preussen Elektra AG v. Schleswag AG, C-379/98, [2002] E.C.R. I-2099.

ITLOS CASES

Southern Bluefin Tuna (New Zealand and Australia v. Japan) Provisional Measures (1999), Case 3 and 4, (International Tribunal of the Law of the Sea), online: ITLOS <http://www.itlos.org/start2_en.html>.

Case concerning the Conservation and Sustainable Exploitation of Swordfish Stocks in the South-Eastern Pacific Ocean (Chile/European Community) (2001), Case 7 – Order 2001/1, (International Tribunal of the Law of the Sea), online: ITLOS <http://www.itlos.org/start2_en.html>.

The MOX Plant Case (Ireland v. *United Kingdom) Provisional Measures* (2001), Case 10 (International Tribunal of the Law of the Sea), online: ITLOS <http://www.itlos.org/start2_en.html>.

Case concerning the Conservation and Sustainable Exploitation of Swordfish Stocks in the South-Eastern Pacific Ocean (Chile/European Community) (2003), Case 7 – Order 2003/2, (International Tribunal of the Law of the Sea), online: ITLOS <http://www.itlos.org/start2_en.html>.

Case concerning Land Reclamation by Singapore in and around the Straits of Johor (Malaysia v. *Singapore), Provisional Measures* (2003), Case 12 – Order of 8 October 2003, (International Tribunal of the Law of the Sea), online: <http://www.itlos.org/start2_en.html>.

INTERNATIONAL ARBITRATION CASES

Pacific Fur Seal Arbitration, (1893) 1 R.I.A.A. 755.

Trail Smelter Arbitration (United States v. *Canada),* (1938) 3 R.I.A.A. 1911, reprinted in (1939) 33 A.J.I.L. 182, (1941) 3 R. Int'l Arb. Awards 1938, reprinted in (1941) 35 A.J.I.L. 684.

Island of Palmas Case, (1928) 2 R.I.A.A. 829.

Lac Lanoux Arbitration (Spain v. *France),* [1957] 12 R.I.A.A. 281, 23 I.L.R. 101.

BP v. *Libya* (1974) 53 I.L.R. 297.

Texaco Overseas Petroleum Co. & California Asiatic Oil Co. v. *Libya,* (1977) 53 I.L.R. 389.

LIAMCO Award, (1981) 20 I.L.M. 1.

Kuwait v. *American Independent Oil Co.,* (1982) 21 I.L.M. 976.

Minors Oposa v. *Secretary of the Department of Environment and Natural Resources (DENR),* (1994) 33 I.L.M. 173.

TABLE OF DECLARATIONS

United Nations Declaration of Principles on International Law Concerning Friendly Relations and Cooperation Among States in Accordance with the Charter of the United Nations, 24 October 1970, 9 I.L.M. 1292.

United Nations Declaration of Principles on International Law Concerning Friendly Relations and Cooperation Among States in Accordance with the Charter of the United Nations, GA Res. 2625, UN GAOR, 25th Sess., Supp. No. 28, UN Doc. A/8028 (1970).

Stockholm Declaration on the Human Environment, 16 June 1972, U.N. Doc. A/CONF.48/14, 11 I.L.M. 1461 (1972).

Development and Environment, GA Res. 2849(XXVI), UN GAOR, 26th Sess., UN Doc. A/RES/2849 (1972).

Permanent Sovereignty over Natural Resources, GA Res. 3171(XXVIII), UN GAOR, 28th Sess., Supp. No. 30, UN Doc. A/9400 (1973) 52.

Declaration on the Protection of Women and Children in Emergency and Armed Conflict, GA Res. 3318 (XXIX), UN GAOR, 29th Sess., Supp. No. 31, UN Doc. A/9631 (1974) 146.

Raw Materials and Development, GA Res. 3201, UN GAOR, 6th Spec. Sess., Supp. No. 1, UN Doc. A/9559 (1974) 3.

Charter of Economic Rights and Duties of States, GA Res. 3281(XXIX), UN GAOR, 29th Sess., Supp. No. 31, UN Doc. A/9631 (1975) 50; 14 I.L.M. 251 (1975).

United Nations Environment Programme, *Draft Principles of Conduct in the Field of the Environment for Guidance of States in the Conservation and Harmonious Utilization of Natural Resources Shared by Two or More States*, UN Doc. UNEP/1G12/12 (1978); 17 I.L.M. 1097, 1099 (1978).

World Charter for Nature, GA Res. 37/7, UN GAOR, 37th Sess., Supp. No. 51, UN Doc. A/37/7 (1983); 23 I.L.M. 455.

International Undertaking on Plant Genetic Resources, 23 November 1983, 22 FAO Conf. Res. 8183, available online: Food and Agriculture Organization <www.fao.org/ag/cgrfa/IU.htm#documents>.

Declaration on the Right to Development, GA Res. 41/128, UN GAOR, 1986 Supp. No. 53, U.N. Doc. A/41/53, 186 (1986).

Protection of Global Climate for Present and Future Generations of Mankind, GA Res. 43/53, UN GAOR, 43rd Session, Agenda Item 148, UN Doc. A/RES/43/53 (1989); 28 I.L.M. 1326.

Protection of Global Climate for Present and Future Generations of Mankind, GA Res. 44/207, UN GAOR, 2d Comm., 44th Sess., Agenda Item 85, UN Doc. A/Res/44/207 (1989).

Bergen Declaration on Sustainable Development in the ECE Region, 16 May 1990, UN Doc. A/CONF. 151/PC/10), reprinted at 1 Yb. I.E.L.. 424 (1990).

Protection of Global Climate for Present and Future Generations of Mankind GA Res. 45/212, UN GAOR, 2d Comm., 45th Sess., Supp. No. 49A, UN Doc. A/45/49 (1991) 147.

Agenda 21, Report of the UNCED, I (1992) UN Doc. A/CONF.151/26/Rev.1, (1992) 31 I.L.M. 874.

Rio Declaration on Environment and Development, Report of the United Nations Conference on Environment and Development, U.N. Doc. A/CONF.151/6/Rev.1 (1992), 31 I.L.M. 874 (1992).

On the Question of Antarctica, GA Res. 46/41, UN GAOR, 46th Sess., Supp. No. 49, UN Doc. A/46/49 (1992).

Vienna Declaration and Programme of Action, adopted at the World Conference on Human Rights, 12 July 1993, UN Doc. A/CONF.157/23.

Declaration on the Rights of Persons Belonging to National or Ethnic, Religious or Linguistic Minorities, GA res. 47/135, UN GAOR, 1993, Supp. No. 49, U.N. Doc. A/47/49, 210.

Draft Declaration of Principles on Human Rights and the Environment, 16 May 1994, available online: <http://fletcher.tufts.edu/multi/www/1994-decl.html>.

UN Population Information Network, *Report of the International Conference on Population and Development,* UN Doc. A/CONF.171/13 (1994).

Copenhagen Declaration on Social Development and the Programme of Action of the World Summit for Social Development, 12 March 1995, UN Doc. A/CONF.166/9 (1995).

Washington Declaration on Protection of the Marine Environment from Land-Based Activities, 1 November 1996, UN Doc. UNEP/OCA/LBA/IG.2/L4, reprinted at (1995) 6 Yb.I.E.L. 883

Draft United Nations Declaration on the Rights of Indigenous Peoples, 26 August 1994, 31 I.L.M. 541 (1995).

OAS, Inter-American Commission on Human Rights, *Draft of the Inter-American Declaration on the Rights of Indigenous Peoples,* OR OEA/Ser/L/V/II. 90 Doc. 9 rev. 1 (1995).

IUCN, *Draft International Covenant on Environment and Development* (Gland, Switzerland: IUCN, 1995), available online: IUCN <http://www.iucn.org/themes/law/pdfdocuments/EPLP31ENsecond.pdf>.

Beijing Declaration and Platform of Action, Fourth World Conference on Women, 15 September 1995, UN Doc. A/CONF.177/20 (1995) and UN Doc. A/CONF.177/20/Add.1 (1995).

Declaration on the Establishment of the Arctic Council, 19 September 1996, 35 ILM 1387 (1996).

Rome Declaration on World Food Security, 13 November 1996, available online: FAO <www.fao.org>.

Organisation of Legality of the Use by a State of Nuclear Weapons in Armed Conflict, [1996], Advisory Opinion, I.C.J. Rep. 226.

New Delhi Declaration, 7 December 1997.

Programme for the Further Implementation of Agenda 21, GA Res. A/RES/S-19/2, UN GAOR, 19th Sess., UN Doc. A/Res/S-19/2 (1997).

International Labour Organisation Declaration on Fundamental Principles and Rights at Work, 19 June 1998, 37 I.L.M. 1237 (1998).

Millennium Declaration, GA Res. 55/2, UN GAOR, 55th Sess., UN Doc. A/Res/55/2 (2000).

Ten-year Review of Progress Achieved in the Implementation of the Outcome of the United Nations Conference on Environment and Development, GA Res. 55/199, UN GAOR, 55th Sess., UN Doc. A/Res/55/199 (2000).

On the United Nations Conference on Environment and Development, GA Res. 55/199, UN GAOR, 55th Sess., UN Doc. A/Res/55/199 (2000).

Doha Ministerial Declaration, Ministerial Conference, Fourth Session, 14 November 2001, WTO Document WT/MIN(01)/DEC/W/1, available online: WTO <ttp://www.wto.org>

Declaration of the World Food Summit, 13 June 2002, available online: FAO <www.fao.org>.

Johannesburg Declaration on Sustainable Development, in Report of the World Summit on Sustainable Development, 26 August to 4 September 2002, UN Doc. A/CONF.199/20.

Johannesburg Plan of Implementation, Report of the World Summit on Sustainable Development, 4 September 2002, UN Doc. A/CONF.199/20.

OAS, *Draft American Declaration on the Rights of Indigenous Peoples,* 17 June 2003, OAS Document GT/DADIN/doc.139/03 (2003).

Permanent Sovereignty Over Natural Resources, GA Res. 1803(XVII), UN GAOR, 17th Sess., Supp. No. 17, UN Doc. A/5217 (1962).

LIST OF ABBREVIATIONS

AEA: Americas Environmental Accord
AP: Additional Procedure

CARICOM- Caribbean Community Secretariat
CBD: Convention on Biological Diversity
CCAD: Central American Commission for Environment and Development
CCD: Convention to Combat Desertification
CDM: Clean Development Mechanism
CEP: Committee on Environmental Policy
CEPAL: United National Economic Commission for Latin America and the Caribbean
CEPF: Critical Ecosystems Partnership Fund
CI: Conservation International
CITES: Convention on International Trade in Endangered Species of Wild Flora and Fauna
CTE: Committee on Trade and Environment
COP: Conference of the Parties

DAC: Development Assistance Committee
DSU: Dispute Settlement Understanding

ECE: Economic Commission for Europe
ECLAC: Economic Commission for Latin America and the Caribbean
ECHR: European Court of Human Rights
ECO: environmental citizens' organizations
ECJ: European Court of Justice
EA: Environmental Assessment
EIA: Environmental Impact Assessment
EMP: Environmental Management projects
ETS: Emissions Trading Scheme
EU: European Union

FAO: Food and Agriculture Organization of the United Nations
FTAA: Free Trade Area of the Americas

GATT: General Agreement on Tariffs and Trade
GATS: General Agreement on Trade in Services
GDP: Gross Domestic Product
GEF: Global Environment Facility
GHGs: Greenhouse Gases
GMOs: Genetically Modified Organisms
GNP: Gross National Product

ICESCR: International Covenant on Economic, Social and Cultural Rights
ICCPR: International Covenant on Civil and Political Rights
ICN: International Competition Network
ICTSD: Information, Communication and Space Technology Division
IDB: Inter-American Development Bank
IGOs: Intergovernmental Organizations
IISD: International Institute for Sustainable Development
ILA: International Law Association
IPCC: Intergovernmental Panel on Climate Change
IPRs: Intellectual Property Rights

JI: Joint Implementation
JPOI: Johannesburg Plan of Implementation

LMO's: Living Modified Organisms
MEA: Multilateral Environmental Accords
MEA: Multilateral Environmental Agreements
MFN: Most Favored Nation

NAAEC: North American Agreement on Environmental Cooperation
NAFTA: North American Free Trade Agreement
NEAP: National Environmental Action Plans
NGOs: Non-governmental Organizations

OAS: Organization of American States
OECD: Organization for Economic Co-operation and Development

PCF: Prototype Carbon Fund
PPMs: Process and Production Methods
PRTR: Pollutant Telease and Transfer Registers
REA: Regional Environmental Accords

SCM: Agreement on Subsidies and Countervailing Measures
SIA: Austainability Impact Assessment
SPS Agreement: Agreement on the Application of Sanitary and Phytosanitary Measures

TBT Agreement: Agreement on Technical Barriers to Trade
TRIPS Agreement: Agreement on Trade-Related Aspects of Intellectual Property

UNCCD: United Nations Convention to Combat Desertification
UNCED: United Nations Conference on Environment and Development
UNCTAD: United Nations Conference on Trade and Development

UNDP: United Nations Development Programme
UNFCCC: United Nations Framework Convention on Climate Change
UNEP: United Nations Environment Programme
UNECE: United Nations Economic Commission for Europe
UNESCO: United Nations Educational, Scientific and Cultural Organization
UNICEF: United Nations Children's Fund
UNIDO: United Nations Industrial Development Organization
UPOV: International Convention for the Protection of New Varieties of Plants

WHO: World Health Organization
WIPO: World Intellectual Property Organization
WWF: World Wildlife Fund
WSSD: World Summit on Sustainable Development
WTO: World Trade Organisation

1

INTRODUCTION TO SUSTAINABLE JUSTICE: IMPLEMENTING INTERNATIONAL SUSTAINABLE DEVELOPMENT LAW

Marie-Claire Cordonier Segger[1] & C. G. Weeramantry[2]

As United Nations Secretary-General Kofi Annan noted, in the 2002 World Summit on Sustainable Development in Johannesburg, South Africa, it is time to face an uncomfortable truth. "[T]he model of development we are accustomed to has been fruitful for the few, but flawed for the many. A path to prosperity that ravages the environment and leaves a majority of humankind behind in squalor will soon prove to be a dead-end road for everyone." In academia or professional practice, it is not enough to simply recognise the immensity of this challenge and then stand aside. It is necessary to debate, develop and implement innovative, integrated solutions on all levels. Kofi Annan continued: "Unsustainable practices are woven deeply into the fabric of modern life. Some say we should rip up that fabric... I say we can and must weave in new strands of knowledge and cooperation."

Sustainable Development: A global concept

A very important aspect of this 'fabric of modern life' is found in our evolving laws and justice systems. These systems are intricately woven upon the shared values, morals and ethics of an increasingly interconnected and interdependent world. Among the shared values, there is found a growing sense of respect for

---

[1] Marie-Claire Cordonier Segger, MEM (Yale), BCL & LLB (McGill), BA Hons (Carl.) Director, Centre for International Sustainable Development Law (CISDL), Chair, CISDL/ILA/IDLO Partnership on International Law on Sustainable Development, Senior Manager, Americas Research Portfolio, International Institute for Sustainable Development & United Nations Environment Programme ROLAC, British Chevening Scholar & SSHRC Fellow, Exeter College, Oxford University Law Faculty, Lecturer, International Development Law Organisation (IDLO) & Member, International Law Association (ILA) Committee on International Law on Sustainable Development. She thanks Ashfaq Khalfan, the other director of CISDL and Markus W. Gehring, CISDL Lead Counsel, for their valuable intellectual contributions to this volume.
[2] H.E. Mr. Judge Christopher Gregory Weeramantry, BA Hons, LL.B, LL.D (London), LL.D h.c. (Colombo, Monash, N.L.S. India), D.Litt h.c. (London), Founder and Chairman of the Board of the Weeramantry International Centre for Peace Education and Research, Judge and Vice-President of the International Court of Justice, a Justice of the Supreme Court of Sri Lanka, Professor of Law in Australia and visiting professor in many other countries, Chairman of a Commission of Inquiry which probed international responsibility for phosphate mining in Nauru, has written extensively on many topics in international law.

M.C. Cordonier Segger & C. G. Weeramantry, eds., Sustainable Justice: Reconciling Economic, Social & Environmental Law
© 2005 Koninklijke Brill NV, Printed in The Netherlands, pp.1-12.

the common interest of all, a sense of responsibility for our common future. This responsibility, in certain instances recognised as a duty, engenders special attention to the needs of the most vulnerable and voiceless, especially the world's poor, and its shared environment.

It has been observed that a great transition is currently occurring in international law.[3] Though this transformation is still opposed by many, it is to be hoped that international law is shifting, through trans-national legal process and the development of governance regimes, from the era of state 'individualism' to the era of the collective community of states. Most rules of past international law have been based on preserving the individual desires and interests of individual states. The international law of the future may, instead, focus on preserving the collective rights of the community of states, as co-stewards of the planet Earth.

For this to occur, a new system of international law, and international justice, must emerge and develop. The norms which make up this system, it is hoped, will be based on the aspiration of freedom and equality for all. In addition, as Judge Charles D. Gonthier proposes, later in this book, there is a need to develop a sense of common responsibility for all members of our community, as symbolised in the third, often under-represented value of the famous French revolutionary cry: "liberté, égalité, *fraternité*." The norms of the emerging system of international law, it is hoped, will be founded upon a spirit of common responsibility for our increasingly interdependent societies and economies, for our shared environment and natural resources, and for the condition of humanity. In short, it is hoped that the world will begin to move towards a more 'sustainable justice'. Such justice should be founded upon good faith recognition of a duty towards the present generation throughout the world, so that their needs can be equitably met, and also respect for the interests of future generations.

Sustainable development, as a concept, emerges from a global aspiration to meet these collective moral obligations. The 1987 *Brundtland Report* describes sustainable development as "development which meets the needs of the present without compromising the ability of future generations to meet their own needs."[4] The 1992 *Rio Declaration* states, in Principle 3, that the right to development must be fulfilled so as to equitably meet the development and environmental needs of present and future generations.[5] It identifies an imperative to meet the development needs of the present and future equitably, and to simultaneously meet environmental needs. Sustainable development provides a 'conceptual bridge' between the right to social and economic

---

[3] See C.G. Weeramantry, *Universalising International Law* (Leiden: Martinus Nijhoff, 2004).
[4] World Commission on Environment and Development, *Our Common Future* (Oxford: Oxford University Press, 1987).
[5] *Rio Declaration*, Report of the United Nations Conference on Environment and Development (1992) UN Doc. A/CONF.151/26/Rev. 1 (1992) 31 I.L.M. 874.

development, and the need to protect the environment. Accommodation, reconciliation and integration are emphasised.

While certainly inspiring, this global concept of sustainable development suffers from a certain degree of vagueness.[6] This vagueness may well have been deliberate, in order to ensure its acceptability to many different local and global perspectives, from many cultures and regions.[7] However, the lack of conceptual clarity, coupled with obstacles from many powerful economic interest groups, has made it quite difficult to implement sustainable development in international policy and especially, in binding international law.

The time has come to seek greater clarity. In 1992 at the United Nations Conference on Environment and Development, heads of State recognised the "need to clarify and strengthen the relationship between existing international instruments or agreements in the field of environment and relevant social and economic agreements or instruments, taking into account the special needs of the developing countries."[8]

Over the past decade, scholars and practitioners from national and international agencies, courts and law faculties around the world have examined and sought to define the relationship sustainable development and international law.[9] Clarity is now urgently needed. Clarity is needed to help avoid or resolve bewildering conflicts and overlaps between economic, environmental and social treaties. Clarity is also needed to make implementation of international law possible, in the many treaties and regimes that have set sustainable development as an object or purpose. And clarity is needed to provide judiciaries, in domestic courts and international tribunals, with guidance to resolve disputes in this area.

A decade later, at the 2002 World Summit for Sustainable Development, heads of State agreed to continue "to promote coherent and coordinated approaches to institutional frameworks for sustainable development at all national levels,

---

[6] See B. Simma, "Foreword" in N. Schrijver and F. Weiss, *International Law and Sustainable Development* (Leiden: Martinus Nijhoff, 2004) at vi, where he states "… perhaps it is inevitable that… an integrative concept such as that of sustainable development which was endorsed as such by the world community as a whole, lacks the kind of clarity… one might be accustomed to in a more limited homogenous group of states… that need not necessarily be considered a disadvantage. Indeed, it may well have been the very lack of conceptual rigor which permitted the entire world community to embrace it."

[7] See M.C. Cordonier Segger and A. Khalfan, *Sustainable Development Law: Principles, Practices and Prospects* (Oxford: Oxford University Press, 2004) [hereinafter *Cordonier Segger & Khalfan*].

[8] *Supra* note 5.

[9] See *Schrijver & Weiss, supra* note 6. For a careful legal examination of the status of sustainable development in international law, see V. Lowe, "Sustainable Development and Unsustainable Arguments" in A. Boyle and D. Freestone, eds., *International Law and Sustainable Development: Past Achievements and Future Challenges* (Oxford: Oxford University Press, 1999). See also W. Lang, ed., *Sustainable Development and International Law* (Boston: Graham & Trotman / Martinus Nijhoff, 1995); K. Ginther, E. Denters and Paul JIM de Waart, eds., *Sustainable Development and Good Governance* (Norwell, Ma.: Kluwer Academic Publishers, 1995); M. McGoldrick, 'Sustainable Development: The Challenge to International Law" (1994) *R.E.C.I.E.L.* 3; and P. Sands, "International Law in the Field of Sustainable Development" (1994) 65 *Brit. Y.B. of Int'l L.* 303.

including, as appropriate, the establishment or strengthening of existing authorities and mechanisms necessary for policy-making, coordination and implementation and enforcement of laws."[10] They even mandated the United Nations Commission on Sustainable Development to take "into account significant legal developments in the field of sustainable development, with due regard to the role of relevant intergovernmental bodies in promoting the implementation of Agenda 21 relating to international legal instruments and mechanisms."[11]

In the context of increasing globalization, this book is part of a concerted international response to that mandate, a diverse collection of perspectives from judges of the highest courts, professionals and scholars of international law.

Sustainable Development in the World's Courts

Some may still argue that the concept of sustainable development is only an aspiration, and not really law– and hence our courts should not concern themselves with it. However, as is demonstrated in the chapters of this book, the concept of sustainable development is a substantive part of international law in a very real sense. It is an object and purpose of many treaties and legal instruments. It has even been suggested that sustainable development has an interstitial normative force.[12] It can drive law-makers (including judges, treaty negotiators and others) to accommodate, to reconcile, even to integrate intersecting and conflicting social, economic and environmental priorities, towards development that can last. And it encompasses a body of principles and practices that are gaining increasing recognition in international law on sustainable development or in short, in 'sustainable development law.'

Sustainable development must, at least in part, be achieved through law. The judiciary, being such an important part of the legal establishment, must necessarily be involved in this. This involvement must be sensitive, and sensible. Sustainable development is currently one of the vibrant topics in the development of both domestic and international law. It is also probably one of the least developed, among the myriad legal topics that come up before the courts. In international law, this is even more so. Sustainable development law is one of the least developed areas of international law. It is, as yet, an infant

---

[10] *Johannesburg Plan of Implementation*, Report of the World Summit on Sustainable Development, Johannesburg (South Africa) (4 Sept. 2002) UN Doc. A/CONF.199/20, available online:
<http://www.un.org/esa/sustdev/documents/WSSD_POI_PD/English/POIToc.htm>
[11] *Johannesburg Declaration on Sustainable Development* and *Johannesburg Plan of Implementation*, Report of the World Summit on Sustainable Development, Johannesburg (South Africa) (4 Sept. 2002) UN Doc. A/CONF.199/20.
[12] V. Lowe, "The Politics of Law-Making: Are the Method and Character of Norm Creation Changing?" in M. Byers, ed., *The Role of Law in International Politics: Essays in International Relations and International Law* (Oxford: Oxford University Press, 2000) at 214-215, where it is proposed that sustainable development can be considered an interstitial norm to resolve conflicting economic development and environmental claims.

concept, so far as modern law is concerned. As an infant concept, it needs to be fostered and nurtured. Treaties and legislation cannot anticipate the nuances of the myriad practical problems that could arise. When cases involving sustainable development arise, tribunals will often find themselves called upon to apply a broad general approach, the detailed implications of which have not yet been considered by scholars or regulators. It is very much like the situation of common law judges, who with only the broadest of general guiding principles, fashioned an intricately nuanced system of law to meet a myriad situations which the formal law giver had not and could not have anticipated. In short, justice systems are at the cutting edge of the development of this concept. Both domestically and internationally, judges will need to show imagination, initiative and vision in handling a matter so deeply fraught with implications for the global future. Only this imagination, initiative and vision can move us toward 'sustainable justice.'

A poignant circumstance is associated with this need to develop more sustainable justice. Disregard for the balance between economic development, social justice and environmental protection, causes harm to two classes of humanity in particular – the poor, and the unborn. Neither of these groups has more than a fledgling ability to assert its rights. Justice systems take up a very particular task in this regard. They must play a role to hold the balance true between powerful interests, on the one hand, and the voiceless, on the other. Justice could be seen to hold an extremely significant fiduciary duty, a trusteeship, in this regard.

Irrational exploitation of natural resources, without regard for the future or the rights of others, is one of the principal contemporary causes of global tension. In many circumstances, it is the seed of future conflicts.[13] Sustainable development law can be described as an insurance against these otherwise inevitable wars. Justice has the working tools with which to handle this enormous responsibility. The basic concepts and procedures are present. Using legal scholarship, new technologies and practical wisdom, judges can access the traditions of thousands of years of human experience in dealing with natural resources, and can rely upon considerable, often underused, equitable jurisdiction. Judges can elevate the legal standing of the sustainable development concept by moving it up the hierarchy of legal norms and principles, preventing it from being lightly dismissed by political, commercial or other interests which seek to advance "development", whatever the cost.

The law, including international and domestic law, can play a very important role in the realisation of more sustainable justice. And in recent years, as is

---

[13] See C.G. Weeramantry, *Universalising International Law* (Leiden: Martinus Nijhoff, 2004) at 447, which states: "True peace is impossible without justice. A principal element of justice is economic justice. Economic justice is impossible without sustainable development. Sustainable development is thus an important prerequisite to peace. If peace is an indispensable object of international law, sustainable development is indispensable to the attainment by international law of its most important goal."

canvassed in recent literature[14] and in the chapters of this book, international legal principles have emerged to help. These principles provide an increasingly firm backbone for a more effective, coherent sustainable development law. International, regional and bi-lateral treaties and tribunals are seeking to balance overlapping economic, social and environmental interests and needs. Local and global regimes, including – and on occasions led by – the tribunals and courts of the world, can contribute an independent, long term perspective to sustainable development decision-making.

Through treaties, tribunal decisions and regulations, justice systems have begun to design and implement innovative procedures in diverse jurisdictions across the world. Elements of a renewed global sustainable development governance system, as identified by the 2002 Johannesburg World Summit for Sustainable Development, continue to be saddled with the nearly impossible –but vitally necessary – role of coordinating these myriad complex efforts. As a result of this activity, some of which will be canvassed in this book, the field of sustainable development law is being practically moulded and adapted to meet a variety of diverse situations and problems, taking it far from being a merely academic and theoretical concept. The next few decades have been offered the exciting task of constructing a law of sustainable development which will help not one geographical region but all, draw upon the nuances not only of one cultural tradition but of all, advance the interests of not merely one section of the global economy but of all and protect the environment not merely for this generation but for others yet unborn.

Sustainable Development Law

In the 2002 Johannesburg Summit on Sustainable Development (the 'Johannesburg Summit'), the need for a coherent approach to sustainable development law was identified and advanced by 202 international scholars, law professors, legal professionals and judges.[15] It was argued that an international law of sustainable development is now emerging.[16] Indeed, a growing *corpus* of legal provisions and instruments can be identified which integrate international environmental, social and economic law.[17]

---

[14] *Cordonier Segger & Khalfan, supra* note 7. See also *Schrijver & Weiss, supra* note 6 at 699.

[15] "International Jurists Mandate for the Implementation of International Sustainable Development Law" in M.C. Cordonier Segger & A. Khalfan, eds., Conference Report from *Sustainable Justice 2002: Implementing International Sustainable Development Law*, co-hosted by the Centre for International Sustainable Development Law, the United Nations Environment Programme, the World Bank, and the International Law Association (June 13-15 2002, Montreal), available online: <http://www.cisdl.org>. See also M.C. Cordonier Segger, A. Khalfan & S. Nakjhavani, *Weaving the Rules for Our Common Future: Principles, Practices and Prospects of an International Sustainable Development Law* (Montreal: CISDL, 2002), which was launched at the 2002 World Summit for Sustainable Development in Johannesburg, South Africa.

[16] On the process of developing norms, see J. Brunnée & S.J. Toope "International Law and Constructivism: Elements of an Interactional Theory of International Law" (2000) 39(1) *Col. J. Trans'l. Law* 19.

[17] See *Cordonier Segger & Khalfan, supra* note 7.

International jurists, professionals and scholars have made great strides in the definition and analysis of legal principles and practices related to sustainable development.[18] International law provides a framework for regimes of cooperation - deliberately woven, implemented, financed and monitored by state actors and many other stakeholders. International law on sustainable development invokes historic, indeed ancient traditions of responsible, sustainable use of natural resources, respect for the earth and consideration for its peoples, for the past, the present and the future. It has important procedural elements related to consultations between environment and socio-economic decision-makers, transparency, participation of civil society and major stakeholders, and impact assessment. It includes a collection of legal instruments for sustainable use of shared resources, bi-lateral, regional and global regimes which set sustainable development as their object and purpose.

As recognised in the Johannesburg Summit, states have assumed "a collective responsibility to advance and strengthen the interdependent and mutually reinforcing pillars of sustainable development - economic development, social development and environmental protection - at the local, national, regional and global levels."[19] In Johannesburg, states also undertook "to strengthen and improve governance at all levels for the effective implementation of Agenda 21, the Millennium development goals and the Plan of Implementation of the Summit."[20] And they reaffirmed their "commitment to the principles and purposes of the Charter of the United Nations and international law, as well as to the strengthening of multilateralism."[21] They expressed support for "the leadership role of the United Nations as the most universal and representative organization in the world, which is best placed to promote sustainable development."[22]

As such, there is a need to advance, strengthen and improve governance for effective implementation of existing international commitments in the field of sustainable development. And sustainable development can serve to strengthen multilateralism, to aid in delivery of the principles and purposes of the Charter and of international law, especially with regard to its three 'pillars' – economic development, social development and environmental protection. International trade, investment and other economic laws aim mainly to achieve economic growth and progress. International law related to human rights, health, indigenous peoples and other social concerns seeks to achieve social justice. International environmental law aims to protect the environment, including the

---

[18] Reviews are provided in *Cordonier Segger & Khalfan, supra* note 7, and in *Schrijver & Weiss, supra* note 6. See also A. Boyle and D. Freestone, eds., *International Law and Sustainable Development: Past Achievements and Future Challenges* (Oxford: Oxford University Press, 1999).

[19] *Johannesburg Declaration on Sustainable Development,* Report of the World Summit on Sustainable Development, Johannesburg (South Africa) (4 Sept. 2002) UN Doc. A/CONF.199/20, available online:
<http://www.un.org/esa/sustdev/documents/WSSD_POI_PD/English/POIToc.htm>

[20] *Ibid.*

[21] *Ibid.*

[22] *Ibid.*

interests of all species. All three must meet the needs of present and future generations, for a development that can last over the long term.

Sustainable development law focuses on these intersections between social, economic and environmental fields of law.[23] A balanced accommodation, reconciliation and even integration of these priorities and norms is increasingly necessary, indeed essential, to achieve development that can last. This proposal is both ancient, and new. Many national laws and tribunals have fully acknowledged a connection between environmental protection, economic development and human rights.[24] On the international level, governments and judges, in binding treaties and international judgments, in 'soft law' declarations and state practice, increasingly perceive these objectives as complementary rather than unrelated or opposing disciplines.

However, as was implicitly recognised in the Johannesburg Plan of Implementation, these laws are not always coherent, either internationally or in the national context. Social, environmental and economic obligations can overlap, or even conflict. When they do, they are not sustainable. As witnessed in recent years, public protests and global tensions, popular struggles against the privatization of essential services, against new rules for trade and investment liberalization, against decisions of international financial institutions, are centered on this concern. Economic laws and policies which do not take social and environmental elements into account are unlikely to be successful in a democratic society. Similarly, environmental laws that ignore social and economic realities, and social laws that violate environmental or economic principles, can waste valuable political and material resources, also leading to failure. The need for a balanced integration of socio-economic development and environment priorities and norms permeates international law and policy on sustainable development. Principle 4 of the 1992 *Rio Declaration* states that in "order to achieve sustainable development, environmental protection shall constitute an integral part of the development process and cannot be considered in isolation from it."[25] Perhaps not all economic or social law requires environmental expertise, nor vice versa.[26] But certain instruments in

---

[23] *Supra* note 18. See also M.C. Cordonier Segger, "Significant Developments in Sustainable Development Law and Governance: A Proposal" (2004) *United Nations Natural Resources Forum* 28:1.

[24] For example, see Indian cases such as *Charan Lal Sadhu* v. *Union of India* AIR 1990 SC 1480 and *Koolwal* v. *Rajasthan* AIR 1998, Raj.2, which address environmental pollution as an issue affecting the human right to life. See also *Leatch v. National Parks and Wildlife Service and Shoalhaven City Council*, 81 LGERA 270 (1993) (NSW Land and Environment Court, Australia); *Vellore Citizens Welfare Forum v. Union of India* [1996] 5 SCC 647 (Supreme Court, India); *Balankulama v. The Secretary, Ministry of Industrial Development, SAER*, vol. 7(2) June 2000 (Supreme Court, Sri Lanka [Supreme Court of the Democratic Socialist Republic of Sri Lanka].

[25] *Rio Declaration on Environment and Development*, United Nations Conference on Environment and Development, U.N. Doc. A/CONF.151/6/Rev.1 (1992), reprinted in 31 I.L.M. 874 (1992) at Principle 4.

[26] This means that not all aspects of international environmental law are international sustainable development law. For example, animal rights, the conservation of 'charismatic mega-fauna', and trans-boundary environmental disputes do not necessarily address sustainable development problems. See A. Boyle & D. Freestone, eds., *Sustainable Development and International Law: Past Achievements and Future Challenges* (Oxford: Oxford University Press, 1999). It is important to be clear on this point. Sustainable development is not about the environment alone. It is not a 'softer' word for international environmental law, and is not

each regime do need to integrate the priorities of others. These tangled obligations, institutions and issues may inspire grand controversy, international debate, tension and conflict, but they are not impossible to resolve.

Indeed, reconciliation and accommodation is taking place every day: in courtrooms and tribunals around the world, in treaty negotiations and implementation, in the drafting or challenging of new regulations, in international organizations.

Great debates have raged as to which legal principles (and underlying these, which values) will guide the reconciliation, accommodation and integration of environmental, social and economic priorities. Based on prior work by the United Nations Commission for Sustainable Development and others,[27] the International Law Association *Committee on the Legal Aspects of Sustainable Development* has elaborated a set of 'Principles of International Law for Sustainable Development. A recent CISDL survey of international treaty and customary sources of international law indicates that many are becoming more widely accepted after the 2002 Johannesburg WSSD.[28] The principles can be found in a later chapter of this book, and need only be briefly mentioned here. They include:
- the duty of states to ensure sustainable use of natural resources,
- the principle of equity and the eradication of poverty,
- the principle of common but differentiated obligations,
- the principle of the precautionary approach to human health, natural resources and ecosystems,

---

simply a euphemism for environmental law in developing countries, either. International environmental law programming is extremely important and must be strengthened. But sustainable development is focused on human communities inasmuch as they depend on their environment, their economy and their society. It addresses a key concept of "needs, in particular the essential needs of the world' poor, to whom overwhelming priority should be given."[26] It requires an accommodation between social, economic and environmental objectives, on all levels. As such, multilateral environmental agreements (MEAs) are only 1/3 the locus of sustainable development efforts. Other aspects of the United Nations system, powerful international actors, particularly those with economic and social mandates, must seek ways to deliver on the overall sustainable development goal.

[27] These included, *inter alia*, WCED, "Report by the World Commission on Environment and Development Experts Group on Environmental Law" in *Our Common Future* (Oxford: Oxford University Press, 1987), *Rio Declaration on Environment and Development* (1992) 31 ILM 874 (adopted 14 June 1992), the concluding Declarations of various large UN Conferences, including the 18th *UNGA Special Session on International Economic Co-operation* (1990), the Vienna *World Conference on Human Rights* (1993), the Cairo *UN Conference on Population and Development* (1994), the Beijing *UN Womens Conference* (1995) and the Copenhagen *Social Summit* (1995); the *Agenda for Development* by the UN Secretary General (1995); the IUCN *Draft Covenant on Environment and Development* (Gland: IUCN, 2000 rev.); the *Report of the Expert Group Meeting on Identification of Principles of International Law for Sustainable Development* (New York: United Nations, September 1995); International Law Association Committee on Legal Aspects of Sustainable Development research reports, including 'The Right to Development in International Law' (1992), 'Sustainable Development and Good Governance' (1995), and 'International Economic Law with a Human Face' (1997); the UNEP *Position Papers on International Environmental Law Aimed at Sustainable Development* (Nairobi: UNEP, 1997 and 2000) (Montevideo Programmes II and III), and the *Earth Charter* (Costa Rica: Earth Council, 2000).

[28] M.C. Cordonier Segger, A. Khalfan, M. Gehring & M. Toering, "Prospects for Principles of International Sustainable Development Law: Common but Differentiated Responsibilities, Precaution and Participation" *R.E.C.I.E.L.* (2003) 12:1 at 45-69.

- the principle of public participation and access to information and justice,
- the principle of good governance, and
- the principle of integration and interrelationship, in particular in relation to human rights and social, economic and environmental objectives.[29]

These fledgling, emerging principles, taken together, may provide certain guidance for jurists seeking ways to balance conflicting or over-lapping social, environmental and economic obligations. Indeed, though more remains to be done, over the past decade in these areas of intersection and conflict, there have been striking international advances in sustainable development law. This book canvasses, from the perspective of authors and experts from all regions of the world, the recent experiences of legal instruments and courts that have sought this difficult balance, in the interests of present and future generations.

Overview of this book

The first part of the book examines the treatment of the concept of sustainable development in international and national courts and tribunals, from the perspectives of learned international and national judges. It includes a chapter by H.E. Judge C. G. Weeramantry of Sri Lanka, on sustainable development as global justice, a chapter by Hon. Mr. Justice C. Gonthier, formerly of the Supreme Court of Canada, which examines 'fraternite' as a global value underlying sustainable development, a chapter by Hon. Mr. Justice U.C. Banerjee, formerly of the Supreme Court of India, on the views and role of this leading court which has issued several extraordinary judgments related to sustainable development, a chapter by Hon. Mr. Justice A. Sachs of South Africa, which reviews this country's cutting-edge jurisprudence to enforce socio-economic rights, and a chapter by Hon. Mr. Justice N.J. McNally, formerly of the highest court of Zimbabwe, which presents his thoughts on poverty eradication as a precondition for sustainable development in Africa.

The second part of the book examines different experiences of integration between economic, social and environmental law in international law and policy. It includes several sections, each addressing different integrated issues and legal instruments which were identified as priorities for implementation of sustainable development law in the 2002 Johannesburg World Summit on Sustainable Development. The first section, on social and environmental elements of economic law, contains a chapter on the way that sustainable development can encourage more mutually supportive relationships between trade and environment law, by Matthew Stillwell of Australia, a chapter on

---

[29] See "ILA New Delhi Declaration of Principles of International Law Relating to Sustainable Development" in Kluwer Academic Publishers *International Environmental Agreements: Politics, Law and Economics* (2002) 2:2 at 209-216, available online: <http://www.kluweronline.com/issn/1567-9764/current>. And see *Schrijver & Weiss, supra* note 6 at 699. See also International Law Association (ILA) Committee on the Legal Aspects of Sustainable Development, *Searching for the Contours of International Law in the Field of Sustainable Development* (New Delhi: ILA, 2002).

sustainable developments in international competition law by Markus Gehring of Germany, and a chapter on international regimes for sustainable corporate law by Marie-Claire Cordonier Segger of Canada, the United Kingdom and Switzerland, and Michael Kerr of Australia. The second section, on sustainable management of land and water, contains a chapter on implementation of the *UN Convention to Combat Desertification and Drought*, by Hama Arba Diallo of Burkina Faso, a chapter on land tenure reform in the drylands, by Marie-Claire Cordonier Segger, Chris Huggins of Kenya and George Sikoyo of Kenya, and a chapter on water tenure reform and public access to water as a basic need, by Sumudu Atapattu of Sri Lanka. The third section, on social and economic elements of biodiversity law, contains a chapter on the need, nature and scope of a new international regime for access and benefit sharing of genetic resources by Jorge Cabrera of Costa Rica and Kathryn Garforth of Canada, a chapter on the regulatory aspects of implementing the Cartagena Protocol on biosafety by Kathryn Garforth, and a chapter on equitable benefit sharing in the Food and Agriculture Organisation's new *International Treaty on Plant Genetic Resources*, by Mary E. Footer of the United Kingdom and the Netherlands, and Emmanuel Opoku Awuku of Ghana. The fourth section, on social and economic elements of climate change law, contains a chapter on emerging issues in climate change law, by Duncan French of the United Kingdom, a chapter one on particular voluntary and regulatory instrument, emissions reduction registries, by Markus Gehring, and a chapter on vulnerability, equity and climate change law, by Xueman Wang of China. The fifth section, on human rights, development and poverty eradication in sustainable development law, contains a chapter on international human rights law and poverty eradication by Sumudu Atapattu, a chapter on human rights obligations in sustainable development financing, by Ashfaq Khalfan of Kenya, and a chapter on social protest against privatization of water, by Bronwen Morgan of the Australia. The sixth section, on international health law and sustainable development, contains a chapter on sustainable development and the right to health, Sumudu Atapattu, a chapter on the trade implications of the World Health Organization's new *Framework Convention on Tobacco Control* by Maya Prabhu of Canada and India, and Sumudu Atapattu, and a chapter on broader ethical and development concerns in health care discourse by Solly R. Benatar of South Africa.

The third part of the book examines a short selection of procedural mechanisms from legal instruments that were highlighted in the World Summit for Sustainable Development as potential best practices and areas for further effort. It discusses how these can strengthen the implementation of sustainable development law. The first section on participation, transparency and access to justice contains a chapter on negotiating and implementing the European *Aarhus Convention*, by Jeremy Wates of the United Kingdom, a chapter on public participation in Americas trade and environment regimes, by Marie-Claire Cordonier Segger and Jorge Cabrera, and a chapter on public participation, access to information and justice in regulatory regimes for clean drinking water by Karin Krchnak of the United States of America. The second section, on financing sustainable development, contains a chapter on the World Bank's efforts in financing sustainable development, by Ko-Yung Tung of China and the United States of America, a chapter on a rights-based approach to programming in the international financial institutions by Jorge Daniel Taillant of Argentina, and a chapter on sustainable livelihoods and financing of legal and judicial reform, by Ashfaq Khalfan. The third section, on compliance and dispute settlement mechanisms, contains a chapter on dispute resolution through the International Court of Environmental Arbitration and Conciliation, by Xabier Ezeizabarrena of Spain, and a chapter on sustainable development in the Inter-American Court on Human Rights, by Romina Picolotti of Argentina, and Marie-Claire Cordonier Segger.

The final part highlights potential future directions for sustainable development law, summarizing several recent developments which may provide guidance for domestic and international decision-makers, regulators, judges and scholars in the field of international law on sustainable development. It contains, a chapter on the 2002 *New Delhi Declaration of Principles of International Law Related to Sustainable Development*, with a commentary by Nico Schrijver of the Netherlands, a second chapter on governing and reconciling social, economic and environmental law, which identifies potential elements of a judicial test for sustainable development, by Marie-Claire Cordonier Segger, and a concluding chapter which presents the 2002 *International Jurists Mandate* for the Implementation of Sustainable Development Law, from the CISDL, UNEP, World Bank and ILA Conference *Sustainable Justice 2002: Implementing International Sustainable Development Law* in Montreal, Canada, June 14-16, 2002.

PART I

SUSTAINABLE DEVELOPMENT IN INTERNATIONAL AND NATIONAL COURTS AND TRIBUNALS

2

ACHIEVING SUSTAINABLE JUSTICE THROUGH INTERNATIONAL LAW

H.E. Judge C. G. Weeramantry[1]

This chapter explores the basic characteristics of a global justice system, setting out a vision for the international law that the author believes should be articulated, advanced, and respected in order to achieve global sustainable development.

International Law in the World Community

In human history, it is clear that power and privilege are rarely, if ever, ceded, except under the compulsion of necessity. Wars, the like of which humanity had not known in thirty centuries, provided this compulsion in the twentieth century. These wars demonstrated the need for a more effective system to govern the conduct of nations. There was the need for the power of a concept to rank above raw power, for the force of a system of cooperation to rank above brute force, for the majesty of a global order to stand above the majesty of the State. These were the thoughts that gripped the minds of practical statesmen at that time, though they had not always been receptive to such ideas.

The desire for the formation of a true international community based not on warfare, but on global cooperation that resulted in the birth of the League of Nations from out of the carnage of World War I. The League was the first global assembly in the long history of the recognized States. Unfortunately, one major war was not enough to compel States into giving up certain privileges. Certain imbalances existed which ultimately prevented the League from becoming an effective international organization that would work towards the advancement of equality and justice for all peoples of the globe.[2]

---

[1] H.E. Mr. Judge Christopher Gregory Weeramantry, BA Hons, LL.B, LL.D (London), LL.D h.c. (Colombo, Monash, N.L.S. India), D.Litt h.c. (London), Founder & Chairman of Board of the Weeramantry International Centre for Peace Education and Research, former Judge and Vice-President of the International Court of Justice, Justice, Supreme Court of Sri Lanka, former Professor of Law, Australia, Chairman of a Commission of Inquiry on phosphate mining in Nauru.
[2] See E. H. Carr, *The Twenty Year's Crisis* (New York: Harper and Row, 1964).

M.C. Cordonier Segger & C. G. Weeramantry, eds., Sustainable Justice: Reconciling Economic, Social & Environmental Law
© *2005 Koninklijke Brill NV, Printed in The Netherlands, pp.15-32.*

After a further devastating loss of life in World War II, the United Nations was conceived from the ashes of the League. The Charter that bound it together achieved the status of a supreme legal instrument effective among all nation-states, producing a universally recognized system of positive law that every member of the world community accepted as binding, with all the force of law.

Two giant steps had thus been taken — one towards establishing a universal body of nation states, and the other towards establishing a universally binding body of legal principles. The international rule of law had descended from the realm of aspiration to the real world. The first step had been taken in the tortuous history of humanity's quest for a legal order which was globally accepted. No longer could such ideas be dismissed as purely visionary. International law had made a quantum leap from utopian vision and non-law towards binding law.

The "realists" and cynics then lowered the timbre of their questioning. No longer did they ask the question "does international law exist?", but came down a notch and instead asked "even if international law does exist, does it matter?" They pointed to the vast spectrum of arenas where power still continued to disport itself as though international law did not exist.[3] It is an indication of how far we have travelled along this road towards the advancement of international law, that today scarcely anyone asks the question "Does international law exist?" Today its existence is largely assumed. However, the international community continues to struggle to ensure that international law is given the respect and authority that it needs, in order to promote peace and the advancement of humanity.

It is a sobering thought that this giant leap forward was not the result of an ordered progression of human thought, but was forced upon the international community by the brutalities of two world wars. Once the thresholds were passed, these wars demonstrated to a disbelieving world the depths of barbarism to which civilized nations can descend, when State sovereignty is free to function without the restraints of a superior legal system to which it owes allegiance. They forced the world to come to its senses on this great issue.

This is where we are now. We are standing at the dawn of a new century and millennium, facing a new series of challenges to the survival of humanity. These challenges, as serious and immediate as the thresholds of the wars last century, relate to hazardous social, economic and ecological thresholds.

---

[3] H. Morgenthau, *Politics among Nations,* 5th ed., (New York: Knopf, 1973).

Current Challenges for International Law

There as several key crisis points which present future challenges for international law.

Almost every day, the international news features problems of refugees in many parts of the world. The tragedies of Somalia, Vietnam and Yugoslavia are well known throughout the international community. Thousands stream across national borders, leaving behind their lifetime's memories, their possessions, and sometimes their loved ones who are too aged or infirm to travel.[4]

Refugee problems are not the problems of refugees alone. They are the problems of the entire civilized world, for we cannot, with any claim to decency or civilization, leave other human beings in the filth and squalor of the refugee camps and the cloud of uncertainty that hangs over their entire future, without some form of international assistance. The international legal system should have some form of relief to offer to them.

Indeed, in recent times, a body of international law has been developed in an effort to protect them. For example, the 1951 *Convention* and the 1967 *Protocol* relating to the status of refugees proscribe required standards of treatment.[5] The United Nations has set up the Office of the United Nations High Commissioner for Refugees.[6] The absolute discretion of States to refuse entry of any foreigners into their countries has to a considerable extent been curtailed by international law in relation to refugees.[7] However, the current framework is still extremely inadequate. While there is insufficient space to enter into details here, this body of law is still far short of the level of achievement required, and it remains very much a crisis area.

The international community also has a related problem foreshadowed for the future - the problem of environmental refugees. International scientific studies have shown that global climate change and the rising of sea levels could pass a certain threshold, flooding a number of low-lying islands in another 50 years or less, so that the occupants of such islands will become refugees, seeking admittance into other States.[8] Desertification, drought and extreme temperature change will also lead to the displacement of thousands, if not millions of people.[9] The problem of environmental refugees may be with us even sooner

---

[4] See E. Feller, V. Türk & F. Nicholson, *Refugee Protection in International Law - UNHCR's Global Consultations on International Protection* (Cambridge: Cambridge University Press, 2003).
[5] *Convention relating to the Status of Refugees*, 28 July 1951,189 U.N.T.S. 150 (entered into force 22 April 1954) and *Protocol Relating to the Status of Refugees*, 31 January 1967, 606 UNTS 267 (entred into force 4 October 1967).
[6] See UNHCR, available online: <http://www.unhcr.ch>.
[7] See, generally, G. Goodwin-Gill, *The Refugee in International Law,* 2nd ed. (Oxford: Oxford University Press, 1996).
[8] See for example United Nations Environment Programme, *Global Environmental Outlook* (Nairobi: UNEP, 2000), and United Nations Development Programme, *Human Development Report* (New York: UNDP, 2001).
[9] *Ibid.*

than we expect. The justice systems of this world must not be caught unprepared.

Indeed, the international environmental pillar of sustainable development is also in crisis. It has been widely acknowledged throughout the world that humanity continues to be endangered by the depletion of the ozone layer, climate change, species extinction, and the pollution of the oceans, rivers and lakes of this world.[10] Human beings, as self interested consumers, have used our inheritance of land and water spaces throughout the world as if these were our private preserves, the absolute property of the present generation.

However, the current generation actually serves as a trustee for the generations yet to come. Unless humanity looks after its environment, it is possible that, through environmental degradation, we might damage our eco-system beyond recovery. We may even drag the future of humanity into destruction — because there is, especially in such fields as nuclear waste, nuclear reactors, nuclear armaments, the destruction of the rainforests, the pollution of the seas, and the damage to the ozone layer, the possibility of irreparable and irreversible damage to the life support system which sustains all of humanity.

The 1972 *Stockholm Declaration on the Environment,*[11] with its 26 principles which offer a foundation for international environmental law, ought to be better known throughout the world. These environmental principles contain an important philosophy for our time. Principle 1 stresses that man has a fundamental right to freedom, equality and adequate conditions of life, not in the abstract, but in an environment of quality that permits a life of dignity and well-being.[12] All the other human rights become worthless if the environment is so damaged as to deny this quality of life, and take away the health of our people. Similarly, the *World Charter for Nature*[13] and the later *Earth Charter* could easily and effectively be brought to the attention of children in schools, as a reminder to them of their duties to the world.

Further, international law must adapt to the fact that we are living in an age dominated by technology. This technology is changing every facet of domestic and international life, and the rate of change is increasing exponentially. Consequently, international law, a slow-moving discipline in the past, has to speed up its rate of change and adaptation. Where formerly international lawyers had two or three generations in which to cogitate upon a major social or technological change, they now must do so in only a number of months or

---

[10] *Supra.* note 7.
[11] *Stockholm Declaration on the Human Environment,* 16 June 1972, U.N. Doc. A/CONF.48/14, 11 I.L.M. 1461 (1972) at Principle 1.
[12] *Ibid.* at Principle 1.
[13] *World Charter for Nature,* GA Res. 37/7, UN GOAR, 37th Sess., Supp. No. 51, UN Doc. A/37/51 (1983); 23 I.L.M. 455.

years. Changes in communications technology, computerization, and bio-medical engineering provide but a few examples.[14]

Some of these changes affect the very foundations on which certain legal principles have been built. The response of the international legal community to such new technology is illustrated in its response to space law and the exploration of the celestial bodies. Had international lawyers not thought as early as 1979 to construct a *Treaty on the Activities of States on the Moon and other Celestial Bodies* (commonly known as the Moon Treaty), we may well have had a new race for colonization of the moon and other celestial bodies.[15] As it currently stands, many States, led by the United States of America, are currently attempting to manipulate or even break the existing international treaty structure in order to militarize space in a new type of arms race. Similar problems are arising with regard to computer privacy, data banks, trans-border data flow, recombinant DNA experimentation, global warming, new drugs and chemicals, and other issues. International law must keep abreast of science, or will watch helplessly from the sidelines while unrestrained technology transgresses all social controls.[16]

A fourth factor is also important, and presents a significant future challenge. Often economic factors can operate just as compulsively as physical force in compelling a country to a particular course of conduct. Economic power can be so great as to enable it to break through the walls of sovereignty. It can influence, even in the minutest detail, the lives of every citizen in every State. It can become an instrument of exploitation from afar, unrestrained by the usual principle that power must be accompanied by responsibility.[17]

In particular, foreign investment is one field in which much work is required to transform the current state of the law and international practice. Throughout the world, there appear to be many unfair, even "unconscionable", contracts between investors or investor countries and debtor countries. There are numerous ways that such contracts can affect human rights, potentially leading to human rights deprivations in certain countries, and even revolutions.[18] Such contracts are drafted by lawyers trained in intricate knowledge of corporate law. However, a proper knowledge and use of broader public international law is needed to address the equitable and human rights aspects of these agreements.

---

[14] See generally, C. G. Weeramantry, *Impact of Technology on Human Rights: Global Case Studies* (Tokyo: United Nations University Press, 1993).

[15] *Treaty on Principles Governing the Activities of States in the Exploration and Use of Outer Space in the Exploration and Use of Outer Space, Including the Moon and Other Celestial Bodies,* 27 January 1967, 610 U.N.T.S. 205, 18 U.S.T. 2410 (entered into force 10 October 1967).

[16] For an early elaboration of this theme by the author, see C. G. Weeramantry, *The Slumbering Sentinels: Law and Human Rights in the Wake of Technology* (London: Penguin Books, 1984).

[17] J. J. Rousseau, *The Social Contract and Discourses* (New York: Dutton, 1950).

[18] See generally S. R. Ratner, "Corporations And Human Rights: A Theory of Legal Responsibility" 111 (2001) *Yale L.J.* 443.

In an age of increasing economic power, of a global marketplace that is steadily increasing its grip on every aspect of peoples' lives, such imbalances can exacerbate severe problems of malnutrition, exploitation of labour, environmental damage, foreign debt, loss of national autonomy, and deprivations of social, economic and cultural rights.[19] However, they appear to pass unnoticed, presenting the appearance of agreements made under firm contractual conditions.

This area requires the most careful and urgent attention. As international law develops, it must recognize the need to develop new principles to handle this area. It will need to recognize the analogy between economic force and physical force. The prohibitions against the illegitimate use of physical force would, where appropriate, be attracted to the illegitimate use of economic force.

This opens up a vast area in which international law will be a prime instrument of service to the global community. New principles and standards will have to be formulated. Much intellectual rigour is called for in this task, for such a concept presents another revolutionary departure from classical principles of international law as articulated by Loewenfeld, among others.[20] While one must move with great caution, the constraint of illegitimate economic power may be an essential area of focus for international law in the future. As with most legal principles which have evolved through balancing competing principles, so also will this task involve a fine sense of judgment between legal principle and practical reality. The changing face of nation state sovereignty is a concurrent thread throughout this discussion. In the many strands that make up the concept of sovereignty, not the least important is the economic strand. Many concentrations of economic force wield more power than most sovereign States. This aspect of sovereignty is being gravely eroded today. While we must acknowledge that in today's world no State can regulate its economic affairs in total freedom from external factors, it is also clear that dependence on external factors can at a certain stage reach such a level as to amount to a negation of sovereignty.

A final major trend of the future that can be identified here is the tendency of international law to break through the barriers imposed upon it by narrow concepts of individual rights. International law cannot be constrained by the narrow concepts of individual rights which flourished in domestic systems under individualist and positivist theories of the nature and functions of law. Under the combined influence of vulnerability and urgency for many of the world's people, ecological problems of global dimensions, a view of planet

---

[19] See generally J. Stiglitz, *Globalization and Its Discontents* (London: Norton, 2003). See also A. Sen, *Development as Freedom* (New York: Knopf, 1999).

[20] H. P. de Vries and A. Loewenfeld, "Jurisdiction in Personal Actions - A Comparison of Civil Law Views" (1959) 44 *Iowa L Rev* 306.

earth as a limited shared resource of all people, and a growing vision of the short-sightedness of current economic planning, the focus of the law's attention has broadened. It can no longer afford to concentrate on the individual, the individual State and the present generation. It needs to set its sights further and broaden the narrow aperture of the lens through which it views the world.[21]

The concept of sustainable development, which looks beyond the mere present into the long-term future and mitigates against maximum, immediate exploitation of common resources at the cost of poor countries, vulnerable groups and future generations, is acquiring a central place in international law. International law must reflect very strongly the need to develop, define and implement this concept. These will be some of the principal formative influences over the international law of the future.

Sustainable Development Law in International Tribunals

There are many reasons for the growing importance of treaty law and it is vital to examine customary international law in the light of the strengths and weaknesses of treaty law.

A considerable strength of treaty law in a world order still based on the sovereign state system is that it postulates the express consent of states and therefore conserves their sovereignty and autonomy. Another source of strength is the specificity of the obligations assumed, thus avoiding to some extent the difficulties attendant on determining whether a given situation falls within the reach of a general principle that is invoked.

But a world whose survival will increasingly depend in the future on active co-operation rather than mere co-existence has need of a system whereby rules that bind the international community do not need to have the specific individual consent of each and every one of the nearly two hundred states comprising the community of nations. If this were the *sine qua non* for a binding rule of international law, we could never obtain the rules that are required to handle the problems of our global village. Treaty law will find itself hopelessly inadequate to handle such matters as the urgent environmental problems which are already on our hands. We must have resort to a set of principles that do not owe their existence to an act of specific state consent but reach beyond state consent to the primordial verities and principles on which the international order is founded. Customary international law provides such a source which will need to be increasingly relied upon in a future where unexpected and urgent problems of an unprecedented nature will keep arising, for which treaty law cannot provide the solutions

---

[21] This idea is central to the concept of preserving our present global community and its resources for use by future generations.

Even if a unanimous consent to a treaty can be obtained, a total global consensus will take time to achieve, and consent at the level of sovereign states is a slow and ponderous process. Moreover, even in the context of a treaty there will be uncertainties in interpretation and application, as well as gaps, and there must be a supplementary source from which these lacunae and interstices in the law can be filled.

The fact that treaty-making is a slow and involved process, that treaties are not all-embracing and do not specifically cover all relevant eventualities, that treaties involve formality in the mode by which they come into existence – all of these combine to highlight the importance of customary international law which postulates a set of principles already in existence, wherefrom one draw the specific rules which may be necessary for handling a given problem or situation. In the words of Oscar Schachter:

> "However, treaties have not fully met the needs of new law. For one thing, the processes of treaty negotiation are often slow and cumbersome. It is easy to see why. The increase in the number of States, the diversity of interests, the novelty of the problems faced, the shortage of competent officials, are factors which combine to delay and complicate the treaty-drafting negotiations and ratifications. The difficulty of obtaining ratifications and accessions, even for States that had supported and signed the treaties has been a discouraging feature. Even when multilateral treaties obtained the requisite number of parties, a substantial number of countries remained outside the treaty, though they had no significant substantive objections and voted for its adoption by the drafting conference." [22]

If treaties require time to evolve, what happens in the time between the rising of the need and the achievement of the treaty? In the world of sustainable development law in particular, we shall have progressively less time in the future than we have had in the past to attend to them, because they are growing increasingly urgent.

There must be a body of legal principle that fills that gap. And customary international law provides just that. Treaties involve formality, and customary international law does not suffer from this impediment. So the latter is still a valuable instrument to us.

---

[22] O. Schachter, "New Custom: Power, Opinio Juris and Contrary Practice" in *Theory of International Law at the Threshold of the 21ˢᵗ Century, Essays in Honour of Krzysztof Skubiszweski* (Cambridge: Cambridge University Press, 1995) at 531.

A sterling example to illustrate this aspect can be drawn from the field of the law relating to modern weapons. To arrive at an international treaty which pronounces that the use of nuclear weapons in any circumstances amounts to a violation of the law is well-nigh impossible under current circumstances. Yet the corpus of customary international law is replete with basic principles which point to this conclusion.[234] What could be more necessary for the survival of humanity than the establishment of such a proposition and what could be more urgent? Yet treaties as a source of the necessary principles are silent whilst customary international law speaks loud and clear. That voice must not be muted. There is therefore, a growing future for customary international law rather than a future of diminishing utility and stature.

The fertility of customary international law as a source of law in domestic jurisdictions that accept international law as part of their legal systems can be well illustrated from numerous jurisdictions.[24] If customary international law has played such a vital formative role in assisting domestic legal systems to handle such a variety of problems, it certainly has the potential in the milieu of international law proper to assist the international legal system to adapt itself to the numerous fundamental changes that system is currently facing.[25]

The World Court, as the principal judicial organ of the United Nations, must be empowered to state and apply international law with an authority matched by no other tribunal must, in its jurisprudence, pay due recognition to the rights of future generations.[26] If there is any tribunal that can recognize and protect their interests under the law, it is this Court.

It is to be noted in this context that the rights of future generations have passed the stage when they were merely an embryonic right struggling for recognition. They have woven themselves into international law through major treaties, through juristic opinion and through general principles of law recognized by civilized nations. Among treaties that may be mentioned, the 1979 *London Ocean Dumping Convention*, the 1973 *Convention on International Trade in Endangered Species of Flora and Fauna*, and the 1972 *Convention Concerning the Protection of the World Cultural and Natural Heritage* expressly incorporate the principle of protecting the natural environment for future generations, and elevate the concept to the level of binding state obligation.

Juridical opinion is now abundant, with several major treatises appearing upon the subject and with such concepts as intergenerational equity and the common

---

[23] See generally the author's Dissenting Opinion in *Legality of the Threat or Use of Nuclear Weapons*, July 8 1996, I.C.J. Rep. 226 (Advisory Opinion).
[24] For an overview, see *supra* note 22, at Chapter 2.
[25] H. H. Koh, "Why Do Nations Obey?" 106 *Yale L. J.* 2259. See also H. H. Koh, "The Globalization of Freedom" (2001) 26 *Yale J. Int'l L.* 305 at 306.
[26] Weeramantry International Centre for Peace Education and Research (WICPER), *The World Court: Its Conception, Constitution and Contribution* (Ratmalana: Vishva Lekha, 2001).

heritage of mankind being academically well established.[27] Moreover, there is a growing awareness of the ways in which a multiplicity of traditional legal systems across the globe protect the environment for future generations. To these must be added a series of major international declarations commencing with the 1972 *Stockholm Declaration on the Human Environment*, and continuing through the 1992 *Rio Declaration on Environment and Development*, and the recent 2002 *Johannesburg Declaration of the World Summit on Sustainable Development*.

When incontrovertible scientific evidence speaks of pollution of the environment on a scale that spans hundreds of generations, it is the opinion of this author that the World Court would fail in its trust if it did not take serious note of the ways in which the distant future is protected by present law. The ideals of the United Nations Charter do not limit themselves to the present, for they look forward to the promotion of social progress and better standards of life, and they fix their vision, not only on the present, but on "succeeding generations". This one factor of impairment of the environment over such a seemingly infinite time span would by itself be sufficient to call into operation the protective principles of international law which the Court, as the pre-eminent authority empowered to state them, must necessarily apply.

Developing Sustainable Development Law

The concept of sustainable development is one of those forward looking legal concepts on which the future happiness of the human family very heavily depends. The betterment of the economic and social conditions of every individual is one of the cardinal missions of all legal systems. "Development" aims at achieving this result at a practical level through such measures as development of economies, development of skills, development of wealth, development of utilization of resources, development of necessary infrastructures, development of living conditions, development of health and development of the overall quality of life.

These are much desired objectives which all too often have been much delayed. International lawyers and policy makers need to get on with the task of achieving them and the law needs to help towards this result. Unfortunately, "development" can take place at the expense of the environment. It can take place at the expense of future generations. It can take place at the expense of the poor and disadvantaged. It can take place at the expense of destroying cultural inheritances and traditional ways of life which have taken thousands of years to achieve. This is the crux of the problem. These values are not disposable, nor are they commodities to be purchased for a pittance. Each of

---

[27] E. Brown Weiss, *In Fairness to Future Generations: International Law, Common Patrimony and Intergenerational Equity* (New York: Transnational, 1989).

these sets of values is important. Each of these represents a human right. Each of these is vital to the human future.

Legal systems, both domestic and international, are expected to foster and advance all of these sets of concerns. Strong legal arguments can be advanced in favour of each of these. Legal systems are thus involved in a delicate balance of competing interests.

There is no longer any room for denying the legal aspects of development. Nor is there room any longer for denying the legal status of sustainability. Out of this juxtaposition of opposing considerations has arisen the concept of sustainable development. It is time that it becomes widely recognised that there is no denying the legal status of the concept of sustainable development – a new synthesis that must result from the clash of opposing interests.

Why can we suggest that sustainable development is part of international law? International law arises initially from the realm of aspiration. All its principles are formulations of aspirations. This formulated idea gradually hardens into concrete law. One excellent example is presented by the Universal Declaration of Human Rights,[28] which began with the formulation of a series of aspirations. As time went on, these aspirations became firmer, they crystallised, they became part of accepted international law and in that way they injected themselves into domestic law, often into constitutions of countries, recognised and enforced by courts and national justice systems. As this chapter seeks to demonstrate, such a process has been initiated for sustainable development. It begins in the realm of the aspirational but as time progresses and its importance becomes clearer, through an iterative process, it becomes more and more a part of the established international legal order and infuses itself into the domestic legal order as well.

It must be recognised that the concept of sustainable development, its place in international and domestic law, and its principles, are still highly contested. There remain several important barriers to the full recognition and enforcement of this concept.

First, it is still very strongly entrenched in modern law that only the living generation have rights under the law. The great majority of our current legal systems, whether Common Law or Civil Law, concentrate almost exclusively on the rights of those who are living here and now. These appear to be the only bearers of rights in modern legal systems. However, this is a very limited view. It does not accord with the philosophies that traditional wisdom has bequeathed to us. Those philosophies teach us that there is a duty on the present generation to look beyond itself to those who are to come after us, as well as to look back at the past and respect those who went before us. This is

---

[28] Dec. 10, 1948, G.A. Res. 217A, U.N. GAOR, 3d Sess., U.N. Doc. A/810 (1948).

very beautifully expressed in the traditional African concept which Bishop Desmond Tutu has explained in his sermons - that the human community consists of three elements - those who went before us, those who are with us here and now, and those who are yet to come.[29] All three together constitute the human community. If one loses sight of any one of those component parts of the trinity, one gains only a lopsided view of the human endeavour. That is a very important tradition which international lawyers must weave into our environmental law framework.

Second, another rather narrow attitude of modern law is to hold that it is only human beings that have any recognisable rights. No other creatures which inhabit this planet which is our common home have any rights recognised by modern legal systems. That was not the case in traditional law. Especially in the Eastern part of the world there was a very deep understanding of the rights of other living creatures to this planet which we all share. In the traditions of many indigenous peoples there were very strong items of State conduct which showed recognition of this principle. The establishment by indigenous rulers of hospitals for animals, as early as the 4th century,[30] showed that there was a strong understanding that human duties are not concentrated on human beings alone, and that one must, in devising a legal system, think a little beyond the confined vision that human beings are the only creatures that matter on this planet.

Third, modern law still seems to concentrate almost exclusively on the rights of individuals. There is a great stress on individualism as though only individuals have rights. However, traditional societies flourished not only on the basis of individual rights but also on the basis of group rights.[31] The group was very important and as one knows even from the history of Europe, the group, whether it be the guild or the manor or the parish, was very important to the life of every individual. There were groups to which every individual belonged and through which the individual felt secure and protected. If you destroy the group, to quote Edmund Burke in his description of the French Revolution, and wipe the State clean of the traditional group organisations, you leave the individual naked and alone to face the might of an all encompassing State.[32] The individual, once he is broken away from the group, has to sink or swim on his own.

Ancient society, in contrast to modern society, recognised that groups had definitive rights. The village had rights. The church or temple had rights. The

---

[29] D. Tutu, *The Rainbow People of God: South Africa's Victory Over Apartheid* (London: Doubleday, 1994). See also Sermon given by Arch Bishop Desmond Tutu, available on line: <http://www.heureka.clara.net/books/tutu-sermon.htm>.

[30] King Buddhadasa of Sri Lanka is recorded as having established such a hospital in the 4th Century. See V. L.B. Mendis, *The Rulers of Sri Lanka* (Colombo: S. Godage & Bros., 2000) at 239.

[31] See generally, C.G. Weeramantry, *Universalising International Law* (Leiden: Martinus Nijhoff, 2004).

[32] E. Burke, "Reflections on the Revolution in France" (Washington: Liberty Fund, 1999), available online: <http://www.baylor.edu/~BIC/WCIII/Essays/reflections.html>.

guild had rights. The manor community had rights. Those important rights were lost sight of during the concentration on individualism that occurred after the European Revolutions. Indeed, when the Indian Constitution was established, Mahatma Gandhi strove hard to obtain recognition of group rights, though he was not successful in the face of the strength of Western concepts of individualism which provided the basic background thinking for many Indian lawyers themselves.

The old international law, if the international law that prevailed until the end of World War II can be so termed, was based upon individualism. It was based upon the individual sovereignty of the different States that are members of the world community. But today's international law does not need to focus so excessively on the individual. It can and will become a socially oriented international law.

Several pressures have forced this recognition, including the pressure of environmental needs, because with ozone depletion, global climate change, extinction of species, regional land degradation, collapse of fisheries and so forth, we have a whole catalogue of possible damage not merely to individual States but to the world at large. Environmental damage does not respect national boundaries. Pollution does not recognise the doctrine of state sovereignty and end at the boundaries of a nation state. Pollution proceeds beyond that and if we are to stop such damage and waste, we must act as a global community and not as a series of separate and individual States asserting their sovereign rights.

In the past, states may have sought to function internationally on the basis of co-existence. Nation states tolerated the existence of the "other" State as a necessity of life. The "other" State was there and governments had to co-exist with one another whether it was desirable or not. States reconciled themselves to that situation and international law worked out rules for co-existence between those States. But humanity has now passed out of the era of co-existence into the era of cooperation; and not merely passive cooperation but active cooperation, because if we are to save our global inheritance we have to do so actively. Lawyers and policy-makers need, for this purpose, to avoid dependence on ideas of sovereignty and the desire of each State to claim complete dominion over everything going on within its borders. States and their governments need to surrender some part of that sovereignty to the rest of the world and to accept common guidance by the global community. Hence, as the environment knows no territorial boundaries, the international community has to live as a cooperative group of States - at the very least so far as environmental law is concerned.

Similarly, the international vision must extend not only to States beyond national frontiers but it must extend in time beyond generational frontiers. The vision must be cast beyond the present generation and must look forward into the future. When lawyers and courts deal with sustainable development law, they are in the realm of future generations. What they are handling are the rights not only of themselves and the present generation, but of generations to come. In the argument of the General Assembly's request for an Advisory Opinion on the illegality of nuclear weapons, counsel appearing for one of the parties argued that if people in the Stone Age had inflicted on natural resources the damage which we are inflicting upon it now, we would still be living with this damage from the Stone Age. Now it is the same with us. What we do now will affect future generations even more remote from us in the future than the Stone Age is remote from us in the past. Just as we would have blamed earlier civilizations for their lack of a sense of responsibility, a lack of moral sense and lack of civilised behaviour, so those arguments could be hurled against us by posterity if we do not take up our responsibilities, with dignity and consideration, now.

Another concept which has worked itself into international law is the concept called the *erga omnes* concept, i.e. the concept of an obligation owed towards the entire world and all its inhabitants. Generally, disputes between two parties are disputes *inter partes*, i.e. disputes between individual parties. There are two parties who come before a Judge and the Judge's task is to determine between those individual parties which party should succeed. But sustainable development challenges are not merely *inter partes*, but may also affect other parties apart from those before the Court. So the Judge, whether domestically or internationally, has to have his eye also on the impact of the Court's decision on the community. Although procedurally it is a matter between the two parties, in substance it is a matter which affects the world. It affects the rights of others outside the limited frame of the parties to the dispute. This *erga omnes* doctrine, which is now being developed in relation to sustainable development, is something that domestic judges may find useful.

Another factor to be considered is that the forces of technology are advancing at an unprecedented rate. This is true of almost any kind of technology. But the rate of the advance of the law that tries to keep this technology in check, to harness it, is extremely slow. The gap between technology and law is continually widening.[33] Our ability therefore to control any technology through law is thus growing weaker day by day. This is a very important phenomenon which all judges and lawyers must take into consideration today. This phenomenon concerns the developing regions even more urgently than most others, because much of the technology used in those regions is not of home growth but comes from the developed nations. Judges and lawyers must, as far as possible, assist in achieving legal control over that technology to ensure that it can serve the interests of all people.

---

[33] See generally, C. G. Weeramantry, *Justice Without Frontiers: Protecting Human Rights in the Age of Technology* (The Hague: Kluwer Law International, 1998).

Finally, international law must draw upon the principles of different civilisations. In the view of this author, this is not yet done adequately. International law on sustainable development might be a little further ahead than some areas. The international community make a much greater commitment to this cause in the future, by drawing upon the thousands of years of wisdom in building up the concept of the common heritage of mankind. That is vital in the context of our ever-shrinking planet which is the common home of everybody. Whatever the forces may be that are resulting in our narrow view of law - be they monetarism or individualism - they are drawing us away from our cultural traditions. It is very important that we restore the links, for otherwise international law will grow further away from the people and the planet it is intended to serve. This is very important if we are to develop the international law of the future in a truly global sense.

Some time ago, the author was Chairman of the Nauru Commission of Inquiry which looked into the question of phosphate mining in Nauru.[34] In consequence of that mining there was not even an inch of topsoil left in the mined out areas and the land was devastated, unfit for any form of human activity. The philosophy behind this result is the idea that if an individual or corporation has certain property rights they can use them to the fullest extent without regard to the traditional ways in which land was respected and protected. There is much guidance that can be gained from traditional wisdom which in these respects surpasses the rather limited vision of modern legal systems. Modern law, rich though it may be, is neglecting an important and fertile source of nourishment when it neglects the traditional wisdom of humanity. In environmental matters, the traditional wisdom of humanity can teach us how we can live in harmony with our environment without destroying it in the manner resulting from the pursuit of legal concepts to the limit of their logic, without applying also the restraining influence of the traditional wisdom of the human family.

We must martial all our resources to this task. The international community has much access to traditional wisdom, and judges as well as lawyers must see how they can best tap into that reservoir of wisdom. It will be very important to the international community in the future. When one analyzes the rich history of these traditions, it is easy to see the force of the argument that humanity is neglecting its richest resource of wisdom if its members do not look back upon tradition and the lessons it can offer in both what should and should not be done. The human family has learnt to live in harmony with the environment for thousands of years and has achieved this in a very successful manner. If we fail to look to the past for its traditional wisdom in facing our environmental problems, we may be depriving ourselves of one of our richest resources. For example, many traditional peoples recognised that the land has a

---

[34] Statements and reports from the UN Nauru Mission, available online: <http://www.un.int/nauru/>.

vitality of its own. Land lives and grows with the people. If the land withers and dies so also do the people, because the health of a community is dependent on the health of the land and the health of the land is lost unless you pay due regard and reverence to that land and look after it as you would look after a living thing. Another part of traditional wisdom involved ensuring that if a resource was used, this was done efficiently. Fauna and flora were comparatively meagre on the African and Australian continents, but every part of the plant and animal was used to maximum advantage. Nothing was discarded. There are many principles ingrained in it which lawyers, judges and policy makers can build into modern international law with great profit - the principle of sustainable use of resources, for example.

As one specific example, it is useful to consider the traditions of the Pacific. The previously mentioned Nauru Commission researched the customs relating to land of the various islands in the Pacific.[35] It came across the evidence given by a Solomon Islander to a Land Reform Commission in the Solomon Islands. His evidence was to the effect that Pacific islanders did not treat land like an article of merchandise as the westerners treat land - an article which, once it is purchased it one can do with it what one will. Land has to be treated with reverence and respect and its 'owners' are obliged to use it in a manner that is respectful to the rights of future generations.

In another illustration, this idea was again encountered when the author was a visiting professor at the University of Papua New Guinea. In Port Moresby, there were pockets of land within the city (the capital) which were not developed. One day in the common room, the conversation turned to the reason why these lands were left undeveloped and they turned out to be land belonging to various family groups. One of the young lecturers in the Law Faculty was a family member of one of those groups and therefore one of the co-owners of this valuable piece of undeveloped land in the heart of the capital. The question was posed: "do you realise you are sitting on a gold mine? Has it ever struck you that if you sold this land you would have a fortune?" This produced an outburst from the lecturer who said "Do you not understand our traditions in this country. This land belonged to our ancestors and belongs to our posterity. How can you suggest that I have the right to sell it? I have to respect the rights of those who have come after me."[36] Such are examples of the traditions of the Pacific countries, traditional wisdom that can be woven into the fabric of modern international law.

This chapter will offer a further example, the Ancient Irrigation system of Sri Lanka, perhaps known from the author's Separate Opinion related to other large water projects. Sri Lanka is covered with a network of thousands of man made lakes and ponds. As Arthur Clarke, the great futurist who lives in Sri

---

[35] See *supra* note 23
[36] *Ibid.*

Lanka, recognises, the system provides a textbook example of many modern dilemmas, including the dilemma of striking a balance between development and the environment. He states that prior to "the Christian era, a series of tremendous irrigation works transformed the island's dry zone into what might have been a fertile paradise. Some of the artificial lakes created are kilometres in circumference and there are thousands of these tanks linked by intricate networks of canals."[37]

These enormous irrigation works - some of them enclosing an extent of water which might run to areas of up to 10 square miles had retaining structures sometimes several miles long and 50 feet high. The Sea of Parakrama for example has a retaining band, 8 1/2 miles long. These enormous structures were linked to 25,000 to 35,000 small tanks. Sri Lankans call them tanks after the Portuguese word tanque, which means a reservoir. These 25,000 - 35,000 small tanks were linked by hundreds of miles of canals to these enormous reservoirs. It is clear that the rulers of that age were extremely concerned with what today, is termed development. As development projects go, this network is even larger than many modern development projects. While they were aimed at development, at the same time they combined development with the protection of the environment. The early Sri-Lankan lawmakers and rulers did not neglect one or the other, but pursued both, striking a happy balance between the two concepts in a manner which has lasted for centuries.

That is precisely the concept which this chapter and text is trying to address: How do you strike a balance between social and economic development, and environmental protection? Respect and consideration for our common future is a part of the culture and responsibility of humanity. International legal scholars are looking for principles and formulas that can reconcile social and economic development and protection of the environment. We must work out these formulas using all the wisdom we can find - and one of the messages that needs to be heeded is this: "Please do not neglect the traditional wisdom of the many rich cultures of our region that we can draw upon for the purpose of developing this very important area of future international law."

Conclusion

The areas referred to in this chapter are representative of the vast field awaiting attention at the hands of international lawyers in the future. A greater interest in the growing discipline of international law is essential, for on its success are centred many of the hopes of humanity for the amelioration of its condition. If international law should fail us at this critical stage in human history, we shall go down to a condition which can outdo the barbarisms of the past. Hence, if we neglect it we are sowing the seeds of our own destruction. Those who stand to lose most if the discipline of international law is neglected are the people of

---

[37] A. Clarke, *The View from Serendip* (New York: Ballantine Books, 1984) at 145.

the poorest and most vulnerable countries. Their very survival depends upon financial and industrial agreements with the more affluent countries, and all these agreements are entered into in accordance with international law. If through neglect, they face a situation where all the legal expertise is on the side of the lender or investor countries, they will necessarily suffer from bad bargains, for there will be no one to look after their interests.

Their traditional neglect of international law at all levels can thus cost them dearly as a nation, and it is from the legal profession itself that the impetus can best emerge to diffuse more information about international law and to ensure that more attention is paid to this aspect as well as to the training of more specialist international lawyers of the future. To students and young scholars, particularly, the message is addressed that it is from among your ranks that the international lawyers must emerge who will in the future guide countries and the world to a position of true equality in the community of nations. If one should fail in this responsibility, one would indeed be failing ones country and the world in the very area in which new talent can serve it to the greatest advantage.

3

FRATERNITY: A GLOBAL VALUE UNDERLYING SUSTAINABLE DEVELOPMENT

Hon. Mr. Justice Charles D. Gonthier[1]

A discussion on sustainable development and globalization is incomplete without an exploration of the values underlying these principles, including the concepts of *"fraternité"*, or solidarity. Sustainable development rests on good governance. Today, that means good governance of diversity. There are two approaches pursued in this chapter; the first is a more formal discussion on the role, scope and relationship of law and morality in good governance. The second discussion goes to the roots of society: the human spirit, its motivation, the concern and commitment to society at every level – in other words, the concept of fraternity and what it means to sustainable development.

The discussion on law and morality is set against the background of the two great expectations which Western societies have of the law today and which it is the challenge of any and every legal system to meet: the first being that moral values find expression in the law and be sanctioned by it. The international conventions and national charters are the highest expression of this. The second is that laws be so conceived and applied as to allow decisions that are perceived as rendering justice in the individual case. The furtherance of a general rule at the cost of injustice in individual cases is less and less accepted as a necessary social burden.

The fact remains, however, that the rule of law, as its name implies, requires set rules to be applied by judges in order that arbitrariness and uncertainty be avoided. If the law is to serve as a guide to social activity, it must have a degree of stability.

This chapter will outline the role of law, what may be expected of it and its limits as an instrument of justice. In order to use it appropriately, in dealing with the environment or otherwise, one must understand these limits. At the

[1] Hon. Mr. Justice Charles D. Gonthier, B.CL., LL.D. (McGill), Chair, Board of Governors of the Centre for International Sustainable Development Law, Wainwright Senior Research Fellow, McGill Faculty of Law, Of Counsel, McCarthy Tétrault LLP, former Justice, Supreme Court of Canada.

M.C. Cordonier Segger & C. G. Weeramantry, eds., Sustainable Justice: Reconciling Economic, Social & Environmental Law
© *2005 Koninklijke Brill NV, Printed in The Netherlands, pp.33-46.*

heart of the discussion is the relationship between law and morality. This will be considered from two aspects: the moral order as a basis of the law and the effect of law on the moral order of society.

The current approach taken by the Canadian legal system to the delineation of law and morality will be explored, as will the differences between law and morality. The case will be made that law must have a moral basis if it is to be respected, and further, that the law should aim to better the moral as well as the physical environment in which we exist. This may assist in understanding to what extent laws <u>are</u> moral and on what basis they may be effective in protecting the environment. This chapter will conclude with a reflection on the moral and legal value of fraternity and its central role in sustainable development and the protection of the environment.

Law and Morality: Delineating Their Differences

It is useful to set out some definitional positions from which a common discussion can begin.

Law is a system for regulating the conduct of the individual as it impacts on other individuals and society. In a narrower range of cases, it can regulate the individual's conduct vis-à-vis himself. For example, section 14 of the *Canadian Criminal Code* prevents an individual from consenting to his own death. Section 71 forbids anyone to accept a challenge to fight in a duel. Section 290 disallows bigamous marriages even where they are consensual.[2] In essence, law regulates conduct and not thoughts.

Morality is a system of rules governing conscience as well as conduct as regards the person towards himself, his creator, other individuals and society (including its institutions). Thoughts are at the heart of morality.

In assessing how these two concepts overlap, there is general agreement that there are areas where laws are entirely absent of morality and others where morality is inherent to the legal rules. An example of the first category would be regulatory laws of a purely arbitrary nature. An example of the second category of laws would be professional discipline codes. Here, morality is integrally intertwined with the regulations.

Approaches to Law and Morality

The bulk of the law dealt with by the Supreme Court of Canada relates to criminal and civil rules. In the civil domain, there are a number of areas where we have accepted without question the introduction of moral elements to the

---

[2] *Canadian Criminal Code*, R.S.C. 1985, c.C-46, ss. 14, 71, 290.

rules. For example, in business relations, recent decisions of the Court have strengthened the concepts of "good faith" and fiduciary obligations. This concept of good faith has recently been codified in the *Quebec Civil Code* in sections 6 and 7.[3] The fact that we naturally accept the inclusion of these moral concepts in the domain of civil law is a positive development.

In the realm of criminal law, there remains considerable debate over whether the law is or should be based on morality. This is not surprising given that criminal law is the area of regulation that places the widest range of sanctions at the disposal of our system of justice and can have the greatest impact on individual liberty. An examination of Canada's criminal law system reveals that its rules are inherently moral and are designed to regulate, protect and foster our moral environment.

Laws are moral in their regulating function because, absent a sound moral basis, laws would have great difficulty securing the compliance of the society they are supposed to regulate. Even the great liberal H.L.A. Hart recognized this when he stated: "In the absence of this [moral] content men, as they are, would have no reason for obeying voluntarily any rules; and without a minimum of co-operation given voluntarily by those who find that it is in their interest to submit to and maintain the rules, coercion of others who would not voluntarily conform would be impossible."[4]

Laws protect our moral environment by reflecting a moral consensus of community tolerance of activities. The law cannot impose the moral views of the majority of what constitutes a "good life" on the rest of the population. Rather, the community sets laws to control behaviour it cannot tolerate because that behaviour is seen as posing a fundamental threat to the community and to its moral environment.

This does not mean that laws serve no exemplary function in moral conduct. The Supreme Court of Canada has made this point in *R. v. Morgentaler*[5], and more recently in *R. v. Keegstra*[6]. In *Keegstra*, a case dealing with the constitutionality of hate speech provisions in the *Criminal Code*, the late Chief Justice Dickson stated: "…s. 319(2) serves to illustrate to the public the severe reprobation with which society holds messages of hate directed towards racial and religious groups. The existence of a particular criminal law, and the process of holding a trial when the law is used, is thus itself a form of expression, and the message sent out is that hate propaganda is harmful to target group members and threatening to a harmonious society. As I stated in my reasons in

---

[3] *Civil Code of Quebec*, S.Q. 1991, c.64 (C.C.Q.), (came into force 1 January 1994).
[4] H.L.A. Hart, *The Concept of Law*, 2nd ed. (Oxford: Clarendon Press; New York: Oxford University Press, 1994) at 189.
[5] [1998] 1 S.C.R. 30 at 70.
[6] [1990] 3 S.C.R. 697 at 769.

R. v. Morgentaler: 'The criminal law is a very special form of governmental regulation, for it seeks to express our society's collective disapprobation of certain acts and omissions.'"

Thomas Aquinas, in his *Summa Theologae,* reminds us that laws attempt to make their subjects good.[7] They can and do, but within the limits tolerated by our multilingual, multiethnic and multicultural societies that have a considerable diversity of moral views. However, it would be imprudent to place too much faith in our legal system as a key mechanism for improving our moral environment, or as the sole mechanism for protecting the physical environment and advancing sustainable development.

Laws can only go so far to protect our moral environment and supporting the good governance which is essential to sustainable development. The law cannot move far beyond the minimum moral consensus without losing its legitimacy. The real protection of our moral and physical environment must come from the responsibility people are prepared to assume in exercising their freedom. We cannot simply assume that legal rights will solve everything. We must put greater emphasis on the duties and responsibilities individuals have to each other and their community. That cannot be accomplished simply through legal edicts. Rather, we must attempt to engender consent. One critical failure of communism was an attempt to meet its goals by imposing compliance. If we wish to foster our moral and physical environment, we must be willing not only to foster this consent but to instill, particularly in young people, a personal commitment to their neighbour and to the community.

In Canada, the *Charter of Rights* has become a focal point for the definition of certain fundamental values of our society and a growing awareness of the need for such public values. It is, however, intended to reflect only a minimum consensus embodied in the law binding on all, the breach of which gives rise to legal sanctions, be it jail time, a fine, an injunction, exclusion from a profession or damages. It is not sufficient for the proper working of society, let alone as a code of personal conduct. This has always been and remains the realm of morality.

The *Charter*, however, has brought within the realm of the law a vast area where previously the law did not dare tread except within narrow limits; matters that society left to be governed solely by morality and sanctioned by conscience: family and religion.

Undoubtedly, this development is a great step. It is a necessary step forward in the evolution of our society and the world – necessary because of the increasing complexity of society and social relationships which carry with them

---

[7] Thomas Aquinae, *Summa Theologae* (Alba: Editiones Paulinae, 1962) at I-II Q. 92.

the need for guidance; necessary because of the increasing diversity of individual backgrounds and values.

The *Charter*, however, is but a small first step; it must be heard as a call for personal dedication to a better society, for this goal cannot be fulfilled by paper declarations. Charters of rights and freedoms are but worthless paper in the absence of duties to satisfy and respect them. Indeed, to my mind, our greatest challenge in the fulfillment of the *Charter*'s promise today is to bring about understanding, the acceptance of this reality and the commitment to living up to it.

Fraternity: The Unspoken Pillar of Democracy

The constitutions of Canada and the United States are founded on precepts of individualism – the guaranteed rights to life, liberty and the security of the person in Canada, and life, liberty and the pursuit of happiness in the United States. By contrast, in France, India, and elsewhere, the motto of the French Revolution, "*liberté, égalité, fraternité*" shapes the legal structures in those countries.

This famous revolutionary cry has been subjected to the vagaries of politics and history over the past two centuries. After having seriously suffered at the hands of colonialism, totalitarianism and the world wars which struck the 20th Century, the principles of liberty and equality were solidly established in the liberal constitutions following the last war. More recently, they were incorporated almost as a matter of course, in the legal orders of the former communist countries over the last decade. Today, more and more citizens throughout the world benefit, at least in theory, from a clear legal protection of their liberty and their right to equality. Freedom – or more precisely freedoms – which are protected have become familiar: freedoms of expression, religion, association; civil liberties; protection against arbitrary arrest and seizure; the right to a fair trial and others are the hard core of human rights at the national and international levels. Their protection continues to improve, through the initiative of international institutions or the creation of new instruments, such as their inclusion in the future European constitution of a European charter of fundamental rights. At the same time, equality has been advanced in many countries by the adoption of laws aimed at prohibiting discrimination and ensuring an equal and fair application of the law. As Professor Jacques Robert has so appropriately commented, "[*translation*] this concern to include the principle of equality at the highest level of the hierarchy of norms certainly constitutes an important enhancement of democracy."[8]

---

[8] Jacques Robert, *Rapport général de 1er Congrès de l'Association des Cours Constitutionelles ayant en Partage l'Usage du Francais (ACCPUF)*, (ACCPUF: Paris, April 1997), at 560.

This victory – in the legal protection of liberty and equality – is not, however, exempt from raising new problems. The tension between basic rights and freedoms and democratic rule which is based upon the will of the majority immediately comes to mind. A jurist might be tempted to answer that the problem is rather a political one: the drafters of the constitution having decided to protect certain rights and their interpretation should not be influenced by such considerations. The judge's experience, however, teaches him or her that whenever the protected rights call to be interpreted, the question of the role of the courts in a democratic society and of the deference that may be called for regarding the will of Parliament necessarily resurfaces.

Moreover, even were we to accept the former answer, the question remains. Indeed, the second problem which arises is purely legal: it is that of the balance to be reached amongst the protected rights themselves when they conflict. Some of the obvious examples arise in the field of <u>heinous</u> or <u>racist</u> propaganda, where freedom of expression and the right to equality conflict. Affirmative action also comes to mind – a policy which opposes two fundamentally different concepts as to the meaning of the right to equality. Such dilemmas arise even more frequently in societies where the greatest variety of claims are made invoking human rights and where we witness what Michael Ignatieff describes as truly a "rights revolution".[9]

In this way, jurists throughout the world are daily faced with delicate issues arising from the recognition given by the law to freedom and equality. Such tensions between the intense complexity of environmental laws and the many conflicting interests at play are at the forefront of concerns of environmentalists in search of sustainable development through good governance of diversity.

One answer may be found in that third facet of the revolutionary cry, which is the complement of the first two and one that is often neglected: fraternity. Brotherhood or "*fraternité*" found its place, though a modest one, in the great human rights movement since the last world war. Fraternity is intertwined with liberty and equality in the very first article of the *Universal Declaration of Human Rights* which proclaims: "All human beings are born free and equal in dignity and rights. They are endowed with reason and conscience and should act towards one another in a spirit of brotherhood." [In French, "*esprit de fraternité*".]

Historically, Greek philosophers feared the concepts of liberty and equality because of their potential damaging effect on fraternity. After the Enlightenment, however, the Greek tradition of fraternity and community action was reversed – fraternity became the distant goal of political action rather than the starting point. The result was that many proximate and

---

[9] Michael Ignatieff, *The Rights Revolution* (Anansi Press: Toronto, 2000).

imperfect fraternities were destroyed or weakened in hopes of creating a more perfect society. Query as to whether this is the same reason why fraternity has been largely ignored in the philosophical writings of North Americans. We may question whether the omission of fraternity from our Constitutions was the triumph of individualism over communalism.

The advent of industrialization and urbanization may be responsible for further hastening the decline of fraternity. The loss of a sense of community is inevitable where society is committed to individual freedom and rights above all. However, while the basis of governance is the individual, individuals do not live in isolation. The emphasis on the individual in western democracies has removed the notions of community and cooperation from the forefront of societal interactions. Yet individuality and association are correlative facets of an essentially undivided experience.[10] In order to obtain true freedom and equality, fraternity must reassert itself in human relationships.

Fraternity and Sustainable Development

Fraternity has been included, some times indirectly, in the constitution of several states. In the clearest cases the principle is expressly stated, normally in their preamble. In other cases, more frequently, fraternity is not mentioned as such but is recognized through other values or related principles, such as solidarity, social justice, the welfare state, human dignity, tolerance or similar concepts. Finally − as in Canada, whose constitution in the British tradition avoids the statement of general principles − one must look to the unwritten constitution and court decisions for fraternity principles.

For jurists, the challenge is to go beyond the concept of fraternity as an ideal or a philosophical or political aspiration, and to identify a truly legal dimension. At the outset, we are struck by several realities.

In the first place, our attempt to give fraternity a specific meaning in this world of ours cannot ignore the many historical realities that have molded its adoption in various countries. Indeed, fraternity as a value has taken on a diversity of colours and sometimes remarkably different meanings from the circumstances of its recognition.

For instance, in Haiti, it became a symbol of the fight against slavery and national independence in the early 19ᵗʰ century. It played the same role in the decolonization of several African countries after the Second World War. More recently, it embodies the will towards reconciliation and the rebuilding of

---

[10] Gordon L. Ziniewicz, *Democracy and Imagination: The Practical Idealism of John Dewey* (Ph.D. Thesis, Boston College, 1992), online: Dr. Z's Philosophy Page <http://www.fred.net/tzaka/six.html> at Chapter 6.

national communities following tragic conflicts in such places as The Former Yugoslavia, South Africa, Cambodia, and to this day, the Democratic Republic of Congo. Elsewhere, also, fraternity or solidarity has been seen as the expression of the attachment of peoples to ancestral tradition or religious values. In the Western World, the recognition of values such as solidarity and the just society inspired the movement to promote and protect the constitutional mechanisms for social and economic protection of the welfare state.

This variety of historic expressions of fraternity leads to a second finding, namely, the flexibility of this value, the number of meanings which it may have and the hopes to which it may give rise in the future. Indeed, while fraternity is an absolute and universal concept in its spirit, it is variable and diverse in its applications. Beyond its national expressions, fraternity extends to the whole of humanity, as evidenced by international humanitarian law, which imposes a minimum respect for human dignity even in the time of war. Fraternity also extends over time, being the basis of obligations towards future generations – particularly those of bequeathing a viable environment and a world order based upon peace amongst nations. These notions of human dignity and obligations to future generations are essential to sustainable development.

The facets of fraternity

To be understood, fraternity must be limited in time and space in each particular context. The link between this concept and the values which it comprises rests on the concept of community.

Fraternity is the value which brings together the abstract notions of liberty and equality in the reality of an existing community which is defined not only in terms of the pursuit of individual interests but also by the sharing of beliefs, values and understanding of history and a desire to ensure the continuity of the community – in other words, an identity. The values upon which it rests and to which it gives rise are many, but one may identify four which are particularly useful to our analysis. These values go beyond the strict framework of written law – their first purpose and effect is to inform and inspire the administration of justice. In this sense, they relate to the spirit of the law rather than its black letter. Indeed, going beyond legal interpretation, fraternity should inspire behavior in those entrusted with the administration of justice so that it may express courtesy and concern for people.

One facet is that of inclusion, which recognizes that certain members of the community, by reason of their vulnerability, require protection and a particular commitment on behalf of others so that they may participate in the life of the community; in this respect, fraternity evokes the idea of empathy. A second facet is that of commitment and responsibility in order for a community to exist. For this reason, the law recognizes that certain relationships between individuals give rise to special responsibilities which sometimes conflict with individualistic notions of liberty and equality. Thirdly, fraternity leads to the recognition of an obligation in many cases to go further in our relationship with others than simply to treat them equally or by respecting their freedom; one must also act with justice and equity and respect their trust. Finally, fraternity within a community evokes the idea of cooperation: the pursuit of common interests by combining one's resources – a notion that itself calls for a redistribution of wealth in so far as this is compatible with the notion of individual responsibility. Inclusion, commitment, responsibility, justice and equity, trust and cooperation, these are values which, when related to the concept of community, should guide our study of fraternity.

In sum, as a first point, one should note the increasing importance of notions related to fraternity in constitutions and in laws. Indeed, though fraternity itself is rarely referred to by the Courts and its mention or its specific mention remains rare in the decisions themselves, a series of notions related to it have long since been referred to. The diversity of terms – such as solidarity, the welfare state, equity, social justice or human dignity – should not obscure their close affinity to fraternity. References to these related notions before the Courts, which until recently were rare, have become more and more frequent. In France, specific mention has been made of the principle of solidarity, particularly since the early 1980s. Most recently, the Supreme Court of the United States upheld the student admission policy of a university aimed at opening access to the university for students from minority groups, on the basic principle that minorities must be represented at the highest levels of decision making, be it government armed forces or business, as they are integral participants in the country.[11]

One of the most significant developments is the emergence of the principle of human dignity as a distinct value entitled to constitutional protection, as well as a conceptual basis for rights and freedoms expressly protected. This understanding is particularly helpful in deciding the legality of limitations applied to rights in the public interest or into establishing a fair balance when protected rights conflict. Most constitutions as well as international treaties on human rights contain provisions allowing such limitations. The interpretation of acceptable limits gives rise to continuing debate.

The concepts of public interest and proportionality applied in this context rest on the notion of fraternity. In Canada, the government may well be justified in placing reasonable limits on some forms of liberty in order to advance a community goal or what the late Chief Justice Dickson described in the *Oakes* case as "the realization of collective goals of fundamental importance."[12] Those

---

[11] See *Gratz et al. v. Bollinger et al.,* 539 U.S. 244 (2003); *Grutter et al. v. Bollinger et al.,* 539 U.S. 306 (2003).
[12] *R v. Oakes,* [1986] 1 S.C.R. 103.

collective goals of fundamental values were described by the Chief Justice as being : "Respect for the inherent dignity of the human person, commitment to social justice and equality, accommodation of a wide variety of beliefs, respect for cultural and group identity, and faith in social and political institutions which enhance the participation of individuals and groups in society."[13]

Finally, in assessing the increasing importance of the values of fraternity in case law, we must underline the increasing role of international and community rights, as well as the international courts which apply them. Even when their decisions are not binding on a national court, the decisions of the European Court of Human Rights and the Court of Justice of the European Community, for example, influence in important ways the national courts in their development of general principles of human rights. The same can be said of treaties and other international instruments which embody fraternity or related values such as the *Universal Declaration of Human Rights* and the *Convention on the Rights of the Child* have been expressly incorporated into constitutions.

Ways of the Future: Fraternity in the 21st Century

The great progress of fraternity and related values in the law raises the question of the outlook for the future of these values. The increasing influence of international norms enhances awareness of the many facets of fraternity. While it applies in the first place between individuals and groups within communities, it also extends to other regions and communities within a given country and beyond to the international level through the establishment of minimal criteria (such as the protection of fundamental rights and the law of war) and the pursuit of common objectives (such as economic development and peaceful resolution of disputes). Fraternity may even extend in time through the concept of intergenerational equity which calls upon us to take into account the rights and interests of future generations through policies, such as respect for the environment, sustainable development, repression of crimes against humanity and the reconstruction of societies devastated by internal conflict. At every level, fraternity gives rise to a variety of duties, but the underlying values remain the same.

There are many challenges, however, which remain.

The integration of ethnic and other minority groups in the political body of a state is not only a requirement for stability but also provides a formative experience for politicians and jurists. The capacity of the law to take into account social diversity and operate as a unifying force rather than a conflicting

---

[13] *Ibid.*

one also improves the capacity of a country to pursue its international relations in a world where we are all minorities who aspire to be recognized.

Another important aspect of the development of fraternity within each country is the recognition and promotion of alternative dispute resolution methods such as conciliation, mediation and arbitration. These methods often go beyond the simple resolution of specific conflicts of the parties involved by allowing them to reconcile their interests over the longer term and avoid future conflict. Obviously, the system of justice must ensure that a balance is maintained so that the desire to promote better relations between the parties is pursued through a dialogue in good faith that does not play on inequality between the parties. The pursuit of the peaceful resolution of conflict, which is at the heart of the spirit of fraternity, exists not only in the context of the resolution of private litigation but is of fundamental importance for the negotiated resolution of the most fundamental constitutional problems. The Supreme Court of Canada's decision in the *Quebec Secession Reference* is a good example. Faced with a potential secession of Québec from the Canadian Federation, the Supreme Court concluded that, even though the Canadian constitution did not expressly provide for a procedure in this respect, the federal institutions and other provinces had an obligation to negotiate in good faith if faced with the expression by a clear majority in a province, in response to a clear referendum question, of an intention of its inhabitants to secede. This would operate in respect of each one's rights under the constitution and in response to a request legitimately expressed.[14] Such an obligation to negotiate in good faith and to take into account the implied obligations arising from the honour of the Crown has also been recognized in the context of relations with native peoples, particularly in the negotiation of agreements and the renunciation of certain rights in order to favour economic development, such as the exploitation of natural resources in aboriginal territory.

Fraternity obviously has its limits; laws based on this value cannot assure the resolution of all disputes between individuals, communities and whole nations. However, it remains our duty to do all we can so that the spirit of fraternity may provide support to the efforts of those who seek to promote harmony. Reverting for a moment to the motto "*liberté, égalité, fraternité*", one should not establish any hierarchy between these three elements. Indeed, if it is true to say that fraternity can only exist between persons who are free and equal, it is also true that liberty and equality cannot be maintained in a society where fraternity does not find its place. The recognition of this interdependence and integration of the essential values of fraternity in the judicial order will remain essential to maintaining peace and democracy in the century to come.

---

[14] *Reference re Secession of Quebec*, [1998] 2 S.C.R. 217.

Conclusion

To accomplish their purpose and to be effective, justice and its administration must rest upon and be the expression of moral values. These values must be expressed and applied according to the rule of law and not the will or wish of persons in authority. Their definition should be the subject of a social consensus on what is essential, but respect diversity in their application according to the variety of cultures, beliefs and religions. The values of liberty, equality and fraternity are the essential expression of the dignity and respect for the human person and therefore are values essential to the integrity of a community and of democracy. These values, in their content, reflect the attributes of the human person and should inspire behaviour and ways of life. While the values may vary with certain limits, each person, individually and collectively in his private life and public life, as well as each society through its institutions, must assume, apply and promote these values. They are everyone's responsibility. The respect for rights entails respect of one's duties.

Good governance is central to ensuring this respect. An approach to governance at all levels – local, regional, national and international – that respects the integral role that individuals can play in ensuring the accommodation of interests and a community approach to activities will lead to greater results in terms of real sustainability. Good governance does not rest exclusively with the state. It is everyone's business and in the final analysis rests on the commitment of every individual.

The depth of that commitment will measure the quality of governance. Indeed, it may be said that in terms of the life of each person, governance rests first and foremost on the actions, decisions and conscience of that person, be it as to his own conduct, his relations with his family, those around him and his immediate community or more generally, his participation in the broader community. Governance also results from the conjunction of the activities of many seeking their own interest which has the consequence of a regulating effect. The stock market is a striking example. Related to such self-interest are the incentives that may be created by public or private initiatives which will tend to influence individual decision making. A fourth element of governance is what is knows as soft laws in the form of codes of ethics, guidelines as to conduct and indeed peer pressure. These are all expressions of moral values which have not consolidated into expression by positive law. One witnesses an increasing tendency for positive law to assume an increased role in this field of moral values. These elements are essential to the protection of the environment and more broadly to sustainable development.

In short, good governance and sustainable development require the accommodation of conflicting interests according to the spirit of the law rather than its letter, particularly with reference to good governance of diversity, which is the challenge of every society and every country today. This spirit must be one of fraternity, which expresses itself directly by rules and norms, but more importantly in the ways, behavior and communication with one's neighbor. Notwithstanding the travails of history, humanity possesses a vast reserve of this value and must live by it.

The concept of accommodation emphasizes the communal aspect of decision-making and development – the balancing of needs and interests of individuals. Freedom and equality cannot come at the expense of one another. If every person pursed their ultimate idea of individuality, no one would achieve it. "Overtly, one must accommodate rather than dominate in order to make room for others to act, since physical space is limited."[15] As noted by the late Chief Justice Dickson, the realization of collective goals is of fundamental importance.

Individual accountability and accommodation will not come on their own, but they can be encouraged and emphasized. "Openness to change, the willingness to change preferences, to expand interests, is allied to the desire to work things out together, to cooperate, to adapt." As stated by the Law Commission of Canada, "the law should facilitate and nurture respectful human interactions."[16] Laws should encourage fair practices in the marketplace, the workplace, the neighborhood and the household to promote a just regime of governance by law.

The growth in the discourse on sustainable development is an important and essential contribution to international law and the international community. The recognition that environmental protection, economic development and societal needs must be approached in an integrated manner is essential to ensuring a secure and healthy future for all of the world's population. This discourse must now move beyond the integration of policies, and look to its implementation and governance.

Behind every policy, every law, and every new development, is a human factor. It is this human factor that is essential to ensuring that sustainable development achieves all it is hoped to achieve. The community mentality – or fraternity – of the citizen population will impact the effectiveness of such policies.[17] Education and knowledge are powerful tools that will enable individuals to better understand the need for greater collaboration and the true impacts of their actions, whether they are one person or a multinational corporation. We have to change from within to have sustainable change – change forced on one

---

[15] Ziniewicz, *supra* note 9.

[16] Law Commission of Canada, *1997 Annual Report – Living Law,* (Minister of Public Works and Government Services Canada: Ottawa, 1997).

[17] *Ibid.*

will not withstand time or pressure; "[t]he point is to assist in converting preference into intelligent preference."[18]

Without the engagement of citizens in the adoption and recommendation of laws, the laws adopted by elected officials will have little practical impact on how things are done.[19] Fraternity and its expression through accommodation are central to ensuring that sustainable development lives up to its promise of ensuring a safe and healthy society for future generations.

---

[18] Ziniwiecki, *supra* note 9 at para. 29.
[19] Law Commission of Canada, *supra* note 15.

4

THE DOCTRINE OF SUSTAINABLE DEVELOPMENT - A DISCUSSION

Hon. Mr. Justice U. C. Banerjee, Judge of the Supreme Court of India[1]

In the Indian sub-continent, jurisprudence and political theories have long recognized the doctrine of sustainable development. These discussions trace back to 'Kautilya's Arthoshastra' in 300 B.C. – where there is mention of preservation of land and its surrounding nature.[2] Indeed, earlier in this volume, Judge Christopher G. Weeramantry, former Vice-President of the International Court of Justice, and a great exponent of the Doctrine of Sustainable Development, has observed that in Sri Lanka centuries ago, the concept of sustainable development had a full play. The concept is ancient, and based on wisdom that deserves constant rediscovery and recognition.

Presently, the doctrine of sustainable development is no longer in the realm of a mere idea to be shaped and focused differently in different circumstances. It stands as an established objective of law and policy, to be placed at par even with the very concepts of democracy, human rights and sovereign equality of states, as noted recently by Vaughan Lowe.[3]

The doctrine of sustainable development, though initially launched internationally in the 1992 *Rio Declaration*,[4] has found its recognition both in major international legal instruments, and in a growing number of judicial decisions since the early nineties.

In *Nuclear Tests Case*,[5] the International Court of Justice rather categorically explained that their order was without prejudice to the obligation of states to respect and protect the natural environment. The Court stated that the

---

[1] Hon. Mr. Justice U.C. Banerjee, Judge, Supreme Court of India, Founder President of NALSAR University of Law, Head of the Indian High-Level Committee to probe into the Godhra incident.
[2] Kautilya, *Arthashastra,* translated by R. Shamasastry (Bangalore: Government Press, 1915) at 1-50.
[3] V. Lowe, "Sustainable Development and Unsustainable Arguments" in A. Boyle and D. Freestone, eds., *International Law and Sustainable Development: Past Achievements and Future Challenges* (Oxford: Oxford University Press, 1999).
[4] *Rio Declaration on Environment and Development and Agenda 21, Report of the United Nations Conference on Environment and Development,* U.N. Doc. A/CONF.151/6/Rev.1, (1992), 31 I.L.M. 874 (1992).
[5] *Case Concerning Nuclear Test*s (New Zealand and Australia / France) [1974] I.C.J. Rep. 457.

M.C. Cordonier Segger & C. G. Weeramantry, eds., Sustainable Justice: Reconciling Economic, Social & Environmental Law
© *2005 Koninklijke Brill NV, Printed in The Netherlands, pp.47-56.*

environment represents the quality of life and health of human beings, and this includes unborn persons as well. Similar is the situation in its judgment concerning Gabcikovo Nagymaros project between Hungary and Slovakia, which was also categorical in the finding that the concept of sustainable development unites both the right to development with the duty to protect the environment.[6] The Separate Opinion, voiced by Judge Weeramantry in that case, is particularly relevant:

> "Had the possibility of environmental harm been the only consideration to be taken into account in this regard, the contentions of Hungary could well have proved conclusive. Yet there are other factors to be taken into account – not the least important of which is the developmental aspect, for the Gabcikovo scheme is important to Slovakia from the point of view of development. The Court must hold the balance even between the environmental considerations and the developmental considerations raised by the respective Parties. The principle that enables the Court to do so is the principle of sustainable development. The Court has referred to it as a concept in paragraph 140 of its Judgement. However, I consider it to be more than a mere concept, but as a principle with normative value which is crucial to the determination of this case. Without the benefits of its insights, the issues involved in this case would have been difficult to resolve. Since sustainable development is a principle fundamental to the determination of the competing considerations in this case, and since, although it has attracted attention only recently in the literature of international law, it is likely to play a major role in determining important environmental disputes of the future, it calls for consideration in some detail. Moreover, this is the first occasion on which it has received attention in the jurisprudence of this Court."

Reference can also be made to a decision by the WTO Appellate Body in the notable *US – Shrimp Case*, between United States and India, Malaysia, Pakistan and Thailand.[7] The Appellate Body expressed its concern for the maintenance of natural resources and for protection of environment. The acceptance of an exception to the GATT under Article XX may not have been granted concurrence by the present author, but the opinion offered a specific recognition of the concept of sustainable development in international treaty law related to trade.

---

[6] *Case Concerning the Gabčíkovo-Nagymaros Project* (Hungary / Slovakia), [1997] I.C.J. Rep. 7.
[7] *United States - Import Prohibition of Certain Shrimp and Shrimp Products* (20 September 1999) WT/DS58/AB/R (Appellate Body Report), WT/DS58/R (Panel Report). See also *United States - Import Prohibition of Certain Shrimp and Shrimp Products: Recourse to Article 21.5 of the DSU by Malaysia* (21 November 2001) WT/DS58/AB/RW (Appellate Body Report), WT/DS58/RW (Panel Report).

The *Brundtland Commission* has asserted that only economic growth can eliminate poverty.[8] The 1992 UNCED[9] and the 2002 WSSD[10] have clearly emphasised that economic growth cannot be based on over exploitation of natural resources, but must be managed in such a way so as to enhance the resource base. These statements reflect a sound global consensus. Thus economic growth is the requirement of the day, and the need of the hour, in order to achieve sustainability, through sustainable development.

It is note worthy, however, that in the pre-UNCED period, there was no call as such for an international participation in the sustainable development. The principal concern of most countries was development. Environment was restricted to certain groups and forums. It was only through the 1992 *Rio Conference*, that environmental protection was extended and united with development concerns. Agenda 21 has been the foremost one in such an international participation and this Agenda stands composed of four sections, namely:
(i)   Social and Economic Dimensions;
(ii) Conservation and Management of Resources;
(iii) Strengthening the Roles of Major Groups;
(iv) Means of Implementation.[11]

The challenges of environment and social and economic development are daunting. The real work to integrate environment and development still lies ahead. The survival of mankind rests on the implementation of the concept of sustainable development. The agreements at the 1992 United Nations Conference on the Environment and Development mark the beginning of an international political will to take the necessary steps to protect the earth. The plans of 193 countries at the 2002 World Summit on Sustainable Development mark a strong reaffirmation of global commitment to implement sustainable development at all levels.

In the area of international law, there is a pressing need for humanity to supplement the framework Conventions adopted at Rio with the adoption of specialized and effective protocols. Several examples are particularly relevant here. At the first meeting of the Parties to the United Nations Convention on

---

[8] World Commission on Environment and Development, *Our Common Future* (Oxford: Oxford University Press, 1987) [*Brundtland Report*].
[9] *Rio Declaration on Environment and Development, supra* note 4. And see *Agenda 21*, in *Report of the United Nations Conference on Environment and Development* U.N. Doc. A/CONF.151/6/Rev.1, (1992), 31 I.L.M. 874 (1992). See also the *Programme for the Further Implementation of Agenda 21* GA Res. A/RES/S-19/2, UN GAOR, 19th Sess., UN Doc. A/Res/S-19/2 (1997).
[10] *Johannesburg Declaration on Sustainable Development*, in Report of the World Summit on Sustainable Development, Johannesburg, South Africa, August 26 to Sept 4, 2002, A/CONF.199/20 (New York, United Nations, 2002). And see the *Johannesburg Plan of Implementation*, in Report of the World Summit on Sustainable Development, Johannesburg (South Africa) (4 Sept. 2002) UN Doc. A/CONF.199/20. Available online: <http://www.un.org/esa/sustdev/documents/WSSD_POI_PD/English/POIToc.htm>. See also the United Nations General Assembly *Millennium Declaration* G.A. Res. 55/9, UN GAOR, 2000.
[11] *Agenda 21*, Report of the UNCED (1992) UN Doc. A/CONF.151/ 26/Rev.1, (1992) 31 I.L.M. 874.

Biological Diversity[12] held in December 1994 at Nassau, Bahamas, India demanded immediate and adequate safeguards against hasty experimentation and use of Genetically Modified Organisms (GMOs), as these could have unimaginable repercussions. The indiscriminate and unregulated use of GMOs poses a threat to the mankind which can only be checked through a legally binding agreement. It is, therefore, necessary to adopt clear comprehensive and legally binding international protocol on bio-safety under the convention on bio-diversity. Similarly, the *United Nations Framework Convention on Climate Change*[13] does not contain specific targets and timetable for the reduction of greenhouse emissions. In view of the horrifying threat of the extinction of mankind as a result of global climatic change, flooding and drought, the Climate Change Convention needs to be supplemented by an adequate and internationally effective protocol containing specific targets to be followed by the States. This would equip the Convention with necessary authorities to implement the concept of sustainable development.

The Indian Supreme Court has been for quite some time, addressed with the issue of environment rather candidly, offering specific directions in order to avoid major bio-diversity crisis. These efforts, starting from the decision of the *State of H.P. vs. Ganesh Wood Products* [14]continue to this date. From the year 1995, in over 20 different decisions, the Supreme Court of India has propagated the doctrine of sustainability. In particular, one judgment of the author, when a Judge of the High Court at Calcutta in India, stated:

> "While it is true that in a developing country there shall have to be developments, but that development shall have to be in closest possible harmony with the environment, as otherwise there would be development but no environment, which would result in total devastation, though however, may not be felt in presenti but at some future point of time, but then it would be too late in the day, however, to control and improve the environment."

> "Nature will not tolerate us after a certain degree of its destruction and it will, in any event, have its toll on the lives of the people. Can the present-day society afford to have such a state and allow the nature to have its toll in future – the answer shall have to be in the negative. The present-day society has a responsibility towards the posterity for their proper growth and development so as to allow the posterity to breathe normally and live in a cleaner environment and have a consequent fuller development."

---

[12] *United Nations Convention on Biological Diversity*, 5 June 1991, 31 I.L.M. 818 (entered into force 29 December 1993).
[13] *United Nations Framework Convention on Climate Change*, 9 May 1992, 31 I.L.M. 849.
[14] *State of H.P.* v. *Ganesh Wood Products* 1995 (6) SCC 363.

"Time has now come therefore to check and control the degradation of the environment and since the Law Courts also have a duty towards the society for its proper growth and further development, it is a plain exercise of the judicial power to see that there is no such degradation of the society and there ought not to be any hesitation in regard thereto. Global maturity in recent years in regard to this concept is now a practical reality and not in the realm of consideration or mere ideas – but what does that expression 'ecology' mean and imply: 'Ecology' in common parlance means the study of home or the household of nature to be kept in order. George I, Clarke in his 'Elements of Ecology' has stated that every living thing is surrounded by materials and forces which constitute its environment and from which it must derive its needs and contact with the environment is inescapable." [15]

As noted by this author in that judgement, there is strong judicial support for the concept of development in India. However, certain schools of thought, however, consider that industrial expansion ought not to be deterred on the concept of ecology. Ecology, it is argued, is simply a price which has to be paid for industrial development in a developing country. Indeed, these schools of thought firmly believe that ecological imbalance is a cost that one should be prepared to pay and not a problem at all. The issue that arises if such a line of thinking is followed through to its logical conclusion, however, is more complex. On the wake of 21st century, when there is a global awareness in regard to maintenance of ecological balance, should the Law Courts be justified in keeping their eyes shut in regard to this concept of ecological imbalance, once the question has been raised before them?

Ecological imbalance is undoubtedly a serious social problem. In this context, the observations made by the Indian court in *Calcutta Youth Front* v. *State of West Bengal* are also rather apposite. In that decision, the Court held:

"An ecological problem, in contrast, is a special type of social problem. To speak of a phenomenon as a 'social problem' is not to suggest merely, or perhaps at all, that we do not understand how it comes about; it is labelled a problem not because, like a scientific problem, it presents an obstacle to our understanding of the world but rather because – consider alcoholism, crime, deaths on the road – we believe that our society would be better of without it." [16]

---

[15] *People United for Better Living in Calcutta-Public and another* v. *State of West Bengal and others* (1993) A.I.R. Calcutta 215.
[16] *Calcutta Youth Front* v. *State of West Bengal* (1986) 2 C.L.J. 26.

There is no manner of doubt that this issue of environmental degradation cannot but be termed to be a social problem and considering the growing awareness and considering the impact of this problem on the society in regard thereto, in the view of this author, the Law Courts should also rise up to the occasion to deal with the situation as it demands in the present day context: Law Courts have a social duty since it is a part of the society and as such, must always function having due regard to the present day problems which the society faces. It is now a well-settled principle of law that socio-economic condition of the country cannot be ignored by a court of law. It is now a well-settled principle of law that while dealing with the matter, the social problems shall have to be dealt with in the way and in the manner it calls for, since benefit to the society ought to be the prime consideration of the Law Courts and ecological imbalance being a social problem ought to be decided by a Court of law so that the society may thrive and prosper without any affection.

Subsequently, the present author had the occasion to consider these concerns again in a similar situation where great efforts were necessary to avoid a biodiversity crisis, whilst on the Bench of Supreme Court of India in *MC Mehta* v. *Union of India*, and stated:

> "Before, however, proceeding with the matter further, a brief backgrounder seems to be rather indispensable having regard to the concept of sustainable development for the capital city. Needless to say while the *Brundtland Report* called out for adaptation globally of a strategy of sustainable development defining it as development that meets the need of the present without compromising the ability of future generations to meet their own needs, the initial linkage between the natural and man made environment and the critical relevance of both environment and development is generally attributed to the *Stockholm Declaration* of 1972 which stands restated and reaffirmed by the UN General Assembly in December, 1986 specifying therein sustained and rapid development for developing nations."[17] (citations omitted).

The *Calcutta Wetland Judgment* was pronounced on the apprehended danger of a severe biodiversity crisis and in the view of this author, as the Law Courts exist for the society and the rule of law is meant to benefit the society, was taken in full discharge of that social duty and obligation and as a guardian-angel of the society. This is a duty cast on to the Law Courts to protect the society from environmental devastation. However, does this duty imply immediate and perpetual stoppage of development activities? The answer cannot but be in the negative. In 21ˢᵗ century, the response of the Courts ought to be assertive

---

[17] *MC Mehta* v *Union of India* (1999) I.C.H.R.L. 58 (29 April 1999). See also *MC Mehta* v *Union of India* (1988) A.I.R. SC 1115 45l (Municipalities Case) and see *MC Mehta* v *Union of India* (1991) A.I.R. SC 382 46 (Environmental Education Case).

though not at the cost of environment – there shall have to be a balance proper between environment and development so that both can co-exist without affecting the other. Inter and intra governmental actions ought to proceed in accordance therewith and not de hors the same. As such, it is unlikely that instead of Courts, some kind of alternative dispute resolution system could provide a better relief to the seeker of environmental protection, human rights or economic development.

The views of this author as regards environmentally sustainable development have been amply stated in two judgments, as noted above. However, the Law Courts of a country cannot formulate an international policy, and this is the place where this concept of sustainable development must gain its stronger and deeper foundations in order to build the necessary global consensus. Sustainable development is not a fixed state of harmony but rather the process of change in which the exploitation of resources, the direction of investment, the orientation of technological development and institutional change are made consistent with future as well as present needs. Several further observations are particularly pertinent in this regards.

Above all, the promotion of the rule of law is the ultimate objective in a sound development process, as this ensures that a civic culture is properly established, through legitimate, acceptance of the enforcement procedures established by a rule of law.[18] In addition, sustainable involves and requires reorientation of the entire perspective of governance not only in its internal affairs but also in the international sphere. Both rich and poor nations exist. Reorientation is necessary to reduce the gap between the rich and the poor, in order to ensure full participation of all countries – large, small, rich and poor, in socio-economic development, and in environmental protection. Such participation is one of the fundamental requirements for achievement of the objective of sustainable development in the matter of population, food, security, loss of species and genetic resources, energy, industry and human settlements. The solutions to challenges in all these areas are found in one goal, sustainable development, and cannot thus be treated in isolation from one another.

Attention is required, however, to be focused on specific priorities. This author proposes, in particular, two pressing concerns.

First, there is a need to address the growing population, particularly in developing countries, and second, there is a priority need to fully realize human rights. Conceptually, population and development are inter-linked – since development is dependent on the population, though the latter cannot be said

---

[18] James C.N. Paul, "The United Nations and the Creation of an International Law of Development" Symposium: The United Nations - Challenges of Law and Development (1995) 36 *Harvard International Law Journal* 307.

to be dependent on the former. In many countries, the population is growing at rates which make reasonable exploitations of improvements in using health, care, food, security or energy supplies, almost impossible. Sustainable development requires the promotion of values that encourage consumption standards that are within the bound of ecological possibility. Sustainable development requires that societies meet human needs, both by increasing productive potential and by ensuring equitable opportunities for all. Meeting these needs should, however, take into account not only the present but future (inter-generational) needs as well. There are thus, to reach a proper and effective sustainable development, two complementary dimensions of the problem. It is necessary to have the education to manage the resources, and also the control to do so. Population explosion acts as a deterrent to the theory of sustainable development. To meet the pressing needs of the population, food and shelter, energy and prospect must be made available. It is the efficient management of these four elements that can, apart from other factors, bring about a state of sustainable development. Education is a requirement so as to ensure that the harmful effects of uncontrolled growth of population are understood by the people at large.

Second, sustainable development must be people oriented. It must promote human dignity and welfare in order to provide for the basic needs of the people as regards shelter, food, health, education and financial capability for sustenance. As such, human rights become the second highest priority, an area where proper and effective remedy ought to accrue so as to attain fuller and more sustainable development. A *Universal Declaration of Human Rights* has taken concrete shape: it stands accepted and adopted throughout the globe.[19] However, the cry for protection continues, irrespective of the ratification and acceptance of major international instruments. A significant need still exists, to recognize human rights in such a way so as to have it enforced in a manner proper and befitting. Development must also work to eliminate all forms of discrimination against women, both as regards employment, education, services and other entitlements. Empowerment of women shall have to be considered in a method and manner conducive to the 21st century situations.

Third, economic policies of individual countries and international economic relations both have great relevance to sustainable development. The reactivation and acceleration of development requires a dynamic and a supportive international economic environment and determined policies at the national level. It will be frustrated in the absence of either of these requirements. A supportive external economic environment is crucial. The development process will not gather momentum if the global economy lacks dynamism and stability and is beset with uncertainties. Neither will it gather momentum if the developing countries are weighted down by external

---

[19] *Universal Declaration of Human Rights* (10 December 1948) G.A. Res. 217A, U.N. GAOR, 3d Sess., U.N. Doc. A/810 (1948).

indebtedness, if development finance is inadequate, if barriers restrict access to markets and if commodity prices and the terms of trade of developing countries remain depressed. The record of the 1980s was essentially negative on each of these counts; these trends need to be reversed. The policies and measures needed to create an international environment that is strongly supportive of national development efforts are thus vital. International cooperation in this area should be designed to complement and support, rather than denouncing, domestic economic policies, in both developed and developing countries, if global progress towards sustainable development is to be achieved.

Thinking toward the future, this author proposes that attention must be focused on four different aspects. First, there is a need for the world to take responsibility for all of its members in the area of sustainable development, through implementation of what can be called the 'one global village' theory. Second, there is great promise offered through the development and introduction of model laws, similar to those promoted by the UNCITRAL. Amongst others, such laws are needed to address pressing concerns related to the preservation of the environment, respect for human rights, implementation of efficient, sustainable economic development laws, and effective fiscal laws. Third, there is a need to adapt the current laws to the exigencies and implications of sustainable development. And fourth, there is a need to introduce local municipal law in line with the model laws and treaties, so that implementation of the model law can be effected and it is possible to settle disputes.

5

ENFORCING SOCIO-ECONOMIC RIGHTS

Hon. Mr. Justice Albie Sachs[1]

One of the most important aspects of the social 'pillar' of sustainable development is the ability of the state to respect and fulfill social and economic human rights. The justiciability of socio-economic rights is extremely significant in this regard, and the South African Constitutional Court has become one of the world's leading judicial decision-making bodies in this area, contributing to the global development of precedence on this issue. One of the most notable features of the *South African Bill of Rights* is the inclusion of socio-economic rights. The sections containing these rights are worth reviewing, and are cited below. This is followed by a brief commentary on these issues, which provides a glimpse of the vision behind the direction taken by South Africa on this issue and how the Constitutional Court has dealt with the judicial enforcement of socio-economic rights and the complexities of this challenge. Finally, a concluding note of analysis is provided.

The South African Bill of Rights

Section 25 -Property
(5) The state must take reasonable legislative and other measures, within its available resources, to foster conditions, which enable citizens to gain access to land on an equitable basis.

---

[1] Hon. Mr. Justice Albie Sachs, B.A., LL.B. (Cape Town), Ph.D. (Sussex), Justice, Constitutional Court of South Africa, Professor Extraordinary, University of the Western Cape, Honorary Professor, University of Cape Town Law Faculty, Member, Constitutional Committee & National Executive, ANC. Formerly, Director of Research, South African Ministry of Justice, Director, South Africa Constitution Studies Centre (University of London),Professor of Law, Eduardo Mondlane University (Maputo, Mozambique), Nuffield Fellow of Socio-Legal Studies, Bedford College, London & Wolfson College, Cambridge, author of numerous books and articles, including Soft Vengeance of a Freedom Fighter (San Francisco: U. Cal. Press, 2000). A recent new edition of his book has just been released which includes a foreword by Archbishop Desmond Tutu and a new epilogue by Justice Sachs, and a film is being made of his life. This paper, which was the basis of a speech by Hon. Justice Albie Sachs given at the 'Sustainable Justice 2002' Conference in Montreal in 2002, shares its thoughts with a speech entitled "Social and Economic Rights: Can they be Made Justiciable?", which has appeared as an article in the SMU Law Review, a Publication of the Southern Methodist University School of Law, Vol. 53, Nu. 4, Fall 2000, SMU. Gratitude is expressed to Chris Pettit of the Weeramantry International Centre for Peace Education and Research (WICPER) in Sri Lanka, for his excellent research assistance in the preparation of this article.

M. C. Cordonier Segger & C. G. Weeramantry, eds., Sustainable Justice: Reconciling Economic, Social & Environmental Law © *2005 Koninklijke Brill NV, Printed in The Netherlands, pp.57-72.*

Section 26-Housing

1. Everyone has the right to have access to adequate housing.
2. The state must take reasonable legislative and other measures, within its available resources,
to achieve the progressive realisation of this right.
3. No one may be evicted from their home, or have their home demolished, without an order of court made after considering all the relevant circumstances. No legislation may permit arbitrary evictions.

Section 27 -Healthcare, food water and social security

(1) Everyone has the right to have access to:
(a) healthcare services, including reproductive healthcare;
(b) sufficient food and water and
(c) social security, including, if they are unable to support themselves and their dependants, appropriate social assistance. .
(2) The state must take reasonable legislative and other measures, within its available resources,
to achieve the progressive realisation of each of these rights.
(3) No one may be refused emergency medical treatment.

Section 28 -Children

(1) Every child has the right
(a) to family care or parental care, or to appropriate alternative care when removed from the family environment;
(b) to basic nutrition, shelter, basic healthcare services and social services.

Section 29 -Education

(1) Everyone has the right
(a) to a basic education, including adult basic education and
(b) to further education, which the state through reasonable measures, must make progressively available and accessible.
(2) Everyone has the right to receive education in the official language or languages of their choice in public educational institutions where that education is reasonably practicable. In order to ensure the effective access to, and implementation of, this right, the state must consider all reasonable educational alternatives, including single medium institutions, taking into account-
(a) equity; .
(b) practicability; and
(c) the need to redress the results of past racially discriminatory laws and practices.

The inclusion of these socio-economic rights in the South African Constitution was unsurprising. As the Constitutional Court stressed in its judgment in the *Soobramoney* case: "We live in a society in which there are great disparities of wealth. Millions of people are living in deplorable conditions and in great poverty. There is a high level of unemployment, inadequate social security, and many do not have access to clean water or to adequate health services. These conditions already existed when the *Constitution* was adopted and a commitment to address them, and to transform our society into one in which there will be human dignity, freedom and equality, lies at the heart of our new constitutional order. For as long as these conditions continue to exist that aspiration will have a hollow ring."[2]

The inclusion of socio-economic rights thus sought to contribute to addressing one of the greatest challenges facing the South African people and their government; the massive legacy of poverty and inequality.

However, the judicial enforcement of socio-economic rights is often said to raise a number of difficult and complex issues. These include the separation of powers; the legitimacy of unelected courts determining policy and expenditure; the problems of institutional capacity, process and evidence; and also the reconceptualisation that is required regarding the nature of rights that expand over time and are expressly made dependent on resources.

The Constitutional Court has dealt with these issues in four different judgments. The first involved objections taken by some parties to the inclusion of socio economic rights in the Constitution.[3] The second related to a case brought by Mr. Soobramoney, a man suffering from renal failure who sought access to dialysis on the grounds of his right to health.[4] The third was brought by Ms Grootboom and the people of her community and concerned shack-dwellers living in appalling conditions and their right to housing.[5] The final case concerned the government's policy to reduce the risk of mother-to child transmission of HIV, in particular restrictions placed on the use of an anti-retroviral drug called Nevirapine, and was brought by the Treatment Action Campaign, a civil society organisation.[6]

Enforcing Socio-Economic Rights in South Africa

The recent and current generations of lawyers in South Africa have fought long and hard for social and economic rights to have the status of enforceable constitutional rights. In 2000, the Constitutional Court heard a case known by the title of the main Plaintiff, Mrs. Grootboom, in which the Court was called upon to determine exactly how it can actually enforce social and economic rights, if at all.[7]

---

[2] *Soobramoney v Minister of Health, Kwa-Zulu-Natal* 1997(12) BCLR 1696(CC) Para. 8 at 5.
[3] *Certification Of the Constitutiotn of South Africa 1986* (1996) (4) SALR 744 (CC) at Para.s 76-78.
[4] *Soobramoney v Minister of Health, Kwa-Zulu-Natal* 1997(12) BCLR 1696(CC).
[5] *Government of the Republic of South Africa & Others v Grootboom & Others* 2000(11) BCLR 1169 (CC).
[6] *Minister of Health & Others v Treatment Action Campaign & Others* (1) 2002 (10) BCLR 1033 (CC).
[7] *Government of the Republic of South Africa & Others v Grootboom & Others* 2000(11) BCLR 1169 (CC).

It is widely agreed throughout the world that shelter, education, nutrition, clean water, and basic health services should be universally available. One of the responsibilities of government, whatever its nature and whatever the society, is to ensure at least the minimum decencies of life for all its citizens. It is controversial, however, whether claims to such decencies should be regarded as enforceable fundamental rights in the constitutional order, in a way similar to the classic freedom or liberty rights and the great civil rights of the citizen: to vote; to speak freely; to be elected; to participate in government; to enjoy a measure of privacy from state intrusion; to have certain rights in relation to property; and generally to be a free person in a free society. The issue has provoked profound debate in many countries, and has been thoroughly explored in South Africa as well.

In the middle 1980's a group of black students at the Law Faculty at the University of Natal in Durban set up a body called the *Anti-Bill of Rights* Committee. There are many oppressors who deny fundamental rights, but why should black students who belong to an oppressed community anticipating a new constitutional order associated with liberation, set up an Anti-Bill of Rights Committee? Some of the expatriates in exile at the time were shocked when they heard of the initiative, but nevertheless understood the students' motivation.

What these students anticipated was a *"Bill of Rights"* that would be, in actuality, a document established in advance by a privileged white minority to ensure that when eventually one-person, one-vote majority rule came to South Africa, and everyone was at last able enjoy the ordinary rights of citizenship, the *"Bill of Rights"* would be in place to block any moves toward major transformation. In effect, it would defend the *status quo*, guarantee property rights, and impose extreme limits on the capacity of the democratic state to take decisive action to achieve meaningful redistribution of wealth. Recall the situation in South Africa at that time; almost 90 percent of the surface area of South Africa was reserved by law for whites only, including all the central business districts and all the beautiful tree-lined suburbs. South Africans were not dealing simply with the kind of inequalities between rich and poor that are found in most societies. Rather, they were confronted with state-enforced separation which ensured the extensive accumulation of resources and power by a racially defined minority. And there was corresponding state-enforced dispossession of the majority, which led to the marginalization of their languages, the loss of their land, and a global reduction of their dignity and status. In that context, a *Bill of Rights* was seen as a *"Bill for Whites."* It would not defend the fundamental rights and freedoms of everybody, but rather, serve as an instrument enacted in advance to ensure that those who *had* would continue to have forever, and those who *had not* would remain without forever.

An immediate need developed for the writing of an article espousing the need for an "Anti-Anti-Bill of Rights Committee." This was done partly for diplomatic reasons, asking what kind of freedom struggle takes up an anti-bill of rights position? A true *Bill of Rights* was vital in the framework of the ultimate answer to apartheid. Apartheid said that black and white could not live together as equals in one country, that they had to have separate institutions, separate rights, arid live in separate areas. The reply was that minorities and majorities could live together as equals provided everyone was constitutionally protected against abuse, irrespective of their language, color, religion, origin, background, or ethnicity. A *Bill of Rights* would thus play an important political role in South Africa, countering any new project to refine and modernize apartheid or any other kind of discrimination or oppression. It was also needed because many liberation movements in different parts of the world had acceded to power and then gone on to abuse the rights of the very people on whose behalf they had fought.

There was another reason as well. South Africa required a clear constitutional framework within which transformation could take place. There was a need for deep change in South Africa; the nation could not just carry on with a small minority enjoying all the good things of life while the overwhelming majority continued to suffer deprivation, malnutrition and indignity. Such a country would not last: it was fundamentally unsustainable. A house so divided against itself just could not stand.

It would be a challenge to ensure that the process of change itself would be fairly conducted according to agreed upon principles that benefited all of society, rather than according to the whim of whoever happened to be in power at any particular time. One important way to achieve this would be to locate transformation within a rights framework. The way to advance this vision involved making social and economic rights integral elements of a future *Bill of Rights.* In this way, the least amongst South Africans (who happened to be the majority under Apartheid) would be regarded as important people. They would be recognized as citizens worthy of being respected and capable of enjoying dignity in the land of their birth.

In the debate and writings that followed, the concept of the "three generations" of rights was introduced to South Africans. The first generation encompasses the classic freedom rights, which emerged from the American and the French Revolutions: the rights of the citizen and the free person. This notion is fundamental to the South African Constitution. People refer sometimes to the "firstness" of the First Amendment, which provides for freedom of speech and freedom of religion. It does not deal with education, with housing, with health. It establishes a particular vantage point or conceptual platform from which to view all the other rights. Social and economic rights are not included.

The second generation of rights emerged in Germany under Bismarck in late 19th century. He established a scheme of welfare rights for German workers. Later reinforced by the impact of the Russian Revolution, these rights came to be central to national policy in the so-called welfare states of the 20th century. The recognition of rights to education, to health, to housing, and to the other minimum decencies of life drew strong support after the Second World War in the form of the Universal Declaration of Human Rights. Such rights, were ultimately entrenched in the International Convention on Economic, Social and Cultural Right*s*, and although this document has not been ratified by all the states in the world, it is widely accepted as containing universally recognized principles of human rights.[8] The phrase "third generation of human rights" was coined by Karl Vasek, a Czech functionary in the United Nations whose object was principally to advance environmental rights, such as the right to a clean, healthy environment. He argued for solidarity rights, which belonged to the whole community, not just to individuals, including the right to development. Initially the recognition of all three generations of human rights was strongly advocated within South Africa.[9] That initiative has now come back to haunt the government and its people, for a number of reasons. The main reason is that government and judiciary are not simply pushing for what they believe should be accentuated in a new South African Constitution. They are interpreting the actual text of an explicit government document containing clear constitutional commitments. Certain critics contend that if one speaks about three generations of rights, one suggests that the second generation is less important than the first generation, and the third generation even less important.[10] Others argue that aspirational and unenforceable socio-economic rights dilute the *Bill of Rights* as a whole, and undermine the classic first generation rights.[11] However, at the International Conference on Human Rights in Vienna, a decade ago, it was accepted that social and economic rights are indivisible from and interdependent with civil and political rights.

Social and economic rights were written into the final text of the South African Constitution in extensive and explicit form. The great battle was not so much over whether social and economic rights should be incorporated, but over

---

[8] The ICESCR has been signed by 148 nations as of December of 2003. See UN Human Rights Commission, available online: <www.unhchr.ch/html/menu3/b/a_cescr.htm> Under international law (Law of Treaties 1898), once a nation-state signs an international treaty or convention, it then has the obligation to work progressively towards the ratification of that treaty or convention and has the immediate obligation of taking steps towards the realisation of the rights articulated within that treaty or convention. A nation-state also has the obligation to refrain from acts that would undermine the object and purpose of the treaty or covenant, both within its sovereign borders and on an international scale. The only way to legally avoid this obligation is to formally withdraw from a treaty or convention.

[9] See African Rights, available online: <http://www.chr.up.ac.za/ggp/coursematerial/goodgovernance/AFRICAN%20RIGHTS.doc>.

[10] See A. Eide & A. Rosas, "Economic, Social and Cultural Rights: A Universal Challenge" in E. Asbjorn, C. Krause and A. Rosas, eds., *Economic, Social and Cultural Rights* (The Hague: Kluwer Academic Publishers, 2001). See also M. Craven, *The International Covenant on Economic, Social and Cultural Rights: A Perspective on its Development* (Oxford: Oxford University Press, 1998).

[11] Ibid.

whether they should be incorporated as justiciable rights in the ordinary way, or as mere *directives* of state policy. When the Irish won independence from Britain and drafted their Constitution, a special approach was developed. They wished to have social and economic rights, but not as the kind of rights that one can go to court over, in order to get an injunction in ones favor in the ordinary way. So they placed them in the Constitution not as a justiciable part of a Bill of Rights, but as directives of state policy; as pragmatic indicators rather than enforceable rights. Thus, a grand preambular section elaborating the functions and the duties of government was included.[12]

India followed, producing a strong Constitution that has stood up to many social fissures and strains, one that has been creatively interpreted by an outstanding Supreme Court.[13] India has simple directives of state policy in its constitution expressing non-justiciable rights, but the Judges of the Supreme Court have used the directives of state policy as a means of interpreting the justiciable rights. Some critics have claimed that they smuggled socio-economic rights in through the back door, down the chimney or through the window.[14]

A very famous case concerning the eviction of pavement-dwellers in Bombay illustrates the recognition of these rights in India. The people facing eviction slept on the streets, sheltered at night under the little barrows from which they traded. The Indian Supreme Court found that the right to life does not just mean the right not to be killed. The concept does not imply only that the state cannot take ones life away without due process: it affirms the principle that one has a right to a livelihood, to some minimum decencies, of which one could not be deprived without due process. The Indian court thus used the directives of state policy as guiding texts for the interpretation of the fundamental right to life as set out in the section of justiciable rights.[15]

The people of South Africa went beyond this. The Constitution expressly included the right of access to adequate housing and access to health and other welfare rights in the text of the Bill of Rights. It was made clear, however, that these rights would not be enforceable in the same self-executing way as other rights. The provisions say that the state in under a duty to make these rights realizable through reasonable legislative and other measures, which must serve progressively to enhance access to these rights, bearing in mind the financial capacities of the state. It should be noted that the section on children's rights provides an unqualified realization of the rights within available resources.

The first major test of these rights came when Mr. Soobramoney approached the Constitutional Court. He was suffering from chronic renal failure,

---

[12] See Irish Constitution, available online: <http://www.oefre.unibe.ch/law/icl/ei00000_.html>
[13] See Indian Constitution, available online: < http://www.constitution.org/cons/india/const.html >
[14] Vijayashri Sripati, "Toward Fifty Years Of Constitutionalism And Fundamental Rights In India: Looking Back To See Ahead" (1950-2000) 14 *Am.U.Int'l.L.Rev.* 413.
[15] *Olga Tellis v. Bombay Municipal Corporation*, 1986 A.I.R. (S.C.) 180.

aggravated heard disease and blood sugar problems. When he collapsed due to his illness initially, he went to a state hospital and received life-saving treatment. But when he returned on a later occasion, he was told that the government can only give *emergency* case once and in cases of chronic patients like Mr. Soobramoney, individuals have to line up in a queue for access to equipment that is expensive to operate and requires a large staff. In practice, South African government resources only allow it to treat thirty percent of the patients who present themselves to the hospitals, and priority is given to those who could benefit in future from renal transplant, which unfortunately ruled Mr. Soobramoney out.

Mr. Soobramoney in his petition to the Court maintained that the Constitution stated that he had a right to life. He claimed that the Constitution dictated that no one shall be refused access to emergency medical treatment, and grants everyone a right of access to healthcare. He then insisted on his constitutional rights.

The case was a most painful matter for the Court to decide, as the court's decision could help prolong his life or else induce his early death. There was no precedent in South African law to help guide the Court's reasoning; the sole guide was the Constitution. The Court decided first that Soobramoney could not claim emergency medical treatment on an open-ended basis that would give him an unqualified right to indefinite medical assistance. The notion of a constitutionally protected, unqualified and immediately realizable right to emergency treatment applied to someone who collapsed with a sudden heart attack, or who was the victim of trauma. Such persons could not be turned away from casualty wards, certainly not from those in state hospitals. If all chronic illnesses were to be treated as emergency medical cases entitled to treatment on demand at state expense, then there would be no funds left over for mother and child care, nothing for health education or immunization, and desperately little for amelioration of AIDS-related illness, tuberculosis, or cancer. That could not have been what the Constitution required. In a concurring judgment, this author stated that being placed in a queue for access to scarce resources is not to find yourself being subject to a limitation of your right, but to be put in a position to enjoy ones right together with others. A society does not ration free speech or the vote, but does ration access to resources. So, provided that the queue is fairly established, and the criteria are rational and non-discriminatory, it was not up to the judges of the Court to say that Mr. Soobramoney should go the head of the queue. That would have involved arbitrarily substituting the distant and untrained judgment of the Court for that of the relevant qualified medical officers, on the spot. The situation was almost the inverse of the well-known case on the right to withdraw treatment here; it concerned the right to have treatment. Yet, the underlying principles were the same. This author quoted from one of US Justice Brennan's minority judgments, following the notion that these agonizing decisions should be taken not as a matter of abstract principle by the court, but by those most intimately involved with the situation, provided that the procedures and criteria they used met constitutional standards of fairness.

Two days later, Mr. Soobramoney died. The public was angry with the Court as the prevailing public opinion was that the Court should have done something, anything to save a life. It mattered not that to have upheld his claim as against others waiting for treatment could well have meant in practice that those with the most money could go to court to get help and leave the disadvantaged without treatment. What the Court insisted upon was that the criteria for selection for expensive treatment be fair and nondiscriminatory. Nevertheless, the NGOs and human rights lawyers, while reluctantly agreeing that the actual decision was inevitable, indicated that they wanted some kind of statement from the Court that would pressurize the state to fulfill social and economic rights, rather than to provide a formulation which would enable the state to avoid its responsibilities.

The *Grootboom* case went beyond the issues in the *Soobramoney* matter and confronted the Court with the question of the enforceability of social and economic rights in what photographers call 'full-frontal mode.' A community of about a thousand persons referred to in South Africa as "squatters," lived in shacks on a piece of water-logged land. More than half were children. They were just some of the millions of people in South Africa without secure tenure, all moving from one backyard or piece of land to another. One day, because of the intolerable conditions, they decided to move to a more hospitable area. It turned out, however, that this newly occupied land had been earmarked for a housing development scheme intended for other poor people like themselves. Thus, in a sense, they could be seen as 'jumping the queue.' They were then evicted from this land and settled on a nearby sports field, since there was nowhere else for them to go. They could not return to the land that they had previously occupied, because others now occupied it. Their case was supported by the Legal Resources Center, an organization initially established to challenge various aspects of apartheid through cases. It felt that this was an appropriate case to test what is meant by the social and economic rights in our Constitution.

The claim of Mrs. Grootboom and the others was based on two provisions of the Constitution. First, it was based on section 26 of the Constitution, which provides that everyone has the right of access to adequate housing, thereby imposing an obligation upon the State to take reasonable legislative and other measures to ensure the progressive realisation of this right within its available resources. Second, it was based on section 28(I)(c) of the Constitution, which provides that children have the right to shelter. The government contended that they had complied with the obligation imposed upon them by section 26 of the Constitution and placed evidence before the Court of the legislative and other measures they had adopted concerning housing.

The Court unanimously held that government had not met its obligations under section 26. In particular, the Court held that the State was obliged to take positive action to meet the needs of those living in extreme conditions of poverty, homelessness or intolerable housing. The Housing Act 107 of 1997 made no express provision to facilitate access to temporary relief for people who had no access to land, no roof over their heads, living in intolerable conditions and in crisis because of natural disasters. These people were in desperate need. The Court held that the absence of a component catering for those in desperate need may have been acceptable if the nationwide housing program would result in affordable houses for most people within a reasonably short time. This was, however, not the case, and housing authorities were unable to state when housing would become available to those in desperate need. The immediate crises was accordingly not being met and the consequent pressure on existing settlements resulted in land invasions by those in desperate need; thereby frustrating the attainment of the medium and long term objectives of the nationwide housing program.

As at the date of the launch of the application, the State had not been meeting the obligation imposed upon it by section 26 of the Constitution within the relevant area. In particular, the programs adopted by the State fell short of the requirements of section 26(2) in that no provision was made for relief to the categories of people in desperate need. The Constitution obliged the State to act positively to ameliorate these conditions. This obligation was to devise and implement a coherent, coordinated program designed to provide access to housing, healthcare, sufficient food and water and social security to those unable to support themselves and their dependants. The State also had to foster conditions to enable citizens to gain access to land on an equitable basis. Those in need had a corresponding right to demand that this be done. However, section 26 (and also section 28) did not entitle the respondents to claim shelter or housing immediately upon demand.

Therefore, the Court issued a declaratory order to substitute the High Court order stipulating that section 26(2) of the Constitution required the State to act to meet the obligation imposed upon it by the section to devise and implement a comprehensive and coordinated program to progressively realise the right of access to adequate housing. This included the obligation to devise, fund, implement and supervise measures to provide relief to those in desperate need within its available resources.

This case was the major test of the enforceability of socio-economic rights under the Constitution and whether the Court could compel the government to provide such rights to the citizenry. It was one thing in the 1980s to tell people fighting for liberation and transformation that a Bill of Rights need not only mean restriction on government's power to act, but could also mean that government has an obligation to right the wrongs of the past. When advocates argued in favor of constitutionalizing social and economic rights, and not simply to make them directives of state policy, it was said that these rights were indivisible from, and as important as, other fundamental rights. Now the Court had to give some kind of concrete meaning to these affirmations, otherwise people would ask what the point is of having social and economic rights in the Constitution at all. There is an oft quoted biblical verse that states something to the effect of, "the first shall be the last, and the last shall be the first." In a sense, South Africans were the last, but now the Constitutional Court was also the first to address such issues. The United States of America (US) was the first to constitutionalize and give judicial protection to fundamental rights of the classic kind that is mentioned here; the liberty rights. The US Supreme Court was also the one of the first to see equal protection as something that needed to be guaranteed by the US Constitution and enforced by the courts. It might be that in retrospect, the separate-but-equal doctrine was not one of the most brilliant features of US jurisprudence, but nevertheless the issues were debated, and eventually *Brown* v. *Board of Education* was decided.[16] The case is regarded by many as providing the greatest legal decision of the 20th century for its sweep, compassion, focus, and its insistence on the role of deep, principled morality at the heart of government. Yet, the discourse in the United States of America today concerning expansion of the concepts of rights so as to include social and economic rights, is extremely limited. The illumination that its judiciary could provide is lost, and not only to Americans, but to the rest of the world as well. In light of recent US government practices, one could say that there is a definite regression in even first generation rights, and second or third generation rights are virtually non-existent.

The South African Constitutional Court believes that 21st-century jurisprudence will focus increasingly on socio-economic rights. The 19th century could be described as the century during which the Executive established control over society; The 20th century as the century where Parliament gained control over the Executive, and the 21st century as the century where the Judiciary will establish principles and norms controlling both Parliament and the Executive. There is growing acceptance all over the world that certain core fundamental values of a universal character should penetrate and suffuse all governmental activity, including the furnishing of the basic conditions for a dignified life for all. It is pertinent to run through some of the problems facing all the governments and peoples of the world today. The first one involves the accountability of governments and the extent to which intervention by an unelected Court is appropriate. If courts decide that families must be given tents, housing, some other form of shelter or accommodation, or any sort of socio-economic rights, that will cost governments money. People

---

[16] See generally, *Brown* v. *Board Of Education* 347 US 483 (1954).

will be tempted to ask: "Who are the judges to require that? They are not accountable." These kinds of decisions are normally the prerogative of democratically-chosen bodies, either the local council, or the provincial or national government. Exactly which organ of government is responsible is a technical question, which depends on a particular Constitutional text and applicable legislation. In general, however, if these organs of state are not performing their duties properly, then the remedy is to refuse to reelect them. If the Court gives a bad judgment, however, judges are independent, and cannot necessarily be removed. Indeed, judges are not so directly accountable. It is difficult to determine whether this problem can be resolved in a formal, abstract, and categorical way. When it comes to matters of deep principle, the lack of accountability of the judiciary actually becomes a virtue. Judges are not running for office, and electoral popularity is of no concern to them in countries where the judiciary is not based on political appointments. In this case, the United States method of filling vacancies through political appointments suffers from major flaws. Judges are required to defend deep core values, which are part of world jurisprudence and part of the evolving constitutional traditions of our country. The lack of accountability of the judiciary in these circumstances actually becomes a "plus." The difficulty, however, is to distinguish between the special cases which deal with these deep values, and the ordinary issues of deciding how to allocate resources among many worthy claimants.

Second, the problem of institutional competence arises. What do courts know about housing, about land, about queues? What do judges in general know about the practicalities of low cost construction, of erecting one's own shelter, of subsidies and sewage? Judges know about fundamental rights, about constitutional law. The eleven judges of the South African Constitutional Court can actively handle legal concepts and ideas, yet have no special expertise on complex socio-economic matters which frequently have a strong technical dimension requiring experts on the spot to work out appropriate procedures and priorities. Recognition of the limited capacities of the judiciary in this area requires a corresponding judicial modesty. Judges cannot be philosopher kings and queens who tell government how to function. However, judges do have a voice "when situations of homelessness go to the core of a person's life and dignity." In this respect the Constitutional Court may be even better equipped than the experts, who are, and correctly so, animated by more bureaucratic and operational considerations. Indeed, the very nature of judicial decision-making is different from theirs. Decisions made by officials and legislatures have to build in compromise; there is nothing inherently wrong with that, compromise is good in public light. It is right that elected officials be directly responsive to the electorate, but judges cannot and should not be, especially when defending fundamental rights. Thus, the compromises bureaucrats appropriately effect, when reconciling different interests are different in nature from the balancing judges set out to achieve when harmonizing competing principles.

Third, there are considerations related to the separation of powers. If judges insist on money being provided for helping Mrs. Grootboom's community, this requires taking money away from other items in the budget. Is that not what parliament should control? Again, one cannot have a purely formal response. There are many cases in which ordinary decisions of the courts have budgetary implications. If for example, courts insist on legal aid for indigent defendants facing long prison sentences, this costs money. Similarly, courts deal with other cases involving allocation of funds, for instance in cases dealing with the rights of prisoners to vote. The independent electoral authority can claim that prisoners could vote in principle, since the legislature had not limited their right, but it could not set up registration centres and polling stations in the prisons, because it would cost too much money to do so. And South Africa's Constitutional Court has held that in fact the right to vote could not be negated merely by a combination of Parliamentary silence, bureaucratic difficulties, and administrative expense. The result becomes that the money is found, and a certain percentage of the prisoners are able to vote.

In the *Grootboom* case*,* however, the Constitutional Court did not just deal with the right to vote, which can be a one-off thing, it dealt with right of access to housing, which is endless. South Africa, like all other nations, has millions of homeless people. When do courts intervene, if at all, and force what could be massive redirection of funds on the Legislature and the Executive? Are social and economic rights just a pie in the sky? Or, are the provisions which set them out no more than beautiful words that in reality diminish the prestige of the Bill of Rights because they are unrealizable and promise something that cannot be achieved? The judges of the Constitutional Court do not take that pessimistic view. At the very least, the whole density, tonality, and sense of rightness of the Bill of Rights*,* is affected by the inclusion of these rights. Is the Constitution about welfare or is it concerned with freedom? It relates to both. Human beings do not want bread without freedom, nor do they want freedom without bread; they want bread and they want freedom. The Bill of Rights must be constructed around the interpretation of both these dimensions, so that each reinforces rather than undermines the other. As Amartya Sen has pointed out, conditions of freedom in poor countries prevent hunger from turning into famine, because there is public accountability for food distribution.[17] Similarly countries with a reasonable standard of living for all tend to be supportive of openness and pluralism.

Second, these rights serve as immediately defensible negative rights. The state is prohibited from taking away housing or destroying education facilities. There have to be programmes of progressive realization of the promised entitlements. Retrogression is constitutionally unacceptable. That principle is relatively easy

---

[17] A. Sen, *Development as Freedom* (New York: Knopf, 1999).

for courts to apply. One cannot just knock down a school or destroy a hospital. Societies and judiciaries are used to negative restraints on the state.

Third, these rights apply in the overall interpretation and development of the common law, for example, in deciding whether or not a contract violates public policy, as well as generally in the interpretation of statues. Thus, they suffuse and influence the whole judicial enterprise in all its manifestations, ensuring that the protection of human dignity is always at the center of what courts do.

Fourth, the South African Constitution gives the Constitutional Court the right to declare that the President or Parliament are in dereliction of a constitutional obligation. This implies that even if the judiciary does not compel the President to act in a particular way, or order Parliament to pass a particular law, it has the power to declare that they have failed to fulfill their constitutional responsibilities. Then, it is incumbent upon the political organs to act. It remains to be seen how this provision will be applied, but it has considerable potential for the future.

Fifth, there is enforcement through monitoring and reporting. The Constitution gives the Human Rights Commission the duty to monitor social and economic rights, and to report annually on its findings. This is common in international instruments of this kind. The monitoring involves both inspection and introspection, and again, it is left to political pressure to ensure compliance with recommendations.

The kinds of factors that might be influential in determining whether courts can grant relief that will impact on the budgets and decision-making of democratically-elected bodies are widespread and deserve to be addressed.

First, is the state directly implicated in the situation in which the applicants find themselves? If the state itself was directly involved in rendering people homeless, then it might be easier to demand that the state remedy the situation it has caused. If for example, the state's machinery is used to evict people and destroy their shacks, a case can be made for saying to the state; "Hold on. You cannot do this. Even if you are not intending to promote homelessness, your machinery is being used to diminish enjoyment of social and economic rights." One can think of other areas where the state might be implicated, for example, in the case of prisoners. If the state deprives an individual of liberty, it must feed them and shelter them. Similarly, people in state hospitals have certain rights to have their needs attended to.

The United Nations committee dealing with social and economic rights refers to a duty of the state to provide a "minimum core" of basic rights for all. Comment 3 of the International Covenant on Economic, Social and Cultural Rights (ICESCR) states: "a minimum core obligation to ensure the satisfaction of, at the very least, minimum essential levels of each of the rights are incumbent upon every State party". The Committee on ESCR reasons that "if the Covenant were to be read in such a way as not to establish such a minimum core obligation, it would be largely deprived of its raison d'être." In the words of the Committee on ESCR, where a State is failing to ensure basic necessities, "it must demonstrate that every effort has been made to use all resources that are at its disposition in an effort to satisfy, as a matter of priority, those minimum obligations. Even where the available resources are demonstrably inadequate, the obligation remains for a State party to strive to ensure the widest possible enjoyment of the relevant rights under the prevailing circumstances. The Committee has also emphasised that severe resource constraints cannot justify taking no measures for the weakest groups in society. "Even in times of severe resources constraints whether caused by a process of adjustment, of economic recession, or by other factors, the vulnerable members of society can and indeed must be protected by the adoption of relatively low-cost targeted programmes." This is far different from suggesting that a simple reference to lack of resources can excuse or justify violations of economic social and cultural rights.

Alternatively, there might be a special claim by certain groups that are particularly vulnerable. This approach appears in the classic *Carolene Products Case* - where the claimants are part of a discrete and insular minority who are politically powerless and need the protection of the court in order to secure their basic dignity and rights.[18] Next, it might be easier to justify intervention where the invasions of rights touch on race and gender, or where they affect an individual's right to life, or are so egregious as to precipitate desperation or extreme urgency. It might be that the consequences are so calamitous that any fair-minded person would say, "Give the people at risk at least some protection, even if it affects the budget. One cannot live in a society that allows human beings to be treated like that." Finally, one can develop procedural rights and rights to information in creative ways to advance the interests of deprived sections of the community.

One can introduce flexible remedies, as was done in *Brown* v. *Board Education*[19], and has been done in India. The judiciary has power to make just and equitable orders. If governments and peoples give maximum flexibility to the organs concerned in terms of how to comply with an order, it logically follows that comply they must. The potential is there for the system of governance of a state and its institutions to be able to guarantee all generations of rights for all individuals. The question now becomes how to live up to that potential.

---

[18] *United States* v. *Carolene Products Co.* 304 U.S. 144 (1938).
[19] *Brown* v. *Board Of Education* 347 US 483 (1954).

6

HUMAN RIGHTS IN THE CONTEXT OF SUSTAINABLE DEVELOPMENT

Hon. Mr. Justice N. J. McNally[1]

Human rights only began to be discussed seriously in political circles towards the end of World War Two. The United States, emerging from isolation, was convinced that its own success as a nation was due to democracy and free speech (defence of civil and political rights); the South and Central Americas were passionately in pursuit of social justice; the USSR doggedly defended the rights of the working classes to health, education and housing; and Lebanon played a surprising and decisive role in defining human rights. The result was the 1948 Universal Declaration of Human Rights. Although a huge political breakthrough, the Declaration was originally a non-binding document.[2]

Indeed, critics have asserted that it was no more than a declaration of intent by those states who have signed the document.[3] Many prefer to credit the International Covenant on Economic, Social and Cultural Rights (ICESCR)[4] and the International Covenant on Civil and Political Rights[5]

---

[1] Hon. Mr. Justice N. J. McNally, former Appellate Judge of the Supreme Court, Zimbabwe, and member of a joint mission to Malaysia for the International Bar Association (IBA), the Centre for the Independence of Judges and Lawyers of the International Commission of Jurists (CIJL), the Commonwealth Lawyers' Association (CLA) and the Union Internationale des Avocats (UIA). This chapter is based on his intervention a conference co-hosted by the Centre for International Sustainable Development Law (CISDL), the United Nations Environment Programme, the World Bank and the International Law Association, 2002 Sustainable Justice: Implementing International Sustainable Development Law, held in Montreal June 14 – 17, 2002. All errors or omissions are the responsibility of the editors.

[2] "In giving our approval to the declaration today, it is of primary importance that we keep clearly in mind the basic character of the document. It is not a treaty, it is not an international agreement. It does not purport to be a statement of law or of legal obligation. It is a declaration of basic principles of human rights and freedoms, to be stamped with the approval of the General Assembly by formal vote of its members, and to serve as a common standard of achievement for all peoples of all nations." Statement by Mrs. Franklin D. Roosevelt (Eleanor), Department of State Bulletin 751 (Dec 19, 1948).

[3] See generally J.Morsink, *The Universal Declaration of Human Rights: Origins, Drafting, and Intent* (Pennsylvania: University of Pennsylvania Press, 2000)

[4] *International Covenant on Economic, Social and Cultural Rights*, adopted and opened for signature, ratification and accession by General Assembly resolution 2200A (XXI) of 16 December 1966 *entry into force* 3 January 1976, in accordance with article 27, available online: <http://www.unhchr.ch/html/menu3/b/a_cescr.htm>.

[5] *International Covenant on Civil and Political Rights*, adopted and opened for signature, ratification and accession by General Assembly resolution 2200A (XXI) of 16 December 1966, *Entry into force:* 23 March 1976, in accordance with Article 49, available online: <http://www.unhchr.ch/html/menu3/b/a_ccpr.htm>.

M. C. Cordonier Segger & C. G. Weeramantry, eds., Sustainable Justice: Reconciling Economic, Social & Environmental Law © 2005 Koninklijke Brill NV, Printed in The Netherlands, pp.73-82.

(ICCPR) as the products of real progress. These Covenants became binding on States Parties in 1976 and were eventually ratified by Zimbabwe in May 1991.[6]

For the purposes of this chapter, it is crucial to understand why there were two covenants and not just one. From the beginning, there had been a dichotomy in people's appreciation of the meaning of the phrase "human rights."[7] The western world, led in this respect by the United States, was largely concerned with the rights of the individual and freedom of the individual.[8] The Soviet Union, and the few members of the Third World who had a voice in international affairs in 1948, were desperate to assert their collective independence from Western dominance.[9] At the same time they were concerned about their poverty relative to the West. Their interests lay in asserting their very basic rights – the right to life, in the sense of freedom from starvation; to decent housing; to a reasonable standard of health and education; and to employment.[10] These were the important rights. Democracy was also essential, but more elusive in this period.

Upon examination, a fundamental practical distinction is found between the two types of rights embodied in the Covenants. For convenience, in this chapter these will be referred to as "individual human rights" and "collective human rights". In many countries individual human rights can be defended and enforced by the courts. If one's right to vote is hindered, that person can obtain relief by way of a court order. If one's freedom of speech is curtailed wrongfully, the court will come to that individual's aid. In addition, the courts jealously guard a person's right to a fair trial. The list continues on through all

---

[6] Available online: <http://www.clea.org.uk/treaties/Iccpr.htm>.

[7] Human rights are universal, but must also be considered in their full legal and moral context. See P. Alston, *Human Rights in Context: Law, Politics, Morals* (Oxford: Clarendon Press, 1996).

[8] As the first chairman of the U.N. Human Rights Commission, Mrs. Roosevelt adroitly coaxed support for language that emphasized individual rights, while it also recognized social and economic rights. Article One paraphrases Jefferson's Declaration, sans Creator: "All human beings are born free and equal in dignity and rights. They are endowed with reason and conscience and should act toward one another in the spirit of brotherhood." Karl E. Meyer, "Enforcing Human Rights" (1999) World Policy J. Vol. XVI: 3, available online: <http://www.worldpolicy.org/journal/meyer3.html>. Mary Ann Glendon: Despite much controversy over their details and the manner of their implementation, it is worth recalling that no nation opposed these "new" rights in principle. Such rights, after all, were already present in many twentieth century constitutions and in legislation like that of the New Deal period in the United States— rights to a minimum standard of living, to work, to social security in the event of unemployment or disability, to form and join unions, and to education. The official U.S. position, as explained by Eleanor Roosevelt, was that it "favored the inclusion of economic and social rights in the Declaration, for no personal liberty could exist without economic security and independence. Unlike the Soviet bloc nations, however, the United States did not consider these rights to "imply an obligation on governments to assure the enjoyment of these rights by direct governmental action."

[9] See E.W. Borhi, "Soviet Economic Penetration and Western Trade", available online: <http://www.cc.jyu.fi/~pete/EWBorhi.pdf>.

[10] There has been disagreement about what constitutes a human right since the signing of the Universal Declaration in 1948. The West stressed the importance of civil and political rights like the right to choose a government, freedom of expression, conscience and belief. But the others gave priority to economic, social and cultural rights, such as the right to work, housing and access to health care. Wednesday, 28 November, 2001, available online: <http://news.bbc.co.uk/1/hi/world/europe/1678895.stm>.

the individual rights normally protected by the Constitution of a country, or the Bill of Rights enshrined in that Constitution.[11]

Although there are exceptions, collective human rights are not always afforded the same protection. In contrast to the United States, where the Supreme Court succeeded striking down segregation in education,[12] poor countries courts have proven unable to affirm peoples right to food, education, clothing, a cure for AIDS (or healthcare) or employment. As a result, collective human rights are often called 'Third Generation Rights' – a name that this author considers to underline their distance away from enforceability by many Courts.[13]

Franklin D. Roosevelt famously called for four freedoms: freedom of speech and belief, and freedom from fear and want.[14] One will note that the first two are individual freedoms while the latter two are collective freedoms. In the end, it was found necessary and appropriate to embody these sets of rights in two separate conventions. Individual human rights were protected by the Covenant on Civil and Political Rights while collective human rights were dealt with by the Covenant on Economic, Social and Cultural Rights.[15]

During the last forty years the focus has been largely on individual human rights in addition to the civil and political liberties aspect of human rights. Indeed, nowadays when people talk about human rights they normally mean individual human rights. When they think of the agencies concerning themselves with human rights, many think of Amnesty International, the Lawyers Committee for Human Rights, or the European Commission on Human Rights.[16] Yet people of developing countries often have a different conception of which agencies are able to deliver upon the premises and promises of human rights.[17] Those most often recognized would be more likely to include the UNDP, UNESCO, UNICEF, WHO, FAO, the World Food Programme, bilateral and multilateral aid agreements, Oxfam, and even *Médecins Sans Frontières*.[18]

---

[11] For example, see the Constitution of the United States of America, the Constitution of Canada and the Indian Constitution, among countless others, though these Constitutions all include an unwritten part that is developed and interpreted by the Courts.

[12] See generally, *Brown* v. *Board Of Education* (1954) 347 US 483.

[13] These third-generation rights -- which also include the right to development and the right to peace -- are "collective," meaning that they vest in the group rather than an individual, which flies in the face of the traditional understanding of human rights.

[14] See Franklin D. Roosevelt, "The Four Freedoms Address to Congress" available online: <http://www.libertynet.org/~edcivic/fdr.html>.

[15] For more on the two covenants see K. Arambulo, *Strengthening the Supervision of the International Covenant on Economic, Social and Cultural Rights* (Antwerp: Intersentia, 1999).

[16] These groups being non-government organizations (NGOs) primarily concerned with the advocating of what in this chapter are referred to as "individual rights;" freedom of speech, freedom of religion, free elections, "democracy," etc.

[17] See "Human Rights, Justice and Reform" available online: <http://www.thirdworldtraveler.com/ Reforming_System/HRJusticeReform.html>.

[18] These agencies are all examples of NGOs that focus on providing basic human needs such as health care, food, shelter, and the "minimum core" requirement articulated in the ICESCR

Civil and Political Rights

Civil and political rights have been drummed into the consciousness of African states, since Ghana became the first of the many British colonies to achieve independence in 1957.[19] Her Majesty's Government and legal professionals became an expert at drafting and exporting constitutions containing Bills of Rights to a series of newly independent African states.[20] However, Britain has neither a written constitution nor a modern Bill of Rights.[21] True to her mercantile tradition, it appears to this author that she has manufactured them only for export.

In Zimbabwe, the native home of this author, the country has had a constitutionally entrenched Bill of Rights since its independence in 1980. [22] There is a certain irony in this, given that none of the colonial powers in Africa – including Britain, France, Portugal, Germany and Italy – have an unblemished human rights record.[23] Indeed, the record in many European countries over the last five hundred years can, in many cases, be characterized as appalling. It is also noteworthy to point out just how recently civil rights were denied to African Americans in the United States.[24] It was said of President Theodore Roosevelt that he had as much use for a constitution as a tomcat has for a marriage licence.[25]

Despite this, as soon as Zimbabwe was granted independence, the attitude towards the country can be characterised as 'never mind what has been done to you in the past, from now on, you must behave like perfect gentlemen.' In effect, what took centuries to achieve in Britain and elsewhere was to be implemented instantly in Zimbabwe. In the early days of independence, a good deal of effort was made in Zimbabwe to adhere to the provisions of the Bill of Rights. This can be attributed in part to the leaders of the revolution, who had

---

[19] See Dr. H. Khamuzu Banda, "The Long Road to Ghana's Independence" available online: <http://www.greatepicbooks.com/epics/september97.html>.

[20] One can see the results of British efforts in a host of African nations including Ghana, Zimbabwe, and South Africa.

[21] The United Kingdom, while governed by a constitutional system, has no real written constitution, but rather a series of constitutional documents that collectively form the basis of UK governance along with the tradition of common law and precedence. The history of UK constitutional documents, available online: <http://www.victoria.tc.ca/history/etext/ menus/Britain-constitution.menu.html>.

[22] See Constitution of Zimbabwe, available online: <http://www.parlzim.gov.zw/Resources/ Constitution/constitution.html>.

[23] The mistakes made by the major colonial powers throughout history are well documented, with the exploitation of Africans during the peak of the slave trade being perhaps the most egregious example. The fact that colonialism is now universally regarded in a negative light, and that the UN Charter and Universal Declaration of Human Rights stress the right to self determination as the bedrock of universal human rights demonstrates how the international community has attempted to overcome the limitations exhibited by the colonial powers.

[24] See *Plessy* v. *Ferguson* (1896) 163 US 537.

[25] This quote was attributed to US Speaker of the House Joseph Cannon, available online: <http://www.cato.org/research/articles/samples-021021.html>.

heavily relied on the provisions of the UN Charter, the Universal Declaration of Human Rights, and the ICCPR, in demanding their own liberation.[26] In so doing, they demonstrated how the concept of human rights had coalesced with the concept of individual human liberties. [27] One may wonder whether the conception of human rights in developed countries has not been distorted by its ubiquitous application to a multiplicity of situations. In least developed countries such as Zimbabwe, many matters that are considered 'human rights issues' in the industrialised world appear trivial, when compared to basic rights, such as access to food, clean water, shelter, basic health and education.

In addition to broadening the definition of human rights to include economic, social and cultural rights, it is the opinion of this author that these liberties should be permitted to possess the same persuasive authority as civil and political rights. An improved definition would be one that appeals as much to conservatives as socialists, as much to republicans as democrats. One may argue that by transcending political opinion, human rights would be in a better position to receive universal approval.

Economic, Social and Cultural Rights

The implementation of economic, social and cultural rights requires not just judicial activism, but more specifically political activism. The myriad of internal concerns in the rich countries of the West makes it appear easy to brush aside with impatience the ceaseless demands of the poor. There are only occasional flashes of recognition of the justice of these demands. Harry Truman said, on the occasion of signing the United Nations Charter on June 26, 1945, "Experience has shown how deeply the seeds of war are planted by economic rivalry and by social injustice." [28] Mahatma Gandhi spoke of poverty as a crime against the poor. [29]

In 1981, the African Union[30] adopted the African Charter of Human and Peoples Rights, which came into force in 1986. [31] The reference to "Peoples Rights" shows that Africa was thinking beyond individual rights to the basic economic and social rights of whole communities.

---

[26] See generally D. Bossart, "Rhodesia to Zimbabwe," available online: <http://www.colorado.edu/conflict/full_text_search/AllCRCDocs/93-31.htm>.

[27] *Ibid.*

[28] Truman's speech at the signing of the UN Charter, available online:
<http://www.trumanlibrary.org/whistlestop/ study_collections/un/large/un_charter/>.

[29] See S. Kapadia, "A Tribute to Mahatma Gandhi: His Views on Women and Social Change", available online: <http://www.mkgandhi.org/articles/kapadia.htm>.

[30] Formerly known as the Organisation of African Unity.

[31] Available online, <http://www1.umn.edu/humanrts/instree/z1afchar.htm>.

In 1986, the General Assembly of the United Nations, in Resolution 41/128, defined "the Right to Development" as a fundamental human right.[32] In 2001, Archbishop Agostino Marchetto, head of the Vatican Delegation to the General Conference of the FAO, said food security "now deserves to be respected as a true and fundamental right of every human person and a vital element of peace and international stability."

Due to the relatively high living standards, many citizens of industrialised countries fail to truly comprehend what it means to live in abject, permanent and inescapable poverty. To this author, cataclysmic events, such as the Japanese attack on Pearl Harbour, the lawless killing and eviction of farmers from their land in Zimbabwe by Mugabe, or the events of 11 September 2001, offer a sudden and terrifying insight into the forces capable of being unleashed by hopelessness, despair or unremitting poverty.

Such events suggest that a balance between civil and political rights and economic, social and cultural rights needs to be realized. Such equilibrium can be more readily achieved once development agencies of the United Nations and the western world are perceived as human rights-agencies. If development is considered a human right, then it follows that a development agency should be acknowledged as a human rights agency.

It is the opinion of this author that before the concept of human rights can be welcomed in the developing world, it must be redefined in such a way that equates collective human rights with individual human rights.[33] Governments in the developing world should be able to perceive the right to development as correlative to the duty to foster democracy and individual freedoms.

One the tendency in certain parts of the industrialised world is to make development aid conditional on the fostering of democracy. First, they must be democratic then, they will be given development aid. This process of reasoning can be viewed as fundamentally flawed. Rather than viewing democracy as a prerequisite to development aid, the two should be recognized as going hand in hand.[34]

---

[32] *Declaration on the Right to Development*, UN GA Res. 41/128 (4 December 1986), Office of the High Commissioner for Human Rights, available online: <http://www.unhchr.ch/html/menu3/b/74.htm>. See in particular *Article 1*: "1. The right to development is an inalienable human right by virtue of which every human person and all peoples are entitled to participate in, contribute to, and enjoy economic, social, cultural and political development, in which all human rights and fundamental freedoms can be fully realized."

[33] "[t]he vision of human rights that most universalists accept and pursue with single-minded devotion, is one that has consistently failed to recognize either economic, social and cultural rights, or rights to peace, development and the environment as "genuine" human rights." J. Oloka-Onyango, "Human Rights and Sustainable Development in Contemporary Africa: A New Dawn, or Retreating Horizons?" *Human Development Report 2000* (New York: UNDP, 2000).

[34] *Cotonou Agreement*, 23 June 2000, ACP-EU, APC online: <http://www.acpsec.org/>.

A Culture of Poverty and Dependency

The pervasive poverty of the Third World is often not fully appreciated by Westerners.[35] Africa's poverty can be characterized as a poverty that is unremitting and endemic. It is reinforced by parasitic diseases, which sap peoples' energy and undermine their initiative. At the psychological level, this author has noted that one can even become fatalistic. If the rain comes, crops can grow, cattle can flourish and the people are well. Without it, crops and cattle may die, and so then might the children. People do not control their environment, rather it controls them. Such a reality pervades the law and politics in African consciousness. Rather than trying to change it, some people accept it and turn to 'forces majeures' or religion to make sense of these events. Witchcraft may even be used, as it is felt that ones ancestors are displeased, and must be appeased. The uncertainty of life makes future planning appear pointless. The only way to prepare for old age is for one to have lots of children who will care for one, once one is unable to do so.

This can be characterized as a 'culture of poverty' leading to a 'culture of dependency.' Many people are forced to seek security and comparative safety by congregating around a leader. This leader may be a tribal chief, a rich businessman or a local politician, and his role is to look after others during bad times. "You are my father and my mother" is an expression one often hears in Zimbabwe. In such context, it is in peoples' interest that their leader is wealthy, and it is comforting that this is demonstrated this by ostentation. As a result, there is less resentment when the leader drives past in a Mercedes-Benz. In a system of patronage, the patron needs money to sustain position, prestige, and power. Nepotism is considered natural, and corruption is regarded as inevitable.

Poverty and dependency find their expression inevitably in a feudal society and political structure. One does not change this by imposing a democratic constitution upon such a state. The status of much of Africa as a feudal or pre-feudal state may require transformation and development, before democracy can flourish. Robert Cooper, in his book *The Post-Modern State and the New World Order*, calls these states "pre-modern."[36] Philip Bobbitt, in *The Shield of*

---

[35] Excluding South Africa, the total income of sub-Saharan Africa amounts to a little more than that of Denmark – to be split among forty-eight nations. World Bank Publications, *World Bank Africa Database* (Washington: World Bank, 2001). The performance of most African economies during the last few decades leaves a lot to be desired. In 1950, GNP per capita for Africa south of the Sahara amounted to 11 per cent of that of the OECD countries. In 1989, the figure had fallen to 5 per cent. World Bank Publications, *World Bank Africa Database* (Washington: World Bank, 1991). In terms of growth, Africa has performed a great deal worse than Latin America or Asia. During the 1980s, GDP per capita in the African countries declined by, on average, 1.3 per cent per annum. See P. Collier, J.W. Gunning & D. Bevan, *Controlled Open Economies: a Neo-Classical Approach to Structuralism* (Oxford: Oxford University Press, 1994). Today, average GDP per capita in Africa is lower than in 1970. See World Bank Publications, *World Bank Africa Database* (Washington: World Bank, 2000).

[36] R. Cooper, *The Post-Modern State and the New World Order* (London: Demos, 2000).

Achilles, warns of "the dereliction of the African continent" while the rest of the planet averts its eyes.[37]

When life is organized along tribal lines, as it is in much of Africa, people will invariably vote for their own tribal leader. To a degree democracy tends to reinforce tribal differences. As a result, African dictators often argue they cannot encourage democracy because it is more important to build national unity across tribal lines.

Finally, it is important to note that in much of Africa, one will find two different legal systems in simultaneous operation. For example in Zimbabwe, there exists the Roman-Dutch law, a version of a western legal system, operating alongside the customary law of the tribes.[38] Concepts like the separation of powers, the independence of the judiciary, and the rule of law do not fit easily into the culture of those governed by customary law where the tribal leader holds ultimate authority. In much of Africa, Islamic Sharia law offers additional richness, and complications.

Poverty and the culture of dependency thus provide, in many ways, an infertile soil in which to plant the seeds of democracy. While western democracies should not abandon the hope of fostering democracy in Africa, there is a need to ensure that the soil receives a great deal of fertilizer, if the delicate democratic plant is to grow and flourish.

Education and Poverty Eradication

Education and poverty eradication are the twin pillars of modernization, the twin chemicals in the fertilizer of democracy. This assertion can be demonstrated quite dramatically by the events surrounding the recent presidential election in Zimbabwe.[39] The vote for change, which was in a very real sense the vote for democracy, came overwhelmingly from the cities and the towns, the educated people and those living in the modern economy. It is ironic that the strongest supporters of democracy are those who would be most affected by economic sanctions if these were imposed against Zimbabwe.[40]

Human Rights in the Context of Sustainable Development

Environmental preservation is essentially a long-term concern, to this author. Survival is a short-term concern; it is a matter of living from day to day. It is difficult to effectively give moral lessons to hungry people. It is difficult to

---

[37] P. Bobbitt, *The Shield of Achilles: War, Peace and the Course of History* (New York: Knopf, 2002).
[38] *Supra* note 21, the *Constitution of Zimbabwe*.
[39] For a collection of articles on the circumstances surrounding the election, available online:
<http://www.hrforumzim.com/special_hrru/ Special_Report_4_2002%20Election/SR4_0.htm - 13k ->.
[40] *Ibid.*

insist on the preservation of the elephant population to villagers whose whole years' crop may be destroyed in a single night by animals coming out of the neighbouring game reserve. It is difficult to require the forests to be preserved if these resources are needed daily for cooking and housing.

These facts are nowadays well known, and it is recognised that for sustainable development, laws must contain some provision whereby peasant populations reap tangible financial rewards for complying with the laws. An example from Zimbabwe is the CAMPFIRE programme.[41] It provides for villagers near a wildlife area to receive significant financial rewards from the licences paid by tourists, big game hunters and photographic safaris. As a result, the villagers develop a practical interest in preserving the wildlife and using the resource sustainably.

Conclusion

The lesson to be learned from this discussion is a simple one but nonetheless important: The Third World is not going to be dragged into the 21st century by the crude technique of the carrot and the stick. It can, by education and careful financial inputs, be brought to a state in which it will be capable of implementing the practices of democracy and individual freedoms. The way forward is sustainable development and its objectives must be education and poverty eradication. Good governance grows out of development. As a result, one cannot demand good governance as a prerequisite for development assistance.

The economic, environmental and social aspects of development need to be recognised as a fundamental human right; not as a reward for good behaviour, but as a powerful inducement for good behaviour.

---

[41] Essays detailing Zimbabwe's CAMPFIRE program, available online: <http://www.resourceafrica.org/directory/2/60/>.

PART II

INTEGRATING ECONOMIC, SOCIAL AND ENVIRONMENTAL LAW IN INTERNATIONAL LAW AND POLICY

(i)

SOCIAL AND ENVIRONMENTAL ELEMENTS OF ECONOMIC LAW

7

TRADE AND SUSTAINABLE DEVELOPMENT
AN OVERVIEW OF KEY ISSUES

Matthew Stilwell[1]

What is the role of trade in achieving sustainable development? Many answers – often contradictory – have been given to this question. Of high relevance to these discussions is the main institution governing the multilateral trading system: the World Trade Organization (WTO). This paper explores a range of issues that arise at the interface of trade and sustainable development, focus specifically on discussions surrounding the WTO. Rather than providing a detailed study of any one of the many issues arising in this area, it offers a brief sketch of the landscape and identifies a range of key issues that merit further consideration by students and scholars of international sustainable development law, with a focus on those that involve a significant environmental dimension.

This chapter has six parts. Following this introduction, the first section provides an overview of the WTO's mandate and relevant agreements and committees. The chapter then explores issues of trade and sustainable development in three main sections: material; legal and policy; and institutional. One section explores issues arising from the real-world relationships or *material linkages* between trade liberalization and the economy, with society and the environment. Economic, social and environmental systems are inextricably connected in the material or physical world. Consequently, trade liberalization may change the pattern or nature of activity in one area while impacting another. Governing these relationships to achieve the goals of society is a role for law and policy. Section four thus explores some *legal and policy* issues, which

[1] Matthew Stilwell, B.Ec, LL.B (Hons) (University of Tasmania), LLM (Columbia University), Director, Institute for Governance and Sustainable Development's European Office, Legal Counsel, UN Environment Programme's Economics and Trade Branch. The views expressed in this article are personal, and do not necessarily reflect the views of IGSD or UNEP. The cut-off date for this article is 1 September 2002. Consequently, issues arising from the World Summit on Sustainable Development (concluding in September 2002) are not considered here. In writing this chapter, the author has drawn heavily on a paper drafted together with his friend and colleague Jan Bohanes (forthcoming), to whom he is indebted for many of the ideas included here. The author would like to thank Jan, Charles Arden-Clarke, Benjamin Simmons, Lisi Tuerk, and David Vivas for their valuable comments on this chapter. He retains full responsibility for any errors.

M. C. Cordonier Segger & C. G. Weeramantry, eds., Sustainable Justice: Reconciling Economic, Social & Environmental Law © 2005 Koninklijke Brill NV, Printed in The Netherlands, pp.87-120.

arise between different fields of law (e.g. international economics, environmental, labour and human rights law) and across different levels of social organization (e.g. between local, national and international law). Legal and policy issues are often created and ultimately resolved by institutions. Section five therefore focuses on some *institutional issues* arising between the WTO and other international institutions.[2] In the final section of the chapter, conclusions are advanced.

The WTO and Sustainable Development

Created by the Uruguay Round of trade negotiations, the WTO is both a set of legal agreements, and an institutional framework to administer the implementation of these agreements, settle trade disputes, and provide a forum for ongoing negotiations. The WTO's founding agreement encourages governments to achieve its economic objectives, "while allowing for the optimal use of the world's resources in accordance with the objective of sustainable development, seeking both to protect and preserve the environment and to enhance the means for doing so in a manner consistent with their respective needs and concerns at different levels of economic development."[3]

The WTO is much more than a "trade" organization in the traditional sense. Whereas the GATT focused primarily on liberalizing trade in goods, the WTO promotes economic liberalization in a range of sectors, and reaches deep into national regulatory systems to address impediments and distortions to international economic activity. While it is institutionally structured to address three primary areas of activity: trade in goods, trade in services, and protection of intellectual property, its agreements also touch on a number of others including investment and government procurement (see Box 1).

Box 1 – Relevant WTO Agreements
- Agreement Establishing the World Trade Organization (WTO Agreement) establishes the WTO's main legal and institutional framework
- General Agreement on Tariffs and Trade (GATT) is the original framework for liberalizing trade in goods
- Agreement on Technical Barriers to Trade (TBT Agreement) provides more specific disciplines regarding national (or sub-national) technical regulations and non-binding standards.
- Agreement on the Application of Sanitary and Phytosanitary Measures (SPS Agreement) applies to certain national measures designed to protect human, animal and plant life or health

---

[2] These three categories – material, legal/policy, and institutional – are not mutually exclusive, and many issues classified within them will have a mixed character; they will arise in the phenomenal world, raise questions of law and policy, and/or require institutional action for their resolution. In this note the author does not examine the generic relationship between these categories, but rather simply use them to help structure the discussion by organizing issues according to their primary character.

[3] *Marrakesh Agreement Establishing the World Trade Organization*, Preamble, April 15, 1994, reprinted in 33 I.L.M. 1144 (1994) [hereinafter "WTO Agreement"].

- Agreement on Subsidies and Countervailing Measures (SCM) disciplines both trade distorting subsidies, and the countervailing measures that may be taken in response
- Agreement on Agriculture promotes liberalization of trade in agricultural goods
- General Agreement on Trade in Services (GATS) establishes binding rules to liberalize international trade in services
- Agreement on Trade-Related Aspects of Intellectual Property (TRIPS Agreement) establishes uniform, minimum standards for the protection and enforcement of intellectual property rights
- The Understanding on Rules and Procedures Governing the Settlement of Disputes (DSU) establishes procedures for the settlement of disputes arising out of the implementation of WTO agreements.

These agreements are administered through a number of councils and committees. Trade and environment issues are considered primarily in the Committee on Trade and Environment (CTE). Trade and development issues are considered primarily in the Committee on Trade and Development (CTD). Environment and development issues are also considered, albeit less directly, in other WTO committees and councils (including those administering the agreements identified in Box 1).

At the WTO's 4th Ministerial meeting in Doha, Qatar, the CTE and CTD were respectively mandated to identify and debate environmental and developmental aspects of upcoming negotiations, to "help achieve the objective of having sustainable development appropriately reflected in those negotiations."[4] The Ministerial Declaration also established a number of other mandates with implications for sustainable development. Many of these are discussed in the following sections, as relevant.

The existing WTO agreements, as well the negotiations and discussions mandated by Ministers at the Doha Ministerial, have implications for the coherent development of the institutional framework for sustainable development. They will play a role in determining the laws and policies developed within the WTO and elsewhere. And they will have significant consequences for the underlying economic, social and environmental systems, as well as the well-being of people relying on them.

Material Linkages – Economic, Social and Environmental

What is the effect of liberalizing trade in agricultural or industrial goods on the economy, communities and the environment? How might liberalizing services – such as healthcare or water provision services – affect human rights to health and food? What are the implications of intellectual property rules for access to life-saving medicines and technology? Answering these and other questions

---

[4] *WTO 4th Ministerial Declaration*, WTO Doc. WT/MIN(01)/DEC/1, para. 51.

requires an understanding of complex interdependencies between trade and other facets of the world.

Trade – defined broadly here as the trans-boundary movement of goods, services and capital – is intimately tied to numerous other economic and social aspects of human behaviour. These, in turn, are intimately connected to each other, and to the natural environment. As a result of these linkages, changes in the character or pattern of activity in one area can change the character or pattern of activity in another. This has the potential to profoundly implicate on human well-being and sustainable development. As with any set of complex systems, the material linkages between trade, other economic activity, society and the environment are multiple and not easily reduced to a set of simple categories or relationships. Nevertheless, some preliminary observations about these relationships are possible, and are relevant as context for discussions of legal, policy and institutional questions in the following sections.

First, while a number of analytic frameworks are conceivable, the most widely accepted framework suggests that trade liberalization can affect the economy, society and environment through four main *mechanisms or media*: by introducing new products*,* disseminating new technologies*,* affecting the structure of economic activity, or by increasing the scale of activity and impacts.[5] While this framework has been applied primarily to trade in goods, it may also provide some insights when examining the effects of liberalization in other areas of economic activity such as services or investment.

Second, the effects of trade liberalization on the economy, society and environment may differ in their *nature*. They may, for example, be *positive or negative (or neutral)*. Done well, trade liberalization can change the economy's structure and scale to promote economic growth, enhance employment and opportunity, and introduce environmentally sound products and technologies. Done poorly, it may collapse infant industries, undermine social cohesion through rapid structural change, or expand domestic market failures into global markets with serious consequences for the environment. Often, both positive and negative effects of some kind will occur simultaneously, requiring policymakers to balance competing objectives in order to optimize outcomes.

Third, the effects of trade liberalization may also differ in *degree*. In some cases, small changes in trade policy will have major implications for economic, social and/or environmental systems. In others, trade liberalization's impacts may be less intense, or take longer to materialize. The extent to which trade liberalization affects underlying systems will depend in part on the other policy measures in place (e.g. policies designed to ensure sustainable use of natural resources). It will also depend in part on the nature of the systems themselves

---

[5] See OECD, *Methodologies for Environment and Trade Reviews*, OECD/GD(94) 103 (Paris: OECD, 1994). See also UNEP, *Reference Manual for the Integrated Assessment of Trade-Related Policies* (Geneva: UNEP, 2001).

(e.g. some natural systems such as fisheries may exhibit non-linear relationships).

Fourth, the effects of liberalization – including its benefits and burdens – are *distributed spatially* across different geographical areas, and to different communities. They may occur primarily within an importing or exporting country, across borders with trans-boundary effects on third countries (e.g. positive or negative economic, social or environmental externalities), or globally (e.g. promoting peace or exacerbating climate change). Liberalizing trade in timber products, for example, can benefit elites but harm local forest communities in exporting countries, provide cheap timber to consumers in importing countries, and affect biodiversity with implications for all.[6] The spatial distribution or locus of effects will influence who bears the benefits and burdens of liberalization, both within and between countries.

Finally, the nature and degree of effects, and who bears the benefits and burdens, will often vary among different *industry sectors and areas of policy*. For instance, the effects of liberalizing trade in agricultural versus industrial sectors may differ markedly. Similarly, the effects of liberalizing trade in goods (e.g. refrigerators or timber) versus liberalizing trade in services (e.g. transportation, tourism or education) will also differ. Understanding these relationships requires careful assessment on a case-by-case basis. Policy makers should be cautious of unthinkingly applying assumptions and experience gained in one area to other areas.

Viewed from these perspectives, trade liberalization is neither inherently good nor bad. Rather, it is one *means* among many available to governments to achieve the *end* of enhancing human well-being and achieving sustainability. From a sustainable development perspective, trade and trade rules must therefore complement other policies helping to optimize individual and collective behaviour to promote human, social and economic development and to protect the environment, with the goal of meeting the needs of present generations with an emphasis on the poorest (intra-generational equity), and of preserving the ability of future generations to meet their own needs (inter-generational equity).[7] Achieving sustainability will require collective action by governments, citizens and business, guided within different jurisdictions and at levels of governance by a coherent and balanced architecture of laws, policies and institutions.

---

[6] D. Downes *et al.*, *Tree Trade: Liberalization of International Commerce in Forest Products: Risks and Opportunities* (Washington: WRI/CIEL, 1999).
[7] For further reference M.C. Cordonier Segger and A. Khalfan, *Sustainable Development Law: Principles, Practices and Prospects* (Oxford: Oxford University Press, 2004).

Legal and Policy Issues – the Importance of Coherence and Balance

Addressing the material linkages between trade, economy, society and environment, and regulating individual and collective human behaviour accordingly, is a role for law and policy. Laws and policies establish the boundaries that keep us on course and prevent us from veering into barbarism or colliding with nature's boundaries. Just as the linkages between systems in the material world are complex, so too are the relationships between different laws and polices.

At the interface of trade and sustainable development arise a whole constellation of legal and policy issues. Some of these have appeared in dispute settlement cases (See Box 2), others have been considered by formal institutional structures, and others still remain to be identified and discussed. This section provides a sketch of some of the main issues with the goal of identifying areas for future investigation. Before addressing some specific issues, it is useful to consider some general comments on the nature of legal and policy issue.

First, it seems almost trite to say that achieving sustainability will require law and policy to be tailored in order to achieve *identifiable outcomes* in the material world. Unfortunately, however, trade policy-making at the multilateral level has to a large extent proceeded on the basis of theory. It has gone largely without a systematic examination of its effects on the economy, society and environment in specific countries and sectors, either by the WTO collectively or by its individual member countries. While some countries have recently undertaken integrated assessments of trade liberalization and trade rules, the majority has not.[8] Better analysis of actual and potential effects "on the ground" will be required before policymakers can accurately identify the role of trade in promoting national development, determine whether to liberalize (and if so the nature and pace of liberalization), and design and implement the associated policies required to direct economic liberalization.

Table 2 – Relevant WTO Disputes

- *US-Gasoline*[9] (1996) involved a successful GATT challenge to US measures that addressed urban motor vehicle pollution by establishing minimum baselines for fuel quality. The Appellate Body determined that the US-treated foreign and domestic fuel suppliers differently, and attempts to consult other governments or count the costs to foreign suppliers were inadequate, and thereby constituted arbitrary discrimination and a disguised restriction on international trade under Article XX.

---

[8] See WTO 4th Ministerial Declaration, *supra* note 3. These assessments have been welcomed by Ministers in paragraph 6 of the Ministerial Declaration.

[9] *United States – Standards for Reformulated and Conventional Gasoline*, AB-1996-1, WT/DS2/AB/R (1997) (Report of the Appellate Body).

- *EC-Hormones*[10] (1998) involved a successful challenge under the SPS Agreement to EC measures banning imports of hormone-treated beef, on the basis that the measures were not sufficiently based on a risk assessment as required by the SPS Agreement (Article 5.1).
- *US-Shrimp*[11] (1998) involved a successful GATT challenge to US measures banning the import of shrimp caught with fishing methods that threatened endangered species of sea turtles. It was determined that the measures treated similarly placed countries differently, lacked flexibility and due process, and did not involve serious multilateral negotiations for sea turtle protection, and thereby constituted arbitrary and unjustifiable discrimination under Article XX.
- *Australia-Salmon*[12] (1998) involved a successful challenge under the SPS Agreement to Australian measures addressing the risk of invasive species by banning imports of uncooked salmon. It was determined that the measures were not sufficiently based on a risk assessment (Article 5.1), and failed to avoid arbitrary or unjustifiable distinctions in the levels of protection it considers to be appropriate in different situations (i.e. between risks from Canadian and ocean-caught Pacific salmon) (Article 5.5) as required by the SPS Agreement.
- *Japan-Varietals*[13] (1999) involved a successful challenge under the SPS Agreement to Japanese measures banning imports of certain fruit crops to address the risk of invasive species. It was determined that the measures were maintained without sufficient scientific evidence (Article 2.2), the provisional measures were not reviewed within a reasonable period, and additional information was not sought for a more objective assessment of risk (Article 5.7).
- *EC-Asbestos*[14] (2001) involved an unsuccessful challenge under the TBT Agreement and the GATT to a French ban on imports of asbestos fibres and products containing them. The French measure was found to be justified as a necessary measure for the protection of human life or health (Article XX(b)). In overturning the panel's decision that the TBT Agreement did not apply, the Appellate Body determined it did not have an "adequate basis" to complete an analysis of the measure under the TBT Agreement.
- *US-Shrimp 21.5*[15] (2001) involved an unsuccessful challenge to US measures to implement the decision in *US-Shrimp*. The US measures were found to be justified under Article XX, subject to certain requirements, including that the US continue to seek a negotiated solution to protect sea turtles.

Second, many issues of law and policies arise *between* different fields of law and policy. Just as linkages exist in the material world, linkages arise among the different systems of law and policy responsible for governing trade, social

---

[10] *EC Measures Concerning Meat and Meat Products (Hormones)*, AB-1997-4, WT/DS26/AB/R, WT/DS48/AB/R (1998) (Report of the Appellate Body).

[11] *United States – Import Prohibition of Certain Shrimp and Shrimp Products*, AB-1998-4, WT/DS58/AB/R (1998) (Report of the Appellate Body).

[12] *Australia – Measures Affecting Importation of Salmon*, AB-1998-5, WT/DS18/AB/R (1998) (Report of the Appellate Body).

[13] *Japan – Measures Affecting Agricultural Products*, AB-1998-8, WT/DS76/AB/R (1999) (Report of the Appellate Body).

[14] *European Communities – Measures Affecting Asbestos and Asbestos-Containing Products*, AB-2000-11, WT/DS135/AB/R (2001) (Report of the Appellate Body).

[15] *United States – Import Prohibition of Certain Shrimp and Shrimp Products, Recourse to Article 21.5 by Malaysia*, AB-2001-4, WT/DS58/AB/RW (2001) (Report of the Appellate Body).

development and environmental protection. Issues may, for example, arise between international economic law and other fields of international law relating to environment, human rights, health policy, labour rights, finance and development. These linkages give rise to a need for integration and coherence in law and policy across these different fields. The UN Sub-Commission on the Promotion and Protection of Human Rights, for example, has recently encouraged "Governments and economic policy forums to take international human rights obligations and principles fully into account in international economic policy formulation."[16]

Third, issues may arise not only between different fields of law and policy, but also *at different levels of governance.* As noted in the previous paragraph, issues may arise between fields of law at one level of social organization or "scale". Issues, for example, may arise between international economic law and the rules embodied in the multilateral environmental agreements (MEAs) ("horizontal linkages"). Issues may also arise among systems at different levels of scale such as between international economic law, and law at the regional, national or sub-national level ("vertical linkages"). An integrated architecture of sustainable development governance must match the level of governance with the level of the issue being regulated, while seeking balance and coherence with related institutional arrangements.[17]

Fourth, issues also arise about the appropriate *balance between markets and regulation.* Many of the legal and policy issues identified below arise from the inherent tension found between liberalizing economic activity by "disciplining" the use of regulations, and the need to regulate at local and international levels in order to achieve economic, social or environmental objectives. In applying and developing trade disciplines, the trading system must balance attempts to enhance market access by, for example, removing or disciplining national measures (known as non-tariff barriers) on one hand, and preserving policy space to regulate to achieve economic, social and environmental objectives, on the other.

Ensuring a coherent and balanced architecture of rules to realize the benefits of economic liberalization while promoting social development and environmental protection – at each level of governance and between levels of governance – remains a major challenge. In all likelihood, it is a challenge that will increase as globalization deepens interdependencies, and as an expanding human population competes for the planet's limited carrying capacities. Drawing on the general discussions of material linkages (above) and legal and policy linkages (above), this section provides a brief sketch – rather than a detailed treatment – of ten of the most prominent issues in the field of trade and sustainable development, commencing with market access.

---

[16] Sub-Commission Resolution 1999/30 (E/CN.4/SUB.2/RES/1999/30).
[17] See M. C. Cordonier Segger, in this volume.

Market access

Expanding market access can have a range of material effects on economic, social and environmental systems, thereby raising a series of legal and policy issues. At the WTO's Committee on Trade and Environment, discussions of market access have focused primarily on the potential benefits of improved access to markets for developed countries. Discussions have noted how improved market access and new trade opportunities can help to reduce poverty, foster economic development, and secure resources to address environmental and social concerns. These discussions were reflected in the Doha Ministerial Declaration, which called on the CTE to give particular attention to the effect of environmental measures on market access.[18]

At a more general level, the purpose of the WTO is to enhance market access for all Members on the basis that freer trade allows states to realize comparative advantages and economies of scale, innovate under the pressure of international competition, and sharing information and ideas, all promoting economic relationships that reduce potential for serious conflict. The advocates of freer trade also argue that it enhances access to environmental goods, services and technologies and spurs demand and capacity for environmental protection.

Conversely, critics argue that freer trade can harm infant industries, exacerbate unequal distribution of wealth and opportunity, increase the scale of negative impacts (such as transport pollution), leverage local market failures into global markets, and reduce economic, social and/or environmental diversity and stability. In particular instances either view, or both, may be correct. Given the interdependency between economic, social and environmental systems, and a range of positive and negative linkages, the challenge is to maximize the contribution of trade to human welfare by ensuring the right kind and level of liberalization, at the right pace, guided by the right policies and laws.

Legal and policy issues regarding market access arise primarily from the tension between liberalizing and regulating economic activity. To liberalize trade, WTO rules discipline a range of national measures (i.e. "non-tariff barriers") to promote trade and prevent protectionism. At the same time, many legitimate national measures affect market access. Consequently, legal and policy tensions between market access and environmental and social protection may arise where regulations – for example those establishing eco-labelling schemes or setting product characteristics – may have the effect of restricting trade opportunities in certain products such as textiles, leather, foot-ware, consumer durables, fish and forest products.[19]

---

[18] See WTO 4th Ministerial Declaration, *supra* note 3, para. 32(i).

[19] On this issue, see V. Jha, A. Markandya & R. Vossenaar, *Reconciling Trade and Environment* (Cheltenham: Edward Elgar, 1999).

This tension is played out in how specific WTO disciplines, such as those in the GATT, TBT and SPS Agreements, are applied to specific national measures. Many of the issues below are specific instances of this tension between market access, national and international "regulatory" measures. To a certain extent issues arising from process and production methods, labelling, scientific uncertainty and precaution, bio-safety and agriculture are specific instances of the general challenge of balancing enhanced market access with the right of governments to regulate at the national and international level to achieve economic, social and environmental goals.

Process and production methods

Should importing countries be permitted to distinguish between timber imports on the basis that some were produced sustainably and others were not? Can countries ban the import of shoes on the basis that their production involved an abuse of labour standards? How do such measures affect exporters, who may be faced with numerous and competing requirements? At the WTO a fundamental debate has turned around whether importing countries should be entitled to ban or regulate products based *not* on their physical characteristics (which may have effects within the importing country), but on factors not reflected in the product's physical composition – such as the social or environmental effects of the *process and production methods* (PPMs) used in exporting countries.

The distinction between regulations based on physical (or "product-related") and PPM (or "non-product related") characteristics has spurred a decade of debate.[20] On one hand, permitting regulation based on the impact of production methods is consistent with environmental management principles, which seek to reduce impacts over a product's whole life cycle (i.e. production, use and disposal). And it recognizes that PPMs may have trans-boundary impacts, or raise ethical concerns within importing countries. On the other hand, PPM-based distinctions enforced in importing countries may confront exporters with a tangle of different and competing requirements, and are open to protectionist abuse. As a matter of policy, reconciling these competing interests requires striking an appropriate balance both between market access and domestic regulation (i.e. between markets and regulation), and between oversight by the international trading system and deference to national policy-making (i.e. "vertical coherence").

The PPM issue arose historically as a matter of law from the GATT's non-discrimination obligations, which oblige countries to avoid discrimination

---

[20] The distinction between product-related and non-product-related PPMs is left aside here. Product-related PPMs serve as a proxy for physical (product-related) characteristics and so are treated within that category for the purposes of this analysis.

between "like" foreign products (Article I's most favoured nation or MFN obligation), and between "like" foreign and domestic products (Article III's national treatment obligation). Under the GATT, the traditional "like product" test involved "employing four general criteria in analyzing 'likeness': (i) the properties, nature and quality of the products; (ii) the end-uses of the products; (iii) consumers' tastes and habits (more comprehensively termed consumers' perceptions and behaviour) in respect of the products; and (iv) the tariff classification of the products…"[21]

In examining PPM-based measures, GATT panels tended to focus on the first of these criteria. They adopted the view that different production methods cannot render two otherwise identical products (such as two shipments of timber, one produced sustainably and one unsustainably) "unlike". Consequently, differential treatment of such "like" products based on their production methods was found to violate GATT non-discrimination obligations. Many outside the trading community have criticized the tendency of GATT panels to discount non-product related characteristics and to downplay other elements of the traditional test when determining likeness. Such actions have been discredited for drawing a bright line in the wrong place, and failing to balance the need to avoid protectionist abuse of PPM measures with the need to ensure governments can make valid regulatory distinctions between products on the basis of non-product related, ethical, social or environmental grounds.

The "bright line" approach of GATT panels does not appear to have been adopted by the WTO Appellate Body. In *EC-Asbestos*, the Appellate Body acknowledged the value of the traditional test, but noted that its general criteria are neither treaty mandated, nor are they a closed list of criteria.[22] Use of the criteria, "does not dissolve the duty or the need to examine, in each case, *all* of the pertinent evidence."[23] It stated:

> "…the kind of evidence to be examined in assessing the "likeness" of products will, necessarily, depend upon the particular products and the legal provision at issue. When all the relevant evidence has been examined, panels must determine whether that evidence, as a whole, indicates that the products in question are "like" in terms of the legal provision at issue. We have noted that, under Article III:4 of the GATT 1994, the term "like products" is concerned with competitive relationships between and among products. Accordingly … it is important under Article III:4 to take account of evidence which

---

[21] *EC-Asbestos, supra* note 12, at para.85.

[22] The author notes that while *EC-Asbestos* did not address PPM-based measures, the Appellate Body's interpretation and application of Article III will likely have implications for future cases involving PPM-based measures.

[23] *EC-Asbestos, supra* note 8, para. 102.

indicates whether, and to what extent, the products involved are – or could be – in a competitive relationship in the marketplace."[24]

While the *EC - Asbestos* case did not directly address PPM-based measures, the Appellate Body's approach to "like products" requires consideration of "all the relevant evidence", which could in future cases conceivably include non-product-related or non-trade concerns (including those arising out of a product's process or production methods), at least to the extent they relate to elements of the traditional test – such as consumer's perceptions and behaviour – or to the nature and extent of a competitive relationship between and among products.

Even if struck down under Article III's "like products" test, PPM measures may still be permissible under Article XX, which permits a higher degree of discrimination between domestic and imported products.[25] Recent decisions in *US-Shrimp* and *US-Shrimp 21.5* suggest that PPM-based measures may, under certain circumstances, be permissible under Article XX. In those cases, the United States' measure effectively required exporting countries to use a production method involving "turtle excluder devices" as a precondition to market entry for their shrimp products. The practical outcome of the Appellate Body's decision in *US-Shrimp 21.5* is to permit the United States to retain its PPM-based measure as long as it continues to satisfy the requirements set out by the Appellate Body, including the requirement to seek a negotiated solution.

Labelling

Labels generally provide consumers with information about a product's characteristics and/or the social or environmental impacts of its production. This provides a market-based incentive for the production of socially and environmentally-sound products and technologies. Labelling schemes may be voluntary (i.e. producers volunteer information to gain market advantage – e.g. that food is organically produced) or mandatory (i.e. producers are compelled by government to provide information – e.g. that a product is genetically modified). Since labelling schemes have the potential to affect market access, they are addressed by a number of WTO agreements, raising questions on how to balance market access with legitimate use of labels at the national level for social and environmental policy purposes.

---

[24] *Ibid.*, paras. 101-103.

[25] *US-Reformulated Gasoline, supra* note 7, at p. 22, stating: "The provisions of the chapeau cannot logically refer to the same standard(s) by which a violation of a substantive rule has been determined to have occurred. To proceed down that path would be both to empty the chapeau of its contents and to deprive the exceptions in paragraphs (a) to (j) of meaning. Such recourse would also confuse the question of whether inconsistency with a substantive rule existed, with the further and separate question arising under the chapeau of Article XX as to whether that inconsistency was nevertheless justified".

Three WTO agreements are particularly relevant: the TBT Agreement, the SPS Agreement and the GATT. The TBT Agreement applies to labelling schemes falling within its definitions of "technical regulations" and non-binding "standards".[26] The SPS Agreement applies to "packaging and labelling requirements directly related to food safety".[27] And the GATT applies concurrently with the TBT and SPS Agreements, to the extent that its provisions to not conflict with these agreements.[28] From these agreements arise a number of legal and policy issues. Four are discussed here.

An initial concern is which of the TBT and SPS Agreements should apply to mandatory labelling schemes, such as those regarding genetically modified organisms, which deal with issues of both food safety and consumer information. Should these be considered "primarily related to food safety" and therefore subject to the SPS Agreement's more stringent science-based disciplines?[29] Or given their diverse policy justifications – including awareness-raising, ethical, religious and environmental concerns, and consumers' right to know – should they be subject to the TBT Agreement's more general requirements? The answer in a specific case would depend on where the line is drawn between the two agreements, and on where the facts fall. The precise relationship between these agreements remains to be considered by the WTO Appellate Body.[30]

Issues also arise around how WTO agreements apply to mandatory labelling schemes. Most of these schemes are covered by the TBT Agreement's definition of technical regulations, which includes "packaging, marking or labelling requirements as they apply to a product, process or production method" (Annex 1). To these regulations the Agreement applies obligations regarding non-discrimination (Article 2.1), trade-restrictiveness (Article 2.2), preferential use of international standards (Article 2.4), notification requirements (Article 2.9), transparency (Article 10), technical assistance (Article 11), and special and differential treatment (Article 12), among others. As yet, the WTO Appellate Body has not considered the application of these provisions to mandatory labelling schemes nor have they resolved a range of issues relating to the TBT Agreement's scope.

Like mandatory schemes, the coverage by the WTO of voluntary labelling schemes has also been much discussed. Many voluntary schemes are

---

[26] TBT Agreement, Annex 1.

[27] SPS Agreement, Annex A.

[28] WTO Agreement, General Interpretive Note to Annex 1A

[29] *See* SPS Agreement, Article 1(4) (stating "Nothing in this Agreement shall affect the rights of Members under the Agreement on Technical Barriers to Trade with respect to measures not within the scope of this Agreement").

[30] For a discussion of how the TBT and SPS Agreements could apply to labeling of genetically modified organisms *see*, M. Stilwell and B. Van Dyke, *An Activists Handbook on Genetically Modified Organisms and the WTO*, online Consumer Council: <www.consumerscouncil.org>.

administered by local governments or non-governmental bodies, and not by the central governments signing WTO agreements. WTO Members have sought to cover local and non-governmental bodies through the TBT Agreement's Code of Good Practice, which parallels many of the obligations applied to technical regulations. WTO Members are to make "such reasonable measures as may be available to them" to ensure local and non-governmental bodies adopt the Code (Article 3.1). What constitutes "reasonable measures" and how, in fact, the Code will be applied to voluntary labelling schemes remains a subject of discussion in the TBT Committee and the CTE.[31]

A fourth issue is whether and how the TBT Agreement applies to labels based on process and production method (PPM) criteria. The views of WTO Members about the scope and coverage of the agreement can be divided (loosely) into three categories. Some (mainly developing countries) are concerned about market access impacts and have argued the TBT Agreement does *not* apply, because to do so would sanctify PPM-based labels; others (notably Switzerland) share the view that the TBT Agreement may not apply, but for opposite reasons – because they support PPM-based labels and are concerned about WTO oversight; and still others (e.g. Canada, the United States and Australia) argue that they *do* fall within the TBT Agreement and are permissible if in conformity with TBT disciplines.[32] Although unresolved, this debate has been given significant attention since the WTO Doha Ministerial Declaration's called on the CTE to pay particular attention to labelling requirements for environmental purposes (paragraph 32 (iii)), and on whether there is a need for further negotiations (paragraph 32).

Scientific Uncertainty and Precaution

Issues of science, uncertainty and precaution are at the center of a number of trade controversies. The impacts of, for instance, a trans-boundary movement of alien species on plant life and health, increased timber trade on forests and biodiversity, and liberalizing transportation or energy services on climate change, are shrouded in uncertainty.

The potential for controversy arises because policymakers must often regulate to protect health and the environment under conditions of scientific uncertainty. At the same time, however, the trading system seeks to prevent these regulations from being used for protectionist purposes by ensuring governments have a sound scientific basis for their actions. While not irreconcilable in theory, these two approaches give rise to considerable tension in practice. They require a careful balance between oversight by the multilateral trading system, and appropriate deference to national policy-makers. Who

---

[31] *See, for example,* WTO document (G/TBT/M/5) for a discussion by WTO Members of how the TBT Agreement may apply to various labelling schemes.

[32] *Ibid.*

determines this balance, and how it is done has given rise to tension in past cases, and will likely continue to do so in the future.

At the heart of this issue is the precautionary principle, which provides that "where there are threats of serious or irreversible damage, lack of full scientific certainty shall not be used as a reason for postponing cost-effective measures to prevent environmental degradation" (Rio Principle 15). While recognizing that the complexity of many environmental and health threats may preclude clear science from emerging in time to take policy action, the precautionary principle advocates against deferring action in the face of potential consequences. The principle is now embodied in many MEAs, and provides the basis for many domestic measures in both developed and developing countries, representing the major legal systems and regions of the world.

The relationship between precaution and multilateral trade rules gives rise to a number of closely related issues. The first and most general issue concerns how much deference the trading system should give to give to national precautionary measures. How, in other words, can an appropriate balance be struck when applying a range of WTO disciplines (including those in the GATT, SPS and TBT Agreements) to national measures taken under conditions of scientific uncertainty and based on the precautionary principle? Precaution will likely continue to be evoked by states when seeking to defend their measures in WTO dispute settlement proceedings. How an appropriate balance is struck between maintaining domestic regulatory space to respond to scientific uncertainty, on one hand, and the need for predictable trading relations, on the other, will thus depend on the interpretation of particular WTO obligations and their application on a case-by-case basis to particular domestic measures.

A second and closely related question is to what extent is the precautionary principle directly reflected at the international level in the WTO's rules themselves? The more WTO agreements embody precaution, arguably the greater the space for national precautionary measures, but the more leeway for protectionist abuse. According to the Appellate Body in *Hormones*, "the precautionary principle has been incorporated in, *inter alia*, Article 5.7 of the SPS Agreement", which addresses the right to take provisional measures where relevant scientific information is insufficient, and "in the sixth paragraph of the preamble and in Article 3.3."[33] At the same time, the Appellate Body notes that the principle "does not ... relieve a panel from the duty of applying the normal (i.e. customary international law) principles of treaty interpretation".[34]

---

[33] *EC-Hormones, supra* note 8, at paras.124 and 253. The extent to which the principle is reflected in other WTO agreements remains unexamined by the Appellate Body. It is worth noting, however, that the TBT Agreement's preamble includes provisions similar to those identified by the Appellate Body in the SPS Agreement as reflecting the precautionary principle.

[34] *Ibid.*

From this statement arises a third issue between WTO rules and the broader field of public international law: to what extent is the precautionary principle a principle of customary international law that should be taken into account when interpreting WTO agreements? Some WTO Members argue the principle has crystallized as customary law and therefore must be used to interpret WTO agreements;[35] others have argued that it is and cannot become customary law and so cannot be used to interpret WTO agreements.[36] The Appellate Body has so far declined to offer a definitive ruling on this issue.[37]

Finally, scientific uncertainty and precaution raises issues of horizontal coherence between different fields of international law. Many obligations in international environmental law – including those directly affecting international trade – are based on the precautionary principle. For instance, the precautionary principle forms the basis of bans on trade in certain listed endangered species under the Convention on International Trade in Endangered Species of Wild Flora and Fauna (CITES).[38] The Cartagena Protocol on Biosafety, similarly, includes explicit reference to precaution in its operative provisions that affect trade.[39] As discussed in the following section on the Cartagena Protocol, in the event of a trade dispute, the relationship between these precautionary obligations and relevant WTO agreements may need to be clarified.

Biosafety

Biosafety raises some specific instances of the more general issues concerning market access and labelling (each discussed above), and the relationship between MEAs and WTO rules (discussed below). Again, the debate arises in large part from the basic tension between exporting countries' desire for market

---

[35] *Ibid.*, at para. 16, Appellate Body noting "[t]he precautionary principle is already, in the view of the European Communities, a general customary rule of international law or at least a general principle of law." *See also Japan – Varietals*, *supra* note 11, at para. 10, Appellate Body noting "[i]n Japan's view, the Panel failed to give due regard to the precautionary principle, which was recognized in both *EC Measures Concerning Meat and Meat Products (Hormones)* and *Australia – Measures Affecting Importation of Salmon.*"

[36] *See EC-Hormones*, *supra* note 8, at para. 43, Appellate Body noting "The United States does not consider that the 'precautionary principle' represents a principle of customary international law; rather, it may be characterized as an 'approach' -- the content of which may vary from context to context."

[37] *Ibid.*, at para. 123, Appellate Body noting that "The precautionary principle is regarded by some as having crystallized into a general principle of customary international *environmental* law. Whether it has been widely accepted by Members as a principle of *general* or *customary international law* appears less than clear. We consider, however, that it is unnecessary, and probably imprudent, for the Appellate Body in this appeal to take a position on this important, but abstract, question." (citations omitted).

[38] *See, for example,* CITES Resolution Conf. 9.24, Annex 4, stating "when considering any proposal to amend Appendix I or II the Parties shall apply the precautionary principle so that scientific uncertainty should not be used as a reason for failing to act in the best interest of conservation of the species."

[39] *See*, Cartagena Protocol on Biosafety, UNEP/CBC/ExCOP/1/L.5 (28 January 2000), preamble and Articles 10 and 11.8.

access, and the need to regulate trans-boundary movement and domestic use of genetically modified organisms (GMOs) to protect health and the environment.

Issues of biosafety, biotechnology and trade in GMOs cut across a number of WTO agreements including the GATT (general provisions on non-discrimination and quantitative restrictions), the TBT Agreement (labelling of GMOs), the SPS Agreement (national measures to protect life and health), TRIPS Agreement (intellectual property rights over plant genetic resources) and Agreement on Agriculture (non-discrimination and non-trade concerns). They also arise between the WTO and the agreements and processes administered by other institutions, including the UN Food and Agriculture Organization (International Treaty on Plant Genetic Resources for Food and Agriculture), the Codex Alimentarius Commission (GMO labelling standards), the Organization for Economic Cooperation and Development (OECD) (work on biotechnology, and agriculture), and a Protocol to the Convention on Biological Diversity (CBD), the Cartagena Protocol on Biosafety.

The Cartagena Protocol provides the most extensive international instrument regulating transboundary movement of certain GMOs (known in the Protocol as "living modified organisms" or "LMOs"). It protects biodiversity from potential LMO risks by, among other things, establishing an "advanced informed agreement" procedure, incorporating a precautionary approach to the trans-boundary movement of LMOs, and establishing a Biosafety Clearing-house to facilitate information exchange and implementation.

As both the Cartagena Protocol and WTO agreements cover the trans-boundary movement of LMOs, a number of issues arise between them. First, the Protocol and the WTO SPS Agreement include differing language on how governments should make decisions under conditions of scientific uncertainty. The Protocol explicitly embodies a precautionary approach (preamble, Article 10.6 and 11.8) and explicitly permits countries to prohibit the import of certain LMOs (Article 10.3). The SPS Agreement, by contrast, merely "reflects" the precautionary principle in certain articles[40] and allows Members to adopt sanitary or phytosanitary measures on a *provisional* basis to be reviewed "within a reasonable period of time" (Article 5.7).

Second, in relation to a specific category of LMOs (known as LMOs "intended for direct use as food or feed, or for processing") the Protocol does not explicitly permit countries to prohibit the import of LMOs, but rather merely states that they may make "a final decision regarding domestic use, including placing on the market, of a living modified organism" (Article 11.1). Decisions made to ban or restrict trade in such LMOs will be closely scrutinized by exporting countries, which may seek to use the SPS Agreement's provisions to

---

[40] For a more detailed discussion of the relationship between precaution and SPS rules, see above.

challenge such a decision. Again, the relationship between these provisions in the Protocol and SPS Agreement has not been the subject of dispute settlement or authoritative interpretive decision.

Third, the two agreements include slightly differing provisions on risk assessment. The Protocol explicitly permits importing countries to require exporters to carry out and pay for risk assessments (Article 15). The SPS Agreement, by contrast, makes no such explicit provision. Rather, it states that Members must base their measures on a risk assessment (Article 3.1). In relation to provisional measures, "Members shall seek to obtain the additional information necessary for a more objective assessment of risk and review the sanitary or phytosanitary measure accordingly within a reasonable period of time" (Article 5.7).[41]

Finally, the Protocol and WTO agreements both include references to packaging/labelling. The Protocol requires parties to consider the "need for and modalities of developing standards with regard to identification, handling, packaging and transport practices" (Article 18). The TBT Agreement seeks to discipline measures for "packaging, marking or labelling requirements" so they do not create "unnecessary obstacles to international trade" (Article 2.2). The Protocol's international standards, as well as national measures implementing them, may thus well raise questions of consistency with provisions of the TBT Agreement, and vice-versa.

There are a number of approaches available to resolve these legal and policy tensions. The WTO could consider using the Protocol as an international standard under the SPS Agreement (Article 3.1 and Annex A) and TBT Agreements (Article 2 and Annex 1). Unnecessary conflicts could also be avoided by interpreting each agreement in light of the other, in accordance with the international law presumption against conflicts.[42] Unnecessary conflicts could also be avoided by promoting cooperation through reciprocal observer status for the Cartagena Protocol and WTO Secretariats in their respective institutions.

In the event of a dispute regarding trade in LMOs, there may be uncertainty as to whether the CBD or the WTO is the appropriate forum for deciding the dispute. To avoid overlapping jurisdiction, WTO Members could agree to

---

[41] Notably, the Appellate Body has stated that Article 3.1 does not require Members to undertake risk assessments themselves, but may rely on risk assessments undertaken by other Members or international organizations. See, *EC-Hormones, supra* note 8, at para. 190. In relation to Article 5.7, the Appellate Body has stated that a provisional measure may not be maintained unless "the *Member which adopted the measure … seek[s]* to obtain the additional information necessary for a more objective assessment of risk" (emphasis added). See *Japan-Varietals, supra* note 11, at para. 89. However, the text of Article 5.7 states that Member<u>s</u> (plural) must seek additional information, which is consistent with the Biosafety Protocol's provisions allowing importing countries to require exporters to undertake risk assessments.

[42] *See* B. Eggers and R. MacKenzie, "The Cartagena Protocol on Biosafety" (2000) 3 *J.I.E.L.* 525 at 541.

follow the recommendation in the 1996 CTE Report to the Singapore Ministerial that Members should consider resolving disputes "over the use of trade measures they are applying between themselves pursuant to the MEA … through the dispute settlement mechanisms available under the MEA". Additionally, in the event of a dispute at the WTO, Protocol Secretariat staff (or other biosafety experts) could be involved in WTO consultations (Article 4 DSU) or mediation (Article 5 DSU), serve as panel members, form an expert group to consider factual issues (Article 13.1 and Appendix 4 DSU), or serve as *ad hoc* experts to advise the panel (Article 13 DSU). Issues relating to dispute settlement are discussed further below.

Agriculture

Because agriculture is so intimately tied to so many other facets of the human and natural world, liberalization of trade in agricultural products may have significant consequences for sustainable development. The Agreement on Agriculture embodies a movement towards a "market-oriented agricultural trading system". The agreement's preamble, as well as Article 20 on further negotiations, notes the need to consider non-trade concerns, including a variety of sustainable development issues such as food security and environmental protection. The agreement has the long-term goal of "substantial progressive reductions in agricultural support and protection …resulting in correcting and preventing restrictions and distortions in world agricultural markets" by addressing three areas: increasing market access, reducing domestic support, and phasing out export competition.

Increasing *market access* involves reducing both tariff and non-tariff barriers to agricultural trade. Reducing tariffs may have a range of positive and negative effects for different actors in different countries. Reducing tariffs will, for example, increase market access for exporting country producers, while exposing producers in importing countries to increased competition. Addressing non-tariff barriers, similarly, raises a range of issues. On one hand, disciplining non-tariff measures, such as national sanitary requirements, may impact health and environment in importing countries. On the other hand, increasing market access is important to developing countries that have based their development strategies in part on exporting agricultural products to northern markets. This balance will likely be influenced by ongoing negotiations, pursuant to Article 20 of the agreement, regarding new rules and disciplines to increase market access.

Reducing *domestic support* – including a range of subsidies and other benefits to farmers – also raises a set of closely interrelated economic, social and environmental issues.[43] Economically, it will reduce the benefits paid to

---

[43] UNEP, *Environment and Trade: A Handbook* (Winnipeg: UNEP/IISD, 2000).

producers in the supporting country, while increasing the competitiveness of foreign producers. Socially, it may affect the viability of recipient agricultural communities, increase the viability of foreign agricultural communities, and reduce the tax burden on non-agricultural communities in the supporting country. Environmentally, it may reduce the over-use of expensive and environmentally harmful inputs such as pesticides and fertilizers in the supporting country while enhancing export opportunities for environmentally sound products produced elsewhere. Of course, the linkages are complex and will play out differently in different ecological, economic, social and institutional contexts. Within the Agreement on Agriculture, some forms of domestic support are protected, including certain subsidies not related to production, payments related to research and structural adjustment programs ("green box" – Article 13(a) and Annex 2), certain payments for limiting production ("blue box" – Articles 6 and 13(b)), and certain trade distorting subsidies that are permitted subject to reduction commitments ("amber box" – Article 13(c) and Part V). WTO Members are discussing whether these classifications should be retained, or whether some other approach should be adopted (e.g. a "development box"). The outcome of these discussions will influence the kinds of national measures that may be taken to protect non-trade concerns such as the environment, food safety, animal welfare, food security and development.

As with domestic support, reducing *export subsidies* raises a complex set of issues. Lowering such subsidies will likely help decrease incentives for overproduction, reduce the dumping of agricultural products on world markets at artificially low prices, and increase the competitiveness of unsubsidized products from developing countries. Although reducing export subsidies may affect recipient producers, it is generally assumed that the net effects will be positive.

WTO Members have agreed (in Article 20) to further negotiations to liberalize trade in agricultural products. In the Doha Ministerial Declaration, they committed themselves to "comprehensive negotiations aimed at: substantial improvements in market access; reduction of, with a view to phasing out, all forms of export subsidies; and substantial reductions in trade-distorting domestic support" (paragraph 13). They also agreed "special and differential treatment shall be an integral part of all elements of the negotiations" so as to "enable developing countries to effectively take account of their development needs, including food security and rural development" (paragraph 13). In addition to the issues raised above, some Members have raised geographical indications, food safety and food labelling as concerns to be discussed in the Agriculture negotiations.

Subsidies

Subsidies are covered by a number of WTO agreements, including the Agreement on Agriculture and the General Agreement on Trade in Services. The primary agreement addressing subsidies, however, is the Agreement on Subsidies and Countervailing Measures (SCM), which disciplines both trade distorting subsidies, and the "countervailing" measures that may be taken by other countries in response to them. It classifies subsidies as prohibited, non-actionable or actionable depending on their trade impact. *Prohibited subsidies* include certain subsidies with serious trade implications, which must be removed immediately once identified. *Non-actionable subsidies* include certain subsidies with limited trade consequences, which are protected from challenge. Between these extremes, *actionable subsidies* are permissible, but may be challenged in WTO dispute settlements if they adversely affect the interests of other WTO Members.

Subsidies can have both positive and negative implications for sustainable development. Used well, they can correct market failures (e.g. failure to reflect positive externalities) and promote behaviour that is environmentally and socially sound. Used poorly, they constitute policy failures that distort otherwise efficient markets, and promote behaviour that is environmentally and socially unsound. In some cases, they may have mixed economic, social and environmental effects; for example, in some cases distorting markets is necessary to protect social and cultural values or environmental resources. When and how subsidies should be applied, the distribution of their costs and benefits on people within and between countries, are complex questions. Consequently, how subsidies are treated by the WTO is an important sustainable development issue.

The SCM Agreement gives rise to a number of legal and policy issues. One concerns how the agreement is applied to environmental subsidies. Until 2000, the agreement established an automatic exemption for some government subsidies to help industries adapt existing facilities to new environmental requirements (Article 8.2(c)). These exemptions, however, were not extended after 2000, raising questions about whether the agreement provides sufficient space for environmental subsidies. While there are no instances of challenges, future environmental subsidies– such as those to promote cleaner production – will be subject to scrutiny as actionable subsidies, and may be found inconsistent with the SCM Agreement.

A second set of issues arises from the potential of the SCM Agreement to yield "triple-win" outcomes – for trade, environment and development – by removing perverse subsidies that distort trade, harm the environment, and limit developing countries' market opportunities. Removing perverse fisheries subsidies, for example, can help to address both trade distortions and over-fishing. At the Doha Ministerial, WTO Members agreed to negotiate to improve WTO disciplines on fisheries subsidies (paragraph 28 and 31 of Ministerial Declaration). The outcome of these negotiations will have important implications for sustainable fisheries management, and may set a precedent for the reduction of subsidies in other areas.

Services

Economic liberalization of services is the goal of the General Agreement on Trade in Services (GATS). According to the GATS, services are traded through four "modes of delivery": cross-border delivery, consumption abroad, foreign direct investment (commercial establishment), and movement of natural persons supplying services. The GATS seeks to liberalize international trade in services by applying rules relating to national treatment, most favoured nation treatment, market access, and transparency.

Economic liberalization of services has the potential to result in positive, negative or neutral economic, social and environmental impacts.[44] Liberalization of services – such as transport, health care, or waste treatment – may have a range of positive impacts where existing services are inadequately provided, or where competition is lacking. By contrast, in the absence of appropriate national legislation, liberalization may ultimately facilitate consolidation of commercial services; increase the cost or reduce coverage to marginal areas of postal, health care, water or education services; or increase impacts of environmentally risky services such as mining, tourism or transportation.

Regulating services to promote positive outcomes and avoid negative ones is a role for national legislation. One key legal and policy issue is finding the appropriate balance (i.e. vertical balance/coherence) between national rules designed to regulate services, and the multilateral GATS disciplines that apply to these rules. As noted in the WTO's Ministerial Declaration on Trade in Services, "measures necessary to protect the environment may conflict with the provisions of the Agreement". This is not only true of existing GATS rules, but also of ones currently under negotiation, such as those to be elaborated under Article IV(4) to ensure certain national regulations do not "constitute unnecessary barriers to trade in services" and are "not more burdensome than necessary to ensure the quality of the service".

The CTE has been asked to examine GATS in the context of sustainable development. It has the mandate to "report, with recommendations if any, on

---

[44] For a discussion of the potential effects of services liberalization on developing countries, see *Communication of Cuba, Dominican Republic, Haiti, India, Kenya, Pakistan, Peru, Uganda, Venezuela and Zimbabwe*, WTO Doc. S/CSS/W/114.

the relationship between services trade and the environment including the issue of sustainable development" and to determine whether any modification of the GATS exception (Article XIV) is required. So far the CTE has focused primarily on the potential material benefits of liberalizing environmental services. It has paid little attention to the potential negative material effects (e.g. environmental impacts of liberalizing energy or transportation services), and the potential legal and policy conflicts between GATS rules and valid national measures. Further work is therefore required to examine the economic, social and environmental implications of services liberalization, and the relationship between GATS disciplines and national regulations.

Just as there are linkages between national and international levels, there are also legal and policy issues arising horizontally at the international level between GATS and other systems of international law, including environmental law and human rights. The CTE's mandate identifies environmental law and calls for "examin[ing] the relevance of inter-governmental agreements on the environment and their relationship to the Agreement." Service liberalization may influence the implementation of the Basel Convention (e.g. impacts of waste management services on transboundary management of hazardous waste), the Convention on Biological Diversity (e.g. impacts of tourism or mining services on conservation of biodiversity) and the Kyoto Protocol (e.g. impacts of energy or transport services on global warming). As well as changing patterns of economic activity – with consequences for society and the environment – GATS disciplines will define and delimit the domestic legal and policy measures available to regulate services in order to implement MEAs. The CTE has yet to offer recommendations on this issue or undertake work examining the possible relationship between the various GATS disciplines on their respective mandates.

Increasingly legal issues are arising between the GATS and human rights law, especially in the area of basic services. The UN Sub-Commission on the Promotion and Protection of Human Rights, for example, has recommended that "the World Trade Organization and its Council for Trade in Services, in conducting its assessments of the impact of GATS in its current and future forms, include consideration of the human rights implications of the international trade in basic services (such as, *inter alia*, the provision of affordable and accessible health and education services) and the further liberalization thereof."[45] It has also encouraged "other relevant United Nations agencies, in particular the World Health Organization and the United Nations Educational, Scientific and Cultural Organization, to undertake analyses, within their respective competencies, of the implementation of GATS on the provision of basic services such as health and education services."[46] The

---

[45] Sub-Commission Resolution 2001/4(E/CN.4/SUB.2/RES/2001/4).

[46] *Ibid.*

relationship between WTO rules and human rights is a relatively new area that merits further consideration by students and scholars of international sustainable development law.

Additional research – on both material and legal/policy implications of services liberalization and rules – is urgently needed in the context of the mandated assessment of the GATS. GATS Article XIX:3 requires an assessment of the application of the agreement. This assessment, according to some WTO Members, should include an assessment of the agreement's potential impacts on the standards of services provided, especially to populations that are poor, vulnerable or socially disadvantaged.[47] This assessment, as well as the ongoing discussions of trade in services at the WTO, provides an important opportunity for the non-trade community (as well as non-trade ministries, parliaments, international organizations and the broader public) to evaluate the role of services liberalization as a means to the broader end of sustainable development.

Intellectual property

Intellectual property is covered by the WTO's TRIPS Agreement. This agreement differs from WTO agreements on goods and services; rather than seeking to liberalize trade, it requires states to establish minimum national standards to protect intellectual property rights such as patents and trademarks, copyright and industrial designs, geographical indications and plant variety protection. Because intellectual property is a driver of innovation and influences technological development and patterns of economic development, the TRIPS Agreement has significant ramifications for sustainability.

Traditionally, intellectual property has provided an instrumental tool at the national level to maximize the benefits of innovation to society by rewarding inventors, and balancing the short-term costs of near-monopoly rights against the long-term dynamic benefits of a more inventive society. The traditional role of intellectual property is, however, changing. There is a tendency at the WTO, and other international organizations such as the World Intellectual Property Organization (WIPO), to extend the scope and geographical coverage of intellectual property rules, with implications for the traditional balance between private rights and the public domain, and between developed countries (which are the primary producers of formal innovation) and developing countries (who are primarily consumers of formal innovation).

This shifting balance plays out in a myriad of more specific issues, including issues relating to public health, biodiversity protection, traditional knowledge, and technology transfer. Among the most controversial of these has been the

---

[47] See *Communication of Cuba, Dominican Republic, Haiti, India, Kenya, Pakistan, Peru, Uganda, Venezuela and Zimbabwe, supra* note 28.

relationship between the TRIPS Agreement and public health. Many developing countries have raised concern that patents required by the TRIPS Agreement are undermining their ability to access affordable medicines to address HIV AIDS, tuberculosis, malaria, and other epidemics. As a result, WTO Members at the Doha Ministerial Meeting adopted a Declaration on the TRIPS Agreement and Public Health calling for the agreement to "be interpreted and implemented in a manner supportive of WTO Members' right to protect public health and, in particular, to promote access to medicines for all".[48] However the Declaration fails to outline how countries with insufficient or no manufacturing capacities in the pharmaceutical sector can make effective use of compulsory licensing. WTO Members have agreed to find an "expeditious solution" to this problem, and will likely negotiate a waiver and a subsequent amendment to the TRIPS Agreement.[49]

A second major issue focuses on the relationship between intellectual property and biodiversity conservation. The importance of this relationship was highlighted in the Doha Ministerial Declaration, which called on the TRIPS Council to "examine, *inter alia*, the relationship between the TRIPS Agreement and the Convention on Biological Diversity".[50] One concern raised by developing countries centered on the fact that patents are being granted in developed countries over genetic resources taken without permission from developing countries, and without efforts to share the benefits of the use of the genetic resources as required by Article 15 of the CBD.[51] Some countries are supporting an amendment of the TRIPS Agreement to address these issues, whereas others believe that a more effective system of contracts between the users and custodians of genetic resources would address the concerns of developing countries.[52] The need for international cooperation is recognized in the CBD's statement that "Contracting Parties, recognizing that patents and other intellectual property rights may have an influence on the implementation of this Convention, shall cooperate in this regard subject to national legislation and international law in order to ensure that such rights are supportive of and do not run counter to its objectives".[53]

Closely related to issues of biodiversity are the implications of the TRIPS Agreement for the rights of indigenous and other local communities over their

---

[48] *Declaration on the TRIPS Agreement and Public Health,* WTO Doc. (WT/MIN(01)/DEC/W/2), at para. 4.

[49] Ibid., at para. 6.

[50] See *WTO 4th Ministerial Declaration, supra* note 3, at para. 19.

[51] See, for example, *Communication from Brazil,* WTO Doc, (IP/C/W/228), paras. 21 and 22 (stating "…patents over a Member's genetic resource, but granted outside its territory raises the issue of potential conflict with the principle of the sovereignty of the Contracting Parties of the CBD over their own genetic resources" and that "amending Article 27.3(b) of TRIPs to accommodate principles of the CBD will be a necessary outcome of the review of that Article. Failure to clarify this relationship may turn out to be detrimental to both instruments.")

[52] See *Communication from the United States,* WTO Doc. IP/C/W/209, at 5-6.

[53] *United Nations Convention on Biological Diversity* 31 I.L.M. 818, at Article 16.5.

traditional knowledge, innovations and practices. The Doha Ministerial Statement calls on the TRIPS Council to examine the Agreement's relationship with "the protection of traditional knowledge" (paragraph 19). This mandate arises from concern that patents are being granted in developed countries over innovations based on traditional knowledge of communities in developing countries, without any effort to share the benefits with them as required by Article 8(j) of the CBD. There is also concern over the absence of appropriate systems offering positive protection for traditional knowledge. This latter subject is currently being discussed in an intergovernmental committee at the World Intellectual Property Organization (WIPO). The involvement of at least three institutions (WIPO, the WTO's TRIPS Council and the CBD) in these discussions raises considerable challenges of coordination and coherence.

The implication of the TRIPS Agreement for agricultural practices is a fourth major sustainable development issue. At least two legal and policy questions arise here. One concerns the implications for agriculture of Article 27.3(b), which requires Members to protect plant varieties either by patents or by an effective *sui generis* system. Some countries have proposed that the International Convention for the Protection of New Varieties of Plants (UPOV) be designated as the effective *sui generis* system for the purposes of the TRIPS Agreement. Others, mostly developing countries, believe that they should maintain flexibility to develop their own *sui generis* systems, and that the most recent version of UPOV (UPOV 1991) may run counter to traditional agricultural practices, such as saving and sharing of seeds by farmers. A second question is the relationship between the TRIPS Agreement and the newly agreed International Treaty on Plant Genetic Resources for Food and Agriculture, which aims to conserve and sustain the use of plant genetic resources for food and agriculture and ensure the fair and equitable sharing of the benefits arising out of their use. WTO Members have yet to explore how this new treaty may affect their discussions of plant variety protection under Article 27.3(b) of the TRIPS Agreement.

Finally, the effect of the TRIPS Agreement on the development, transfer and dissemination of technology has also been identified as a major concern for sustainable development. As noted in Agenda 21, "access to and transfer of environmentally-sound technology are essential requirements for sustainable development".[54] The TRIPS Agreement includes in its objectives "the ... transfer and dissemination of technology, to the mutual advantage of producers and users of technological knowledge and in a manner conducive to social and economic welfare" (Article 7). The agreement also contains specific provisions requiring developed countries to establish incentives for technology transfer to the least developed countries (Article 66.2). Despite these references, many developing countries remain unconvinced that the Agreement, in fact,

---

[54] *Agenda 21*, UN. Doc. A/CONF.151/26, adopted 14 June 1992, at para 34.7.

promotes technology transfer. To explore the relationship between various WTO rules on technology transfer the WTO Members have agreed to establish a Working Group on trade and technology transfer (paragraph 37 Ministerial Declaration), and to review of the TRIPS Agreement in light of its objectives and principles, including the Article 7 reference to technology transfer (paragraph 19 Ministerial Declaration).

Multilateral Environmental Agreements (MEAs)

MEAs are inter-governmental accords designed to address shared environmental problems such as climate change, biodiversity loss and ozone depletion. The policies and rules embodied in MEAs and the WTO intersect in many ways; they touch on issues of scientific uncertainty and precaution, intellectual property, biodiversity conservation, and protection of traditional knowledge, as well as on transboundary movement of living modified organisms, endangered and invasive species, and hazardous wastes and chemicals, to name a few. Clarifying competences, realizing synergies and resolving tensions between these evolving regimes is an essential step towards developing a coherent framework of governance for sustainable development. A number of MEA-related trade issues are addressed in other sections of this paper. This section addresses one key subject: the WTO's ongoing negotiations on the relationship between WTO rules and "specific trade obligations" in MEAs.

Negotiations on the relationship between existing WTO rules and specific trade obligations set out in MEAs are mandated by paragraph 31(i) of the Doha Ministerial Declaration. Many of the measures in the MEAs designed to protect the environment have trade implications. Indeed, among the primary purposes of some MEAs is regulating the trans-boundary movement of a particular category of product, such as hazardous waste, LMOs , or dangerous chemicals. By establishing procedures for prior informed consent, national technical regulations and border measures (such as bans or quotas), MEAs help to address the externalities associated with the production, trans-boundary movement and use of these products. Trade-related measures variously serve to regulate trade in environmentally harmful products; remove economic incentives that encourage environmental destruction; promote compliance with MEA provisions; and encourage broad country participation to reduce the potential of non-parties undermining a treaty's objectives.

While many MEAs embody trade-related environment measures, none use the term "specific trade obligations," giving rise to a definitional challenge for the WTO that affects the negotiation's scope. Although the WTO has a mandate to provide protection for the "balance of rights and obligations" embodied in WTO agreements, the organization does not offer any similar protection for the balance of rights and obligations embodied in the MEAs. In addition, the negotiations only address the least controversial aspects of trade-related measures in MEAs – i.e. those that are specifically mandated and apply only between parties. They do not take up non-specific measures and measures applying to non-parties to the MEA, which have been the source of greater controversy within the trading community. When addressing this aspect of the Doha mandate, it is hoped that WTO Members can build on past WTO practice, including the 1996 CTE Report stating WTO Members should consider resolving disputes "over the use of trade measures they are applying between themselves pursuant to the MEA ... through the dispute settlement mechanisms available under the MEA". They may also wish to consider the outcome of the *Shrimp 21.5* Appellate Body decision that upheld certain trade measures (unilaterally applied) "as long as ... ongoing serious good faith efforts to reach a multilateral agreement" exist.[55]

In addition to these issues, a number of the other environmental mandates in the Doha Ministerial Declaration raise legal and policy issues of relevance to the MEAs. These include negotiations for "procedures for information exchange" between MEAs and WTO bodies, "criteria for observer status" (discussed in the next section), the call for the CTE to pay particular attention to "labelling requirements for environmental purposes" and "the effect of environmental measures on market access" (paragraph 32 of Ministerial Declaration) which may, for instance, influence the development of labelling and documentation for LMOs under the Cartagena Protocol on Biosafety[56] Similarly, mandates on fisheries subsidies (paragraph 28 and 31), reduction of tariff and non-tariff barriers to environmental goods and services (paragraph 31(iii)), and the relationship between trade and transfer of technology (paragraph 37), may also affect issues covered by MEAs.

Institutional Issues

Legal and policy issues such as those discussed above are often created and ultimately resolved by organizations and other institutional arrangements. Institutions perform the function of developing, interpreting and executing rules to achieve agreed objectives.

An examination of institutional linkages and issues is required when more than one institution is responsible for defining objectives and related laws and policies in a particular arena (e.g. trade and the environment).

---

[55] *US-Shrimp 21.5, supra* note 13, para. 153
[56] See *Cartagena Protocol on Biosafety, supra* note 25, Article 10.

Institutional linkages exist at a number of levels. At the national level, relationships exist among trade and other non-trade ministries. At the international level, relationships exist among formal bodies of trade and other non-trade organizations. They also exist among the secretariats of international institutions.

Of the many institutional issues, this paper discusses three in brief: integrated assessments; information exchange and observer status; and compliance, enforcement and dispute settlement.[57]

A.   The role of Integrated Assessments

Assessments provide a powerful tool for examining the material effects of trade liberalization on economic, social and environmental systems. In addition, they can be used to explore the legal and policy implications of trade rules on other systems of law and policy at the local, national, regional and international level. And they can help to identify opportunities to increase institutional cooperation among and between the various levels.

"An integrated assessment," according to UNEP, "considers the economic, environmental and social impacts of trade measures, the linkages between these effects, and aims to build upon this analysis by identifying ways in which the negative consequences can be avoided or mitigated, and ways in which positive effects can be enhanced."[58] The UN Sub-Commission on the Promotion and Protection of Human Rights has encouraged governments "to undertake comprehensive and systematic studies, in consultation with United Nations and regional human rights mechanisms and relevant civil society organizations, of the human rights and social impacts of economic liberalization programmes, policies and laws."[59]

Assessments can be conducted before, during or after trade negotiations. The focus can be on implications for a sector (such as agriculture, forestry, fisheries or mining), a country or other geographic region, or a particular social or environmental system. The ultimate goal of assessments is to enable countries to implement integrated policies that optimize the sustainable development gains from economic liberalization. The importance of assessing the impacts of trade rules and liberalization was recognized in the WTO's 4th Ministerial Declaration, which encourages "expertise and experience [to] be shared with Members wishing to perform environmental reviews at the national level" (paragraph 33).

---

[57] For further discussion of dispute settlement see M.C. Cordonier Segger, in this volume.

[58] See *UNEP Reference Manual, supra* note 4, at iii.

[59] Sub-Commission Resolution 1999/30 (E/CN.4/SUB.2/RES/1999/30).

Assessments at the national level can be complemented by multilateral assessments of WTO Agreements. The GATS for example, calls on future negotiation to be guided by guidelines that are prepared in light of "an assessment of trade in services in overall terms and on a sectoral basis with references to the objectives of this Agreement."[60] At both the multinational and national level, assessments of trade liberalization and trade policy form an essential tool for gathering information about the real and potential contributions of trade to sustainable development.

B.   Information exchange and observer status

As well as the negotiations on "specific trade obligations" identified in section IV.J above, the WTO has mandated negotiations for procedures for information exchange between MEAs and WTO, and criteria observer status in WTO bodies.

Procedures for information exchange are an important vehicle for enhancing cooperation and communication between international trade, environment and other institutions. The Doha Ministerial Declaration calls for negotiations on "procedures for regular information exchange between MEA Secretariats and the relevant WTO committees" (paragraph 31(ii)), and also welcomes the "WTO's continued cooperation with UNEP and other inter-governmental environmental and developmental organizations (paragraph 6). Negotiations on this issue should build from existing practice, and develop predictable procedures allowing MEAs and WTO to share information across the range of issues with the goal of making trade and environmental policy more mutually supportive.

Reciprocal observer status provides opportunities for governments and secretariat staff to increase their understanding of different regimes, exchange information and perspectives, and identify practical opportunities to increase coherence. The Doha Declaration establishes negotiations on "criteria for granting observer status" to MEAs in relevant WTO bodies (paragraph 31(ii)). The goal of these negotiations is to make it easier and quicker for MEAs to receive observer status in WTO bodies. In establishing mechanisms to increase cooperation between MEAs and the WTO, members of the WTO may wish to examine their organization's agreements with other international organizations such as that between the WTO, World Bank and the International Monetary

---

[60] *See* GATS Article XIX, and also the *Guidelines and Procedures for the Negotiation on Trade in Services*, adopted by the Special Session of the Council for Trade in Services on 28 March 2001, paragraph 14, (S/L/93). See also *Communication from Cuba, Dominican Republic, Haiti, India, Kenya, Pakistan, Peru, Uganda, Venezuela and Zimbabwe to the Council for Trade in Services*, *supra* note 28, calling for assessment of the economic and social impacts of the GATS. In relation to other WTO agreements, *see*, Agreement on Agriculture, Article 20 (noting that ongoing reform should take into account "the experience … from implementing the reduction commitments", and TRIPS Agreement, Article 71.1 (which provides for future reviews of the TRIPS Agreement "having regard to the experience gained in its implementation").

Fund. This accord establishes a High Level Working Group on Coherence to oversee cooperation between the three organizations, prepare joint reports, and promote a range of cooperative activities, including participation at meetings, information sharing, and contacts between staff on specific projects.

C.   Compliance, enforcement and dispute settlement.

Another set of institutional linkages arises out of the provisions for compliance, enforcement and dispute settlement included in MEAs and the WTO. Generally, *compliance* refers to a situation in which parties to honour their treaty obligations, and compliance measures would include measures, such as technical cooperation and technology transfer, designed to achieve this goal. *Enforcement* refers to multilateral measures designed to respond to a party's failure to comply, and would include suspension of certain rights and privileges or trade-related measures. D*ispute settlement* refers to procedures designed to address bilateral (or plurilateral) disputes between parties, and would include provisions for consultation, good offices, mediation, arbitration or judicial settlement.[61] In each of these areas there are overlaps between the institutional mechanisms in MEAs and the WTO, giving rise to the potential for synergies and conflicts.

The area most likely to give rise to challenges to institutional coherence is dispute settlement. MEA and WTO provisions may apply simultaneously to the same countries and activities. A lack of clarity about the relationship between dispute settlement systems gives rise to the risk of forum shopping and raises the potential for conflicting outcomes. The importance of coherence between MEA and WTO dispute settlement systems was recognized by WTO Members in Item 5 of the CTE's agenda, which empowers the CTE to offer recommendations on the "relationship between the dispute settlement mechanisms in the multilateral trading system and those found in multilateral environmental agreements".

In the absence of any recommendations by the CTE, the relationship between WTO and other dispute settlement systems remains unclear. Determining which forum should decide which matter requires an examination of factors including explicit treaty language on dispute settlement[62], general treaty language on the relationship between treaties[63], and general principles of law, such as the duty of good faith and *res judicata* (the principle that the same matter cannot be decided twice). How these factors play out in a particular dispute will require an analysis of all relevant rules and evidence.

---

[61] The terms *compliance, enforcement* and *dispute settlement* are not mutually exclusive, nor are they used consistently in the literature. For example, it is possible that a measure (such as technical assistance) may be used for both compliance and enforcement purposes.

[62] See, for example, *SPS Agreement*, Article 11.3.

[63] *WTO Dispute Settlement Understanding*, Article 22.1.

While explicit guidance by states is preferable, there are less direct approaches that can reduce the potential for conflict. According to the joint UNEP-WTO paper strengthening compliance mechanisms in MEAs would "enhance the effective implementation of MEAs, and ... prevent MEA-related disputes from arising in the WTO dispute settlement system".[64] Additionally, the WTO could "put less focus on judicial settlement of disputes, and more on mediation and conciliation combined with technical assistance and capacity building for implementation."[65] In the event a MEA-related dispute does arise at the WTO, the DSU also includes a number of mechanisms allow for the dispute settlement system to consider environmental factors. These include the use of procedures for good offices, mediation and consultation (Article 5) to encourage dispute avoidance and to ensure participation by MEA Secretariats and other experts; use of experts on an *ad hoc* basis under Article 13(1); establishment of Expert Review Groups under Article 13(2) and Appendix 4 to provide non-binding advisory opinions; and increased use of environmental experts as panellists.

Conclusion

Moving human behaviour onto sustainable development pathways is a complex and important task, requiring common goals and collective action by multiple institutions and actors. Economic integration is bringing markets, societies and cultures together, benefiting some, but leaving many marginalized. The scale of human impacts has breached planetary ecosystem limits, unbalancing the climate and depleting biodiversity, with uncertain implications for all. World population has trebled in the last 70 years to 6 billion people, and is projected to peak at around 9 billion in 2050. Achieving a minimum level of well being for all in 2050 and beyond, while avoiding serious environmental and social dislocation, will require significant foresight, careful planning, and a degree of humility. It will entail agreeing objectives, such as those included in Agenda 21 and the UN Millennium Declaration, and ensuring that all policies, laws and institutions – including those in the field of international trade – work systematically towards them.

Achieving this requires articulating more clearly what trade is for. Historically, trade liberalization has been regarded by some in the trading community as an end in itself, with environment and development seen as secondary and often conflicting objectives. This has limited scope for meaningful dialogue, obscured issues, and hindered movement towards a synthesis for sustainable development. Recently, some more enlightened members of the trading community have begun to discuss the need for a new synthesis – for an analytic

---

[64] Joint Paper by WTO and UNEP Secretariats, entitled *Compliance and Dispute Settlement Provisions in the WTO and in Multilateral Environmental Agreements*, WTO Doc. WT/CTE/W/191, para.141.

[65] *Ibid.*

framework that retires the tired "trade, environment, development" triumvirate, elects sustainable development as its governing principle, and employs trade meaningfully as a means of securing specific and measurable sustainable development goals.

At the international level, many of these sustainable development goals have already been agreed in documents such as Agenda 21 and the UN Millennium Declaration. Indeed, the WTO's preamble identifies trade liberalization as a means to the end of "raising standards of living ... in accordance with the objective of sustainable development, seeking both to protect and preserve the environment" with "positive efforts designed to ensure that developing countries, and especially the least developed among them, secure a share in the growth in international trade commensurate with the needs of their economic development." Yet, as noted earlier, insufficient effort has been made at the multilateral level to systematically assess the effects of trade and trade liberalization on real people and communities. Work is now underway by various UN bodies, such as UNEP, UNDP and the UN Human Rights bodies, to identify the role of trade in helping to achieve goals in their respective areas. These efforts, undertaken in cooperation with the WTO, should be institutionalized and expanded.

At the national level, insufficient attention has been given (particularly in developing countries) to clearly identifying the relationship between trade and national development priorities, and to assessing the impact of past and proposed future trade liberalization. Rather the agenda has been set and driven from the top-down, and largely by developed countries in pursuit of relatively narrowly defined economic interests. It is essential to the long-term legitimacy of the trading system for this tendency to be reversed. At all levels, an ongoing effort will be required to understand the complex interdependencies between trade and other facets of the world we live in. In light of this understanding, trade and trade rules must complement other activities and policies to promote human, social and economic development and to protect the environment; they must be reformed and developed in light of this objective, and mindfully of other systems of law, policy and institutions, to form part of a more balanced and coherent system of governance for sustainable development.

8

SUSTAINABLE COMPETITION LAW

*Markus W. Gehring**

How could competition rules[1] foster rather than frustrate broader sustainable development goals? Modern society has seen 'competition laws' proliferate as anti-trust laws become increasingly central to economic regulation.[2] Propositions that the World Trade Organization (WTO) become an umbrella association for international competition disciplines have led to debates at the 5th WTO Ministerial Conference in Cancún.[3] Concurrently, sustainable development has been recognized as an overarching goal,[4] recently re-affirmed by over 140 countries in Johannesburg, South Africa.[5] Fundamental questions arising from such developments include: how do national competition regimes integrate sustainable development goals, and how can international rules help?

* Markus W. Gehring, LL.M (Yale), B.C.L. (Hamburg) i.p., Lead Counsel for Trade, Investment and Competition Law, Centre for International Sustainable Development Law (CISDL), Researcher, Concerted Action on Trade and Environment (funded by the European Commission), Tutor of Public International Law, University College, Oxford Law Faculty, was head of the CISDL Delegation in Cancun, Mexico at the WTO 5th Ministerial Conference. He would like to thank A. L. Chua, Professor at Yale Law School, V. Chetty, Director at Edward, Natham and Friedland, South Africa and R. Pittman, U.S. Department of Justice. He also wishes to acknowledge A. Klevorick, J. M. Balkin, R. W. Gordon, S. V. Levinson and the participants in the Law and Globalization seminar, Spring 2003 at Yale Law School.
[1] The term anti-trust law is more widely used in North America, while other jurisdictions more frequently refer to the same legal field and key issues as 'competition law'. International bodies, such as the OECD, the WTO and the UNCTAD refer to competition law as does the new cooperative International Competition Network of national competition authorities. For further information, see the ICN, available online: <http://www.internationalcompetitionnetwork.org>.
[2] See Frédéric Jenny, "Globalization, Competition and Trade Policy: Convergence, Divergence and Cooperation" in Yang-Ching Chao, Gee San, Changfa Lo and Jiming Ho, eds., *International and Comparative Competition Law and Policies* (The Hague: Kluwer Law International, 2001)at 31- 33. [Jenny] And see Eleanor Fox, "International Competition Law" in Andreas F. Lowenfeld, *International Economic Law* (Oxford: Oxford University Press, 2003). [Fox] Andrew I. Gavil, William E. Kovacic & Jonathan B. Baker, eds. *Antitrust Law in Perspective : Cases, Concepts and Problems in Competition Policy* (St. Paul, Minnesota: Thomson/West, 2002) at 38. [Gavil]
[3] *WTO Ministerial Declaration, Ministerial Conference* (held on 14 November 2001) WTO Doc. WT/MIN(01)/DEC/W/1, online: WTO <http://www.wto.org>. [*WTO Ministerial Declaration*]
[4] See Richard L. Revesz, Philippe Sands & Richard B. Stewart, eds., *Environmental Law, the Economy, and Sustainable Development* (Cambridge: Cambridge University Press, 2000). See also Marie-Claire Cordonier Segger & Ashfaq Khalfan, *Sustainable Development Law: Principles, Practices and Prospects* (Oxford: Oxford University Press, 2004).
[5] *Johannesburg Plan of Implementation*, Report of the World Summit on Sustainable Development, Johannesburg (South Africa) (4 Sept. 2002) UN Doc. A/CONF.199/20. Available online <http://www.un.org/esa/sustdev/documents/WSSD_POI_PD/English/POIToc.htm> at para. 2.

M.C. Cordonier Segger & C. G. Weeramantry, eds., Sustainable Justice: Reconciling Economic, Social & Environmental Law
© 2005 Koninklijke Brill NV, Printed in The Netherlands, pp.121-134.

Competition advocates propose that by improving economic governance, competition law, in itself, *indirectly* supports sustainable development.[6] By stimulating innovation and constant product improvement among companies, competition law and policy help to achieve sustainable development. In accordance with this view, monopolies and cartels evade markets, resulting in economic injustice, higher prices and lower quality of goods for consumers. As a result, one may conclude competition law seeks to support greater equity facilitating economic growth while helping to eradicate poverty. Should consumers demand such goods, more competitive conditions may also lead to companies developing safer, healthier, more environmentally sound or socially just products. While companies protected by cartels or secure in a monopoly position have little incentive to change their practices, companies faced with competition may seek to develop new product lines, or improve the old ones, to meet the environmental and social expectations of consumers.

Supporters of competition laws offer additional arguments. Good competition policy enforcement, as with sound environmental management, requires a high degree of openness, accountability and monitoring. Such systems depend on good governance, a principle of sustainable development law. In addition, enforced competition rules can provide incentives for companies to improve their efficiency, avoiding wasteful practices and ensuring the sustainable use of natural resources. Finally, and perhaps most significantly for the international trade community, in the absence of sound and enforceable competition rules, a liberalization program might result in few benefits. Such laws are crucial for countries with open markets and foreign companies attempting to enter such markets. In their absence, the first company or companies to enter such a market can block future entrants, denying competing goods and services to consumers. This would confine the gains to a monopoly or international cartel thereby frustrating the rationale for having an open market.

Such arguments are certainly worthy of consideration. However, they do not answer the central concerns: whether a sustainable international competition law agenda is possible, and if so, how this can be achieved. It is not easy to establish and maintain a competition authority. In addition to considerable political support human resources and financial investments, mechanisms for monitoring and enforcement are also required. For sustainable development advocates, theories alone may not prove sufficiently persuasive. Convincing decision-makers to invest scarce political capital to make competition law a priority may necessitate finding ways for competition law to *directly* support sustainable development.

This leads to one of the thorniest issues in competition law and policy: whether other public concerns should influence competition decisions. This chapter

---

[6] Karl M. Meessen, "Competition in the Doha Round of WTO Negotiations" in N. Schrijver and F. Weiss, *International Law and Sustainable Development* (Leiden: Martinus Nijhoff, 2004) at 217, 227.

seeks to stimulate an informed, constructive debate on what kinds of national, regional and international competition law regimes are needed in the future.

What is Sustainable Competition Law?

Sustainable development law is found in the intersection of environmental, social and economic law.[7] More sustainable competition law will take social and environmental priorities into account, rather than focusing purely on economic priorities and imperatives. International competition disciplines or network guidelines should not seek to outlaw existing diversity of national competition rules or exceptions related to sustainable development. Rather they should explore the linkages and develop a positive agenda for competition law that supports sustainable development.

If the global community were to implement international competition, the lack of central institutions with the authority to balance competing priorities would necessitate mechanisms to ensure consideration of environmental and social objectives to be built into international competition treaties themselves. There is also a need to ensure that countries have the possibility to use competition law to support their sustainable development objectives. Doing so requires countries to provide spaces to explore linkages and policies related to the international goal of sustainable development. Further research and analysis is necessary to define and refine the nature of this linkage.

Building on substantive work addressing these issues in the area of trade and investment negotiations,[8] at least three ways to integrate the concept of sustainable development into national competition law and policy can be identified. Might these provide a way forward for international or regional competition law cooperation as well?

First, substantive international competition rules with sustainable development goals may be implemented (though economic laws and disciplines may provide too blunt an instrument to achieve important social or environmental goals in many areas). Second, express exceptions or exemptions can be granted where these rules might limit the abilities of countries to use social and environmental measures.

---

[7] This becomes clearer at the international level, where international regimes regulate specific aspects and intersecting with other regimes. Thus, for example, the WTO, international human rights treaties and certain Multilateral Environmental Accords (MEAs) intersect and a mutually supportive solution needs to be found. For further analysis see Marie-Claire Cordonier Segger & Ashfaq Khalfan, *Sustainable Development Law: Principles, Practices and Prospects* (Oxford: Oxford University Press, 2004), or see Markus Gehring & Marie-Claire Cordonier Segger, eds., *Sustainable Developments in World Trade Law* (The Hague: Kluwer Law International, 2005).

[8] See Daniel C. Esty, *Greening the GATT: Trade, Environment and the Future,* (Washington: Institute for International Economics, 1994).

Third, enhanced application of competition rules may be negotiated, where fair competition favours small and medium size companies and more environmentally favourable effects.

Such a 'sustainable competition law' research agenda might include consideration of the following questions:

- **Cartels:** What is the sustainable development impact of global or regional cartels? How can these affect environment and human rights? What measures need to be taken by key sectors to ensure cooperation on issues of sustainable development?

- **Mergers and acquisitions:** What sustainable development considerations are at stake with regard to global mergers and acquisitions of multinational enterprises? How can such decisions affect the environment and human rights? What are the key economic sectors, and what measures can ensure that new international competition policies support greater sustainability on these occasions?

- **Exceptions:** Which international competition law exceptions support sustainable development, and which do not? How do countries ensure consumer rights, social justice, environmental protection and other sustainable development priorities will continue to be reflected in special national competition rules that are not necessarily common on an international level? Which exceptions might be disciplined, creating win-win-win competition/environment/social laws?

The Doha 'Development Agenda' Mandate on Competition:

"23. Recognizing the case for a multilateral framework to enhance the contribution of competition policy to international trade and development, and the need for enhanced technical assistance and capacity-building in this area as referred to in paragraph 24, we agree that negotiations will take place after the Fifth Session of the Ministerial Conference on the basis of a decision to be taken, by explicit consensus, at that Session on modalities of negotiations.

24. We recognize the needs of developing and least-developed countries for enhanced support for technical assistance and capacity building in this area, including policy analysis and development so that they may better evaluate the implications of closer multilateral cooperation for their development policies and objectives, and human and institutional development. To this end, we shall work in cooperation with other relevant intergovernmental organisations, including UNCTAD, and through appropriate regional and bilateral channels, to provide strengthened and adequately resourced assistance to respond to these needs.

25. In the period until the Fifth Session, further work in the Working Group on the Interaction between Trade and Competition Policy will focus on the

clarification of: core principles, including transparency, non-discrimination and procedural fairness, and provisions on hardcore cartels; modalities for voluntary cooperation; and support for progressive reinforcement of competition institutions in developing countries through capacity building. Full account shall be taken of the needs of developing and least-developed country participants and appropriate flexibility provided to address them."[1]

Where should dialogue take place?

While competition has a significant international dimension, global debates on sustainable competition law have only just begun. At present, central questions revolve around the forum and modalities of such debates. Multinational enterprises act in domestic markets and often it is only these companies which have the economic power to engage in uncompetitive activities. The OECD has produced a number of non-binding instruments dealing with hard-core cartels, cooperation between competition authorities, pre-merger notification and reporting.[9] Some bilateral accords also exist, which formalize cooperation between competition authorities. However, there is no truly international competition law.

The Doha 'Development Agenda' Mandate

The WTO Doha Ministerial Declaration contains a mandate to decide, by explicit consensus of the members, on the modalities to start global negotiations.[10] Hence, discussions - and any subsequent negotiations - take place under the aegis of the WTO, through Ministerial meetings (such as Cancun, Mexico, in 2003) and informal inter-governmental dialogues. However, it must be noted that the objectives and goals of competition law are actually very different from traditional trade law disciplines. The competition dossier is demanding; it requires extraordinarily sophisticated domestic institutions (competition authorities), backed by legislation, jurisdiction and quasi-judicial independence. Many of these competition authorities are highly independent, and have the power to directly review, investigate and sue large private corporations. Any new mechanisms for international cooperation need to reflect these specific conditions.[11] While many countries (or regions, in the case of the EU) have such domestic authorities, many others do not; this is especially true of the least developed countries.

---

[9] A March 30 1998 recommendation states that Members should make every effort to enforce their own anti-cartel laws, and increase co-operation. A 1999 book states that the primary purpose of competition law is to improve economic efficiency so that consumers enjoy lower prices, in addition to gaining access to more choice, and improved product quality. See OECD/World Bank, *A Framework for the Design and Implementation of Competition Law and Policy* (Paris: World Bank and Organisation for Economic Co-operation and Development, 1999).

[10] *WTO Ministerial Declaration, supra* note 3.

[11] Jenny, *supra* note 5. See also Mitsuo Matsushita, "International Cooperation in the Enforcement of Competition Policy" (2002) 1 *Wash. U. Global Stud. L. Rev.* 463.

The current WTO discussions have followed a cautious approach, and may be further delayed in the future. While a tentative multilateral framework of principles may prove the object of debate, the only measures of substance arising from this would address the so-called 'hard-core' cartels (those that engage in price-fixing, bid-rigging and market sharing) at the international level. One option includes a TRIPs-style agreement, with consensus on core elements or provisions to establish baseline-operating conditions. Such an agreement on trade related aspects of anti-competitive measures may only contain basic principles and procedural safeguards. The provisions to restrict or control hard-core cartels would only be relevant in cases of truly global cartels (which do not primarily operate in one region or country) or cartels in newly opened markets which lack effective competition authorities. Support mechanisms, such as a peer review process (or Competition Review Mechanism, modeled on the Trade Policy Review Mechanism) could provide countries with an objective review of their compliance and enforcement records while also fostering transparency. Cooperation measures are also possible without launching a concerted programme of WTO negotiations. Such negotiations usually lead toward 'convergence' or commitments to ratchet down government measures. Different countries have presented arguments supporting either side. However, for many least developed countries (particularly those without a competition policy, or those in the first stages of establishing a Competition Authority), significant technical assistance will be an essential precondition to meaningful participation in negotiations. As a result, while the WTO discussions to date have helped clarify some points they have not led to a consensus on whether to begin negotiations under the Doha mandate.

A concerted process is needed to examine the links between sustainable development and competition law, in the interests of ensuring that new rules can support the WTO's stated sustainable development goals. It is necessary for countries to maintain their ability to integrate public interest consideration into their laws, create exceptions, and enforce competition laws in a particular way. In summary, sustainable competition law has to be possible on an international level.

Competition Law Principles and Sustainable Development

The few international competition laws found to generally exist do not contain specific rules or disciplines, nor do they create international competition authorities. Rather they affirm principles for cooperation between parties, since dispute settlement procedures are usually unavailable. From a sustainable development perspective, this appears to be a positive step. The principles currently under discussion appear more likely to be compatible with sustainable development objectives, rather than adverse to it. These include:

Transparency: Given that international debates centre around transparency there is a basic need for competition procedures and rules to be clear and understandable for all economic actors, including foreign competitors. As regulated in the WTO Agreement on Technical Barriers to Trade,[12] national focal points seeking information are being discussed by the WTO.

Non-discrimination: There is growing international concern about the principle of non-discrimination in competition law. While key to the trade in goods agreements, some developing countries believe this principle does not correspond with other doctrines of competition law.[13]

Procedural fairness: Procedural fairness is an integral part of multilateral efforts seeking to establish a form of international competition regime. Some basic guarantees, such as independent judicial review, have been discussed.

Provisions on global hard-core cartels: Resisting global hard–core cartels is one of the primary reasons for supporting international competition laws. Since truly global cartels can only partly be controlled by domestic and regional rules, international cooperation is necessary to ensure the enforcement of their competition policy. Further research is needed to go beyond the obvious linkages and define how hardcore cartels affect the potential for sustainable development.

These basic principles are very much in line with the tenets of sustainable development, which could include transparency and openness, good governance and rule of law, as well as other goals.[14] Indeed, on the level of principles, the requirement of non-discrimination with respect to competition law poses the only question. For example, most competition laws contain special exceptions for anti-competitive activities that strengthen export competitiveness.[15] From an international perspective, this could already constitute discrimination as such exceptions are hardly available to the international competitor. However, as demonstrated by the concrete formulation of this principle in the Canada-Costa Rica Free Trade Agreement, such provisions do not necessarily need to contravene sustainable development considerations, if drafted with sensitivity.[16]

---

[12] Part of the *Final Act Embodying the Results of the Uruguay Round of Multilateral Trade Negotiations* (Dec. 15, 1993) Legal Instruments--Results of the Uruguay Round vol. 31, 33 I.L.M. 1 (1994).

[13] See *Communication from India*, (held on 26 September 2002), WTO Doc. WT/WGTCP/W/215.

[14] See International Law Association, *Declaration of Principles of International Law Related to Sustainable Development*, 2002 Annual Conference, New Delhi, India, as cited in N. Schrijver and F. Weiss, *International Law and Sustainable Development* (Leiden: Martinus Nijhoff, 2004), also available online: ILA <www.ila-hq.org>. See also UNEP & IISD, *Environment and Trade: A Handbook* (Winnipeg: IISD, 2000), available online: UNEP <http://www.unep.ch/etu/etp/acts/aware/handbook.pdf>.

[15] See for example sec. 44 (1)(g) *Commerce and Fair Trading Act*, New Zealand.

[16] *Canada-Costa Rica Free Trade Agreement*, 23 April 2001, entered into force 1 November 2002.

Competition Law in the International Competition Network (ICN)

At its core, competition law is about building effective institutions at the domestic or regional levels. These are institutions that can challenge potential monopolies, review proposed mergers and acquisitions, prevent concentration of ownership, and break up price-fixing or other anti-competitive behaviour. An international agenda in this area should focus mainly on securing cooperation between these institutions. It should not limit governments' abilities to regulate or negotiate too much 'convergence' between distinct competition regimes. It is not clear whether, over the short or even medium term, the WTO members will reach a consensus on the modalities of a negotiation in this area. In addition, and perhaps more significantly, it also remains unclear whether the WTO is the best institution to promote the development of, or strengthen domestic competition authorities in developing countries. This is a priority in the area of competition law and sustainable development. Without such institutions, developing country negotiators would have no domestic experience to draw upon in order to negotiate effectively in regional level discussions, let alone at the WTO.

A new forum called the International Competition Network (ICN) was recently launched to assist developing and developed countries with practical competition enforcement and policy issues.[17] Through dialogue it seeks to become a forum to improve worldwide cooperation while enhancing convergence on international competition law and policy. The EU does not consider the ICN as an alternative to the discussions in the WTO, but rather a forum for technical assistance. Similarly, scholarly commentators do not view it as a substitute to other multilateral efforts, including through the WTO.[18] It has working groups on Mergers, Capacity Building & Competition Policy Implementation, Antitrust Enforcement in Regulated Sectors, Funding and Memberships. The ICN may prove to offer a useful and more consensus-oriented alternative venue to accomplish much of the 'international cooperation on competition' agenda.

---

[17] The founding conference of the International Competition Network (ICN) was held in Naples, Italy, September 28-29, 2002. Its second annual conference was in Merida, Mexico, June 23-25, 2003. It provides antitrust agencies from developed and developing countries with a focused network for addressing practical antitrust enforcement and policy issues. It facilitates procedural and substantive convergence in antitrust enforcement through a results-oriented agenda and an informal, project-driven organization. It seeks to "bring international antitrust enforcement into the 21st century." According to the ICN, "[b]y enhancing convergence and cooperation, [it] promotes more efficient, effective antitrust enforcement worldwide." The network states that "[c]onsistency in enforcement policy and elimination of unnecessary or duplicative procedural burdens stands to benefit consumers and businesses around the globe." The organization has already announced a series of best practice proposals aimed at improving merger review and competition advocacy. For further information, visit http://www.internationalcompetitionnetwork.org/index.html..

[18] See recently Roland Weinrauch, *Competition Las in the WTO – Rationale for a Framework Agreement* (Vienna: Neuer Wissenschaftlicher Verlag, 2004), at 160 p. [Weinrauch]

Such government networks[19] are an important new international phenomenon in many inter-governmental and global settings, including this new area of international competition law and policy. This raises an important question: are new global competition regimes with the potential to lead to binding legal rules in important areas of public policy, better discussed in international organizations and negotiations, or in network structures? Much depends on the capacity of these networks to use all available tools and participatory mechanisms to ensure that their deliberations remain open and accessible. From a sustainable development point of view, several considerations are particularly significant.

First, if a network plays a policy development role, how does it ensure the maximum transparency, public participation and access to justice in such a network? In an enhanced international organization, such as the WTO, debates can be opened to extreme (domestic and international) public scrutiny. Each decision is open to analysis by academics, interested parties and even civil society groups. There exist advantages and disadvantages to the informality of an inter-governmental network mechanism. A closed, less transparent context may benefit authorities from developing countries with less experience in competition law, by supporting greater degrees of capacity-building and peer learning.   However, the lack of external transparency may also make accountability harder to achieve should discussions lead to policy decisions. High levels of transparency lend an air of legitimacy to the network by avoiding perceptions of 'regulatory capture' by special interests. This enables the network to earn the support of important allies.

Secondly, how does the network ensure that a delicate balance of independence and legislative oversight is preserved in a governmental network structure? Competition authorities are necessarily highly independent bodies empowered with an almost judicial authority. International recommendations distributed through a network may lie virtually outside the scope of democratic oversight, thereby affecting the perception of independence. Will decision-making through a network preserve and strengthen this independence in all countries, or will it result in less accountability? Such a balance may be particularly necessary in areas of competition law where social, economic, or even environmental policy issues are affected.

Thirdly, there may be 'unintended consequences' for development. In existing international organizations, it is already hard for smaller countries to secure adequate representation. Lack of capacity, careful analysis and representation can lead to the imposition or even transplanting of inappropriate national laws, standards and institutions. In the area of competition law, such a dynamic may

---

[19] See Anne-Marie Slaughter, *A New World Order* (Princeton: Princeton University Press, 2004) at 16.

already exist.[20] Depending on the priority given to this concern, an informal or even official government network could serve as a capacity-building mechanism, or increase this lack of participation.

The challenge to the ICN, and the WTO, becomes acute when seeking integrated and coherent sustainable development laws. If an environment or development ministry has only one or two experts on economic issues, they cannot participate effectively in a national, let alone an international, policy-making body, except to be on the receiving end of competition law information and policy decisions. Both networking and negotiations require much more than international principles to succeed; they require a sustained, concerted effort of knowledge and capacity-building and joint research as well as national, regional and international analysis.

International Cooperation on Sustainable Competition?

In the short term, neither WTO negotiations nor the ICN alone, provide the 'perfect' institutional framework to negotiate international cooperation on competition law so as to promote sustainable development. Rather, progress may be needed in both forums.

The ICN serves an important purpose. It provides a short-term option to build links between competition authorities which allows for an exchange of highly technical information, bridging gaps between different levels of competition authority development, as well as building consensus on important issues. It remains to be seen how a network structure can address the linkages between competition law and sustainable development, and whether adequate mechanisms can be set in place to ensure a place for debate on the myriad policy issues raised in this context. When characterized by inclusivity and expertise, the network structure may serve to facilitate the development of a global epistemic community on key international issues. Indeed, with regards to sustainable development issues, government networks should be capable of developing innovative mechanisms to include and involve civil society. This can lead to richer debates, higher levels of capacity and more informed public scrutiny in developed and developing countries. Such inclusion may help to ensure that their decision-making or information distribution is more equitable and balanced.

Eventually, for the negotiation of binding decisions affecting important national and international public policies, debates may need to shift to a real international organisation, such as the WTO or an appropriate regional forum.

---

[20] Most of the developing (and economy in transition) world's competition laws, for example, are direct copies of the US or the EU statutes (the Czech Republic only recently replaced the Sherman Act to the relevant EU regulations). While this may not be a bad development for competition, it may be intrusive for other legal developments.

The WTO may play a decisive role since it is the only global economic institution able to provide binding decisions, which may prove increasingly important in this area. In the interest of subsidiarity, however, it seems clear the WTO would only be obliged to deal with truly global competition issues. While the WTO may provide a series of basic norms, regional institutions may provide more appropriate forums for cooperation in certain sectors or given specific issues.

In line with the old truism, 'an ounce of prevention is worth a pound of cure,' it is the opinion of this author that the WTO and the ICN coordinate with other international experts and organizations to ensure greater information exchange, develop capacity and build a body of substantive analysis and knowledge on sustainable development and competition law. Before errors are made, explicit spaces must be provided for research and dialogue in order to adequately analyze the linkages between competition law, social and environmental policies.

As a minimum pre-condition to these debates, both the WTO discussions and the ICN should carefully seek mechanisms to facilitate transparency and civil society participation. These mechanisms will need to be innovative in order to respect the unique nature of this area of law and the powerful economic interests at play.

Strong competition rules underpin a healthy, open economy, fostering innovation and leading to lower prices and better products for consumers. On the national level, there exist different approaches to achieving more sustainable competition law. In certain instances, through exceptions or other provisions, national competition rules also recognize other important national public policy objectives. Maintaining a diversity of national approaches towards competition law is important especially with regard to different economic structures, such as small economies. Social provisions are well established in many national competition laws. Most developing countries find them necessary while many developed countries still use them. While a few special ecological provisions can be found in competition laws the application of such rules have the potential to positively or negatively impact the environment. The linkages between such policies require further investigation.

Competition law, in a global economy where markets continue to become more open, cannot remain exclusively national if they want to remain effective. Global competition rules and instruments can help address anti-competitive economic behaviour on a global level, by designing a mix of global cooperation instruments that will encourage competition and lead to more sustainable global economies. Should the WTO ministers decide to negotiate international competition rules, it should be made clear that countries can include sustainable development considering the social and ecological impacts of their policies.

International cooperation regimes in this area are necessary and valuable. However, a more liberal international approach to global governance could prove more feasible and legitimate than either WTO negotiations or governmental networks alone. Information exchange, policy dialogue and capacity building through a new international competition network may be extremely useful in developing international consensus on important upcoming issues. This consensus may even be a necessary precondition for eventual negotiations on these issues in the WTO or elsewhere. Transparent rules for cooperation may be useful, both between competition authorities at different levels of development, and with other members of civil society. Indeed, high levels of engagement of interested experts, civil society organizations and others might bring significant advantages, though the participation (or sponsorship) of private law firms will require careful management.

Competition and Sustainable Development 'Cut Both Ways'?

At present, it appears competition law and policy holds potential to either favour or jeopardize the international goal of sustainable development.[21]

On the one hand, the aim of sustainable development should provide enough of a justification to refrain from following straightforward competition rules in specific instances. Certain exceptions already exist to ensure governments retain the freedom to regulate in light of their social or environmental priorities. For example, this happens when a specific segment of a market is guaranteed in order to promote the development of a desirable new technology. The European Court of Justice (ECJ) recently upheld a German law that guarantees a certain percentage of the German energy market for alternative, renewable energy sources.[22] Considering renewable energy to be a legitimate social goal, the ECJ ruled the measure will be exempted from European Union competition laws, which have the potential to curb the use of such policies.[23] This recognition also exists in developing countries. India's competition law puts a strong emphasis on consumer protection, and Jamaica's courts recognize valid exceptions where full application of anti-trust measures would jeopardize legitimate sustainable development goals.[24] Regional bodies of the Caribbean Community (CARICOM) have developed community legislation that boosts member state codes.[25]

---

[21] Marie-Claire Cordonier Segger, *Sustainable Development Implications of Competition Law and Policy*, IISD WTO Policy Briefing Paper Series (Geneva / Winnipeg: IISD, 2003).
[22] *PreussenElektra AG v Schleswag AG* C-379/98[2002] E. C. R I-2099.
[23] *Ibid.*
[24] WTO Working Group on the Interaction between Trade and Competition Policy, *Overview of Members' National Competition Legislation - Note by The Secretariat*, WT/WGTCP/W/128/Rev.2 (4 July 2001), App. 3 (counting the EU and its members as separate, given that all EU member states have competition laws). See also Jenny, *supra* note 2.
[25] *Ibid.*

On the other hand, fostering further competition in certain markets could also be positive for sustainable development. As argued above, if particular global players hold a near-monopolistic position in an industry, competition law may prove beneficial by encouraging many small or medium sized enterprises to engage in experimentation and make more sustainable technologies viable. Again, in the energy sector, global energy giants presently offer cheap, reliable fossil fuels by externalizing many public costs. One may argue that these actors could 'crowd out' smaller players who could viably develop new renewable energy sources such as solar, wind or small-scale hydro.[26] By fragmenting these markets, competition law and policy could allow small companies to make a profit, thus encouraging the development of small-scale alternatives.

Other questions can also be considered. When the merger between the two largest companies demonstrates the ability to unfairly limit competition, anti-trust law permits a consideration of the public interest and the interest of the consumer. [27] Could investigations and trials be extended to consider the social or environmental impacts of business ventures, if this is also deemed to be in the public's interest? If the neglect of sustainability priorities comes to be characterized as unfair competition, international anti-trust law may one day provide a tool for sustainable development. Policies to encourage sustainable consumption patterns have a strong link with competition policy and law. Consumer information and education, as well as clear procedures for consumer participation in regulatory processes, can help to ensure fair and open competition.[28] In this respect, can competition laws that prevent misleading advertising or ensure accurate labelling be helpful to ensure greater respect for the rights of consumers?

Finally, the issue of competition dispute resolution should also be examined through future research. The WTO 'Doha Agenda' appears silent on the point,[29] but disputes on whether domestic competition laws conform to internationally negotiated obligations would need to be settled, presumably by existing, binding WTO panel procedures. Questions arising from such an issue include: how would this affect the independence of competition agencies, and enforcement decision-making processes? Might it not raise fears of the WTO second-guessing individual decisions of competition authorities?

---

[26] Segger, *supra* note 19.

[27] Gavil, *supra* note 2.

[28] Joseph F. Brodley, "The Economic Goals of Antitrust: Efficiency, Consumer Welfare, and Technological Progress"(1987) 62 N.Y.U.L. Rev. 1020.

[29] *WTO Ministerial Declaration, supra* note 3.

Conclusions: A Need for Inquiry, Dialogue and Capacity Building

In conclusion, what is sustainable international competition law in a world of increasing globalization?[30] If there are potential sustainable development benefits from stronger international competition law, legal researchers and countries should investigate. Should negotiations of some kind proceed, ignorance of the law is never a good idea. Many developing countries do not have any experience with competition law or policy, even at the domestic level.[31] For WTO negotiations to be successful for developing countries, significant capacity building will be necessary to ensure positive gains and to address automatic (deserved) resistance to the unknown. Indeed, the Doha Declaration goes on to recognize the needs of developing and least-developed countries for "technical assistance and capacity-building in this area, including policy analysis and development," so that these actors can evaluate the development implications for themselves. It commits to "work in cooperation with other relevant intergovernmental organizations, including UNCTAD, and through appropriate regional and bilateral channels, to provide strengthened and adequately resourced assistance to respond to these needs."[32] This recognizes the need for legal research and policy analysis focusing on the needs and concerns of the developing countries in these debates. Furthermore, it recognizes that assistance and is needed to build the capacity of negotiators on the issue. Being prepared benefits all during debates or negotiations. During the Ministerial Conference in Cancún, there was neither the political will nor the general agreement that international competition rules will automatically benefit all members. However, there seems to be an emerging position that a WTO Framework Agreement could lay out some very general principles. The ICN may reach certain limits, where deeper cooperation would need an international organisation, so the EU continues to consider a comprehensive global competition agreement be feasible.[33]

The policy implications are clear. There is a broader global context that must be taken into account. Public concerns, such as sustainable development, can and should potentially influence competition decisions. Different countries have adopted laws that provide for this type of influence. On an international level, any new agreement should be drafted so that countries retain their regulatory abilities to include and increase the standards of their socio-economic and environmental objectives related to their competition laws.

---

[30] Mario Monti, the then Competition Commissioner of the EU put the challenge as follows: "Recognising that consumers and companies alike are increasingly citizens of a globalised economy, we have the difficult mission of ensuring that international integration of markets leads to maintained competitive outcomes, thus making the globalisation process both economically more efficient and socially more acceptable." in 1st OECD Global Forum on Competition, 2001, online: OECD < http://www.oecd.org/dataoecd/0/49/2434501.pdf >.

[31] See United Nations Conference on Trade and Development, *Model Law on Competition - Draft elements and Commentaries for Articles of a Model Law or Laws on Competition* (Geneva: UNCTAD, 2002) at 5.

[32] Doha Ministerial Declaration, *supra* note 3.

[33] See Weinrauch, *supra* note 17, at 165.

9

CORPORATE SOCIAL RESPONSIBILITY: INTERNATIONAL STRATEGIES AND REGIMES

Michael Kerr[1] & Marie-Claire Cordonier Segger[2]

Sustainable development is not about the environment alone - it is about the promotion of integrated environmental, social and economic progress towards a common goal. This integrated concept has tangible expression in both international and 'soft' law. It evolved to address some of the most pressing concerns of human society, including the current unsustainable patterns of production and consumption,[3] worldwide population growth,[4] ozone depletion, climate change, and loss of biodiversity, as well as the need for stronger labour rights and standards, better health services, prohibitions on child labour, proscription of discrimination against women, and protection for communities impacted by corporate activities.[5] These critical issues must be addressed if the global community is to continue to grow and progress in a sustainable manner.

The modern corporation, which has now come to dominate global economic activity, has a pivotal role to play in the sustainable development agenda. A study

---

[1] Marie-Claire Cordonier Segger, MEM (Yale), BCL & LLB (McGill), Director, Centre for International Sustainable Development Law (CISDL), Chair, CISDL/ILA/IDLO Partnership on International Law on Sustainable Development, Senior Manager, Americas Research Portfolio, International Institute for Sustainable Development & United Nations Environment Programme ROLAC, British Chevening Scholar & SSHRC Fellow, Exeter College, Oxford University Law Faculty, Lecturer, International Development Law Organisation (IDLO) & Member, International Law Association (ILA) Committee on International Law on Sustainable Development.. The chapter is based on thoughts developed in research for an earlier article, M.C. Cordonier Segger, "Sustainability and Corporate Accountability Regimes: Implementing the Johannesburg Summit Agenda" (2003) 12:3 *RECIEL* with permission of the author.
[2] Michael Kerr, B.A (Monash), LL.B. (Hons.)(Bond), Legal Research Fellow for Sustainable Corporate Law, Centre for International Sustainable Development Law (CISDL) & Consultant, International Trade and Corporate Social Responsibility. The authors gratefully acknowledges the excellent substantive contributions and research of Rachel Bendayan and Hari Suthan, CISDL Associate Fellows.
[3] United Nations Environment Programme, *Global Environmental Outlook Report* (Cambridge: Cambridge University Press, 2000).
[4] *Ibid.*
[5] *Johannesburg Plan of Implementation*, Report of the World Summit on Sustainable Development, Johannesburg (South Africa) (4 Sept. 2002) UN Doc. A/CONF.199/20. Available online: <http://www.un.org/esa/sustdev/documents/WSSD_POI_PD/English/POIToc.htm>. See also the nine principles of the *Global Compact*, available online: < http://www.unglobalcompact.org/Portal/?NavigationTarget=/roles/portal_user/aboutTheGC/nf/nf/theNinePr inciples>.

M.C. Cordonier Segger & C. G. Weeramantry, eds., Sustainable Justice: Reconciling Economic, Social & Environmental Law ©
2005 Koninklijke Brill NV, Printed in The Netherlands, pp.135-154.

undertaken by the Washington based Institute for Policy Studies[6] found that of the 100 largest economies in the world, 51 are corporations, while only 49 are countries.[7] The study also showed that the sales of the top 200 corporations are the equivalent of 27.5 percent of world economic activity.[8]

However, the success of the corporation as a business institution has not been without its costs. In the course of production of goods and services, corporations have made a significant contribution to many environmental and social problems. Consequently, governments, intergovernmental agencies, environment and social development groups, civil society and increasingly, the private sector, have become active participants in global efforts to address the environmental and social impacts of corporations. Due to the sheer size of companies and their importance within the global economy, this is an essential step on the road to sustainable development.

At the forefront of these efforts has been a world wide trend towards 'corporate social responsibility' and 'corporate accountability.' Although these terms have no single definition, a common understanding of 'corporate social responsibility' (CSR) is the need for corporations to integrate environmental and social considerations along with traditional economic considerations in their production and governance practices.[9] The notion of 'corporate accountability' is, in many respects, the 'flip side' of the CSR coin. It is concerned with the need for corporations to explain and accept responsibility for their actions. Traditionally, corporate regulatory regimes in many jurisdictions have focused on ensuring that corporations, particularly company directors, are accountable to their shareholders. A more expansive notion of corporate accountability ensures that companies are accountable to a wider group of stakeholders such as employees, customers and the communities in which they operate.[10]

This chapter will discuss four major strategies that have been pursued to ensure that corporations are environmentally and socially responsible and that they are held accountable for their actions in the event they breach these responsibilities.[11]

---

[6] S. Anderson & J.Cavanagh, *Top 200: The Rise of Corporate Global Power* (Washington: Institute for Policy Studies, 2000).

[7] The study obtains this finding by comparing the corporate sales of the largest 200 corporations as listed by *Fortune* in 1999, with the Gross Domestic Product (GDP) of the world's nations for the same year.

[8] *Supra* note 6 at 3.

[9] See for example, the Canadian Government's definition of CSR, available online: <http://strategis.ic.gc.ca/epic/internet/incsr-rse.nsf/vwGeneratedInterE/Home>. This states that it is important to recognise that there are many notions of CSR, some of which concentrate purely on the financial responsibility of the company to maximise profits on behalf of the investors). See also Friedman's widely cited claim that the social responsibility of business is to make profits as cited in R. Lansdowne & J. Segal, "The Social Responsibility of Modern Corporations" (1978) 2 *U.N.S.W.L.J.* 336 at 337. For a perspective on the varying ways of conceptualising CSR, see J. Tolmie, "Corporate Social Responsibility" (1992) 15(1) *U.N.S.W.L.J.* 268.

[10] Canadian Democracy and Corporate Accountability Commission, *Final Report- the New Balance Sheet: Corporate Profits and Responsibility in the 21ˢᵗ Century* (Toronto: CDCAC, 2002) at 2.

[11] Not all strategies are discussed. For example, there is no discussion of the strategy to remove environmentally harmful subsidies that promote unsustainable corporate activity or economic instruments, such as pollution taxes, that can also promote CSR.

These strategies include the use of (1) voluntary initiatives to promote improved corporate environmental and social performance; (2) legal proceedings to impose foreign direct liability for environmental damage or human rights violations; (3) law reform in national corporate regulatory regimes; and (4) international treaties and conventions.

Strategy 1: Voluntary Initiatives to Promote Improved Corporate Environmental and Social Performance

In 1992 the United Nations officially encouraged the use of voluntary initiatives through Agenda 21.[12] Before this time, only a handful of formal voluntary initiatives existed. Over the past decade however, they have increased in popularity to the point where they now number in their thousands[13] and are viewed, at both the national and international level, as the preferred instrument to improve corporate environmental and social performance. Common aims of such initiatives, as can be seen below, include: minimizing negative environmental impacts of corporate activity; increasing ecological efficiency in the production of corporate goods and services; encouraging corporate adherence to internationally recognized labour and human rights standards; and encouraging adherence to public triple bottom line (economic, environmental and social) reporting.

Voluntary initiatives take many different forms. The United Nations Environment Program (UNEP) for example, has sought to divide voluntary initiatives into five major categories.[14]

First, they identify industry initiatives in which industry has exclusive management responsibility including defining the targets, if any, to be reached and whether or how to report progress publicly. These initiatives may be industry-specific, cross sectoral, or otherwise exclusive to the company, as well as national or international in their reach. For example, the 'code of conduct' adopted by the global footwear company, Nike, governing the company's product facilities in the areas of environment, health, safety and which prohibits the use of child and forced labour.[15]

Second, they focus on government initiatives, through which governments set the goals to be met (usually in consultation with industry and other stakeholders) and monitor the performance of the companies that volunteer to take part. For example, participants in the Australian Greenhouse Challenge, which is designed to abate the greenhouse gas emissions of Australian industry, - sign voluntary

---

[12] U.N. Conference on Environment and Development, *Agenda 21* U.N. Doc. A/CONF.151.26 (1992) at Chap. 30.
[13] UNEP, *Voluntary Initiatives: Current Status, Lessons learnt and Next Steps.* (Geneva: UNEP, 2000) at 3, available online: <http://www.uneptie.org/outreach/vi/reports/voluntary_initiatives.pdf>.
[14] *Ibid.* at 5.
[15] Available online: <http://www.nike.com/nikebiz/nikebiz.jhtml?page=25&cat=code#code [*Code of Conduct*].

agreements with the government that provide a framework for undertaking and reporting on actions to abate emissions.[16]

Third, they examine joint government / industry initiatives, negotiated agreements or covenants, in which government and industry negotiate the objectives, as well as how to monitor and report progress. They may be company or industry sector specific, or cover cross-sector issues. Other stakeholders usually have only a consultative role. The long term agreement between the Dutch government and the Dutch textile industry to improve energy efficiency is one prominent example.[17]

Fourth, they identified third-party initiatives, through which third parties (non-government, non-business) develop and run the initiative, although companies or industry associations may be involved in an advisory capacity or as members of the organization. For example, the forest certification scheme coordinated by the Forest Stewardship Council (FSC) which is focused on ensuring the environmentally appropriate, socially beneficial and economically viable management of the world's forests.[18]

Fifth, they have noted UN and other international voluntary initiatives, through which the UN or other intergovernmental organizations act as catalysts for the development and implementation of initiatives. For example, the UN Global Compact designed to bring companies together with UN agencies as well as labour and civil society in order to support nine principles of the UN global compact in the areas of human rights, labour and the environment.[19] A further example is the Global Reporting Initiative (GRI) whose mission is to develop and disseminate global Sustainability Reporting Guidelines. These guidelines are used by organizations for voluntary reporting on the economic, environmental, and social dimensions of their activities, products, and services.[20]

The Benefits of Voluntary Initiatives

There are numerous benefits associated with the use of voluntary initiatives as an instrument for bringing about improved corporate environmental and social performance. For instance, they can be implemented faster than economic or regulatory instruments, which ordinarily must undergo a lengthy legislative process before implementation. Voluntary initiatives are therefore useful to address an immediate environmental or social issue. [21]

---

[16] Australia's Greenhouse Challenge, available online:
<http://www.greenhouse.gov.au/challenge/about/index.html>. There is considerable cross over between categories 2 and 3. For example, the UNEP discussion paper places the Australian Greenhouse Challenge within category 2 when it could just easily fall within category 3.
[17] Available online: <http://www.eceee.org/library_links/proceedings/1997/pdf97/97p3-167.pdf>.
[18] Certification criteria of the FSC, available online: <http://www.fscoax.org>.
[19] See Global Compact, available online: <http://www.unglobalcompact.org/Portal/Default.asp>.
[20] Initiated in 1997 by the Coalition for Environmentally Responsible Economies (CERES), the GRI became independent in 2002, and is an official collaborating centre of UNEP.
[21] *Supra* note 13 at 3.

In addition, many voluntary initiatives are designed, implemented and administered by an individual corporation or an industry association. As a result, governments are not burdened with the administration and enforcement costs that are associated with regulatory or economic instruments.[22] Voluntary initiatives also offer a degree of flexibility to private participants and governments.[23] Unlike regulatory and economic instruments, the targets or processes associated with voluntarily initiatives can be quickly adjusted to suit the different needs of participants or to meet evolving environmental or social problems.

Finally, voluntary initiatives allow for significant cultural change within a corporation.[24] This is because the initiatives are adopted voluntarily by the corporations concerned and are not made in response to prescriptive regulatory standards. This creates a sense of ownership and acceptance of the initiative among corporate directors, management and employees.

Limitations of Voluntary Initiatives

Whilst carrying some clearly recognizable benefits, the effectiveness of voluntary initiatives in bringing about improved corporate environmental and social performance has been questioned. Both UNEP[25] and the OECD[26] have published discussion papers and reports outlining the limitations of voluntary initiatives. The OECD's most recent (2003) report, *Voluntary Approaches for Environmental Policy: Effectiveness, Efficiency and Usage in Policy Mixes*[27] is perhaps the most critical analysis to date. This report, which analysed a significant number of national and international environmental voluntary initiatives, found that the majority had failed to bring about a change in corporate behaviour beyond that of 'business as usual.' It states that "[w]hile the environmental targets of most but not all voluntary approaches seem to have been met, there are only a few cases where such approaches have been found to contribute to environmental improvements significantly different from what would have happened any way. Hence, the environmental effectiveness of voluntary approaches is still questionable."[28]

Critics of voluntary initiatives often focus on the fact that voluntary initiatives are non-binding. This has meant that such initiatives are unable to incite all companies to improve their environmental and social performance and thus, on their own, can not deal with negligent or consistently poor performers. Other criticisms have

---

[22] *Ibid.*
[23] *Ibid.*
[24] *Ibid.*
[25] *Supra* note 13.
[26] OECD, *Voluntary Approaches for Environmental Policy: An Assessment.* (Paris: OECD, 1999). For a more recent OECD report on voluntary initiatives, see OECD, *Voluntary Approaches for Environmental policy: Effectiveness, Efficiency and Usage in Policy Mixes.* (Paris: OECD, 2003).
[27] OECD, *Voluntary Approaches for Environmental policy: Effectiveness, Efficiency and Usage in Policy Mixes.* (Paris: OECD, 2003).
[28] *Ibid.* at 14.

focused on the fact that many voluntary initiatives lack clearly defined and quantitative targets, are poorly monitored and do not contain any meaningful enforcement mechanism to ensure compliance.[29]

Perhaps the most significant limitation is their ineffectiveness in bringing about changes in corporate environmental and social performance when used in isolation. This was one of the key messages of UNEP's discussion paper, *Voluntary Initiatives: Current Status Lessons Learnt and Next Steps (2000).* This states that: "[t]ypically, the successes and failures of an initiative result not so much from its own design as from the strengths and weaknesses of outside pressures (e.g. fear of regulatory action or liability claims, anticipation of new tax burdens or new market opportunities). Voluntary initiatives should not be proposed and adopted as substitutes for regulation or used as justification for dismantling regulatory capacity."[30]

When voluntary initiatives are adopted as substitutes for regulation or used as justification for dismantling regulatory capacity, 'regulatory capture' is said to have been achieved by industry.[31] Some authors have commented on the increasing trend, particularly in North America and Europe, to view CSR as an option to be pursued only through voluntary measures. This, they feel, operates as a break on the implementation of new legislation or regulation in response to hotly contested CSR issues.[32] These observations suggest there is a degree of regulatory capture of efforts to promote CSR and increased corporate accountability which threatens to stall further progress in the improvement of corporate environmental and social performance.

Strategy Two: Foreign Direct Liability for Environmental Damage or Human Rights Violations

Foreign direct liability is the instrument used by civil society to enforce minimum standards and seek corporate accountability in cases of the worst conduct. This approach uses domestic courts (often in the corporate headquarter State) to find companies directly liable for violating international law, or to force significant punitive settlements.[33] Successful law-suits have generally taken place against global 'rogue' corporations: those whose profits come from operating below the minimum standard in countries without strong regulatory regimes or enforcement.[34] Several

---

[29] *Supra* note 13, *Ibid.* at 3.

[30] *Supra* note 13 at 11(Quote from Robert Gibson, University of Waterloo, Canada- UNEP Workshop participant).

[31] *Supra* note 13 at 43.

[32] H. Ward, *Legal Issues in Corporate Citizenship* (International Institute for Environment and Development: London, 2003) at 1.

[33] S. Zia-Zarifi, "Suing Multinational Corporations in the U.S. for Violating International Law" (1999) 4 *UCLA J. Int'l L. & Foreign Aff.* 81.

[34] See B. Frey, "The Legal and Ethical Responsibilities of Transnational Corporations in the Protection of International Human Rights" (1997) 6 *Minn. J. Global Trade* 181-87, which illustrates corporate accountability scenarios, duties, and liability, and asserts the inadequacy of voluntary codes without government regulation.

barriers faced by victims have led them to sue parent companies, rather than local subsidiaries. First, such corporations may organise themselves so that the local subsidiaries are insolvent, not worth suing or are uninsured. Furthermore, the claimants often have no means of obtaining substantial access to justice in their home courts, particularly when contingency fee or legal aid arrangements are not in place; and finally, minimal worker's compensation schemes can preclude claims against an employer.[35]

The main legal stumbling block to such suits has been the *forum non conveniens* principle of private international law, under which common law courts exercise jurisdiction to halt a claim on the grounds that the claimants' domestic courts provide a 'more appropriate' venue (forum). Narrow judicial interpretations can also limit the extraterritorial scope of domestic legislation. Procedural barriers, such as establishing standing, presenting the existence of personal jurisdiction over the defendant, and defeating dismissal for comity have also inhibited many claims.[36] Whereas these hurdles have bared recovery in the past, recent litigation in the United States (US), the United Kingdom (UK) and other countries indicate a turning tide. A handful of cases now proceeding through courts demonstrate that corporations may be held directly liable for violating norms of customary international law or for committing the tort of negligence.[37]

The United States Alien Tort Claim Act

In the U.S., the *Alien Tort Claims Act* (ATCA) grants the federal court jurisdiction over 'any civil action by an alien for a tort committed in violation of the law of nations or a treaty of the United States.'[38] It achieved its status as an instrument of corporate liability in 1980, when the Second Circuit decided *Filartiga v. Pena-Irala*.[39] The statue gained further prominence when *Kadic v. Karadzic*[40] held that the ATCA could be used against private individuals. A successful claim under the ATCA must present three elements: (1) an alien sues (2) for a tort (3) committed in violation of the law of nations.[41]

---

[35] In *Cape Plc.* case, all these factors applied. It is noteworthy also that *Adams and Others* v. *Cape Industries Plc and Another* [1990] 1 Ch 433, to 572, in which a group of United States asbestos victims unsuccessfully attempted to enforce a Texas judgement against Cape's UK assets. Cape had no assets in the United States and had liquidated its subsidiary. The Court of Appeal expressly endorsed the conclusion the court of first instance that Cape had deliberately engineered the restructuring while 'reducing if not eliminating the appearance of any involvement therein of Cape or its subsidiaries.'

[36] See M. Shaughnessy, 'Human Rights and the Environment: the United Nations Global Compact and the Continuing Debate About the Effectiveness of Corporate Voluntary Codes of Conduct', (2000) 16 *Colo. J. Int'l Envtl. L. & Pol'y* 159, at 165.

[37] H. H. Koh, "Transnational Public Law Litigation" (1991) 100 *Yale L.J.* 2347, at 2349; but see also G. A. Christenson, "Customary International Human Rights Law in Domestic Court Decisions" (1995) 25 *G.A. J. Int'l & Comp. L.* 225, at 230-31.

[38] Alien's Action for Tort (also referred to as the Alien Tort Claims Act), 28 U.S.C. § 1350 (1994). See also S. Zia-Zarifi, *supra* note 33.

[39] *Filartiga* v. *Pena-Irala*, 630 F.2d 876 (2d Cir. 1980).

[40] *Kadic* v. *Karadzic* 70 F.3d 232 (2d Cir. 1995).

[41] *Ibid.* at 239, 241.

However, the statute, part of the first *Judiciary Act* of 1789, was rarely invoked for the first 190 years of its existence.[42] But, since most of the 100 world's largest corporations are from the US, the act is now being used to address egregious human rights violations. In the *Burma v. Unocal* case,[43] the federal district court in California upheld access to U.S. courts for citizens of Burma who claimed that Unocal had effectively 'enslaved' them during the construction of an oil pipeline through their country. Also, workers in Saipan's (Mariana Islands) garment industry recently brought suit against U.S. corporations for violations of the U.S. *Fair Labor Standards Act.*[44] Although few ATCA cases against corporations have been litigated on the merits, many suggest that meritorious cases will still proceed, forcing the door open for increased corporate liability.[45]

The Tort of Negligence in the United Kingdom

The US trend for accountability is also echoed in the United Kingdom, specifically in a series of recent cases on access to justice for foreign victims of multinational corporations.[46] While claims brought against Unocal and Shell in U.S. courts used the *1789 ATCA*, the UK trilogy *of Thor, Rio Tinto and Cape Industries* were based on more conventional tort/negligence principles. These cases, however, indicate a change in the attitude of the English courts towards compensation claims brought against a parent company of a corporation in domestic courts.

The most recent and definitive judgment was given by the House of Lords In *L v. Cape Industries,* [47] where more than 3,000 South African workers sued Cape Industries for damages and loss of life caused by asbestos related cancer. Cape Industries Plc's asbestos mining and processing business originated in South Africa and it maintained an interest there until 1989, when it began to operate only in the UK. The victims argued that as a parent company which exercised *de facto* control over its foreign subsidiary, and being aware that its operations involved risks to the health of the employees of that subsidiary, Cape Industries Plc. owed a duty of care to those workers. The company tried to avoid the case on the basis of *forum non conveniens,* but the court held that due to the difficulty of pursuing the case in South Africa, it could proceed in England.[48] Some suggested at the time that '[i]t is not

---

[42] Despite several superficial changes to the ATCA's wording, no substantive changes have been made since the statute was enacted as part of the first Judiciary Act, ch. 20, § 9, 1 Stat. 73, 77 (1789). See A. Burley, 'The Alien Tort Statute and the Judiciary Act of 1789: A Badge of Honour, 83 *Am. J. Int'l L.* (1989), 81.

[43] *Nat'l Coalition Gov't of the Union of Burma* v. *Unocal, Inc.*, 176 F.R.D. 329 (C.D. Cal. 1997). See also *Doe v. Unocal Corp.*, 963 F. Supp. 880 (C.D. Cal. 1997). But also see *Doe v. Unocal Corp.*, 110 F. Supp. 2d 1294 (C.D. Cal. 2000).

[44] *Does I thru XXIII* v. *Advanced Textile Corp.*, 214 F.3d 1058 (9th Cir. 2000).

[45] See *Zarifi, supra* note 33.

[46] R. Felix et al., "Three Minerals, Three Epidemics' Asbestos Mining and Disease in South Africa" in M.A. Mehlman & A. Upton, eds., *The Identification and Control of Environmental Diseases: Hazards and Risks of Chemicals in the Oil Refining Industry* (Princeton: Princeton Scientific Publishing, 1994) 265.

[47] See *Lubbe and Others* v. *Cape Industries Plc.*[2000] 1 W.L.R. 1545.

[48] Following the Connelly ruling, the British Lord Chancellor proposed legislation to reverse the effect of the decision, *inter alia*, because of concern that it might cause MNCs to shift their operations away from the UK. It is of interest that subsequently in a merger between Rio Tinto and Australian mining company, CRA, CRA shifted its head office to London.

that this decision has suddenly increased everyone's liabilities, it has just made it more likely that the cases will be heard in England.'[49]

However, the fact that the directors of the parent company were aware of the hazards associated with asbestos exposure was the turning point of the judgement, and this in following with the decisions in *Connelly* v. *Rio Tinto Plc*[50] and *Sithole & Others* v. *Thor Chems. Holdings Ltd. & Another*[51] where the conduct and motives of the defendant were deemed valuable in the assessment of duty of care.

Interlinked with legal liability in tort for negligence is the principle that practising 'double standards' in relation to health and safety should not be legally defensible. Whether a risk of injury can be foreseen does not depend on local laws or regulations. If standards are less stringent overseas, a corporation still has, or ought to have had, awareness of the risks. Compliance with local standards may ensure no prosecutions for contravention of local laws but is not a defence to a claim brought in negligence. As stated by Sir Anthony Tuke, former Chairman of Rio Tinto: 'It is not enough for international companies to shelter behind the laws of the countries in which they operate; their responsibilities go beyond that.[52]

The legal developments secured by these cases and similar cases in other jurisdictions,[53] are an important development towards greater corporate accountability. Those legal advances provide a salutary warning against the application of double standards. In light of such cases, multinationals may need to take active measures to ensure that worldwide operations comply with international standards.[54]

Strategy 3: Law Reform in National Corporate Regulatory Regimes

Despite the regulatory capture exhibited in some North American and European jurisdictions, certain countries are exploring measures to enshrine notions of 'CSR' and 'corporate accountability' into their domestic corporate regulatory regimes. This represents a fundamental shift in the way many jurisdictions view national corporate laws. Indeed, traditionally, environmental and social issues have been considered 'outside' the scope of corporate law belonging instead in other

---

[49] See "Forum Non Conveniens in America and England: A Rather Fantastic Fiction" 103 *LQR* (1987), 398, 400.
[50] *Connelly* v. *Rio Tinto Plc* (1997), 3 WLR 376 [*Rio Tinto*]
[51] See *Sithole & Others* v. *Thor Chems. Holdings Ltd. & Another*, The Times 15 February 1999, Court of Appeal (Civil Division).
[52] Rio Tinto Corporation, *1992 Annual Report* (London: Rio Tinto, 1992).
[53] Cases involving foreign direct liability for human rights abuses and environmental violations have also been heard in Australia, Europe and Canada. For further discussion on these cases, see generally M.C. Cordonier Segger, "Sustainability and Corporate Accountability Regimes: Implementing the Johannesburg Summit Agenda" (2003) 12(3) R.E.C.I.E.L 295- 309. Also see generally H. Ward, *Legal Issues in Corporate Citizenship* (London: International Institute for Environment and Development, 2003).
[54] O. Kamminga and S. Zia-Zarifi, eds., *Liability of Multinational Corporations under International Law* (London: Kluwer Law International, 2000).

regulatory regimes.[55] Furthermore, this effort is also an indication that CSR is ready to move away from its 'voluntary identity' and be integrated as a mandatory consideration in the governance of the modern corporation.

Reporting and Disclosure

The "frontier battleground" of this shift has been in the areas of mandatory corporate reporting and disclosure.[56] Mandatory sustainability reporting requirements for corporations have now established a firm foot hold in the national corporate legal regimes in many jurisdictions. Some examples include:

South Africa- As a consequence of recommendations flowing from the King Committee on Corporate Governance in 2002, all companies with securities listed on the JSE Securities Exchange South Africa, financial entities defined in legislation regulating the South African financial services sector, and public sector enterprises and agencies must now comply with a Code of Corporate Practices and Conduct which, *inter alia*, requires each entity to issue an annual sustainability report. According to paragraph 5.1.3 of the Code, "[d]isclosure of non financial material [in the report] should be governed by the principles of reliability, relevance, clarity, timeliness and verifiability with reference to the Global Reporting Initiative (GRI) Sustainability Reporting Guidelines."[57]

France- Article 116 of the *Law on New Economic Regulations* (2001) requires all companies listed on France's 'premier marché' to report against a number of sustainability indicators relating to human resources, community issues, labour standards and key health, safety and environment issues.[58]

Norway- According to the *Accounting Act* (Regnskapsloven) (1999), which directs company directors on what to include in their annual financial report:

---

[55] For example, in many common law jurisdictions, corporate law as it is taught and practised is concerned with the legal relationship between a narrow category of corporate actors. Along with the corporation itself, corporate law is viewed primarily to be concerned with the rights, interests, duties and liabilities of "corporate insiders": shareholders and the directors. Although it may concern itself with some outside actors, such as creditors or others who enter into contracts with the corporation, corporate law in common law jurisdictions does not concern itself with the corporation as a social or environmental actor. See for example, R. Tomasic et al., *Corporations Law in Australia* (Sydney: Federation Press, 2nd ed., 2002) at 67.

[56] *Supra* note 32 at 3.

[57] The executive summary of the *King Report 2002* is available online at <http://www.gcgf.org/WABA/philip%20Armstrong%20(executive%20summary%20).pdf>. The JSE Securities Exchange (South Africa) listing rules require annual disclosure of the extent of a listed company's compliance with the Code of Corporate Practices and Conduct and the reasons where relevant for non compliance. The sustainability Reporting requirements are contained in section 5 of the Code of Corporate Practices and Conduct.

[58] Law on New Economic Regulation (Nouvelles Regulations Economiques – NRE) article 116, paragraph 4. The reporting indicators are available in English in M. Mansley, *Open Disclosure: Sustainability and the Listing Regime* (London: Claros Consulting, 2003) available online: <http://www.foe.co.uk/resource/reports/open_disclosure.pdf>. The 'Premier Marche' is the main listing market on the French stock exchange now known as Euronext Paris. It is made up of large French and foreign publicly listed companies.

a) "An account must be given of the working environment and an overview must be given of implemented measures that are of importance to the working environment. In addition, separate information is required about injuries, accidents and absence due to illness."

b) "An account must be given of the matters relating to the enterprise, including resources used in production and products, which contributes to an impact on the external environment and of the measures which have been implemented or are being planned to prevent or reduce negative impacts on the environment."[59]

In addition, mandatory corporate environmental reporting laws requiring varying levels of reporting have been enacted in Australia, Belgium, Denmark, Sweden and the Netherlands.[60]

There is now also an emerging body of legislation applicable to the financial sector requiring investment fund mangers to disclose their social or environmental policies. The UK was the first to introduce this form of disclosure when, in 1999, UK Parliament approved the Pension Disclosure Regulation. The Regulation amended the *Pensions Act* 1995 (UK), requiring all trustees of UK occupational pension funds to disclose *"the extent, (if at all), to which social, environmental or ethical considerations are taken into account in the selection, retention and realization of investments."* Australia, Belgium, and Germany have followed the UK's lead and introduced broadly parallel legislation. [61]

Foreign Direct Liability- Proposed Legislative Initiatives

Numerous corporate law reform proposals have sought to incorporate the principles of foreign direct liability into national legislation. In Australia, the Australian Democrats proposed the *Corporate Conduct of Conduct Bill* 2000 (Cth), which was designed to, *inter alia,* impose environmental and human rights standards on Australian corporations and their related entities when operating in a foreign country.[62] In addition, the Bill would also allow persons, both natural and corporate, who have suffered loss and damage as a consequence of the activities of an Australian company to bring actions in the Federal Court and seek injunctions and, or, compensation.[63] Although the Bill is still listed as "current," it is unlikely to be passed into law whilst the current coalition government is in power. A

---

[59] For further information about the environmental reporting provisions contained in Norway's Accounting Act go to http://www.enviroreporting.com/others/norway_act.pdf.

[60] A useful summary of these initiatives can be found in M. Mansley, *Open Disclosure: Sustainability and the Listing Regime*. London: Claros Consulting 2003 available at
<http://www.foe.co.uk/resource/reports/open_disclosure.pdf>.

[61] *Supra,* note 31 at 3.

[62] *Corporate Code of Conduct Bill* 2000 (Cth), clause 3(1).

[63] *Corporate Code of Conduct Bill* 2000 (Cth), clause 17.

Parliamentary Inquiry led by coalition government members rejected the Bill claiming it was unnecessary and unworkable.[64]

Proposals for this form of legislation are not confined to Australia. In the United States, a similar bill, aimed at transnational operations of U.S companies, was unsuccessfully proposed by Congresswoman Cynthia McKinney.[65] Likewise, the *Corporate Responsibility Bill* (UK), a private members bill tabled in 2002 in the UK Parliament, included an extra territorial element that would have enable affected communities abroad to seek damages in the UK for human rights and environmental abuses committed by UK companies or their overseas subsidiaries.[66] Although legislative proposals of this kind have yet to be accepted into national legislation, their strong support among the NGO community and by some members of government is an indication that proponents for this form of legislation will continue to persevere. [67]

Directors Duties

The most important reforms in corporate law are taking place in the areas of company directors' duties. Under corporate law, directors manage the affairs of a company and have a duty *to act in good faith and in the best interests of company*. Notwithstanding some statutory variations, this duty is widely recognised in common law jurisdictions, including the United States, and has now been adopted by an increasing number of civil law jurisdictions around the world.[68] The crucial role of directors in determining corporate culture is highlighted by the observations of an Australian Parliamentary Committee which in 1989 investigated the social and fiduciary duties and responsibilities of company directors in the Australian (common law) jurisdiction. The Committee stated that: "[d]irectors are the mind and soul of the corporate sector. They are crucial to how it operates and to how its great power is exercised. They determine the character of the corporate culture.

---

[64] Parliamentary Joint Statutory Committee on Corporations and Securities, *Report on the Corporate Code of Conduct Bill*. Canberra: Senate Printing Unit, 2001 at 46. Although, some level of support for the objects of the Bill was expressed by the Australian Labor Party, when in opposition.

[65] *Corporate Code of Conduct Act* H.R 2782, 107th Cong (2001), is available online at
<http://www.theorator.com/bills107/hr2782.html>.

[66] The *Corporate Responsibility Bill* (UK) (Bill 129) is available on line at
<http://www.publications.parliament.uk/pa/cm200203/cmbills/129/2003129.pdf>.

[67] For evidence of the support for the Australian Bill see generally Parliamentary Joint Statutory Committee on Corporations and Securities, *Report on the Corporate Code of Conduct Bill*. Canberra: Senate Printing Unit, 2001. For evidence of support for the UK Bill go to <http://www.corporate-responsibility.org>.

[68] For a discussion of this directors' duty within its wider common law setting see Canadian Democracy & Corporate Accountability Commission (CDCAC), *Canadian Democracy & Corporate Accountability: An Overview of Issues*. (Toronto: CDCAC, 2001) at 30 -33. For an example of this duty in the United States see Sections 512 and 1712 *Pennsylvania's Business Corporation Law* (15.Pa.C.S). Most statutory variations to this duty are 'permissive' in nature and are not intended to impose a separate fiduciary obligation on the directors to consider interests outside those of the company's interests. For example, in New Zealand, section 132 of the *Companies Act 1993* (NZ) clarifies that the duty of a director to act in the best interests of a company does not inhibit a director to make provision for the benefit of employees of the company in connection with the company ceasing to carry on the whole or part of its business. For an example, of this directors' duty in a civil law jurisdiction see *Russian Law of Joint Stock Companies* 1996 (Russia), Article 71. For a wider discussion of its adoption in civil law jurisdictions see OECD, *Experiences From the Regional Corporate Governance Roundtables*. (Paris: OECD 2004) at 44-45.

Their actions can have a profound effect on the lives of a great number of people, be they shareholders, employees, or the public generally. They can weaken and even suppress market forces. They can disturb and destroy an environment."[69]

If, as this Australian Committee observed, directors "are the mind and soul" of the corporate sector and are "crucial to how its great power is exercised", the interpretation of the directors duty to act in the best interests of the company is a key determining factor in how corporations will behave. The traditional interpretation of this duty, particularly in common law courts, is that a director's duty is to the company. The company's shareholders are the company and therefore no interests outside of those of the shareholders can be considered by the directors.[70] This interpretation tends to codify the shareholder primacy principle and has led to a concern that environmental and social interests are incompatible with the interests of shareholders focused on profit maximisation.[71]

This narrow interpretation has been somewhat adjusted through case law[72] and statute in some common law jurisdictions to clarify that directors can consider other interests than just the shareholders'. For example, thirty-two states in the United States have now enacted 'constituency statutes', which explicitly permit directors to consider the interests of non-shareholders.[73] Some of these statutes are broadly worded so that directors can consider the effects of their decisions on employees, customers, the community and society in general.[74] Arguably, this could extend to a consideration of environmental impacts given the social consequences of environmental degradation.

However, some commentators feel that U.S constituency statutes are "red herrings" and have done little to advance the interests of non-shareholders under U.S corporate law.[75] Whilst these statutes represent a statutory variation of the directors' duty to act in the best interests of the company, the laws do not oblige directors to act in a socially or environmentally responsible fashion while pursuing company objectives. Of the thirty-two constituency statutes in place all but one are permissive in nature.[76] In other words, the directors may take the interests of non-

---

[69] Senate Standing Committee on Legal and Constitutional Affairs, *Company Directors' Duties: The Social and Fiduciary Duties and Responsibilities of Company Directors.* (AGPS: Canberra, 1989) at 7 [*Director's duties*].

[70] See for example, *Dodge* v *Ford Motor Company* (1919) 204. *Mich.*459, 170 N.W. 668, 3 A.L.R. 413.

[71] *Supra* note 9 at 23.

[72] *Tech Corp. Ltd* v *Miller* (1973) 33 DLR (3d) at 313-14. This decision of the Supreme Court of British Columbia clarifies that company directors, in common law jurisdictions, when acting in the best interests of the company may consider non-shareholder interests such as company employees and the communities in which the company operates.

[73] For reference to each of thirty-two statutes see, E. Adams and J. Matheson, "A Statutory Model For Corporate Constituency Concerns" 49:4 *University of Minnesota Law School Emory Law Journal.* (2000) 1085-1135

[74] See for example, Minnesota' constituency statue Minn. Stat. Ann. 302A.251 (West 1998)

[75] See J. Springer, "Corporate Constituency Statutes: Hollow Hopes and False Fears" (1999) *New York University School of Law Annual Survey of American Law* at 123.

[76] The Connecticut statute is the one exception. *Connecticut Corporate Statute* 33-756(d) requires a director of a corporation, which has a class of voting stock registered pursuant to Section 12 of the *Securities Exchange Act* of 1934, in determining what he reasonably believes to be in the best interests of the company to consider, *inter alia*, the interests of company employees, the community and societal considerations. However, these matters need only

shareholders into account, but need not do so. As a consequence, constituency groups do not have enforceable rights should their interests be ignored.[77] In the case of the only mandatory constituency statute in place in Connecticut, the additional non-shareholder interests need only be taken into account in a small number of business decisions relating to plans of merger, sale of assets and an approval of business combination. These statutes therefore do not represent a marked departure from the statutory and general law duties of directors currently in place in most jurisdictions.

In the UK, amendments proposed to the company directors' duties arguably represent the greatest expansion of directors' duties seen in any jurisdiction.[78] The proposed statutory amendments will codify the duties of company directors by requiring them to act in a way that will most likely promote the success of the company. When deciding on what will most likely promote that success, the director *must* take account of all "material factors" that it is practicable for him to identify. This includes, *inter alia*, the company's need to have regard to the impact of its operations on the communities affected and on the environment in circumstances where a "person of care and skill" would consider such a matter relevant.[79]

The proposed UK variation on the directors' duty, unlike most statutory variations in the US, is mandatory as opposed to being merely permissive in nature. Also, the duty will apply to all decisions of a company director. The real implications of this new duty are not yet known. Will it be effective in incorporating environmental and social considerations into corporate decision making? Will it enable directors to overlook environmental and community interests in most circumstances as they are not deemed relevant or practicable to identify? Will it give socially responsible shareholders enforceable rights in the event company directors overlook environmental and community interests in deciding what will promote the success of the company? Could the duty establish grounds for persons in communities negatively affected by corporate activity to seek compensation or injunctive relief when company directors have failed to consider their interests? These questions will remain unanswered until the new duty is drafted into law and its meaning is examined by the courts.

Although the new duty does not go as far as some would have liked,[80] if implemented it will represent the first occasion in any jurisdiction, in which

---

be considered in a small number of business decisions relating to plans of merger (s 33-817), sale of assets (ss 33-830 and 33-831) and approval of business combination (ss 33-841 and 33-844).

[77] *Supra* note 73 at 108.

[78] See the UK government 'white paper', 'Modernising Company Law' (Cm 5553), published on 16 July 2002. It is available at <http://www.dti.gov.uk/cld/review.htm>.

[79] *Director's duties*, *supra* note 77 at schedule 2, paragraph 2 of the White Paper.

[80] For example, the Corporate Responsibility Coalition (CORE) unhappy with a number of aspects of the proposed corporate law reforms, has drafted a *Corporate Responsibility Bill* outlining a stricter, and arguably more effective, version of the proposed directors duty. To visit the CORE website and view a copy of Bill, which has been twice tabled as a private members bill in UK Parliament go to <http://www.corporate-responsibility.org>.

environmental and community interests are a mandatory consideration for company directors while fulfilling their duties and responsibilities to the company. This is quite symbolic, as it is from early English law that the fiduciary duties of directors can be originally traced. Accordingly, if the UK moves to amend its corporate laws governing the duties of company directors as proposed, it is very likely that other jurisdictions will follow.

Consistent with the principle of 'integration' that permeates the concept of sustainable development, these first steps towards the integration of environmental and social considerations into economically focused corporate law regimes represent an exciting and necessary step forward for sustainable development law.[81]

Strategy 4: International Treaties and Conventions

Just as national corporate regulatory regimes are evolving to enshrine notions of CSR and corporate accountability, it is becoming clearer that international treaties will soon play an important role in addressing one of the core concerns with regard to sustainable development: the impact of corporate activities on the environment and on the human rights of vulnerable communities.

The prevailing concept of a state's territorial sovereignty under international law has traditionally dictated that the regulation of corporate activities in areas of environment and human rights falls within the national rather than international sphere.[82] This has impeded the potential for international environmental and human rights treaties to impose liability on corporations that are responsible for environmental damage or human rights abuse.[83]

But recent events suggest that a shift is occurring. International schemes and conventions have been recently negotiated on the regional level and in areas of particular urgency, with the participation of corporations and civil society organizations, to address the liability of both states and corporations. These treaty mechanisms are international, but effect direct changes in the marketplace and involve corporations at each stage. In international sustainable development law, this has happened in the International Maritime Organization,[84] and in negotiations

---

[81] The principle of integration is evident in principle 4 of the *Rio Declaration on Environment and Development* which states that in order to achieve sustainable development, environmental protection shall constitute an integral part of the development process and cannot be considered in isolation from it. Furthermore, *Agenda 21* at paragraph 8.14 states that "to effectively integrate environment and development in the policies and practices of each country, it is essential to develop and implement integrated, enforceable and effective laws and regulations that are based upon sound social, ecological, economic and scientific principles."

[82] D. Ong, "The Impact of Environmental Law on Corporate Governance: International and Comparative Perspectives" (2001) Vol. 12 No.4 *European Journal of International Law* at 696.

[83] *Ibid.* at 697. There are exceptions. A number of international conventions exist that impose civil liability on operators of nuclear facilities in the event of transboundary nuclear incident.

[84] See IMO Legal Committee, *Draft International Convention on Liability and Compensation for Damage in Connection with the Carriage of Hazardous and Noxious Substances by Sea* I.M.O. Doc. LEG 67/3 (18 May 1992); *Convention on the Prevention of Marine Pollution by Dumping of Wastes and Other Matter* 1046 U.N.T.S. 120, 11 *I.L.M.* 1294 (Nov. 13, 1972).

for the 2000 Cartagena Protocol on Biosafety to the 1992 Convention on Biological Diversity.[85] Another prime example is the 1973 Basel Convention, where negotiations have resulted in a new Protocol which, when it enters into force, can directly impose liability on corporate actors.

The Basel Convention Protocol on Liability and Compensation

The Basel Convention on the Control of Transboundary Movements of Hazardous Wastes and their Disposal entered into force in 1992.[86] It seeks to first, reduce to a minimum the amount of transboundary shipments of hazardous waste by encouraging their treatment and disposal as close to their points of origin as possible; and second, to reduce the amount of hazardous waste in total.

In 1999, parties to the Convention agreed on a Protocol on Liability and Compensation.[87] The new regime seeks to reinforce observance of the standards and procedures of the Basel Convention, and provide redress after environmental damage has occurred.[88] Furthermore, it provides a comprehensive regime for liability, as well as adequate and prompt compensation for damage resulting from the transboundary movement of hazardous wastes and other wastes and their disposal (including illegal traffic in those wastes).[89]

In addition to the strict liability regime, the Liability Protocol assigns liability to any person "for damage caused or contributed to by his lack of compliance with the provisions implementing the Convention or by his wrongful intentional, reckless or negligent acts or omissions."[90] This includes legal persons, extending liability beyond states to corporations. The reference to 'person' rather than 'Party' underscores the direct liability of corporations which engage in such activities, and makes it clear that they are responsible for insurance. This mechanism ensures that sustainable development costs are internalised.[91] Contracting Parties can bring their claim for damages against corporations in the court of another Party where '(a) the damage was suffered; or (b) the incident occurred; or (c) the defendant has his

---

[85] Governments in other negotiations, such as the *United Nations Convention on Biological Diversity* (5 June 1992) 31 *I.L.M.* 818 (entered into force 29 December 1993), and its 2000 *Cartagena Protocol on Biosafety Cartagena Protocol on Biosafety* (15 May 2000) 39 *I.L.M.* 1027 (entered into force 11 September 2003), available online: <http://www.biodiv.org> have highlighted the complexity of the issue, in relation with the determination of causality assessment, type of damage, type of responsibility, conflict of laws in case of transboundary damage. They suggest that a fund could be formed, financed by biotechnology companies, to address possible hazards. See "First Meeting of the Intergovernmental Committee for the Cartagena Protocol" 9:171, *ENB* (14 December 2000), available online: <http://www.iisd.ca/biodiv/iccp1/14_thursday.html> .

[86] *Basel Convention on the Control of Transboundary Movements of Hazardous Wastes and Their Disposal* [*Basel Convention*] (1989) 28 *I.L.M.* 649 (opened for signature 22 March 1989, entered into force 5 May 1992).

[87] See *Protocol on Liability and Compensation for Damage Resulting from Transboundary Movements of Hazardous Wastes and Their Disposal* (Basel, 10 December 1999) Art. 1 (not yet in force)[*Basel Liability Protocol*].

[88] See S. Murphy, "Liability in the Basel Convention" (1994) 88 *Am. J. Int'l L.* 24.

[89] See *Basel Liability Protocol, supra* note 86 at Art. 3.

[90] *Ibid.* Art. 5.

[91] These guarantees must satisfy the minimum limits established in Annex B to the Protocol. *Supra* note 86, Article 14. Note that there is no limit for Article 5 fault-based liability.

habitual residence, or has his principal place of business.'[92] This provides access to justice for states, and grants clear jurisdiction to domestic courts. Any person liable under the Protocol is allowed to seek contribution from any other person liable under the Protocol, or from any person with whom the liable party has an express contractual agreement.[93] Liability may also be reduced or disallowed if the injured party caused or contributed to the damage.[94]

The European Institutions

On a regional level, a new, legally binding instrument will be drawn up on civil liability for transboundary damage caused by industrial accidents in the member states of the United Nations Economic Commission for Europe (UNECE),[95] by Parties to the UNECE Conventions on the Protection and Use of Transboundary Watercourses and International Lakes and on the Transboundary Effects of Industrial Accidents.[96] The instrument will build upon the Convention on civil liability for damage resulting from activities dangerous to the environment (Lugano Convention)[97] and will have the potential to prevent accidents from happening in the first place.[98]

The *Treaty Establishing the European Community* and the binding decisions of the European Council and Commission have led to bodies which have developed directly applicable legal obligations for corporations. The Council and Commission issue labour and human rights related regulations and directives with which private companies must comply, and as mentioned above, many cases have been heard where obligation was directly imposed. European Community law is, arguably, a type of international law, but it enforces direct rights and duties on corporations. This follows both from the language of the Treaty of Rome itself[99] and from the acceptance of the 'direct effect' doctrine by both the European Court of Justice and the EU member states.[100] Indeed, the understanding that EU law can, when it is clear enough, have direct effect on individuals within member states, is now a cornerstone of the EU legal system.[101] It might be argued that this 'new legal order of international law' makes the EU unique and demonstrates that other, seemingly

---

[92] *Supra* note 87 at Art. 17.

[93] *Ibid.* Art. 8.

[94] *Ibid.* Art. 9.

[95] UNECE, Report of the Joint Special Session ECE/MP.WAT/7 and ECE/CP.TEIA/5 (11 October 2001).

[96] *Ibid.*, *UNECE Convention on the Protection and Use of Transboundary Watercourses and International Lakes* (Helsinki, 17 March 1992); *UNECE Convention on the Transboundary Effects of Industrial Accidents* (Helsinki, 17 March 1992).

[97] Convention on Civil Liability for Damage Resulting from Activities Dangerous to the Environment (Lugano, 21 June 1993).

[98] UNECE, 'Press Release: Civil Liability – Agreement Reached on New Legally Binding Instrument' (ECE/ENV/01/04, 4 July 2001).

[99] *Treaty of Amsterdam Amending the Treaty on European Union, the Treaties Establishing the European Communities and Related Acts* (Amsterdam, 10 November 1997), [hereinafter 'EC Treaty'], at Article 249 establishes EU regulation as 'binding in its entirety and directly applicable in all Member States.'

[100] See ECJ 5 February 1963, Case 26/62, *Van Gend en Loos* v. *Nederlandse Administratie Der Belastingen,* [1963] ECR 3, at 12.

[101] See J.H.H. Weiler, "The Transformation of Europe" (1991) 100 *Yale L.J.* 2403, at 2413-15.

more ordinary treaty regimes can at best provide for the indirect sort of liability seen in the environmental or bribery conventions.[102] But in the alternative, perhaps the European Community's practice shows that states can conclude treaties providing for direct corporate responsibility and implement those treaties effectively. As such, it could serve as a model for further international developments, in the *Johannesburg World Summit of Sustainable Development* (WSSD) and other processes. From this point of view, "the leap of faith is one of political will; the legal doctrine follows inevitably."[103]

The Johannesburg Plan of Implementation- Towards an Intergovernmental Agreement on Corporate Responsibility and Accountability

Each of the above examples relates primarily to the imposition of civil liability on corporations for environmental damage, just as the prior discussion of litigation in US or UK courts related primarily to liability for violations of health or human rights. However, whilst being an important component of corporate accountability, they do not concern all aspects of the accountability agenda, such as sustainability reporting and issues with regards to access to justice. Furthermore, they do not encompass the wider notion of CSR which requires a company to integrate environmental and social considerations into all aspects of corporate activity ranging from the way they produce goods and services to their internal governance practices. However, an international treaty or agreement that might encompass these wider notions of CSR and corporate accountability could one day be a reality.

The *Johannesburg World Summit of Sustainable Development (WSSD) Plan of Implementation* at paragraph 49 encourages action at all levels to: "Actively promote corporate responsibility and accountability, based on the *Rio Principles*, including through the full development and effective implementation of intergovernmental agreements and measures, international initiatives and public-private partnerships, and appropriate national regulations, and support continuous improvement in corporate practices in all countries."[104]

One of the key questions is what might an "intergovernmental agreement or measure" that actively promotes corporate responsibility and accountability, based on the *Rio principles*, look like? For 'effective implementation', a key component of a new agreement, of course, would be its control or enforcement mechanisms. Such an agreement might need to take care to include the social (including human rights) and environmental aspects of corporate responsibility and accountability.

Approach 1- International convention requiring domestic law implementation

---

[102] See *Van Gend en Loos, supra* note 100 at 12.

[103] S.R. Ratner, "Corporations and Human Rights: A Theory of Legal Responsibility" (2001) 111 *Yale L.J.* 443.

[104] *Johannesburg Plan of Implementation*, Report of the World Summit on Sustainable Development, Johannesburg (South Africa) (4 Sept. 2002) UN Doc. A/CONF.199/20. Available online:
<http://www.un.org/esa/sustdev/documents/WSSD_POI_PD/English/POIToc.htm>.

One approach, based on the model of the corporate accountability convention proposed by some NGOs in the lead up to WSSD,[105] could be to require signatory states to implement law reforms within their own domestic corporate regulatory regimes. Such law reforms might include: mandatory sustainability reporting requirements (with reference to the Global Reporting Initiative), new directors' duties to fully consider environmental and social issues in corporate decision-making, the imposition of liability on directors for corporate breaches of international and national environmental and social laws. Signatory states could also be required to guarantee the rights of redress for citizens whose interests are affected by corporate activity, including access for affected people anywhere in the world to pursue litigation where parent corporations claim a 'home', are domiciled, or listed. Although there may not be the political support amongst many states for such a convention at this present stage, it is arguably one of the more effective means of ensuring corporate responsibility and accountability internationally. The convention could also be a vehicle for the implementation of uniform financial reporting, corporate governance and accounting standards that are so clearly lacking at the international level.[106] Accordingly, it would be a fully integrated economic, environmental and social instrument. The convention could be implemented under the auspicious of the U.N or even through negotiation of a special agreement pertaining to corporate governance through the framework of the World Trade Organisation.

Approach 2- Implementation through commonly agreed international principles

Rather than relying on domestic implementation, a second means of implementation could be for the 'intergovernmental agreement' to establish a set of commonly agreed principles of corporate conduct, perhaps building upon the existing nine principles of the UN global compact[107] or the guidelines for multinational enterprises established by the Organisation for Economic Cooperation and Development (OECD).[108] The agreement could set up a free-standing body or tribunal composed of representatives of the parties authorized to adjudicate over corporate violations of the principles and impose sanctions. This body might, for instance, have the power to order or authorize states to fine the offending company or increase tariff barriers on the exports and imports of the firm; to order or request that international arbitral bodies, such as the International Centre for the Settlement of Investment Disputes (ICSID),[109] to refuse to hear claims brought by those companies; to order or request intergovernmental bodies

---

[105] Outline of the proposed convention, available online:
<http://www.foe.co.uk/resource/briefings/corporate_accountability.pdf>.
[106] There is presently no binding international agreement that standardizes financial reporting, corporate governance standards and accounting standards between nation states. This is remarkable given the push towards a 'global market place' of recent decades.
[107] Global Compact, supra note 19.
[108] The OECD Guidelines for Multinational Enterprises, available online:
<http://www.oecd.org/document/28/0,2340,en_2649_34289_2397532_1_1_1_37425,00.html>.
[109] Convention on the Settlement of Investment Disputes between States and Nationals of Other States (Washington, 18 March 1965).

that include corporate participants to preclude participation of violating entities; or to prohibit international organizations from signing contracts with offending firms. These types of procedures might also allow for findings of violations against the State of incorporation of a particular enterprise, or even against the enterprise itself.

However, the current political environment and the global nature of this concept suggest that states would be unlikely to contemplate such a robust enforcement process in the near future.[110] Instead, a more 'palatable' variation of this might be to authorize the special tribunal or body to receive and review reports from states, NGOs, or multinational corporations, or even hear complaints about conduct from local community representatives or NGOs. The findings flowing from the complaint, while not judicial in nature, would create a public - and, one hopes, objective - record of the activities of certain companies, allowing other actors, especially civil society groups, to mobilize action against them.

Conclusion

Each of four strategies have important roles to play in ensuring that companies are environmentally and socially responsible and that they are held accountable for their actions in the event they breach those responsibilities. An approach that relies on one strategy (e.g. voluntary initiatives) to the exclusion of others will be bound by the limitations of this 'blinkered approach' and will ultimately fail to achieve the objectives of CSR and corporate accountability. The lessons learnt from the implementation of existing voluntary initiatives tell us that what is required is an appropriate mix of voluntary and regulatory measures.

This chapter also reveals that some strategies- such as the use of foreign direct liability outlined in strategy two- have up to now been more suited to pursuing human rights and social objectives. On the other hand, strategies similar to strategy four, have up to this point been largely confined to pursuing environmental objectives within the CSR agenda. The fact that some strategies are focused on environmental as opposed to human rights and social issues, and visa versa, only reinforces the importance of the need for the global community to act on its commitments arising from WSSD to "actively promote corporate responsibility and accountability based on the *Rio Principles,* through intergovernmental agreements and measures." Of all the initiatives outlined above, the implementation of an intergovernmental agreement has perhaps the greatest potential to unify the global community in a targeted effort to promote both environmentally and socially responsible behaviour within the business community the world over. Although such an agreement may be a few years away, it is important to recognise the urgency of the growing list of issues that now underpin the sustainability agenda and the important role corporations have in ensuring that sustainable development becomes a reality.

---

[110] J.L. Johnson, "Note: Public-Private-Public Convergence: How The Private Actor Can Shape Public International Labor Standards" (1998) 24 *Brooklyn J. Int'l L.* 291.

(ii)

SUSTAINABLE MANAGEMENT OF LAND AND WATER

10

CHALLENGES TO IMPLEMENTING INTERNATIONAL SUSTAINABLE DEVELOPMENT LAW ON DESERTIFICATION

Hama Arba Diallo[1]

The United Nations Conference on Environment and Development (UNCED), held in Rio de Janeiro in 1992, succeeded in placing the concept of sustainable development as a combination of economic growth, environmental protection and social improvements, high on the international political agenda.[2] Furthermore, UNCED affirmed the increasing importance of international environment law in codifying and promoting the concept of sustainable development.[3]

Since the Rio Conference, a multiplicity of international, legally binding environmental instruments has been negotiated, agreed upon, and entered into force. Among these instruments is the *United Nations Convention to Combat Desertification in Those Countries Experiencing Serious Drought and/or Desertification, Particularly in Africa* (UNCCD),[4] which aims to prevent, rehabilitate and reclaim degraded land. In other words, the purpose of this Convention addresses sustainable use of natural resources and the prevention of a serious social, economic and environmental problem, rather than addressing simple environmental protection like many other instruments of international environmental law. The management of natural resources, even in the case of the UNCCD, has traditionally been considered strictly within national law and priorities.[5] However, the international community's increasing recognition that

---

[1] Mr. Hama Arba Diallo, Executive Secretary, *United Nations Convention to Combat Desertification and Drought, Particularly in Africa*. This chapter is based on his keynote address to the Conference, Sustainable Justice 2002: Implementing International Sustainable Development Law, in Montreal, Canada, June 12 – 14, 2002. All errors and omissions are the responsibility of the editors of this collected volume.

[2] Report of the United Nations Conference on Environment and Development, *Rio Declaration on Environment and Development*, 1992, UN Doc. A/CONF.151/5/Rev. 1, 31 I.L.M. 874 online: UN <http://www.un.org/documents/ga/conf151/aconf15126-1annex1.htm>. *[Rio Declaration]*

[3] *Ibid.* at principle 1, 4, 7 (for example).

[4] United Nations Convention to Combat Desertification in Those Countries Experiencing Serious Drought and/or Desertification, particularly in Africa (17 June 1994, Paris) 33 I.L.M. 1328 (entered into force 26 December 1996). [UNCCD]

[5] N. Schrijver, *Permanent Sovereignty over Natural Resources: Balancing Rights and Duties* (Cambridge: Cambridge Univ. Press 1997) at 390.

M.C. Cordonier Segger & C. G. Weeramantry, eds., Sustainable Justice: Reconciling Economic, Social & Environmental Law
© *2005 Koninklijke Brill NV, Printed in The Netherlands, pp.157-162.*

all states are ecologically, as well as economically, interrelated has posed a new challenge to this approach. In the context of the UNCCD, more than one hundred countries are affected by desertification, causing economic uncertainty intra- and inter-state migration, and conflicts over scarce resources. The consequences of desertification impact also countries outside the affected areas, which has prompted a growing consensus for a global response.[6] At 179 signatories (two options: put the numbers of signatories at 191 to 15 September 2004 or leave the text as such introducing a footnote providing this information), the number of Parties to the Convention, demonstrates a worldwide commitment to jointly address desertification and mitigate the effects of drought.[7]

The focus of the Convention is on dryland areas that cover more than one third of the world's total land area.[8] The fragile drylands are highly prone to land degradation; for example in Africa, 73% of the agricultural drylands are estimated to be already degraded.[9]

The geography of poverty coincides strongly with that of desertification. According to the World Bank, of the 1,3 billion people living on less than one dollar per day, nearly 75% live in rural areas.[10] These people include many of the world's poorest, most marginalised, and politically weak citizens. For instance, nearly half of the population of the African continent, 325 million people, lives in drylands.[11] Poverty and environmental degradation are linked in a complex, often mutually reinforcing relationship. Poor people are forced to over-exploit land resources in order to survive, and the resulting impoverishment of land decreases the potential for subsistence and income creation. From this viewpoint, poverty is both the cause and consequence of desertification.

Correspondingly, combating desertification and reducing poverty should be considered as interrelated objectives. Thus, the Convention has a strong sustainable development aspect. The potential of the UNCCD to respond directly to the economic, social and environmental challenges related to poverty alleviation in drylands suggests that it is essentially a tool for developing the poorest and marginalized rural areas.[12]

---

[6] *Ibid.*
[7] UNCCD, "The Convention," online: UNCCD <http://www.unccd.int/convention/menu.php>.
[8] UNDP (1999) 'Drylands Population Assessment II' Paper prepared by Siobhan Murray, Lauretta Burke, Dan Tunstall, World Resources Institute and Peter Gilruth, UNDP Office to Combat Drought and Desertification, November, 1999.
[9] Chapter 12 of Agenda 21 /UNCED
[10] MDBs/IMF Report to G8, *Global Poverty Report*, (Okinawa Summit, July 2000).
[11] G. Hyden & M. Bratton, eds., *Governance and Politics in Africa* (Boulder: Lynne Rienner Publishers, 1993).
[12] A. Boyle & D. Freestone, eds., *International Law and Sustainable Development: Past Achievements and Future Challenges* (Oxford: Oxford University Press, 1999).

International legally binding sustainable development conventions, such as the UNCCD, are one source of international law.[13] In this capacity, these instruments seek international commitment to jointly agreed guidelines and principles, governing the conduct of countries in the areas covered by each convention. These guidelines and principles materialize in specific arrangements between various stakeholders at the national, sub-regional, regional and global levels.

Obligations under the UNCCD

The United Nations Convention to Combat Desertification requires that countries affected by desertification implement the Convention by developing and implementing national, sub-regional and regional action programmes. The preparation of these programmes is specified in the treaty's five Regional Implementation Annexes for Africa, Asia, Latin America and the Caribbean, Northern Mediterranean and the Central and Eastern Europe, respectively.[14]

The Rio Conference emphasized acknowledging human beings as the center of sustainable development. This approach paved way for the demand of integrating citizens in the political decision-making. In accordance with these principles, the UNCCD stresses the need for action programmes to adopt a democratic, bottom-up approach. They should emphasize popular participation and the creation of an "environment" designed to allow local people to help themselves reverse land degradation. Governments will remain responsible for creating this enabling environment. They must make politically sensitive changes, such as decentralizing authority, improving land-tenure systems, and empowering women, farmers, and pastoralists. They should also permit non-governmental organizations to play a strong role in preparing and implementing the action programmes. In contrast to many past efforts, these action programmes must be fully integrated with other national policies for sustainable development.

On the other hand, developed countries that are Parties to the Convention are obliged to encourage the mobilization of substantial funding for the action programmes. They should also promote access to appropriate technologies and know-how. The Convention's action programmes are developed through consultations among various stakeholders in the affected countries, the donor community, and intergovernmental and non-governmental organizations.[15] This process will improve coordination and channel development assistance to where it can be most effective. It will also produce partnership agreements that

---

[13] W. Lang, ed., *Sustainable Development and International Law* (London: Graham & Trotman/Martinus Nijhoff, 1995).
[14] United Nations Convention to Combat Desertification, "Action Programmes for Combatting Desertification," online: UNCCD < http://www.unccd.entico.com/english/basicfacts4.htm>.
[15] UNCCD, *supra* note 4, at Art. 10- 2 f).

spell out the respective contributions of both affected and donor states and of international organizations.

In addition, the Convention contains obligations related to, *inter alia*, collection, analysis, exchange of information as well as technical and scientific cooperation.[16]

Challenges for Meeting the Obligations of the UNCCD

Despite the rapid expansion and wide range of contemporary international environment law, relatively little is known about the practical impact of sustainable development conventions on government behaviour. Some observers suggest that the gap between law in books and state actions may now appear wider than at any other time in history. In accordance with the principle of sovereignty and the demands set by national priorities, countries differ in their status of implementing obligations and applying principles of international environment law, including those related to sustainable development conventions.

In the context of the United Nations Convention to Combat Desertification, to-date 65 affected countries have prepared and in most cases formally adopted their national action programmes to combat desertification.[17] Seven sub-regional and four regional action programmes have been finalized.[18] While the national action programmes spell out the frameworks for concrete action to combat desertification, the sub-regional and regional action programmes emphasize the exchange of information as well as the technical and scientific cooperation among the respective countries.

An assessment of recent political trends and policies related to the targeting of development assistance reveals an increasing political interest in the interrelationships between poverty reduction and land degradation. The major cooperating partners consider the fight against poverty to be an overriding goal of international development cooperation and recognize the close linkages between poverty and desertification. The severity and concentration of poverty in rural dryland areas is also thoroughly recorded in the publications of international organizations and research institutions.

However, statistics show a steady decline in resources allocated for sectors related to rural development during the last decade. According to the OECD, resources allocated by DAC members to the agricultural sector fell from 12,1 %

---

[16] *Ibid.* at Article 16.
[17] *Supra* note 13.
[18] *Ibid.*

in 1979 to 5,3 % in 2000 of total bilateral commitments.[19] The unpredictability and scarcity of financial resources has been a major challenge to the UNCCD.

The World Summit on Sustainable Development was expected to foster poverty reduction through adopting pragmatically oriented policies and programmes on various branches of sustainable development. Strengthening rural development, particularly agriculture in rural dryland areas, was recognised as a high priority in the Summit.[20] Correspondingly, it was also agreed in principle to seek to reverse the negative trend of resource allocation to rural development, as this was seen as necessary to ensure that political commitments are reflected in practical action in the years to come.[21] This has required a critical assessment of the current targeting of development assistance, as well as a renewed commitment to long-term activities aiming at poverty reduction. The creation of a dedicated area of the Global Environment Facility for land degradation is an important first-step in this regard. [22]

Another challenge facing sustainable development in the context of international legally binding instruments is how to avoid the overlapping of activities and ensure optimal efficiency in implementing the numerous sustainable development conventions. Developing countries have reported to experience serious difficulties in trying to meet the numerous simultaneous obligations under these instruments.

With regard to the Rio Conventions on combating desertification, biodiversity and climate change, the respective Conferences of the Parties have frequently brought up the need for establishing closer cooperation and identifying synergies and linkages between the three Conventions.[23] For this purpose, a Liaison Group has been established with the aim of providing a forum for exchange of views and information among the secretariats to the Conventions. Further, the Joint Work Programme between the Convention on Biodiversity (CBD) and the UNCCD, focusing on biodiversity in dryland areas, was finalised in the course of 2001. [24] A corresponding work programme is also under way between the United Nations Framework Convention on Climate Change (UNFCCC) and the UNCCD. [25]

---

[19] K. Fukasaku, *Overview, Miracle, Crisis and Beyond* (Paris: OECD Development Center, 2004).
[20] Johannesburg Plan of Implementation, *Report of the World Summit on Sustainable Development,* (4 Sept. 2002) UN Doc. A/CONF.199/20, online: UN
<http://www.un.org/esa/sustdev/documents/WSSD_POI_PD/English/POIToc.htm>
[21] *Ibid.*
[22] M.C. Cordonier Segger, "Significant Developments in Sustainable Development Law and Governance: A Proposal" *United Nations Natural Resources Forum*: 28:1 (2004). [Cordonier Segger]
[23] *Rio Declaration, supra* note 2.
[24] *Convention on Biological Diversity*, Conference of the Parties to the Convention on Biological Diversity, UNEP/CBD/COP/7/INF/28 (2004).
[25] Cordonier Segger, *supra* note 21.

In addition to the cooperation at the level of the secretariats, several countries, which are Parties to the UNCCD, have, since 2000, held national workshops on the synergistic approach. These workshops have gathered together the national focal points for all three Conventions with the aim of identifying concrete areas of cooperation for implementing the Conventions.

Conclusion

We are witnessing an accelerated development of international law in general, and international environmental law in particular. Several characteristics of this emerging law for sustainable development can be identified. First, in environmental law we are moving beyond law that is focused strictly on physical parameters of problems to be regulated; we are beginning to take into consideration its economic dimension, which is what sustainable development is all about. Second, there is growing recognition of the need for the widest possible partnership between nations and peoples to address issues of environment and sustainable development. Third, environmental governance should be reviewed to strengthen its institutional structure based on an assessment of future needs to be able to face wide-ranging environmental threats in a globalizing world. Fourth, the process of implementing international law in the field of sustainable development is unique in nature. We have a history of introducing innovative means and mechanisms of implementation. What we see in recent environmental treaties is not only the setting of ambitious goals, but also the provision of supportive means for the achievement of those goals, whether financial mechanisms, or provisions for the transfer of resources or of technology. Fifth, it is also expected that more attention will be paid to dispute avoidance within the general framework of dispute settlement and resolution.

Much more attention is being given to the institutionalization of implementation capacity or capacity building. Indeed, during negotiations on international legal instruments more time is spent discussing how to set up implementing mechanisms to ensure that scientific information is continually brought forward, or through the design of reporting mechanisms. Looking at the work and activities undertaken by multilateral environmental agreements we can say that the implementation review process has become a regular, even central part of international environmental co-operation. In fact, almost every MEA uses some kind of formal reporting system, many engage in implementation review, and an increasing number use or are developing a compliance review institution.

Concerning the UNCCD, the implementation of international sustainable development law has undergone various steps from the analysis of information contained in the national communications to the assessment of the compatibility of achievements and the obligations contained in the Convention.

11

LAND TENURE REFORM IN THE DRYLANDS: HOPES AND CHALLENGES

Marie-Claire Cordonier Segger[1], Chris Huggins[2] and George Michael Sikoyo[3]

"Property rights serve human values. They are recognized to that end, and are limited by it."
- Chief Justice Joseph Weintraub, Supreme Court of New Jersey, USA

Land is a critical productive asset on which many livelihoods depend, particularly in the developing world. For the poorest drylands populations, land degradation is a major factor that affects the ability to achieve food security and enhance livelihoods. Drylands are parts of the world where rainfall is very low and rates of evaporation are high. The type of ecosystem in the drylands is determined by the amount of water present. This variation leads to the great diversity of landscapes possible such as the plains, grasslands, savannahs, steppes or pampas. The hyper-arid areas, which include deserts, are not considered as part of drylands. Drylands make up a significant amount of the world's land mass (54% of the world's productive land is drylands) and population. They are important sources of food security, biodiversity and global ecosystem functions, and they are vulnerable to degradation. Nearly all drylands and their inhabitants face constant risks from land degradation. Many factors contribute to land degradation. As the essence of the drylands is climate

[1] Marie-Claire Cordonier Segger, MEM (Yale), BCL & LLB (McGill), BA Hons (Carl.), Director, Centre for International Sustainable Development Law (CISDL), Chair, CISDL/ILA/IDLO Partnership on International Law on Sustainable Development, Senior Manager, Americas Research Portfolio, International Institute for Sustainable Development &United Nations Environment Programme ROLAC, British Chevening Scholar & SSHRC Fellow, Exeter College, Oxford University Law Faculty, Lecturer, International Development Law Organisation (IDLO) & Member, International Law Association (ILA) Committee on International Law on Sustainable Development.
[2] Chris Huggins, M.A.(Strathclyde) M.A. (Glasgow), Research Fellow, African Centre for Technology Studies (ACTS).
[3] George Michael Sikoyo, MSc. (Ecological Economics), BSc. Forestry (Hons), Dip.(Education), Research Fellow, African Centre for Technology Studies (ACTS). A later version of this collaborative chapter appeared as a Global Drylands Imperative challenge paper, M.C. Cordonier Segger & C. Huggins, *Land Tenure Reform in the Drylands* (Nairobi: UNDP, 2003). The authors would like to thank Phillip Dobie, the Director of the United Nations Development Programme Drylands Development Centre in Nairobi, Kenya, and Camillo Ponzani, for their roles in initiating the project, also Joana Talafre of the Canadian International Development Agency, without whose support this research would not have been possible, and Sumudu Atapattu, Judi Wakhungu and Hari Suthan for their valuable comments and intellectual contributions. A sincere vote of thanks is also extended to the UNDP for their interest and support in making this research possible, though the views expressed are those of the authors alone.

M.C. Cordonier Segger & C. G. Weeramantry, eds., Sustainable Justice: Reconciling Economic, Social & Environmental Law
© 2005 Koninklijke Brill NV, Printed in The Netherlands, pp.163-194.

variability, successful drylands use requires a balance of adaptability and resilience. Land degradation occurs when this balance is lost. Through poorly managed intensification of land use and deforestation, productive drylands can be degraded into unproductive land. This land cannot support any agriculture, nor can it even support pastoralism. The fragility and delicate balances necessary to maintain the world's drylands, coupled with their multiple resources and variety of stakeholders, underscore the importance of care in sustainable dryland management and development. This task requires significant investments in human capital and resource management systems, including land tenure reform efforts. The issue of land tenure reform, in particular, is highly relevant. Land tenure systems which impose unequal access to and control of resources for marginal populations, or undermine effective land management institutions can contribute to the degradation of dryland areas. Conversely, effective, secure access to land resources can provide an essential incentive for land users to invest in sustainable land use practices.

International attention to the related issues of land reform and land degradation occurs mainly in the context of the 1994 *UN Convention to Combat Desertification*.[4] Recently, discussion of these issues has been re-invigorated following the recommendations of the world's governments at the 2002 *World Summit for Sustainable Development*[5] in Johannesburg, South Africa.

This chapter therefore seeks to highlight the land tenure reform, desertification and hope for the world's drylands. It aims to provide the challenges of land reform in the drylands as well as show its importantance for sustainable development. The different land tenures in the drylands are mentioned and relevant case studies of land tenure practices from around the world are given. Finally, the chapter provides the lessons for decision-makers and concludes with the practical courses of action for land tenure reform in the drylands.

1. The Challenges of Land Tenure Reform in the Drylands

Land tenure systems are a legal construct – a bundle of rights designed and enforced by the societies, which grant them. However, a number of challenges and questions remain for these societies. How to properly characterize all these different yet vitally important rights? Which rights pertain to which land user, how can they be recognized, and how can they be made secure enough to catalyze crucial investments for the drylands?

---

[4] *UN Convention to Combat Desertification in Countries Experiencing Serious Drought and/or Desertification, Particularly in Africa*, 33 ILM 1328 (1994).
[5] *Johannesburg Plan of Implementation*, Report of the World Summit on Sustainable Development, Johannesburg (South Africa) (4 Sept. 2002) UN Doc. A/CONF.199/20. Available online:
<http://www.un.org/esa/sustdev/documents/WSSD_POI_PD/English/POIToc.htm>.

The rights in question take myriad forms. They can be held by individuals, firms, organized groups and the state at all levels. Their precise nature often depends on context-specific statutes and by-laws, which may pose restrictions on land and resource-use. In many countries, dry areas were (until recently) seen as 'wastelands', of little economic interest to central authorities. For this reason land rights remain ambiguous in many drylands, often with multiple and overlapping legal regimes – usufruct (claim by use), customary, religious - sometimes contradicting with each other and with the legislation of the state. This can lead to conflict.

The creation of property rights in land is also complicated by the co-existence of formal and customary legal systems. Often, traditional legal arrangements are unwritten, and therefore may be 'invisible' to external institutions. Many societies in developing countries have deeply embedded preferences for customary law approaches to questions of rights to access, use, inherit or transfer title over land. Locally-developed and adapted to specific ecological conditions, these laws can be fundamental expressions of culture and tradition, derived from a combination of spiritual beliefs, geography, economics and history. In these instances, urban 'modern' biases must be adjusted to consider the views and needs of rural peoples, especially in developing countries.

In many developing countries in particular, property rights with regard to land are ill-defined, often due to the competing or conflicting nature of customary and statutory rights.[6] When rights to resources are not well-defined, the poorest and most marginalized segments of society, especially women and children, suffer the most – exacerbating their daily struggle to meet basic needs. In such situations, more powerful members of society can use their access to information, political influence, and money to access land resources at the expense of the poor. In some countries, communities face the sporadic nationalization of land holding by the state, undermining the incentive for individuals or legal entities to invest in the land. In fact, even where land tenure systems do function, they often have unequal effects on the society.

Simply providing title to land, however, does not in itself guard against this process. The very act of deciding who owns land is frequently manipulated by powerful groups, with the result that the state ends up legitimizing and enforcing inequalities. It is not surprising; therefore, that the pattern and process of land ownership and distribution in many countries is simply a reflection of deeply embedded power relations. Indeed, it would be naïve to suggest that this pattern could be fully transformed without a sustained effort to address the structural conditions which created it.

---

[6] S. Moyo, (2003) "The Land Question in Africa: Research Perspectives and Questions." Paper Presented at *Codesria Conferences on Land Reform, the Agrarian Question and Nationalism* (Gaborone, Botswana, October 2003 and Dakar, Senegal, November 2003).

Providing legal title to land users in a transparent manner is not necessarily a solution to these challenges. It allows for the land to be used as collateral for loans, but also often leads to default to usurious lenders, leading to concentration of land ownership. Furthermore, providing title in the name of the 'head of the household', typically considered as the male, often leads to sale of land, which may in fact have been worked by women. This situation is exacerbated in most communities in the developing world where barriers contrived by tradition and culture can make the situation worse for women and youths.

The issue of land-use-specific tenure also needs to be considered. Much of the theory and practice of land tenure is implicitly predicated on the assumption that land users use one piece of land, as in most temperate agricultural systems. In areas where rainfall is too low to support crop production and where people lack economically accessible groundwater, however, there is an ecological imperative for mobility; to follow the rains wherever they may fall. In the case of mobile land use, the key challenge in land tenure reform is to ensure that there are reciprocal agreements of access between land users. Land titling on the basis of title in the name of an individual in such a system would be inappropriate, as it would confer right of disposal, potentially taking a part of the resources out of the land use system. This is precisely what is happening in many areas which are only of marginal agricultural potential - in particular where the state is investing in water development, often in uneconomic schemes and under pressure from better connected groups – to the detriment of the traditional land users. Such policies enhance conflict between agriculturalists and pastoralists, which is another major challenge for land tenure reform in drylands.

Furthermore, there might be the most progressive land tenure legislation on the books in a capital, but if it is not implemented at the local level it will not bring sustainable land use practices or equity. As such, land tenure - and in particular land tenure reforms – are not only a legal issue but also one of governance. Security of tenure, therefore, is guaranteed more by the political neutrality of the bodies which write and enforce legislation and the transparency of land reform processes - a function of a balance of power, hence the central importance of genuine broad-based participation in land reform processes. Facilitating these conditions is a great challenge; but is a precondition for meaningful change.

As should be apparent from the issues raised, the questions of access to, as well as ownership and distribution of land, are politically complex. Experience suggests that secure land tenure systems can help encourage productive investment, create incentives for conservation, improve livelihoods and stimulate economic development in both rural and urban areas of countries with large areas of drylands. On the other hand, there is also evidence that inappropriate land tenure systems - those which result in unequal access to and control of resources for marginal populations - are a major obstacle to poverty reduction. Efforts to implement land reforms often challenge vested interests and provoke social tension, while the failure to pursue land reform can spark conflict or even rebellion. Failure to implement meaningful reforms, however, can contribute to the continued degradation of dryland areas[7], which in turn will create the social conditions under which it is difficult to carry out such reforms - a vicious circle.

Amongst the many important issues several key challenges can be identified for policy-makers. It will be a challenge to ensure that land tenure systems and land tenure reform processes are truly participatory, accessible, and transparent. It will also be a challenge to identify institutional structures that can be established at local, national and international levels to support legal aspects of land tenure security and reform. It will be a challenge to address, through national processes, the overlaps and contradictions between formal and informal, customary and modern land tenure systems, and 'hybrid' systems. It will also be a challenge to promote and protect the right of marginalized groups, including women, to control their land. Finally, one of the most serious challenges is the need to implement land tenure systems and land tenure reform processes that take a holistic, comprehensive and co-ordinated view of the institutional and physical environment.

Land Tenure Reform: Definition and Importance

The nature of tenure security has long been the subject of debate, especially as regards the drylands, where underlying ownership is dynamic and often disputed. It is also important to understand western notions of property rights because these continue to dominate both theory and practice of land tenure reform across the globe.

Tenure security and livelihoods can be seen from the four points of view which influence tenure policy and land reforms in developing countries.[8] One focuses on 'property rights', underscoring the value of tradable titles to an economy, where tradable assets provide the key to credit and incentives to various kinds of investment in land. A second draws attention to 'agrarian structure' and inequities of property ownership. A third advocates for 'common property' and argues for the recognition and support of traditional, community-based property systems, many of which are still operative in the world's drylands.

---

[7] Desertification means the conversion of useable drylands into unproductive land that cannot support agriculture or settlement and is caused mainly through intensification of land use and deforestation.
[8] See L. Ellsworth, *A Place in the World: Tenure Security and Community Livelihoods, A Literature Review* (Washington DC: Ford Foundation, 2002).

From this view, the commons is a source of non-tradable livelihoods for the poor. The fourth point of view is that of the 'institutionalists', who focus on how the larger political economy is constantly reshaping property regimes, providing or denying tenure security to those people claiming a particular property right.

Another major influence, especially during the 1970's and 1980s, is the "Tragedy of the Commons" paradigm.[9] According to this argument, pastoralists raising their herds in "a pasture open to all" will seek to maximize their gain, by increasing the number of animals they own. This eventually results in land degradation: but for each individual herder, the direct benefits of the extra animals outweigh the indirect costs imposed by degradation – which is borne by the community as a whole. The fact is, however, that very few pastures are "open to all". Customary regulations have emerged in most places to ensure that communities know where, when, and how they can graze or cultivate. These systems may not be perfect, but they do provide some form of environmental management. Problems emerge when such systems are undermined by processes of conflict, modernization, and competing forms of governance. In such cases, regulations may not be enforced, meaning that the 'tragedy of the commons' idea becomes, at least partially, a reality.

Land tenure reform refers to changes in the way in which societies confer bundles of property rights and obligations to land holders - that is, it focuses on the terms and conditions on which land is held, used, and transferred. Clear land reform legislation will include provisions that clarify contradictions between potentially overlapping institutions. These laws should establish the purposes of the land reform; set forth the legal grounds for rights to land; create unambiguous, stable, property rights in land; and set a framework for the distribution of these rights to new holders.

The need for effective land tenure reform is well recognized in international sustainable development law, including the 1994 *Convention to Combat Desertification in those Countries Experiencing Serious Drought and/or Desertification* (UNCCD) and several international human rights instruments. It has also been given recent attention by World Leaders in the Johannesburg Declaration and its Johannesburg Plan of Implementation.

The 1994 UNCCD obliges state parties to take measures to control and prevent the spread of desertification in their territories or to transfer technical support and funds to states that suffer from desertification. The UNCCD recognizes that desertification problems are often manifestations of structural social and economic problems, including poverty and lack of access to land, and poorly defined or inequitable land tenure regimes. It also recognizes that past failures

---

[9] See G. Hardin, "The Tragedy of the Commons" 162 *Science* (1968) at 1243-1248.

to combat desertification have been linked to a lack of local resource-user involvement and to incompatibility with indigenous cultures and land tenure systems. The UNCCD contracts a domestic obligation for countries to improve these laws in the future and to ensure that they do not further contribute to further degradation.

The Declaration of the 2002 WSSD

States committed to: "[p]rovide access to agricultural resources for people living in poverty, especially women and indigenous communities, and promote, as appropriate, land tenure arrangements that recognize and protect indigenous and common property resource management." [10]

To help protect and manage the natural resource base of economic and social development, states also committed to: "[a]dopt policies and implement laws that guarantee well defined and enforceable land and water use rights and promote legal security of tenure, recognizing the existence of different national laws and/or systems of land access and tenure, and provide technical and financial assistance to developing countries as well as countries with economies in transition that are undertaking land tenure reform in order to enhance sustainable livelihoods." [11]

And finally, for sustainable development for Africa, states committed to:"[p]romote and support efforts and initiatives to secure equitable access to land tenure and clarify resource rights and responsibilities, through land and tenure reform processes that respect the rule of law and are enshrined in national law, and provide access to credit for all, especially women, and that enable economic and social empowerment and poverty eradication as well as efficient and ecologically sound utilization of land and that enable women producers to become decision makers and owners in the sector, including the right to inherit land." [12]

Several other international 'soft law' instruments are relevant. Global Plans of Action developed at the United Nations Conference on Human Settlements in 1996 recognized land reform as essential to achieving sustainable development.[13] In addition, most major international and regional human rights instruments guarantee a right to property or peaceful enjoyment of

---

[10] *Johannesburg Plan of Implementation*, Report of the World Summit on Sustainable Development, Johannesburg (South Africa) (4 Sept. 2002) UN Doc. A/CONF.199/20. Available online: <http://www.un.org/esa/sustdev/documents/WSSD_POI_PD/English/POIToc.htm>. [*Johannesburg Declaration*].

[11] *Ibid.*

[12] *Ibid.*

[13] See Report of the United Nations *Conference on Human Settlements* (Habitat II), U.N. Doc. A/CONF.165/14 (1996).

possessions.[14] These rights, often already exist in international and domestic legislation but lack effective implementation or monitoring systems. Nowhere is this more evident than in the continuing effort to put the legal rights available to rural women with regard to landed property into practice. Land distribution programmes still often assume the recipient will be a male without proper investigation of equity and economic rights of women. Due to its complexity, a 'rights-based approach to land tenure reform' is still elusive in practice. But in many regions, calls for the realization of a range of land-related human rights, such as the right to free movement, to information, to the means to have an adequate diet and to a sustainable environment, are becoming stronger and better recognized.

International *recognition* of the importance of land tenure, clear resource rights, and land reform is not, however, sufficient for effective land tenure reform. Indeed, global influence at the local level may have negative impacts on access for some groups. For example, international investment and trade regulations associated with the WTO and International Financial Institutions are part of a process by which land is becoming increasingly commodified through various processes, which are often 'embedded' in struggles over valuable mineral and biological resources.[15] Protected areas are an important part of these contested forms of globalization.

As demonstrated by the 2002 WSSD Declaration, it is now widely understood that the unequal distribution of land and weak tenure systems both contribute to poverty in many rural areas, especially in developing countries. Even with international assistance, many developing countries lack the institutional structures, legal capacity and information systems needed to carry out sustained reforms. The principles that shape these policies seem logical and easy to implement on paper. In reality, land tenure reform is a formidable, multidimensional task.

---

[14] The United Nations *Universal Declaration of Human Rights*, GA Res. 217 (III), UN GAOR, 3d Sess., Supp. No. 13, UN Doc. A/810 (1948) at Art. 17 (contains a commitment to such rights. While a Declaration is not binding in international law, it has been convincingly argued that many principles enshrined in this Declaration are *jus cogens* norms) See also, the *European Convention for the Protection of Human Rights and Fundamental Freedoms* 312 U.N.T.S. 221 (1950) at Prot.1 (recognizes the right to peaceful enjoyment of property); the *American Declaration of the Rights and Duties of Man* O.A.S. Res. XXX, adopted by the Ninth International Conference of American States (1948) at Art. 23, reprinted in *Basic Documents Pertaining to Human Rights in the Inter-American System* OEA/Ser L. V/II.82 Doc. 6 rev. 1 at 17 (1992) (recognizes the right to property and in a binding corollary); the *American Convention* 9 I.L.M. 673 (1970) at Art. 21; the *African Charter of 1981* CAT/C/XX/Misc.1 (1997) at Arts. 14, 20, 21 and 22; the (binding) *International Convention on Civil and Political Rights* 999 U.N.T.S. 171 (1966) (self-determination); the *International Covenant on Economic, Cultural, and Social Rights* GAOR, 2200 A (XXI) (1966) at Art. 6.1, Arts. 11 (living and housing) and 15 (intellectual property rights).

[15] S. Moyo, "The Land Question in Africa: Research Perspectives and Questions" (2003) Paper Presented at *Codesria Conferences on Land Reform, the Agrarian Question and Nationalism* (Gaborone, Botswana, October 2003, and Dakar, Senegal, November 2003)

In developing countries and economies in transition, land tenure reform can take several forms: redistribution of land to the landless, securing tenure rights for landless individuals, or restoring rights in lands that were forcibly taken during colonial rule or under state control.

Arguments for pro-poor land reform and secure property rights.[16]

1. Land reform can increase economic and agricultural productivity, as better compensation for effort motivates people.
2. Individuals and groups with little or no security of tenure have greater incentives to make the long-term investments necessary for sustaining and increasing agricultural productivity.
3. Land reform addresses social equity and maintains or restores political stability by improving the status and dignity of landless populations.
4. Land tenure reform can create the conditions for improved environmental and resource management. For example, by guaranteeing rights to land over generations, people are encouraged to cooperate and avoid conserve its resources, as they are more likely to derive the future benefits.

However, many land tenure reform efforts are hindered by factors such as inadequate funding, weak infrastructure, lack of integration with other policy priorities (such as land-use planning), resistance by incumbent elites, corruption, and political struggle. These can affect the success of such programs. The costs of establishing an appropriate legal and physical infrastructure, including a registry system, are often high. Social realities also complicate legal arrangements especially in developing countries and countries with economies in transition. For example, terrace sharecropping, carried out by tenants in traditional relationships that transcend generations, challenges new legal systems. Similarly, the use of grasslands by migratory peoples in many countries for forage or seasonal transversal - not settlement - sits uncomfortably with legal concepts of "possession" of land. In addition, even if people can secure rights to land, their ability to use it may depend on access to scarce water resources.

Before examining case studies of land reform from different countries, this chapter will review certain characteristics of land tenure on the drylands, identifying some of the points that make the drylands unique social and ecological environments.

---

[16] M. Kirk, U. Löffler & W. Zimmermann, *Land Tenure in Development Cooperation* (Wiesbaden: GTZ, 1998).

Land Tenure in the Drylands

The drylands of the world are challenging environments. Low levels of average rainfall, in addition to the variable nature of the rainfall- long droughts may be followed by destructive flash-floods- pose numerous constraints on farmers. As a result, it becomes difficult to plan for optimal land holdings, seed, fertilizer and labour inputs because rainfall is so uncertain. In response to these environmental realities, dryland communities have tended to use three key livelihood strategies: flexibility (e.g. adjusting the location and amount of land cultivated or grazed according to rainfall), adaptability (e.g. switching crops or income-generating activities as necessary), and diversity (increasing the number of livelihood options available, both 'on-farm' and off).[17] Some specific examples of livelihood tactics are provided in Box 3 below.

Strategies employed at the local level to cope with the variable character of dryland environments[18]

Strategies employed by farmers include:
• Labour invested in soil-and-water conservation systems.
• Production of crops in a cross-section of ecological zones in order to spread risk and benefit from the differences in micro-environments.
• Opportunistic responses to climatic variability, such as the planting of crops in river flood-plains (flood-recession agriculture).

Some of the adaptive strategies used by **pastoralists** include:
• Keeping a number of small livestock herds, distributed over a wide area of the environment (herd splitting)
• Diversifying herd composition
• Use of kinship networks to redistribute livestock and thus spread the risk and benefits more evenly

There are many other strategies used by both agriculturalists and pastoralists, including:
• Gathering wild foods
• Diversifying into alternative productive strategies, such as wage labour, trade in honey, charcoal burning, or the selling of medicinal products
• Adapting and re-interpreting ethnic or group identities and alliances to improve access to natural resources

---

[17] See M. Mortimore, B. Adams & F. Harris, "Poverty and Systems Research in the Drylands" (2000) 94 IIED Gatekeeper Series 1, available online: International Institute for Environment and Development, < http://www.iied.org/docs/gatekeep/GK94.pdf >.
[18] Adapted from J. Lind & C. Huggins, *Conflict and Local Adaptation to Environmental Change in Africa: A Background Paper* (Nairobi: African Centre for Technology Studies ACTS, 2000) [on file with authors].

Rather than statutory laws, customary systems are the *de facto* systems of land tenure in operation in many dryland zones. In Africa, for example, many people hold their land under indigenous customary systems irrespective of the formal legal position.[19] As described above, these are characterized by systems of multiple resource use that are complex but particularly common in dryland areas. Specific areas of resource abundance, including dry-season grazing areas and pastures reserved for times of drought, wooded areas and seasonal rivers are often key to livelihoods in the drylands and hence have special land tenure regimes. These areas form 'lifelines' for local communities, and are often managed under systems of multiple resource use.[20]

Water is a prime determinant of access to dryland areas; and ownership of water sources is usually vested in the local community (e.g. lineage group, or village) rather than the household. Finally, communal tenure is a common feature of customary land tenure systems in the drylands, with overall authority for land use vested in the traditional leaders of the cultural group (typically older men). In agricultural areas, common pool resources are used predominantly by the poorer segment of society, providing a safety-net for those with minimal private land holdings.

Pastoral land tenure systems utilize concepts radically different from those generally employed by 'modern', 'western' systems. Resource rights are generally identified by group membership - such as clan or tribe – rather than by geographical boundary. Many pastoral groups have 'home areas' but also have dry season territories (which may be far away) as well as 'buffer zones' which border competing groups. Terms of access to these 'buffer zones' may be kept deliberately flexible, to allow creative use of such areas which avoids potential conflicts. Boundaries, therefore, do not function in ways that are understood by modern legal systems.[21] Indeed, the 'territories' utilized by pastoral communities tend to change in size and shape over seasons and years, depending on climatological variation and negotiations between competing communities.

However, many changes are occurring. Common resource areas are indirectly threatened by the commercialization of production and trade, urban links, and political systems attempting to replace or undermine the traditional leaders. In some cases, customary leaders have sold land rights as individuals, and the

---

[19] M. Rukuni, "Land Tenure and Sustainable Development in Africa" Paper Presented at the *Scandinavian Seminar College Conference on African Perspectives of Policies and Practices Supporting Sustainable Development* (Brussels, Belgium, May 27, 1999).

[20] See C. Huggins & F. N. Gichuki, "Irrigation in the Drylands of Kenya: Impacts on Local Uses of Natural Resources" Paper Presented at the *Regional Biodiversity Forum* (Mombasa, February 2000).

[21] See J. Unruh, "The Relationship Between Indigenous Pastoralist Resource Tenure and State Tenure in Somalia" (1995) 36 *GeoJournal* 1.

whole community has become landless in the eyes of the law. In other cases, the regulations for use of communal areas break down due to a combination of factors. Frequently, powerful actors manage to gain influence in weakened management institutions, and modify access regulations to suit their interests. Women and youth, in particular, tend to have little say in such issues.

In many countries, land tenure has been vested formally in the state, and local populations have been assigned non-transferable user rights (or largely ignored by the legal regime). This was the case across much of the Sahel, where the 'tragedy of the commons' argument was used to justify state control. In practice, active state control over drylands is frequently limited to specific, resource-rich areas, such as forests (e.g. for timber, or as conservation areas), or rivers (e.g. irrigation, hydropower). Similarly, private interests tend to be limited to such key resource areas.

In practice, land tenure is pluralistic, and customary and modern systems can be permeable, influencing each other and borrowing from each other in innovative ways. Often, individuals will try to enforce their property rights by switching from one system to another as it suits them, or even using both simultaneously.

Case Studies of Land Tenure Reform Practices

According to the FAO and other agencies, land reform is back on the agenda because rural populations, including drylands dwellers, have put it there.[22] Those people maintained their demand for access to land and other resources, especially in situations of under-utilized, 'idle', lands and grossly unequal land holdings. While the protests of the rural poor have never ceased, today there are several trends that give added weight to their demands.

Awareness plays a key role. Globalization means that rural populations are participating in the world development debates in ways that were impossible a decade ago. In effect, the Internet allows some rural populations and their civil society partners to inform the world of land reform issues. From the invasions of land seekers in Malawi and Zimbabwe, the *Movimento Sem Terra* in Brazil and the continuing demand for restitution of property taken by previous regimes in South Africa to the transformation of economies and land use systems in the former Soviet Union and Aral Sea Basin, these new levels of publicity and awareness bring new dimensions to land reform.

In particular, global or cross-border coalitions are forming to address common challenges. For example, there is a new recognition by the women's movement and development practitioners alike, that rural women make up the bulk of

---

[22] J. Riddell, *Contemporary Thinking on Land Reform* (Rome: FAO, 2000). See also J. Riddell *et al.* "Recent FAO Experiences in Land Reform and Land Tenure" in *Land Reform, Land Settlement and Co-operatives* (Rome: FAO, 1997).

agricultural producers but are the last to be included in land reform and rural asset distribution programmes.[23] As a result, international working groups are now forming to address these issues, building the capacity of women to organize and participate.

Also, many countries have undergone radical political transformations during the last decade or so, including former USSR states as well as many single-party states in Africa, which have liberalized their political – and economic- environments. Land reform is often one of a package of fundamental processes which are designed to improve equity and economic productivity in such countries.

Within land tenure reform processes, dryland areas face particular challenges. In some countries, increased population and multiplying land uses (partly due to industrialisation) in high-potential areas are causing dryland areas to become more important for production. In others, pro-poor policies highlight the difficulties of remote dryland communities, located far from markets and without significant representation at governmental levels.

Land tenure systems are designed and overseen primarily at the national level, and this is where land tenure reform takes place. As such, the following case studies have focused mainly on national attempts to reform land tenure systems. Many attempts could be highlighted, but this chapter covers experiences in different regions of the world, including the former USSR, Central Asia, Southern Asia, Central America, and the Horn of Africa. Each case study illustrates an important trend, and together, they demonstrate some of the significant challenges faced in diverse drylands circumstances around the world.

Modern legal systems are struggling to understand and support evolving customary land tenure regimes

In some dryland areas, customary systems provide flexible, well-adapted solutions to local land tenure needs. However, customary land tenure systems are coming under increasing stress due to population increase, expansion and commercialisation of agriculture, as well as other 'modernisation' processes. For example, in West Africa, customary systems were often respected by government. However, official attempts to mediate conflicts over access to land from a Western legal viewpoint can use terminology and structures that do not reflect the nuances of customary land tenure systems. Policy-makers will discuss land tenure in terms of 'customary' or 'modern'. In fact, an evolutionary process is underway, through which some communal lands are being

---

[23] C. Walker, "Land Reform and Gender in Post-Apartheid South Africa" (1998) *UNRISD News* 18:4 6.

'individualised' but in locally-specific ways, which differ from typical understandings of privatisation and modernisation.

In areas such as the savannah zones of West Africa, customary land tenure systems are particularly strong. These customary systems dynamically adapt to changing social and economic circumstances. For example, as arable land becomes more scarce, informal land markets are emerging, even though this is against 'tradition'. Pastoralists are increasingly moving into agricultural zones, and developing economic relationships with cattle-keeping farmers, which can be mutually beneficial but also, at times, conflictual.

Attempts by the state to mediate land disputes have encountered difficulties due to the complexities of customary systems. Customary systems are usually unwritten, have flexible geographical boundaries, and change depending on power-relations within the community. Often, legal and academic authorities over-simplify and generalise the customary rules of some groups onto others. Attempts to register land titles are likely to be problematic, as land titling may not take secondary user rights (e.g. to access tree products, or water sources) into account, privileging the rights of some over others.

In one area, customary 'land chiefs' are entrusted with the management of vacant land. Newcomers can apply to the land chiefs, and offer 'gifts' to use such land each year. There is often competition between the different land chiefs to attract livestock keepers to their areas, in order to gain cattle as 'gifts'. Recently, the state has forbidden access to land by pastoralists who are not citizens; they even attempted to expel them. Conflict has erupted, and the policy has sparked division between leaders who benefit from the herders and those who do not. State policies are seen by some as a way for central authorities to eventually take responsibility for land away from customary leaders. These experiences suggest several lessons.

First, in many instances, customary tenure systems are subject to change due to social and economic pressures. As such they can be controlled by powerful actors at the expense of more marginal people, and can become contested. Participatory research is necessary to understand how local systems can be enhanced by laws and policies in order to protect marginalised groups, such as widows. In addition, land titling, often seen as a solution to tenure insecurity, is not necessarily appropriate in dryland areas where communities enjoy multiple overlapping user-rights to a variety of resources. However, some aspects of the titling process such as historical research and mapping of land uses, could improve land tenure security in dryland areas if local people are given access to this information. As customary land rights systems are so complex and numerous, it is impossible to legislate for all. A more realistic approach is to provide a legal framework to validate local agreements. Such a framework would make local systems enforceable if they adhered to agreed procedures, such as witnessing of agreements, or written formalisation of agreements in a local *lingua franca*.

Landscape-sensitive approaches are a necessity for effective land tenure reforms.

Many pastoral and agro-pastoral societies have been largely misunderstood, ignored and increasingly marginalised from mainstream development efforts. Development efforts are generally piecemeal and focus on the project level, rather than taking a landscape-level approach. There appears to be a lack of coordination and awareness of the 'big picture' including cross-border movements in the sustainable management of drylands. The lack of detailed information by policy makers on pastoral livelihoods and its links to landscapes, coupled with institutions imposed on these communities, often creates a costly information gap resulting in policy mismatches between the local level, national level and neighboring countries that share the same landscape. The pastoralists' almost total reliance on the common resource pool makes them vulnerable to unfair land tenure arrangements. This is compounded by the fact that their experiences with the administration over the years have created an element of mistrust.

African pastoralists have for a long time been deemed as having land tenure systems structurally incapable of efficient land use. The notion that pastoralism is a primitive form of production has ensured that subsequent land tenure arrangements have not been sensitive to the realities of African ecosystems. The resultant land tenure reforms, with their focus on private land ownership agreements, have dispossessed many pastoralists of their traditional access to range land. In the process communities have become more vulnerable to drought and famine.

Historically, pastoralists had varying rights to resources within the commons. In most cases herders recognize private ownership of specific key resources (e.g. leaf-fall, firewood, and fruits). Among most pastoral groups, an assembly of initiated male leaders handles land administration and dispute resolution. Colonial and post-colonial changes in administration can result in differing policy directions at varying periods of time such as privatization, African socialism, and land adjudication/consolidation. The subsequent 'confusion' alienates communities from the state. This can be exacerbated by policies that tend to favour one community against the other resulting in conflict, which often crosses international borders. These experiences suggest several lessons.

First, the development of land tenure arrangements that take the whole landscape into consideration - irrespective of cross border administration regimes - should be enhanced. This could be done through participatory and inclusive processes from the site levels to the regional level. In addition, there is need at the regional level to broaden areas of cooperation to include land tenure reforms because of the political, social, and economic linkages. This could be effected through memoranda of understanding and protocols.

Fertile mountain terraces can become drylands if they are not managed for food security and flood control[24]

In some areas, such as the Near East, highlands cultivation uses traditional terraces which help anchor soil to the mountainsides and store rainfall runoff. However, traditionally maintained terraces can fall into disrepair or become abandoned for a variety of reasons, including the increasing importance of off-farm income; the lack of clearly defined responsibility between landowners and tenants; and the lack of money to invest in terrace maintenance. Less terrace maintenance can cause increased runoff, eroding the slopes and causing destructive floods in the *wadi* (ephemeral stream) beds. In effect, the management practices can turn the slopes into veritable drylands. The lack of adequate decision-support tools and opportunities for participation, which can enable policy makers to understand farmers' investment behavior and lead to more acceptable, relevant policies, further inhibits the reversal of terrace degradation and restoration, affecting food security and povery alleviation.

In many highland areas of the Near East, such as highland Yemen or Syria, land is cultivated by owner families in the terraces, but sharecropping is also significant on over a third of the land. Terraces cultivated by landowners are often better maintained and more productive, demonstrating better maintenance than sharecropping tenants. While the responsibilities for maintenance, repair and other costs are defined in the customary rules of land use in the area, uneven distribution of power (often favouring landlords to the detriment of the cropper) has led to 'silent resistance', where the properties are not well maintained. More clearly defined responsibilities, through clear and enforced local agreements to cover maintenance and other costs, would help to address this issue.

When the land tenure systems are better defined, incentives exist for farmer investment in appropriate technologies. For example, gabion and rock construction techniques for erosion prevention in *wadi* beds have been

---

[24] See M. Alsanabani *et al.* "Impact of Land Tenure and Other Socioeconomic Factors on Mountain Terrace Maintenance in Yemen" CGIAR System-Wide Program on Property Rights and Collective Action, International Food Policy Research Institute, Washington, DC. (Series: CAPRi Working Paper, no. 3). See also the *Oriental Institute Archaeological and Environmental Investigation of Yemeni Terraced Agriculture* available online: Center for Archaeology of the Middle East Landscape, <http://www.oi.uchicago.edu/OI/PROJ/CAMEL/YEMEN/Yemen.html>; see the International Centre for Agricultural Research in the Dry Areas 2000 *ICARDA Annual Report: Improving Rural Livelihoods in the Yemeni Mountains through Integrated Natural Resource Management,* online: ICARDA's Research Portfolio <http://www.icarda.cgiar.org/Publications/AnnualReport/2000/Project%204.1/Project4.1.html>.

introduced to farmers in several locations, providing bank protection. These can withstand flash floods: once there is security against flooding, crop improvement investments are more likely. Also, degraded livestock range can be improved. Once land terrace management is enhanced and productivity increased, investments can be made in improved veterinary services and extension services in order to improve livestock health and reduce losses. Water harvesting techniques for domestic purposes can also be introduced in Yafa'a to reduce the burden on women who regularly travel long distances to gather water. These experiences suggest several valuable lessons.

First, proper enforcement of customary land use rules, which define maintenance and cost-sharing responsibilities, could significantly increase the investment in land improvement and terrace maintenance. Farmers are often seeking options for more profitable use of their terraces. Further on-farm participatory research is needed, to identify appropriate technologies, such as fruit trees and improved water harvesting (including micro-dams for supplemental irrigation). Causes of low productivity should be analyzed and the information made available to farmers and policy makers, as these can be actively engaged. Finally, research and sharing of gender-appropriate technologies and water management approaches could also help local farm families cope with the changing socio-economic environment.

Challenges of Market-Based Reform in Countries with Economies in Transition

In many countries with economies in transition, market-based land reform has been recently initiated, founded on the theory that markets can arbitrate supply and demand of land. A market-led land reform requires willing sellers and buyers. It is not clear that liberalisation always brings investors. Can market forces ensure that those who are most motivated and better suited to be farmers obtain the land, while inefficient land holders and absentee land owners are phased out? Many believe that the new land markets still require some state intervention. By themselves, markets will not do much to transfer land to the poor. If the former owner must be compensated at near market value by the purchaser, a poor farmer cannot repay out of farm profits alone. Even when land changes hands, land is often sold back former owners if markets are unregulated. Careful re-distribution of public lands, or state expenditure on land reclamation and subsequent allotment as private property can make assets available to those too disadvantaged to enter into normal land market transactions. Support is also needed for institutions to administer the necessary land acquisition and distribution mechanisms, and to advise prospective land owners.

For example, the Aral Sea, bordered by Uzbekistan and other states, was once one of the largest freshwater lakes in the world. But the appropriation of the area for Soviet central planning has degraded the sea and surrounding areas, with resulting land degradation. The Aral Sea Basin Capacity Development Project sought to restore the land as well as establish new land tenure systems. Pre-Soviet tenure was varied, based on local traditional and Islamic law. This land was appropriated as Soviet *Sovkhoses* (state) or *Kolkhozes* (coop) property in the 1930s. As a result of the development of irrigated cotton monoculture, accompanied by the deterioration of land quality, the increase of water consumption for irrigation and a number of arid years, the flow of water into the sea in the 1980s practically ceased. The shoreline has retreated a distance of 60-80 km, exposing 33,000 square km of seabed. Salt-laden sand dust destroys up to 15,000 hectares of pastureland every year in the sea zone, and soil productivity has plummeted. The result is the deterioration of the population's health in the crisis zone: infant mortality; lung disease; cancers; tuberculosis; and typhoid. Salt and dust storms have raised the level of particulate matter in the atmosphere by over 5 percent, seriously affecting the Earth's climate.

The post-Soviet Constitution for the area neither establishes nor prohibits property rights. Some auctioning of Aral Sea basin has been attempted, though many of these auctions failed, except for those covered by reforestation projects. Most fertile land rights are now held by *Kolhozes* called "*Shirkat*" farms (village + crops). Some agricultural pseudo-privatization has taken place, through conversion to non-transferable leases of 49 years or less. Farmer selection for this program of conversion is based on "demonstrated managerial and farming skills." Some farm houses and gardens are also now held under private land use right as "*Dekham*" farms. A non-commercial bank was formed to facilitate redevelopment and crop conversion, but a lack of real liquidity of collateral inhibits access to capital. In response, a new collateral system is being formed based on transfer of buildings and use rights. The value of these land use rights are to be established by "committee of experts." These experiences suggest several important lessons.

First, it is important to keep a realistic timeline for land reform efforts in vulnerable areas. A very slow conversion from monoculture can result, when expectations of quick profits from foreign investment hampers long-term investments. Second, real estate is made up of more than the houses. The dual legal status of lots vis-à-vis their infrastructure can be difficult to manage. Clarifications of the legal status of both aspects of the 'bundle of rights', and the institution of management reforms which keep the two together, could contribute to stronger adoption of market-based reforms. Third, public trust is needed to strengthen market processes. State ownership can mean continued politicization of stewardship issues. As such, increased public trust is needed to support the process of auctions and bring in greater investment to the region, leading to higher values for the land, hence greater stewardship.

The Challenges of Land Tenure Security in Developing Countries with an Uncoordinated Institutional Environment

Many developing countries, for example in Eastern and Southern Africa, have initiated processes of land tenure reform in recent years. These processes have the potential to empower local communities and improve access to land for dryland communities. However, governments still often hesitate due to the political difficulties of the tasks. Due to the sensitive politics of land reform, the issues surrounding a reform process can be debated mainly by politicians, without sufficient dialogue with civil society or relevant government departments. Stakeholders can rarely participate in policy formulation processes, and results of official inquiries into land tenure may be kept confidential. For the first time, customary tenure systems, including communal ownership arrangements, are being supported (rather than ignored or outlawed) by some legal initiatives. However, conflict between the interests and mandates of key government departments are reducing the success of such initiatives.

The recent experiences of Ethiopia provide an example. A long history of insecure, fluctuating, and ambiguous land tenure regimes has had negative impacts on public and civil service confidence in this sector. Since the promulgation of the national Constitution in the mid 1990s, land tenure has – on paper - been improved. The Constitution affirms that the land belongs to the people first, and the State second. Secondary land use rights, including the customary rights to access grazing land, water, forests, and other natural resources, are protected by the Environmental Policy.

However, many problems remain. The government has yet to formulate a comprehensive land policy, and many aspects of the Constitution have yet to be clarified and implemented. Land remains state-owned, leading to feelings of uncertainty over future tenure security. There is a general lack of policies supportive of common property regimes as are found in dryland areas. There are some conflicts in the mandates and activities of various government departments, and development has been unco-ordinated as a result.

For example, development projects often contradict the constitutional rights of dryland peoples to access land and express their cultural identity. Expansion of large-scale commercial farms in dryland areas has prevented local people from accessing prime dry season grazing land, making survival during drought increasingly difficult. Agricultural projects, often donor-funded, have heightened communal tensions leading to an exacerbation of conflict in the area. These experiences suggest several lessons.

First, there is a need for integration of activities and mandates between different levels of government – a harmonization along the 'vertical' institutional axis. For example, there is urgent need for local bylaws that provide effective legal instruments to enforce national and regional policies. In addition to 'vertical' integration, 'horizontal' integration between sectors is also vital. Formulation of a comprehensive land use policy is a useful instrument for this task, as the legislation and policies of various sectors (e.g. environment, forestry water) should be revised to follow it. The ultimate source of authority, of course, should be the constitution. Finally, it seems clear that land reform is a sensitive issue that should be addressed with caution but also with frankness. It should be tackled in a steady, transparent manner and all stakeholders should be involved, in order to build confidence in the process.

Collective and Private Land Tenure Reforms can Undermine Communal Co-operation

Some systems of land reform seem to be in danger of creating a sense of the "tragedy of the commons", by making it harder for people to cooperate in traditional or modern structures to manage their common resources. Many regions have historically complex and varied land tenure systems. Applying generic "westernized" and "entrepreneurial-focused" land reform systems in areas previously under communal regimes may not always be the best solution. For example, instead of creating a system of entrepreneurship as planned in one region of Asia, people felt like the land tenure reform forced them into a situation where they were all "eating from the same ricepot."

In part of Central Asia, reforms aimed at rewarding farmers for increased agricultural production by initiating leases to small plots have instead created a tragedy of the commons. The system's small plot leases can be sought for a period of up to 30 years, and are both transferable and inheritable land use rights, which provides for privatization of stocks to small-holders. Unfortunately, the system failed to specify which rights were derived from the post commune "collective ownership" and has led to inconsistent transfers to villages and local political structures. Likewise, the system has failed to provide villagers with actual documentation of use rights, which has created even more chaos. *De facto* common property regimes were encouraged.

In response to the incomplete and ineffective land reform in this area, locals began to demonstrate entrepreneurship through self-empowerment. They sought new and, in some cases, highly innovative mechanisms to establish "co-operative management systems." But for inspiration, they turned to ancient traditional patterns of subsistence and organization, turning the village into the basic unit of use and control for these systems. These experiences suggest several lessons. First, voluntary entrepreneurship might be preferable to compulsory systems. In some cases, a compulsory rights contract system, which is imposed from above by the state onto villages and rights-holders, is difficult for local people to assimilate. Local initiatives which 'bubble up' from villages can be recognized and supported. In Asia, this self-organizational dynamic can be harnessed to encourage and develop stronger entrepreneurship through careful program design. Second, there is often a need to phase in accountability when phasing in rights. Systems need to be put in place to encourage transparency and accountability when land tenure reform is attempted in arid areas of Asia. The higher administration can otherwise seem omnipresent, leading to governance challenges and potential for rent-seeking. Greater decentralization of authority coupled with clear lines of responsibility, capacity building, and local empowerment could help.

"Privatizing Pastoralism" Can Lead to Unregulated Resource Use

Recently, a process of transition to a market system- including the abolition of the collectives- has been taking place in certain countries of Central Asia. The new land tenure systems rely mainly on the re-emergence of customary regulation and autonomous cooperation, especially based on kinship relationships. At higher levels, this appears to leave a gap between the formal legal and political structures, and the resumed customary forms. More certain authority and greater stability might be needed to bridge this gap. For example, herd stocks were re-privatized to small-holders, (though the land itself often remained state-owned), re-creating pastoralist grazing livelihoods. Considerable urban-to-rural migration by former collectives' technical personnel took place, to take up the newly privatized small-holdings. The relatively inexperienced former personnel started to overgraze near sedentary settlements.

Under Central Asian pre-socialist systems, for example, Mongolia, the country was ruled by the hereditary aristocracy or Buddhist clergy. The ownership was public, considered to reside in the monarchy. Tenant rights were held within customary fifes. The formation of new republics shifted ownership rights in land to the new state. Bond herding ended, and small herding dominated. Further fragmentation of region-plots was induced in order to reduce nomadism, which was seen as 'destabilising' the community. For example, livestock ownership limits were used to phase-in collectivization of herders into state farms. Collectivization processes effectively reintroduced yield-focused stewardship.

In the land tenure reform process, Central Asian lands previously occupied by collectives were also restored to the families of former pastoralist herders, transforming the land use patterns. But without the collectives' surplus-marketing functions and other mechanisms, the increased incentive of small-holders was to build their herds, leading to increasing degradation of the open access resource. In addition, some winners in the privatization process became absentee herders. In Mongolia, 95% of the land is vulnerable to desertification. A 1994 Land Law allows certain leasing arrangements and supports the regulatory authority of provincial Governors, but implementation needs to be more consistent in order to contribute to greater security of tenure and access to grazing for all pastoralists. The Land Law and its Civil Code also need to recognize and incorporate customary use patterns more fully. These experiences suggest several lessons.

First, it is not clear that a pure 'back to the roots' strategy is really possible. Central Asian pastoralism is still under considerable ecological stress after de-collectivization. More careful regulation of the new systems of land use, and support for customary grazing regulations would strengthen the current system of private tenure. Second, hybrid systems may be either a 'saving grace' or a 'coup de grace.' Present arrangements encourage hybrid nomadic-sedentary patterns. But it is necessary to find ways to prevent the hybrid arrangement from leading to pressures from both sides. One way forward would be to develop incentives that are cooperative in nature, or training to help establish a culture of negotiated land use. Finally, in-equities play an important role in success or failure. Increasing wealth gaps amongst herders has potential to foster social and political volatility. While a political movement is forming to encourage full private ownership of pastures, another option would be careful use of incentives to cooperate in better distribution of costs and benefits.

Conflict in the Drylands Zones Limits Options for Land Tenure Reform

Due to ethnic conflict in some drylands, such as in South Asia, land tenure in war-affected regions has unique challenges. In war-affected areas, many people cannot access their land due to insecurity. In these conditions, land pressures can increase for minority populations and other groups due to the ethnic conflict and insecurity. Clearer and better-defined systems would support reconciliations and development efforts, and contribute to confirm old and create new socio-political alliances among the communal (ethnic) groups. Improved access to and possession of priority claims for resources can help to determine different coping strategies for villages in complex emergencies and in the peaceful areas.

One poignant example is the case of Sri Lanka, state-led land colonization had an important impact on the entitlements of Tamils, triggering grievances towards the government and the majority ethnic group.[25] Grievances over land resource distribution in large-scale settlement schemes have been major reasons for 'ethnicised conflict' in the East.[26] Research findings confirm that resource entitlements in many areas of Eastern Sri Lanka are 'ethnicised.' Access to resources is unequally distributed among the three communal groups, which reinforces grievances among those who feel at the losing end.

---

[25] J. Goodhand & P. Atkinson, *Conflict and Aid: Enhancing the Peacebuilding Impact of International Engagement* (London: International Alert, 2001). See also J. Goodhand & N. Lewer, "Sri Lanka: NGOs and Peace-Building in Complex Political Emergencies" (1999) 1 *Third World Quarterly* 69-87.
[26] B. Korf, "Ethnicised Entitlements in Land Tenure of Protracted Conflicts: The Case of Sri Lanka" (Paper presented at the 9th Biennial IASCP Conference, June 2002). See also S. Klingebiel & J. Rösel. *Hauptbericht zur Evaluierung 'EZ-Wirkungen in Konfliktsituationen' Fallstudie Sri Lanka.* Referat 310 (Bonn: Bundesministerium für Wirtschaftliche Zusammenarbeit und Entwicklung BMZ, 1999).

State-run programs for the sustainable management of land resources in Sri Lanka offer valuable lessons for land reform. Two projects can be highlighted. First, Integrated Rural Development Programs address land degradation issues through local livelihood projects. These seek to reduce land degradation in critical areas, and to raise the living standards of the poorest communities - those who depend on the land for their sustenance. Second, Sri Lanka runs a Landslide Hazard Mapping Project, which seeks to regulate the development of housing and infrastructure on a sustainable basis in the Badulla and Nuwara Eliya Districts. The project was specifically designed to (a) provide landslide hazard assessment, (b) ascertain socio-economic problems of resettlement and (c) create awareness among resident communities about the adverse impacts of improper land uses. These projects offer hope for conflict situations, and their experiences suggest several useful lessons:

First, it is important to focus on the poor, and their challenges. In combating land degradation, there is a need to recognize the importance of concentrating initially on the poorer segments of the farming population within the critical areas. Second, sometimes progress can be achieved by moving the reforms from land to land-users. In early projects in Sri Lanka, the focus was on the land, to conserve and stabilize areas that had been degraded. In later projects the emphasis has shifted from the land to the land users. This new focus has generated considerable improvements, by recommending a set of soil conservation measures to land users, and providing them with incentives in the form of subsidies and cash payments. Such subsidies need to be adjusted or more carefully targeted to ensure they do not favour the more affluent farmers. Finally attention must be paid to the sustainability of the effort itself. By and large land users have been encouraged to change their current land use practices mainly through the provision of material incentives. The project can build-in provisions to encourage increasing self-sufficiency for farmers vis-a-vis external agents, to ensure that interest in conservation measures continues once assistance ceases.

Water Development in the Drylands can Change Land-uses and Bring Conflict

In the Senegal river basin during the late 1980s, plans to construct a major dam, which would change the flow of water in the region and allow for increased agricultural opportunities, had explosive consequences. The market value of some land increased greatly, and the political elite in Mauritania therefore moved to disenfranchise many of the inhabitants, especially those with secondary user rights. This legal move was accompanied by a campaign to strip many of the affected people of their citizenship, which angered neighbouring Senegal, and triggered a tit-for-tat cycle of expulsions and violence.

This case is just one of many recorded conflicts over land in West Africa and elsewhere, where land is, "one of the most commonly recurring causes of conflict throughout recorded history".[1] But the conflict was triggered by an anticipated change in land use, from low-input, seasonal cultivation and grazing, to intensive commercial farming, and as such it was a 'modernization' conflict. It shows that the fate of drylands, and the people who rely upon them, are intimately linked to the utilization of water resources. The dam project was initiated in good faith, with the aim of increasing irrigated agriculture, generating electricity, and making the river navigable. However, the project's impacts on dryland land uses indirectly contributed to massive social upheaval, inequitable land reform, and a situation of potential international conflict. In addition, land degradation in the region, combined with devastating drought, transformed land-use changes into a high priority for the governments in the region.[1] A more sustainable drylands scenario could have minimized the political and economic pressure for the dams and thus avoided conflict.

These challenges and experiences suggest several lessons. One lesson is that land reform can be used for exclusive and inequitable purposes: upholding the "rule of law" becomes a less inspiring vision when the political situation means that the rule of law itself is unjust. More recently, greater political will has emerged in the region for equitable land use regimes. In some instances, pastoral land use zones have been established, mechanisms for conflict resolution have been designed, and customary rules have been supported by law, with the support of international institutions. International legislation, including the UNCCD, has also proved a powerful incentive for change.[1]

Land Tenure Reform Requires Effective Legal Systems and Good Governance

In order to provide foundations for continued economic recovery and rural growth in many parts of Central America it is necessary to improve tenure security, both for productivity and equity. Poverty reduction strategies in the region highlight land regularization as a priority to revive economic growth and improve the livelihood of the poor. But for these projects to be effective in the long term, the legal nature of the reform must be secure. And greater public participation and awareness is necessary, including for innovations aimed at improving the lot of women.

Nicaragua, like other countries in the region, suffers land degradation due to deforestation, drought and natural disasters (such as Hurricane Mitch). With a population density of 30 inhabitants per km2, land is relatively land abundant, but land tenure systems are either concentrated or highly insecure.[27] In 1979, more than 52 percent of Nicaragua's total area was owned by 4 percent of Nicaraguan families, and there were also significant foreign holdings in the

---

[27] J. M. Paige, *Coffee and Power: Revolution and the Rise of Democracy in Central America* (Cambridge, Mass.: Harvard University Press, 1997).

country.[28] Drylands make up about 15% of the territory and are home to 50% of the population. In the 1980s, large tracts of lands were re-distributed through agrarian reform programs. However, these included much land the government did not legally own, sowing seeds of continuing property rights insecurity.

The legal system appeared to be the weakest link in the formal titling process, leading to efforts to ensure that it was significantly bolstered and transformed to protect emerging property interests. Although some adjudicatory functions were handled by a specialized administrative office, many property claims are referred to the courts, which are notoriously slow to produce rulings and often unable to guarantee enforcement. Recent case studies still illustrate that the poor spent considerable amounts of money or even had to sell portions of their lands to hire lawyers to defend their land claims in dubious legal cases.[29]

However, legal issues are not the only problems. Gender-sensitive land reform laws, in order to ensure equal treatment of women, have ensured titles are issued jointly to husband and wife.[30] But although 80% of new titles in Nicaragua were issued jointly, less than 20% of these are held jointly today. Surveyed landholders may not be aware of the exact nature of their documents, or wives might actually sign away their part. For this aspect, greater awareness-raising efforts are needed, or issuance of joint titles may have limited impact on actual decisions and thus not serve to improve women's position. These experiences suggest several lessons.

First, legal validity and official recognition of the titles issued is essential. Unless definitive and enforceable resolutions to the present conflicts over property and compensation can be reached, these benefits will remain nothing more than speculation. Second, formal titling must be supported by steady improvements in the financial, technical, educational, and political resources. There is also a need to ensure local community participation in titling programs, and it is essential to resolve property and compensation disputes, with all the legal and political changes that this will entail.

---

[28] A. Lacayo Oyanguren, *The CIA Factbook on Central America* (Washington: CIA, 1996). See also J. Jonakin, "The Impact of Structural Adjustment and Property Rights Conflicts on Nicaraguan Agrarian Reform Beneficiaries" (1996) *World Development* 24:7 at 1179-1191.

[29] M. Merlet & D. Pommier, *Estudios Sobre Tenencia de la Tierra. Nicaragua.* (Managua, Nicaragua: Institut de Recherches et d'Applications des Méthodes de Développement IRAM, 2000).

[30] C. D. Deere & M. Leon, *Who owns the Land? Gender and Land Titling Programs in Latin America* (mimeo: on file with authors, 2000). See also D. Wachter, *Farmland Degradation in Developing Countries: The Role of Property Rights and an Assessment of Land Titling as a Policy Intervention* (Madison: University of Wisconsin, 1992).

Drylands Land Reform Lessons for Decision-Makers

The formulation of land tenure systems must be a strategic process, involving analysis of the dynamic nature of dryland livelihoods in the 21st century. The case studies above reveal a series of general lessons learned. Drylands have complex ecologies and can shift quickly from a productive to unproductive state - and vice versa. In many regions, drylands are occupied by the poorest of peoples, who depend on these lands for their livelihoods. The needs of poor dryland communities are often overlooked in policymaking, particularly when the decision-making process is concentrated in urban areas. There is now an urgent need to focus on the poorest of the poor, drawing upon specific lessons from past experiences.

Working with Legal Pluralism and 'Hybrid' Legal Systems

In many areas, modern and customary land tenure systems co-exist. Modern legal systems of access to and ownership of forests and water sources often contradict customary laws which often provide complex, variegated access to individual resources. This contradiction sometimes threatens local communities and the management systems they have successfully adapted over centuries. Codification of customary regimes poses enormous administrative and conceptual challenges for many countries. Legal systems, including land tenure reform attempts, must try to fit local circumstances by addressing the ecological, socioeconomic, land-use, historical and cultural characteristics of the people living in the drylands. The local level may often be the most effective place to for tackle specific tenure systems.

There are many examples of the re-emergence of customary regulation and autonomous cooperation based on kinship and families. Hybrid or 'pluralist' systems of land tenure reform eventually result. In these instances, sensitive governance and active community participation becomes key to ensuring equity and addressing transition challenges from informal to formal ownership, ensuring inclusion of all those most affected.

Eating from a Common Rice-Pot: Tragedy of the Commons in the Drylands?

Several issues related to the concept of the "tragedy of the commons" emerge. The applicability of the term varies widely. While customary tenure systems are never perfect, and are generally being eroded by processes of 'modernisation', they can be more resilient than many outsiders believe. They may seem inactive because they are often 'invisible' and unwritten. Only if they break down completely, or are highly contested, do they represent a tragedy of the commons, in which 'open access' leads to unsustainable use of resources.

Even carefully planned 'modern' property regimes can lead to such a tragedy if they are not acceptable to local people. There is strong need for further exploration of whether and how collective or individual rights can be effective, particularly in situations where rights are insecure and tragedy is looming. Locally-tailored solutions should be sought and supported.

Land use planning which takes care of the various stakeholder interests is essential. Planning should be a participatory, on-going *process*, inclusive of all stakeholders. Furthermore, instruments for the implementation of national land use policies need to be harmonized including administration and information systems. Harmonization of the sectoral policies and legislation – e.g. laws on water, forests, and environment - need to be addressed, integrating the concerns and livelihood needs of drylands communities.

Effective institutions to resolve conflicts or disputes are required including transparent local land/resource tribunals incorporating legitimate customary practice, third party mediation and processes for equitable allocation of natural resource rights. Conflicts with deep and unresolved historical and inter-ethnic inequalities in land distribution and resource access require special attention including building of trust and consensus between different interest groups and cultivation of political will.

Managing Fragile Environments – the Need for Holistic Strategies

New land management practices, especially when drawing from adapted traditional systems, have the possibility of improving livelihoods and addressing poverty and food security. Most successful land tenure efforts in dryland environments have been implemented as part of a wider 'package' of land management improvement, including institutional strengthening and technical backstopping. These examples of best practice have also taken the environmental realities – the physical distribution of natural resources across a wide landscape – and the social, cultural, and economic realities, as their starting point; rather than assuming that existing top-down administrative structures can succeed. In addition, they have been co-ordinated with policy processes and development programmes which create an enabling environment for alternative sources of livelihood which provide income for investment into drylands. Inclusiveness, transparency and accountability are the hallmarks of successful approaches.

Land and Tenure Do Not Always Lead to Collateral

Legal titles to land do not necessarily open up opportunities for credit in poor agricultural areas. If there is little confidence that broader legal systems will enforce loan/debt recovery (due to high transaction costs involved), or land markets do not appear to be functioning, formal title often has little and only collateral value. These conditions lead to low demand and few investors. In addition, land 'ownership' as a means to credit access is not always appropriate in drylands where communities enjoy overlapping user rights to a variety of resources including arable land, grazing and forests.

Land Tenure Security Requires More Than Titles

Legislation is just one of the mechanisms necessary for land tenure security. Processes such as recognition of informal rights of use and occupation, codification of tenancy, sharecropping agreements and establishment of cooperative ownership should be supported by land administration and management institutions, which are vital for effective governance. It is crucial that land administration institutions be accessible to ordinary people in drylands and that they recognize the complexity of land rights on the ground.

Well-functioning rights and land institutions underpin economic development and help reduce corruption and social conflict. Democratic land use planning is crucial in order to mediate effectively between the competing interests of land users. In addition to land tenure security, specific conditions must be in place to encourage investment, such as better access to input and product markets, including savings and credit; appropriate technologies for increased sustainable productivity, and opportunities to diversify both within and beyond pastoral and agro-pastoral livelihoods.

Practical Courses of Action for Land Tenure Reform in the Drylands

Poverty, land degradation and desertification lead to loss of livelihoods, especially for vulnerable drylands dwellers. This chapter suggests that these are manifestations of deeper structural social and economic problems, including land pressure, lack of access to land, poorly-defined land tenure regimes, and poorly managed land reform efforts. Several preconditions can be recognized, which lead to specific sustainable development recommendations.

How to ensure that land tenure systems and land tenure reform processes are truly participatory, accessible, and transparent?

There is a need to commit to transparency and public participation in land tenure management and reform. The efforts must be coupled with strong commitments to accountability, transparency and public information-sharing. This helps to ensure sustainability of the effort, and reduces the possibility that laudable goals are subverted by other interests. Decision-makers can explore multi-stakeholder approaches to identifying and responding to land use and land reform challenges. Past failures to combat desertification have been linked to a lack of local resource-user involvement and to an absence of solutions compatible with indigenous cultures and land tenure systems.

What institutional structures can be established at local, national and international levels to support legal aspects of land tenure security and reform?

In many cases, especially in emerging and transforming economies, land markets may require some state intervention. By themselves, markets will not do much to transfer land to the poor. Careful re-distribution of public lands, or state expenditure on land reclamation and subsequent allotment as private property can make assets available to those too disadvantaged to enter into normal land market transactions. Support is also needed for institutions to administer the necessary land acquisition and distribution mechanisms, and to advise prospective land owners.

It is important to develop effective, accessible information systems which provide data on land use patterns, land values, availability of water, the identity of traditional land-users and title-holders. An accessible land registration system is also vital. In the best cases, this also involves public information efforts to encourage those with valid claims to come forward. Finally, establishing forums for public consultation and involvement in decision-making and peaceful dispute resolution is also crucial.

How can national processes address the overlaps and contradictions between formal and informal, customary and modern land tenure systems, and 'hybrid' systems?

It is helpful to develop systems of land tenure which respect local and customary traditions. Community traditions of self-organization can be harnesses, and these innovative approaches have emerged as a key to successful land tenure reform. Policies can also explore creative approaches to the use of customary land systems, including in some instances their codification. It is important however that the communities coming under such codified systems be highly involved in the process as well as 'self-identifying', since issues of communal identity are often complex and contested.

How can the rights of marginalized groups, including, women to control over land be promoted and protected?

Special emphasis should be placed on the development of ways to ensure that marginalized groups -- be they pastoralists, nomadic groups, poor dryland communities, or women -- are able to benefit from land distribution programs. Legal means – such as joint titles for married couples – could be accompanied by awareness-raising and civic education exercises. Gender-sensitive technologies and natural resource management systems – addressing access to water, for example – also have great potential.

How can land tenure systems and land tenure reform processes take a holistic, comprehensive and co-ordinated view of the institutional and physical environment?

Land issues can have international repercussions where resource degradation (e.g., land or water) or tensions arising from it spill into neighbouring countries. Regional approaches are useful, and developed countries and other donors can and must increase their commitment to provide technical support, skilled personnel and funding to local administrative units responsible for areas suffering from land degradation. Also, policies need to be set in place to protect and manage the natural resource base for economic and social development. Land reform efforts are particularly successful when built on the foundations of broader natural resource management and income-generation programmes to enhance sustainable livelihoods in vulnerable areas.

Conclusions and Future Directions

Given the current levels of international assistance on these issues, many developing countries lack the institutional structure, financial resources, human skills, and information systems needed to carry out sustained land tenure reform. These constraints have already been present for many years. Are there innovative ways to escape the deadlock on these issues? How might new resources must be harnessed? What capacity is there to increase legal and academic attention to these issues and to support the further development of the necessary skills within the ranks of policymakers and administrators?

A special focus is needed to ensure sustainable development for Africa. As revealed above, African drylands face some of the most difficult challenges, partly as a legacy of colonialist land tenure systems and inadequate reform efforts. Decision-makers should promote and support efforts and initiatives to secure equitable access to land tenure. Policies need to clarify resource rights and responsibilities, through land and tenure reform processes that respect the rule of law and are enshrined in national law, and provide access to credit for all, especially women. These policies must focus on enabling economic and social empowerment and poverty eradication as well as efficient and ecologically sound utilization of land. They need to ensure that women producers can become decision makers and owners in the sector, giving women the right to inherit land.

Land degradation, reduced access to land, climate variability, water scarcity, and desertification have turned some communities into "environmental" refugees-- that is, people have left their lands due to a lack of access to viable natural resources, though they often have no other secure lands to go to. Little attention has been placed on this issue to date. The definition of refugees contained in the 1951 Geneva Convention on Refugees is not sufficiently broad to include the case of environmental refugees. While some early projections of the scale of this phenomenon were overly pessimistic, and paid insufficient attention to the coping strategies available to people suffering from environmental stress, the concept remains a valid one. Clearly, environmental change may only be one factor in a variety of problems causing migration; still, the question of whether "environmental" migrants deserve special treatment, and how this intersects with other human rights principles warrants considerable exploration. Such long-term issues require attention at the level of international law as well as national laws and constitutions.

How will drylands be affected by movements of people in the coming decades (either due to economic forces, conflict or population growth)? There is little prospective thinking underway on the intersection of nature, society and economy in drylands. Also, while much attention is paid to rapid urbanization (especially in Africa), it seems that the focus is on capital cities, while insufficient attention is paid to population drift towards secondary rural towns which will be the 'frontline' of the phenomenon in the future.

Many studies implicitly reject the idea that sedentarization is a desirable objective of land reform. In some places, negative perceptions of dryland livelihoods – especially pastoralism – have been tempered by evidence of their viability. However, there has been a lack of committed follow-up in terms of creating an enabling environment for livelihood diversification and protection of the ecological and institutional foundations of pastoralism. However, some governments still explicitly or implicitly see sedentarisation as a desirable goal. Evidence from communities that have both gained and suffered economically from such processes would considerably enrich this discussion.

The status of customary land laws also warrants considerable further exploration. In most instances, governments lack a sophisticated understanding of the content, values and principles in customary laws. Greater understanding of these systems could help generate more sophisticated ideas for synergy between customary and formal legal systems. In some instances, states can consider the possibility for formally acknowledging a system of legal pluralism, particularly where such systems already function side-by-side in practice. One particular legal issue that emerges many times is - what are the alternatives to the registration of collective rights under the names of individuals? How can formal legal systems based on individual rights accommodate the notion of collective rights and ensure the distribution of benefits among communities, without inadvertently reinforcing inequities that may persist within the communities? This debate could be informed by lessons from the work on intellectual property rights for traditional communities, which addresses benefit-sharing for members of communities who possess valuable ethno-botanical knowledge, for example.

This chapter raises many questions and challenges. There are few simple or straightforward answers. The principal future challenge facing policy-makers, academics, nongovernmental organizations and members of dryland communities is to engage in a sustained, inclusive, and honest process of dialogue.

12

WATER TENURE REFORM AND PUBLIC ACCESS TO WATER AS A BASIC NEED

Sumudu Atapattu[1]

Water is a basic human need. It is essential for domestic, industrial and agricultural use. While the *International Covenant on Economic, Social and Cultural Rights* does not specifically mention access to water as a human right,[2] it does embody the right of people to "an adequate standard of living for himself and his family, including adequate food, clothing and housing, and to the continuous improvement of living conditions."[3] This right cannot be realized if people lack access to clean water and basic sanitation.

Despite water being essential for human survival, over one billion people today lack access to clean drinking water.[4] More than double that number lack access to sanitary facilities.[5] Scarcity of water is becoming a major problem in many countries, particularly developing countries and is closely related to poverty,[6] rapid population growth, and urbanization. It has also led to many conflicts in developing countries.

Furthermore, with recent privatization efforts, water has become a commodity which, like any other commodity, can be traded in the open market. Faced with higher tariffs and less water, people resort to unhealthy practices, resulting

---

[1] Sumudu Atapattu, LL.M, PhD (Cantab), Adjunct Faculty & Visiting Scholar, University of Wisconsin-Madison Law School, Lead Counsel for Human Rights and Poverty Eradication, Centre for International Sustainable Development Law (CISDL), Consultant, Law & Society Trust, (Colombo, Sri Lanka) & former Senior Lecturer, Faculty of Law, University of Colombo, Sri Lanka. The CISDL would like to thank Professor Madeleine Cantin Cumyn and Professor Robert Godin, at the McGill Faculty of Law, for their invaluable advice and encouragement in the development of this research.
[2] See, however, the discussion, *infra*.
[3] *International Covenant on Economic, Social and Cultural Rights*, GA res. 2200A (XXI), 21 UN GAOR Supp. No. 16, UN Doc. A/6316 (1966), at art.11.
[4] See, WHO/UNICEF Joint Monitoring Programme for Water Supply and Sanitation, *World Health Organization, Global Water Supply and Sanitation Assessment 2000 Report*, online: WHO <http://www.who.int/water_sanitation_health/Globalassessment/GlobalTOC.htm.>..
[5] *Ibid.* It is estimated that about 1.1 billion people in the world lack access to fresh water while 2.4 billion lack adequate sanitation. See, Ismail Serageldin, "Beating the Water Crisis," (Oct.1996) 8.3 *Our Planet*, online: Our Planet <http://www.ourplanet.com/imgversn/83/serag.html> .
[6] See World Conservation Union, *Water Resources Management for Poverty Alleviation- Background Document for the IUCN WSSD meeting in Dakar, Senegal*, online: IUCN <http://www.iucn.org/wssd/files/africa/dakar_water_poor.doc>.

M.C. Cordonier Segger & C. G. Weeramantry, eds., Sustainable Justice: Reconciling Economic, Social & Environmental Law
© *2005 Koninklijke Brill NV, Printed in The Netherlands, pp.195-216.*

in water-borne diseases (sometimes even death[7]), which, in turn, has had a huge impact on public health expenditure. With globalization, increased attention has been paid to the involvement of the private sector in areas that have been traditionally regulated by public bodies, such as water and sanitation. Whether water should be treated as a social good or an economic good has become a hotly debated issue in recent years.

This chapter discusses the main issues in water tenure systems and the legal characterization of water in common law and civil law systems as well as the arguments made in favour of privatization of water management. It also discusses General Comment No 15 on Human Right to Water adopted by the UN Committee on Economic, Social and Cultural Rights in 2002 and relevant international instruments both binding and non-binding. It focuses on access to water for basic human needs and for a sustainable livelihood not on access to water for other uses such as industry or generation of power or for purely economic purposes – in relation to the latter issue, it is reasonable to consider water as an economic good. It then discusses what the progressive realization of the human right to water means and its implications for states. The chapter then canvasses two case studies to highlight two diametrically opposing approaches to the management of water. It concludes by discussing options for future legal developments in the field of freshwater management and human rights law. The relationship between water supply and the General Agreement on Trade in Services (GATS) is beyond the scope of this chapter.

Main Issues in Water Tenure Systems

Property over water:

While traditionally governments have been at the forefront in providing water to the public, several tenure systems as well as legal principles have developed over the years in relation to the appropriation of water. These systems and principles are inextricably linked to water management systems. The water tenure systems differ somewhat under civil law, common law and customary law. The main principles that have evolved over the years are the *absolute ownership doctrine,* which is common to the traditional common law,[8] and the concept of *res communes,* which is often present in the civil law.[9] Many customary approaches have also regarded water as a common property not

---

[7] About five million people, mostly children, die each year as a result of water borne diseases, see *infra.*
[8] Claire Skrinda, « Le statut juridique de l'eau dans les autres provinces canadiennes, » *Le Statut Juridique de l'eau en droit québécois* Madeleine Cantin Cumyn, Michelle Cumyn et Claire Skrinda, Mémoire A la Commission sur la gestion de l'eau au Québec [Consultation publique tenue A Montréal entre les 23 et 30 Novembre, 1999] à la p. 37, Annexe III, en ligne : BAPE
<http://www.bape.gouv.qc.ca/sections/archives/eau/docdeposes/memoires/memo248.pdf.>
[9] *Ibid*

susceptible for individual ownership.[10] While it is difficult to generalize as each tribe or community had their own practices and tenure systems regarding water and water management, "ownership of water sources was usually invested in the local community rather than the household."[11] Even then, water was rarely "owned' by these groups. Access by others was often allowed, and a distinction was made between different water uses – domestic use and water for cattle. Among highly mobile societies water use was negotiated through agreements.[12]

According to Claire Skrinda, "traditionally, in both civil and common law, the law relating to water resources classified water according to the form, location, and the movement of water."[13] She comments that issues relating to water law arose around two topics: landowners' rights with regard to water on his property or flowing through his property, and public rights regarding water used for navigation and later, power. It is noted, however, that the law relating to groundwater resources remained troublesome both under common law and civil law.[14]

After an analysis of leading common law cases regarding water, Skrinda concludes that while a court may declare that a person has a right to use a water resource, rarely does this right extends to a right in the water itself and that "to a large extent, water in the common law has not lost its essential characteristic of *res communis*."[15] In addition, the earlier common law approach has been replaced by a "reasonable use" principle. It is noted that the basic features of usufructuary rights have been formulated under two common law doctrines – the riparian doctrine and the prior appropriation doctrine, both of which exist in Canadian jurisprudence. While the former relies on the concept of reasonable use to allocate water amongst competing users, the latter uses a more "first come, first serve" approach. In the final analysis Skrinda concludes that water is *res communes*, irrespective of origin or destination.[16] In other words, this means that water cannot be subject to private ownership.

Closely related to the *res communes* concept is the public trust doctrine. According to the public trust doctrine, common property is vested in the state for the benefit of the public. Although the public trust doctrine originally applied to navigable waters in the United States,[17] other jurisdictions have now

---

[10] C. Huggins, "Rural Water Tenure in East Africa: A comparative study of legal regimes and community responses to changing tenure patterns in Tanzania and Kenya" (Madison: University of Wisconsin, Land Tenure Centre, 2000) online: LTC <http://www.wisc.edu/ltc/live/bashorn0005a.pdf>.

[11] *Ibid.* at 5.

[12] *Ibid.*

[13] *Supra* note 8 at 43.

[14] *Ibid.* at 43-44..

[15] *Ibid.* at 48.

[16] *Ibid.* at 55.

[17] Jan S. Stevens, "Current Developments in the Public Trust Doctrine and Other Instream Protection Measures" in Kathleen Marion Carr, and James D. Crammond, eds., *Water Law: Trends, Policies, and Practice,* (Chicago: American Bar Association Section of Natural Resources Energy and Environmental Law, 1995) at 141.

extended the application of this doctrine to all natural resources. Thus, in *M.C. Mehta* v. *Kamal Nath and Others*, the Supreme Court of India held that in accordance with the public trust doctrine, the Government should be considered the trustee of all natural resources that are by nature destined for public use and enjoyment.[18] The Court reviewed cases from the US and noted that under English common law, this doctrine extended only to traditional uses such as navigation, commerce and fishing and said that now the doctrine has been extended to all ecologically important lands, including *freshwater*, wetlands and riparian forests.[19]

Coupled with the concept of sustainable development,[20] the public trust doctrine means that the state is under an obligation to hold natural resources for the benefit of the present generation as well as future generations. The Supreme Court of Sri Lanka took this one step forward by stressing that the "principle of shared responsibility" should be applied in relation to natural resources, asthe ancestors had done in the past.[21] The case dealt with the legal challenge to a proposed leasing of a phosphate mine to a multinational company, bypassing the environmental law of the country. The Court stressed the need to conserve natural resources for the benefit of future generations and stressed the responsibility of everybody in exploiting natural resources, not just that of the state, which the public trust doctrine implies. The principle of shared responsibility is wider in scope than the public trust doctrine. These principles and concepts have important ramifications for designing a legal regime for freshwater.

The California Supreme Court laid down several principles in relation to the public trust doctrine in the *National Audubon Case*:[22]   First, there is an "affirmative duty to take the public trust into account in the planning and allocation of water resources, and to protect public trust uses whenever feasible…[23] Second, [U]nnecessary and unjustified harm to trust interests"

---

18 *M.C. Mehta* v. *Kamal Nath & Others* [(1997) 1SCC 388], excerpts in *Compendium of Summaries of Judicial Decisions in Environment Related Cases* (SACEP/UNEP/NORAD Publication Series on Environmental Law and Policy No. 3, 1997), online: <ESCAP
http://www.unescap.org/drpad/vc/document/compendium/in1.htm> .
19 *Ibid*.
20 A classic definition of sustainable development was put forward by the World Commission on Environment and Development in 1987: "Development that meets the needs of the present without compromising the ability of future generations to meet their own needs," The World Commission on Environment and Development, *Our Common Future* (Oxford: Oxford University Press, 1987).
21 *Bulankulame and others* v. *Secretary, Ministry of Industrial Development and others*, (2000) 3 SriLR 243, SC Application No 884/99 (FR), SC Minutes 6.2.
22 *National Audubon Society v. Superior Court*, 33 Cal. 3d 419 (Cal. Sup. Ct. 1983). *[National Audubon Society]*
23 *National Audubon Society, ibid* at 419. Jan Stevens points out that "in California the State Water Resources Control Board has continuing supervisory powers over water uses both under the public trust and the state constitution," see J. Stevens, "Current Developments in the Public Trust Doctrine and Other Instream Protection Measures" in K. Marion Carr and J. D. Crammond, eds., *Water Law, Trends, Policies and Practice* (Chicago: American Bar Association Section of Natural Resources Energy and Environmental Law, 1995) at 147.

should be avoided.[24] Third, the state has the power and the affirmative duty to exercise continuing supervision over the taking of appropriated water, even when allocation "decisions were made after due consideration of their effect on the public trust."[25]

This case lays down an important principle, namely that public authorities have an affirmative duty to take the public trust doctrine into account in the allocation of water resources as well as the obligation to exercise continuing supervision over appropriated water.[26] In another case the California Supreme Court reiterated, "running waters of the state of California are public property."[27] Any person who wishes to "obstruct" them has to do so under permission of the state, subject to any conditions that the state may impose.[28]. Although the case dealt with the issue of fisheries, the principle therein can be equally applied to appropriation of water. In another case, the Appellate Court held that "[a]ll water rights, including appropriative, are subject to the overriding constitutional limitation that water use must be reasonable ....[and] all permits.... are subject to the continuing authority of the Board to prevent unreasonable use.[29] It thus seems that reasonable use is an established principle in Californian law and resonates well with the concept of sustainable development.

Both civil law and common law systems as well as customary practices indicate that water should be governed as a common property, rather than vesting individuals with proprietary rights. This approach accords well with the public trust doctrine and is probably the only way to ensure that the one billion people in the world today without access to potable water get some relief.

In a study conducted on water rights under civil law and common law systems (comparing United States with Venezuela), Franco Garcia concludes that water rights follow a climatic pattern – where there is a water surplus, the private ownership doctrine is generally accepted, while in arid and semi-arid zones, water is generally considered to be public property.[30] He refers to the *common law rule of absolute ownership*,[31] the *rule of unlimited use* under English law and the *doctrine of land ownership* in the United States. By contrast, the *rule of reasonable use* while recognizing the ownership of groundwater by the owner of the land, limits the proprietor's right of use of the water. A variation of this rule is the *doctrine of correlative rights,* according to which the owner of the land is entitled to

---

[24] *Supra note 22* . at 446.
[25] *Ibid.* at 447.
[26] *Supra* note 18 at 147.
[27] *Schaezlein v. Cabaniss*, 135 Cal. 673, 470-71 (1902), cited in J. Steven, *supra note 23*
[28] *Ibid.*
[29] *Ibid.*
[30] J. M. Franco-Garcia, *Water Rights under Civil Law and Common Law Systems* (Venezuela and the United States as a case study)(Madison, Wisconsin, 1965) (unpublished dissertation, on file with author).
[31] This doctrine recognizes ownership of ground water by the owner of overlying land. It places no restrictions on the owner's right of the use of water.

his reasonable share of the water, if there is not enough water to supply the needs of all.[32]

The *doctrine of public property*, on the other hand, vests groundwater in the public and as a result, governments have a duty to ensure that groundwater rights are under administrative control. According to the *doctrine of prior appropriation*, the person who has beneficially used groundwater for a certain period of time is considered the rightful owner of the water. This is used in several countries in Africa and the Middle East. Misuse of the water would result in the loss of the water rights and leads to the *doctrine of prescriptive rights,* where owners of the land have not been using the groundwater for a certain period of time.

These principles offer different options to policy makers with regard to water management. With the advent of the principles of sustainable use and exploitation of resources, the rights of an owner of land to the groundwater are no longer unlimited.

The management of water resources has become a controversial issue in recent years, particularly due to the privatization efforts of the World Bank. If water resources (and for that matter, all natural resources) are vested in the state as a result of the public trust doctrine, then there is a duty on the state to manage this resource for the benefit of the public, not only the present generation, but also generations to come. This, in turn, leads to good governance issues of transparency and accountability, as well as giving the opportunity to potentially affected people to participate in the decision-making process. Thus, participatory rights of people, particularly indigenous and marginalized groups, become important. If a government is corrupt, this will reflect adversely in relation to water management issues as well. The principle of shared responsibility also has much potential as it stresses the duty of every person, not just that of the state, to manage natural resources in a sustainable manner.

Privatization of water supply and management

If water is to be regarded as *res communes*, then privatization of water supply and management could be considered by some to be contrary to this concept. It is also true that governments no longer have the necessary funds to invest in public service areas that were not traditionally subject to privatization. This section discusses the approach of the World Bank, where a market based approach to water management has been taken.

The supply of safe drinking water, water resources management and wastewater treatment are priority areas for the World Bank and figure high on its agenda. It has supported many water-related projects with varying degrees of success.

---

[32] *Ibid.*

According to the World Bank Operational Manual the "Bank involvement in water resource management entails support for providing potable water, sanitation facilities, flood control, and water for productive activities in a manner that is economically viable, environmentally sustainable, and socially equitable."[33]

A report of the Bank on Water Resources Management proposes a new approach to managing water resources by adopting a comprehensive policy framework and treating water as an economic good.[34] It further proposes the decentralization of management and delivery structures, greater reliance on pricing, and fuller participation of stakeholders. With regard to water policy objectives, the report provides that one of the goals should be the greater involvement of the private sector, non-governmental organizations and user groups in relation to water supply and sanitation. The Bank's overarching objective is to reduce poverty by supporting efforts to promote sustainable development. The Bank gives priority to countries where water is scarce or where problems of water allocation or environmental degradation are serious.[35]

The report further provides that the reform of water resource management policies will have consequences for the institutions that deal with water resources. Toward this end, the Bank assists "governments in establishing a strong legal and regulatory framework for dealing with pricing, monopoly organizations, environmental protection and other aspects of water management."[36]

The Bank strongly supports decentralization of water resources management. The report provides that "[b]ecause of their limited financial and administrative resources, governments need to be selective in the responsibilities they assume for water resources."[37] The Bank supports governmental efforts of decentralizing responsibilities to local governments as well as transferring service delivery functions to the private sector: "[t]he privatization of public water service agencies, or their transformation into financially autonomous entities, and the use of management contracts for service delivery will be encouraged."[38]

It thus appears that the main thrust of the Bank's involvement in the water resource management sector has been to encourage the privatization of water service agencies, thereby ending the government monopoly in this service sector. The Bank further provides that while public sector programs have been

---

[33] The World Bank, *The World Bank Operational Manual: Water Resources Management* (Feb.2000), OP 4.07.
[34] The World Bank, *Water Resources Management*, 3rd ed. (Washington: World Bank, Aug. 1995) at 3, online: WB <http://www.worldbank.org>.
[35] *Ibid.* at 5.
[36] *Ibid.*
[37] *Ibid.* at 6.
[38] *Ibid.* (emphasis added).

carried out in relation to accessing water and sanitation services, they have fallen short of their objectives. As a result, they note, more and more governments are turning to the private sector for help: "Lessons from experience show that private sector involvement can improve service delivery at the same time that it reduces the burden on constrained public finances."[39]

Designed properly with the involvement of all the stakeholders, particularly the public, there is no doubt that privatization of water management and supply can reap real benefits to the public. Unfortunately, this has failed in many instances, as the experience of various countries has shown. Privatization can result in high tariffs on members of the public. It can place a heavy burden on people from developing countries who can barely sustain themselves above the poverty line. Now that water is accepted a basic human right, governments have a duty to ensure that this right is respected.

Are the concepts of *res communes* and privatization of water mutually contradictory? In adopting General Comment No 15 on Right to Water, the UN Committee on Economic, Social and Cultural Rights emphasized that "[w]ater should be treated as a social and cultural good, and not primarily as an economic commodity."[40] The General Comment further provided that:

> "State parties should ensure that the allocation of water resources, and investments in water, facilitate access to water for all members of society. Inappropriate resource allocation can lead to discrimination that may not be overt. For example, investments should not disproportionately favour expensive water supply services and facilities that are often accessible only to a small, privileged fraction of the population, rather than investing in services and facilities that benefit a far larger part of the population."[41]

While the General Comment does not prohibit privatization *per se*, it does warn of the possible consequences of expensive water supply services and facilities, including possible discrimination against marginalized groups.

Water figured high on the agenda of the World Summit on Sustainable Development (WSSD), which concluded in 2002. Under the Plan of Implementation adopted at the Summit, the parties agreed to achieve the Millennium Development Goal on safe drinking water and access to basic sanitation.[42] The parties also undertook plans to develop "integrated water

---

[39] "Private Sector Providers in CWSS," The World Bank Group: Water Supply and Sanitation, online: World Bank: <http://www.worldbank.org/watsan/topics/psproviders.html>
[40] Economic and Social Council, "The Right to Water: General Comment No. 15" Arts. 11 and 12 of the International Covenant on Economic, Social and Cultural Rights, 29th Sess., Agenda Item 3, Distr. General, UN Doc. E/C. 12/2002/11 (2002), online: UNHCHR <http://www.unhchr.ch/html/menu2/6/gc15.doc>.
[41] *Ibid.* at para. 14.
[42] *Johannesburg Plan of Implementation*, Report of the World Summit on Sustainable Development, Johannesburg (South Africa) (4 Sept. 2002) UN Doc. A/CONF.199/20, available online: <http://www.un.org/esa/sustdev/documents/WSSD_POI_PD/English/POIToc.htm>

resources management and water efficiency plans by 2005"[43] to, *inter alia*, facilitate the establishment of public-private partnerships and other forms of partnerships that give priority to the needs of the poor. The Plan of Implementation also requires respecting local conditions, involving all concerned stakeholders, and monitoring performance and improving accountability of public institutions and private companies.[44] Thus, despite severe opposition to privatization by developing countries, privatization of water has been included as a possible option in the documents of the WSSD. Indeed, the legal systems of many developed countries have engaged in debates on the advisability of privatization of sub-soil water resources. While privatization often leads to improved efficiency, and minimizes wastage, rising costs of water negatively impact the poor. However, in many instances, the public sector is no longer in a position to provide basic facilities and services to its people, indicating an increased role for the private sector. One way to ensure that the poor have access to water is by providing subsidies to these people.

The problems associated with lack of access to safe drinking water and sanitation facilities are clear enough. Governments are spending more and more money on public health problems caused by water-borne diseases, which are rampant in developing countries. Most of these diseases are preventable. More than 5 million people, most of them children, die every year from water-related illnesses.[45]

The main argument against water privatization is that it is often associated with high costs. Driven by the force of profits, private companies are seen by some as not accountable to the government or the people. Those living in developing countries view with suspicion and alarm the privatization of the supply of such an essential resource as water.

Another criticism is that these policies are formulated behind closed doors without giving those who are most likely to be affected - the poor and the vulnerable - any opportunity to be heard. It often seems that governments in developing countries do not have any choice but to accept these conditions, which could exacerbate existing conditions of the poor. As one writer points out:

The UN Millennium Declaration urges states to take steps to halve by the year 2015, the proportion of the people who are unable to reach or to afford safe drinking water, available online: <http://www.un.org/millennium/declaration/ares552e.htm, visited on 10/7/02>.
[43] *Johannesburg Plan of Implementation*, Report of the World Summit on Sustainable Development, Johannesburg (South Africa) (4 Sept. 2002) UN Doc. A/CONF.199/20, available online: <http://www.un.org/esa/sustdev/documents/WSSD_POI_PD/English/POIToc.htm>
[44] *Ibid.*
[45] S. Grusky, "IMF Forces Water Privatization on Poor Countries" available online: <http://www.waternunc.com/gb/ProblemofWater.htm >.

"The goal is to render water a private commodity, sold and traded on the open market, and guaranteed for use by private capital through global trade and investment agreements. These companies do not view water as a social resource necessary for all life, but an economic resource to be managed by market forces - like any other commodity.

A closer and well-documented examination of their [transnational water companies] practices tells a very different story: higher customer rates, dramatic corporate profits, corruption and bribery, lower water quality standards, and overuse of the resource for profit. While the companies argue that the privatization of water services is socially beneficial, the consequences of corporate control are that social and environmental concerns come second to the economic imperative of maximum profits for the shareholders."[46]

The UNDP Human Development Report 2003 identifies several reasons why governments often finance and provide basic social services, such as health care and water: such services are public goods and their market price alone does not capture their intrinsic value and social benefits; to ensure that basic social services are available equitably; as access to basic social services is a fundamental human right, governments have an obligation to ensure that these services are provided to the people.[47] The Report, however, notes that the public provision of social services is not always the best solution, particularly where institutions are weak and accountability for the use of public resources is low, which is often the case in developing countries.[48] The Report identifies several reasons why the private sector is playing a growing role in developing countries in relation to social services: lack of government resources, low quality public provision and pressure to liberalize the economy. Despite the recent push towards privatization, "only about 5% of the world's people (about 300 million) receive their water from private companies."[49] Most such privatization of water and sanitation services has occurred through public-private partnerships in urban areas. The Report, however, notes that private companies are unlikely to provide water services in rural areas in low-income countries, as they are generally considered unprofitable.[50]

---

[46] M. Barlow, "Water as Commodity - The Wrong Prescription" *Institute for Food and Development Policy*, Food First <http://www.foodfirst.org/pubs/backgrdrs/2001/s01v7n3.html.

[47] UNDP, *Human Development Report: Millennium Development Goals: A Compact Among Nations to End Poverty*, (New York: Oxford University Press, 2003) online: UNDP <http://hdr.undp.org/reports/global/2003/>.

[48] *Ibid.*

[49] *Ibid.*

[50] *Ibid.*

A Human Right to Water? [51]

As noted above, international human rights instruments do not specifically mention water as a human right, although reference is made to an adequate standard of living, including adequate food, clothing and housing as well as the right to health. In an attempt to rectify the lacuna in the law, the UN Committee on Economic, Social and Cultural Rights adopted General Comment No. 15 in late 2002 declaring water as a human right: "Water is fundamental for life and health. The human right to water is indispensable for leading a healthy life in human dignity. It is a pre-requisite to the realization of all other human rights."[52] The Committee was of the opinion that the right to water is clearly implicit in the rights contained in the Covenant.

As a result of the General Comment, the argument can be made that the right to water has been elevated to the status of a stand alone protected right, on par with other rights recognized in the Covenant. This interpretation, however, is not universally accepted.[53] The Committee noted the significance of the right as follows:

> "The human right to water entitles everyone to sufficient, safe, acceptable, physically accessible and affordable water for personal and domestic uses. An adequate amount of safe water is necessary to prevent death from dehydration, to reduce the risk of water-related disease and to provide for consumption, cooking, personal and domestic hygienic requirements."[54]

The Committee noted that the word "including" in Article 11 indicates that the catalogue of rights there was not exhaustive and that "right to water clearly falls within the category of guarantees essential for securing an adequate standard of living, particularly since it is one of the most fundamental conditions for survival."[55] It is also inextricably linked to the right to health.

The Committee also noted that the right to water contains both *freedoms* and *entitlements*. The freedoms include the right to maintain access to existing water supplies and the right to be free from interference. Entitlements include the right to a system of water supply and management that provides equality of opportunity for people to enjoy the right to water. It further noted that "water should be treated as a social and cultural good, and not primarily as an economic good."[56]

---

[51] For a comprehensive discussion of legal provisions relating to water, see *Legal Resources for the Right to Water: International and National Standards* (Geneva: COHRE, January 2004).

[52] *Supra,* note 40.

[53] *See infra* note 60.

[54] *Supra,* note 40, at para. 2.

[55] *Ibid,* at para. 3.

[56] *Ibid,* at para. 11.

While the adequacy of water may vary according to different conditions, the Committee identified three factors that must be satisfied in all circumstances: availability, quality and accessibility. The latter has four overlapping dimensions: physical accessibility, economic accessibility, non-discrimination, and information accessibility.

Like all other human rights, the right to water must be guaranteed on the basis of non-discrimination and equality. Similarly, it imposes three types of obligations on states parties – *obligations to respect* (refraining from interfering directly or indirectly with the enjoyment of the right to water); *obligations to protect* (preventing third parties from interfering with the enjoyment of the right to water) and the *obligations to fulfill* (taking positive measures to assist individuals and communities to enjoy the right, ensuring appropriate education regarding hygienic use of water, protection of water sources and methods to minimize water wastage).

In addition, the UN Committee on Economic, Social and Cultural Rights recognized the importance of water in 2000, when it adopted the general comment on health.[57] It noted that health is an inclusive right and extends to factors that determine good health, including access to safe drinking water and adequate sanitation, food, nutrition and housing and healthy environmental conditions. This is a clear recognition of the link between health and access to water.[58] It further notes that functioning health and health-care facilities, goods and services and programs have to be available to the people. . This includes the underlying determinants of health, such as safe and potable drinking water and adequate sanitation facilities.[59]

What is the significance of the recognition of water as a human right? In addition to the discussion above regarding the obligation of states to progressively realize this right on a basis of equality and non-discrimination, it also means that access to water is a *legal entitlement*, not a commodity or service provided on a charitable basis.[60] It also means that states parties will have to report to the Committee on the progressive realization of this right. Furthermore, the mechanisms available in the UN human rights system will be used to monitor the progress of states in realizing this right and hold governments accountable where violations have taken place. Since it is now considered a human right, access to water cannot be denied if people do not have the means to pay.

---

[57] UN Committee on Economic, Social and Cultural Rights, "General Comment No 14: The Right to the Highest Attainable Standard of Health," Art. 12 of the International Covenant on Economic, Social and Cultural Rights, 22nd Sess. Agenda Item 3, UN Doc. E/C.12/2000/4, at para. 11(2000).

[58] *Ibid.*

[59] *Ibid*, at para. 12(a).

[60] See, WHO, *The Right to Water*, Health and Human Rights Publication Series, No 3 (Geneva: WHO, 2003), online: <http://www.who.int/water_sanitation_health/en/rtwrev.pdf>.

However, not everybody views this development in a positive light. While not denying that water is a basic human need, some argue that treating it as a stand alone right would lead to a legal obligation to physically provide water to people in order to satisfy basic human needs. Canada, in particular, is alarmed at the prospect of being under a legal obligation to export water to places that face a scarcity of water.[61]

Other international instruments

Several human rights as well as environmental instruments recognize the importance of water for survival. The *Convention on the Rights of the Child,* for example, refers to the provision of adequate nutritious food and clean drinking water in the context of realizing the right to health.[62] The *Convention on the Elimination of All forms of Discrimination Against Women* refers to the right of women, *inter ali*a, to enjoy adequate living conditions, particularly in relation to housing, sanitation, electricity and water supply.[63]

The *UN Convention to Combat Desertification in Countries Experiencing Serious Drought and/or Desertification, Particularly in Africa*,[64] requires parties, *inter alia* to adopt an integrated approach addressing physical, biological and socio-economic aspects of the processes of desertification and drought; to promote cooperation among affected countries in the fields of environmental protection and the conservation of land and water resources as they relate to desertification and drought.[65] This Convention is particularly important as it recognizes the crucial relationship between land and water as well as its impact on sustainable development:

> "Mindful that desertification and drought affect sustainable development through their interrelationships with important social problems such as poverty, poor health and nutrition, lack of food security, and those arising from migration, displacement of persons and demographic dynamics…"[66]

The *UN Convention on the Law of the Non-navigational Uses of International Watercourses of 1997* deals with the resource allocation and utilization of the

---

[61] Discussions with Canadian officials at the CSD meeting, April 2004, New York.
[62] *Convention on the Rights of the Child*, G.A. Res. 44/25 annex, 44 U.N. GAOR Supp. (No. 49) at 167, U.N. Doc. A/44/49 (1989) Art. 24, 2 (c).
[63]*Convention on the Elimination of All Forms of Discrimination against Women*, G.A. res. 34/180, 34 U.N. GAOR Supp. (No. 46) at 193, U.N. Doc. A/34/46 (1979) Art. 14, 2(h).
[64] Implementation of the United Nations Convention to Combat Desertification in Those Countries Experiencing Serious Drought and/or Desertification, Particularly in Africa, U.N. GAOR 58th Sess., Agenda Item 94(b), U.N. Doc. A/C.2/58/L.7/Rev.1 (2003)..
[65] *Ibid*, Art. 4, General Obligations.
[66] *Ibid*, Preamble.

waters of an international watercourse.[67] Article 5 of the Convention requires states to utilize a watercourse in an equitable and reasonable manner. In particular, states are required to ensure optimal and sustainable utilization of the resource, consistent with protecting the watercourse, while taking into account the interests of all the states concerned. The factors to be taken into account to ensure equitable and reasonable use include: the ecological features of the watercourse, socio-economic needs of the states, the population dependent on the watercourse, the effects of the use on other states, existing and potential users of the watercourse, and the conservation of the watercourse.[68] States are also under an obligation not to cause significant harm to other states in utilizing an international watercourse. Where significant harm has nonetheless occurred, the author state must take all appropriate measures to mitigate such damage and where appropriate, offer compensation. The obligation not to cause significant damage to the environment of other states is part of customary international law, binding on all states.

These Conventions are, of course, only binding on those states that have ratified them. In addition, several non-binding instruments contain references to the right to water. Among them, Agenda 21 is significant. [69] It devotes a chapter to the protection of freshwater resources and the adoption of an integrated approach to the development, management, and use of water resources.[70] Its general objective is to ensure that adequate supplies of water of good quality are maintained for the entire population, while preserving the hydrological, biological and chemical functions of ecosystems. It also recognizes the adverse effects of pollution and the need to adopt an integrated approach to water. Agenda 21, however, regards water as both a social good and an economic good: "Integrated water resources management is based on the perception of water as an integral part of the ecosystem, a natural resource and a social and economic good, whose quantity and quality determine the nature of its utilization."[71]

In recognition of the growing inequities caused by lack of access to clean drinking water, the UN pledged in the Millennium Declaration that the international community would take steps to halve the number of people without access to clean water and sanitation by the year 2015.[72]

The *Indigenous Declaration on Water* released at the Third World Water Forum in Kyoto, Japan in 2003, refers to water as being sacred: "Our relationship with

---

[67] International Law Commission, *UN Convention on the Law of the Non-navigational Uses of International Watercourses, 1997* GA Res. 51/229, UN GAOR, UN Doc. A/51/869. (1997). The Convention defines an international watercourse as a watercourse that is geographically divided between different states.
[68] *Ibid*, Art. 6.
[69] U.N. *Conference on Environment and Development, Agenda 21*, U.N. Doc. A/CONF.151.26 (1992) *Agenda 21*, Chapter 18, Principle 2.
[70] *Ibid*, Chapter 18.
[71] *Ibid*.
[72] *Supra* note 42 at 1.

our lands, territories and water is the fundamental physical, cultural and spiritual basis for our existence. This relationship to our Mother Earth requires us to conserve our freshwaters and oceans for the survival of present and future generations." The Declaration further notes that water is being treated as a commodity and a property interest that can be bought, sold and traded in the global market. Through the right of self-determination, the Declaration notes, the indigenous peoples have the right to freely exercise full authority and control over natural resources, including water. The Declaration warns that indigenous peoples will not accept any agreements on water privatization and liberalization, and would fight against such agreements or proposals.

Similarly, the *Abuja Ministerial Declaration on Water* adopted in 2002,[73] notes that the need for adequate supplies of freshwater will remain a major national, regional and international priority in the years to come: "An adequate supply of freshwater is the most important prerequisite for sustaining human life, for maintaining ecosystems that support all life, and for achieving sustainable development."[74]

Progressive realization of the human right to water

The right to water, like other ESC rights, is subject to progressive realization. However, several obligations toward achieving the full realization are of immediate effect: the guarantee that the right will be exercised without discrimination [Article 2(2)] as well as the obligation to take steps toward full realization of the rights in the Covenant. General Comment No 3 of the CESCR deals with the nature of state obligations and stresses that the undertaking in Article 2(1) "to take steps," is not qualified or limited:

> "Thus while the full realization of the relevant rights may be achieved progressively, steps towards that goal must be taken within a reasonably short time after the Covenant's entry into force for the States concerned. Such steps should be deliberate, concrete and targeted as clearly as possible towards meeting the obligations recognized in the Covenant."[75]

The General Comment noted that Article 2 requires parties to take all appropriate means, including the adoption of legislative measures to give effect to the obligations under the Covenant. It stressed that "all appropriate means" must be given its full and natural meaning. Each state party must decide the means most appropriate with respect to each right and indicate in their reports

---

[73] *The Abuja Declaration on Water: A Key to Sustainable Development in Africa*, Launch of the African Ministerial Conference on Water (AMCOW), 29 April 2002.
[74] *Ibid.* at 2, para. 5. The Declaration further notes that "almost half the people of the African continent, particularly women and children, suffer from water-related diseases." The economic and humanitarian implications of this need no emphasis.
[75] *Ibid.* at para. 2.

not only the measures that have been taken, but also the basis on which they were considered appropriate. Appropriate measures may include consideration of administrative, financial, educational and social measures, in addition to legislative measures.

The Comment further noted that the term progressive realization is used to describe the intent of Article 2. It "constitutes a recognition of the fact that full realization of all economic, social and cultural rights will generally not be able to be achieved in a short period of time… While it is, on the one hand, a necessary flexibility device, it must also be read in light of its overall objective of the Covenant: to establish clear obligations for the full realization of the rights in question. "It thus imposes an obligation to move as expeditiously and effectively as possible towards that goal."[76] Article 2(1) obligates states to take necessary steps consistent with " the maximum of its available resources." States must demonstrate that every effort was made to use all resources that are at its disposition to satisfy the minimum obligations in the Covenant. Even where available resources are totally inadequate, states must strive to ensure the widest possible enjoyment of the rights under the prevailing circumstances. This provision indicates that even with limited resources, states must strive to ensure the enjoyment of rights recognized in the Covenant.

General Comment No 1, which deals with reporting by state parties, is also relevant here. It pointed out that "the Covenant attaches particular importance to the concept of "progressive realization" of the relevant rights and, for that reason, the Committee urges state parties to include in their periodic reports information which shows the progress over time, with respect to the effective realization of the relevant rights."[77] Both qualitative and quantitative data are required to make an adequate assessment of the situation.

Case Studies

Two case studies will be discussed here: the recent water policy in Quebec and the privatization of the water supply service in Cochabamba, Bolivia. These two case studies have been selected in order to highlight two diametrically different approaches that have been taken with regard to the management of water resources.

---

[76]Committee on Economic, Social and Cultural Rights, *General Comment 3: The nature of States parties obligations* (Art. 2, para.1 of the Covenant) 5th Sess., Compilation of General Comments and General Recommendations Adopted by Human Rights Treaty Bodies, U.N. Doc. HRI\GEN\1\Rev.1 (1994) at para 9..

[77] Committee on Economic, Social and Cultural Rights, *General Comment 1: Reporting by State Parties*, 3rd Sess. , UN Doc. E/1989/22, (1989) at para. 7.

New water policy in Quebec[78]

In the fall of 2002, the Quebec Government adopted its Water Policy with the following objectives: ensuring the protection of this unique resource; managing water with a view to sustainable development; and better protecting public health and ecosystems. It also affirmed that water is an integral part of the Quebecers' collective heritage. Both surface and groundwater are recognized in the Civil Code of Quebec as being common to all, subject to rights of use or limited appropriation rights. "This "common to all" status implies that all members of society have the right to access water and use it in a manner consistent with its nature, and that the government has a responsibility to regulate water use, establish priority uses and preserve its quality and quantity, while taking the public interest into account."[79]

Similar to the approach taken by the Supreme Court of Sri Lanka when it advocated the principle of shared responsibility, the Government of Quebec urges its citizens to become more involved in the management of this vital collective heritage and to play a larger role in water management.

The policy also highlights the importance of water governance reform in order to achieve the objectives identified in the Policy. It notes that it is necessary to develop and enunciate a shared, comprehensive vision of water resources. It further highlights the need for increased participation by different users as well as accountability of water management players. In order to achieve this, the Policy identified five courses of action:
- Revision of the legal framework pertaining to water;
- Implementation of watershed-based management;
- Acquisition of knowledge and information about water;
- Introduction of economic instruments for governance; and
- The strengthening of Quebec's partnerships and relations.

The Policy notes the need to revise the legal framework in order to implement the Policy, particularly to ensure that water is recognized as a collective heritage. It also seeks to establish mechanisms to implement the user pays and polluter pays principle, as well as economic mechanisms (charges, taxes, permits etc) to support them. It stresses the importance of participating in international instruments in the area of water. While not advocating the privatization of water resources and supply *per se*, the Policy does seek to establish a framework for the delegation of *management functions* to the private sector. This seems to indicate that at least with regard to management aspects of water, the private sector will play a significant role. If done with proper oversight by the Government, this should not be a cause for concern. While the Policy is not

---

[78] This section draws from information available at: Environnement Quebec, *Quebec Water Policy,* online: Gouvernement du Quebec < http://www.menv.gouv.qc.ca/eau/politique/index-en.htm>.
[79] *Ibid.*

very clear on how this will be done, the question arises whether this would be against the declared policy of the Government of Quebec that "water is an integral part of the Quebecers' collective heritage." Careful thought should be given as to how the government would get the private sector involved in the management of water.

The Preamble to the *Act to Establish the Fonds National De L'Eau* recognizes that water resources are essential to the environmental, economic and social well-being of Quebec and that "water resources, both surface water and groundwater, constitute a common heritage which is important to conserve to meet the needs of present and future generations."[80] It establishes a fund which "shall be dedicated to the financing of measures taken by the Minister of the Environment to ensure water governance and in particular, to the financing of measures conducive to the protection and development of water resources and to ensuring a sufficient quality and quantity of water in a perspective of sustainable development."[81]

Privatization of water in Cochabamba, Bolivia[82]

In stark contrast to the discussion on the reform of the water sector in Quebec, which identified water as the collective heritage of the people of Quebec, one finds the privatization of water resources in Bolivia a story of violence and the marginalization of the poor.

Privatization was a key component of the Sanchez administration's (1993-97) economic policy. The World Bank and the IMF pushed the Bolivian government to sell many of its public enterprises to international investors in order to increase economic efficiency. Succumbing to pressure, the Bolivian government privatized the Cochabamba's – Bolivia's third largest city - water system in 1999.

Protests broke out in February and March 2000 when the price of water skyrocketed by 200-300% in many cases, just weeks after the city's water system was privatized. Protests led to violence and even death at the hands of the police and the military. Protests spread from Cochabamba to other parts of Bolivia with 50 people detained, dozens injured and six people dead. In April the President imposed martial law and a state of emergency severely curtailed people's civil rights. A teenage protestor was shot and killed by the police. Freedom of association and freedom of the press were also severely restricted. Finally, on April 10, the President announced the termination of the water contract with the private company and turned over the control of the city's

---

[80] *Act to Establish the Fonds National De L'Eau* , RSQ 2003, c. F-4.002, Preamble .
[81] *Ibid*, s. 1.
[82] This section draws from "Water Privatization Case Study: Cochabamba, Bolivia, Public Citizen", online: Public Citizen < http://www.citizen.org/documents/Bolivia>. .>

water system to the protestors' organization – Coalition for the Defense of Water and Life. The company is now suing the Government for $ 25 million in compensation.[83]

This story, unfortunately, is not unique to Bolivia. Many countries have had similar experiences. India, South Africa, Ghana, Mozambique, the Philippines to name but a few of them, have faced parallel situations. These countries have experienced higher tariffs, which people can ill afford. They have also experienced rises in water-borne diseases as people resort to unhealthy practices. In South Africa, for example, in late 2000, a cholera epidemic claimed several lives and infected at least 100,000 people who were forced to drink untreated water, as they could not afford pipe borne water. Since the implementation of the project to privatize water, access to water by poor communities depends on affordability - no money, no water. As a result many people have been cut off and denied access to water.

In recent times, even peaceful protests were met with violence. In April 2002, when non-violent demonstrators walked to the Mayor's house protesting against evictions and water and electricity cut-offs because people could not afford them, the Mayor's bodyguard fired into the crowd, wounding two. While the committee members were arrested no action was taken against the bodyguard.

An independent network of community groups, known as the Anti-Privatization Forum, has been established in several Johannesburg townships. Mass marches of workers and people are common as is the theft of water and electricity.[84] In addition, protests against privatization of water have occurred in India, El Salvador, Zambia, Brazil, the Philippines and Costa Rica.[85]

While privatization has definite benefits such as increased efficiency, it does pose considerable threats to poor communities. Increased prices are a major problem these communities have to face. Lack of concern for environmental aspects, and lack of transparency and accountability are also major issues facing developing countries. Many argue that water, being essential for human survival - as a social good - should not be placed at the hands of the private sector whose main concern is profit maximization. Others argue that being considered a "free good" has resulted in wasteful practices and the looming water crisis. Thus, they argue that water should be considered both a social good and an economic good.[86]

---

[83] "Bolivia: Cleaning Up the Bechtel Mess," *Defend the Global Commons*, Vol 1, No. 2 at 11 (August, 2002)., online: Public Citizen < http://www.citizen.org/documents/JoDefendeng.PDF. >
[84] *Ibid.*
[85] *Ibid.*
[86] Peter Gleick, *et al.*, "The New Economy of Water: The Risks and Benefits of Globalization and Privatization of Fresh Water," Pacific Institute (2002) online: Pacific Institute < http://www.pacinst.org/reports/new_economy_of_water/new_economy_of_water_ES.pdf>.

In a study undertaken by the Pacific Institute, it is argued that privatization of water is not necessarily bad. However, certain safeguards have to be put in place to ensure that the process of privatization and its benefits actually trickle down to those who need it most - the poorer segments of society. They provide the following principles and standards for privatization of water supply systems and infrastructure:

1. Continue to manage water as a social good
(a) meet basic human needs for water;
(b) meet basic ecosystem needs for water
(c) basic water requirements for users should be provided at subsidized rates when necessary for reasons of poverty.
2. Use sound economics in water management
(a) water and water services should be provided at fair and reasonable rates;
(b) subsidies, if necessary, should be economically and socially sound
(c) private companies should show that new water supply projects are less expensive than projects to improve water conservation and efficiency
3. Maintain strong government regulation and oversight.
(a) Governments should retain or establish public ownership or control of water sources;
(b) Public agencies and water service providers should monitor water quality. Governments should define and enforce water quality laws
(c) Contracts should lay out the responsibilities of each partner
(d) Clear dispute resolution procedures should be developed prior to privatization
(e) Provide for independent technical assistance and contract review
(f) Negotiations over privatization contracts should be open, transparent, and include all affected stakeholders.[87]

These recommendations, however, presuppose that the government in question will be in a sufficiently strong position to exert pressure on the private sector. In many developing countries, unfortunately, this will remain unattainable. This is particularly challenging if private sector participants are multinational companies.

Options for Future Legal Developments in the Field of Freshwater Management and Human Rights Law

As the above discussion revealed, two main trends can be identified with regard to water supply and management, which appear on its face to be mutually contradictory. One trend is to regard water as a *res communes* or a collective heritage of people not subject to ownership rights except where law recognizes user rights and appropriation rights. This category recognizes the main

---

[87] *Ibid.*

responsibility of governments in ensuring equal access to water irrespective of the socio-economic conditions of people. It also highlights the responsibility of all people in protecting water resources and adopting wise management strategies. The principles of public trust and shared responsibility as well as sustainable development play an important role here.

In stark contrast, the other trend highlights the need to privatize water resources and management. The World Bank has actively sought the increased participation of the private sector in the management of water in an effort to increase efficiency and minimize waste. These goals are seen by many as being necessary, as in many instances the lack of access to water has resulted not so much from scarcity of water but due to wasteful practices and inefficiency, particularly in developing countries. On the other hand, privatization efforts have led to higher tariffs in many parts of the world, which have had an adverse impact on the poor.

While being commendable, the recognition of water as a human right does not solve the main problem faced by many developing countries: a lack of resources to ensure equal access to water, exacerbated by a scarcity of water. It is primarily for this reason that governments have increasingly turned to the private sector. While General Comment No 15 does not explicitly prohibit privatization of water, privatization seems to be against the recognition of a human right to water in at least one respect. The reality of the poor being unable to afford higher tariffs that could result from privatization, may lead to the breaching of the principles of equal access and affordability.

However, privatization of management of the supply of water and the recognition of water as a human right does not have to be mutually exclusive or contradictory. While the recognition of water as a human right does accord states with specific obligations with regard to its implementation, there is nothing to stop them from involving the private sector in giving effect to its obligations. However, states must ensure that the right to water is guaranteed on the basis of non-discrimination and must prevent third parties from interfering with this right.[88]

So what are the options for the future? Since water is now considered a part of international human rights law, states have an obligation to progressively realize this right. They will have to ensure it is recognized in national legislation as a fundamental right and that it is afforded on the basis of equality without discrimination. They must also ensure that redress, including legal redress is available at the national level in the event that this right is not available to people. If states resort to the option of privatization, they must ensure that this does not result in unequal access to water and the marginalization of the poor.

---

[88] J. Liu, "Issue Focus: The Human Right to Water" (Feb. 2003) *ESCR in Focus*, Vol. 2, Iss. 1.

States also have the obligation to ensure access to information and the participation of all stake-holders in the decision making process. This means that privatization should not be a closed process; rather all potentially affected parties should be involved in the decision making process. As has been pointed out, public participation and transparency are essential if sustainable development is to be achieved.[89]

---

[89] *Gunaratne* v. *Homagama Pradeshiya Sabha* (1998) 2 SLR 11 (SL SC) 5 S. *Asian Envt'l L. Rep.* 151 (1994). [Supreme Court of Sri Lanka].

(iii)

SOCIAL AND ECONOMIC ELEMENTS OF BIODIVERSITY LAW

13

GLOBAL ACCESS, LOCAL BENEFITS: AN INTERNATIONAL ACCESS AND BENEFIT-SHARING REGIME?

Jorge Cabrera[1] and Kathryn Garforth[2]

This chapter outlines the role of the *Convention on Biological Diversity*[3] (CBD), as well as other national, regional, international and non-state initiatives in creating access to genetic resources and benefit-sharing (ABS) systems. The different regimes offer insights into the relationship between international sustainable development law and ABS. They also generate ideas for elements that should be included in an international regime on ABS, as proposed at the World Summit on Sustainable Development in 2002 and negotiations for which were launched at the seventh Conference of the Parties to the CBD in 2004. As a preliminary result of this legal research, it can be suggested that such an international regime is needed to fill the gaps in the existing ABS framework, particularly those gaps relating to sustainable use of biodiversity, fair and equitable benefit-sharing, and monitoring and remedies. This would provide the best potential for a system that adequately addresses the environmental, social and economic aspects of sustainable development.

Defining the Issue

Access to genetic resources and benefit-sharing incorporates all three strands of sustainable development, namely, the environment, society and the economy. With regards to the environment, genetic resources need to be protected both for their inherent value and also for their potential contributions to human well-being, particularly in the areas of natural heritage conservation, agriculture

---

[1] Jorge Cabrera Medaglia, B.C.L & LL.M (University of Costa Rica), Lead Counsel for International Sustainable Biodiversity Law, Centre for International Sustainable Development Law (CISDL), Professor, University of Costa Rica Faculty of Law & UNED University, Tutor, WIPO Intellectual Property Law, Legal Advisor, National Biodiversity Institute (INBio) of Costa Rica, former Co-chair, UN Convention on Biological Diversity Expert Panel on ABS & Chair, CBD Sub-Working Group on IPRs.
[2] Kathryn Garforth, LL.B. (Osgoode Hall), M.E.S (York), Research Fellow, Centre for International Sustainable Development Law (CISDL). This chapter was prepared with contributions from Michelle Toering former Officers of the CISDL Secretariat, and Hari Suthan, Associate Fellow, CISDL as well as Ashfaq Khalfan and Marie-Claire Cordonier Segger, CISDL Directors.
[3] *Convention on Biological Diversity*, 5 June 1992, 31 I.L.M. 818 (entered into force 29 December 1993) [CBD].

and medicine. With regards to society, genetic resources have been conserved, used, and developed by local and indigenous communities for centuries if not millennia. These groups often have unique knowledge of the resources. Their contributions can be very valuable and must be recognized and encouraged. Furthermore, human rights law protects both the rights of such groups to food and health as well as their right to share in scientific advancements and its benefits.[4] With regards to the economy, research into and commercialization of genetic resources is necessary to feed a growing population and to treat new and re-emergent diseases. Intellectual property rights (IPRs) are a recognized component of commercial endeavors. They can contribute to the environmental and social aspects of international sustainable biodiversity law by providing incentives for protection. The concern, however, is that IPRs will block access to genetic resources and will undervalue the input of local and indigenous communities.

Access to Genetic Resources and Benefit-Sharing in the United Nations *Convention on Biological Diversity*

The *Convention on Biological Diversity* attempts to weave together the three strands of sustainable development. It aims to use the economic incentives created by the potential commercial value of genetic resources towards the conservation of these same resources. It does this by creating a framework for access to genetic resources and equitable benefit-sharing. These goals are reflected in the objectives of the Convention as set out in Article 1:

> "The objectives of this Convention, to be pursued in accordance with its relevant provisions, are the conservation of biological diversity, the sustainable use of its components and the fair and equitable sharing of the benefits arising out of the utilization of genetic resources, including by appropriate access to genetic resources and by appropriate transfer of relevant technologies, taking into account all rights over those resources and to technologies, and by appropriate funding."

The remainder of the Convention elaborates how these objectives should be achieved. Articles 8 and 15 are particularly important in laying the foundation for ABS.

Article 8, entitled '*In-situ* Conservation', and specifically subsection (j), has generated significant discussion in regards to the social aspect of ABS. It mandates the Contracting Parties, "as far as possible and as appropriate", to

---

[4] See the *International Covenant on Economic, Social and Cultural Rights*, 19 December 1966, 993 U.N.T.S. 3 (entered into force 23 March 1976) at arts. 11 and 12 (for food and health, respectively); see also the United Nations *Universal Declaration of Human Rights*, GA Res. 217 (III), UN GAOR, 3d Sess., Supp. No. 13, UN Doc. A/810 (1948) at Art. 27 (for scientific advancements).

protect indigenous and local knowledge and innovations as well as encourage their use with the participation of, and benefit-sharing for, these communities.

Article 15(1) recognizes state sovereignty over natural resources in the context of access to genetic resources. This is very important as it enables states to control access to these resources, allowing for the possibility of profiting from providing access. It also constituted somewhat of a shift in international law. Previously, international law had held that plant genetic resources, at a minimum, were the common heritage of humanity.[5] Under Article 15, access to genetic resources is to be on mutually agreed terms subject to prior informed consent.[6] Article 15(7) provides a framework for the implementation of the third objective of the Convention, namely fair and equitable sharing of benefits.[7]

While it is beyond the scope of this chapter to explore them in any detail, Articles 16 to 21 of the Convention also relate to ABS.[8] The articles on access to and transfer of technology and the handling of biotechnology and distribution of its benefits affect the interface of intellectual property rights and genetic diversity in particular.[9]

Emergent Regimes on Access to Genetic Resources and Benefit-Sharing

The CBD was largely responsible for establishing that there *should* be access to genetic resources and benefit-sharing. Since then, the question has become *how* to have ABS. In the past twelve years, numerous national, regional, international and non-state regimes have been initiated to implement ABS. There is much to be learned from examining the successes and failures of these initiatives as scholars and policy-makers look towards the creation of an international regime.

National regimes

According to the Secretariat to the CBD, more than 50 countries have adopted, or are in the process of adopting, ABS policies and legislation.[10] These policies generally take one of four forms. First, they can consist of access provisions contained in framework environmental or sustainable development legislation. Second, they can consist of particular access provisions in nature conservation

---

[5] See *International Undertaking, infra* note 23 at Art. 1.
[6] CBD, *supra* note 3 at Art. 15(4) and (5).
[7] For more details on Art. 15(7), see section on 'The Fair and Equitable Sharing of Benefits, below.
[8] For more details on Art. 16, see section on 'Technology Transfer', below.
[9] CBD, *supra* note 3 at arts. 16 and 19.
[10] Secretariat for the Convention on Biological Diversity, *International Regime on Access and Benefit-Sharing: Proposals for an International Regime on Access and Benefit-sharing*, 7 January 2003, UN Doc., UNEP/CBD/MYPOW/6 at 8, online: Convention on Biological Diversity <http://www.biodiv.org> [*Proposals for an International Regime*].

or biodiversity laws. Third, access provisions can be incorporated into existing laws through amendment; and fourth, specific laws can be drafted to set out new access and benefit-sharing rules.[11]

South Africa's proposed *National Environmental Management: Biodiversity Bill*[12] is one of the newest national initiatives on this issue, falling into the second category of the typology above. It includes provisions on ABS within the context of broader conservation legislation. The Bill is divided into ten chapters covering a range of issues including: the establishment of a National Biodiversity Institute to replace the current National Botanical Institute (Chapter 2); a regulatory framework for integrated management of South Africa's biodiversity (Chapter 3); and provisions on the prevention, control and elimination of alien species (Chapter 5).

Of most interest here is Chapter 6 on 'Bioprospecting, Access and Benefit-Sharing'. Chapter 6 is meant to regulate the bioprospecting of genetic resources and "ensure the equitable sharing of benefits arising from the commercialisation through bioprospecting of traditional uses or knowledge of indigenous biological resources, with persons or communities practising these traditional uses or knowledge".[13] Section 76 of the Bill requires individuals to have a permit in order to engage in bioprospecting. Furthermore, under section 77, bioprospectors must have entered into a benefit-sharing agreement in order to use traditional knowledge.

The Biodiversity Bill has come under fire for its perceived lack of continuity with the policy indicated in the government's Biodiversity White Paper.[14] Furthermore, the Bill does not meet some of the requirements of the CBD. It only requires benefit-sharing arrangements with holders of traditional knowledge, thus excluding other potential knowledge-holders. Section 77(2) also prohibits holders of traditional knowledge from unreasonably refusing to enter into benefit-sharing agreements where the knowledge to be used is in the public domain.[15] This may well run contrary to the type of prior informed consent required under the CBD.

---

[11] *Ibid.* at 9.
[12] South Africa, *National Environmental Management: Biodiversity Bill*, 8th draft, Gazette 24311, Notice 49, 24 January 2003, online: South African Government Online <http://www.gov.za/bills/index> [*Biodiversity Bill*]. See also J. Cabrera Medaglia, "The Legal Frameworks and Public Policy on Access to Genetic Resources and Benefit Sharing: The Case of Costa Rica" (report presented to the University of California, Davis, 2002). One of the first measures was Costa Rica's creation of a National Biodiversity Institute (INBio) in 1989. Other examples include the Republic of Korea, India and Bolivia, see *Proposals for an International Regime, supra* note 10 at 9.
[13] *Biodiversity Bill, supra* note 12 at s. 75(1).
[14] R. Wynberg and M. Burgener, "A Critical Review of Provisions Relating to Bioprospecting, Access and Benefit-Sharing in the Biodiversity Bill" (discussion paper presented to IUCN South Africa, February 2003) online: Contact Trust <http://www.contacttrust.org.za/CTDocs/netbio/2003BBRWMB.doc>.
[15] *Ibid.*

Regional regimes

One of the difficulties with national ABS regimes is that they may encourage a 'race to the bottom' mentality. That is, if two neighbouring countries share similar genetic resources and one offers access at a lower cost than the other, the 'cheaper' state is likely to garner more interested customers, other things being equal. Various writers have discussed the creation of a 'biodiversity cartel' to circumvent this problem.[16] While the feasibility of such a cartel on a worldwide scale seems doubtful, some parts of the world have established regional regimes governing ABS.[17] The efforts of the Andean countries are one such example.

The Andean Pact Decision 391[18] was the first subregional legislative measure on access to genetic resources and benefit-sharing in response to Article 15 of the CBD. The "Common System on Access to Genetic Resources" is a "general norm that establishes applicable minimum rules in all the member states."[19] Decision 391 regulates access to genetic resources, the equitable distribution of benefits derived from their use, and recognizes the contributions of indigenous people through the access contracts.

In addition to establishing a framework for Member states to regulate access within their borders, Article 10 of Decision 391 requires Member states to "define mechanisms for cooperation on matters of mutual interest connected with the conservation and sustainable use of genetic resources and their derivatives and related intangible components."[20] The Decision also requires Member states to notify each other immediately "of all applications, resolutions and authorizations of access and of the suspension and termination of contracts signed."[21] Such notification must be given to the Board of the Andean Community on Genetic Resources, which is composed of representatives from each of the designated national authorities. The Andean Community has the

---

[16] See D.S. Tilford, "Saving the Blueprints: The International Legal Regime for Plant Resources" (1998) 30 Case W. Res. J. Int'l L. 436-440; Walter V. Reid et al., "A New Lease on Life" in World Resources Institute, *Biodiversity Prospecting: Using Genetic Resources for Sustainable Development* (Washington, D.C.: World Resources Institute, 1993) at 44-46.

[17] Many of the most biodiverse countries in the world have also united as the Group of Like-Minded Megadiverse Countries to present a single negotiating position at CBD meetings. For more information, see www.megadiverse.org.

[18] Andean Pact, Decision 391, *Common System on Access to Genetic Resources* (1996). [*Decision 391*]. Examples of other regional regimes include the *Central American Agreement on Access to Genetic Resources and Bio-chemicals and related Traditional Knowledge* (draft 2001), the Framework Agreement of the Association of South-East Asian Nations (draft 2000), and the *African Model Law for the Protection of the Rights of Local Communities, Farmers and Breeders, and for the Regulation of Access to Biological Resources* (2000) by the Organization of African Unity. See also *Proposals for an International Regime, supra* note 10 at 6-7.

[19] P. Molina, "Fact sheet: Access to Genetic Resources in the Andean Community" (paper presented at the South-South Biopiracy Summit "Biopiracy - Ten Years Post-Rio" August 2002) Online: Biowatch South Africa <http://www.biowatch.org.za/pmolina.htm>.

[20] *Decision 391, supra* note 18 at Art. 10.

[21] *Decision 391, supra* note 18 at arts. 48 & 49.

task of ensuring that the Decision is carried out effectively and that appropriate mechanisms and information sharing systems are put in place to promote respect for the terms of the decision and the sustainable and equitable use of and access to genetic resources.

Decision 391 includes an effective framework for addressing the concerns of Member states, the scope of access to be contracted for, and the mechanisms necessary to ensure protection of the resources from the states' perspective. It falls just short, however, of protecting the rights of indigenous and local communities. The Decision separates the "tangible component" of genetic resources (plants, animals, microorganisms) from the "intangible component" (indigenous knowledge). The Decision also guarantees the direct participation of indigenous and local communities in access agreements to their knowledge, and requires the distribution of benefits gained through access to the "intangible component". No such requirements exist for access to tangible components. As such, indigenous organizations feel that the Decision excludes them from an important step in the process of determining access. They believe that local populations, in whose territories resources are often located and who are guardians of associated knowledge, should be parties to the initial access contract to the tangible genetic resources. They should not be limited to merely participating in the determination of which activities will be permitted once access to the resources has been granted.

Existing international regimes

As will be discussed below, the *Plan of Implementation of the World Summit on Sustainable Development*[22] suggested the creation of a multilateral regime on ABS. Apart from this recommendation and the language of the CBD, the only other legally-binding multilateral instrument on issue is the Food and Agriculture Organization's *International Treaty on Plant Genetic Resources for Food and Agriculture.*[23]

The Treaty on Plant Genetic Resources was preceded by the *International Undertaking on Plant Genetic Resources*[24], a non-legally binding resolution of the Food and Agriculture Organization (FAO) passed in 1983 and amended three

---

[22] United Nations, *Report of the World Summit on Sustainable Development* WSSD Res. 2, 17th plenary meeting, UN Doc.A/CONF.199/20 (2002) 6-72, online: United Nations: Johannesburg Summit 2002, online: Johannesburg Summit 2002
<http://www.johannesburgsummit.org/html/documents/summit_docs/131302_wssd_report_reissued.pdf >.
[23] International Treaty on Plant Genetic Resources for Food and Agriculture, FAO Res. 3/2003, 3 November 2001 (entered into force 29 June 2004). [*ITPGRFA*].
[24] *International Undertaking on Plant Genetic Resources*, FAO Conference Res. 8/83, 22d Sess. UN Doc. C/83/Rep (1983) [*International Undertaking*].

times between 1989 and 1991[25]. In light of the CBD, the FAO began negotiations in 1993 to turn the International Undertaking into a legally binding treaty.[26] These negotiations were successfully completed in November 2001 resulting in the International Treaty on Plant Genetic Resources for Food and Agriculture.

The objectives of the Treaty are contained in Article 1:

> "the conservation and sustainable use of plant genetic resources for food and agriculture [PGRFA} and the fair and equitable sharing of the benefits arising out of their use, in harmony with the Convention on Biological Diversity, for sustainable agriculture and food security."

The centerpiece of the Treaty is "a 'multilateral system for access and benefit-sharing', which for certain categories of PGRFA … guarantees facilitated access in return for benefit-sharing".[27] In establishing the multilateral system, countries had to be careful not to undermine the sovereign rights of states over their natural resources as enshrined in Article 15 of the CBD. Article 10 of the Treaty achieves this by basing the existence of the multilateral system on the exercise of sovereign rights.

The multilateral system created by the Treaty only covers, as the name suggests, plant genetic resources for food and agriculture.[28] Furthermore, the system includes only those species of PGRFA listed in Annex I of the Treaty.

> "This is because certain countries that are generally rich in biodiversity – even if not particularly so in PGRFA – wanted to limit the application of the multilateral system, thereby leaving the potential for bilateral arrangements under Article 15 of the CBD to be applied for all other plant genetic resources, including medicinal plants and others that may have potential value under bilateral deals."[29]

Thirty-five species are listed in the Annex, including most of the major food crops. In addition, under Article 11(2), only those genetic resources (of the species listed in the Annex) that "are under the management and control of the Contracting Parties and in the public domain" are a mandatory part of the multilateral system. All other holders of PGRFA are invited to include their resources in the system.

---

[25] *Agreed Interpretation of the International Undertaking*, FAO Conference Res. 4/89, 25th Sess., UN Doc. C/89/24 (1989); *Farmers' Rights*, FAO Conference Res. 5/89, 25th Sess. (1989); FAO Conference Res. 3/91, 26th Sess. (1991); being Annex I, II, and III respectively to the *International Undertaking*.

[26] H. David Cooper, "The International Treaty on Plant Genetic Resources for Food and Agriculture" (2002) 11 R.E.C.I.E.L. 1 at 2 [Cooper].

[27] Cooper, *supra* note 26 at 4; *ITPGRFA, supra* note 22 at Art. 10(2).

[28] *ITPGRFA, supra* note 23 at Art. 3.

[29] Cooper, *supra* note 26 at 5.

Article 12 of the Treaty governs the terms of access to the genetic resources covered in Annex I. Access is to be provided to other contracting parties as well as to legal and natural persons under their jurisdiction.[30] State parties should provide facilitated access, which is subject to a number of conditions in Article 12(3). These conditions include, *inter alia*, that facilitated access should be free or with only minimal cost to cover expenses,[31] and that access must respect existing property rights – both intellectual and otherwise.[32] Article 13 addresses the sharing of benefits arising from the use of the PGRFA in the multilateral system. Accordingly, benefits are to "be shared fairly and equitably through … the exchange of information, access to and transfer of technology, capacity building and the sharing of benefits arising from commercialization".[33] Article 13 goes on to provide more detail on what each of these mechanisms entails.

The final element to be discussed is the role of IPRs in the multilateral system. This was one of the most contentious issues during negotiations. All parties agreed that IPRs should not be applied to the resources as received from the multilateral system.[34] The difficult part was whether IPRs should be available for 'components' or 'derivatives' of PGRFA from the multilateral system. Developing countries were willing to agree to IPRs on derivatives, e.g. new plant varieties derived from the resources obtained from the system, but not on parts or components, e.g. genes or proteins. The solution was to use vague language in discussing the relationship between IPRs and the PGRFA in the multilateral system paving the way for conflicts of interpretation in the future.[35]

Non-state initiatives

Apart from the state-led regimes, there are numerous ABS efforts that have been initiated by universities, corporations, civil society, and other international organizations. One of the largest of these regimes is that of the Consultative Group on International Agricultural Research (CGIAR) and its International Agriculture Research Centres (IARCs).[36] The work of this organization points

---

[30] *ITPGRFA, supra* note 23 at Art. 12(2). This Article is subject to Art. 11(4) which provides for an assessment of the inclusion of PGRFA held by natural and legal persons in the multilateral system two years after the Treaty enters into force. This assessment will be used to decide if natural and legal persons will continue to have facilitated access.

[31] *ITPGRFA, supra* note 23 at Art. 12(3)(b).

[32] *ITPGRFA, supra* note 23 at Art. 12(3)(f).

[33] *ITPGRFA, supra* note 23 at Art. 13(2).

[34] *ITPGRFA, supra* note 23 at Art. 12(3)(d).

[35] Cooper, *supra* note 26 at 8-9; *ITPGRFA supra* note 23 at Art. 12(3)(d).

[36] CGIAR is arguably a state-led initiative because many of its funders are state agencies. It was not instigated by states, however, and its governing body is not composed of state representatives. For these reasons, it has been included here. Other non-state initiatives include voluntary codes of conduct such as the *Micro-Organisms Sustainable Use and Access Regulation International Code of Conduct,* Belgian Co-ordinated Collections of Micro-organisms (1999), online : <http://www.belspo.be/bccm/mosaicc/>, as well as the GlaxoSmithKline corporate policy on ABS, see *Proposals for an International Regime, supra* note 10 at 7.

to another problem area for ABS regimes: how to manage access to genetic resources and benefit-sharing for those resources that are conserved *ex situ*.

CGIAR is a fairly informal body, created in 1971 at the instigation of the Ford and Rockefeller Foundations and now funded by various states, corporations, multilateral agencies such as the World Bank, and private foundations.[37] There are 16 IARCs scattered about the globe and while the CGIAR is the central coordinating body, each of the IARCs operates largely independently. Eleven of the IARCS also have genebanks. The geographic origins are unknown for much of the material in the genebanks, but it can be assumed that the state where the IARC is located is not the same as the state of origin for much of the germplasm. The other relevant feature of the IARCs is that the material in the genebanks is available for use by non-IARC scientists. This has created difficulties in recent years with accusations that other researchers have attempted to obtain intellectual property rights over material obtained from an IARC genebank.[38]

The features of CGIAR and the IARCs raise a variety of questions. On what terms should access to the genetic material in the IARC genebanks be granted? Should IPRs on the material be allowed? If yes, in what form, i.e. on whole, unaltered organisms obtained from an IARC, on parts thereof (genes, proteins, etc.), or on derivatives therefrom? How should the benefits of any use of the genetic resources be shared with the state or community that first provided them? CGIAR and the IARCs have attempted to resolve these problems through a variety of means.

First of all it is important to note that the CBD only applies to genetic resources collected in accordance with the Convention's provisions.[39] Given the much longer history of the IARCs than the CBD, very few of the resources in the IARC genebanks fall within the purview of the Convention. Instead, CGIAR and the IARCs have had to develop their own solutions.

The first big step was the 1994 agreements between the individual IARCs and the FAO[40] which placed the bulk of the Centres' germplasm under the auspices of the FAO to be held "in trust for the benefit of the international community".[41] These Trust Agreements included provisions that the Centres would not claim legal ownership of the germplasm nor seek IPRs over the

---

[37] CGIAR, "Co-sponsors and Members", online: CGIAR <http://www.cgiar.org/members/index.html>.

[38] Rural Advancement Foundation International & Heritage Seed Curators Australia, "Plant Breeders Wrongs: An Inquiry into the Potential for Plant Piracy through International Intellectual Property Conventions" (1998), online: ETC Group <http://www.etcgroup.org/documents/occ_plant.pdf>.

[39] CBD, *supra* note 3 at Art. 15(3).

[40] "The Agreement Between [name of Centre] and the Food and Agriculture Organization of the United Nations (FAO) Placing Collections of Plant Germplasm under the Auspices of FAO" in System-wide Genetic Resources Programme, *Booklet of CGIAR Centre Policy Instruments, Guidelines and Statements on Genetic Resources, Biotechnology and Intellectual Property Rights*, vers. 1 (Rome, 2001) at 2-7 [Trust Agreements].

[41] *Ibid.* at Art. 3(a).

germplasm or related information.[42] Access to the genetic resources is provided under Article 9 and where this involves transfer of the resources or related information to outside parties, the Centres must ensure that these parties are bound by the same restrictions on ownership and IPRs.[43]

The Centres provide access to the resources in their genebanks via Material Transfer Agreements (MTAs). In 1998, CGIAR and the Centres developed a standard MTA which includes a reiteration of Article 3(b) on ownership and IPRs from the Trust Agreements.[44] The MTA is included on the packaging accompanying the resources sent to a third party and, according to the MTA, "acceptance of the material constitutes acceptance of the terms of this agreement". The MTA does not, however, prevent the recipient from applying for IPRs on parts of the material or derivatives therefrom, as the MTA only applies to the germplasm as received from the Centre.[45]

The Trust Agreements with the FAO were to be in accordance with the International Undertaking. When the Treaty on Plant Genetic Resources replaced the International Undertaking, it included provisions accommodating the Trust Agreements. Article 15(1) calls upon the IARCs to sign agreements with the Governing Body of the Treaty, agreements that will supersede the Trust Agreements with the FAO.[46] Now that the Treaty has entered into force, the IARCs will develop new MTAs to reflect the Treaty's provisions on facilitated access and benefit-sharing.[47] Also, under Article 11(5), the Multilateral System created by the Treaty shall include the PGRFA in Annex I held by the IARCs.

This multiplicity of solutions to the CGIAR-IARC situation does not resolve all questions, but it does go a long way to putting the genetic resources of this institution on much more stable footing.

The Bonn Guidelines & the World Summit on Sustainable Development

In May 2000, the Parties to the CBD held their fifth conference. At that meeting, they "established the Ad Hoc Open-Ended Working Group on Access and Benefit-Sharing with the mandate to develop guidelines and other approaches for submission to the Conference of the Parties at its sixth meeting".[48] The Ad Hoc Open-Ended Working Group met and developed the draft Bonn Guidelines on Access to Genetic Resources and the Fair and

---

[42] *Ibid.* at Art. 3(b).
[43] *Ibid.* at Art. 10.
[44] "Material Transfer Agreement (MTA)" in *Booklet of CGIAR Centre Policy Instruments, supra* note 40 at 13.
[45] Crucible II Group, *Seeding Solutions*, v.1 (Ottawa: International Development Research Centre, 2000) at 66.
[46] Cooper, *supra* note 26 at 6.
[47] *ITPGRFA, supra* note 23 at Art. 15(1)(b).
[48] *Proposals for an International Regime, supra* note 10 at 2.

Equitable Sharing of Benefits Arising Out of Their Utilization. The Guidelines were adopted, with some amendments, at the sixth Conference of the Parties (COP6).[49]

As their name suggests, the Bonn Guidelines are meant to serve as a point of reference for policy, legislative and contractual matters related to ABS. In essence, they expand upon the key provisions in the CBD on ABS, particularly those addressing mutually agreed terms and prior informed consent. The provisions on prior informed consent include basic principles and elements, suggested procedures and processes, and the requirement that consent be granted by a competent authority.[50] Mutually agreed terms for benefit-sharing also includes certain basic requirements, although by its very nature, it is a much more open and flexible concept.[51]

The Bonn Guidelines were also referred to in the Plan of Implementation of the World Summit on Sustainable Development (WSSD).[52] Chapter IV of the Plan of Implementation addresses the protection and management of the natural resource base of economic and social development. In particular, paragraph 44 focuses on biodiversity, and subsection (n) encourages the implementation and further development of the Guidelines. Subsection (o) calls for action to "[n]egotiate within the framework of the Convention on Biological Diversity, bearing in mind the Bonn Guidelines, an international regime to promote and safeguard the fair and equitable sharing of benefits arising out of the utilization of genetic resources". The Parties to the CBD answered this call at their seventh conference, reaching a decision to launch negotiations for an international regime.[53]

Suggestions for an International ABS Regime

What is the Problem? What are the Needs?

The call for an international regime on ABS begs the question 'why is this necessary?' Again, the answer involves environmental, social, and economic factors – the three elements of sustainable development.

From an environmental perspective, historical access to genetic resources has not always encouraged conservation of the resource or its ecosystem and at times has even led to the destruction of the resource. "In one particularly

---

[49] Being the Annex to *Access and benefit-sharing as related to genetic resources,* CBD COP Dec. VI/24 A, 2002, UN Doc. UNEP/CBD/COP/6/20 [*Bonn Guidelines*].
[50] *Bonn Guidelines, supra* note 49 at IV(C).
[51] *Bonn Guidelines, supra* note 49 at IV(D).
[52] *Supra* note 22.
[53] *Access and benefit-sharing as related to genetic resources (Article 15),* CBD COP Dec. VII/19 D, UN Doc. UNEP/CBD/COP/7/21.

egregious example, the entire adult population of *Maytenus buchananni* – source of the anticancer compound maytansine – was harvested when a mission sponsored by the U.S. National Cancer Institute collected 27,215 kg in Kenya for testing in its drug development program".[54]

Socially-speaking, access to genetic resources has not always respected the human rights or ethical values of the source communities. For example, in the mid-nineteenth century, British botanical collectors smuggled cinchona seeds out of Peru, Bolivia and Ecuador despite local laws prohibiting the export of the seeds and plants. The rationale for these expeditions was that the native populations did not recognize the value of cinchona in treating malaria, that local bark-cutting practices were endangering the resource and that the English were undertaking a humanitarian mission by bringing cheap quinine to the world when, in fact, little of this was accurate.[55] Instead, the British succeeded in securing their own supply of cinchona by undercutting the Andean monopoly on the product.

Finally, even though genetic resources are an important source for medical research, less than .0001% of the profits from pharmaceutical products based on traditional medicine have been returned "to the local plant users who assisted preservation, research and discovery efforts".[56] Without the economic incentive of benefit-sharing to aid in conservation efforts, genetic resources and biodiversity are that much more vulnerable to destruction.

These examples all pre-date 1992 and international agreement on the CBD and its provisions on ABS. As we have seen, these provisions have been further developed in the Bonn Guidelines. Despite these developments, many of the problems and controversies of ABS continue to exist. Different individuals and organizations have different reasons for wanting to negotiate and international regime on ABS.[57] The remainder of this section will focus on one such justification: the gaps in the existing system of ABS.

Gaps in the Current System

An international regime on ABS needs to ensure that it creates a complete system for addressing ABS. The current combination of the CBD, the Bonn Guidelines, and the types of national, regional, international, and non-state

---

[54] World Resources Institute, *Biodiversity Prospecting: Using Genetic Resources for Sustainable Development* (Washington, D.C.: World Resources Institute, 1993) at 3-4.

[55] L. Brockway, *Science and Colonial Expansion: The Role of the British Royal Botanic Gardens* (New York: Academic Press, 1979) at 110-124.

[56] Marianne Guérin-McManus *et al.*, "Bioprospecting in Practice: A Case Study of the Suriname ICBG Project and Benefits Sharing under the Convention on Biological Diversity" (1998) at 2, online: Convention on Biological Diversity <http://www.biodiv.org/doc/case-studies/abs/cs-abs-sr.pdf>.

[57] K. Garforth and J. Cabrera, "Sustainable Biodiversity Law: Global Access, Local Benefits. A Scoping Study on Future Research Priorities for Access to Genetic Resources and Benefit-Sharing" (13 August 2004) at 24, online: CISDL <http://www.cisdl.org/pdf/CISDL_ABS_Scoping_Study.pdf>.

initiatives discussed above is falling short of this goal. In particular, there are three main lacunae in the current ABS framework. The first gap is a lack of measures linking access to genetic resources with the sustainable use of biodiversity. The second gap is in addressing the third objective of the CBD, i.e. "the fair and equitable sharing of benefits arising out of the utilization of genetic resources".[58] Particular shortcomings here include the areas of technology transfer and the obligations for user countries. The final area that is lacking is monitoring and remedies. Two case studies examining the impact of ABS on local communities will help to highlight how some of these issues are addressed in practice.

Case Study #1: The Fijian coastal villages of Verata[59]

Where:
Fiji – particularly the 8 coastal villages in the county of Verata.

When:
Project planning began in 1995, implementation started in 1997.

Who:
The University of the South Pacific in Suva, Fiji.
The Strathclyde Institute of Drug Research at Strathclyde University in Glasgow, Scotland. (The Institute acts as a broker between collectors of biological samples and interested companies.)
The people of Verata.
NGOs: the South Pacific Action Committee for Human Ecology and Environment, the Rainforest Alliance, and the Worldwide Fund for Nature/South Pacific.

Why:
To help a community concerned with the environmental impacts of
resource extraction link bioprospecting to conservation.
To increase the capacity of the University of the South Pacific to conduct research on medicinal plants.
To collect biological samples for screening by the Strathclyde Institute.

---

[58] CBD, *supra* note 3 at Art. 1.
[59] The information in this case study comes from three sources: W. Aalbersberg, *Marine Bioprospecting: The Pathway for Organism to Product and the Implication for Indigenous Resource Owner*, IAS Technical Report No. 99/08 (Institute of Applied Sciences, The University of the South Pacific, 1999); W. Aalbersberg *et al.*, "The Role of a Fijian Community in a Bioprospecting Project" (1998), online: Convention on Biological Diversity <http://www.biodiv.org/doc/case-studies/abs/cs-abs-fj.pdf>; Environmental Policy Studies Workshop, *Access to Genetic Resources: An Evaluation of the Development and Implementation of Recent Regulation and Access Agreements* (New York: Columbia University: 1999), online: Convention on Biological Diversity <http://www.biodiv.org> [Environmental Policy Studies Workshop].

How:

A project team met with the people of Verata to discuss the possibility of bioprospecting in their community and to see if there was support for the idea. With support obtained, the Strathclyde Institute negotiated a contract with the University of the South Pacific and the University negotiated a contract with the community of Verata. These documents were subject to comment by stakeholders and reviewed by lawyers for the community before being finalized. Under the contracts, Strathclyde retained 40% of all funds it received from licensing the samples. The other 60% went to the University, which passed the funds on to Verata.

Project implementation included participatory workshops on resource management issues. From these workshops, the community implemented conservation measures including marine taboo areas where no extraction was allowed. Community members were also trained as sample collectors and carried out the sampling for the project. Locals were also trained in biological and socioeconomic monitoring based on local concepts. Monitoring was totally implemented by the community. In 1999, the community of Verata established a Trust Fund to manage the funds received from the Strathclyde Institute.

What:

The outcomes of the project include: (1) the recovery of species thanks to conservation measures and (2) investment in community projects through the Trust Fund.

Case Study #2: Suriname and the Interior Maroon Tribes[60]

Where:

Suriname – particularly the Maroon tribes of the interior.

When:

Began in 1993 and benefits from the Forest People Fund are ongoing.

Who:

The Saramaka tribe of Suriname, and the International Cooperative Biodiversity Group, a U.S. government funded program, who gave a grant to the Virginia Polytechnic Institute and State University, Conservation International (CI), Bedrijf Geneesmiddelen Voorziening Suriname – a state-owned pharmaceutical company, the Missouri Botanical Gardens. Also, Bristol-Myers Squibb Pharmaceutical Research Institute, and Dow Chemical, who joined the project in 1998.

---

[60] The information in this case study comes from two sources: M. Guérin-McManus *et al.*, *supra* note 56; and M. Guérin-McManus, K.C. Nnadozie, & S.A. Laird, "Sharing Financial Benefits: Trust Funds for Biodiversity Prospecting" in S.A. Laird, ed. *Biodiversity and Traditional Knowledge: Equitable Partnerships in Practice* (London: Earthscan Publications Ltd., 2002) 333.

Why:

To promote environmental, economic, scientific, political, and cultural sustainability through bioprospecting; to record and secure the value of tribal knowledge; to develop the identification and documentation of Suriname biodiversity and the capacity for doing so; to increase local capacity for pharmaceutical research and production; to develop commercial drugs from plant extracts; to compensate tribal communities through a trust fund established from immediate payments that will also administer a portion of future royalties.

How:

A research agreement was signed between the research organizations and the funding program. Conservation International explained the research project, its objectives, requirements, potential benefits and intention of participants to the Samaraka in order to obtain prior informed consent to begin bioprospecting. A letter of intent was signed by CI and the Granman of the Saramaka tribe. It included provisions that CI would act as a fiduciary for the Saramaka tribe, that the Granman granted permission to CI to begin ethnobotanical research in cooperation with the Saramaka people, and that the basis of an ongoing relationship was informed consent. Collectors were required to update the Granman on the project and be granted permission to continue before each expedition. The project trained and employed tribal community members and other citizens in botanical and ethnobotanical sampling. The project also included screening samples for anti-malarial activity which is important to the people of Suriname. Multifaceted benefit-sharing included a long-term research agreement which controlled ownership, licensing and royalty fee structure for any potential drug developments; a Statement of Understanding further defining the distribution of royalties; the Forest People's Fund; and other non-monetary compensation like technology transfer that provided immediate benefits. The Forest People's Fund is a trust fund created from an initial endowment from Bristol Myers Squibb. The purpose of the Fund is to support small-scale, sustainable economic development and health projects that are designed and proposed by the communities themselves. The fund also creates immediate benefits for the community from the bioprospecting project.

What:

The outcomes of the project include: (1) local employment for shamans, field collectors and support staff, (2) sustainable development from trust fund projects, (3) prevention of loss of traditional knowledge, (4) increased local and national interest in conservation.

ABS and Sustainable Use of Biodiversity

Access to genetic resources and benefit-sharing has great potential to encourage the conservation and sustainable use of natural resources. If an area were to become a sustainable source for a genetic resource, it could mean the protection of the ecosystem rather than its conversion to a less diverse environment. The key is for an international ABS regime to make the link between ABS and sustainable use.

As described, Article 1 of the CBD sets out the objectives of the Convention which include the sustainable use of the components of biodiversity as well as the sharing of benefits arising from the use of genetic resources by means such as appropriate access to these resources. Article 11 of the Bonn Guidelines echoes these objectives:

> "The objectives of the Guidelines are the following:
> (a) To contribute to the conservation and sustainable use of biological diversity;
> (b) To provide Parties and stakeholders with a transparent framework to facilitate access to genetic resources and ensure fair and equitable sharing of benefits."

Article 11 of the CBD is a general provision requiring the Contracting Parties to provide incentives for the conservation and sustainable use of biodiversity. Article 15(2) goes further requiring the Contracting Parties to "endeavour to create conditions to facilitate access to genetic resources for environmentally sound uses." Similarly, paragraph 51 of the Bonn Guidelines suggests incentive measures that could be helpful in the implementation of the Guidelines. It proposes that states identify and mitigate or remove any perverse incentives that may block the conservation and sustainable use of biodiversity through ABS. It also suggests the creation and use of markets as a way to conserve and sustainably use biodiversity.
Beyond these quite vague suggestions, however, there is nothing that explicitly points to the sorts of measures that countries can take to encourage the environmentally sound use of genetic resources through access to these same resources.

The link between conservation and access to genetic resources is very strong in both the case studies in this section. The projects in both Fiji and Suriname involved the creation of trust funds that have been used to support environmental protection and conservation projects. The bioprospecting project in Fiji went even further by incorporating resource management workshops into the project implementation. An international regime on ABS should build on these examples by exploring in more detail the types of measures that encourage conservation through access to genetic resources and benefit-sharing.

The Fair and Equitable Sharing of Benefits

Benefit-sharing under the CBD is based on principles of justice, namely fairness and equity.[61] Article 15(7) of the Convention requires Contracting Parties to take measures:

> "with the aim of sharing in a fair and equitable way the results of research and development and the benefits arising from the commercial and other utilization of genetic resources with the Contracting Party providing such resources. Such sharing shall be upon mutually agreed terms."

The provision also requires that the benefit-sharing measures be in accordance with the technology transfer provisions of the Convention, discussed below.

The Bonn Guidelines echo the principles of justice and fairness[62] but also go quite a bit further in defining possible measures for benefit-sharing. These include paragraph 16(d) and its discussion of the obligations of Contracting Parties with users of genetic resources, paragraphs 45 through 50 on the relationship between mutually agreed terms and benefit-sharing, and finally, Appendix II which lists types of monetary and non-monetary benefits that can be included in benefit-sharing agreements.

The focus here will be on the promotion of technology transfer and the benefit-sharing obligations of user countries as possible components of an international ABS regime that responds to the principle of fair and equitable benefit-sharing.

Technology Transfer

Technology transfer is not a new concept. It has been the subject of discussion and negotiation at the United Nations for over 25 years.[63] Likewise, it is a recurring theme in multilateral environmental agreements, which tend to reiterate the need for technology transfer from developed to developing countries. For the most part, the promise of technology transfer has not been met.

Article 16 of the CBD addresses technology transfer. It recognizes "that both access to and transfer of technology among Contracting Parties are essential

---

[61] CBD, *supra* note 3 at Art. 1.
[62] *Bonn Guidelines, supra* note 49 at para. 11.
[63] UNCTAD, Draft International Code of Conduct on the Transfer of Technology, U.N. Doc. TD/CODE/TOT/47 (1985), online: United Nations Conference on Trade and Development <http://r0.unctad.org/stdev/compendium/documents/totcode%20.html>. Negotiations on the Technology Transfer Code began in 1976 and continued into the mid-1980s without ever reaching a final conclusion.

elements for the attainment of the objectives of this Convention".[64] The Contracting Parties are obliged to undertake "to provide and/or facilitate access for and transfer to other Contracting Parties of technologies that are relevant to the conservation and sustainable use of biological diversity or make use of genetic resources and do not cause significant damage to the environment."[65] Article 16 also calls for the transfer of technology to developing countries to be on fair and most favourable terms.[66]

Technology transfer arises in a number of places in the Bonn Guidelines. It is listed as one of the objectives of the Guidelines,[67] as part of fair and equitable benefit-sharing in the responsibilities of users of genetic resources,[68] and as a type of non-monetary benefit that may be shared[69].

The two case studies illustrate different approaches to technology transfer. In Fiji, the Strathclyde Institute was unable to commit to technology transfer but did help to train local scientists. At the same time, community members received the training they needed to better manage their local resources, which can be understood as a form of technology transfer. In Suriname, technology transfer was included as one facet of the project's non-monetary benefit-sharing arrangements.

While the provisions on technology transfer in the CBD are quite lengthy, ultimately they leave the implementation of technology transfer up to the Contracting Parties. The international regime needs to go beyond these statements and explore more explicit guidelines to promote technology transfer, particularly of technologies relating to genetic resources. The international regime should also investigate more specific ways to resolve the technology transfer gap in the existing ABS framework to the benefit of developing countries. Finally, technology transfer in an international regime should relate to the first gap in the current ABS framework. It should help make the connection between access to genetic resources and the conservation and sustainable use thereof.

At the same time, it must be recognized that the existing technology transfer provisions in the CBD were some of the most contentious articles during the negotiations. At the Earth Summit in Rio de Janeiro in 1992, the U.S. refused to sign the Convention largely due to the technology transfer provisions in Article 16 and the fear that they would run roughshod over intellectual property

---

[64] CBD, *supra* note 3 at Art. 16(1).
[65] *Ibid.*
[66] *Ibid.* at Art. 16(2).
[67] *Bonn Guidelines, supra* note 49 at para. 11(g).
[68] *Ibid.* at para. 16(b)(ix).
[69] *Ibid.* at Appendix II.

rights.[70] One of the benefits of an international regime on ABS that consists of a variety of binding and non-binding elements is that non-agreement on contentious issues like technology transfer need not result in the failure of the entire regime.

Benefit-Sharing Obligations of User Countries

As discussed, Article 15(7) of the CBD places an obligation on all Contracting Parties to take measures with the aim of fair and equitable benefit-sharing. Paragraph 16(d) of the Bonn Guidelines elaborates the responsibilities that Contracting Parties should consider acting upon in developing ABS pursuant to Article 15 of the CBD. These include developing ways to inform potential users of genetic resources of their obligations regarding access, implementing measures to prevent use of genetic resources provided without the prior informed consent of the providing Party, and creating voluntary certification schemes.[71]

Despite the fact that these obligations fall on all Contracting Parties, countries that are providing access to their genetic resources have largely carried the burden of implementing ABS to date. These states, many of which are developing countries, have had to confront the difficulties of regulating a novel and complex subject. An international regime on ABS needs to close the gap between provider and user Parties in the implementation of ABS. It should place obligations on the user Parties to help develop, implement, and comply with measures on access to genetic resources and benefit-sharing.

One of the suggested obligations on user Parties is the certificate of disclosure of origin. This measure has already received a lot of attention and has been implemented by some states.[72] As set out in paragraph 16(d)(ii) of the Bonn Guidelines, disclosure of origin involves "[m]easures to encourage the disclosure of the country of origin of the genetic resources and of the origin of traditional knowledge, innovations and practices of indigenous and local communities in applications for intellectual property rights". This measure is important for monitoring access and use of genetic resources, and for deterring biopiracy but its potential for closing the gaps of the existing ABS framework are somewhat overstated. The difficulties that countries have experienced in the formation of their access laws, and thus in providing access to genetic resources, will not be solved through disclosure of origin obligations.

---

[70] N.D. Hamilton, "Who Owns Dinner: Evolving Legal Mechanisms for Ownership of Plant Genetic Resources" (1993) 28 Tulsa L.J. 587 at 623.

[71] *Bonn Guidelines*, *supra* note 49 at para. 16(d)(i), (iii), (v).

[72] Secretariat for the Convention on Biological Diversity, *Compilation of Submissions on Access and Benefit-Sharing as Related to Genetic Resources Received by the Secretariat Pursuant to Decisions VI/24 A-D of the Conference of the Parties*, 30 September 2003, UN Doc., UNEP/CBD/WG-ABS/2/INF/1, online: Convention on Biological Diversity <http://www.biodiv.org>.

Monitoring and Remedies

A common weakness of national ABS systems is a lack of monitoring to determine the impacts of bioprospecting projects.[73] Part of the explanation for this weakness may lie in the third and final gap of the current ABS framework. The CBD does not contain any provisions specifically addressing the monitoring of ABS contracts while paragraph 55 of the Bonn Guidelines discusses only potential monitoring elements of national ABS systems.

Despite this gap in the existing international framework, the Fijian case study includes a very strong monitoring component, encompassing both biological and socioeconomic elements. This monitoring is entirely carried out by the community. The Suriname project includes formal and informal evaluations that involve activity reports and coordination of plans. An international regime should include the adoption of mechanisms such as codes of conduct and declarations of principles which would improve the possibility of monitoring and controlling the flow of genetic resources.

The international regime should equally attend to the need of provider countries for legal remedies in cases of non-compliance. These remedies should be effective and within reach for developing countries and their institutions. Article 14 of the CBD on 'Impact Assessment and Minimizing Adverse Impacts' provides that the Conference of the Parties will examine the issue of liability and redress for damage to biodiversity. However, this provision is not specific to ABS and Article 15 makes no mention of Contracting Parties taking measures to regulate non-compliance with their ABS regimes. Paragraph 61 of the Bonn Guidelines goes further and allows Parties to take "effective and proportionate measures" for violations of their national ABS measures including those on prior informed consent and mutually agreed terms. To be effective, the remedies in an international regime should include facilitated access that will help level the playing field between the users and providers of genetic resources.

The Meaning of an International ABS Regime in International Sustainable Development Law

The Plan of Implementation from the WSSD points to the next step in the development of access to genetic resources and benefit-sharing – the creation of an international regime. The Parties to the CBD have taken this step, agreeing to launch negotiations for an international regime and drafting the terms of reference for these negotiations. If such a regime is to be consistent with the sustainable development objectives of the Convention on Biological Diversity then it should aim to develop and enhance understanding of the inter-

---

[73] Environmental Policy Studies Workshop, *supra* note 59 at vi.

linkages between biodiversity-related policies and law at the national, regional and international levels.[74] This means that an international regime must be integrative in at least two different ways – it must meld the social, environmental and economic goals of sustainable development, as well as incorporating the lessons learned from the implementation of ABS efforts in different national, regional and international fora.

An international ABS regime that focuses on filling in the gaps of the existing ABS framework will go a long way to achieving this goal. The creation of such a regime will involve drawing on different local, national, regional and international experiences in implementing the current ABS framework, some of which we have highlighted here. By these means, a regime can be built that is informed by the past successes and failures of access to genetic resources and benefit-sharing and includes more specific mechanisms to ensure continued progress in this field.

---

[74] M. C. Cordonier Segger & A. Khalfan, *Sustainable Development Law: Principles, Practices and Prospects* (Oxford: Oxford University Press, 2004).

14

SUSTAINABLE AGRICULTURAL RESOURCES AND FOOD SECURITY: THE SEED TREATY AND EQUITABLE BENEFIT SHARING

Mary E. Footer[1] & Emmanuel Opuku Awuku[2]

Since the beginning of agriculture, the world's farmers have developed through selection and breeding roughly 10,000 plant species for use in basic food and fodder production. Crop germplasm or plant genetic resources for food and agriculture (PGRFA) provides the raw material that plant breeders and farmers need to develop new varieties in order to face potential future challenges such as climate change, unknown pests and plant diseases and to ensure a nutritious diet. Indeed, the engineering of these materials has been hailed as essential to address food security and malnutrition in developing countries.[3] Newly engineered crops are being used in developing countries such as Argentina, South Africa, China, the Philippines and India.[4]

---

[1] Mary Footer, BA (Hons.), LL.M. (University of London, UCL), Member, International Trade Law Committee of the ILA, Deputy-Director of the Amsterdam Center for International Law, Associate Professor of Law, Universiteit van Amsterdam.

[2] Emmanuel Owoku Apuku, M.A. Law (Voronezh University, Russia), Ph.D. LLM (University of London, SOAS), MCIArb. (Chartered Institute of Arbitrators, UK), Member, International Trade Law Committee, ILA, Senior Programme Officer, Commonwealth Secretariat, Legal and Constitutional affairs Division. The views expressed in the chapter do not necessarily represent the views of the Commonwealth Secretariat, and the fact of Dr. Awuku's employment with the Commonwealth Secretariat does not imply any endorsement of his views by the Secretariat. The chapter is based on two presentations given by the authors at the 71st[5] Conference of the International Law Association, Berlin, 16-21 August 2004, before the Committee on International Law on Biotechnology, of which they are both Members.

[3] For example, the West African Rice Development Association (WARDA), a public international agricultural research centre in Cote d'Ivoire, has used 'embryo rescue' to enable African and Asian varieties of rice to cross-breed. This innovation in rice production promises several advantages over conventional African varieties, including earlier maturity, improved pest resistance, tolerance to drought and acid soils, and greater height, making it easier to harvest by hand. See *Democratizing Biotechnology: Genetically Modified Crops in Developing Countries. Biotechnology for Africa?*, Briefing Paper 10, Institute of Development Studies, University of Sussex, Available online: <http://www.ids.ac.uk/biotech>.

[4] Alan Larson, *Trade and Development Dimension of U.S. International Biotechnology Policy*, Available at: http://usinfo.state.gov/journals/ites/0903/ijee/larson.htm

M.C. Cordonier Segger & C. G. Weeramantry, eds., Sustainable Justice: Reconciling Economic, Social & Environmental Law © 2005 Koninklijke Brill NV, Printed in The Netherlands, pp.241-258.

At the same time, agricultural biodiversity, which is the basis for food production and which has been developed and safeguarded by farmers since the dawn of humankind, is in sharp decline due the effects of modernisation, changes in diets and increasing population density. Today, it is estimated that approximately 150 crops feed most of the world's population but only twelve crops provide 80% of dietary energy (rice, wheat, maize, and potato alone provide some 60% of all staple foods).[5]

This chapter discusses the legal aspects of access to genetic resources and benefit sharing, with a focus on plant genetic resources for food and agriculture or PRGFA and within that context, the issue of farmers' rights. From a rights point of view, the issue of access to PGRFA is multi-faceted. It involves issues of sovereign rights, rights of individuals and the rights of indigenous and local communities, including farmers. The 1992 United Nations Convention on Biological Diversity (CBD)[6] provides a general context, and there are many other initiatives of both a public and private character in the field of genetic resources at the international, regional and domestic level. This chapter focuses principally on the International Treaty on Plant Genetic Resources for Food and Agricultural (ITPGRFA) of the Food and Agriculture Organisation (FAO), which entered into force in June, 2004.[7]

The development of equitable benefit sharing of PGRFA for agrobiodiversity and food security

As has been discussed in earlier chapters of this book, the entry into force of the CBD hastened the assertion of sovereignty over genetic resources and the exercise of jurisdiction by States over access to those resources, setting out, in Article 1 UN CBD, a basic commitment to "fair and equitable sharing of the benefits arising out of the utilization of genetic resources...." Additionally, Article 8(j) UN CBD encourages the equitable sharing of the benefits arising from the utilization of knowledge, innovations and practices of indigenous and local communities embodying traditional lifestyles relevant for the conservation and sustainable use of biodiversity.

As discussed in the previous chapter, a framework for the implementation of access to genetic resources is provided throughout the UN CBD.[8] It

---

[5] 'International plant genetic resources treaty enters into force', FAO Newsroom report, 29 June 2004, available at: http://www.fao.org/newsroom/en.

[6] United Nations Convention on Biological Diversity, 5 June 1992, 31 I.L.M. 818 (1992) (entered into force 29 December 1993) [Hereinafter CBD or UN CBD].

[7] International Treaty on Plant Genetic Resources for Food and Agriculture, adopted on 3 November 2001 by Res. 3/01, FAO Conference, 31st Sess. (entered into force 29 June 2004); available online: <www.fao.org/waicent/faoinfo/agricult/cgrfa/IU.html.> [Hereinafter ITFPGRA or 'Seed Treaty'].

[8] In particular, Article 15 CBD which is linked to provisions on access to and transfer of technology (Article 16 CBD), exchange of information (Article 17 CBD), technical and scientific cooperation (Article

endorses the sovereign rights of States over their biological resources and the consequent authority of national governments to regulate access to genetic resources. States are also under an obligation to facilitate access to genetic resources, to make that access subject to the prior informed consent of Parties and to ensure that access is on mutually agreed terms. Thus, in the CBD regime international treaty law strikes a balance between a State's authority to regulate access to genetic resources and it obligation to facilitate access by others to those genetic resources.

States parties to the CBD enjoy a wide discretion as to how to regulate access and it has already led to national and regional law on access to genetic resources and benefit sharing. The variety of regulation covers a broad spectrum of statutory and contractual rights (such as bioprospecting arrangements between governments and individual entities). The scope of national and regional access legislation may also extend to the regulation of traditional knowledge, including the prior consent of local and indigenous communities for access to genetic resources and their subsequent utilisation. National access and benefit sharing legislation does not cover *ex situ* collections of genetic resources acquired before the entry into force of the CBD[9] and this is particularly important for PGRFA with respect to collections of seed germplasm which are held in national agricultural research centres or NARCS, agricultural research stations, marine biological institutes, botanical gardens and similar institutions.

Access and Benefit Sharing through the Multilateral System: The 'Seed Treaty'

The ITPGRFA or 'Seed Treaty' is the successor to a non-binding international instrument, the 'International Undertaking' that was adopted as a 1983 FAO Conference Resolution.[10] A fundamental revision of the International Undertaking proceeded from the early 1990s onwards,[11] in an attempt to harmonise it with the 1992 UN CBD and possibly add it as a protocol to that treaty, in the same way as the 2001 Cartagena Protocol on Biosafety.[12] Its subsequent (re-)negotiation was intertwined with the UN

---

18 CBD) and the handling of biotechnology and distribution of its benefits (Article 19, paragraphs 1 and 2 CBD), *supra* note 6.

[9] Article 15, paragraph 3 CBD, *supra* note 6.

[10] The 1983 FAO International Undertaking on Plant Genetic Resources (International Undertaking, or IU) was adopted by Res. 8/83, FAO Conference, 22nd Sess. See M. E. Footer, "Intellectual Property and Agrobiodiversity: Towards Private Ownership of the Genetic Commons" (1999) 10 *Yearbook of International Environmental Law* (Oxford: Oxford University Press, 2000) 48-81, at 62-68 for an overview.

[11] M. Footer, *ibid.*, 62-68.

[12] 2001 Cartagena Protocol on Biosafety to the Convention on Biological Diversity, 29 January 2001, 39 I.L.M. 1027 (2001) (in force: 11 September 2003).

CBD, beginning with Resolution 3 of the 1992 Nairobi Conference, which addressed the interrelationship between the CBD and the promotion of sustainable agriculture.[13]

The resolution foresaw the strengthening of the FAO Global System for the Conservation and Utilisation of Plant Genetic Resources for Food and Agriculture (the FAO Global System),[14] the cornerstone of which would be a new agreement that would have to address two outstanding matters. The first was 'access to *ex situ* collections not acquired in accordance with [the] Convention' and the second was 'the question of farmers' rights'. The 1993 FAO Conference provided the framework for the revision of the International Undertaking along these lines[15] and led to a series of negotiations under the auspices of the FAO Commission on Plant Genetic Resources, which began in 1994 and continued until the adoption of the Seed Treaty on 3 November 2001.[16]

The scope and coverage of this newest FAO treaty differ markedly from those of the previous International Undertaking, reflecting the overall orientation of the CBD. The guiding principles are the promotion of sustainable agriculture and food security. Its main objectives are the conservation and sustainable use of plant genetic resources for food and agriculture and equitable benefit-sharing for sustainable agriculture and food security.[17] The key to the Seed Treaty is the establishment of a multilateral system for facilitated access to a specified list of plant genetic resources for food and agriculture.[18] The multilateral system is balanced by benefit-sharing in the areas of information exchange, technology transfer, capacity building and commercial development. It also contains a section on farmers' rights, that is derived from an interpretation which was previously annexed to the International Undertaking,[19] but is now taken up as a separate provision in a legally-binding international instrument. [20]

---

[13] 1992 Nairobi Conference for the Adoption of the Agreed Text of the Convention on Biological Diversity; Res. 3 was adopted on 22 May 1992 and related to 'The Interrelationship between the Convention on Biological Diversity and the Promotion of Sustainable Agriculture', and 31 I.L.M 846 (1992).

[14] Established by FAO Res. C 9/83, FAO Conference, 22nd Sess., it was intended that the FAO Global System should provide an intergovernmental framework for the safe conservation, promotion of unrestricted availability and sustainable utilisation of PGRFA for present and future generations. See J. Esquinas-Alcazar, "The Global System on Plant Genetic Resources" (1993) 2 *RECIEL* 152 *et seq.*

[15] Res. C 7/93, FAO Conference, 22nd Sess. See generally K. ten Kate and C. Lasén Diaz, "The Undertaking Revisited: A Commentary on the Revision of the International Undertaking on Plant Genetic Resources for Food and Agriculture" (1997) 6:3 *RECIEL* 284-292.

[16] 2001 ITPGRFA or Seed Treaty, *supra* note 6; see further M. E. Footer, "Our Agricultural Heritage: Agricultural Sustainability, Common Heritage and Intergenerational Equity" in N. Schrijver and F. Weiss (eds.), *International Law on Sustainable Development: Principles and Practice* (The Hague: Martinus Nijhoff, 2004) at 433 – 466.

[17] Article 1, ITPGRFA 2001, *supra* note 6, which is further supported by the preambular text to the Treaty (recital 4).

[18] Ibid and Annex 1 to ITPGRFA 2001, *supra* note 6. See further M. Footer, *supra* note 15 at 433 – 466.

[19] Res. C 4/89, FAO Conference, 22nd Sess. already recognised the contribution of farmers to the conservation and development of plant genetic resources but another text of even date, the 'Agreed

The most significant and innovative part of the Seed Treaty is the inclusion for the first time in the history of plant genetic resources of a 'Multilateral System of Access and Benefit-Sharing' (the Multilateral System).[21] This 'Multilateral System' is a consequence of a policy reversal in the field of plant genetic resources for food and agriculture, which has seen crop germplasm pass from the domain of common heritage of humankind to that of national sovereignty over biological resources. Its inclusion in the Seed Treaty continues to recognise this sub-species of plant genetic resources as a common concern of humankind and also the fact that all countries depend to some extent on PGRFA which originated elsewhere.[22] Just like the provisions regulating access under the CBD, Parties retain full authority to regulate their own PGRFA but where the Seed Treaty differs from the CBD is that it places strict limitations on the ability of Parties to restrict access to that PGRFA from other states.

Having said that, while the Treaty covers all genetic material for food and agriculture, Parties are under an obligation (at a minimum) to guarantee access to the genetic material of 35 crop genera and 29 forage species that are in the public domain and are considered essential for global food security and human nutrition.[23] The listing includes crops like rice, maize, wheat, cassava and potatoes which are important to agrobiodiversity and food security; a notable omission is soybean, which China managed to successfully have excluded from the basic list of food crops.[24]

Access must be provided only for the purpose of utilisation and conservation in pursuit of research, breeding and training for food and agriculture and must be accorded expeditiously.[25] States that are parties to the Seed Treaty must also make all available 'passport' data and any other associated available non-confidential descriptive information.[26] There is a standstill provision which allows a developer (breeder or farmer) in a country of origin of crop germplasm the right to delay access for a period during

---

Interpretation of the International Undertaking: Farmers Rights', Res. C 5/89, FAO Conference, 25th Sess. (the 'second interpretation') expressly recognised 'farmers' rights'.

[20] Article 9, ITPGRFA 2001, *supra* note 6. On the concept of farmers' rights generally, see Martin A. Girsberger, *Biodiversity and the Concept of Farmers' Rights in International Law: Factual Background and Legal Analysis* (Bern, Berlin, Bruxelles, Frankfurt am Main, New York, Wien: Peter Lang AG, 1999).

[21] Articles 11, 12 and 13, ITPGRFA 2001, *supra* note 6. See also C. Fowler, "Accessing Genetic Resources: International Law Establishes Multilateral System" (2004) 51 *Genetic Resources and Crops Evolution* 609-620.

[22] M. Footer, *supra* note 15, at 433 – 466. For a critique of this approach, see I. Mgbeoji, "Beyond Rhetoric: State Sovereignty, Common Concern, and the Inapplicability of the Common Heritage Concept to Plant Genetic Resources" (2003)16 *Leiden Journal of International Law* 821-837.

[23] Article 11, paragraphs 1 and 2, ITPGRFA 2001, *supra* note 6. The actual listing of the 35 crop genera and 29 forage species is contained in Annex I to the Treaty.

[24] M. Footer, above n. 15, with details in fn. 11.

[25] Article 12, paragraph 3(a) (b) ITPGRFA 2001, *supra* note 6.

[26] Article 12, paragraph 3(c) ITPGRFA 2001, *supra* note 6.

which that crop germplasm is under development at the time when access is requested.[27]

One of the most controversial points throughout the seven years of negotiation was the issue of plant genetic information and technology, which was protected by intellectual property rights and confidentiality clauses, i.e. proprietary technologies. A compromise solution was worked out, which essentially favours the maintenance of essential crop germplasm in the public domain by forbidding the grant of any intellectual property right over the accessed PGRFA. The Seed Treaty makes it clear that recipients of PGRFA through the Multilateral System cannot claim intellectual property rights that might otherwise limit facilitated access to the PGRFA, or their genetic parts or components, in the form received from the Multilateral System.[28] In addition, PGRFA accessed under the Multilateral System must also be made available to other interested parties by the recipient under the conditions laid out by the Treaty.[29] The inclusion of these provisions was hailed as a victory by scientists and research institutions from countries with strong, government-backed research and breeding capabilities as well as many developing countries. However, countries like the US, Canada and Japan strongly opposed the inclusion of limitations on the grant of intellectual property rights, fearing that this would stifle innovation. Where PGRFA is already protected by intellectual property, or indeed any other property rights, access can only take place in conformity with the treaty or other statutory instruments regulating the particular kind of property rights.[30]

The benefit sharing provisions under the 2001 Seed Treaty form part of what some people have termed a 'grand bargain'[31] which seeks to redress the asymmetry in plant genetic resources and bargaining power between developed and developing countries. Parties that facilitate access through the Multilateral System have the right to receive some form of benefits. As a starting point, the Seed Treaty takes the approach that all benefits arising from use, including commercial use, of PGRFA acquired through the Multilateral System are to be shared equitably through one of four mechanisms: (i) exchange of information (catalogues and inventories, information on technologies, and the results of technical, scientific and socio-economic research); (ii) access to and transfer of technology, (iii) capacity-building (the establishment of programmes for scientific and technical education and training in conservation and sustainable use of PGRFA); and (iv) sharing of monetary and other benefits arising from

---

[27] Article 12, paragraph 3(e) ITPGRFA 2001, *supra* note 6.
[28] Article 12, paragraph 3(d) ITPGRFA 2001, *supra* note 6.
[29] Article 12, paragraph 3(g) ITPGRFA 2001, *supra* note 6.
[30] Article 12, paragraph 3(f) ITPGRFA 2001, *supra* note 6.
[31] K. ten Kate and S. A. Laird, "Biodiversity and Business: Coming to Terms with the 'Grand Bargain'" (2000) 76:1 *International Affairs* 241-264 at 244.

commercialisation.[32] These mechanisms must take account of the priorities in the FAO's rolling Global Plan of Action,[33] which will depend on the effective implementation of the benefit-sharing provisions, and the funding strategy to be set up under the Treaty in the form of a Trust Account.

The part of the mechanism that will no doubt attract the greatest attention is the sharing of monetary and other benefits, including those arising from the involvement of the private sector in developing countries in research and technology development or quite simply the commercialisation aspect of benefit-sharing. A standard Material Transfer Agreement or MTA will be used in order to facilitate access to crop germplasm through the Multilateral System.[34] This particular development lags behind that of the CBD where an *Ad Hoc* Open-ended Working Group has been actively working on producing a set of international guidelines and approaches on access and benefit-sharing, which have subsequently been submitted to COP-7.[35] The proposed MTA will need to include the requirement that an equitable share of the benefits arising from the commercialisation of product, incorporating material accessed through the Multilateral System, is paid to the Trust Account, which must be set up by the Governing Body, conform the Treaty. [36] The Governing Body, which has not yet met, will set the level, form and manner of payment under the commercialisation provisions of Article 13.2(d) of the Seed Treaty, in line with commercial practice. [37]

Farmers' rights

The Seed Treaty also recognises the contribution of farmers to conserving and enhancing plant genetic resources for food and agriculture but it does

---

[32] Article 13, paragraph 2, paragraphs (a) through (d) ITPGRFA 2001, *supra* note 6.

[33] FAO Global Plan of Action for the Conservation and Sustainable Use of Plant Genetic Resources for Food and Agriculture (Article 14), ITPGRFA 2001, *supra* note 6. Originally set up in 1983 as one of the instruments in the overall FAO Global System, above n. 15, the Global Plan of Action was formally adopted by 150 countries, following the adoption of the FAO, *Report on the State of the World's Plant Genetic Resources for Food and Agriculture*, prepared for the Fourth International Technical Conference on Plant Genetic Resources, Leipzig, Germany, 17-23 June 1996, and known as the Leipzig Declaration. The main task of the Global Action Plan is to provide a periodic reporting system (by FAO Member governments) in order to keep track of the state of the world's plant genetic resources.

[34] The Expert Group on the Terms of the Standard Material Transfer Agreement, or MTA, Brussels, met in Brussels from 4-8 October 2004, and is charged with developing the relevant contractual basis for access and transfer of individual crop germplasm in the Multilateral System. Available online: <http://www.fao.org/ag/cgrfa/docsmta1.htm> for details.

[35] See UN CBD, work of the *Ad Hoc* Open-ended Working Group on Access and Benefit-Sharing, available online: <www.biodiv.org>.

[36] Article 13, paragraph 2(d) (ii), first full paragraph, in conjunction with Article 19, paragraph 3(f), 2001 ITPGRFA 2001, *supra* note 6.

[37] Article 13, paragraph 2(d)(ii), second full paragraph, ITPGRFA 2001, *supra* note 6.. See, for some of the problems to which this could give rise, B. Koo, P. G. Pardey and B. D. Wright, "Conserving Genetic Resources for Agriculture: Counting the Cost" Brief 6 of the International Food Policy Research Institute (IFPRI) Series *Research at a Glance: Biotechnology and Genetic Resource Policies* (University of Minnesota and IFPRI, Washington, D.C., January 2003).

not define 'farmers' rights' as such.[38] Instead, it provides broad guidelines to Parties concerning the scope of the rights to be protected but devolves overall responsibility for the realisation of those rights to the Parties themselves in a similar fashion to other economic and social rights. According to the Seed Treaty it is the duty of national governments inter alia to take measures 'to protect and promote Farmers Rights' that include *de minimis* the protection of traditional knowledge, farmers' entitlement to a part of benefit-sharing arrangements and the right to participate in decision-making regarding the management of plant genetic resources.[39]

Noteworthy is the absence in the treaty of any mention of farmers' rights over their landraces. In fact, the 'recognition' of farmers' contribution to plant genetic resource conservation and enhancement does not include any property rights at all. In this context, the only rights that are recognized are the residual rights to save, use, exchange and sell farm-saved seeds. It is therefore questionable the extent to which the Seed Treaty contains sufficient guarantees to farmers for the protection and promotion of their rights.

Similarly, it is also intended that benefits arising from the access and benefit sharing provisions of the Multilateral System should primarily be directed to farmers who conserve and sustainably use crop germplasm. However, it is hard to see how this will work in practice, not least because it may prove difficult to identify the 'farmers'. [40] Not surprisingly, scholarly debate continues in relation to the potential consequences of the commercial and non-commercial aspects of the Multilateral System and its ultimate beneficiaries.[41]

Farmer's Rights and the Linkage to Indigenous and Community Rights

In addition to farmers' rights under the Seed Treaty, there is also a need to focus on recognizing and protecting the rights of indigenous peoples and local communities, in the interest of food security and sustainable development. Issues of indigenous and local peoples' rights have featured strongly in international legal and policy debates. The World Commission on Environment and Development stressed the importance of traditional knowledge in the sustainable development process, and observed that 'tribal

---

[38] Article 9, paragraph 1, ITPGRFA 2001, *supra* note 6 simply follows the text contained in the interpretations to the earlier International Undertaking in '[recognizing] the enormous contribution that the local and indigenous communities and farmers of all regions of the world' make to the conservation and development of PGRFA. It is not a definition.

[39] Article 9, paragraph 2, ITPGRFA 2001, *supra* note 6.

[40] It is also possible that similar problems may arise with respect to collaborative partnerships, which are provided for in Article 13, paragraph 2(d)(i) ITPGRFA 2001, *supra* note 6.

[41] M. Footer, *supra* note 15 at 433 – 466.

and indigenous people will need special attention as the forces of economic development disrupt their traditional lifestyles'.[42] Agenda 21 recommends that governments should adopt policies and/or legal instruments that will protect intellectual and cultural property of indigenous peoples.[43]

As such, for sustainable development, local communities should have control of and access to agricultural bio-diversity, so that they can continue to develop their farming systems. Further, such local farmers must have the right to benefit from biological resources and related knowledge.

However, there are a number of barriers preventing the poor from accessing fully the benefits of modern technology including inadequate regulatory procedures, poorly functioning markets and seed delivery systems, weak domestic plant breeding capacity, inadequate research capacities, and complex intellectual property issues.[44] The remainder of this chapter focuses on intellectual property rights issues as they relate to access to genetic resources and the rights of farmers in developing countries.

Western biotechnological, pharmaceutical and human health care industries have increased their interest in natural products as sources of new biochemical compounds for drug, chemical and agro-products development. Although the interest in traditional knowledge and medicines from developing countries has increased in the past few decades, few if any benefits yet accrue to the source countries and the traditional communities. Many have argued that their contributions to plant breeding, genetic enhancement, biodiversity conservation and global drug development are not adequately recognized, compensated or even protected.[45]

In this respect, the situation of local farmers in developing countries is particularly important. Over a long period of time, farming communities in developing countries have bred and developed their crop varieties, improved on the varieties through selective breeding and sold them locally under names which have found widespread local acceptance. In recent decades, some of these local varieties have also been exported. Intellectual property protection in developing countries, however, is poor and, in many cases, the government is opposed to the granting of monopoly rights in agricultural crops.

---

[42] World Commission on Environment and Development, *Our Common Future* (Oxford: Oxford University Press, 1987) at 12.
[43] Agenda 21, Chapter 26.4 (b), in N. A. Robinson (Ed.) *Agenda 21: Earth's Action Plan* (New York: Oceana Publications, 1993) at 509.
[44] "Biotech and Developing Countries" (May 2004) *Bridges Journal* ICTSD 8:5.
[45] J. Mugabe, "Intellectual Property Protection and Traditional Knowledge" in *Intellectual Property and Human Rights: A Panel Discussion to Commemorate the 50th Anniversary of the Universal Declaration of Human Rights*, Geneva, on 9 November 1998 (Geneva: WIPO, 1999) at 97-122.

In such situations, an agricultural biotechnology company from a developed country can acquire samples of the crop. As these varieties are not produced using biotechnology, the company can make use of the exemption for plants and animals allowed under the WTO Agreement on Trade-Related Aspects of Intellectual Property Rights (TRIPs)[46] by claiming that these are natural varieties where no inventor can be identified. This is legally correct as most developing countries do not provide intellectual property protection for their plant varieties. The agricultural biotechnology company can then genetically engineer a close substitute for the natural variety, which maintains its desirable consumer characteristics. This genetically modified variety can be patented and its name copyrighted, which makes it eligible for intellectual property protection under TRIPs. This means that the biotechnology firm can license the production of crop in any climatically friendly country, export the product in competition with natural varieties and prevent the natural varieties from being sold in importers' markets using their natural names.[47] Some examples of this in practice include Jasmine rice from Thailand and Basmati rice from India, variants of two rice varieties that have been patented and copyrighted by United States firms.[48]

Some view this system as 'bio-piracy', arguing that if a patent law is intended to reward inventiveness and creativity systematically but fails to honestly apply the criteria of novelty and non-obviousness, which are called for in the granting of patents related to indigenous knowledge, the law is flawed and needs to be changed. Such authors suggest that such a system cannot be the basis for granting patents or establishing exclusive marketing rights.[49]

While the TRIPs Agreement establishes minimum standards on patents, industrial designs, trade secrets, copyrights, trademarks and geographical indications, thereby comprising the most comprehensive body of international law on intellectual property rights, it cannot adequately cover or protect traditional knowledge and innovations of indigenous and local peoples.[50] For many developing countries, the rights of indigenous and local

---

[46] Annex 1C of the Agreement on Trade-Related Aspects of Intellectual Property Rights (TRIPs). The TRIPs Agreement provides for a common set of rules to protect and enforce intellectual property rights. Its purpose is to reduce distortions and impediments to international trade, to promote effective and adequate protection of intellectual property rights, and to ensure that measures and procedures to enforce intellectual property rights do not themselves become barriers to legitimate trade.

[47] W. A. Kerr, J. E. Hobbs and R. Yampoin, "Intellectual Property Protection, Biotechnology and Developing Countries: Will the TRIPS be Effective?" (1999) *AgBioFroum* 2: 3 and 4, at 203-211.

[48] *Ibid.*

[49] V. Shiva, "Biopriacy: Need to Change Western IPR Systems" (28 July 1999) *The Hindu* (New Delhi). Available online: <http://www.hinduonline.com/today/stories/05281349.htm>.

[50] A general distinction is made between the knowledge systems of the formal sector, of both private and public institutions, and those of the informal sector, of communities and individuals. The formal sector knowledge systems are codified, recorded in writing and defended through national and international law, e.g. the TRIPS Agreement and multilateral treaties, such as the Patent Co-operation Treaty, and the Berne and Paris Conventions. The knowledge systems of the informal sector are not protected through intellectual property rights. They are often oral, built on trust, and defended through the norms and practices of traditional institutions. P. Mulvany, "TRiPs, Biodiversity and Commonwealth Countries:

peoples' are a major concern. Local communities have accumulated a broad technological knowledge base to conserve and sustainably use plant genetic resources.

Article 27 (3) (b)[51] of TRIPS speaks of the protection of plant varieties through an 'effective sui generis system'. However, it is not clear whether this term has been sufficiently defined to be useful in the context of the TRIPs Agreement and in any case, it is very difficult to determine what an effective sui generis system for plant varieties would entail. The International Convention for the Protection of New Varieties of Plants (UPOV),[52] introduced in 1978 provides one interpretation. Developing countries have been urged to adopt this treaty, and implement its interpretation of sui generis plant variety protection systems. However, very few developing countries have become members of UPOV, for two principal reasons.

First, while the 1978 version of the Convention allows farmers to re-use propagating material from the previous seasons' harvests, and to freely exchange seeds of protected varieties with farmers,[53] the 1991 version of the Convention is more stringent.[54] A farmer who produces a protected variety from locally developed or farmed seeds can be found guilty of patent infringement, unless a national law provides otherwise. Second, it has been argued that the 1991 UPOV Convention is inadequate for the protection of traditional knowledge of indigenous and local peoples, as it does not appropriately recognize the contributions of indigenous and local peoples toward plant breeding programmes.[55]

Capacity building priorities for the 1999 review of TRIPs Article 27. 3(b)" (1998) A Discussion Paper, Commonwealth Secretariat at 9.

[51] Article 27(3)(b) of TRIPS states that: 'Members may also exclude for patentability ... (b) plants and animals other than micro-organisms, and essentially biologically processes for the production of plants or animals other than non-biological and microbiological processes. However, members shall provide for the protection of plant varieties either by patents or by an effective sui generis system or by any combination thereof.'

[52] The Union internationale pour la protection des obtentions végétales (UPOV) or International Union for the Protection of New Plant Varieties was established by the International Convention for the Protection of New Varieties of Plants of 2 December 1961, 815 *UNTS* 11609 (1972), as amended. The 1978 Act of the UPOV Convention, which entered into force on 8 November 1981, ensures that Member States acknowledge the achievements of breeders of plant varieties, by making available to them exclusive property rights on the basis of a set of uniform and clearly defined principles. To be eligible for the protection, varieties have to be 1) Distinct from existing commonly known varieties; 2) Sufficiently homogenous; 3) Stable; and 4) New in the sense that they must not have been commercialised. Like all intellectual property rights, the rights of plant breeders are granted for limited periods of time, at the end of which the varieties protected by them pass into the public domain. Authorisation from the holder of the right is not required for the use of the protected variety in research, including its use in breeding further new varieties.

[53] *Ibid.*

[54] A further amendment to the UPOV Convention took place on 19 March 1991 and entered into force on 24 April 1998.

[55] J. Mugabe, P. Kameri-Mbote & D. Mutta, "Traditional Knowledge, Genetic Resources and Intellectual Property Protection: Towards a New International Regime" (2001) Working Paper of the International Environmental Law Research Centre, 20001-5, Geneva, available at: www.ielrc.org/content/w0105.pdf

As one alternative solution, at the global level, the TRIPS Agreement could offer protection to traditional knowledge through Article 22(1) on geographical indications, which 'identify a good as originating in a territory of a WTO member, or a region or locality in that territory, where a given quality, reputation or other characteristic of the good is essentially attributable to its geographic origin'. Like trademarks, these allow producers to differentiate between themselves and to segment the market, thus achieving higher returns provided consumers are willing to pay a price premium for their distinct product. Geographical indications have certain characteristics that are more in line with the ways in which traditional communities use their knowledge. They are based on collective traditions and a collective decision-making process; they protect and reward traditions while allowing evolution; they emphasize the relationships between culture, land, resources and environment; they are not freely transferable from one owner to another; are not subject to unconditional control by a private owner; and can be maintained as long as the collective tradition is maintained.

Similarly, collective marks or certification marks, which are usually owned by associations of producers, could also be used to protect goods based on traditional knowledge. For example, in the United States the Intertribal Agriculture Council licenses use of its annually-renewable 'Made by American Indians' mark for the promotion of agricultural or other Indian-made products that have been produced and/or processed by enrolled members of recognized tribes.[56]

As another alternative, national legislation could be used to fill the gap. With such legislation in place, jurisprudence could develop that recognises and enforces traditional knowledge and farmers' rights. The African Union (formerly the Organisation of African Unity) has designed a draft 'African Model Legislation for the Protection of the Rights of Local Communities, Farmers and Breeders, and for the Regulation of Access to Biological Resources'.[57] It provides that a written contract shall be entered into by the state and the collector, but with the full participation and approval of the concerned local community or communities. It further suggests an institutional arrangement for developing a system of registration of items protected by community intellectual property rights and farmers' rights according to their customary practices and law. Other provisions pertain to the development of national information systems to compile and document

---

[56] United Nations Conference on Trade and Development, *System and National Experiences for Protecting Traditional Knowledge, Innovations and Practices* 22 August 2000 TD/B/COM.1/EM.13/2 at 12.
[57] African Union, *AU Model Law for the Protection of the Rights of Local Communities, Farmers and Breeders, and for the Regulation of Access to Biological Resources.* (2000, Algeria) Available online: <http://www.grain.org/brl_files/oau-model-law-en.pdf>.

information on local knowledge and innovation practices of communities and guidelines for collectors of resources.[58]

At the national level, several developing countries have enacted legislation to regulate and protect their plant varieties, and have also ratified the TRIPs Agreement thereby giving effect to Article 27(3)(b) relating to the protection of plant varieties. Developing country scholars have argued that traditional knowledge held by indigenous and local communities now forms part of the product discovery process of the industrialized world, but that this knowledge is not recognized and adequately protected by conventional intellectual property protection systems.[59] Their suggestion is that sui generis legislation systems need to be developed that would name the sources of genetic material and traditional knowledge used in new products and allow for the sharing of benefits arising from the use of such genetic material and knowledge. Three particular examples can be provided.

First, the Kenya *Seeds and Plant Varieties Act*, 1972 amended in 2002,[60] confers power to the Minister to regulate transactions in seeds, including provisions for the testing and certification of seeds; for the establishment of an index of names of plant varieties; to impose restrictions on the introduction of new varieties; to control the importation of seeds; to authorise measures to prevent injurious cross-pollination; to provide for the granting of propriety rights to persons breeding or discovering new varieties; to establish a tribunal to hear appeals and other proceedings.

Second, in a similar way, the Belize *Protection of New Plant Varieties Bill*, 2000,[61] gives effect to breeders` rights. Both the Kenya and the Belize legislations recognise breeder's rights and provide for the protection of new plant varieties.

Third, the India *Protection of Plant Varieties and Farmers' Rights Act*, 2001,[62]goes further by recognising not only the rights of breeders but also the rights of farmers. The legislation also stresses the importance of recognizing and protecting the rights of the farmers in respect of their contribution made at any time in conserving, improving and making available plant genetic resources for the development of new plant varieties. In this respect, a farmer is also defined as any person who "conserves and preserves .... any wild species or traditional varieties or adds value to such wild species or traditional varieties through selection and identification of their useful

---

[58] UNCTAD, *System and National Experiences, supra* note 55, at 14.
[59] Mugabe, Kameri-Mbote & Mutta, *supra* note 54.
[60] The Seeds and Plant Varieties Act, 1972, as last amended and published on June 7, 2002 in the Official Kenya Gazette, Supplement No.49.
[61] Protection of New Plant Varieties Bill, 2000, Belize, Gazette 18th March 2000.
[62] The Protection of Plant Varieties and Farmers' Rights Act (PPVFR), Act 53 of 2001, India.

properties."[63]   The legislation further provides that "the farmer who is engaged in the conservation of genetic resources of land races and wild relatives of economic plants and their improvement through selection and preservation shall be entitled in the prescribed manner for recognition and reward from the National Gene Fund; provided that material so selected and preserved has been used as donors of genes in varieties registrable under this Act."[64] The Indian legislation also provides for and regulates benefit sharing with respect to any variety registered under the Act [65] and provides for claims being made on behalf of any village or local community as regards their contribution in the evolution of any variety.[66]

Future Directions

What are the prospects for the legal protection of PGRFA, at national and regional levels, as well as under the 1992 UN Convention on Biological Diversity, the TRIPs Agreement and more particularly the 2001 FAO 'Seed Treaty'? The latter in particular holds out the potential for the promotion of sustainable development through the use of a truly multilateral system for access and benefit sharing plant genetic resources for food security but can it work?

The current international regime, which regulates the use of genetic materials for agriculture, is complex and continues to suffer from fragmented governance and conflicting interests. It will not be easy to ensure that seeds and crop germplasm development can be used in a sustainable manner that respects the rights of indigenous communities and local farmers, supports food security, and also provides for sustainable agricultural development.

While the entry into force of the 'Seed Treaty' may provide an important new instrument for sustainable development, several important issues remain to be resolved. The Seed Treaty's Multilateral System also includes PGRFA, which are held in the *ex situ* collections of the international agricultural research centres or IARCs, which are members of the Consultative Group on International Agricultural Research or CGIAR, as well as in the *ex situ* gene bank collections of other international institutions.[67] These *ex situ* collections alone cover some 660,000 accessions of crop germplasm.[68] The importance of the CGIAR collections cannot be underestimated. This informal association of 57 public and private sector members, drawn from developed and developing countries, private foundations and development banks, has historically worked on the basis of sharing resources and

---

[63] *Ibid*, Chapter I, Section 2(k).
[64] *Ibid.*, Chapter VI, Section 39(1)(iii).
[65] *Ibid.* Part IV, Section 26.
[66] *Ibid.* Part VI, Section 41.
[67] M. Footer, *supra* note 15 at 433.
[68] *Ibid.*

knowledge, and has always been guided by the core principle that crop germplasm held in those research stations was collected from the fields and forests of farming communities in the developing countries of the Southern Hemisphere but that it is held 'in trust' for the benefit of the international community, in particular, for developing countries.

The Seed Treaty continues to recognise these *ex situ* collections of PGRFA as being held 'in trust' by the IARCs but they will now be guided by a new system of agreements to be concluded between them and the Governing Body under the Treaty.[69] As a general principle, the *ex situ* collections of crop germplasm, which are listed in Annex I of the Seed Treaty and are held by the IARCs, will henceforth fall under the Multilateral System and will be subject to the Seed Treaty provisions.[70] Financial benefits flowing from the exchange of germplasm in the *ex situ* collections that fall under the Multilateral System, i.e. the Annex I listings held by the IARCs, will accrue to the funding mechanism to be set up under the Treaty (the Trust Account), again with monetary and other benefits being used for conservation and sustainable use of the PGRFA in national and regional programmes located in developing countries, which are centres of genetic diversity, and least developed countries. [71]

---

[69] ITPGRFA 2001, *supra* note 6, Article 15, paragraph 1.
[70] ITPGRFA 2001, *supra* note 6, Article 12, paragraph 1(a).
[71] *Ibid.*

Conclusions

Access to genetic resources and benefit sharing has several important legal aspects, in both domestic and international law. These laws hold the potential to recognise the value of biodiversity and plant genetic resources for food and agriculture, financing and encouraging their sustainable use. They could also result in un-kept promises, with difficult consequences for the world's most vulnerable peoples and their food security and survival. A rights-based perspective is essential, as access to these special resources is multi-faceted. It involves sensitive questions of sovereign rights, rights of individuals and the collective rights and needs of important claimants and stewards, especially indigenous peoples, community and local farmers'. Coordination and coherence will be extremely important. The United Nations Convention on Biological Diversity provides a general context, but there are many other initiatives of both a public and private character in the field of genetic resources at the international, regional and domestic levels. Of particular relevance, in this regard, is the International Treaty on Plant Genetic Resources for Food and Agricultural (ITPGRFA) of the Food and Agriculture Organisation (FAO), which has recently entered into force. At present, this is an emerging and rapidly evolving area of sustainable development law, particularly with regards to the legal provisions for the sustainable use of plant genetic resources for food and agriculture. Much will depend on the nature, scope and sensitivity of implementation efforts which have just begun. It is a crucial field of study for the next decades. The human rights, survival and food security of peoples, their ecosystems and their economies, lives depend on its successful and sustainable implementation.

15

WHEN BIOSAFETY BECOMES BINDING: IMPLEMENTING THE CARTAGENA PROTOCOL

Kathryn Garforth[1]

This chapter provides an overview of decision making under the *Cartagena Protocol on Biosafety*.[2] It is intended to serve as an introduction to some of the key links between sustainable development law and biosafety, paving the way for a more in-depth analysis in the future. The chapter focuses on precaution and sound science in decision-making, and offers ideas from existing biotechnology and biosafety regulatory frameworks.

The Biosafety Protocol is an interesting example of sustainable development law, as it is part of a growing trend towards hybrid multilateral agreements.[3] These treaties are not purely economic, environmental or social- rather, they incorporate elements of all these areas of sustainable development. The Biosafety Protocol has strong links to trade law via the Protocol's focus on transboundary movement of Living Modified Organisms (LMOs) and their socio-economic implications; links to environmental law through the Protocol's foundation in the precautionary principle and use of sound science; and links to social and human rights law through its elements of public awareness, public participation, and public right to know.

---

[1] Kathryn Garforth, LL.B. (Osgoode Hall), M.E.S (York), Research Fellow, Centre for International Sustainable Development Law (CISDL). The author would like to thank Marie-Claire Cordonier-Segger, CISDL Director and Worku Damena, Associate Legal Affairs Officer, Secretariat of the Convention on Biological Diversity for their substantive intellectual contributions.
[2] *Cartagena Protocol on Biosafety to the Convention on Biological Diversity*, 29 January 2000, 39 ILM 1027 (entered into force 11 September 2003) [*Biosafety Protocol*].
[3] U.P. Thomas, "The CBD, the WTO, and the FAO: The Emergence of Phytogenetic Governance" in Philippe G. LePrestre, ed., *Governing Global Biodiversity: The Evolution and Implementation of the Convention on Biological Diversity* (Aldershot: Ashgate, 2002) 177 at 200.

M.C. Cordonier Segger & C. G. Weeramantry, eds., Sustainable Justice: Reconciling Economic, Social & Environmental Law
© 2005 *Koninklijke Brill NV, Printed in The Netherlands, pp.259-270.*

Biosafety and the Cartagena Protocol

What is 'Biosafety' and Why Is It a Concern?

Biosafety is not defined in either the Cartagena Protocol or the *Convention on Biological Diversity*[4] (CBD). However, according to the Secretariat to the CBD, "[b]iosafety is a term used to describe efforts to reduce and eliminate the potential risks resulting from biotechnology and its products."[5]

The potential risks can be grouped into the three areas of sustainable development. Environmental concerns include the potential for living modified organisms released into the environment to become pests, to out-compete and replace their wild relatives, to increase dependence on pesticides, or to spread their introduced genes to weedy relatives, potentially creating 'super-weeds.'[6] Social concerns include threats to human health from new allergens in the food system, threats to traditional agricultural practices such as seed-saving, and ethical concerns over patenting life and the treatment of animals.[7] Finally, economic concerns include concentration of the life sciences industry in Western industrialized countries and potential international trade difficulties caused by the challenge of integration or mutual recognition of different national biotechnology policies and practices.[8] Potential social, economic and environmental impacts must be further studied.[9]

Evaluating the true risks of environmental and health concerns hinges upon improvements in the science of biosafety. As experience is gained with genetically modified organisms (GMOs), we also gain knowledge of their benefits and pitfalls. In the case of food crops, modern varieties of plants may be so far removed from their wild relatives that they become less hardy and well-suited for persisting as pests in the wild.[10] Furthermore, introduced traits such as herbicide resistance are unlikely to confer an advantage to a wild plant as it is unlikely to be exposed to the herbicide outside an agricultural setting. More research is needed, however, on the release of plants with traits such as disease resistance or stress tolerance, as these are characteristics that may

---

[4] *Convention on Biological Diversity*, 5 June 1992, 31 I.L.M. 818 (entered into force 29 December 1993) [*CBD*].
[5] "Frequently Asked Questions on the Biosafety Protocol", online: Convention on Biological Diversity, <http://www.biodiv.org/biosafety/faqs.asp?area=biotechnology&faq=2>.
[6] R. Salazar & M. Valverde, *Biosafety, Consumer Protection and International Trade* (Costa Rica: November 2000), online: Canadian Institute for Environmental Law and Policy <http:// www.cielap.org/biotechsp.pdf>.
[7] *Ibid.*
[8] *Ibid.*
[9] D. Stabinsky, "Bringing Social Analysis Into a Multilateral Environmental Agreement: Social Impact Assessment and the Biosafety Protocol" (2000) 9 *Journal of Environment & Development* 260 [Stabinsky].
[10] The Royal Society of Canada, *Elements of Precaution: Recommendations for the Regulation of Food Biotechnology in Canada* (Ottawa: The Royal Society of Canada, 2001), 2001) at 121, online: <http://www.rsc.ca/foodbiotechnology/indexEN.html> [*Elements of Precaution*].

increase fitness in the wild, resulting in "super-weeds" could spread and become very difficult to eliminate.[11]

Gene flow is the movement of genes between individual organisms and it is a normal part of the process of evolution. In the case of genetically modified organisms, gene flow can result in the spread of introduced genes to other non-modified individuals. This raises the concerns mentioned above, and could also create difficulties for patent litigation where the modified genes are patented. Physical and spatial barriers can help to reduce gene flow although enforcing their use can be challenging.[12] Further research is needed in the areas of both science and policy to determine the extent of the gene flow problem and ways to resolve it. This work is particularly important as countries prepare for the introduction of crops that have been modified to produce industrial or pharmaceutical chemicals.

The introduction of new genes into an organism destined for human consumption also raises concerns about allergies. Genes produce proteins and increasing exposure to proteins not previously consumed by humans could pose a problem, particularly in a system where the use of genetically modified products cannot be traced.[13] Still, genetically modified foods are not necessarily unique in this respect since organisms obtained through more conventional breeding techniques can also produce novel proteins. To date, the consumption of genetically modified foods by a large number of people over a period of at least five years is not believed to have elicited allergic reactions.[14] However, further research on human allergies and genetic modification is required in order to reduce the risks in the coming years.

What is the Cartagena Protocol?

In 1992, world leaders met at the Earth Summit in Rio de Janeiro and agreed to the *Convention on Biological Diversity*. Included in the Convention is Article 19 on the handling of biotechnology and distribution of its benefits. In paragraph 3, the parties agreed to:

> "consider the need for and modalities of a protocol setting out
> appropriate procedures, including, in particular, advance

---

[11] GM Science Review Report, *An Open Review of the Science Relevant to GM Crops and Food Based on the Interests and Concerns of the Public* (July 2003), online: GM Science Review
<http://www.gmsciencedebate.org.uk/report/pdf/gmsci-report1-pt1.pdf>.
[12] *Elements of Precaution, supra* note 10 at 125. In North America, the most widely grown crop varieties are not native to the area so there are few wild or weedy relatives available to reproduce with genetically modified varieties. In a country like Mexico, which is a centre of diversity for corn, the potential for the introduced genes in genetically modified corn to spread is much higher. This could jeopardize the wild corn varieties, which are important sources of biodiversity, though this is only likely where the genes do increase the fitness of the corn.
[13] *Elements of Precaution, supra* note 10.
[14] *Ibid.*

informed agreement, in the field of the safe transfer, handling and use of any living modified organism resulting from biotechnology that may have adverse effect on the conservation and sustainable use of biological diversity."

After a long and contentious negotiating process, fraught with several stops and starts, the promise of Article 19(3) was brought to fruition when the parties agreed to the Biosafety Protocol in January 2000. As a protocol to the CBD, the objective of the Biosafety Protocol is very similar to the objectives of the CBD. The Protocol aims "to contribute to ensuring an adequate level of protection in the field of the safe transfer, handling and use of living modified organisms resulting from modern biotechnology that *may have adverse effects on the conservation and the sustainable use of biological diversity*".[15] This objective is rooted in the precautionary principle as set out in Principle 15 of the Rio Declaration[16] and it seeks to fulfill the first two objectives of the CBD, namely conservation and sustainable use of biodiversity.[17]

The Core of the Protocol: Procedures for Advanced Informed Agreement and Living Modified Organisms for Food, Feed or Processing

The Protocol divides living modified organisms (LMOs) into several categories. The two main groups of concern are LMOs that are intended for introduction into the environment of an importing Party, and LMOs for use as food, feed or for processing (LMOs-FFP). The first group of LMOs is subject to the Advance Informed Agreement (AIA) procedure contained in Articles 7 through 10 of the Protocol. This procedure requires the Party that intends to export LMOs to notify, or to require the exporter to notify, the Party that is destined to be the importer.[18] The notification must include, as prescribed in Annex I of the Protocol, descriptions of the organism in question, intended use, and the regulatory status of the LMO in the country of export. The importing party is then required to acknowledge receipt of the notification by indicating "[w]hether to proceed according to the domestic regulatory framework of the Party of import or according to the procedure specified in Article 10."[19] Article 10, in turn, sets out a decision-making procedure that parties can use to determine whether to approve or prohibit the import, or request additional information. The procedure includes a risk assessment and allows the party of import to use precaution to avoid or minimize the potential adverse effects of the LMO where there is scientific uncertainty.[20] The AIA procedure applies

---

[15] *Biosafety Protocol, supra* note 2 at Art. 1, emphasis added.
[16] See the secction 'Key Considerations for Decision-Makers', below for the text of Principle 15.
[17] *CBD, supra* note 4 at Art.1.
[18] *Biosafety Protocol, supra* note 2 at Art. 8(1).
[19] *Ibid.* at Art. 9(2)(c).
[20] *Ibid.* at arts. 10(1) and 10(6).

primarily to LMOs such as seeds, fish and other modified organisms intended for release into the environment.[21]

The second procedure concerns living modified organisms for direct use as food, feed, or for processing, in other words, LMOs like corn and soy that are traded as commodities intended for consumption rather than for release into the environment.[22] Article 11 requires a party that makes a decision concerning domestic use of an LMO-FFP that may be subject to transboundary movement to notify the other parties of the decision via a Biosafety Clearing-House established elsewhere in the Protocol.[23] The purpose of this provision was to be "relatively speedy [in comparison to the AIA] while allowing an importing country to exercise some degree of sovereignty and control over the regulation of imports of LMO-FFP commodities."[24] This procedure therefore allows countries to make their own decisions regarding the import of LMOs-FFP and these decisions can be based on precaution.

Key Considerations for Decision-Makers

Precaution & Sound Science in Biosafety Decision-Making

The objective of the Protocol begins by stating that it is "[i]n accordance with the precautionary approach contained in Principle 15 of the Rio Declaration on Environment and Development."[25] Principle 15 reads, in turn:

> "In order to protect the environment, the precautionary approach shall be widely applied by states according to their capabilities. Where there are threats of serious or irreversible damage, lack of full scientific certainty shall not be used as a reason for postponing cost-effective measures to prevent environmental degradation."[26]

As already described, both the AIA and the LMOs-FFP decision-making procedures allow parties to use precaution in determining whether to allow the importation of living modified organisms:

> "Lack of scientific certainty due to insufficient relevant scientific information and knowledge regarding the extent of

---

[21] A. Cosbey & S. Burgiel, *The Cartagena Protocol on Biosafety: An Analysis of Results* (2000), online: International Institute for Sustainable Development <http://www.iisd.org/pdf/biosafety.pdf> at 10 [Cosbey].

[22] *Ibid.*

[23] The provisions on the Clearing-House can be found in *Biosafety Protocol, supra* note 2 at Art. 20.

[24] F. Pythoud & U.P. Thomas, "The Cartagena Protocol on Biosafety" in Philippe G. LePrestre, ed., *Governing Global Biodiversity: The Evolution and Implementation of the Convention on Biological Diversity* (Burlington, VT: Ashgate Publishing Co., 2002) 39 at 48 [Pythoud].

[25] *Biosafety Protocol, supra* note 2 at Art.1.

[26] *Rio Declaration on Environment and Development* UN Doc. A/CONF.151/5/Rev.1 (1992), 31 ILM 874 (1992).

the potential adverse effects of a living modified organism on the conservation and sustainable use of biological diversity in the Party of import, taking also into account risks to human health, shall not prevent that Party from taking a decision, as appropriate, with regard to the import of that living modified organism … in order to avoid or minimize such potential adverse effects."[27]

The inclusion of the precautionary principle in the Protocol was not without controversy, however, as there are various definitions of the principle, little consensus on what it actually means, and debate over whether or not it is a principle of customary international law.[28]

The counterpoint to the use of the precautionary principle in decision-making is the need for risk assessment to be based on sound science. Both the AIA and the LMOs-FFP procedures incorporate risk assessment into their processes. Annex III to the Protocol contains guidelines for risk assessments under the Protocol including the principle that "[r]isk assessment should be carried out in a scientifically sound and transparent manner."[29] It is only once the risk assessment has been completed without resolving the scientific uncertainty or, where there is insufficient science to conduct the assessment in the first place, that parties can then turn to precaution and base their decision concerning the importation of an LMO on the desire of the party to protect the environment.[30]

The implementation of the Cartagena Protocol and its incorporation of the precautionary principle raise interesting questions concerning their relationship with world trade law. The *Agreement on the Application of Sanitary and Phytosanitary Measures*[31] that formed part of the outcome of the Uruguay Round of GATT negotiations also allows for the use of precaution. Article 5.7 states:

"In cases where relevant scientific evidence is insufficient, a Member may provisionally adopt sanitary or phytosanitary measures on the basis of available pertinent information, including that from the relevant international organizations as well as from sanitary or phytosanitary measures applied by other Members. In such circumstances, Members shall seek to obtain the additional information necessary for a more

---

[27] Art. 11(8). This paragraph is nearly identical to Art. 10(6) which allows for precaution in the AIA procedure. The ellipses in the above quote cover a specific reference to LMOs-FFP while the corresponding paragraph in Article 10 refers specifically to the LMOs covered by the AIA.

[28] See Pythoud, *supra* note 24; M-C Cordonier Segger & M. Gehring, "The WTO and Precaution: Sustainable Development Implications of the WTO Asbestos Dispute" (2003) 15 *Journal of Environmental Law* 289.

[29] *Biosafety Protocol, supra* note 2 at Annex III, para. 3.

[30] IUCN, *An Explanatory Guide to the Cartagena Protocol on Biosafety* (Cambridge, UK: International Union for Conservation of Nature and Natural Resources and FIELD, 2003) at para. 340 [IUCN].

[31] *Agreement on the Application of Sanitary and Phytosanitary Measures*, being part of Annex IA to the *Agreement Establishing the World Trade Organization*, 15 April 1994, 33 I.L.M. 1144 [SPS Agreement].

objective assessment of risk and review the sanitary or phytosanitary measure accordingly within a reasonable period of time."

This embodiment of precaution is much more limited than under the Biosafety Protocol. It places a positive obligation on parties to seek the information required to complete the scientific evidence and then review their measures in light of this information. The Biosafety Protocol *allows* states to review their decisions on importation of LMOs and also allows exporting parties to request such a review but there is no positive obligation comparable to that in the SPS Agreement.[32] The Protocol also allows parties to shift the burden of compiling evidence on the safety of an LMO to the exporter[33] whereas the SPS Agreement requires the party wishing to impose measures to consider the existing evidence and acquire additional information. As experts have commented, "the WTO agreements make it quite difficult for an importing country to use [precaution] arguments effectively to prevent the importation of agricultural commodities".[34]

At the same time, however, the Biosafety Protocol also helps to clarify what precaution might mean in the context of the SPS Agreement and beyond. The Protocol requires both risk assessment and risk management, and explains in Annex III what is involved in conducting a risk assessment.[35] Furthermore, the Protocol explicitly allows parties to consider socio-economic concerns in their decision-making,[36] a point on which the SPS Agreement is silent.[37] Finally, as some have argued, the Protocol established the precautionary principle as a principle of international environmental law and potentially of customary international law as well.[38] Should this be accepted it could clarify the status of the principle in the WTO, which to date has not recognized precaution as a principle of international law.[39]

Decision-Making under the Advance Informed Agreement Procedure

As described briefly above, Article 10 of the Protocol governs decision-making under the AIA procedure. Article 10 contains a complicated set of provisions that make reference to other parts of the Protocol. The Article must also be interpreted in light of other articles of the Protocol that are tied to its

---

[32] *Biosafety Protocol, supra* note 2 at Art.15.
[33] *Biosafety Protocol, supra* note 2 at Art.15(2).
[34] Pythoud, *supra* note 24 at 45.
[35] *Biosafety Protocol, supra* note 2 at arts.15 and 16; Cosbey, *supra* note 21 at 13.
[36] *Biosafety Protocol, ibid.* at Art. 26. See also Stabinsky at 261.
[37] Cosbey, *supra* note 21 at 14.
[38] *Ibid.*
[39] See *EC Measures Concerning Meat and Meat Products (Hormones)*, adopted on 13 February 1998, WT/DS26/AB/R, WT/DS48/AB/R

procedure. It is impossible to explore the full scope of Article 10 here so this discussion will focus on when it applies, and how it relates to Article 26 and the SPS Agreement.

The first step in understanding the decision procedure in Article 10 is to determine when the provision actually applies. For this, it is necessary to look at two other articles. Article 7(1) says that "the advance informed agreement procedure in Articles 8 to 10 and 12 shall apply prior to the first intentional transboundary movement of living modified organisms for intentional introduction into the environment of the Party of import." This means the decision procedure does not apply to non-intentional and non-transboundary movements of LMOs, or the regulation of LMOs-FFP or other types of LMOs that are governed by other parts of the Protocol.[40] Turning to Article 9, it is found that a party of import must inform the exporter "[w]hether to proceed according to the domestic regulatory framework of the Party of import or according to the procedure specified in Article 10." Thus the decision procedure in Article 10 does not apply to all instances when the AIA procedure is in effect, either. In fact, part of the purpose of Article 10 was to act as a safety net for those countries that have not yet enacted their own domestic biosafety legislation.

Once a state chooses to use Article 10, it must base its decisions on a risk assessment as outlined in Article 15 and Annex III. As discussed above, where the risk assessment is insufficient to resolve any scientific uncertainty, the importing state may use precaution in its decision-making. What is not referred to in Article 10 however, but addressed in Article 26, is the fact that parties making decisions about importation "may take into account, consistent with their international obligations, socio-economic considerations arising from the impact of living modified organisms on the conservation and sustainable use of biological diversity …"[41] There are two points about this provision. The first is that it relates to all decision-making under the Protocol, not just decision-making under the AIA procedure. The second is that it does not allow for an open-ended consideration of all socio-economic issues but only those that relate to the objective of the Protocol in ensuring the conservation and sustainable use of biodiversity.[42]

Returning to the SPS Agreement, various parts of its provisions require member states to consider economic factors both when determining domestic levels of sanitary and phytosanitary protection as well as when instituting measures to meet these desired levels of protection. These economic factors include "the potential damage in terms of loss of production or sales in the

---

[40] See in particular Articles 5 and 6 which cover LMOs for pharmaceuticals and transit and contained use.
[41] *Biosafety Protocol, supra* note 2 at Art. 26.
[42] IUCN, *supra* note 30 at para. 628.

event of the entry, establishment or spread of a pest or disease"[43] and "the objective of minimizing negative trade effects"[44]. No mention is made of social considerations. Seeing as the Biosafety Protocol requires socio-economic considerations to be compatible with states' other international obligations, decision-makers in states that are party to both agreements must be careful to ensure that implementation of the Protocol does not come into conflict with commitments under the WTO.

How will National Biosafety Regulations be Designed and Implemented?

A national biosafety framework is a combination of policy, legal, administrative and technical instruments that is set in place to address the environmental safety and human health aspects of the products and processes of biotechnology. Some frameworks focus specifically on biotechnology – they regulate the process by which new organisms and products are created. Other frameworks regulate the new products or organisms themselves, regardless of whether they are produced by biotechnology or other means.

Although national biosafety frameworks vary from country to country, they usually contain a number of common elements:

- A government policy on biosafety, often part of a broader policy on biotechnology.
- A regulatory system.
- A mechanism to handle requests for permits for certain activities, such as releases of GMOs into the environment.
- A mechanism for monitoring and inspections.
- A system to provide information to stakeholders about the national biosafety framework.[45]

A survey of some of the existing national regulatory frameworks helps to illustrate the current state of the law.

---

[43] SPS Agreement, *supra* note 31 at Art. 5.3.

[44] SPS Agreement, *supra* note 31 at Art. 5.4.

[45] UNEP Training Manual, *Implementing National Biosafety Frameworks*, online: Biosafety in Central and Eastern Europe <http://www.biosafety-cee.org/attachments/CEE%20-%20Training%20-%20%20manual.doc>. For background information and guidance on the development of government policies on biosafety, see, for example, M.A. McLean *et al.*, "A Conceptual Framework for Implementing Biosafety: Linking Policy, Capacity and Regulation" (2002) online: International Service for National Agricultural Research <http://www.isnar.cgiar.org>.

South Africa

South Africa passed the *Genetically Modified Organisms Act, 1997*[46] prior to the conclusion of the Biosafety Protocol. The Act has numerous goals, and seeks "[t]o provide for measures to promote the responsible development, production, use and application of genetically modified organisms; to ensure that all activities involving the use of genetically modified organisms (including importation, production, release and distribution) shall be carried out in such a way as to limit possible harmful consequences to the environment; … to lay down the necessary requirements and criteria for risk assessments".[47] The government also promulgated regulations under the Act, which set out the activities involving GMOs that require a permit. These activities include the importation and exportation of GMOs and the general release and marketing of GMOs.

Canada

Though Canada has not yet ratified the Biosafety Protocol, the Canadian government has developed a Canadian Biotechnology Strategy to govern the regulatory principles of biotechnology in Canada. Under this Strategy, different types of GMOs are governed by different pieces of federal legislation.[48] The *Seeds Act*[49] has been designated as the relevant legislation for genetically modified plants, and regulations on the release of seed have been adapted to cover the release of GM plants. These regulations require that an application to release modified seeds include information on things like the introduction and expression of the novel trait and the potential risks of the novel plant to the environment and human health before the plant can be approved for unconfined release.[50] That said, the applicant may be exempted from providing the environmental and human health information.[51] The Canadian Food Inspection Agency has also developed a regulatory directive on *Assessment Criteria for Determining Environmental Safety of Plants with Novel Traits*.[52] The information required under the directive is much the same as that required under the *Seeds Act* regulations including the potential exclusion of environmental and human health information.

---

[46] *Genetically Modified Organisms Act*, No. 15 of 1997, online: Gauteng Legislature <http://www.gautengleg.gov.za>.
[47] *Ibid.*, preamble.
[48] More specifically, products of biotechnology are regulated by specific statutes, or, if there is no designated statute, they fall under the *Canadian Environmental Protection Act, 1999*, S.C., c. 33.
[49] *Seeds Act*, R.S.C. 1985, c. S-8 [*Seeds Act*].
[50] *Seeds Act*, C.R.C., c. 1400, especially ss. 108-111.
[51] *Ibid.*, s. 110(4).
[52] Canada, *Regulatory Directive Dir94-08: Assessment Criteria for Determining Environmental Safety of Plants with Novel Traits* (1994), online: Canadian Food Inspection Agency <http://www.inspection.gc.ca/english/plaveg/pbo/dir/dir9408.shtml>.

Brazil

The Brazilian Act No. 8,974 of 1995 covers a wide area of biotechnology applications including stem cell research and the release of genetically modified organisms. The Act makes it a criminal offense to release or dispose of GMOs into the environment except under the standards set by the National Technical Commission on Biosafety (CTNBio).[53] Decree No. 1,752 of 1995 sets out the hierarchy, jurisdiction and structure of CTNBio including its role in proposing a National Biosafety Policy, and establishing standards and regulations for activities such as the making, transportation, consumption and release of GMOs. CTNBio also issues the Biosafety Quality Certificates required by organizations seeking to develop activities related to GMOs.[54]

These brief case studies are all drawn from policies and legislation that were developed prior to the conclusion of the Biosafety Protocol. Both South Africa and Brazil have only recently ratified the Protocol while Canada has signed but not yet ratified the Protocol. This means that even for those countries that already have some sort of biosafety regulatory framework in place, changes will likely be necessary in order to properly implement the Protocol.

The case studies illustrate one of the first choices faced by decision-makers in this area: whether to regulate the product or the process. In some countries, modern biotechnology and the products thereof are not seen to be fundamentally different from products created by older techniques such as cross-breeding. These countries, like Canada, choose to regulate the new product no matter how it was created. Other countries do perceive biotechnology to be fundamentally different from earlier human technologies, so they have laws, like Brazil's Act No. 8,794, which specifically regulate the process of biotechnology. This decision is as much a cultural issue as it is an economic or environmental one.

Finally, biotechnology and biosafety are two rapidly changing fields. Legislators must walk a fine line between drafting laws that are too precise, making them out of date by the time they are implemented, and drafting laws that only paint the broad brush strokes, leaving the details to the regulators and reducing the value of the democratic process. As a result, it is important for decision-makers to be aware of this balancing act and keep in mind that whatever laws they create on this issue will need to be regularly reviewed. The Biosafety Protocol itself acknowledges the continual change in the fields of biotechnology and biosafety. It provides for an assessment and review of the Protocol, including

---

[53] Brazilian Act No. 8,974 of 1995 at Art. 13(V).
[54] Decree No. 1,752, December 20, 1995 at Art. 8.

its procedures and annexes, five years after entry into force and at least every five years thereafter.[55]

Future Challenges

Building strong and lasting biosafety institutions depends on a number of factors. These include the continued development of the science of biosafety in conjunction with the continued development of the precautionary principle. Further discussion, debate and application of the precautionary principle will help to clarify its proper use both in the context of biosafety and beyond. At the same time, more research on the impacts of living modified organisms can reduce the need for decisions based on precaution.

It may be challenging to keep an open dialogue between countries and to respect the policy choices of other jurisdictions, but this sort of research can best be done through coordination and cooperation rather than through individual states acting in isolation. The Biosafety Clearing-House is a good step towards this goal as it provides decision makers with relatively easy access to information on biosafety initiatives in other countries. States can use these tools to survey other ideas and help decide what would and would not work for them.

Ultimately, decision-makers must keep in mind that biosafety law intersects with all three areas of sustainable development – the economic, the environmental and the social. Strong biosafety institutions will reflect not only the business and the science of biotechnology, but its cultural dimensions as well.

---

[55] *Biosafety Protocol, supra* note 2 at Art. 35.

SOCIAL AND ECONOMIC ELEMENTS OF CLIMATE CHANGE LAW

16

CLIMATE CHANGE LAW: NARROWING THE FOCUS, BROADENING THE DEBATE

Duncan A. French[1]

It is well recognized that the climate change phenomenon has never been just an 'environmental' issue, as traditionally conceived. As a consequence, the climate change 'regime,' from the outset, had a breadth and a contextual richness that went far beyond international environmental law *stricto sensu*. It is important to recognize when discussing the climate change regime that this is not simply a reference to the 1992 UN Framework Convention, the 1997 Kyoto Protocol and the work of the subordinate bodies established there under. To construe it in this way would not only be a gross simplification of the developing polity, but would also ignore the variety and complexity of the interactions and issues that permeate the climate change agenda. At the outset, it is important to acknowledge the role of the myriad of official, semi-official and non-official commercial, scientific and 'public-interest' communities that interact with and seek to influence the legal and political developments. It is beyond the scope of this chapter to detail the nature of the climate change regime, though special mention may be made of the Intergovernmental Panel on Climate Change (IPCC), whose reports have proved an increasingly scientific basis for international action.[2]

Climate change has an obvious symbiotic relationship with the concept of sustainable development. The preamble to the Convention affirms that "responses to climate change should be coordinated with social and economic development in an integrated manner with a view to avoiding adverse impacts on the latter, taking into full account the legitimate priority needs of developing countries for the achievement of sustained economic growth and the eradication of poverty." Some have even gone so far as to say that the

---

[1] Duncan French, B.A. (East Anglia), LL.M (Nottingham), Ph.D (Wales, Cardiff), Lecturer in Law, University of Sheffield, United Kingdom, Senior Research Fellow, Centre for International Sustainable Development Law (CISDL), Co-Rapporteur of the International Law Association Committee on International Law on Sustainable Development..

[2] IPCC, *Third Assessment Report,* online: IPCC online: <http://www.ipcc.ch>. As the IPCC's Third Assessment Report stated in 2001, '[t]here is new and stronger evidence that most of the warming observed over the last 50 years is attributable to human activities' and '[e]missions of greenhouse gases…due to human activities continue to alter the atmosphere in ways that are expected to affect the climate.'

M.C. Cordonier Segger & C. G. Weeramantry, eds., Sustainable Justice: Reconciling Economic, Social & Environmental Law
© *2005 Koninklijke Brill NV, Printed in The Netherlands, pp.273-284.*

international response to climate change, along with the 1992 Convention on Biological Diversity, "affirm the place of 'sustainable development' in international law" [sic].[3]

It is not the intention of this brief chapter either to seek to evaluate to what extent this is true or to dwell, at the conceptual level, on the nature of the interaction between climate change and sustainable development.[4] Instead, the chapter will set down five specific elements where the two issues arguably intersect, and where, in particular, the tenets of sustainable development – to the extent that such tenets exist – elaborate upon the strict textual requirements of climate change law.

Before focusing on these elements, however, three general observations can be made. The first is that the Climate Change Convention represents one of the most important attempts at integrating sustainable development and global environmental concerns. This is, of course, important at the instrumental level, since it embraces both Northern and Southern concerns in a delicate balance, neither giving undue pre-eminence to the global over the regional, national or local, nor – at the same time – ignoring the magnitude of the global problem. It encourages continuing dialogue between and within developed and developing states and seeks to promote active negotiations between the parties.

At a more substantive level, however, the Climate Change Convention represents evidence of the importance, if not legal necessity, of adopting a more integrated approach to international issues. Most may not want to go as far as former Vice-President Weeramantry in his separate opinion in *Gabcikovo-Nagymaros* (1997), where he puts forward his idea of sustainable development acting almost as a *legal* bridge between the right to development and the right to environmental protection,[5] but nevertheless most would accept the emerging normative significance of Principle 4 of the Rio Declaration in this regard. As Principle 4 notes, "environmental protection shall constitute an integral part of the development process and cannot be considered in isolation from it." Integration is at the heart of sustainable development and, as this chapter will make clear, it may be sustainable development's most important contribution to the legal debate.

---

[3] P. Sands, "International Law in the Field of Sustainable Development" (1994) 65 *Brit. Y.B. Int'l L.* 303 at 304.

[4] See further, D. French, *International Law and Policy in the Field of Sustainable Development* (Manchester: Manchester University Press, forthcoming).

[5] International Court of Justice, *Case Concerning the Gabcikovo-Nagymaros Project (Hungary/Slovakia)*, Separate Opinion of Vice-President Weeramantry, [1997], online: ICJ, < http://www.icj-cij.org/icjwww/idocket/ihs/ihsjudgement/ihs_ijudgment_970925_frame.htm >. See also V. Lowe, "Sustainable Development and Unsustainable Arguments" in A. Boyle and D. Freestone, eds., *International Law and Sustainable Development* (Oxford: Oxford University Press, 1999), 19 at 30-3: "it is a convenient, if imprecise, label for a general policy goal which may be adopted by states…It is clearly entitled to a place in the Pantheon of concepts that are not to be questioned in polite company, along with democracy, human rights, and the sovereign equality of states."

The climate change regime, however, is more than an example of integration in the abstract; it also has broader political significance. Consequently, the second general comment is that the climate change regime arguably represents the most politically important collaboration yet at bringing together social, economic and environmental factors within one framework. The question then becomes whether the necessary political will and legal mechanisms are available for it to succeed?

The international community is very good at dividing issues into manageable pieces. Since the emergence of the League of Nations and the United Nations system, there has been a trend towards the increased fragmentation and simplification of international law into subject-specific fields. Of course, such fragmentation has generally proven to be exceedingly beneficial in the development of international law; as demonstrated by the development of a workable and surprisingly efficient international legal system and, just as important, the emergence of an exceedingly competent international civil service. However, a negative aspect of this development has been the general lack of integration between subject areas, not only in terms of the substantive content of international law, but also the personnel who make up the international system.

Consequently, the international community has not been good – and remains poor – at being able to 'think outside the box.' The adoption of the Climate Change Convention and subsequent developments is a real attempt by the international community to try to move beyond this compartmentalization and take a much more holistic approach to an issue, as is, in any event, mandated by sustainable development. The success or otherwise of such an endeavour is, of course, debatable. But what is quite clear is that most states recognize the broader political implications of getting the climate change problem *right*, even if they cannot agree upon the measures necessary.

The decision of the United States to formally announce its intention not to ratify the Kyoto Protocol despite its earlier signature is therefore an unfortunate episode in the development of the climate change regime. Much has been written about the United States' decision. This chapter simply adds that whether one agrees with the US approach or not, it highlights a wider recognition that climate change is as much an economic and developmental question as it is an environmental one. It is – ultimately – an issue of sovereignty. With the most dramatic effects of climate change still very unclear, how a State decides to respond to climate change will inevitably have an impact upon its future development. On one level at least, the Bush Administration is right to recognize the magnitude of becoming a party to Kyoto. However, most would argue that the US rejection of the Protocol fails to take into account the wider context. It is only through the setting of challenging targets within an international framework that a scientifically appropriate and – as important – equitable solution can be negotiated for what is an inherently international issue. In the words of the Convention: "change in the Earth's climate and its adverse effects are a common concern of humankind." As has been noted elsewhere, sovereignty can no longer just be internally focused; it must 'not be treated as a static, immovable fact, but rather as a flexible tool through which states can more effectively act in an increasingly interdependent global society'.[6]

The third general comment is that by adopting the 2001 Marrakech Accords, which seek to elaborate upon the framework provisions of the Kyoto Protocol, the climate change regime has a real chance to become more than just a paper exercise (if and when it enters into force). Just as the Biodiversity Convention has the potential to be a very practical and holistic example of sustainable development 'in action' (and there is some evidence that the initial difficulties in implementation may be starting to subside), the full implementation of the Kyoto Protocol will dramatically alter the nature of the climate change regime. The largely discursive nature of the regime up to this point will become a much more serious endeavour, with real rules to implement and *enforce*. But there is also a real risk, discussed below, that hard rules, if not appropriately formulated, can ignore wider societal concerns. How such rules are made 'sustainable' will be crucial to the acceptability and ultimate success of the Kyoto Protocol.

The general acceptance of the role of sustainable development within the climate change regime includes a number of *particular* issues where climate change and sustainable development intersect. The relationship with sustainable development is more obvious for some of these issues than others. However, all share a common theme in that the science and politics of climate change do not, by themselves, provide definitive answers to these issues. In some ways, climate change is too restricted a sphere of discussion to deal with broader problems of society. The technological imperative of much of the climate change agenda needs the more contextual application of sustainable development to tackle such societal concerns. Five of these elements are the topic for the remainder of this chapter.

'State Responsibility': A Hard or Soft Approach?

One issue where sustainable development is likely to play an important role may seem, on first analysis, somewhat of a strained choice. However, the issue of the legal responsibility of states for climate change raises, in a very obvious way, the interaction between sustainable development and climate change. Nevertheless, this interaction has so far been largely ignored, and apart from the declarations made on signature of the Convention by a number of small-

---

[6] D. French, "A Reappraisal of Sovereignty in the Light of Global Environmental Concerns" (2001) 21 *L.S.* 376 at 399.

island developing States,[7] the question of state liability itself has been sidelined by the wider legal and political process.

In reality, the strict application of the law of state responsibility as recently codified by the International Law Commission to a broad scientifically and politically complicated area such as climate change is never likely to occur. Nor, in the long-term, would such a strict application of the law be particularly helpful to the international response to climate change, since it would create division rather than a more united sense of purpose.

Instead, in place of the traditional 'hard' rules relating to responsibility as a means of holding states to account for internationally wrongful acts, responsibility has become a 'softer' concept allowing the international community to build a broad consensus around the need for international cooperation. The notion of 'common concern' has become the leading metaphor in the debate, suggesting a more coordinated, more voluntary, approach. In particular, the commonality of the responsibility is the recognition that, to a greater or lesser extent, all states are responsible. However, common concern places a thin veneer of responsibility on the whole international community (or certain defined groups therein), but with no express legal obligation on any particular state, both in terms of its historic responsibility for the anthropogenic exacerbation of climate change and in terms of its responsibility for remediation and/or adaptation. This *de facto* exclusion of questions of legal liability for past actions in place of a more neutral focus was a political necessity to ensure broad participation in the climate change regime. Common concern places negotiation above legal accountability.

However, the issue of legal responsibility will not be sidelined forever, particularly as the effects of climate change become more obvious and more serious than they are today. This was recognized by those small island developing states that had added declarations to their signature. Such declarations should also prevent developed states, in the future, from arguing that the issue of state responsibility has been 'estopped' from being raised because of the decision to adopt a multilateral approach to the issue (*viz.* the Framework Convention). However, as noted above, there is nothing necessarily virtuous or politically astute about placing strict application of the law above political reality, and the need to find an acceptable balance between holding States to account and moving the political process forward will become an increasingly important aspect of the climate change negotiations.

---

7 See the identical declarations made by Fiji, Kiribati, Nauru and Tuvalu: 'signature of the Convention shall, in no way, constitute a renunciation of any rights under international law concerning state responsibility for the adverse effects of climate change, and that no provisions in the Convention can be interpreted as derogating from the principles of general international law'. Papua New Guinea added a similar declaration to its instrument of ratification.

The issue of state responsibility – along with so many other issues related to climate change – raises the necessity of incorporating a sustainable development perspective within the wider debate. In particular, the integration of socio-economic and environmental needs, as mandated by sustainable development, will provide a useful framework in which the international community can negotiate a balanced approach to past responsibility and future action. Developing states – particularly those states whose very existence is threatened – need significant assistance. Forcing developed states to accept as a legal obligation their responsibility, however, without also recognising the structural dependency that *all* States presently still have on the burning of fossil fuels, would jeopardise international cooperation, which is the only way of finding a possible solution.

Sustainable Development and the Contextualization of Climate Change

One of the most important points of contact between sustainable development and climate change is in the 'contextualization' of the climate change regime; in particular, the further elaboration of the numerous cross-cutting issues intrinsic to both the Framework Convention and the Kyoto Protocol. Key amongst them include the operation of the Clean Development Mechanism and the numerous international assistance funds (as operated by the Global Environment Facility), the implementation of the Conference of the Parties' strategies on the transfer of environmentally sound technologies and capacity-building, and the use of forestry and other land-use changes in developing countries as a means of reducing or capturing greenhouse gases.

The potential problem with all of these issues can best be summed up by the question: to what extent will the implementation of the climate change regime be placed within the wider sustainable development context in which such measures are expected to operate? In particular, to what extent will the flexibility provided for under the Framework Convention and Kyoto Protocol be implemented with regard to the social and economic context, particularly of developing countries?

It is beyond the scope of this chapter to go into great detail on any of the crosscutting issues. It is, however, sufficient to note that the problem highlights a key tension within the climate change debate. Is the goal of the climate change regime – as an environmental regime – to secure the stabilization, and then reduction, of greenhouse gases, in the most cost-efficient manner possible? Or does the climate change regime – taking into account, in particular, the structural nature of the issues involved – have a broader purpose?

While developed states would reject the argument that the climate change regime is an experiment in distributive justice in disguise, and developing states would almost certainly contest the extent to which they have received adequate benefits thereunder, it is quite clear that the climate change regime is not simply another multilateral environmental agreement. Its 'ultimate objective,' global nature, and economic focus all point towards a regime that is larger and more wide-reaching than one that is simply environmental in purpose.

On the face of it, significant concern is already paid to the developmental context. The 2001 Strategy (or 'Framework') on capacity-building, for instance, states that 'capacity-building must be country-driven, addressing the specific needs and conditions of developing countries and reflecting their national sustainable development strategies, priorities and initiatives.' Similarly, the Framework on the transfer of environmentally sound technologies notes that, to be effective, it must be a 'country-driven, integrated approach [involving] cooperation among various stakeholders.' This seems to be the right rhetoric, but of course the devil is in the detail. Win-win solutions (as regards tackling climate change and improving the situation of developing countries) or even the more idealistic win-win-win-win solutions (the third and fourth 'wins' recognizing that such action should be both pro-poor and environmentally sound) are noble aspirations but very difficult to achieve in practice.

The concern, of course, is that rather than a bottom-up community-orientated approach to sustainable development, the imperative of climate change will result in a rather singular vision of sustainable development that possesses little in the way of context and is imposed largely by developed states. In particular, issues such as the practical operation of the Clean Development Mechanism and the reliance on Southern forests as sinks as a technological solution to climate change will be implemented with little regard for the Southern context.[8] So, for example, adaptation measures much needed in many developing states will be sidelined by the political expediency of short-term emission reduction measures; and international funding of climate change will be so fixated on climate change abatement that it will ignore the wider socio-economic picture in which such funding occurs. These are very real issues and will ultimately determine the success or otherwise of the climate change regime.

Integration of Inter-Linkages

The Conference of the Parties at its meeting in Marrakech in 2001 noted in its Ministerial Declaration the need to recognise and improve upon the handling of inter-linkages between climate change and other sustainability-related issues; in particular, desertification, poverty and biodiversity loss. As the preamble to the

---

[8] See *Kyoto Protocol to the United Nations Framework Convention on Climate Change*, U.N. Doc. FCCC/CP/1997/7/Add.2, 37 I.L.M. 32 (1998) at Art. 12: '[t]he purpose of the clean development mechanism shall be to assist Parties not included in Annex I in *achieving sustainable development* and in contributing to the ultimate objective of the Convention, and to assist Parties included in Annex I in achieving compliance with their quantified emission limitation and reduction commitments…' (emphasis added).

Ministerial Declaration notes, '*Believing* that addressing the many challenges of climate change will make a contribution to achieving sustainable development.'[9]

Of substantive interest is the Ministerial Declaration's call to find greater synergies within multilateral environmental agreements to deal with 'problems of poverty, land degradation, access to water and food and human health.'[10] This is both a call for greater integration between the 'issue-areas' themselves and, as important, integration between the international and regional institutions concerned with such issues. Integration is more easily achieved *within* an institution, but real progress towards achieving sustainable development also requires much more integration *between* institutions.

Moreover, this is not just a question of more closely integrating climate change with other environmental and social issues, though that is obviously important. There is also a real need to consider how to integrate climate change considerations within the operation of international – as well as regional and national – economic institutions and operations. How should the future trade negotiations initiated at Doha seek to accommodate climate change? What should the response of the World Bank programme and the International Monetary Fund be to climate change as the effects of climate change become more apparent? International legal principles in the field of sustainable development will become increasingly relevant as the vulnerability of developing states to climate change grows and the need for adaptation becomes more pertinent. In particular, the largely ignored topics of over-consumption and production will finally be brought within the main debate.

Differentiation and Commonality Post-2012

An interesting issue yet to be faced – though one that the United States argues the international community should consider sooner rather than later – is the necessity for emission reduction obligations to be imposed on developing, as well as, developed countries. The United States has made its position very clear on this point; it refuses both on economic and environmental grounds the present exclusion of developing [non-Annex I] State Parties from the emission reduction obligations contained within Annex B of the Kyoto Protocol.[11]

But even if agreement were reached to adopt a broader approach to emission reductions, how might such obligations be set? Though the issue is not presently on the negotiation agenda, this is not a purely speculative discussion as there will inevitably be a debate prior to the start of the second commitment

---

[9] Input to the World Summit on Sustainable Development, Decision 1/CP. 7 The Marrakesh Ministerial Declaration, UN Doc FCCC/CP/2001/L.27/Rev.1 (2001), preamble.
[10] *Ibid.*
[11] U.S. Environmental Protection Agency, *Climate Change Review,* at 13-14, online: EPA <http://yosemite.epa.gov/OAR/globalwarming.nsf/content/ResourceCenterPublicationsPositionPapers.html>.

period post-2012, as to whether developing states should begin to reduce emissions so as to further the ecological integrity of the Kyoto Protocol. One should not also ignore the fact that if developing countries were to accept emission reduction targets, their allocations would potentially be available for purchase by developed states under international emissions trading.

On what basis, however, should such obligations be negotiated? How might the principle of common but differentiated responsibility as used elsewhere within the climate change regime and in international environmental law more generally relate to the future allocation of greenhouse gas emissions? Should differentiation be based on harm caused, on the percentage of global emissions actually emitted by a state, on the continuing necessity of leadership by the North, on the socio-economic status of the South, on some form of *per capita* equation, or on some other factor?

In other words, when and on what basis should the current principles of the leadership and past trends of developed states be superseded by a more universal conception of global responsibility? However, this in turn requires a balanced approach to climate change that takes into account wider legal and political norms, central to which is sustainable development. As Principle 3 of the Rio Declaration notes, environmental and developmental 'needs' must both be 'equitably' met.[12] What this means is subject to significant political debate, though the reliance on equity in this context surely requires a careful balancing of interests between, among other things, the necessity of early precautionary action and recognition that poverty reduction is a primary obligation of developing countries. How these – and other interests – are reconciled is a political judgment that will ultimately require international compromise.

Sustainable Development and the 'Ultimate Objective'

Finally, in relation to climate change and sustainable development, what should one make of the 'ultimate objective' of the Climate Change Convention? As Article 2 of the Framework Convention notes, "The ultimate objective of this Convention and any related legal instruments that the Conference of the Parties may adopt is to achieve, in accordance with the relevant provisions of the Convention, stabilization of greenhouse gas concentrations in the atmosphere at a level that would prevent dangerous anthropogenic interference with the climate system. Such a level should be achieved within a time-frame sufficient to allow ecosystems to adapt naturally to climate change, to ensure that food production is not threatened and to enable economic development to proceed in a sustainable manner."[13]

---

[12] Report of the United Nations Conference on Environment and Development, UNCEDOR, Annex 1, UN Doc A/CONF.151/26 (Vol. I) (1992) at principle 4, online: <
http://www.un.org/documents/ga/conf151/aconf15126-1annex1.htm>.
[13] *United Nations Framework Convention on Climate Change*, U. N. Doc. A/AC.237/18 (Part II) (Add. 1), Misc 6 (1993), Cm 2137; 31 I.L.M. 848 (1992).

What is the role of international law in such radical societal change? This is a difficult and complex issue, beyond the scope of the present paper, but key to unravelling the nuances of the provision is the notion of equity. Equity, as already mentioned, has legal and political implications. That may be why it is both a useful concept and a controversial one.[14]

As noted in the 2002 New Delhi Declaration of Principles of International Law Relating to Sustainable Development adopted by the International Law Association, equity is 'central to the attainment of sustainable development' and at its heart involves fairness between and within generations.[15] Intra-generational equity, 'the right of all peoples within the current generation of fair access to the current generation's entitlement to the Earth's natural resources,' may be a less-discussed concept, but it is arguably as important to the 'attainment of sustainable development' as inter-generational equity, 'the right of future generations to enjoy a fair level of the common patrimony.' Both are unquestionably vague notions, but ones that nevertheless provide a useful framework through which to try to conceive a better understanding of the 'ultimate objective' of the Climate Change Convention.

Fairness is difficult to define, but it inevitably requires as a minimum an integrated approach to all relevant considerations. This, however, raises a broader question about integration as a normative principle of international law. When one talks about integration, does one actually mean integration (in terms of a process of considering all relevant factors, while the decision may not in itself be considered as 'integrated' in isolation), or does one actually mean synthesis (the objective of achieving an 'integrated' result)? Is integration an obligation of process or a normative obligation of result? Professors Patricia Birnie and Alan Boyle argue that the decision of the International Court of Justice in *Gabcikovo-Nagymaros* supports the view that it is "the process of decision-making [that is] the key legal element in sustainable development, rather than the nature of the development."[16]

Many might contest this conclusion and argue that, in fact, the latter interpretation is significantly preferable as it sees integration as a substantive principle of public international law. However, international law works best when it is acting within the *realpolitik*. Why try to make international law something that it is not? The limited state practice that does exist in this area

---

[14] See D. French, "International Environmental Law and the Achievement of Intragenerational Equity' (2001) 31 *Envtl L. Rep.* 10469 at 10475-10477.
[15] Conference of International Law Association, "New Delhi Declaration of Principles of International Law Relating to Sustainable Development" (2002) Resolution 3/2002, online: ILA, < http://www.ila-hq.org/pdf/Sustainable%20Development/Sus%20Dev%20Resolution%20+%20Declaration%202002%20English.pdf>. Also appears in N. Schrijver & F. Weiss, eds., *International Law and Sustainable Development* (Leiden: Martinus Nijhoff, 2004) at 699.
[16] P. Birnie and A. Boyle, *International Law and the Environment,* 2nd ed. (Oxford: Oxford University Press, 2001) 96.

suggests, moreover, a rather narrower interpretation of integration. It is difficult to justify legally the notion that states are somehow under a *legal* obligation to *achieve* an integrated result. In any event, at what level should such integration occur: the project level, the programmatic level, or the societal level? Too much remains uncertain for integration to be anything more, at the present stage, than a requirement that the environment be considered in the same decision-making process as economic and social factors.

Conclusion

This chapter has tried to highlight why the climate change regime is not only an important topic in its own right, but is also intrinsically related to sustainable development. As noted above, while the climate change regime should not be seen as an attempt at distributive justice, it is fundamentally misconceived to focus the debate solely upon the environmental aspect. Sustainable development requires the adoption of a broader 'sustainability' perspective, one that recognises the various inter-linkages between climate change, economic development and social progress. The nature and extent of the 'sustainability' of the climate change regime will determine not only its own effectiveness, but also the likelihood of it being taken as a model for future international cooperation regimes.

17

COUNTING CREDITS: EMISSIONS REDUCTION REGISTRIES AS A FIRST STEP TOWARD CLIMATE CHANGE REGIMES IN NORTH AMERICA

Markus W. Gehring[1]

Several states in the USA have adopted legislation to establish CO2 emission registries. Based on case studies comparing the registry in the UK emission trading scheme, the registry for the new EU emission trading directive and several State emission registries in the US, this chapter addresses the following questions: Can the U.S. State registries be viewed as a first step towards State carbon trading schemes? How do these compare to the UK and the EU emission registries, and how will they relate? Do current registries allow entries from other emission reduction efforts outside the registries jurisdiction? Is linkage between the different systems possible, and if so, how? This chapter presents a comparative study of state emission registries in the U.S., the registry in the UK emission-trading scheme and the registry for the new EU emission-trading directive.

Climate Change and the Need for Global Cooperation

Climate change is a global social and environmental concern, it requires immediate action at all levels. Greenhouse gases - especially carbon dioxide – act like a blanket over the Earth's surface, inducing changes in the climate.[2]

[1] Markus W. Gehring, LLM (Yale), BCL (Hamburg) i.p., Lead Counsel for Trade, Investment and Competition Law, Centre for International Sustainable Development Law (CISDL), Researcher, Concerted Action on Trade and Environment (funded by the European Commission), Tutor of Public International Law, University College, Oxford Law Faculty. He wishes to thank Michelle Toering, a student of the McGill Faculty of Law, and Elliot Siemiatycki, student at McGill University, for their research assistance and valuable contributions. He must also Brennan van Dyke, Regional Director for North America of the United Nations Environment Programme, for excellent intellectual guidance and support in the research.
[2] The main GHGs are water vapour, carbon dioxide, ozone, methane, nitrous oxide, and halocarbons and other industrial gases. Emissions of carbon dioxide (mainly from burning coal, oil, and natural gas), methane and nitrous oxide (due mainly to agriculture and changes in land use), ozone (generated by automobile exhaust fumes and other sources) and long-lived industrial gases such as CFCs, HFCs, and PFCs are changing how the atmosphere absorbs energy - at an unprecedented speed. See J. T. Houghton *et al.*, eds., *Climate*

M.C. Cordonier Segger & C. G. Weeramantry, eds., Sustainable Justice: Reconciling Economic, Social & Environmental Law
© 2005 Koninklijke Brill NV, Printed in The Netherlands, pp.285-300.

While the world's climate has always varied naturally, the vast majority of scientists now believe that rising concentrations of "greenhouse gases" (GHGs) in the earth's atmosphere are overriding these processes, leading to potentially irreversible climate change. These concentrations are human-induced – the results of economic and demographic growth over the last two centuries since the industrial revolution.[3]

Projected impacts of climate change

Despite uncertainties about where climate changes will occur, the rate of change, and the magnitude, there is little debate on at least two key issues. First, because of the rapid build-up of GHGs, the earth's temperature will warm significantly, precipitation patterns will change, and sea levels will rise. The Third Assessment Report of the Intergovernmental Panel on Climate Change (IPCC), released in 2001, confirms that the climate will change more rapidly than previously expected, provoking many difficult consequences.[4]

Second, the adverse impacts of projected changes in climate will pose major challenges for all countries. Although a few people may benefit from climate change, the IPCC warns that more will suffer, with potentially dramatic negative impacts on human health, food security, economic activity, water resources and physical infrastructure.[5] While no one will escape the effects, poorer people and developing countries are the most vulnerable to negative impacts.

It is imperative to find solutions – ways to reduce greenhouse gas emissions cheaply and effectively. Under the United Nations Framework Convention on Climate Change (UNFCCC), the Kyoto Protocol specifies legally binding commitments by most industrialized countries (defined as Annex I countries) to reduce their collective GHG emissions by 5.2 percent compared to 1990

Change 2001: The Scientific Basis, Contribution of Working Group I to the Third Assessment Report of the Intergovernmental Panel on Climate Change (IPCC) (Cambridge: Cambridge University Press, 2001).
[3] Climate Change Secretariat, *A Guide to the Climate Change Convention and its Kyoto Protocol* (Bonn: UNFCCC, 2000), online: World Bank Group < unfccc.int/resource/guideconvkp-p.pdf >.
[4] Global mean surface temperatures are projected to increase by 1.4 - 5.8°C by 2100. Global mean sea levels are expected to rise by 9 - 88 cm by 2100, flooding many low-lying coastal areas. Changes in rainfall patterns are also predicted, increasing the threat of drought or floods. Overall, the climate is expected to become more variable, with a greater threat of extreme weather events (intense storms, heat-waves, etc). There is also the risk of abrupt and large-scale "surprises", for instance, the weakening or complete shut down of the ocean thermohaline circulation (such as the Gulf Stream), or the collapse of the Greenland and West Antarctic ice sheets. See R. T. Watson and the Core Writing Team, eds., *Climate Change 2001: Synthesis Report* (Cambridge: Cambridge University Press, 2001).
[5] Farming could be seriously disrupted with falling crop yields in many regions. Tropical diseases, such as malaria or dengue fever, are expected to spread into new areas. Fresh water, already in short supply in many arid and semi-arid regions, is likely to become even scarcer. While sea levels rise changing weather patterns could trigger large-scale migration from more seriously affected areas. See James J. McCarthy *et al.*, eds. *Climate Change 2001: Impacts, Adaptation & Vulnerability.* Contribution of Working Group II to the Third Assessment Report of the Intergovernmental Panel on Climate Change (IPCC) (Cambridge: Cambridge University Press, 2001).

levels by the period 2008-2012. How does emerging CO2 registry environmental legislation connect to these broader policy goals of reducing the GHG emissions, and preventing potentially devastating climate change?

From greenhouse gas inventory to reduction registry

There is general international consensus that GHG emissions need to be monitored. Indeed, 'GHG Inventories' are presently required by international obligations.[6] However, it is still unclear how these inventories relate to the new GHG registries, which are set up to record reduction efforts by all actors. The purpose of this chapter is to compare different reduction registration systems, and explore how these relate to GHG inventories and to the registries used for carbon emission trading.

The development of emission reduction registries is not directly linked to GHG inventories. GHG inventories are approximate assessments of the overall amount of GHG emissions from a given jurisdiction. Inventories are used to establish GHG baselines for UNFCCC obligations. Most inventories reveal that overall GHG emissions are still increasing. In contrast, the general aim of emission registries is to monitor reduction efforts generated by specific facilities or activities. Reduction efforts might be indirectly reflected in a given inventory as registries monitor GHG reductions. But these appear to focus on recording potentially valuable assets (for example, emission reduction credits) for future emission trading schemes, rather than on meeting UNFCCC obligations *per se*.

It has been argued that registries actually promote GHG emission reductions, because they raise awareness about reduction potential and reduction technology. However, their establishment (analyzed in more detail below) can also be seen as a mere regulatory fig leaf (sham regulation). Establishing a registry (mainly to record voluntary actions) can make it appear that something is being done, without making the tough choices inherent in an effective emission reduction program.

The history of carbon emission inventories

Debates concerning climate change as an environmental problem began in the U.S. in the late 1970s[7] It was almost a decade until discussions translated into action at the international level. During the UNFCCC negotiation at the beginning of the 1990s, there was little consensus among countries on how to address the problem. One of the very few binding obligations in the UNFCC was the agreement that all parties of the UNFCCC would install national GHG

---

[6] Climate Change Secretariat, *A Guide to the Climate Change Convention and its Kyoto Protocol* (Bonn: UNFCCC, 2000), online: UNFCC<http://unfccc.int/resource/guideconvkp-p.pdf>.
[7] US Council on Environmental Quality, *Annual Report 1980, Environmental Quality 1979* (Washington: CEQ, 1980).

inventories (Art. 4.1 a, UNFCCC).[8] In accordance with Articles 4 and 12 of the Convention, and the relevant decisions of the Conference of the Parties (COP), Parties to the Convention "submit national greenhouse gas inventories of anthropogenic emissions by sources and removals by sinks of greenhouse gases not controlled by the Montreal Protocol, to the UNFCCC secretariat."[9]

For Annex I Parties, two sequential processes have been established: annual reporting of national greenhouse gas inventories, and annual review of the inventories. These processes are supported by decisions, guidelines and tools-including computer software. Many countries have fulfilled the very basic obligation to submit inventories. The US submitted their third national inventory report in 2002.[10] The national inventory reports of GHGs have followed a common format since the year 2000 and are thus easier to summarize.[11]

These reports have a very general approach and contain estimated numbers of the overall emissions. Although there are guidelines and recommendations from the IPCC on how to set up a national GHG inventory[12] there cannot be any listed single source reductions. This is one of the gaps that the registries are meant to fill.

Example of a successful trading registry

There are a number of existing emission trading registries in North America for non-GHGs pollutants. The acid rain and the NOx trading registry in Ontario is an example of an existing, functioning emission reduction registry.[13] One of the principal lessons from the Ontario example is that a registry can become an essential tool for emission trading if it has a clear statutory basis and the registry is conceptually integrated into the emission trading regime. The Ontario system

---

[8] *United Nations Framework Convention on Climate Change*, U.N GAOR Intergov't Negotiating Comm., 5th Sess., U.N. Doc. FCCC/1992 (1992), reprinted in 31 I.L.M. 848 (1992) (entered into force Mar. 21, 1994) art. 4. [UNFCCC]: Commitments - 1. All Parties, taking into account their common but differentiated responsibilities and their specific national and regional development priorities, objectives and circumstances, shall: (a) Develop, periodically update, publish and make available to the Conference of the Parties, in accordance with Article 12, national inventories of anthropogenic emissions by sources and removals by sinks of all greenhouse gases not controlled by the Montreal Protocol, using comparable methodologies to be agreed upon by the Conference of the Parties;

[9] See UNFCCC Secretariat, "Greenhouse Gas Emissions," online: UNFCC<http://unfccc.int/program/mis/ghg/index.html>.

[10] *U.S. Climate Action Report- Third National Communication of the United States of America*, (Washington D.C.:; U.S. Department of State, May 2002) online:< http://unfccc.int/resource/docs/natc/usnc3.pdf>.

[11] COP UNFCCC - Fifth session - Bonn, 25 October - 5 November 1999 - Review of the Implementation of Commitments and of other Provisions of the Convention UNFCCC - guidelines on reporting and review, Agenda items 4 (a) and 4 (h) FCCC/CP/1999/716 February 2000. online:<http://unfccc.int/resource/docs/cop5/07.pdf>.

[12] IPCC, *Revised 1996 IPCC Guidelines for National Greenhouse Gas Inventories*, online: IPCC<http://www.ipcc-nggip.iges.or.jp/public/gl/invs1.htm>.

[13] See Ontario Emissions Trading Regulation (O.Reg. 397/01), effective 31 December 2001 & Ontario Emissions Trading Code and Technical descriptions of NOx/SO2 emission reductions, online: <http://www.ene.gov.on.ca/envregistry/016576er.htm>.

has also gained experience in recognizing NOx reduction credits generated in the U.S.A. As the NOx credits are required to fulfill a statutory requirement, they receive considerably more scrutiny from all parties concerned. Though there were many concerns about unified verification, accountability and transparency for credits generated outside Canada, the Ontario regulation contains very explicit requirements for the establishment of the baseline and the calculation of the emission reduction. Based on this experience, it appears easier to create the trading system first (at least in principle) and then institute the registry. An emission reduction registry can only truly begin to function if there is consensus as to what is being traded.

Case Studies: Registries as the Backbone of an Emission Trading Scheme

The UK Experience

The UK emissions trading scheme is the world's first economy-wide greenhouse gas emissions trading scheme.[14] The UK emissions trading scheme (ETS) was officially launched on April 2nd of 2002, with the opening of the Emissions Trading Registry. This is a government-run electronic register of the participants' accounts and trades. A total of 34 organisations ('direct participants' in the scheme) have voluntarily taken on a legally binding obligation to reduce their emissions against 1998-2000 levels, delivering over 4 million tonnes of additional carbon dioxide equivalent emission reductions in 2006.[15]

The scheme is also open to the 6,000 companies with climate change agreements. These negotiated agreements between business and government set energy-related targets. Companies meeting their targets will receive an 80% discount from the Climate Change Levy, a tax on the business use of energy. These companies can use the scheme either to buy allowances to meet their targets, or to sell any over-achievement of these targets.[16] The general principle is the creation of a market, which allows companies, which generate emission reductions to benefit financially by selling their "credits",[17] whilst companies

---

[14] The UK is the first country to introduce an economy wide domestic emissions trading scheme. It is based on a cap and trade system, where companies reduce their emissions over time in order to reach a fixed emissions target while having enough of allowances to cover their emissions. If companies find themselves below their targets they will be able to sell the excess allowances and if they are above their targets they will have to buy allowances. While the scheme is voluntary, companies involved have been offered financial incentives by the government.

[15] In 1997, at the Kyoto Summit on Climate Change, the EU signed up to an agreement to reduce Greenhouse Gas Emissions by 8% on 1990 levels during the years 2008 - 2012. The UK share was a commitment to reduce by 12.5% on 1990 levels during the years 2008 - 2012.

[16] In March 1998 Lord Marshall was asked to produce a report on economic instruments and the business use of energy. This initially led to the introduction of the Climate Change Levy, now followed by a further measure recommended by Lord Marshall, the introduction of an Emissions Trading Scheme.

[17] The terminology of '*Credit*' used in draft framework document for the UK Trading Emissions Scheme is 'The commodity derived from domestic or international emission reduction projects representing a single

who have failed to reduce will be financially penalised by having to buy "credits" to make up their shortfall.[18]

The UK trading scheme is mainly based on a policy that was not put in the form of a law. The principal part of the policy regulates, seen as the backbone of the emission-trading scheme is the registry.

It may be an over-simplification to perceive the whole system as being based solely on a functioning registry, as has been done in the past.[19] While it is the role of government is to be responsible for the registry, many other trading activities are carried out by private entities. While it is still quite early to draw final conclusions, the UK carbon emission trading experiences seem to indicate that the registry regulation is essential to emission trading.[20] The system mainly works through the Internet. The contractual nature of trading depends on registry rules. Participants in the system feel that the rules governing the registry are an essential element of the ETS. The UK follows a soft-touch approach with regard to trading, while maintaining a high level of verification and accountability. When recognized, the emission-trading scheme becomes part of a broader climate change program that is clearly embedded in British GHG emission reduction efforts.[21] There is no need for companies to register their reductions because these emission reductions become relevant through the 'credits' that remain unused for the company.

This system is diametrically opposed to the current registry efforts in the US states. In contrast to the American registries, which aim to register real world

---

tonne of carbon dioxide equivalent and able to be traded in the Scheme.' See Department of the Environment, Transport and the Regions (DETR), *Draft Framework Document for the UK Emissions Trading Scheme* UKETS 01(01) (May 2001), at 7, online: DETR < http://www.ghgprotocol.org/docs/UKETS_trading2.pdf>.

[18] The companies who volunteered to participate set their targets through an auction process, which was completed on 12 March 2002. Companies in the auction bid in accordance with the level of emissions reductions they would make below their baseline level in 2006. These bids have been used to set emissions targets for the next five years. The auction finished at a price of £53.37 per tonne of carbon dioxide equivalent emission bid into the auction.

[19] Anthony Hobley *et al.* "The EU Emission Allowance Trading Scheme: A Prototype for Global GHG Emissions Allowance Trading?" [May 2001] Environmental Finance, 17, online: IETA <http://www.ieta.org/Documents/New_Documents/B&M17_20.pdf>.

[20] DEFRA, *The UK Emissions Trading Scheme - Auction Analysis and Progress Report*, (Oct. 2002), online: DEFRA <http://www.defra.gov.uk/environment/climatechange/trading/pdf/trading-progress.pdf>.

[21] The UK Climate Change Programme, published in November 2000, sets out how the UK Government and the devolved administrations propose to meet these climate change targets. The programme sets out a range of integrated policies, including an emissions trading scheme, that are designed to reduce greenhouse gas emissions across all sectors of the economy and to prepare the UK for significant emissions reductions needed in the future. The programme could reduce UK emissions up to 23 per cent below 1990 levels by 2010, levels well beyond the Kyoto target. The UK emissions trading scheme will be voluntary and open to all organizations operating in the UK. The trading scheme will not stand in isolation; it will compliment and inject flexibility into related policy instruments. For example, energy-intensive companies that have entered into climate change agreements in order to receive an 80 percent discount from the Climate Change Levy will also be able to trade in order to meet emissions targets. The government also proposes that the trading scheme link to other trading initiatives such as the renewable energy obligation and Energy Efficiency Commitment. See DEFRA, *Climate change-The UK Programme,* (updated Feb. 2001), online: DEFRA <http://www.defra.gov.uk/environment/climatechange/cm4913/index.htm>.

reductions of GHGs, the UK includes these reductions as part of the individual company's calculation. The more reductions a company creates, the more it can sell off unused emission credits. The reduction registries in the US would have to convert the registered reductions into additional 'credits'. In the case of the UK, it is not permitted to create credits outside the system and thus international exchange is only possible through the swapping of credits within the system.[22] This means that even if the most significant impediments were disregarded (the withdrawal of the US from the Kyoto Protocol), there would be few ways to devise a functional link between the American US states registered emission reductions and the UK GHG credits.

Canadian Experience with Reporting

The first part of the overall backstop legislation has recently been adopted in a public notice published on March 13, 2004 pursuant to the Environmental Act of Canada:[23] This states: "[n]otice is hereby given, pursuant to subsection 46(1) of the Canadian Environmental Protection Act, 1999, that, with respect to emissions of GHGs identified in Schedule 1 [List of the six Kyoto GHGs] and for the purpose of conducting research, creating an inventory of data, formulating objectives and codes of practice, issuing guidelines or assessing or reporting on the state of the environment, any person who operates a facility described in Schedule 2 [Defines a 100 kilotonnes CO2 equivalent threshold] to this notice during the 2004 calendar year and who possesses or who may reasonably be expected to have access to information described in Schedule 3 [lists the reportable information such as company name, process and emissions according to source] shall provide the Minister of the Environment with this information no later than June 1, 2005."

In the first phase, only those facilities that emit more than 100 kilotonnes of CO2e per year are required to report their emissions. This includes major industrial facilities that produce electricity, heat or steam using fossil fuels, certain power generating facilities, integrated steel mills, facilities involved in smelting and refining metals, petroleum refineries, and chemical producers. Many of these have already begun registering their GHGs.[24]

Statistics Canada will be the implementing agency for this registry legislation. It was allegedly chosen because of its highly reliable and cost effective reporting,

---

[22] Both companies have subsidiaries in two different emission trading schemes. They both want to sell credits in one scheme and need more credits in the other, which allows them to exchange an appropriate number of credits.
[23] Notice with respect to reporting of greenhouse gases (GHGs) for 2004, C. Gaz., 2004. Vol. 138, No. 11, online: <http://canadagazette.gc.ca/partI/2004/20040313/html/notice-e.html#i3>.
[24] Government of Canada, The Green Lane, *First Phase of Mandatory Greenhouse Gas Emissions Reporting* [Backgrounder], (12 March, 2004) online: <http://www.ec.gc.ca/press/2004/040312_b_e.htm>.

and its positive working relations with industry, federal, provincial and territorial governments and NGOs.[25] The 2004 reports is due on June 1, 2005.

The EU Plan for Registry Regulation

The European Union plans for January 2005 to establish a common GHG emission trading scheme (EU ETS), based on a European Directive that entered into force on 25 October 2003..[26] A directive is a European framework legislation that requires either a national statute or laws to be implemented. This will give countries considerable discretion over how they enact the trading scheme, which industrial sectors they include, etc.

In the process of designing the EU's ETS, it was recognized that EU-wide trading would only be possible with a common registry system. In addition, it was decided that while the ETS will be based on a European Directive, a European Regulation must establish the Registry itself. Regulations are directly applicable, with force of law, in all current EU member states. (There is some discussion as to whether the new member states will be included in the carbon market, as most of them are Annex I countries recognized as Economies in Transition.) The draft regulation is currently undergoing preparation.[27]

The Commission plans that each member state will establish an individual register that is fully compliant with the UNFCCC rules, in particular Decision 19/CP.7 of the Conference of the Parties to the UNFCCC. Art. 1 of the draft Regulation lays out the purpose: "Regulation lays down general provisions, functional and technical specifications and operational and maintenance requirements concerning the standardised and secured registries system consisting of registries, in the form of standardised electronic databases containing common data elements, and the Community independent transaction log. It also provides for an efficient communication system between the Community independent transaction log and the UNFCCC independent transaction log." The planned transaction logs are electronic databases on the Community and UNFCCC levels that record the issue, transfer and cancellation of allowances. They will be operated and maintained by the EU Commission and the UNFCCC Secretariat respectively. The independent Community

[25] Natural Resources Canada, Selection of Statistics Canada as the Vehicle for a Mandatory GHG Emissions Reporting System [Backgrounder] (12 March, 2004) online: NR Canada <http://www.nrcan-rncan.gc.ca/lfeg-ggef/English/reportingvehicle/index.htm>.
[26] Commission of European Communities, *Directive 2003/87/EC of the European Parliament and of the Council of 13 October 2003 establishing a scheme for greenhouse gas emission allowance trading within the Community and amending Council Directive 96/61/EC,* online: Commission of European Communities <http://europa.eu.int/eur-lex/en/com/pdf/2001/en_501PC0581.pdf>. See also *Proposal for a Directive of the European Parliament and of the Council amending the Directive establishing a scheme for greenhouse gas emission allowance trading with the Community, in respect of the Kyoto Protocol's project mechanisms 96/61/EC,* COM (2003) 403 final.
[27] See draft of 24. June 2004 of the Commission Regulation (EC) No …/2004 of xx/xx/2004 for a standardised and secured system of registries pursuant to Directive 2003/87/EC of the European Parliament and of the Council and Decision 280/2004/EC of the European Parliament and of the Council.

transaction log will maintain a communication link with the national registries, according to Art. 6 of the Draft Regulation. It is envisioned that the Community transaction log will have a communication link directly with the UNFCCC transaction log, after the later has been established.

Certain details still depend on the so-called "Linking Directive", which will link the EU's ETS with the Kyoto trading system. Nevertheless the Draft Regulation already contains all the necessary provisions, for example to register CDM credits.

A Commission Decision establishes binding guidelines in all Member States for the monitoring and reporting of GHG emissions.[28] This highly technical document contains activity-specific reporting rules for different industrial activities such as coke ovens, metal ore roasting, production of cement, glas, ceramic or pulp and paper. Most of these standards are based on fossil fuel consumption.

The European experiences to date demonstrates that a common registry is highly desirable but that it should be part of a broader emission trading design, as much of the functioning of the trading scheme depends on the common rules of one coherent, harmonized registry system. The difference between the EU and US registries is similar to those found between the latter and the UK. A Linking Directive has been prepared that will provide a mechanism to relate the EU ETS to the Kyoto Protocol flexibility mechanisms. Some linkage would only be conceivable under a (currently unlikely) change of the US position vis-à-vis the Protocol.[29]

The California Climate Action Registry

California confirmed its position as a US leader in environmental legislation with the establishment of the California Climate Action Registry (the registry) in 2001US.[30] Technical changes were made to the statute in SB 527, which was signed by Governor Gray Davis on October 13, 2001, finalizing the structure for the Registry. Senator Byron Sher was the author of both bills. Several issues have been raised by this initiative.

First, there are additional climate change laws in California. How will the different regimes relate to each other, in the law and in practice? Second, the

---

[28] Commission of European Communities, *Commission Decision of 29 January 2004 establishing guidelines for the monitoring and reporting of greenhouse gas emissions pursuant to Directive 2003/87/EC of the European Parliament and of the Council,* online: EU Commission
<http://europa.eu.int/comm/environment/climat/pdf/c2004_130_en.pdf>.

[29] The U.S. states cannot act independently; they are constitutionally prevented to engage in international affairs.

[30] See U.S. SB 1771, *An Act to Add Chapter 6 (commencing with section 42800) to Part 4 of Diviision 26 of the Health and Safety Code, and to add Chapter 8.5 (commencing with Section 25730) to Division 15 of the Public Resources Code, relating to Air Pollution.* Sept. 30, 2000. Cal. 2000.

goal of 'securing' emission reduction benefits[31] appears problematic. Will the new registry serve to encourage emission reduction, or simply seek to ensure that early actors are not penalized should later legislation come into force? Third, there are still many questions pending related to the management of the registry. Fourth, there are still questions related to the voluntary nature of the new registry, and its dependence on the Internet as a forum for communication and secure registrations.

A general reporting protocol, and the registry's online emission calculation and reporting tool (CARROT) will seek to provide the framework for effective registry participation. Other suggestions have been raised regarding ways to ensure greater credibility for the system, for instance, through independent verifying companies. In addition, concerns still exist regarding the planned contractual relations between and with the registry members. Finally, at this point there appears to be no Emissions Trading System planned, leading many to question the overall purpose and value of the new tool.

Other US experiences include the Wisconsin Voluntary Emission Reductions Registry[32] and the New Hampshire Greenhouse Gas Emissions Reductions Registry.[33] Similar questions have been raised about these registries, as have also been raised about the California system. Finally, the North East Climate Registry (Item 9 of the New England Governors/Eastern Canadian Premiers (NEG/ECP) Climate Action Plan) provides an innovative example of trans-border cooperation, through Greenhouse Gas Early Action Demonstration Projects and legal initiatives by individual states in the region.

---

[31] California Health and Safety Code, *California Climate Action Registry*, 26 § 42800-42801.01, Part 4, (2000)::
"(a) It is in the best interest of the State of California, the United States of America, and the earth as a whole, to encourage voluntary actions to achieve all economically beneficial reductions of greenhouse gas emissions from California sources. (b) Mandatory greenhouse gas emissions reductions may be imposed on California sources at some future point, and in view of this, the state has a responsibility to use its best efforts to ensure that organizations that voluntarily reduce their emissions receive appropriate consideration for emissions reductions made prior to the implementation of any mandatory programs."
[32] U.S., Chapter NR 437 *Voluntary Emission Reduction Registry.*, Department of Natural Resources, Wisc., NR437.01 "Applicability; purpose. (1) APPLICABILITY. This chapter applies to any person who wants to register emission reductions or avoided emissions of greenhouse gases or air contaminants, or carbon sequestration, if the emission reduction, emission avoidance or carbon sequestration occurs before it is required by law or results in emissions which are lower than those allowed by law."
[33] U.S., RSA 125-L:3, *Voluntary Greenhouse Gas Emissions Reductions Registry*, New Hamp., 2001, Part Env-A 3801.01. It states "the purpose of this chapter is to ensure, to the greatest extent possible, that efforts to reduce greenhouse gas emissions undertaken voluntarily by New Hampshire sources prior to the implementation of any mandatory federal program are recognized through the establishment of a registry for early reductions of greenhouse gas emissions. Participation in the New Hampshire voluntary greenhouse gas emissions reductions registry does not guarantee that recognition or credit will be awarded towards any future mandatory federal greenhouse gas reduction program."

Policy Implications: Compatibility for International Carbon Emission Trading

The voluntary registry vs. the non-voluntary registry?

The current state registries appear only peripherally inspired by the Kyoto Protocol. In most cases, the state registries appear more like to be driven by a concern that national legislation might not recognize emission reduction gains since 1990. In addition, such legislation seems to be established to record and 'safeguard' (or protect, for later credit) any reductions achieved early. While the educational exercise is valid, it would be helpful to have a stronger international connection.

It appears that the purposes of the two systems are almost opposite. In particular, the 'safeguarding' nature of the state emissions reduction registries makes it difficult to view these initiatives as a building block. However, neither of these systems actually constitutes stumbling blocks. It can be argued that the experience gained by the regulatory bodies and private actors, as well as the awareness raised by participation in such a system, are still valuable for a future ETS with a strong emission registry.

Do current registries allow entries from other emission reduction efforts outside the registries jurisdiction? Is linking between the systems possible?

At the moment, linkages of emissions reduction credits can only take place in one direction. Credits can only be taken into account from outside the USA, into the US, as the US is not party to the Kyoto Protocol. Any 'exportation' of carbon credits from non-parties will have no effect on compliance. Thus it is highly unlikely that either the UK or the EU would allow such importation. The technical standard for registration of reductions does not seem very different. While theoretically possible to 'import' credits from a Kyoto Protocol party, the current legislation makes it economically irrational, as the credits are likely to yield considerably higher prices in signatory countries.

What legal instruments are needed to facilitate international emissions trading?

The comparative review reveals that clear registry provisions are necessary to ensure stable, predictable and transparent carbon financing arrangements. The international system should provide the necessary guidance for any country or state level ETS. There is a fundamental difference between GHGs and acid rain or ozone depleting substances. Both the latter are localizable or at most, regional contaminants. Their effects, unlike GHGs, are felt partly by those responsible for them. GHGs, on the other hand, lead to global impacts and cannot be isolated nor contained to one country or region. Only through wide spread participation can emission trading realize its potential as a valuable tool to fight climate change. While the Marrakech Accords, under the Kyoto Protocol, provide enough details to enable effective national and sub-national legislation, linking instruments are necessary to ensure that the system as a whole can function optimally. There is a need for greater research and careful design of linking initiatives between the various emissions reduction registries currently proliferating in the international carbon management system.

Conclusions

Based on the brief case studies and analysis above, it can be concluded that while certain regions and countries have accomplished much in a short time, the first approaches to carbon reductions in the U.S. are still too timid. Such cautious preliminary steps will not take the world far enough in the direction that is required. The focus of the state carbon emission registries appears to be on 'safeguarding' reductions achieved by early actors, facilities or projects. It provides a first, but largely insufficient step to tackling the problem of climate change-causing emissions on a state, national and certainly international level. The design and promulgation of clear national legislation linking to international agreements would allow for considerably greater market advantages for participating actors, be they state governments, local governments, businesses or NGOs.

New US state registries do not currently violate international agreements, as they are not harming the country's ability to meet its UNFCCC stabilization commitments, nor are they affecting its commitments to prepare inventories. The Convention stipulates a strong commitment to "achieve stabilisation of greenhouse gas concentrations in the atmosphere at a level that would prevent dangerous anthropogenic interference with the climate system," as stated in Article 2 of the UNFCCC. As such, the 186 states, including the U.S., which have approved, acceded to, accepted, or ratified the UNFCCC, are bound by their commitment to this goal of stabilisation. Countries that have ratified the UNFCCC are obliged to act in accordance with their obligations, even through their participation in carbon registries. However, the actions of these U.S. states would be considerably more effective, especially over the long term, if they took preliminary steps to apply the existing Kyoto Protocol rules.

In order to make the different systems eventually compatible, certain factors could already be taken into account in the establishment and testing of U.S. State registries. First, emission reduction registry schemes should establish and adhere to minimum conformity guidelines concerning monitoring, verification, accountability and other common standards. This would enable, and facilitate, eventual cooperation with other registries. Secondly, legally binding rules will eventually be needed to govern the registry and the actions of the participants. Careful attention to the guidelines and procedures being set in place now will result in greater gains over the long term. Third, as the registered reductions become part of ETS, regulations will be required to govern the transfer of old reductions, which should include deduction factors where appropriate.

Finally, this chapter highlights one key insight into this rapidly developing new carbon legislation. A registry for emissions reductions is the opposite (i.e. mirror image) of the registry for ETS. A company reduces its emissions, and therefore gains credits. But the credits are actually the reflection of the 'cap' in a carbon trading system. Without effective, predictable and enforceable national or State-level caps in sight, it is hard to see how the early registration of reductions can support the establishment of ETS.

This concern does not completely undermine the value of state level initiatives being tested throughout the U.S. today. Current emissions reduction registries will only carry the desired financial and other advantages for their participants if emission reduction provisions are eventually instituted. As such, the proliferation of such registries can be seen as a relatively non-controversial 'first step.' They are not yet close to the necessary comprehensive programs, but nonetheless, can be considered sincere developments that generate useful experience with the registration system, provide a way to record the benefits of a future program, and generate important value in terms of awareness and education. Emission reduction registries will only make complete sense when an emission reduction-trading scheme is in place. The current political climate, especially in the U.S., elevates even very minor initiatives concerning climate change to the level of an important contribution.

Table: State Registry Programs Currently Running or Under Design

	California	New Hampshire	New Jersey	Wisconsin
Purpose	Non-regulatory method by which businesses can be encouraged to voluntarily reduce greenhouse gas emissions.	To help sources establish a baseline against which any future federal GHG emissions reduction requirements may apply.	NJ expects that companies will generate GHG credits with the expectation that GHG credits will become valuable in the future. As a pro-active GHG focused policy, a registry may increase this speculative value by laying the foundation for future policies.	To ensure, to the greatest extent possible, that efforts undertaken voluntarily by persons in Wisconsin to reduce or avoid emissions of GHGs or air contaminants or to sequester carbon are publicly recognized and that these reductions are considered under future mandatory federal or state emission reduction programs.
Implementation Timing	January 2001, new law enacted Spring 2001, Board appointments and organization plan being developed	Adopted Chapter Env-A 3800 "Voluntary Greenhouse Gas Reductions Registry" on 2/23/01	Amended the Open Market Emission Trading Program to include GHGs	The WI legislature directed the DNR to establish a multi-pollutant emissions registry-currently engaged in the rulemaking process. In effect summer 2003.
Are Emissions Reductions Reported, or Only Emissions Inventories?	Emissions only	Emission reductions	Emission reductions	Emission reductions
Is Participation Mandatory or Voluntary?	Voluntary Program administered by a non-profit	Voluntary Program administered by the state	Voluntary Program administered by a private	Voluntary Program administered by the state

	California	New Hampshire	New Jersey	Wisconsin
	managed by a stakeholder board of directors	environmental agency – The Department of Environmental Services	firm-Moosakin Corporation	environmental agency – The Department of Natural Resources
What GHG Emissions are Included in Reporting?	GHGs (CO_2), CH_4, N_2O, HFCs, PFCs, SF_6 after three years of involvement	GHGs (CO_2, CH_4, N_2O, HFCs, PFCs, SF_6)	GHGs (CO_2, CH_4, N_2O, HFCs, PFCs, SF_6), NOx, VOC	GHGs (CO_2, CH_4, N_2O, HFCs, PFCs, SF_6) NOx, SO_2, VOC, $PM_{2.5}$, CO, Lead, Mercury
Is Reporting at the Entity or Facility/Project Level?	Mandatory corporation wide reporting	Project level. Corporate wide suggested but not required.	Project level	Optional corporate wide and project level
What is the Reporting Scope: Direct and/or Indirect?	Both direct and indirect emissions reported	Both direct and indirect emission reductions	Both direct and indirect emission reductions	Both direct and indirect emission reductions
Are Trades of Emission Reductions Tracked?	No	No	Yes but not for GHGs	No
What Types of Recognition (Public and Regulatory) Are Available?	Yes	Yes	Yes	Yes
What are the Requirements for Verification?	Certification is necessary	Verification required by third party or NH DES	Verification by PE required	No must certify but third party is optional.
Are Mass Emissions Reported or is There an Output Based Metric	Mass and rate-based	Mass-based	Mass-based	Mass and rate-based
Are There Specific Data Protocols?	Board will adopt protocols that facilitate recognition in future regulatory	Defers to EIA 1605(b) and others as determined by the agency – WRI GHG	Articulated by the DEP	IPCC, EPA EIIP, AP42, WRI GHG Protocol and others

	California	New Hampshire	New Jersey	Wisconsin
	regimes. Aims to be consistent with WRI GHGProtocol	Protocol		
Reporting Forms/Software	Registry will review available software, including EPA's software, to see whether it will meet registry requirements	Has developed reporting forms - Defers to EIA 1605(b)	Reporting forms - Private firm administering registry	Reporting forms and guidance under development
Cost of Participation	Reasonable fees to be determined	None	For NOx and VOC, from $0.20 - $12.50 per DER (ton) Vary for GHGs from $0.00 - $0.03/DER (ton).	None

Source: Northeast States for Coordinated Air Use Management, "Greenhouse Gas State Registry Collaborative," online: NESCAUM <*http://www.nescaum.org/Greenhouse/Registry/state_matrix.html*>.

18

DEVELOPING GLOBAL CLIMATE REGIMES

Xueman Wang[1]

Climate change is not only an environmental problem. It affects almost every sector of national economics -- ranging from energy to industry, forestry and agriculture -- and links to issues of population, excess consumption and poverty. The solution to the climate change problem lies in a fundamental shift in the composition of social and economic activities – a shift to sustainable development.

The United Nations Framework Convention on Climate Change (UNFCCC),[2] adopted in 1992, recognizes the interdependence between climate change and social economics. It aims to stabilize atmospheric concentration of greenhouse gases (GHG) at a safe level to allow "economic development to proceed in a sustainable manner."[3] This means that the objectives of the Convention can only be achieved in the context of systematic, continuing and comprehensive efforts to ensure the success of sustainable development.

The Kyoto Protocol, adopted in 1997, represents the first step of substantive action to be taken by developed countries to combat climate change.[4] The principle goal of the Protocol is for developed country parties to reduce their GHGs by a minimum of 5% below 1990 levels during the commitment period of 2008 to 2012. Recognizing the potentially high costs of implementation, the Protocol, based on cost-effective principles, creates three market mechanisms to enable developed countries to reach their targets offshore: clean development mechanisms (CDM), joint implementation (JI) and emissions trading. It also allows an offset of emissions by the uptake of carbon in forests and farmland (carbon sinks). All these mechanisms are designed to reduce the

---

[1] Xueman Wang, LL.M. (Wu Han, China), M.A. (Fletcher School, Tufts), Lead Counsel for Climate Change and Vulnerability Law, Centre for International Sustainable Development Law (CISDL), Legal Officer, Secretariat for the Convention on Biological Diversity, former Legal Officer, Climate Change Secretariat. Views expressed in this paper are of the author, and do not represent those of either Secretariats.
[2] U.N. Doc. A/AC 237/18 (Part II) (Add. 1) 31 I.L.M. 848. Adopted at the 1992 UN Conference on Environmental and Development in Rio de Janeiro.
[3] *Ibid,* at Art. 2.
[4] COP 3 Report, doc. FCCC/CP/1997/7 Add.1, Adopted at the third Conference of the Parties to the UNFCCC in Kyoto, Japan, 1997.

costs of emissions reduction and to avoid any possible harmful impacts on market competitiveness and economic development.

The Marrakech meeting held in 2001 finalized the rules, procedures and modalities related to various mechanisms under the Protocol. With the effectiveness of these mechanisms under the Kyoto Protocol still to be tested, an important challenge facing the international community will be to decide on action to be taken beyond the accord, bearing in mind that it envisages an evolving process, with negotiation of emission reduction targets for the second commitment period due to start in 2005.[5] The whole Protocol is also scheduled for review at the second Convention of the Parties, which, depending on the date of entry into force of the accord, may take place around the same time.

In further developing an international regime, three issues, among others, are important: adaptation and vulnerability of developing countries; shared responsibility for future commitments; and partnership with the private sector.

Developing countries are particularly susceptible to the adverse effects of climate change. There are a number of activities being initiated to deal with this vulnerability, including research and monitoring of climate change impacts, assessment of vulnerability and adaptation options, capacity-building, and improving early warning systems for rapid response to extreme weather events. Funding for these activities is crucial; the Marrakech Accords established three funds: the special climate change fund, the least-developed countries fund, and the adaptation fund under the Kyoto Protocol. The Global Environmental Facility (GEF) will manage these funds. It is encouraging to see that some developed countries have already declared they will collectively contribute US$410 million annually in extra financing for developing countries by 2005.[6]

The second issue, which is fundamental to elaborating the future climate regime, is the development of criteria by which to distribute responsibility for tackling global warming. Under the Climate Change Convention and the Kyoto Protocol, parties are divided into two main groups: countries with economies in transition, and industrialized countries; 41 of which are currently listed in the Convention as Annex I, including members of the Organization for Economic Co-operation and Development (OECD) in 1992. All other countries not listed in the Convention's Annexes (i.e. mostly the developing countries) are known as non-Annex I countries. They currently number 145.

While article 4.2(a) of the Convention recognizes that developed countries must take the lead in modifying long-term emissions trends, the ultimate objective of

---

[5] *Ibid* at Art. 3.9.
[6] Climate Change Secretariat, *Guide to the Climate Change Convention and its Kyoto Protocol* (Bonn: UNFCC, 2002), online: UNFCC <http://unfccc.int>.

stabilization of atmospheric concentration requires that both developed countries make deeper cuts, and that developing countries engage in action to constrain their fast-growing emissions. The dilemma facing these countries is apparent. On the one hand, emission reduction requires that countries adopt comprehensive policy measures to convert to low-carbon energy systems, which may lead to high costs and economic loss in the short term. States, and developing countries in particular, understandably worry that reduction costs will harm their market competitiveness and hinder their economic development. On the other hand, however, the costs of inaction will be even higher. The rising temperatures caused by climate change will have profoundly adverse effects on human health, economic growth and ecological systems, thus placing developing countries in a particularly vulnerable position.

An international regime to tackle climate change must find a balanced approach by integrating socio-economic and environmental needs, in addition to creating incentives and lowering the costs of emission reduction. Global action to reduce emission must not depress economic growth. The distinct needs of developing countries must be recognized and reflected in the future allocation of greenhouse gas reduction targets. Technological innovation and the role of the market should be further explored while transforming to low-carbon energy systems.

In developing the future global regime, the following questions need to be answered. How would an international regime accommodate the respective needs of different groups of countries while ensuring that all do their "fair share"? What would be the criteria in determining the distinct responsibilities between the North and South and among the developing countries? What strategies would create incentives for investment and technology flows, enabling developing countries to integrate climate concerns into their development strategies? Duncan A. French discusses several of these issues in the following chapter, "Narrowing the Focus, Broadening the Debate".

Finally, if the new global climate regime is to be considered effective, it must involve a wide range of actors, including industry as a leader of the private sector. One of the main reasons for the success of the Montreal Protocol in dealing with depletion of the ozone layer was the active participation of major manufacturers such as Dupont and ICI, who broke ranks with the rest the CFC manufacturers. On the issue of climate change, oil giant Royal Dutch/Shell, convinced that action on global warming is necessary and inevitable, has promised to cut its greenhouse-gas emissions to 10% below their 1990 level within three years. The private sector, from the bottom up, is becoming a driving force in shaping the climate policy, which reinforces the need for governments to send a strong, clear and consistent signal to the industry. Business is likely to respond favourably to a system that includes elements such as certainty of rules, reward for success, greater reward for greater risk, cost reductions, increasing revenues and public credit for good works.

In conclusion, combating global warming is a long process and will require the efforts of generations. The challenge in dealing with climate change has always been finding a balance between the environment and development needs, as well as between long-term gain and short-term pain. The Kyoto Protocol is a starting point in obliging developed countries to undertake legally-binding emission reduction targets and exploiting market means to allow flexibility in fulfilling their obligations. Moving beyond the Kyoto Protocol requires the future global regime to grow under the framework of sustainable development by helping developing countries to increase their ability to adapt to the adverse effects of climate change; by engaging wider groups of countries (both developed and developing) to take abatement measures to cut or constrain emission growth; and by encouraging industry to actively participate in global action to combat climate change.

HUMAN RIGHTS, DEVELOPMENT AND POVERTY ERADICATION

19

INTERNATIONAL HUMAN RIGHTS LAW AND POVERTY ERADICATION

*Sumudu Atapattu**

During the past few decades, unprecedented development in terms of technology and the standard of living occurred in developed countries. However, 1.2 billion people in the world today live on less than US$1.00 a day.[1] Starvation and malnutrition have led to many health problems, particularly in children, thereby irreparably damaging future generations. This significant gap between the rich and the poor led UN Secretary General, Kofi Annan, to declare in his Millennium Report that "[a]bsolute poverty is an affront to the dignity of humankind", and to urge states to pledge to halve the number of poor by 2015. [2]

The basic right of everyone to an adequate standard of living,[3] recognized more than 50 years ago by the international community, has eluded the majority of the world's community.[4] Hundreds of millions of people continue to live in poverty without adequate food and water and without adequate housing and sanitation. There is no doubt that poverty is a major violator of human rights, as it leads to the deprivation of other rights such as those relating to health, education, work and privacy. It also leads to the denial of procedural rights by

---

* Sumudu Atapattu, LL.M, PhD (Cantab), Adjunct Faculty & Visiting Scholar, University of Wisconsin-Madison Law School, Lead Counsel for Human Rights and Poverty Eradication, Centre for International Sustainable Development Law (CISDL), Consultant, Law & Society Trust, (Colombo, Sri Lanka) & former Senior Lecturer, Faculty of Law, University of Colombo, Sri Lanka. Paper prepared for the Sustainable Justice 2002 conference organized by the Centre for International Sustainable Development Law, Montreal, Canada, together with the World Bank and UNEP, June 14-16, 2002.
[1] See World Bank, *World Development Report 2000/01* (Washington: World Bank, 2001), which highlights that more than 2 billion people live on less than US $ 2.00 a day.
[2] K. Annan, "We the Peoples: The Role of the United Nations in the 21st Century" (New York: United Nations, 2000), available online: United Nations <http://www.un.org/millennium/sg/report/full.htm>.
[3] See *Universal Declaration of Human Rights*, GA Res. 217 (III), UNGAOR, 3d Sess., Supp. No. 13, UN Doc. A/810 (1948) Principle 25, which states: "Everyone has the right to a standard of living adequate for the health and well-being of himself and of his family, including food, clothing, housing and medical care and necessary social services…".
[4] *International Covenant on Economic, Social and Cultural Rights*, 19 December 1966, 993 U.N.T.S. at 3, Art.11. Twenty years later, States Parties "recognized the right of everyone to an adequate standard of living for himself and his family, including adequate food, clothing and housing, and to the continuous improvement of living conditions."

M.C. Cordonier Segger & C. G. Weeramantry, eds., Sustainable Justice: Reconciling Economic, Social & Environmental Law
© *2005 Koninklijke Brill NV, Printed in The Netherlands, pp.307-312.*

limiting the rights to participate in the decision-making process, to obtain information, and to have access to justice.

The international community has recognized the link between poverty and sustainable development, most importantly by proclaiming in the 1992 *Rio Declaration on Environment and Development* that:

> "All states and all people shall cooperate in the essential task of eradicating poverty as an indispensable requirement for sustainable development, in order to decrease the disparities in standards of living and better meet the needs of the majority of the people of the world."[5]

Thus, poverty is a condition that cuts across a wide spectrum of issues - social, economic and environmental - and, as a result, requires a holistic approach. The progressive realization of economic, social and cultural rights is imperative, if the present plight of the poor is to be ameliorated.

Human Rights and Poverty Eradication

Against this background, it is essential to identify cross-cutting issues and develop a research agenda within the framework of international sustainable development law. Indeed, the close relationship that exists between international human rights law, international environmental law and international economic law in relation to the issue of poverty eradication cannot be overlooked.

Human rights and international financial institutions

Throughout the development of the International Monetary Fund (IMF) and the World Bank (the Bank), it can be noted that the latter institution, in particular, has responded to a much broader mandate than originally envisaged. It has developed programs on poverty alleviation, rule of law, governance, environmental protection and infrastructure development in developing countries. These efforts recognize that "creating the conditions for the attainment of human rights is a central and irreducible goal of development."[6]

However, the IMF and the World Bank have strongly resisted assuming any responsibility for the protection of human rights in recipient countries, alleging a desire not to be human rights policemen. As a result, they have been reluctant

---

[5] *Rio Declaration on Environment and Development*, Report of the United Nations Conference on Environment and Development (1992) A/CONF.151/26 (Vol. I), princ. 5.
[6] J. D. Talliant, "Human Rights and International Financial Institutions." Paper presented at the CISDL Conference on Sustainable Justice: Implementing International Sustainable Development Law, A conference of the CISDL, the UNEP & the World Bank (Montreal, June 14, 2002). Report available online: www.cisdl.org, paper resulted in a chapter which appears in this volume..

to impose conditionalities to their development aid. Developing countries are also wary of such conditions to aid since they perceive them as another way for the North to hinder free trade by controlling the activities of, and imposing their ideology on, the South. Still, the re-emerging debate on economic, social and cultural rights faces an alarming increase in global poverty, a widening gap between rich and poor countries, and, in developed countries, an increasing gap between the rich and the poor. As a result, multilateral development agencies have been compelled to look at developmental issues, and particularly at poverty. At issue, however, is whether these institutions should seek to secure minimum levels of human dignity based on universally accepted human rights.

The adoption in 1999 of the *Poverty Reduction Strategy Papers* (PRSP) by the Bank and the IMF is the latest attempt to address global poverty. These papers are intended for the poorest country members of the Bank and the IMF. The proposed strategy seeks to make development a more country-owned process, and to gain more country participation in the development of its lending portfolio. The Bank has clearly attempted to make the PRSP process more participatory by including civil society participation. However, they make no attempt to describe the goals of the exercise in rights language; while geared to focus on poverty, the process is not approached from a rights-based perspective.

Poverty reduction involves a myriad of human rights issues, including access to education and basic health services. In this respect, basic human rights are being addressed, albeit indirectly, through the PRSP process by the Bank. However, the move towards strengthening participatory mechanisms is also an indirect way of addressing other human rights issues; the shoring up of procedural rights is nonetheless an important step in achieving other substantive rights.

Economic, Social and Cultural Rights and the Role of National Human Rights Commissions

To speak of international human rights and poverty eradication is, in effect, to address economic, social and cultural rights (ESC rights). Marginalized groups must be able to claim their ESC rights; but to reduce poverty, it is also essential that they become aware of their rights.

There is an increasing body of jurisprudence from the UN Committee on ESC rights, which holds that these rights are justiciable. While litigation remains a primary mechanism to enforce them, alternative mechanisms should be considered, as courts can be inaccessible due to their cost and cumbersome procedures. In addition, some judges and lawyers may not acknowledge that ESC rights are justiciable. An alternative mechanism of interest is the national human rights commission which has advisory and monitoring functions that will ensure accessibility for marginalized groups. It can also intervene in courts as *amici curiae* and its position as between government and civil society would facilitate a dialogue on these rights.

Finally, human rights law should not be reserved to lawyers. Marginalized groups must become aware of their rights in order to claim them. Empowering marginalised groups through education and awareness may, in addition, incite them to change attitudes and behaviours, develop capacities and implement mechanisms that achieve sustainable development.

Potential of International Sustainable Development law and human rights law to contribute to poverty eradication

Whether international sustainable development law and/or human rights law contribute to poverty eradication is a difficult question to answer and depends on the circumstances of each case. The critical issue is what to do when circumstances keep changing.

With regard to the nature of poverty, and the reasons why people are poor, it is important to realize that poverty is a multi-dimensional issue. For example: deprivation of capabilities and lack of basic rights and freedoms are but part of the problem. Addressing some dimensions and not others may prove ineffective; on the other hand, a holistic solution may not be applicable in practice. With regard to the link between poverty eradication and sustainable development, the issue is whether a world without poverty would be ecologically sustainable. Further, it will be important to define whether "development" will necessarily refer to the lifestyle of Western Europe and North America.

There have been several "flavours" in the past: economic growth; social development; socio-economic development; human development; the basic needs approach; endogenous development; and now sustainable development. While all of these seem to have made a contribution, it is no secret that the number of poor seems to be growing, and development has in that sense remained elusive. While many gains have been made, there has been a miserable failure to reach the targets of each decade. Could it be that governance is the new development flavour of the decade?

The application of well-balanced international sustainable development law regimes may be very challenging for today's highly sectoral implementing institutions. Governance for sustainable development seeks to build institutions that make and implement sustainable development decisions, and which are economically, socially and environmentally balanced. The alternative approach, which is also more practical, is to build the capacities of existing institutions but with improved coordination.

An even bigger challenge is empowerment, which requires the transformation of existing power structures,. The role of governance in this case is to build the capacity of the poor so they can take greater control of their own lives and livelihoods. Good governance, then, becomes the exercise of authority through democratic policies, processes and institutions so that the power relationship among the social actors is a positive sum game. To operationalise governance in this sense, its role in the distributive function - who gets what, when and how - and the constitutive function - who sets the rules, how and when - must be addressed by international sustainable development laws and human rights laws. But these laws must go further and help change power relations by assisting communities to articulate their concerns, mobilize among themselves, distribute power among their members, and affirm their rights in courts.

Sustainable development law and human rights law must also articulate the moral basis of their doctrine and principles to differentiate between causes and symptoms of the problems they seek to address. There is a need for a new global human order - a shift from "human havings" to "human beings", and this can be achieved by sustained support for new moral leadership at all levels, a redefinition of human progress de-coupled from gross consumption, and a revamping of incentives, and disincentives.

The Brundtland Commission Report recognized that sustainable development is a "systems problem."[7] There is, therefore, a need for a systemic approach to the solution. The crises we face are not those of water, energy, health, agriculture or biodiversity, on the one hand, and poverty, human rights and governance, on the other; they are one interlocking crisis. However, the system within which we operate - the socio-ecological system - is both dynamic and co-evolutionary, and behaves more like a complex adaptive system, showing characteristics of self-organization, irreducible uncertainty, surprise and non-linear behavior, and, hence, inherent unpredictability. Existing laws are difficult to apply within such a system, and sustainable development law will have to confront these challenges.[8]

Conclusion

Several issues of interest must be raised in an international debate regarding the linkages between sustainable development, poverty and human rights. In particular, PRSPs can be critiqued for imposing additional conditions on developing countries, especially in relation to further restrictions on access to trade. South Africa was taken as a good example on the issue of justiciability of ESC rights; but as the jurisprudence currently raises these rights, without

---

[7] World Commission on Environment and Development, *Our Common Future*. (Oxford: Oxford University Press, 1987).
[8] *Ibid.*

corresponding duties, rights might easily risk becoming simply claims on an overburdened state. Both over-consumption and under-consumption must be addressed, and can be found to be linked to poverty and to have a negative impact on achieving sustainable development. Furthermore, lack of participation among those who are the objects of development can be seen to be a negation of human rights. And, finally, human rights education should be mentioned, as it has been found to play an important role in achieving sustainable development.

20

INTERNATIONAL HUMAN RIGHTS LAW AND LEVELS OF FINANCING FOR DEVELOPMENT

Ashfaq Khalfan[1]

A critical challenge for the international community is to address intersections between international law and policy in the economic, social and environmental fields. These intersections have often been ignored, or priorities in certain fields have been used to over-ride those in others. One instance is development financing, where human rights legal obligations have generally been ignored, or at best, seen as relevant only when development projects cause violation of human rights, in particular civil and political rights. However, the ambit of human rights is far broader and indeed provides a little-recognised legal framework for the process of resource mobilisation for development. The existence of a legal framework for development financing is especially relevant because most international economic and environmental agreements that relate to development financing are in the form of declarations, rather than treaties, or exist in extremely vague forms in international treaties. Indeed, even recent political declarations have tended to shy away from concrete obligations. For example, in *Agenda 21,*[2] while although a comprehensive plan was agreed upon, certain States opposed the inclusion in the declaration of the necessary financial amounts that had been calculated by the Secretariat of the Rio Summit. The *UN Millennium Declaration,* which specifies clear targets for human development does not address resource mobilisation.[3] The most recent and relevant declaration, the *Monterrey Consensus on Financing for Development,*[4] discussed below, shares many of these characteristics.

---

[1] Ashfaq Khalfan, B.A (Hons.), B.C.L., LL.B. (McGill), Director, Centre for International Sustainable Development Law (CISDL), Programme Director, Water Rights, Center on Housing Rights and Evictions (COHRE). The author would like to acknowledge comments on an earlier draft by Jane Glenn (McGill University Faculty of Law), Philip Alston (New York University Faculty of Law), Adelle Blackett (McGill Faculty of Law), Peter Leuprecht (McGill Faculty of Law), Markus Gehring (CISDL Lead Counsel for Sustainable Trade, Investment and Competition Law), Caroline Dommen, (3D – Trade, Human Rights, Equitable Economy) and Jeff King (CISDL Research Fellow).
[2] *Agenda 21*, 1992 Report of the UNCED, I (1992) UN Doc. A/CONF.151/26/Rev. 1, (1992) 31 I.L.M. 874.
[3] *Millennium Declaration*, G.A. Res. 55/9, UN GAOR, 2000. This Declaration included, *inter alia*, a commitment to halve by the year 2015 the proportion of the world's population whose income is less than $1 a day, at para. 19.
[4] *Monterrey Consensus on Financing for Development* UN Doc. A/Conf. 198/11, 22 March 2002. Although the World Summit on Sustainable Development (WSSD) also addressed development financing issues, the

The failure to mainstream human rights obligations in international initiatives related to financing for development is unfortunate, since legal obligations in the politicised and contested world of development financing can form the basis for ensuring that expectations are met, for reducing arbitrary decision-making and for forming the basis for mutual accountability among and within States. This chapter will discuss the implications of human rights laws the levels of financing that should be directed towards development. This chapter outlines State obligations under the *International Covenant on Economic, Social and Cultural Rights (ICESCR)* and other instruments to raise the resources necessary for the realisation of economic, social and cultural rights at the national level, from the maximum of their available resources, with particular focus on the most vulnerable communities.[5] States are legally obliged to ensure that at least 'core obligations' corresponding to the most basic needs are immediately realised. International obligations also exist to guarantee respect for such rights in other countries, and to implement, individually and collectively, an international anti-poverty strategy that takes 'core obligations' into account in developing countries.

This chapter also addresses the status and implications of the right to development, and addresses two complex issues: whether trade and investment liberalisation can serve to meet States' obligations under the ICESCR; and the extent to which international obligations in relation to economic, social and cultural rights are conditional upon compliance by recipient States with these rights. The chapter then briefly analyses the *Monterrey Consensus on Financing for Development* from a human rights perspective.

Effect of Human Rights Obligations on Levels of Development Financing at the Domestic Level

Positive obligations to raise resources for development are a component of obligations to realise economic, social and cultural rights such as the rights to adequate food, water, housing, education, work and an adequate standard of living. All States have committed to the realisation of these rights by ratifying some or all of the relevant treaties, which include the *Charter of the United Nations*,[6] the *International Covenant on Economic, Social and Cultural Rights*

Monterrey Consensus provisions were largely reproduced in the provisions of the Johannesburg Programme of Implementation (JPOI). The JPOI is contained in Report of the World Summit on Sustainable Development, Johannesburg, South Africa, August 26 to Sept 4, 2002, A/CONF.199/L.1 (New York, United Nations, 2002). The negotiators at the WSSD understandably did not wish to re-open issues for discussion on which extensive negotiations had been completed only eight months earlier.

[5] While the present chapter focuses only on financial resources, it is worth considering a range of other resources, such as natural and information resources that can also be applied towards development efforts, see R. Robertson, "Measuring State Compliance with the Obligation to Devote the 'Maximum Available Resources' to Realizing Economic, Social and Cultural Rights" (1994) 16 *Human Rights Quarterly* 695.

[6] *Charter of the United Nations,* 26 June 1945, Can. T.S. 1945 No. 7.

(ICESCR),[7] the *Convention on the Rights of the Child,*[8] the *International Convention on the Elimination of All Forms of Racial Discrimination*[9] and the *Convention on the Elimination of All Forms of Discrimination Against Women.*[10] The core aspect of these treaties is best reflected in the *ICESCR,* currently ratified by 148 States, which stipulates "Each State Party to the present Covenant undertakes to take steps, individually and through international assistance and co-operation, especially economic and technical, to the maximum of its available resources, with a view to achieving progressively the full realisation of the rights recognised in the present Covenant, including particularly the adoption of legislative measures."[11]

Each State party to the *ICESCR* is required to realise economic, social and cultural rights progressively.[12] The extent of these obligations has been the subject of authoritative interpretation by the United Nations Committee on Economic, Social and Cultural Rights (CESCR), a body of independent experts established by the United Nations Economic and Social Council.[13] The *ICESCR* commits States to move expeditiously towards the realization of the rights,[14] and they are required to use what resources are available in an equitable and effective manner.[15] Certain rights must be realised immediately: there must not be discrimination in implementation of the rights; and steps must be taken immediately with a view to the progressive realisation of these rights. These steps should be deliberate, concrete and targeted as clearly as possible towards meeting the obligations recognised in the Covenant.[16] Other immediate obligations include the duty to *respect* these rights by not taking any action to prevent their realisation by individuals and groups, and to *protect* these rights by

---

[7] *International Covenant on Economic, Social and Cultural Rights (ICESCR),* 19 December 1966, 993 U.N.T.S. 3.

[8] *UN Convention on the Rights of the Child,* GA Res. 44/25, UN GAOR, 44th Sess., Annex, Supp. No. 49, UN Doc. A/44/49 (1989) 167.

[9] *International Convention on the Elimination of All Forms of Racial Discrimination* (1969), 660 U.N.T.S. 195.

[10] *Convention on the Elimination of All Forms of Discrimination Against Women,* 4 January 1969, Can. T.S. 1982 No. 31.

[11] *ICESCR, supra* note 7, Art. 2 (1).

[12] *ICESCR, ibid.,* Article 2.1. A similar formulation on economic, social and cultural rights exists in the Universal Declaration on Human Rights, *Universal Declaration of Human Rights,* Dec. 10, 1948, G.A. Res. 217 A, UN GAOR, 3d Sess., pt. I, Resolutions, at 71, UN Doc. A/810 (1948), which states in Article 22: "Everyone, as a member of society, has the right to social security and is entitled to realization, through national effort and international co-operation and in accordance with the organization and resources of each State, of the economic, social and cultural rights indispensable for his dignity and the free development of his personality."

[13] The Committee sought the authorisation of the United Nations Economic and Social Council, which is one of the primary United Nations made up of Member States, to develop General Comments, and received encouragement from the Council to "continue using that mechanism to develop a fuller appreciation of the obligations of States Parties under the Covenant." Economic and Social Council Resolution 1990/45, para. 10, quoted in Philip Alston, "The Committee on Economic, Social and Cultural Rights" in Philip Alston (ed.), *The United Nations and Human Rights* (Oxford: Clarendon Press, 1992), 473-508 at 494.

[14] Committee on Economic, Social and Cultural Rights, *General Comment No.14: The Right to the Highest Attainable Standard of Health,* UN ESCOR, 2000, UN Doc. E/C.12/2000/4, at para.31. See also the *Limburg Principles on the Implementation of the Covenant on Economic, Social and Cultural Rights* (1987), U.N. Doc. E/CN.4/1987/17, Annex, (1987) 9 Human Rights Quarterly 122 at para. 21. The *Limburg Principles* were developed by a number of leading experts in the field of international economic, social and cultural rights.

[15] *Limburg Principles, ibid.,* at para. 23 & 27.

[16] Committee on Economic, Social and Cultural Rights, *General Comment No.3: The Nature of State Parties Obligations,* UN ESCOR, 1990, UN Doc. E /1991/23, paras. 1 & 2.

taking measures to ensure that individuals are not deprived of their rights.[17] The *ICESCR* further requires that available resources be appropriately targeted to benefit the poor, particularly the most vulnerable groups.[18] Certain obligations in this area are also included in a non-progressive form in other treaties. The right to life, as set out in Article 6 of the *International Covenant on Civil and Political Rights (ICCPR)*,[19] requires positive measures which, according to the United Nations Human Rights Committee, should include measures to eliminate epidemics.[20]

A benchmark for more immediate action by States is the concept of 'minimum core obligations' which are set out by the United Nations Committee on Economic, Social and Cultural Rights as follows:

> "[A] minimum core obligation to ensure the satisfaction of, at the very least, minimum essential levels of each of the rights is incumbent upon every State party. Thus, for example, a State party in which any significant number of individuals is deprived of essential foodstuffs, of essential primary care, of basic shelter and housing or of the most basic forms of education is *prima facie* failing to discharge its obligations under the *ICESCR*… In order for a State party to be able to attribute its failure to meet at least its minimum core obligations to a lack of available resources, it must demonstrate that every effort has been made to use all resources that are at its disposition in an effort to satisfy, as a matter of priority, those minimum obligations."[21]

Core human rights obligations create national obligations for all States, and international responsibilities for developed States, as well as others that are "in a position to assist."[22] The possible absence of resources and insufficient international assistance, does not excuse the State from its domestic obligations. Even in cases of severe resource constraints, "the vulnerable members of society can and indeed must be protected by the adoption of relatively low-cost targeted programmes."[23] Such vulnerable groups include those excluded on the basis of race, gender, age, disability and other such characteristics, as well as the

---

[17] Committee on Economic, Social and Cultural Rights, *General Comment No.12: The Right to Adequate Food*, UN ESCOR, 1999, UN Doc. E/C.12/1999/5 at para.15.

[18] CESCR, *General Comment No.3, supra* note 16 at para. 12.

[19] (1976), 999 U.N.T.S 171.

[20] See Human Rights Committee, *General Comment No. 6*, UN GAOR, 1982, Supp. No. 40, UN Doc. A/37/40 at para. 5. The Human Rights Committee is the body of independent experts, established under the *ICCPR*, to monitor its implementation.

[21] *General Comment No.3, supra* note 16 at para. 10. See also the list of obligations in *General Comment No. 14, supra* note 14 at para. 43-44. In this comment, at para. 47, the CESCR has stated that such core obligations are 'non-derogable' and that a state party cannot, under any circumstances whatsoever, justify its non-compliance with core obligations

[22] Committee on Economic, Social and Cultural Rights, *Poverty and the International Covenant on Economic, Social and Cultural Rights*, UN ESCOR, 2001, UN Doc. E/C.12/2001/10. See also below.

[23] *CESCR, General Comment No.3, supra* note 10 at para. 12.

poor in general. Furthermore, the most basic needs can be widely protected even in times of recession or adjustment, for example, by transferring resources from curative medical facilities to primary health care programmes, from highly trained doctors to paramedical personnel, from tertiary education to primary and secondary education, and from subsidies for vocal and powerful groups to subsidies for weaker and less articulate groups.[24] The United Nations Committee on Economic, Social and Cultural Rights notes that inappropriate resource allocation can lead to discrimination that may not be overt, such as when investments disproportionately favour expensive services and facilities that are often accessible only to a small, privileged fraction of the population, rather than investing in lower-cost services and facilities that benefit a far larger part of the population.[25] While it is preferable for such obligations to be carried out by executive and legislative actions, the judiciary can play a role in ensuring that human rights are upheld in budgetary allocations, as seen by jurisprudence in South Africa, [26] Columbia[27] and India[28] among others. [29]

Although the above analysis focuses mainly on resource mobilization for realising economic, social and cultural rights,[30] such resources must be raised and utilised in a manner consistent with all human rights, including civil and

---

[24] This point is cited by the CESCR, *ibid.,* and refers to the United Nations Development Programme, *Human Development Report 1990* (New York: Oxford, 1990) at 4. See for an empirical application of the right to health to public health budgets: H. Hofbauer and G. Lara, *Health Care: A Question of Human Rights, Not Charity* (Mexico City: FUNDAR, Centro de Análisis e Investigación, 2002), http://www.fundar.org.mx and S. Cassiem and J. Streak, *Budgeting for Child Socio-Economic Rights: Government Obligations and the Child's Right to Social Security and Education* (Cape Town: IDASA, 2001).

[25] Committee on Economic, Social and Cultural Rights, *General Comment No.15: The Right to Water* UN ESCOR, 2002, UN Doc. E/C.12/2002/11, para. 16.

[26] See *Treatment Action Campaign* v. *Minister of Health,* 2002 SA 8 (CC) in which the Court required the state to provide detailed treatments to reduce mother to child transmission of HIV. Conversely, the Court decided that the state's failure to provide free renal dialysis was justified after reviewing the resources available in *Soobramany v. Minister of Health, KwaZulu-Natal,* 1998 (1) SA 765 (CC). The court stated: "to be reasonable, measures cannot leave out of account the degree and extent of the denial of the rights they endeavour to realise. Those whose needs are the most urgent and whose ability to enjoy all rights therefore is at most peril must not be ignored by the measures aimed at achieving realisation of the right."

[27] The Colombian Constitutional Court stated that since provision of health care is subordinate to the existence of economic resources, and is partial and progressive in nature, available resources should be used in a rational and equitable fashion in cases in which the restoration of health is actually possible. It therefore approved the removal from hospital of a girl who was in a stable but irreversible condition on the basis that hospital beds and room should not be occupied by persons whose state of health was not expected to improve, so as to deprive other persons of care. Constitutional Court, Judgement No. T-484 of 11 August 1992, *Revista Mensual, Jurisprudencia y Doctrina,* 1992, Vol. 21, PP. 1008-1109. Conversely, the state was required to provide treatment to an AIDS sufferer in a precarious economic state. Constitutional Court, Judgement No. T-505 of 28 August 1992, *Revista Mensual, Jurisprudencia y Doctrina,* 1992, Vol. 21, PP. 1101-1106.

[28] The Indian Supreme Court held that the State is required to provide *at least the minimum conditions ensuring human dignity,* and ordered the government to provide suitable accommodation for a disabled woman living in a mental home, *Vikram Deo Singh Tomar* v. *State of Bihar,* (1988) Supp. SCC 734 at 736.

[29] See for a series of case studies, M. Langford, *Litigating Economic, Social and Cultural Rights: Achievements, Challenges and Strategies* (Geneva: Centre on Housing Rights and Evictions, 2003), online: COHRE <www.cohre.org>.

[30] Naturally the funding of civil and political rights, as set out in the *International Covenant on Civil and Political Rights,* 19 December 1966, 999 U.N.T.S 171 are of key importance from the point of view of indivisibility, and is linked to the effective implementation of the *ICESCR,* see the *CESCR Poverty Statement, supra* note 22 at paras. 10-12.

political rights. As pointed out by the United Nations Committee on Economic, Social and Cultural Rights, the recognition of the rights to food, health, and education, for example, requires the fulfilment of civil and political rights (for example the right to free expression), and of the rights to political participation and decision-making, and non-discrimination.[31] Human rights law also requires the need for sustainability be taken into account, given the impact of environmental degradation and pollution on the right to food and health. According to the Committee, the notion of sustainability is intrinsically linked to the right to food, or food security, implying that food must be accessible for both future and present generations. [32]

International Obligations in Relation to Economic, Social and Cultural Rights

A series of treaties set obligations that indicate an obligation to engage in international cooperation for development in order to realise economic, social and cultural rights. The *Universal Declaration on Human Rights (UDHR)*, which provides for civil, political, economic, social and cultural rights, includes the provision: "Everyone is entitled to a social and international order in which the rights and freedoms set forth in this Declaration can be fully realized."[33] The *UDHR* carries more legal weight than ordinary General Assembly resolutions, and has been said to form part of international customary law binding on all States.[34] This is because it interprets the UN Charter, has been treated by most States as a standard-setting mechanism, and has been treated by the International Court of Justice as a source of international custom. Similarly, under the UN Charter, member States commit to take joint and separate action in co-operation with the UN Organisation to promote higher standards of living, full employment, conditions of economic and social progress and development, and the observance of human rights and fundamental freedoms for all.[35] Having received near-universal acceptance, the commitments in the UN Charter and the *UDHR* indicate that a legal obligation, however imprecise, exists for all members of the United Nations.[36] This commitment was recognised at the Millennium Summit of 2000 where States unambiguously declared: "We recognize that, in addition to our separate responsibilities to our individual societies, we have a collective responsibility to uphold the principles of human dignity, equality and equity at the global level."[37]

---

[31] *CESCR Poverty Statement, ibid.* at paras. 10-12.
[32] General Comment, No. 12, *supra* note 17, at para. 7.
[33] *Supra* note 12, Art. 28.
[34] See A. Eide & G. Alfredsson, "Introduction" in A. Eide & G. Alfredsson, eds. *The Universal Declaration of Human Rights: A Common Standard of Achievement* (The Hague: Martinus Nijhoff, 1999) at xxx-xxxii.
[35] *Charter of the United Nations,* supra note 6, arts. 55 & 56.
[36] According to Rosas, writing in 1995, "That there are some rights and obligations at this level, too, cannot be denied, but what specific impact they can have on the policies of States and international institutions is yet to be determined." A. Rosas, "The Right to Development" in A. Eide, C. Krause & A. Rosas, eds. *Economic, Social and Cultural Rights: A Textbook,* 1st ed., (Dordrecht: Martinus Nijhoff, 1995) at 251.
[37] *Millennium Declaration, supra* note 3, Article 2.

Obligations to provide international cooperation and assistance are most clearly contained in Article 2(1) of the *ICESCR*,[38] where States commit to take steps "individually and through international assistance and co-operation" to achieve progressively the full realisation of the rights recognised in the Covenant. In addition, in Article 11(1) of the *ICESCR*, State parties agree to "take appropriate steps to ensure the realisation of this right (the right to an adequate standard of living), recognising to this effect the essential importance of international cooperation based on free consent." In Article 11(2), State parties agree to take "individually and through international cooperation" measures needed to recognise the right of everyone to be free from hunger. According to the Committee on Economic, Social and Cultural Rights, "international cooperation for development and thus for the realization of economic, social and cultural rights is an obligation of all States. It is particularly incumbent upon those States that are in a position to assist others in this regard."[39] However, while the existence of some legal obligation in relation to international cooperation is therefore clear, the particular content of this obligation requires further analysis.[40]

International obligations, although different from domestic obligations, may similarly be classified according obligations *to respect*, *to protect* and *to fulfil* economic, social and cultural rights. The last aspect, 'to fulfil' is controversial. It is difficult to show that these *ICESCR* creates a legally binding obligation upon any particular State to provide any particular form of assistance to another.[41] The countries that negotiated the *ICESCR* did not agree that developing countries could claim aid as a legal right, which is relevant as a supplementary means of interpreting the terms of the Covenant. Some developing States said that there was a strong obligation on the developed world, partly on grounds of interdependence, but also, as stated by Mali, as reparation to the developing world for the "systematic plundering of their wealth under colonialism."[42] But the only formal suggestion that a legal obligation existed came from Chile, which stated that "international assistance to underdeveloped countries had, in a sense become mandatory."[43] The United States, which has not ratified the Covenant, stated it essential that the Article indicated the necessity of

---

[38] See text accompanying note 11 above.
[39] Gen Comment No. 3, *supra* note 12 at para. 14.This commitment exists in Articles 2 (1), 11, 15, 22 & 23 of the *ICESCR*.
[40] M. Craven, *The International Covenant on Economic, Social and Cultural Rights: A Perspective on its Development* (Oxford: Clarendon, 1995) at 147 & 149. See also for a detailed discussion of this topic, International Council on Human Rights Policy, *Duties sans Frontieres: Human Rights and Global Social Justice* (Geneva: ICHRP, 2003), online: ICHRP <www.ichrp.org>.
[41] See Craven, *ibid* at 149, and P. Alston & G. Quinn, "The Nature and Scope of States Parties' Obligations under the International Covenant on Economic, Social and Cultural Rights" (1987) 9 Human Rights Quarterly 156 at 186-191.
[42] Alston & Quinn, *ibid.* at 189.
[43] *Ibid.*

international assistance, but no more.[44] Some States that did ratify the *ICESCR*; France, the Soviet Union and Greece were emphatic that assistance could not be mandatory.[45]

According to Article 32 of the *Vienna Convention on the Law of Treaties*, the preparatory work to a treaty is only a supplementary means of interpretation, one to which there should only be resort if the primary means of interpretation leave the meaning ambiguous. These means of interpretation are specified in Article 31 of the Vienna Convention. They specify that a treaty should be interpreted in good faith in accordance with the ordinary meaning to be given to the terms of the treaty in their context and in the light of its object and purpose. Other relevant factors to take into account include any subsequent practise in the application of the treaty that establishes the agreement of the parties regarding its interpretation, as well as any relevant rules of international law applicable in the relations between the parties.[46] There is no practise that suggests agreement between State parties on the interpretation of the *ICESCR* on the extent of international cooperation obligations. However, the ordinary meaning of the *ICESCR*, taken together with provisions of the UN Charter and the *UDHR* relating to international cooperation, as discussed above, suggest a positive legal obligation. Alston and Quinn argue that although it is unlikely that the Covenant creates any particular States to provide any particular form of assistance, it would be unjustified to argue that the relevant commitment is meaningless. They suggest that in the context of a given right it may, according to the circumstances, be possible to identify obligations to cooperate internationally that would appear to be mandatory on the basis of the undertaking contained in Article 2(1) of the Covenant. One example might be to consider situations where the economic actions of one State or group of States cause substantial injury to other States.[47] It has similarly been suggested that a State could be viewed as not complying with its *ICESCR* obligations if the amount of aid it provided to other countries declined over a number of years.[48] This is relevant since the percentage of Gross National Product (GNP) of the developed countries dedicated to international aid declined from 0.33% in 1992 to 0.22% in 1997.[49] Finally, the text of the *ICESCR* clearly mandates

---

[44] *Ibid.* at 188-189. The United States may therefore not be bound by the full spectrum of the international obligation discussed in this chapter. However, as it has ratified other treaties recognising economic, social and cultural rights, it is not possible to entirely rule out any obligation upon it. Furthermore, as a signatory to the ICESCR, it is bound by good faith obligations to refrain from any act that would frustrate the object and purpose of the treaty.

[45] *Ibid.* at 190.

[46] *Limburg Principles, supra* note 14 at para. 4, *Vienna Convention on the Law of Treaties,* 23 May 1969, 8 I.L.M. 679 (entered into force: 27 January 1980), Arts. 31-32.

[47] P. Alston & G. Quinn, *supra* note 41 at 191.

[48] Craven also suggest that standards could be set by the CESCR with reference to the resources required to meet the challenge of global poverty, *supra* note 40 at 150.

[49] However, overall amounts have been slightly increasing since 1997, though not yet at 1992 levels. See B. Bramble, "Financial Resources for the Transition to Sustainable Development" in F. Dodds, ed. *Earth Summit 2002: A New Deal* (London: Earthscan, 2000) at 139. See also the result of the Monterrey Conference on Financing for Development, discussed below.

international cooperation to ensure an equitable distribution of world food supplies in relation to need.[50]

The United Nations Committee on Economic Social and Cultural Rights has elaborated on this notion by adding the concept of an 'international minimum threshold':

> "When grouped together, the core obligations establish an international minimum threshold that all developmental policies should be designed to respect. In accordance with General Comment No. 14, it is particularly incumbent on all those who can assist, to help developing countries respect this international minimum threshold. If a national or international anti-poverty strategy does not reflect this minimum threshold, it is inconsistent with the legally binding obligations of the State party."[51]

This statement by the CESCR is consistent with its previous interpretations of the Covenant. Minimum core obligations in the domestic context were explained by the CESCR as necessary since: "If the Covenant were to be read in such a way as not to establish such a minimum core obligation, it would be largely deprived of its raison d'être."[52] An analogous argument may apply at the international level. Unless the wealthier States are obliged to assist those developing countries that are unable to realise their core economic, social and cultural rights obligations, references to international cooperation in the *ICESCR* would be of little relevance in light of the *ICESCR*'s purpose, which is to ensure the realisation of economic, social and cultural rights for all in accordance with their commitments in the *UN Charter* and the *UDHR*. Preambulatory paragraph 3 of the *ICESCR* states, "Recognizing that, in accordance with the Universal Declaration of Human Rights, the ideal of free human beings enjoying freedom from fear and want can only be achieved if conditions are created whereby everyone may enjoy his economic, social and cultural rights, as well as his civil and political rights."

The notion of the international minimum threshold suggests a process to delineate the extent of international obligations relative to domestic obligations. If international anti-poverty strategies must 'enable' developing countries to meet their core obligations, the international community is responsible for the extent of assistance necessary to supplement domestic resources in order to

---

[50] Article 11.2 of the ICESCR, *supra* note 7, requires that States "individually and through international co-operation, [undertake] the measures, including specific programmes, which are needed … to improve methods of production, conservation and distribution of food, …. by developing or reforming agrarian systems in such a way as to achieve the most efficient development and utilization of natural resources; and to ensure an equitable distribution of world food supplies in relation to need."

[51] *CESCR Poverty Statement, supra* note 22 at para. 20. See text accompanying note 46 above on the relevance of the 'object and purpose' of a treaty in its interpretation.

[52] General Comment No. 3, *supra* note 16 at para. 10.

meet such core obligations. Although the *ICESCR* does not place any particular obligation on any one country to provide aid to another country, it requires that the State parties to the Covenant individually and collectively take necessary actions consistent with the Covenant to ensure, as stated in the *UDHR,* that international co-operation and assistance be directed towards the establishment of a social and international order in which the rights and freedoms set forth in the *ICESCR* can be fully realised.[53]

In assessing the implications of the 'core obligations approach,' the international programme found in the *Millennium Declaration*[54] is of relevance. These commitments, known as the Millennium Development Goals (MDGs), are to be realised by 2015, include, *inter alia*: a commitment to halve the number of people in absolute poverty and hunger, to halve the number of people who cannot access safe drinking water, to provide basic education for all and reverse the spread of major diseases.[55] Obligations to eliminate absolute poverty, hunger and to provide basic education and safe drinking water, for example, are all minimum core obligations. Under the *ICESCR,* such obligations should be immediately addressed. In spite of their consequent limitations, the Millennium Development Goals are useful to this analysis since the resources needed to reach them have been quantified. The Zedillo Report,[56] produced by a panel of eminent persons commissioned by the UN Secretary General, has estimated that meeting the MDG targets would require, together with appropriate economic and social policies, roughly an additional US $50 billion investment in human needs and capacities over current spending.[57]

An inter-related obligation is the requirement that, in the same manner as domestic resources, international assistance (aid and debt relief) be targeted towards the most vulnerable populations.[58] This obligation is of significant concern since it has been estimated that historically and presently, international assistance is not focused on the most needy countries, and the most needy populations within them. For example, in 1995, it was estimated that twice as much overseas development assistance (ODA) per capita went to countries with the wealthiest 40% of people in the developing world as opposed to the

---

[53] As stated in the *Limburg Principles, supra* note 14 at para. 30. See also Office of the High Commissioner for Human Rights, *Draft Guidelines on a Human Rights Approach to Poverty Reduction Strategies* (Geneva: OHCHR, 2002), Guideline 15: Right to International Assistance and Cooperation.

[54] *Supra* note 3.

[55] *Ibid.* at para. 19.

[56] The panel notes that this estimate does not include increased costs of servicing distant populations, potential synergies in public spending and possible improvements in efficiency. It further states that the $50 billion estimate is given only to indicate the magnitude of the financing requirements, "but there is no doubt that the figure is substantial." See *Report of the High-Level Panel on Financing for Development to the Secretary General,* 26 June 2001, U.N. Doc. A/55/1000.

[57] *Ibid* at 68-72.

[58] The CESCR has stressed, for example in the context of the right to housing, that international assistance should be focused on the most disadvantaged groups, *General Comment No. 4: The Right to Adequate Shelter,* E/1992/23-E/C.12/1991/4.annex III at para. 19. The *Limburg Principles, supra* note 10, state; "international cooperation must be directed towards the establishment of a social and economic order in which the rights and freedoms in the Covenant can be fully realized (cf. Art. 28, *UDHR).*"

poorest 40%. Less than 7% of bilateral ODA was directed to human development concerns - primary health care, basic education, safe drinking water, etc.[59] The obligation to target aid to the poorest is particularly clear under the *ICESCR* since failures to target aid cannot be excused by claiming a 'lack of available resources.'

In contrast to obligations to *fulfil* economic, social and cultural rights discussed above, State obligations to *respect* and *protect* economic, social and cultural rights of persons in other countries are more clearly established in the ICESCR. The references to international cooperation in the *ICESCR* establish, at the least, that States cannot carry out actions that would clearly create obstacles to the realisation of economic, social and cultural rights. As a result, international lending institutions, by virtue of the commitments of their member States, are required to respect economic, social and cultural rights in the context of their imposition of structural adjustment programmes.[60] Similarly, it has been suggested that States have a positive duty to ensure that all bodies subject to their control respect the enjoyment of rights in other countries. Therefore, they must apply these principles in voting within international organisations and in regulating multinational companies based in their countries.[61] The obligations under the *ICESCR* require that measures be urgently taken to remove global structural obstacles to the realisation of economic, social and cultural rights.[62] The *ICESCR* arguably requires that unsustainable foreign debt be cancelled.[63] The effect of such debts on economic, social and cultural rights is clear for many of the least developed countries whose annual debt repayments have, at times, amounted to between 69% to 200% of their combined health, education and social expenditure.[64]

The example of the Heavily Indebted Poor Country Initiative (HIPC) can be used to illustrate the impact of these obligations.[65] The HIPC Initiative is implemented by the World Bank and the International Monetary Fund (IMF), with the participation of many bilateral donors. The terms of this initiative allow for the reduction of the public debt of the 43 poorest nations to levels that are considered 'sustainable.' Debt relief is conditional upon compliance with economic reforms set out by the IMF and World Bank. The use of the proceeds of debt relief is to be guided by Poverty Reduction Strategy Papers

---

[59] M. Ul-Haq, *Reflections on Human Development,* (New York: Oxford, 1995) at 35.

[60] Committee on Economic, Social and Cultural Rights, *General Comment No.2: International Technical Assistance Measures,* UN ESCOR, 1990, UN Doc. E/1990/23, at para. 9.

[61] Craven, *supra* note 40 at 148. In relation to membership in international organisations, see *General Comment No. 2, ibid.*

[62] *General Comment 12, supra* note 17 at para. 41.

[63] Poverty Statement, *supra* note 22 at para. 21. *General Comment No.2,* of the Committee on Economic, Social and Cultural Rights, *supra* note 60, referred in 1990 to the possible need for debt relief initiatives.

[64] *Joint Report by the Independent Expert on Structural Adjustment Programmes and the Special Rapporteur on Foreign Debt,* UN Commission on Human Rights, UN ESCOR, 2000, UN Doc. E/CN.4/2000/51 at para 17 [hereinafter *Joint Report*].

[65] A number of suggested indicators for international assistance are suggested in the *Draft Guidelines: A Human Rights Approach to Poverty Reduction Strategies, supra* note 53, Guideline No. 15 at 55-57.

(PRSPs) produced by the relevant State, developed transparently and with the broad participation of civil society. The PRSP process, initially suggested by OXFAM, a prominent development NGO, and the United Nations Children's Fund (UNICEF), aims to serve as a contract between debtor and creditor governments to ensure that debt relief is directly used for poverty reduction.

While the HIPC initiative clearly aids the realisation of basic economic, social and cultural rights, it has been critiqued from a human rights perspective by two experts appointed by the UN Commission on Human Rights.[66] The experts note that the initiative excludes many of the least developed countries, and uses a definition of 'debt sustainability' that is not related to the levels of need within the country. For example, debts are judged to be sustainable if they are equivalent to 150% of a country's annual exports, or 250% of yearly taxation. This is an arbitrary cut-off that does not admit countries based on their ability to repay their debts in light of social needs within the State.[67] At the least, a human rights approach requires that the actual needs of the population be taken into account in determining whether a country can repay its debts.

The experts also note that the plan will continue to maintain conditionality requirements, suggesting that the HIPC scheme is therefore simply a backdoor for the IFI's to maintain control over the national development policies of poor countries.[68] While the conditionality issue is dealt with in more detail below, at the minimum, the *ICESCR* requires that conditions by donor agencies are not inconsistent with human rights. Examples of inconsistent conditions could include, for example, introducing unaffordable user charges for basic services such as water, sanitation, health and education, without any subsidies or exemptions for the poorest sectors of the population.

The Right to Development

The right to development gives further support to the domestic and international human rights listed in the above discussion. The General Assembly *Declaration on the Right to Development*[69] defines the right to development as emanating for the civil, political, economic, social and cultural rights included in the *ICCPR* and *ICESCR*.[70] It re-affirms these rights as an applicable part of general international law, and not just binding on the parties of the two Covenants. It has also been seen as a means to extend the effective implementation of existing standards of human rights.[71] The Declaration

---

[66] *Joint Report, supra* note 64 at para. 17.

[67] *Ibid.* at para. 7 & 9-12.

[68] *Ibid.*

[69] GA Res. 41/128, UN GAOR, 1986. This Declaration was adopted by a vote of 146 for and one against (the United States) and eight abstentions (most of these were developed countries).

[70] Arts. 1 (1) & 6.2. The right is also recognised by the *African Charter on Human and Peoples' Rights*, 27 June 1981, 21 I.L.M. 59 (1982) (entered into force 21 October 1986), Art. 22 and is therefore binding on parties to it.

[71] I. Brownlie, *The Human Right to Development* (London: Commonwealth Secretariate, 1989) at 14-15.

includes an obligation to provide for the participation of all people in development, and the fair distribution of the benefits resulting from development on the basis of equality of opportunity for all.[72] The Declaration recognises that "States have the duty to cooperate with each other in ensuring development and eliminating obstacles to development."[73] Other important elements of the Declaration may include an *implicit* duty upon developed States to provide development assistance to developing States.[74]

The precise meaning and legal status of the right to development, as set out in the *Declaration on the Right to Development,* is not completely clear. A General Assembly resolution on its own does not become part of customary international law binding on States unless there consistent and general recognition by States that a principle is binding as a matter of law. It is questionable whether the right to development, as contained in the *Declaration on the Right to Development* is now a principle of customary law.[75] Nevertheless, it is in the process of becoming international law. The right to development has been repeatedly recognised in various United Nations Declarations, although there is disagreement over its content.[76] In addition, since the *Declaration on the Right to Development* was formulated with reference to the United Nations Charter and the International Covenants, it may potentially be seen as a logical implication of those treaties.[77]

One may also argue that the 'right to development' exists in instruments besides the *Declaration on the Rights to Development.* Equitable development, within and between States, is necessarily required to realise many of the human rights recognised in treaty law, such as the *ICESCR* and in established customary law.[78] As such, it may be stated that there is a legally binding right to development, which would include at least some of the provisions in the *Declaration on the Rights to Development.*

---

[72] *Declaration on the Right to Development, supra* note 69, Arts. 2 (3) and 8.

[73] *Declaration on the Right to Development, ibid,* Art. 3.3. There has been concern as to who the rights-holder is. International Court Justice Bedjaoui has clarified that the State is the primary subject – but that the individual is the ultimate beneficiary, cited in Brownlie, *supra* note 71 at 16. In addition, since the *Declaration* draws on the *ICESCR,* States would be bound to engage in development for the benefit of their citizens in accordance with human rights principles.

[74] Brownlie, *ibid* at 9.

[75] Rosas, *supra* note 36 at 251.

[76] The right was re-affirmed by consensus at the 1993 World Conference on Human Rights in the *Vienna Declaration and Programme of Action,* U.N. Doc. A/CONF.157/23, para. I/10. The right, adapted to include the rights of future generations, is also recognised in Principle 3 of the *Rio Declaration on Environment and Development,* 14 June 1992, U.N. Doc. A/CONF.151/26, 31 I.L.M. 874.

[77] This would be analogous to the principle of effective and implied powers in the law of treaties. Brownlie, *supra* note 71 at 14-15.

[78] A similar point is made by the CESCR in *General Comment No. 3, supra* note 16 at para. 14.

Trade Liberalisation, Investment Inflows and International Assistance Obligations

It is often argued that the best way for developing countries to raise the finances necessary for their development is to pursue the economic benefits of trade and investment liberalisation rather than relying on overseas development assistance. Such processes can generate new resources and create employment thereby reducing poverty and the resulting burden on States as well as empowering individuals. This argument has some validity, in that human rights obligations do not normally prescribe any particular method for their realization. What is important is that the rights are realised by any means effective. According to the CESCR, "the rights recognized in the Covenant are susceptible of realization within the context of a wide variety of economic and political systems, provided that the interdependence and indivisibility of the two sets of human rights is respected."[79]

Human rights institutions have noted that that international trade and investment systems must be reformed to support, rather than undermine, human rights. The Draft Guidelines on a Human Rights Approach to Poverty Reduction Strategies, prepared by the Office of the UN High Commissioner for the Human Rights, indicate that international assistance includes more than financial and technical assistance; it also includes an obligation to work actively towards equitable multilateral, trading, investment and financial systems that are conducive to the reduction and elimination of poverty.[80] According to the Committee on Economic, Social and Cultural Rights, it is imperative that measures be urgently taken to remove global structural obstacles to the realization of rights, such as the widening gap between rich and poor, and the absence of an equitable multilateral trade, investment and financial system.[81]

It should be emphasised, however, that just as one cannot rely solely on overseas development assistance as a means to realise economic, social and cultural rights, one cannot conversely rely solely on the expected benefits of trade and investment liberalisation. There is significant evidence that such liberalisation has not yet led to an equitable distribution of resources.[82] In relation to agriculture, for example, developed countries have maintained high tariffs on agricultural products and provided subsidies to their producers that have harmed the ability of farmers in poorer countries to sell their produce.

---

[79] *General Comment No. 3, ibid.* at para. 8.

[80] *Supra* note 53 at 54. For more detail see C. Dommen, "Raising Human Rights Concerns in the World Trade Organization Actors, Processes and Possible Strategies"(2002) 24:1 *Human Rights Quarterly* as well as OHCHR, *Economic, Social and Cultural Rights: Liberalisation of Trade in Services and Human Rights: Report of the High Commissioner*, 25 June 2002, UN Doc. E/CN.4/Sub.2/2002/9 and OHCHR, *Economic, Social and Cultural Rights The impact of the Agreement on Trade-Related Aspects of Intellectual Property Rights on Human Rights*, 27 June 2001, UN Doc. E/CN.4/Sub.2/2001/13.

[81] *CESCR Poverty Statement, supra* note 22 at para. 21.

[82] See, for example, G. Soros, *On Globalization* (New York: Public Affairs, 2002), *Economist,* "Argentina's Collapse" March 2, 2002, at 26-28.

Overall agricultural subsidies in the developed countries rose from US$ 182 billion in 1995 to $300 billion in 1998.[83] In addition, given that many economic, social and cultural rights obligations are immediate, States cannot claim to be meeting these obligations by relying on anticipated or future gains that would result from trade. Although there is disagreement on the extent of the overall benefit of trade liberalisation, it is generally accepted that there will be short-terms costs related to economic restructuring as States begin liberalization. Indeed, it is not a given that trade liberalisation will bring about improvement in all situations. Some developing States will be negatively affected by competition from countries where producers have more access to State support and access to credit on easy terms, enjoy greater institutional support for training workers, have ready access to technological innovation, and can depend on integrated marketing systems for distributing their merchandise.[84] Indeed, the experience of the Newly Industrialised Countries in East and South-East Asia has shown that investments in health care and education were a prerequisite for such countries to benefit from trade liberalisation.[85] It is therefore necessary that efforts to fulfil minimum core obligations be addressed through a variety of international measures, including appropriately structured trade liberalisation, targeted international assistance and debt relief, rather than any one of these measures.[86]

International Assistance Obligations: Conditional upon Compliance?

A key issue is whether the international community's obligations to cooperate for the realisation of human rights are nullified if a recipient State is misusing resources, engaging in officially sanctioned corruption or neglecting vulnerable populations. There is no simple answer to this long-standing issue. One primary concern is the effect of effects of withholding assistance. International assistance obligations are owed to peoples in developing countries, not their governments. It would therefore be inconsistent with human rights law to penalise individuals for the acts of their governments. In such cases, financial and technical assistance should also be provided through good governance initiatives to assist developing States willing to improve their ability to use resources effectively and efficiently. Where necessary, international assistance can be channelled directly to the affected populations through non-governmental organisations, or to individual government departments. A general policy to bypass a developing country government would weaken its

---

[83] W. Bello, "*High Stakes for the 1999 Review of the Agreement on Agriculture,*" (1998) 2 Bridges Between Trade and Sustainable Development 2 at 2.
[84] D. Barkin, "Wealth, Poverty and Sustainable Development" in J. Harris, *Rethinking Sustainability: Power, Knowledge and Institutions* (Ann Arbour, University of Michigan, 2000) at 89.
[85] A. Sen, *Development as Freedom* (New York: Alfred Knopf, 1999).
[86] Indeed, the WTO Doha Declaration recognises that the trade regime should consider issues of external indebtedness of developing countries. World Trade Organization, *Ministerial Declaration, 14 November 2001, Doha,* WT/MIN (01)/DEC/W/1, at para. 36.

ability to address structural poverty over the long-term, and should therefore occur only when necessary.

Conditionality is problematic as a means to promote human rights because it relies on the dependency of Southern States on the North, itself is a profound and fundamental violation of human rights. Conditionality in this context helps legitimize and reinforce such unequal relationships.[87] In addition, developed countries are not necessarily in a better position to evaluate human rights performance than developing countries, and often have political and economic interests that create conflicts of interest in such evaluation. There have been powerful critiques of the use of sanctions by Western States in response to (mainly civil and political) human rights violations. Such actions have been characterized as often being inconsistent, relying on legal fictions of trickle-up effects, being carried out for appearances sake and often of benefit to the sanctioning State.[88] These concerns have to be balanced against the counter-argument that failure to address mis-spending will often make the donor State complicit in violation of human rights, particularly where assistance is provided in the form of loans whose re-payment would burden the developing country in the future.[89] In addition, it is unrealistic to expect that any State can justify to its taxpayers the provision of international assistance if a high proportion of this assistance is effectively wasted. Finally, even the critics of conditionality, such as An-Na'im, accept that realising basic human rights is such important that one can justify, at least in the short term and as a last resort, the use of international power relations to secure human rights and create the space for national movements to take responsibility of ensuring the promotion of human rights.[90] Therefore, the challenge is to consider what types of international institutions can ensure that such decisions on international assistance are taken in a fair manner that represents both donor and recipient States and which have the effect of ensuring that international assistance is used towards the realisation of human rights.

Significant amounts of debt relief and official development assistance are now being channelled through processes that allow for greater degrees of 'national ownership,' in accordance with nationally developed Poverty Reduction

---

[87] A. An-Na'im, "Problems of Dependency, Human Rights Organizations in the Arab World (An Interview with Abdullahi An-Na'im):" (2000) 214 *Middle East Report* 20 at 22.

[88] K. Tomasevksi, *Responding to Human Rights Violations 1946-1999* (The Hague: Martinus Nijhoff, 2000).

[89] Indeed, there is a strong legal argument for the proposition that States are not bound to pay public debt contracted by previous dictators that was clearly not used to benefit the population, where the lender was aware or should have been aware that this was the situation. See A. Khalfan, J. King & B. Thomas, *Advancing the Odious Debt Doctrine: Legal Aspects* (Montreal: CISDL, 2002), online: Centre for International Sustainable Development Law <www.cisdl.org/pdf/debtentire.pdf>.

[90] An-Na'im, *supra* note 87 at 22, reluctantly accepts the need "to be pragmatic in the short term about using the existing power relations to promote some level of protection of human rights and create the space for internal constituencies and activism to emerge. However, it is necessary to invest in the process of developing truly autonomous human rights movements that work at the local level, are protected by local constituencies, organise around their own priorities, enlist political support within their own communities and pressure their own governments."

Strategy Papers (PRSPs), which are required to be developed transparently and with the broad participation of civil society. As discussed above, the PRSP process has been critiqued on the basis that the evaluation of these papers by the International Financial Institutions (IFIs) and by individual donor States (in relation to bilateral assistance) is not independent. The programme limits the participation of UN bodies only to the IFIs (and thereby excludes United Nations specialised agencies such as the United National Development Programme).[91] Therefore, the PRSP process requires reforms in order to ensure either better representation of developing States in the IFIs or establishment of an independent body appointed with representation of donor and recipient States.

Certain elements of the Cotonou Agreement[92] between the European Union (EU) and the African, Caribbean and Pacific nations (ACP) which mitigate unilateral decision-making by donor States may be helpful in considering future models. The Cotonou Agreement explicitly recognizes the need for respect for human rights. The performance of ACP States of their obligations under the Agreement is monitored by a Council comprised of Ministers of all the EU and ACP parties. Where sanctions are proposed, the Agreement specifies a mediation and dialogue process over a period of three months, after which disputes over the application of the Agreement may be taken to an internationalised arbitration. Both parties agree on an arbitrator, failing which the arbitrator is appointed by the President of the Permanent Court of Arbitration.[93] An emerging potential model is the New African Partnership for Development (NEPAD), commenced in 2001 by the Organisation of African Unity (now known as the African Union) with the support of the major developed States. NEPAD is intended to stimulate significant public and private investment in Africa's development from developed countries. African countries, on their part, commit to improve their own governance through the development of a Peer Review Mechanism. One of objectives of NEPAD is to ensure stronger protection of human rights in each country. NEPAD does not systematise the realisation of human rights within its development plans. However, if this model eventually succeeds, it could provide a framework in which States can effectively discharge their domestic and international human rights obligations relating to financing for development.[94]

---

[91] *Joint Report by the Independent Expert on Structural Adjustment Programmes and the Special Rapporteur on Foreign Debt*, *supra* note 64 at para. 7 & 9-12. This has important political implications. The Boards of the IFIs are dominated by developed countries, as votes are allocated according to financial contributions. United Nations specialised agencies are under the control of the UN political organs in which each member State has one vote.

[92] *Partnership Agreement between the Members of the African, Caribbean and Pacific Group of States (ACP) of the one part, and the European Community and its Member States, of the other part* 2000/483/EC (Cotonou, 23 June 2000) *Official Journal L 317 of 15.12.2000*.

[93] *Cotonou Agreement, ibid.*, Arts. 9 & 96-97.

[94] The objectives, structure and goals of NEPAD are described online: New Partnership for Africa's Development <www.nepad.org>.

The international human rights treaty bodies, which are composed of independent experts from developed and developing countries, could play a useful role in contributing to an environment that is less politicised and better geared towards the effective realisation of human rights. Arjun Sengupta, the Independent Expert on the Right to Development appointed by the United Nations Commission on Human Rights, has suggested the formulation of 'development compacts' – where increased assistance would be conditional upon effective compliance with human rights by the developing countries, which would be monitored by national human rights commissions. Such a system would, to some extent address the 'dependency argument' raised by An-Na'im. However, in 1999, at the United Nations Human Rights Commission, a number of Southern States rejected a 'rights-based approach to development,' arguing that it undermines human rights by creating conditionalities to development, itself a basic human right.[95] The position of these countries most probably reflects mistrust of the *bona fides* of Northern States and inter-governmental organisations in respect to conditionality, rather than opposition in principle to implementing human rights in development work. In this respect, it is noteworthy that a number of these States, in particular India, recognise economic, social and cultural rights at the domestic level. Such mistrust may be mitigated by confidence-building measures (such as independent arbitration and Northern States accepting clear time-bound commitments). However, the position of these States indicates that significant amount of work needs to be done to establish joint and mutual partnership approaches to integrating human rights into development financing.

Human Rights Assessment of the Monterrey Consensus on Financing for Development

The Monterrey Consensus was adopted at the United Nations International Conference on Financing for Development, held from 18-22 March 2002, by the representatives of all UN member States. It is the first global declaration devoted entirely to the means of raising financing for development. The negotiating process involved States as well as representatives of business and civil society. States did not generally raise human rights at the Conference or at the preparatory process that agreed the text. The document does not address the implications of human rights law, except for one brief reference to respect for human rights, including the right to development, at the domestic level.[96] Nevertheless, from the point of view of the substance of human rights, the document can be described as not inconsistent with human rights law in some areas, and consistent with human rights laws in relation to domestic measures

---

[95] These countries included Algeria, Bhutan, China, Cuba, Egypt, India, Iran, Malaysia, Myanmar, Nepal, Pakistan, Sri Lanka, Sudan and Vietnam. See P. Alston, "Peoples' Rights: Their Rise and Fall" in P. Alston, ed. *Peoples' Rights* (Oxford: Oxford University, 2001) at 285. This position is not supported by the General Assembly *Declaration on the Right to Development, supra* note 69, which clearly states in Articles 1.1 and 6.1 that the right to development comprises all civil, political, economic, social and cultural rights.
[96] *Monterrey Consensus on Financing for Development, supra* note 4 para. 11.

(in particular references to emphasizing attention to vulnerable groups). However, the document falls short by failing to specify targeted commitments to put in place adequate resources to achieve human rights obligations.

The Introduction to the Monterrey Consensus acknowledges 'dramatic' shortfalls' in resources required to meet the Millennium Development Goals (MDGs) and 'other' internationally agreed development goals.[97] In regard to mobilizing domestic resources, the document lists necessary elements such as good governance, 'sound economic policy,' anti-corruption, transparency and supervisory mechanisms, avoidance of inflation, human rights (including the right to development) and market-oriented policies.[98] These are all consistent with a human rights approach. In particular, the document addresses elements consistent with the obligation to focus on the most vulnerable, by referring to the need for investments in economic and social infrastructure, attention to disadvantaged communities (such as the rural sector, women, children, the elderly), worker training, social safety nets, investments in housing and incorporation of the informal sector into the formal economy, "wherever feasible."[99] The latter phrase, which allows excessive discretion for the State, is regrettable. There are, unfortunately, no benchmarks for resource mobilization for the State to finance development for the poor. Actions such as the 20/20 Initiative (which suggested that States would devote 20% of their budget to basic social services, and aid donors would commit at least 20% of their assistance these social services), are not taken up in the text.[100]

The document is relatively conservative from a human rights perspective on the second chapter which deals with foreign direct investment (FDI) and other private flows. The text, unfortunately, states that FDI is important because it can transfer technology, create jobs, stimulate entrepreneurship, "and ultimately *eradicate* poverty."[101] As discussed above, such a claim may be misleading by implying that FDI could be relied upon to fulfil the international assistance obligations. Investment structured towards productive employment may assist in realising economic, social and cultural rights, but would not be of assistance to those persons unable to work, who do not have skills, or indeed lose their employment as a result of increased competition. At best, it can only be a partial solution.

In contract to investment, the Monterrey Consensus does not make unwarranted claims about contribution that trade can make to development. The chapter on international trade as an engine for development cautiously

---

[97] *Ibid.,* at para. 2. As noted above, although the MDGs fall short of human rights obligations, it represents at least a starting point, See text accompanying note 54.
[98] *Monterrey Consensus, ibid.,* at paras. 10-11.
[99] *Ibid.,* at paras. 16-19.
[100] The 20/20 Initiative was proposed at the World Summit for Social Development. See Bramble, *supra* note 49 at 147.
[101] *Monterrey Consensus, supra* note 4 at para. 20.

states that "a rule based, universal equitable multilateral trading system *as well* as meaningful trade liberalization *can* substantially stimulate development."[102] The text recognizes certain issues that need to be addressed to support economic development in Southern countries. It affirms the necessity to put the needs and interests of developing countries at the heart of the World Trade Organisation (WTO) Programme for implementation of commitments made at the 2001 Doha Ministerial conference in relation to the marginalisation of least developed countries (LDCs).[103] It should be noted, however, that such commitments in Doha were made "without prejudging the outcome of negotiations."[104] The text also reiterates calls for developed countries to "work towards the objective" of quota- and duty-free access to LDC exports and indicates the need for effective and predictable trade-related capacity building.[105] Both of these are measures that could help provide important sources of finance for development in Southern countries.

The Monterrey Consensus also addressed a number of key trade concerns of developing countries, but does not commit to any substantive actions. It includes a commitment to "continue to assess" the IMF Compensatory Financing Facility in relation to falling commodity prices – a major challenge for the least developed countries.[106] It acknowledges issues of particular concern of developing countries, such as the need for provisions in WTO law for 'special and differential treatment for developing countries' to be made more concrete.[107]

In the chapter on international and financial technical cooperation for development, the document "Strongly endorses ODA [overseas development assistance] as a complement to other sources, particularly for countries with least capacity to attract private investment. It is a crucial instrument for education, health, rural development, etc. For countries like Africa, LDCs etc., it is critical to the achievement of the Millennium Development Goals and other internationally agreed development targets."[108] The document therefore usefully notes the need for a contextual approach to determine the necessity for direct international financing measures, taking note of the lesser ability of some States to benefit from trade and investment. In relation to new sources of financing, the document *'urges'* developed countries to make concrete efforts towards *the* target of 0.7% of each development country's Gross National Product (GNP) towards assistance developing countries, with 0.15-0.2% of GNP directed to LDCs.[109] Although States are not clearly committed to

---

[102] *Ibid.,* at para. 26
[103] *Ibid.,* at para. 29-31.
[104] World Trade Organization, *Ministerial Declaration, 14 November 2001, Doha,* WT/MIN(01)/DEC/W/1, at paras. 13 & 42.
[105] *Monterrey Consensus, supra* note 4 at para. 34.
[106] *Ibid.,* at para. 37.
[107] *Ibid.,* at para. 28.
[108] *Ibid.,* at para. 39.
[109] *Ibid.,* at para. 42.

actually reach this target within a specified time-frame, it is significant that this long-standing target is re-affirmed as authoritative, in spite of significant opposition during the negotiations to this point from the United States, which had described the target as out-dated. The reservation of 0.15-0.2% of GNP for LDCs is salutary given the concern expressed above about the provision of aid mainly to the wealthier developing countries. However, it can be argued from a human rights perspective that, as a means to fulfil core obligations, the proportion of aid going to LDCs should be much higher.[110]

The document also notes the need to target aid to the neediest within each recipient country.[111] The text makes a concerted effort to address concerns about conditionality, by emphasising at various points the need for national ownership[112] and calls for the untying of aid.[113] These are positive steps, although as noted in below, there is a need to make far more progress on the establishment of partnerships on this issue, rather than decision-making that ultimately rests with donor States.

The chapter on external debt has some significant innovations. It notes that debtors and creditors must share responsibility for *preventing* and *resolving* unsustainable debt situations.[114] The text states that debt relief, "where appropriate", should be pursued vigorously and expeditiously, in various fora, and it invites further national and international measures, including debt cancellation "where appropriate."[115] One of the most important points was the document's call for *future* reviews of debt sustainability to bear in mind the impact of debt relief on progress towards the achievement of the development goals contained in the Millennium Declaration.[116] The document stresses the importance of "continued flexibility" with regard to the eligibility criteria, and the importance of reviewing computational assumptions underlying debt sustainability at the completion point, taking into account worsening growth prospects, natural disasters, conflict and terms of trade.[117] As noted above, debt sustainability analyses currently do not officially take into account the actual needs of the population in determining whether a country can repay its debts. The new text therefore calls for a more contextual and human development-

---

[110] While one could argue that *most* aid should go to LDCs, one cannot say that *all* aid should go to LDCs. While it may be assumed that middle-income developing countries are in a position to realise core obligations through domestic resources and greater redistribution, one should not ignore instances of mass poverty caused by epidemics (such as AIDS in Botswana) or severe economic downturns (such as in Argentina) that cannot be addressed by the State. In other instances where pockets of severe poverty is the result of deliberate neglect of slum dwellers, lower castes or other minorities, for example, it may be argued that international assistance directly to such excluded communities is particularly necessary.

[111] *Ibid.,* at para. 40.

[112] *Ibid.,* at para. 40 &43.

[113] *Ibid.,* at para. 43.

[114] *Ibid.,* at para. 47.

[115] *Ibid.,* at para. 48.

[116] *Ibid.,* at para. 49.

[117] *Ibid.,* at para. 49. The phrase "continuing to…" is often used in the document, as a way to prevent change, while allowing developing countries to make their point.

oriented approach to addressing debt sustainability. Although this text is only a recommendation to the International Financial Institutions, and individual donor States, its political weight was shown by the fact that it was one of the most hotly debated topics at the preparatory conferences, and was only agreed in its final form after adept negotiating by South Africa on behalf of the Group of 77 and China (the negotiating block of developing countries).[118] A related aspect on debt is the Monterrey Consensus's encouragement of exploration of innovative mechanisms to address middle-income country debt.[119] This phrase may recognise that failures to realise core obligations due to debt is not a LDC phenomenon alone. However, the vagueness of this phrase militates against such an interpretation.

The chapter on systemic issue-coherence and consistency of the international monetary, financial and trading systems encourages policy and programme coordination at the international level to meet the MDGs through sustained economic growth, poverty eradication and sustainable development.[120] The document notes international financial institutions should take into account social costs of adjustment programmes and minimize negative impact on the vulnerable segments of society.[121] This point speaks very clearly to a concrete requirement on such institutions under human rights law, as indicated above. States unambiguously commit in the text to negotiate and finalise as soon as possible a UN Convention against corruption.[122] While the effectiveness of this Convention remain to be seen, it has significant possibilities for generating resources for development by repatriating stolen wealth to its countries of origin and creating disincentives to corruption.

In summary, the text of the Monterrey Consensus offered few new commitments. Nevertheless, there is some progress on the normative level that does bode well for the observance of human rights related to development financing at the domestic and international level. A note of caution is in order here. The Monterrey Consensus is only politically rather than legally binding. Nevertheless, it provides normative guidance that will certainly be deployed strategically in negotiations between governments. Indeed, Monterrey proved to have an immediate impact on the willingness of most developed countries to increase their international assistance. At the conference the United States publicly announced that it would its annual ODA by $5 billion annually, phased in from 2004 to 2006 (an increase of 0.05% of its GNP), while the European Union (EU) promised that all its members will reach the EU's short-term 0.33% target by 2006, thereby increasing the total to 0.39% of GNP. These numbers are bound to change, but it is clear that the downward trend in ODA

---

[118] This and other observations about the Monterrey process are based on the author's perceptions while attending the final preparatory committee meeting and the Monterrey Conference.
[119] *Monterrey Consensus, supra* note 4 at para. 51.
[120] *Ibid.,* at para. 52.
[121] *Ibid.,* at para. 56.
[122] *Ibid.,* at para. 65.

has been halted, although not yet rising towards the 0.7% GNP UN target. This is a tangible improvement, although it remains to be seen whether such assistance will be targeted to where it is needed most. It should also be pointed out that these new additions will provide only an estimated one-third of the additional $50 billion in aid required to meet the Millennium Development Goals.

Conclusions

A human rights perspective on development financing provides a number of important prescriptions for action by the international community. In the first section, the chapter demonstrated that the *International Covenant on Economic, Social and Cultural Rights* and related treaties provides clear legal obligations upon States to raise resources at the national level, to the maximum of their available resources, and with particular focus on disbursing these to the most vulnerable communities. States are legally obliged to ensure that at least 'core obligations' corresponding to the most basic needs are immediately realised. In situations of resource scarcity, obligations remain to re-focus existing resources to low-cost programmes to benefit the poorest. In regard to the controversial area of international assistance obligations to help finance development, it was noted that there is a strong argument to state that there are concrete legal obligations upon the international community. The concept of a 'minimum international threshold' linked to core obligations has clear implications for total levels of international assistance and debt relief, and also requires that these should be focused upon the poorest peoples. It was noted that the *Millennium Development Goals* fall short of this threshold. Duties to avoid harming the enjoyment of economic, social and cultural rights at the international level also have clear implications, *inter alia,* for the voting of States in international bodies, debt collection and structural adjustment measures.

This chapter considered the relevance of the *Declaration on the Right to Development* to financing for development. It was noted that international assistance obligations exist independently of the *Declaration* – an important fact given that it is unlikely whether the right to development, as contained in the *Declaration,* is now a principle of customary law. However, it was noted that the *Declaration* is in the process of becoming customary law, which is important given its potential contribution to human rights obligations related to financing for development.

Two tangled issues raised by the analysis of domestic and international legal obligations were addressed. The first was the question of whether international obligations could be fulfilled through the expected benefits of trade and investment liberalisation. It was noted that appropriately structured trade and investment liberalisation could be considered a essential tool to fulfil international assistance obligations. However, given that States must realise core obligations immediately rather than in the future, it would not be consistent with the *ICESCR* and related obligations if States simply relied on expected gains from liberalisation, particularly since the trading system is not necessarily structured in favour of development that would benefit the poorest. It was therefore noted that a full range of international assistance and cooperation measures, including aid, debt cancellation and trade liberalisation would be required so as to fulfil human rights obligations within a short time frame.

The second tangled issue was whether international assistance obligations persist when the recipient States are violating domestic obligations in relation to development financing. It was concluded that international assistance remained obligatory in such instances as the developed States can provide assistance to good governance initiatives, when demonstrably necessary, choose to channel all aid through non-governmental channels. However, due to concerns about the partiality of donor States and the legitimation of unequal relationships between Northern and Southern States, unilaterally imposed conditionalities must give way to joint approaches that emphasise mutual obligations, potentially with the use of national and international human rights institutions.

The 2002 Monterrey Consensus on Financing for Development was analysed from a human rights perspective. It was noted that it calls for a number of positive changes in the direction of human rights observance, but that it has insufficient commitments to ensure sufficient resources and appropriate mechanisms to ensure their effective delivery. There was no commitment in the Consensus for States to consistently take into account human rights obligations. The result of the Conference may have been different had human rights considerations been more visible at the Conference. Very few civil society organisations with a human right background participated. The civil society organisations present used human rights as a rhetorical term without spelling out its legal and political implications. An illustration of this approach was the title of the civil society alternative Summit, which was termed 'Global Forum on Financing the Right to Equitable and Sustainable Development.' International law does of course require that development be equitable and it does restrict many forms of activity that cause environmental degradation through environmental and human rights treaties and customary laws.[123] However, there is no formal 'right to equitable and sustainable development' and as suggested in this chapter, the right to development is not the strongest tool to promote human rights in development financing. In order to achieve their objectives, civil society organisations would have been well advised to concentrate on ensuring that existing human rights were effectively implemented rather than using loose terminology in a purely rhetorical fashion

---

[123] See M. Cordonier Segger and A. Khalfan, *Sustainable Development Law: Principles, Practices and Prospects* (Oxford: Oxford University Press, 2004).

or trying to improve currently recognised human rights in a forum not intended for this purpose.

Although the Monterrey Consensus does not systematically take account of human rights obligations, its contents do not preclude their implementation in practise. There are a number of ways in which this can happen. States and inter-governmental organisations (IGOs) must acknowledge human rights obligations in their domestic and international financial policies as the first step to carrying out a full assessment of their policies. They must develop the capacity of their officials to assess the contents of human rights obligations at the national and international level. Although neglect of human rights in the context of development financing is partly ideological, to a great extent it also has to do with widespread lack of knowledge and a perception that economic, social and cultural rights are merely aspirational and lack precise and immediate obligations. Finally, States and IGOs must substantively integrate human rights into their financial decision-making. Civil society can assist in such work by playing a monitoring role, identifying the most vulnerable communities and empowering them to claim their rights, contributing its own efforts to development and using national and international complaints mechanisms and the media to ensure that development financing occurs in a manner consistent with human rights. Businesses can support and assist the implementation of human rights laws, and, as far as possible, provide assistance to communities in which they operate.

A final point that can be considered is that human rights, as an ideology that claims (with some justification) to be universal,[124] is instrumentally and politically useful as a means to address the North-South divide on critical and contested development issues such as aid conditionality and equity between States. This chapter has proposed an approach that notes that State sovereignty is limited by human rights obligations, but these limits apply at both at the national and at the international level. Human rights, by virtue of their legal and obligatory character, could provide the framework for mutual obligations and mutual accountability that address the concerns of developed and developing countries.

---

[124] However, one should take note of relevant critiques by Kenyan human rights scholar Makau Mutua of the international human rights movement, which he criticises as Euro-centric and imperialistic. Makau therefore pleads for a human rights movement that is inclusive, multicultural and deeply political (in the sense of jettisoning the pretence that human rights groups practise law, not politics). See M. Mutua, "Savages, Victims and Saviors: The Metaphor of Human Rights" (2001) 42:1 *Harvard International Law Journal*. Most developing countries have emerging human rights movements that have the ability to influence their States. It will be necessary for such organisations to develop greater regional and international presence.

21

SOCIAL PROTEST AGAINST PRIVATIZATION OF WATER: FORGING COSMOPOLITAN CITIZENSHIP?

Bronwen Morgan[1]

Water, for many people, is an intuitive 'last bastion' against privatization. The notion of profiting from the distribution of something so vital raises political hackles and upbraids moral sensitivities more easily than any of the other basic goods and services that make up the package of infrastructure underpinning so much of daily activity.

The importance of access to water leads activists to label as 'weapons of mass destruction' restriction valves – new technologies inserted into the systems of those whose water bills are unpaid that cause them to spend twenty minutes to fill a glass of water. Yet this sense of outrage changes over time. The degree to which private sector involvement in water services waxes and wanes: both the UK and the US involved the private sector extensively in the 19th century, both shifted definitively for most of the 20th, and only recently has the UK turned back again.[2] Moreover, while private sector involvement has become relatively routinised in the UK at this point, it remains an issue of intense controversy in the international context. Despite the sense of cycling between public and private that one gets from looking at things in the *longue durée*, though, the current international context of water service provision raises new issues that offer an intriguing glimpse into questions of emerging shared cosmopolitan identities, in ways that link producers and consumers across national boundaries.

[1] Bronwen Morgan, B.A.Hons, LL.B. Hons (Sydney), Ph.D. (U.Cal., Berkeley), Harold Woods Research Fellow in Law, Wadham College & Centre for Socio-Legal Studies, University of Oxford, UK. This article is based on research funded by the ESRC and the AHRB under Research Grant 143-25-0031, in the Research Programme on Cultures of Consumption, and their support is gratefully acknowledged. Working papers relating to this project will be published in 2005 on online: <www.consume.bbk.ac.uk/research/morgan.html>.
[2] J. Hassan, *A History of Water in Modern England and Wales* (Manchester: Manchester University Press, 1998)

This chapter aims to explore how what Craig Calhoun calls "new ways of imaginatively constituting identity, interests and solidarities"[3] arise in the context of water. These new ways arise not only in relation to networks of transnational producers but also, and critically, amongst the many consumers on the receiving end of their services, a core portion of whom are activists protesting the emerging shape of transnational provision of water services. Ultimately, the chapter hopes to provide some tentative directions forward that may build bridges between the currently rather different constitutive practices of cosmopolitan protesters and producers.

At one level the involvement of the private sector in the provision of water services is simply an example of a well-trod debate about the appropriate threshold between market and state. However this debate in a globalised world raises a new dimension, for a politics of north-south distributional justice now overlays the traditional issues of efficiency and distribution as they might arise in any longstanding national context. Such a politics is explicitly acknowledged by international institutions: the provision of clean water and sanitation to the billions of individuals who currently lack them worldwide has become a major focus of international coordinating efforts to reach the Millennium Development Goal targets set by the UN in 2000.[4] In response to this, empire lives on in the image of a drop of water brimming at the lip of a tap. Britain and France host the 3 largest water companies in the world that in their drive to expand access to the business of providing water services now provide water to over 300 million individuals in over 200 different countries.[5] While this still leaves some 85% of the world's population unaffected by Thames, Suez or Vivendi, as they are most popularly known,[6] the proportion is nonetheless significant and provides a window onto an emerging trajectory that might be termed 'global water welfarism'.

Global water welfarism entails a vision of a regime where public aid supplements the private investment of multinational corporations to solve the social and environmental problems of global water provision, catalysed by a hopeful mix of corporate social responsibility and the probing eye of government and civil society monitors. In this vision, mass provision of social services across state boundaries is both an opportunity to extend global capitalism and at the same to soften its harsher effects. The vision of benign welfarism is, of course, a bitterly contested one. The debate it sparks can be seen as an echo of older debates on the question of whether national welfare state policies established in post-war industrial democracies served merely to

---

[3] C. Calhoun, "Constitutional Patriotism and the Public Sphere" in P. De Greiff and C. Cronin, eds., *Global Ethics and Transnational Politics* (Cambridge: MIT Press, 2002) at 277.
[4] United Nations Millennium Declaration, Resolution 55/2 adopted by the United Nations General Assembly, available online: <http://www.un.org/millennium/declaration/ares552e.htm>.
[5] Figures collated from the websites of the companies, available online: <http://www.rwethameswater.com> and <http://www.suez.com; www.veoliaenvironnement.com>.
[6] The actual names of the companies are RWE-Thames, Suez and Veolia Environnement.

legitimate the basic structures and results of capitalism, or to genuinely modulate it as a form of political economy. But it has an added bite in the global context. For the separation between regulation and operation that has come to dominate conventional wisdom about state-market relations in a national context serves these new developments well. Even in national contexts, the regulatory role assigned to the state has often come to mean supporting a market framework rather than modulating it or softening its harsher effects. For example in the UK in the mid-1990s, the regulator Ofwat refused to alter the policy of prepaid meters imposed on poor consumers by the water companies.[7] In that case, a lawsuit and a related political battle ultimately resulted, with the help of a change of government, in legislative prohibition of disconnection.

But in the global context, the possibility of infusing the regulatory role of the state with such concerns – concerns that are in essence motivated by social justice – is considerably more limited. For that infusion depends on having a bounded community, or a clear sense of the scope of those to whom obligations of social justice are owed. That the impact of UK private company actions on poor UK consumers is an appropriate issue for resolution by a UK regulator or the UK parliament is not controversial. By contrast, while the impact of multinational companies on poor citizens of developing countries may be an issue with powerful moral traction, its institutional resolution is much more difficult. This is at least in part because it is difficult to articulate the bounded communities to whom obligations are owed and from whom entitlements can be claimed in this context. As a result, the market-state relationship in the international context tends to be premised on 'public-private partnerships' where the public regulatory role limits itself to providing market-strengthening support, and where it is difficult and controversial to expand that role even where the political will exists.

The result over time is that multiple legislative reforms in many different countries combine to create a web of institutional support for an increasingly integrated global market where a few large companies can invest in multiple locations using roughly the same template, but there is little in the template for addressing issues of social justice. On top of this, public regulatory support for this market framework results in at least some of its resulting benefits (and in some cases, eg where concession contracts are pegged to the dollar, most of the benefit) flowing *out* of the state providing the regulatory support rather than to its own constituents. Now of course, the side benefits to the local citizens (upgraded infrastructure, expanded access, improved water quality) are meant to compensate for profit repatriation beyond borders, and much of the political conflict over private sector participation revolves around arguments about whether such side benefits actually accrue. Similarly, much written to date on

---

[7] M. Drakeford, "Water Regulation and Pre-payment Meters" (1998) 25 *Journal of Law and Society* 588 at 596.

particular experiences of private sector participation in providing water services in a transnational context has tried to evaluate the successes or failures of particular contracts, projects and concessions. Instead, it is important to bring to the surface the questions of identity and membership that are often presumed, assumed or tacitly desired in assessing these successes and failures.

In particular, critical accounts of privatization frequently project an emerging shared cosmopolitan identity amongst those mobilising against privatization. Now, we should not forget that such a shared identity already exists in the configuration that supports what one might call the 'post-Washington consensus with a human face', embodied for the author's purposes by global water welfarism. For global water welfarism is premised on an economistic global society, and cosmopolitanism is quite firmly established here, at least if one speaks of a community of shared interests, albeit not necessarily one of 'thick' ideals or common identities.[8] Tellingly, the first cited usage of 'cosmopolitan' was by John Stuart Mill in 1848 in his classic *Political Economy*, where he observed that 'capital is becoming more and more cosmopolitan'.[9] The important question, though, is *whether social protest against privatization can establish a social imaginary for cosmopolitan citizenship and transnational solidarity*. More specifically, does this protest forge links, establish practices that build social relations based on common experience, or functionally integrate activities of mutual support, all in ways that transcend economism? Does it generate a narrative that is at once embedded in concrete practices yet makes sense of them in ways that go beyond present practice – especially ways that bind dispersed actors on grounds other than a promise of access to the fruits of increased economic growth?

The answer of this chapter is that it does, but only at a rhetorical and symbolic level, and not at the level of translating it into implemented reality. The promise that shared cosmopolitan identities might emerge from practices of social protest against private sector participation is thus limited. Yet the promise is still real, and it has much to contribute to future possible trajectories of state-market relations, perhaps not only in relation to water. It lays the ground for developing an institutional imagination, one that infuses technocratic management with an expressive dimension that enables a meaningful and practical dialogue between protestors, workers, consumers and producers. To reach these possibilities, which are elaborated in the final section, we must however first understand the tension that limits this cosmopolitan promise.

A crucial tension

The social protest generated around private sector participation in water services simmers in a particular kind of crucible, one shaped by an important

---

[8] As above.
[9] B. Robbins, *Secular Vocations: Intellectuals, Professionalism, Culture* (Verso, 1993) at 182.

tension between the symbolic resonance of water and the techno-bureaucratic rationality of its delivery in the context of modern urban infrastructure. This context, in the sprawling mega-cities of the future, is the one where private sector participation is most salient. It is here, especially but not only in developing country mega-cities, that the urban margins are swelled by recent influxes of rural peoples whose relationship to water has historically been the cashless nexus of a subsistence existence where water is integrated into livelihoods rather than bundled up as a commercial service, that the tension is most highly strung. In such contexts, images of water as a communal natural resource held in common, as a human right and fundamental need, even as a sacred fluid and physical mystery, are brutally ill-at-ease with the legal and regulatory frameworks that ensure the sustainability and efficiency of massive capital investments into the physical infrastructure that makes access to water the effortless turn of a tap.

A particularly vivid illustration of this can be drawn from an ill-fated concession contract signed with International Water, a multinational consortium including both USA's Bechtel and the UK's United Utilities, in Cochabamba, Bolivia in 1999. The conflict arising from this has become a leitmotif in the narratives unfolding around this issue. Here, there is simply an attempt to highlight the tension involved, rather than telling a full story. Under the concession, collecting rainwater, a practice carried out for centuries by indigenous people in the semi-rural areas at the margins of Cochabamba became subject to a (paid) permit system under the exclusive authority granted to International Water to operate the concession in a pre-determined geographical area. The intuitive absurdity of this can, however, be better understood (even if not justified) when it is understood that there are really two competing frameworks shaping what counts as common sense in operation. The notion that rainwater is a freely available natural resource, even a gift from God, makes sense when the relationship between the recipient and the natural resource is unmediated and direct. But once water becomes a service, provided by a third party and mediated by larger technical infrastructure which is itself essential to the universality of provision in a particular spatial area, then at least from the perspective of the service provider, requiring a permit for rainwater collection may come as a normal incident of an exclusivity clause in the regulatory framework. Such clauses are from their point of view widely accepted as a legitimate part of long term infrastructure concessions in order to ensure the predictability of the cost flows on which tender prices are based.

Now there are of course potential points of intersection between these two views of what is 'common sense' about water provision. For example, the capacity of the villagers to pay for the rainwater permits can and should be integrated into the cost structure of the concession contract. More of these intersections in due course: what is important for now is the implication of this tension. It is this: water is *rhetorically and symbolically* powerful as a frontier issue, a threshold to defend against ever-encroaching commodification and the spread of economic rationality. This makes possible a powerful politics of challenge, one which is manifesting itself through webs of protest that make common claim to defending water as a human right and a public trust, at a level of urgency that justifies civil disobedience. But transforming these politics of challenge into implementation faces significant hurdles. In particular, the modalities built by the webs of social protest seem to be relatively ineffective in building alternative models of managing water.

To see this, consider what happened in Cochabamba after the 'water war' that ejected the multinational water operator and had the government rescind the concession contract. The city's municipal council took back water services and created a 'social model' of management, with as many as six members of civil society on the board elected directly from the community. But in the process of implementing the changes, internal disagreements in the original civil society coalition led to the number of elected members being halved, voting turnout in two of the three remaining zones has been exceptionally low, and attempts to coordinate international technical assistance for a 'public sector social approach' fell through. Many of the most energised activists have since turned their attention to the conflicts over gas now salient in Bolivia. While the issues underlying both gas and water are importantly related, the links between them do not facilitate day-to-day problem solving in particular sectors. And thus the problem of access to water languishes.

Human right or commodity?

One way of putting this challenge is to complicate the slogan that animates so much of the social protest around private sector participation in water services: 'water is a human right and not a commodity'. The clarity of this dichotomy is muddied (albeit not erased) when the practical implications of the notion of a human right to water are fleshed out. Socio-economic rights, which would include a right for every individual to access "sufficient, safe, acceptable, physically accessible and affordable water" as the UN Committee on Economic and Social Human Rights words it, by their nature make direct claims of entitlement on finite resources.[10] In practice the resource allocation dilemmas that result are necessarily implemented by regulatory norms that protect consumer (public) interests by establishing minimum standards of provision. These kinds of human rights, then, have an inevitable regulatory face, and strategies to implement them will centre on the articulation of substantive regulatory standards, benchmarking and monitoring. Nor is a human right to water necessarily incompatible with private provision. Even imposed as a mandatory obligation on national state governments, it can be given technical

---

[10] United Nations Committee on Economic, Social and Cultural Rights, General Comment No 15 (2002), The Right to Water (Articles 11 and 12 of the International Covenant on Economic, Social and Cultural Rights) (26 November 2002).

and practical flesh via the entrepreneurial initiative of well-resourced private actors such as multinational water companies in combination with a regulatory framework controlled by public actors. In short, the rhetoric of a human right to water once implemented and fleshed out in practice has a tendency to dissolve into a series of strategies eerily resembling consumer rights – an important dimension of a market state but hardly a frontier against its expansion.

Yet it should not be suggested that consumer rights and human rights in this domain can be too easily conflated. The urgency of the rights claim is not necessarily stifled by the web of a complex regulatory framework. Distributive justice and universal access, to take two core dimensions of socio-economic rights, can be and are fleshed out through rules on cross-subsidies or through detailed codes of procedure governing disconnection practices by companies. And neither facet is typically core to consumer rights agendas. Moreover, the challenge of what a human right to water might mean on the ground is being taken up by NGOs: two publications have recently appeared[11] from environmental and socio-economic human rights organisations that elaborate the practical, legislative and regulatory dimensions of a human right to water in ways that initiate very interesting conversations. Such conversations may well modify the regulatory expectations and hopes of commercial providers in ways that begin to build a bridge between the aspirations of struggle generated by protest and the routine of instantiating those aspirations.

Important limits remain. For the *texture* and *tone* of such conversations create difficulties in underpinning a social imaginary capable of fostering cosmopolitan identities that offer alternatives to global economism. For example, the compatibility of human rights-mandated cross-subsidies with the disciplines of the General Agreement on Trade in Services may well be the welfare state redistributive policy issue of the global economy. Yet it is hardly the stuff of cosmopolitan citizenship. Otherwise put, while the increasing interpenetration of regulatory issues, human rights and consumer entitlements may *instrumentally* appear more and more a part of a single coherent (fairly technocratic) conversation, it is a trajectory that still sits uneasily with that deeper, more elusive level that has so far been alluded to, as the symbolic and rhetorical power of water as an ultimate frontier of privatization. That power is far more than 'mere' rhetoric. The elusive but vital facet of the call for a human right to water that gives it a clarion quality has to do with its *identity-conferring dimensions*. The call suggests that, at least potentially, struggles around water may help diffusely related, territorially dispersed citizen-consumers who share little but the need for water, to construct a series of practices that might build

---

[11] World Conservation Union, *Water as a Human Right?* IUCN Environmental Policy and Law Paper No 51, (Gland: IUCN, 2004); Centre on Housing Rights and Eviction (COHRE), *Legal Resources for the Right to Water: National and International Standards* (Geneva: COHRE, January 2004). See also right to water, Wateraid, available online: <http:www.righttowater.org.uk>.

identity across borders. If such practices are possible, something akin to class consciousness could emerge, adding to the rhetorical appeal of water's frontier nature both an expressive dimension and a praxis of action.

Unruly consumers

The question of whether the rhetorical promise of water can be substantiated, then is a question of whether some of the more unruly practices of social protest against the commodification of water might generate solidarities of an identity-conferring type. Do they, to keep the question metaphorical for a moment longer, generate stories that link communities in ways other than the promise of economic growth through intensified market competition? More specifically, does such protest forge links between otherwise disparate individuals, does it establish practices that build social relations based on common experience, does it functionally integrate activities of mutual support? There are examples where this does indeed happen. In both South Africa and New Zealand, activist groups have mobilised to engage in deliberate strategies of mass non-payment, followed by mutual support in assisting those who are disconnected as a result to illegally reconnect to the network.[12] New Zealand consumer activists have sought ways to disrupt business-as-usual routine both locally (sending cheques written on bricks to a local company whose corporatisation they oppose, having ascertained that this counts as legal tender) and internationally (hosing the Bolivian embassy down with a fire-engine owned by one of the activist groups to express solidarity with Bolivian activists in Cochabamba). Bolivian and Canadian water activists have met face-to-face to share strategies and tactics: in one instance the North Americans conveyed to the Bolivians news of a prior similar struggle over water privatization in Tucuman, Argentina that was said to inspire the Bolivian activists to persist with the mass blockades they had imposed on their town.[13] All of these practices, particularly those that throw their participants into conflict with the law, have some potential to foster a collective sense of shared purpose, and to link the narrower issues of water to larger structural issues of the appropriate limits of capitalism. Activists speak with passion about the energy and sense of purpose that they acquire from these experiences and links, and the possibilities for building coalitions across different areas of essential services, so that health, education, transport, electricity and so on can all become linked sites of alternative communities.

There are also important limits, though to this apparent community-building, and it is water that shows them up most vividly. The kinds of coalitions that have been idenfitied are at their most powerful when they are saying a clear and un-nuanced 'no'. The issue which most unites the multiplicity of groups

---

[12] Drawn from the author's primary research in this area. Working papers will be available online: <http//www.consume.bbk.ac.uk/research/morgan.html>, *supra* note 1.
[13] *Supra*, note 1.

engaged in these protest circles, including those mobilising around water, is opposition to the General Agreement on Trade in Services, which imposes a generalised framework of market-strengthening rules across borders. But in health, and in education, even in information technology, there are possibilities of alternative provisioning that provide outlets for cooperative creativity of a more routinized, yet positively life-changing kind. Guerilla schools can be established, alternative health networks built, wireless networks expanded, yet water activists often face the unappealing choice between going back to the well or venturing into large-scale infrastructural construction. With water, more sharply than with any other shared good or service, we are face to face with the fiercely asymmetrical crucible of producer-consumer relations in a globalized world. In such a context, it is imperative to face up to the divide between the turbulent struggle of articulating a social imaginary that goes beyond economism and the routine of its instantiation. Struggle easily acquires a greater lure than routine, and the transition from one to the other in the context of the current debates over water is complicated by the intervention of scale and the bureaucratic rationality of modern industrial solutions to the problem of access to water. Scale really matters – teamwork with one's colleagues and neighbours to provide water from springs and wells can have positive identity-conferring potential that simply dissolves when large-scale pipe networks and treatment systems are built and must be managed with all their attendant risks and complexities. That 'social' models of participatory management lose their appeal when 'scaling up' is not necessarily an indication of flagging commitment to the building of collective identity. It may be simply that the time freed by the luxury of an onsite tap sparkles with an array of alternative uses that pose stiff competition to the prospect, say, of representing consumers on the Customer Committee of UK regulator Ofwat.

It is in this sense that there is a limited truth to the comments often made by water company executives that local citizens in different countries do not care who manages their water, but rather only care that something clean, safe and affordable comes out of the tap. For where routine is at issue rather than struggle or turbulence, the capacity to enact what Rogers Smith calls new 'stories of peoplehood' will be crucially dependent on local context.[14] Robert Putnam's oft-cited argument about the social capital of Northern Italy depends on a four-century trajectory of repeated routine practices.[15] Closer to the water sector, the equally oft-cited example of the Brazilian city of Porto Alegre's participatory budgeting process, a remarkable example of routine technocratic practices infused with a sense of deliberative community, cannot easily if at all be replicated.[16] Its resilience and energy are embedded in culturally and

[14] R. M Smith, *Stories of Peoplehood: the Politics and Morals of Political Membership* (Cambridge: Cambridge University Press, 2003)
[15] R. Putnam, *Making Democracy Work : Civic Traditions in Modern Italy* (Princeton: Princeton University Press, 1993)
[16] B. de Sousa Santos, "Participatory budgeting in Porto Alegre: Toward a redistributive democracy" (1998) 26 *Politics & Society* 461-510.

historically specific trajectories of Brazilian labour union history, regional characteristics and the emergence of the Workers' Party.[17] The same could be said of the southern zone of Cochabamba, where the multiplication of water user committees at grass-roots level is both enhancing local identities and at the same time building bridges between the remunicipalised water company and local communities.[18] That this co-exists with the more dispiriting facets of the Cochabamba story earlier mentioned is itself proof of the contingency of building lasting shared identities from struggle.

In short, there is very limited potential to *routinise* the building of transnational communities of shared identities, at least in ways that would transcend incompletely specified ideals or temporarily overlapping interests. Only existing embedded communities tend to sustain and enliven routine to a point where they build shared identity. Absent such communities, and a history of their involvement in water management, the bureaucratization of the details of water service delivery render the 'stuff' delivered from taps into the H_2O that Ivan Illich distinguishes so carefully from the "water of dreams". H_2O is homogenous, substitutable, industrial and calibrated according to cost. The nature of its provision alienates those who drink it from the daily routine practices of that delivery and provision, and enacts the very separation that causes nothing but the end-product to matter. Those routine practices are so familiar to us in the industrialised world that it may seem churlish to question their worth: who would, after all, choose to go back to collecting water from the river as the Conservative MP Dr. Arthur Shadwell once advised 19th century activists demanding an entitlement to water in London to do?[19] No-one, and justifiably so; yet the *cumulative* effect of separating consumption from production, regulation from operation, collective choices from individual goals, can be corrosive. What Illich's maddeningly vague phrase the "water of dreams" captures, is the largely unconscious or imperfectly articulated need for a sense of collective identity to underpin and stabilise the dispersed and disaggregated activities that combine to produce a hoped-for common good. If this dimension of assumed identity is inaccessible, its absence creates a residual undertow, a falling away of taken-for-granted stability. It is this that energises the patterns of conflict we see around water privatization. That energy must, if there is to be a way forward, be harnessed in ways that bridge the tension between struggle and routine.

---

[17] *Ibid.*
[18] Author's primary research, *supra* note 1.
[19] V. Taylor and F. Trentmann, "Liquid Politics: Water Politics in Victorian England and the Formation of the Consumer" Paper presented in the Conference *Knowing Consumers: Actors, Images, Identities in Modern History,* Universität Bielefeld, *Zentrum für interdisziplinäre Forschung,* 27 - 28 February 2004 at 44. Available online: <http://www.consume.bbk.ac.uk/ZIF%20Conference/TaylorTrentmannZiF.doc>.

Forward to where?

The way forward must be one that respects the deep challenge posed by social movement opposition to bureaucratization of the life world. This will necessitate going beyond received 'solutions' which rely too heavily on institutional reproduction from radically different contexts. The depoliticised split between regulation and operation that characterises institutional solutions offered in the national contexts of industrialised states is an example of just such an unreflective solution. We need rather to infuse technocratic citizenship with an affective dimension. This requires that we recognise the routine challenges of implementing ideals (hence it is necessarily technocratic to some degree) but that we embed those routines in practices which confer identity, establish a social imaginary, make new citizens out of us in unexpected ways. There are two routes forward here, the first institutional and the second expressive. Both demand repeat work – though the former is more obviously routine – work that builds the glue that holds networks together, and that makes people relate to faraway situations and understand themselves relationally in newly connected ways.

Institutional imagination and expressive creativity is needed to do this kind of work. What would it mean to give institutional form to the idea of transnational solidarity? What if, as one partnership initiative coming out of the UN Sustainable Development Conference in Johannesburg 2002 has proposed,[20] every citizen in the industrialised world paid an extra cent per cubic metre on their water bill, and the funds collected as a result were channelled to the developing country's water and sanitation needs? The mechanics of how this might work may seem defeating, but need not be. After all, Australian city consumers are in the process of adding 5% to their water bills to compensate the country's farmers for cutting back their irrigation usage in order to provide an ecological reserve for the country's river systems, a reserve to which those rivers are now legally entitled. This kind of creative amalgam of mutually painful and admirably transparent compromises across whole sectors of society could be 'scaled up': it would provoke contentious conversations about lines of accountability and who should benefit, but such conversations would be constitutive of just the kinds of identities that are being gestured towards.

Or what if local governments in the industrialised world bottled some of the clean, safe tap water their citizens enjoy and sold it at something more than cost as a 'social venture' to fund public-public partnerships with a paired municipality in a developing country? The process of building relationships to establish such partnerships, and of making decisions about precisely what kind of technical assistance might be of best aid to that municipality, would require

---

[20]PS-Eau, *Cent per M3: Financing Water by Water and Global Solidarity Mechanisms* (PS-Eau: Johannesburg, 2002). A Partnership Initiative presented to 2002 Johannesburg World Summit on Sustainable Development, lead partner PS-Eau, a French non-governmental organisation. Copy of draft plan on file with author.

people across boundaries to acquire a knowledge and understanding of each other's contexts and conditions that could underpin far more than the fleeting high generated by the colour and clash of anti-globalisation politics. 'Fair trade' water might catalyse 'socially responsible development' North-South partnerships which in turn could facilitate cross-certification of sustainable local water systems according to benchmarks developed in rural Chile, thereby inverting the 'learning' so often assumed to flow from North to South.

These wonderings could be thought of the 'technical assistance' dimension of alternative social imaginaries. Just as the bureaucracy of privatization arguably plays a crucial role in building the hegemonic version of globalization,[21] so a more subaltern sense of integrated identity and shared understandings could develop around routine collaborations – not a straightforward oppositional identity, but one premised on challenging overlaps, trajectories that are 'modern but different'. And here the analogy with the bureaucracy of privatization has a second productive echo. Marketing and communication strategies are of growing importance for hegemonic globalization. The stories and images generated around the perceived benefits of this trajectory of development may ring hollow to many, but they speak sense and clarity to just as many more. What is important is the cultivation of a *positive* narrative or expressive dimension to encapsulate what activists are seeking, one that is neither a platitudinous 'humanitarian' spin on technocratic solutions nor overly reliant on rigid dichotomous rhetoric.

The European constitutional process illustrates how difficult this is. While the Nice Charter of Rights[22] goes some way to colouring the grey thicket of its all too numerous pages, it, like the claim that water is a human right, is vulnerable to that core tension between struggle and routine. And bridging that tension can have strange effects. Another initiative emerging from Johannesburg, along with the 'cent/m3' idea outlined above, is a Draft Declaration on the Right to Access Essential Services[23] which would notionally be submitted to the UN. This strange document blends visions of market efficiency, ecological purity and sensibilities of democratic process and social justice into a weird transmogrification addressed emphatically to the "user-consumers of the planet". Is this all that can be brought to a vision of cosmopolitan citizenship? Can we bring the carnivalesque dimension of protest, the expressive creativity of documentaries like Thirst, to the work of building alternatives? That of course is the hope of the annual World and European Social Fora, as also of

---

[21] D. Hall, "Investing in the bureaucracy of privatisation - a critique of the EU water initiative papers", PSIRU Working Paper, unpublished. Available upon request from PSIRU: Public Services International Research Unit, University of Greenwich, online: <http://www.psiru.org>.

[22] Charter of Fundamental Rights of the European Union, 2000 OJ (C 364) 1, agreed at Nice, France (entered into force Dec. 7, 2000).

[23] Institut de Gestion Deleguee, Draft *Declaration on the Right to Access Essential Services* (Johannesburg: Institut de Gestion Deleguee, 2002). Partnership submitted to the 2002 Johannesburg Summit, lead partner is Institut de Gestion Deleguee (Institute of Delegated Management), a French NGO. Copy of draft initiative on file with author.

the provocatively long Universal Forum of Cultures that took place this year over five months in Barcelona.[24] In the narrower context of water alone, the alternate enormity or undesirability of alternative provisioning makes integration of these facets with routine institution-building and day-to-day governance very difficult indeed. But as currently detached from the structures of power as the Social Fora and the Barcelona Conversation might still be, they are at least spaces where conversations can take place about *the overall trade-offs* between the costs and benefits of multiple policy sectors. Here, beyond sector-specific transnational politics, active deliberation and participation can transcend the devolved and disaggregated spaces that tend to be the only ones open at a routine level – certainly to consumers – in a global yet interconnected world. This is how to build a cosmopolitan citizenship that is more than simply technocratic.

Conclusion

The story of water is an exemplar of key forces shaping the struggle to put a 'human face' on globalisation that is analogous to the nationally-based 'welfare state' politics of last century. But a planet of user-consumers is one where 'community' is a market stripped even of the nation-building aspiration of forbears such as the Bismarckian welfare state. Michael Mann has argued that historically speaking, authoritarian forms of government are a much more likely and much less fragile route to social stability than liberal democratic routes.[25] The practices of social protest around the privatization of water challenge the assumption that global water welfarism in its technocratic corporate capitalist form is an appropriate route to social citizenship. Water is a potential frontier of what freedom and collective self-realisation might mean in the 21st century. While liberal democratic citizenship may well be impossible to reproduce on a global level, the echoes of those ideals remain vital as motivation and inspiration. They can spur a dream, not of democratic world government, nor of elaborate global regulatory networks providing social benefits, but of new forms of local experiments that link together to become larger than the sum of their parts. These intertwinings of institutional imagination and expressive creativity could be thought of as a search for regulatory justice. The environmental justice movement, after all, has brought a new and important dimension to the often highly technocratic dialogues around environmental regulation. For the debates on privatization in a global context, regulatory justice may be the building block of cosmopolitan identities that link communities in ways other than the promise of economic growth through intensified market competition. If so, fleshing out what it means is an important task, a vital step towards enabling the politics of protest to flower into new stories instead of morphing into stones.

---

[24] Available online: <http://www.barcelona2004.org/eng/>.
[25] M. Mann, "Ruling Class Strategies and Citizenship" in M. Bulmer and A.M. Rees, eds., *Citizenship Today: the Contemporary Relevance of TH Marshall* (London: UCL Press, 1996).

(vi)

HEALTH LAW AND SUSTAINABLE DEVELOPMENT

22

SUSTAINABLE DEVELOPMENT AND THE RIGHT TO HEALTH

*Sumudu Atapattu**

A close relationship exists between environmental protection (or degradation) and health issues. Indeed, a separate branch of medical science has emerged called environmental health, and warnings of health problems caused by environmental degradation now abound. This close relationship envisages the interaction of several branches of the law, namely international law and human rights law as well as other disciplines such as environmental protection, economic development and medical science. Sustainable development is the point of convergence between all these issues and disciplines.

Many techniques and principles have also emerged in order to deal with the ever-increasing impact of environmental degradation on human health. The environmental impact assessment process (EIA) and the precautionary principle are good examples. Although called an *environmental* impact assessment, the report often covers a much wider area and discusses the sociological impact of the proposed project. Such an assessment recognizes the role of human beings in both destroying and protecting the environment. [1] Accordingly, the starting point of this chapter will be Principle 1 of the 1992 *Rio Declaration on Environment and Development*: "Human beings are at the centre of concerns for sustainable development."[2]

---

* Sumudu Atapattu, LL.M, PhD (Cantab), Adjunct Faculty & Visiting Scholar, University of Wisconsin-Madison Law School, Lead Counsel for Human Rights and Poverty Eradication, Centre for International Sustainable Development Law (CISDL), Consultant, Law & Society Trust, (Colombo, Sri Lanka) & former Senior Lecturer, Faculty of Law, University of Colombo, Sri Lanka. Paper prepared for the Sustainable Justice 2002 conference organized by the Centre for International Sustainable Development Law, Montreal, Canada, together with the World Bank and UNEP, June 2002.
[1] This is reflected in the *Declaration of the United Nations Conference on the Human Environment, 16 June 1972, 11 I.L.M. 1416 [Stockholm Declaration]* (The Preamble notes that "Of all things in the world, people are the most precious. It is the people that propel social progress, create social wealth, develop science and technology and, through their hard work, continuously transform the human environment").
[2] 31 ILM 874 (1992)

M.C. Cordonier Segger & C. G. Weeramantry, eds., Sustainable Justice: Reconciling Economic, Social & Environmental Law
© *2005 Koninklijke Brill NV, Printed in The Netherlands, pp.355-364.*

Environmental protection and human health

Many environmental law instruments deal with the link between environmental degradation and human health. Starting with the 1972 *Stockholm Declaration on the Human Environment*, these instruments affirm the notion that we must improve the quality of the environment to protect human health and to ensure an adequate standard of living for human beings.

Principle 1 of the *Stockholm Declaration* provides as follows: "Man has the fundamental right to freedom, equality and adequate conditions of life, in an environment of a quality that permits a life of dignity and well-being...."[3] Although it does not affirm a human right to a healthy environment, as some commentators contend, this principle does confirm that an environment of a particular quality is necessary for man to enjoy his rights to freedom, equality and adequate conditions of life. It is not, however, clear what is meant by "adequate conditions of life" although it seems to imply an adequate standard of life, in which event, it is clearly related to human health.

Principle 7 of the *Stockholm Declaration* affirms the protection of human health in the context of marine pollution. It urges states to take all possible steps to prevent pollution of the seas by substances that are liable to create hazards to human health, and to harm living resources and marine life.[4] The *World Charter for Nature*[5] – the first ever document to lay down the rights of nature – follows an ecocentric approach and as such emphasizes the integrity of nature without referring directly to human beings. It does, however, refer to areas degraded by human activities and provides that such areas should be rehabilitated for the well-being of the population. Principle 14 of the *Rio Declaration on Environment and Development*[6] calls upon states to cooperate and discourage or prevent the relocation and transfer to other states of any activities and substances that cause severe environmental degradation or are found to be harmful to human health. Furthermore, the *Draft Declaration of Principles on Human Rights and the Environment*[7] – the first of its kind – specifically refers to human health and the environment in several of its provisions. Principle 7 provides that all persons have the right to the highest attainable standard of health free from environmental pollution.[8] This document also affirms the right of all persons

---

[3] 11 ILM 1416 (1972)

[4] Principle 7, Stockholm Declaration, *ibid.*

[5] *World Charter for Nature,* GA Res. 37/7, UN GAOR, 37 U.N. GAOR, Supp. No. 51, U.N. Doc. A/37/51 (1982).

[6] *Rio Declaration on Environment and Development* UN Doc. A/CONF.151/5/Rev.1 (1992), *reprinted in* 31 ILM 874 (1992) [*Rio Declaration*].

[7] Included as an annex to the Review of Further Developments in Fields with Which the Sub-Commission Has Been Concerned, Human Rights and the Environment: Final Report Prepared by Mrs. Fatma Zohra Ksentini, Special Rapporteur, UN ESCOR Commission on Human Rights, Sub-Commission on Prevention of Discrimination and Protection of Minorities, U.N. Doc. E/CN.4/Sub.2/1994/9 (1994).

[8] UN Commission on Human Rights, Sub-Commission on Prevention of Discrimination and Protection of Minorities, Human Rights and the Environment, Final Report of the Special Rapporteur, UN Doc. E/CN.4/Sub.2/1994/9 (6 July 1994).

to a secure, healthy and ecologically sound environment and notes that human rights, an ecologically sound environment, sustainable development and peace are interdependent and indivisible. Finally, the *Earth Charter*,[9] noting that environmental, economic, political, social and spiritual challenges are interconnected, calls upon states to guarantee the right to potable water, clean air, food security, uncontaminated soil, shelter and safe sanitation. It also calls upon states to ensure that information of vital importance to human health and environmental protection, including genetic information, remains available in the public domain.

Sustainable Development

Sustainable development itself has evolved as a mechanism to deal with the "conflict" between economic development and environmental protection. While a precise definition of sustainable development is difficult, it is generally considered to encompass both substantive and procedural elements.[10]

The relevant substantive elements include the principle of equity; intra- and inter-generational rights; and the principle of integration. The procedural elements include the right to information; the right to participate in the decision-making process (public participation); the environmental impact assessment process; and the right to effective remedies.

The principle of equity (though not confined to the environmental field) is closely related to the principle of intra- and inter-generational equity. These principles seek to ensure that those of the present generation as well as generations to come will have an equitable share of natural resources in relation to their development as well as in relation to environmental protection.

Relevant Human Rights Provisions

While international human rights instruments do not yet recognize a right to an environment, several of their provisions have been invoked in relation to environmental issues. Regional human rights instruments, on the other hand, have addressed this issue. The human rights provisions that have been invoked are the right to life, the right to health, the right to privacy and the right to an adequate standard of life. Environmental problems can be a threat to all of the mentioned rights, including, in some instances, the right to life.[11]

---

[9] Online: The Earth Charter Initiative <http://www.earthcharter.org> (last modified: 23 May 2002). This is a document prepared by civil society groups and has not been endorsed by the international community. Although an Earth Charter was proposed to be adopted at the UN Conference on Environment and Development, this did not happen; the Rio Declaration was adopted instead.

[10] See S. Atapattu, "Sustainable Development, Myth or Reality?: A Survey of Sustainable Development under International Law and Sri Lanka Law" (2001) 14 Geo. *Int'l. Envtl. L. Rev.* 265.

[11] See e.g. J. Gasana, "Remember Rwanda?" *World Watch* 15:5 (September/October 2002) 24.

Articles 11 and 12 of the *International Covenant on Economic, Social and Cultural Rights*[12] (ICESCR) are a good example. Article 11 deals with the right of every individual to an adequate standard of living for himself and his family, including adequate food, clothing and housing, as well as the continuous improvement of living conditions. Article 12 addresses the right of every individual to the enjoyment of the highest attainable standard of physical and mental health and the continuous improvement of living conditions.

Articles 27 and 24 of the *Convention on the Rights of the Child*[13] (CRC) echo articles 1 and 12 respectively of the ICESCR. Article 27 states that every child has a right to a standard of living adequate for the child's physical, mental, spiritual, moral and social development. Article 24 refers to the improvement of all aspects of environmental and industrial hygiene and article 24(c) refers in particular to the dangers and risks of environmental pollution.

While international human rights instruments have been slow to adopt provisions in relation to environmental rights, General Comment No. 14[14] of the UN Committee on Economic, Social and Cultural Rights (which monitors the implementation of the ICESCR), clearly identifies the link between environmental degradation and the right to health. Recognizing that the right to health is closely related to and dependent upon the realization of other human rights, the General Comment proceeds to note that food and nutrition, housing, access to safe and potable water and adequate sanitation, safe and healthy working conditions *and a healthy environment* are indispensable for the realization of the right to health.

The General Comment also notes the right to healthy natural and workplace environments and the need to prevent and reduce exposure to substances such as radiation, harmful chemicals or other detrimental environmental conditions that directly or indirectly impact upon human health.

The Committee interprets the right to health as an inclusive right, extending not only to appropriate health care but also to the underlying determinants of health: access to safe and potable water and adequate sanitation, food, nutrition and housing, and healthy occupational and environmental conditions. Thus, the Committee has recognized that the elements of a healthy environment are a prerequisite to the enjoyment of the right to health.

Environmental instruments, on the other hand, have consistently recognized the link between environment and health and, more recently, between health

---

[12] *International Covenant on Economic, Social and Cultural Rights,* 993 U.N.T.S. 3 (1976) [*ICESCR*].
[13] *Convention on the Rights of the Child,* 28 I.L.M. 1456 (1989).
[14] UN Committee on Economic, Social & Cultural Rights, *General Comment 14: The Right to the Highest Attainable Standard of Health* UN Doc. E/C.12/2000/4 (2000) Art. 12.

and development. *Agenda 21*[15] contains a separate chapter on protecting and promoting human health and notes that health and development are intimately connected. It further notes that "the linkage of health, environmental and socio-economic improvements require intersectoral efforts."[16] Addressing the primary health needs of the population is identified as integral to the achievement of sustainable development. The *Framework Convention on Climate Change*,[17] the *Vienna Convention for the Protection of the Ozone Layer*,[18] and the 1992 *Rio Declaration* all identify the link between environment and health.

In one of its resolutions, the UN General Assembly recognized that "all individuals are entitled to live in an environment adequate for their health and well-being."[19] The World Health Organization (WHO) has also recognized this link and works on the impact of environmental degradation and chemical contamination -amongst others- on human health. The *Framework Convention on Tobacco Control* (FCTC), while primarily aimed at protecting human health, also addresses the issue of environmental degradation caused by tobacco, the health impact of environmental tobacco use (passive smoking) as well as air pollution caused by tobacco smoke.[20]

The Relationship between Sustainable Development and the Right to Health

While the link between environment and health is obvious, one may wonder about the link between sustainable development and health. As noted above, sustainable development seeks to reconcile environmental protection and economic development. One aspect of this, is the principle of integration - integrating environmental concerns into the development process. There is ample evidence of the health problems caused by unsustainable development. Thus, sustainable development would mean developing in such a way that there are minimal adverse effects on, *inter alia*, human health. However, protecting human health is not the only objective of sustainable development.

Several documents also note the link between sustainable development and human health. The *Declaration of the Environment Leaders of the Eight on Children's Environmental Health*[21] states that "The protection of human health remains a fundamental objective of environmental policies to achieve sustainable

---

[15] See *U.N. Conference on Environment and Development, Agenda 21,* U.N. Doc. A/CONF.151.26 (1992).
[16] N.A. Robinson, *Agenda 21: Earth's Action Plan Annotated* (New York: Oceania Publications, 1993) at 56.
[17] *Framework Convention on Climate Change,* 31 I.L.M. 851 (1994).
[18] *Vienna Convention for the Protection of the Ozone Layer,* 26 I.L.M. 1529 (1988).
[19] GA Res 45/94, 4th December 1990.
[20] Document A56/INF.Doc/7, 21 May 2003, available online:
<http://www.who.int/tobacco/areas/framework/ final_text/en>.
[21] *Declaration of the Environment Leaders of the Eight on Children's Environmental Health*, Online: U of T G8 Information Centre, available online:
<http://www.library.utoronto.ca/g7/environment/1997miami/children.html>.

development. We increasingly understand that the health and well-being of our families depend upon a clean and healthy environment."[22]

Given that a healthy environment is necessary to allow human beings to "develop", the protection of the environment becomes imperative for sustainable development. In order to reconcile the present debate on the right to development and the right to a healthy environment, it seems that a right to sustainable development must be recognized. This, in turn, would protect many other human rights, such as the right to life, the right to health, and the right to an adequate standard of living. The *UN Framework Convention on Climate Change* made reference, for the first time, to the *right to sustainable development*. This is a significant development. The Rio Declaration does not contain a definition of sustainable development, although several of its principles refer specifically to it, and it seems to underlie the whole Declaration. It does, however, endorse the link between human health and environmental protection. Principle 1 notes that "Human beings are at the centre of concerns for sustainable development. They are entitled to a healthy and productive life in harmony with nature."[23]

The International Law Association's *New Delhi Declaration of Principles of International Law Relating to Sustainable Development*[24] is also important in this regard. While not going as far as articulating a distinct right to sustainable development, the document does recognize the link between environmental protection, development, and respect for human rights. It also notes that sustainable development should be integrated into all relevant fields of policy. Noting that the realization of economic, social, and cultural rights, civil and political rights, and peoples' rights is central to the pursuance of sustainable development, the Principles further lay down the objective of sustainable development as follows:

> "[The 70th Conference of the International Law Association] [e]xpresses the view that the objective of sustainable development involves a comprehensive and integrated approach to economic, social and political processes, which aims at the sustainable use of natural resources of the Earth and the protection of the environment on which nature and human life as well as social and economic development depend and which seeks to realize the right of all human beings to an adequate living standard on the basis of their active, free and meaningful participation in development and in the

---

[22] *Ibid.*

[23] This formulation has been heavily critiqued for its manifestly anthropocentric nature. See M. Pallemaerts, "The Future of Environmental Regulation: International Environmental Law in the Age of Sustainable Development: A Critical Assessment of the UNCED Process" (1996) 15 *J. L. & Com.* 623.

[24] Resolution 3/2002, 6 April 2002, online: International Law Association http://www.ila-hq.org/pdf/Sustainable%20Development/Sus%20Dev%20Resolution%20%2B%20Declaration%202002%2 0English.pdf. [*the Principles*].

fair distribution of benefits resulting therefrom, with due regard to the needs and interests of future generations."[25]

Without educating the public, both in developing countries or developed countries, about the possible effects of unsustainable practices, it is not possible to achieve sustainable development. Thus, education and access to information play an important role in the struggle for sustainable development. These rights, in turn, feed into another important right, the right to participate in the decision-making process.

Tobacco as a Case Study

Tobacco poses a pressing threat to human health and the environment. The statistics in relation to tobacco are staggering. It is estimated that by 2030, 10 million people will die from tobacco related illnesses and 7 million of these people would be from developing countries.[26] The situation is all the more tragic given that it is a preventable problem. While the medical community is grappling with the enormous task of treating tobacco-related diseases, the legal community is grappling with complex legal issues posed by tobacco. Concepts such as voluntary assumption of risk, freedom of choice, and freedom of expression (on the part of tobacco companies) and the ensuing public health problems have created a major dilemma for the law.

Tobacco is a legal product, which may be deadly when used for its intended purpose. Since its producers are multinational corporations making billions of dollars, banning the production of tobacco completely might be problematic. The FCTC, drafted under the auspices of the WHO, therefore aims to control it. The Convention gives leeway to states to implement measures at the national level, such as controlling advertising, and banning the advertising and sale of tobacco to children. Environmental Tobacco Smoke (ETC) is another problem where the victim, often a child, does not consent to the smoke, has no control over it, yet is forced to inhale it (through second hand smoking) in clear violation of her human rights. ETC also contributes to air pollution. Tobacco cultivation, too, has resulted in much environmental degradation, leading to deforestation and soil erosion in some countries. Thus, tobacco poses a particular challenge to environmental lawyers, public health personnel, and trade lawyers.

With regard to environmental tobacco smoke, the Declaration notes that it is a significant public health risk to young children and that such children are more likely to suffer from reduced lung function, infections of the lower respiratory tract, and respiratory irritations. It also discusses the link between global climate change and health effects and points out that "Our children and future

---

[25] *Ibid.*
[26] WHO Tobacco Free Initiative, available online: <http://www.afro.who.int/tfi/>.

generations face serious threats to their health and welfare from changes in the Earth's climate due to the build up of greenhouse gases in our atmosphere..... Future generations will face many potential impacts of climate change with serious health, environmental and economic consequences."

This document, although not binding, clearly makes a link between sustainable development and human health, with children's health in particular. It urges member states to take action to protect children and future generations within the context of poverty alleviation and economic and social development in the global transition to sustainable development.

Subsequent to this Declaration, the WHO convened an International Consultation on Environmental Tobacco Smoke (ETS) and Child Health in 1999. It concluded that ETS is a substantial threat to child health, causing severe problems, including death in certain instances, and that almost half of the world's children are exposed to ETS. The Consultation recognized the need to take swift action and to have strong public policies aiming to ensure the right of every child to grow in an environment free of tobacco smoke. The report of the Consultation[27] points out that children's exposure to ETS is involuntary and can be taken as a violation of the human rights recognized in article 6 (right to life) and article 24 (right to health) of the CRC. The report calls for a two-pronged approach to this problem, involving complementary legislation and education. With regard to smoking in private homes, the report recognizes the limited utility of legislation and calls upon states to carry out a comprehensive awareness-raising program on the health impact of ETS.

The Role of Education and Other Procedural Rights

Article 13 of the ICESCR embodies the right to education, and the State Parties "agree that education shall be directed to the full development of the human personality and the sense of its dignity, and shall strengthen the respect for human rights and fundamental freedoms."[28] Similarly, article 28 of the CRC deals with the right of the child to education. Furthermore, the UN Decade for Human Rights Education also endorses this right.

The right to receive and impart information and the right to participate in the decision making process are recognized in the *International Covenant on Civil and Political Rights.*[29] They are also recognized in environmental instruments. The *Rio Declaration*, for example, endorses these rights in Principle 10:

---

[27] World Health Organization, Division of Noncommunicable Diseases, Tobacco Free Initiative, *International Consultation on Environmental Tobacco Smoke (ETS) and Child Health: Consultation Report,* WHO/NCD/TFI/99.10 (1999), online: Tobacco Free Initiative <http://tobacco.who.int/page.cfm?sid=50>.
[28] *ICESCR, Supra* note 9 at Art. 13.
[29] *International Covenant on Civil and Political Rights* 999 U.N.T.S. 171, Can. T.S. 1976 No. 47, 6 I.L.M. 368 (1976).

"Environmental issues are best handled with participation of all concerned citizens, at the relevant level. At the national level, each individual shall have appropriate access to information concerning the environment that is held by public authorities, including information on hazardous materials and activities in their communities, and the opportunity to participate in decision-making processes. States shall facilitate and encourage public awareness and participation by making information widely available. Effective access to judicial and administrative proceedings, including redress and remedy shall be provided."[30]

Moreover, General Comment No 14, which is referred to above, notes the relevance of these principles in relation to the right to health and provides that a further important aspect is the participation of the population in all health-related decision-making at the community, national and international levels. Information and participation are inter-related rights, since without adequate information that is timely and accurate, people are not in a position to make informed decisions, thus the importance of fora where they can participate in information sharing and the decision-making process. Information and participation are, therefore, twin rights which are intrinsically inter-related and encompass the entire gamut of other rights.

Conclusion: Sustainable health law?

A close relationship exists between environmental protection, human health, human rights, and economic development. Sustainable development is the point of convergence. It is within a framework of sustainable development that one should seek to achieve environmental protection, human rights protection (social rights) and economic development. If a population is unhealthy as a result of environmental degradation or due to issues such as tobacco consumption, is it possible to achieve economic development? Who is to benefit from such development? The answer lies in seeking a balance between these competing claims by achieving sustainable development.

---

[30] *Rio Declaration, supra* note 4 at princ. 10.

23

THE WHO FRAMEWORK CONVENTION ON TOBACCO CONTROL: WHEN THE WHO MEETS THE WTO

Maya Prabhu[1] & Sumudu Atapattu[2]

This chapter provides an abbreviated overview of the Framework Convention on Tobacco Control (FCTC).[3] Negotiated under the auspices of the World Health Organization (WHO), the FCTC is the first international legal instrument designed to reduce tobacco-related deaths and diseases around the world. It is a comprehensive multilateral treaty which encompasses everything from tobacco smuggling to tobacco advertising, taxes, warning labels, designs and the extent of liability of tobacco companies. The WHO's 192 Member States unanimously adopted the FCTC at the 56th World Health Assembly on May 21, 2003 and it was open for signature until June 29, 2004; thereafter countries that have not signed may accede to the Convention. The Convention will enter into force and become a legally binding document 90 days after the 40th ratification or equivalent instrument. As of June 30, 2004, 168 WHO Member States and the European Community (EC) have signed on with 23 countries having ratified, accepted, approved or acceded to the Convention.

The FCTC is a compelling case-study for international sustainable development law for a number of reasons. First, the globalized market for tobacco has implications for every area of sustainable development, including health, labour, the environment and the economy. As such the FCTC is at the intersection of all three legal regimes - social, economic and environmental - which make up the corpus of sustainable development law.[4]   Second, the international

---

[1] Maya Prabhu, A.B. (Harvard), M.Sc. (LSE), M.D. (Dalhousie), LL.B. (McGill), Lead Counsel for International Sustainable Health Law, Centre for International Sustainable Development Law (CISDL).
[2] Sumudu Atapattu, LL.M, PhD (Cantab), Adjunct Faculty & Visiting Scholar, University of Wisconsin-Madison Law School, Lead Counsel for Human Rights and Poverty Eradication, Centre for International Sustainable Development Law (CISDL), Consultant, Law & Society Trust, (Colombo, Sri Lanka) & former Senior Lecturer, Faculty of Law, University of Colombo, Sri Lanka.
[3] *World Health Organization Framework Convention on Tobacco Control* opened for signature 21 May 2003 (not yet in force), A56/8, available online: < http://www.who.int/tobacco/framework/final_text/en/> [FCTC].
[4] *Johannesburg Declaration on Sustainable Development* (South Africa) (4 Sept. 2002) Art. 5, available online: <http://www.un.org/esa/sustdev/documents/WSSD_POI_PD/English/POI_PD.htm>.

M.C. Cordonier Segger & C. G. Weeramantry, eds., Sustainable Justice: Reconciling Economic, Social & Environmental Law
© *2005 Koninklijke Brill NV, Printed in The Netherlands, pp.365-380.*

regulation of tobacco illustrates contradictions between states' own agendas, as they often pursue restrictive policies domestically and more liberalized policies internationally. Finally, the FCTC represents the first time the WHO has exercised its considerable treaty-making powers in the name of public health, as an explicit counterbalance to another international legal regime. In specific, the FCTC is a response to the World Trade Organization's (WTO) very success in reducing barriers to the international tobacco trade, at the expense of significant health externalities. Thus, the FCTC marks a new chapter in the health vs. trade debates, debates which the authors believe are only likely to be amplified in the future.

This chapter can only serve as a brief introduction to the tobacco issue in the context of sustainable development law, and will pave the way for a more comprehensive CISDL research paper this year. However, in outlining the FCTC, this chapter will survey the tensions between a liberalized international market for tobacco and the public health imperative that such a market creates. It will also address the means by which ISDL principles can mediate those tensions between countries' obligations to shield citizens from the economic and social consequences of tobacco use and their obligations to pursue more open international markets. Finally, it will consider strategies and institutions by which signatories to the FCTC can translate its international aspirations into national law.

The FCTC: The Need for a Binding International Health Law Regime

The milestone significance of the FCTC is best understood by noting that, historically, international health law has been the purview of public health experts rather than legal ones. The reasons for the historic disconnect between international health concerns and international law are manifold. Among the most important is that, until recently, neither the international health nor international legal communities saw international health law as an outcome-determining factor for public health progress. Health problems have tended to be seen as technical problems to be solved rather than social issues to be legislated; accordingly it has been medical, pharmaceutical and engineering breakthroughs which, rightfully, have been given credit for the greatest advances in modern medicine.

Thus, it has primarily been health organizations, such as the WHO, rather than judicial decision-making bodies, which have driven global public health policy. Though the WHO has been given tremendous international legal powers under its Constitution, including the authority to adopt treaties addressing any matter in its domain,[5] international health law has tended to be derived from "soft law processes," through recommendations and regulations, rather than through legally binding rules. Interpretation and dispute settlement of those recommendations and regulations, too, have tended to be governed by informal processes. This soft law "ethos" is based on the assumption that international health law can be better achieved through cooperation and consensus building rather than a hard legal approach. Thus, the WHO Constitution does not give the WHO any enforcement powers to use in connection with violations of binding rules of international law.[6]

However, a changing global context has necessarily drawn international health concerns closer to international economic and social law. Most of the focus on health and international law has been directed towards the control of infectious diseases, national security threats and the provision of affordable medicines. But an equally important, though under-discussed issue, is how globalization has led to the growth in power and reach of non-state actors who have a substantial role in public health.[7] While many new actors, such as non-governmental organisations (NGOs), have been staunch advocates for public health,[8] the impact of certain transnational corporations has been more controversial. The direct negative health effects of the increasingly globalized production and market of tobacco, alcohol, and other products with adverse effects on health have been well documented.[9] The question that arises is whether international law can be used to regulate the health effects of these

---

[5] *WHO Constitution* (1948) 14 U.N.T.S. 186, Art. 19, available online:
<http://www.who.int/rarebooks/official_records/constitution.pdf> [WHO Constitution].
[6] See generally, D. P. Fidler, *International Law and Public Health: Materials on and Analysis of Global Health Jurisprudence* (New York: Transnational Publishers 2000); D. P. Fidler, *International Law and Infectious Diseases* (Clarendon Press 1999); D. P. Fidler, "The Future of the World Health Organization: What Role for International Law?" (1998) 31 *Vand. J. Transnat'l. L.* 1079; D. P. Fidler, et al., "Emerging and Re-Emerging Infectious Diseases: Challenges for International, National, and State Law" (1997) 31 *Int'l Law.* 773; D. P. Fidler, "Globalization, International Law, and Emerging Infectious Diseases" (1996) 2 *Emerging Infectious Diseases* 77; D. P. Fidler, "The Globalization of Public Health: Emerging Infectious Diseases and International Relations" (1997) 5 *Ind. J. Global Legal Stud.* 11; D. P. Fidler, "Microbialpolitik: Infectious Diseases and International Relations" (1998) 14 *Am. U. Int'l L. Rev.* 1; A. L. Taylor, "Controlling the Global Spread of Infectious Diseases: Toward a Reinforced Role for the International Health Regulations" (1997) 33 *Hous. L. Rev.* 1327.
[7] G. Walt, "World Health: Globalisation of International Health" (1998) 351 *Lancet* 434.
[8] The campaign led by Medicins sans Frontieres (MSF) against the major pharmaceutical companies over access to HIV/AIDS drugs in developing countries, is but one example of the newfound power among pro-patient NGOS.
[9] R. Beaglehole & D. Yach, "Globalisation and the Prevention and Control of Non-Communicable Disease: The Neglected Chronic Diseases of Adults" (2003) 362 *Lancet* 903; D. Yach & D. Bettcher, "The Globalization of Public Health, I: Threats and Opportunities" (1998) 88 *Am. J. Public Health* 735; D.W. Bettcher et al., "Global Trade and Health: Key Linkages and Future Challenges" (2000) 78 *Bull. World Health Org.* 521.

products, just as law has been used to regulate these industries at the domestic level.

Tobacco: The Relationship to Sustainable Development

There is no greater area of structural conflict between trade liberalization and public health than that of tobacco control. There is a strong link between increased tobacco consumption and free trade and tobacco-related foreign direct investment.[10] All the benefits of liberalized trade (increased access to cheaper consumer products) apply in reverse to cigarettes because public health is harmed when cigarettes are made more attractive and less expensive. Empirical evidence confirms that trade openness leads to increased tobacco consumption especially in low income countries.[11] And with increased consumption there is an inevitable increase in tobacco-related deaths.

Tobacco use is the leading cause of preventable death in the world today. It is currently responsible for the death of one in ten adults worldwide (about five million deaths each year). If current smoking patterns continue, it will cause some ten million deaths each year by 2025. As is often noted by public health professionals, tobacco is the only consumer product that, when used as recommended, eventually kills half its regular users.

There are tremendous development implications for the tobacco trade, not the least because developing countries will face the brunt of the tobacco epidemic. Although tobacco use has declined in many high-income countries in recent decades, there have been sharp increases in tobacco use, especially among men, in low and middle-income countries in recent years.[12]

By 2030, the World Bank predicts that smoking will kill about one in six adults globally per year. That most of the projected deaths will occur in low and middle-income countries is not by happenstance. As markets in industrialized countries have declined, transnational tobacco companies have aggressively

---

[10] D.W. Bettcher et al., *Confronting the Tobacco Epidemic in an Era of Trade Liberalization*, WHO/NMH/TFI/01.4 (Geneva: World Health Organization, 2001); see also A.L. Taylor & D.W. Bettcher, "WHO Framework Convention on Tobacco Control: A Global Good for Public Health" (2000) 78 *Bull. World Health Org.* 920 [A.L. Taylor & D.W. Bettcher]; D. Bettcher & I. Shapiro, "Tobacco Control in an Era of Trade Liberalisation (2001) 10 *Tob. Control* 65.
[11] A.L. Taylor & D.W. Bettcher, *supra* note 10, at 924.
[12] WHO, *WHO Tobacco Free Initiative, No World Tobacco Day 2004: Rationale*, available online: < http://www.who.int/tobacco/areas/communications/events/wntd /2004/rationale/en/>.

exploited the potential for growth in tobacco sales in developing countries, thus raising the tobacco-related disease burden there at an alarming rate.[13]

A prime example of this targeting is China, where tobacco companies have been intensely promoting their products. As of 1998, it was estimated that of the world's 1.1 billion smokers, 300 million are in China. Smokers in the US consume 450 billion cigarettes a year, while those in China consumed approximately 1.7 trillion during the same period. Lung cancer in China has been increasing at a rate of 4.5% a year.[14]

Meanwhile, in richer countries such as Canada, the UK, and Australia, smoking is on the decline.[15] While smoking rates in some industrialized countries are decreasing at about 1% a year, those in developing countries are increasing at around 3% per year. It is estimated that, if current trends persist for the next 30 years, 7 million people from developing countries will die every year from smoking-related diseases.[16]

Tobacco has implications for every aspect of sustainable development:

Economic Impact: There is a significant economic impact at both the household and macro levels. Country-specific analyses of the tobacco industry by the World Bank in collaboration with the WHO find that tobacco addiction imposes high opportunity costs on many poor households, who spend significant proportions of their income on tobacco instead of on nutrition and other needs.[17] Tobacco-causing diseases lead to high public health costs. Yet, tobacco control is highly cost-effective and compares favorably with interventions such as immunization.[18] Moreover, it reduces the need for future expenditure on disease treatment and health promotion.

---

[13] V. Ernster et al., "Women and Tobacco: Moving from Policy to Action" (2000) 78 *Bull. World Health Org.* 891; C.W. Warren et al., "Tobacco Use By Youth: A Surveillance Report from the Global Health Youth Survey Project" (2000) 78 *Bull. World Health Org.* 868; P. Krishnan et al., "Commentary" (2003) 361 *Lancet* 1669.
[14] C. Chelala, "Dispatches: Tobacco Corporations Step Up Invasion of Developing Countries" (1998) 351 *Lancet* 889 [Chelala].
[15] O. Shafey, S. Dolwick, G. E. Guindon (eds.), *Tobacco Control Country Profiles* (American Cancer Society, Atlanta, GA, 2003).
[16] Chelala, *supra* note 14, at 889.
[17] WHO, *Intergovernmental Negotiating Body of the WHO Framework Convention on Tobacco Control, Activities Since the Previous Session*, WHO Doc.A/FCTC/INB5/4/ (Geneva) (12 Sept. 2002), available online: < www.who.int/gb/fctc/PDF/inb5/ einb54.pdf> ; The World Bank Group, *Curbing the Epidemic: Governments and the Economics of Tobacco Control* (Washington, D.C.: The World Bank, 1999) at 2, available online: <http://www.worldbank.org/tobacco/reports.htm > [World Bank Tobacco].
[18] *Ibid,* World Bank Tobacco.

Labor Impact: Tobacco kills people at the height of their productivity, depriving families of breadwinners and nations of a healthy workforce. Tobacco users are also less productive while they are alive due to increased sickness. A 1994 report estimated that the use of tobacco resulted in an annual global net loss of US$200 thousand million, a third of this loss being in developing countries.[19] A tremendous part of the health and economic costs related to tobacco are endured by small farmers and their families that grow the tobacco crop. Precarious labor conditions, including the use of child labour and exposure to highly toxic products, and a highly negative impact on the environment, make tobacco an issue inextricably linked to poverty and other development issues.[20]

Environmental Impact: Tobacco growing harms the environment. It leads to the degradation of the environment caused by the tobacco plant leaching nutrients from the soil, pollution from pesticides and fertilizers and deforestation as a result of the fire curing of some common varieties of tobacco. A recent study that assessed the amount of forest and woodland consumed annually for curing tobacco concluded that nearly 5% of overall deforestation in respective growing countries was due to tobacco cultivation.[21] Tobacco smoke and passive smoking also contributes to air pollution, especially indoors, and exacerbates respiratory ailments.

The Trade Context for the FCTC

The increased international trade in tobacco also illustrates the tension between domestic and international goals. The intersection of US policy on trade and tobacco is one of the best examples. Domestically, the US government exercises its legal powers to regulate tobacco consumption in order to prevent and reduce tobacco-related diseases in its population. Simultaneously, the same US government uses national and international trade law to open the markets of developing countries for cigarettes in order to increase US tobacco companies' exports.

The health and tobacco debates date back to the late 1980s. At that time, the US negotiated bilateral agreements with several Asian countries to open foreign markets to US tobacco products under threat of US sanctions. In each case, tobacco manufacture and sales were controlled by state monopolies. The US

---

[19] See World Health Organization, *WHO Tobacco Free Initiative, Why is Tobacco a Public Health Priority*, available online: <http://www.who.int/tobacco/about/en/>.
[20] See World Health Organization, *Press Release, WHO, World No Tobacco Day 2004: The Vicious Circle of Tobacco and Poverty* (28 May 2004), available online: <http://www.who.int/mediacentre/releases/2004/pr36/en/>.
[21] See World Health Organization, *WHO Tobacco Free Initiative, No World Tobacco Day 2004: Rationale* available online: < http://www.who.int/tobacco/areas/communications/events/wntd /2004/rationale/en/>.

government succeeded in negotiating the elimination of excise taxes and distribution practices that discriminated against US tobacco products. The new market openness resulted in an overall increase in demand for tobacco, with the highest increase in poor countries.[22]

One exception to this pattern was in Thailand. The facts surrounding this matter are fully described elsewhere,[23] but are described briefly below in order to highlight several issues relating to international tobacco regulation.

Under its domestic Tobacco Act of 1966, Thailand prohibited the importation of cigarettes and other tobacco preparations, but authorized the sale of domestic cigarettes. Cigarettes were subject to an excise tax, a business tax and a municipal tax. In 1989, the US asserted that the import restrictions were inconsistent with general elimination of quantitative restrictions called for under Article XI of the GATT; it argued that the restrictions could not be justified under either the exceptions allowed for under that same Article, or by Article XX(b), which provides for measures necessary for the protection of human life or health. The US also argued that the internal taxes were inconsistent with GATT Article III:2, vis-à-vis the "National Treatment on Internal Taxation and Regulation."

Thailand, in turn, asserted that import restrictions were justified under Article XX(b) because the government had adopted health measures which could only be effective if cigarette imports were prohibited. It argued that the chemicals and other additives contained in US cigarettes made them more harmful to human health than Thai cigarettes.

WHO submissions to the GATT dispute panel confirmed that cigarettes manufactured in developed countries contained more additives and flavoring to make them easier to smoke, especially by women and adolescents. However, the WHO did not find any scientific evidence to show that one type of cigarette was more harmful to health than another. And ultimately, the GATT Dispute Panel found that the import restrictions were inconsistent with Article XI and not justified under that Article's exceptions. It further concluded that the import restrictions were not "necessary" for the protection of human life or

---

[22] A.L. Taylor et al., "Trade Policy and Tobacco Control" in P. Jha & F. Chaloupka (eds.) *Tobacco Control in Developing Countries* (Oxford: Oxford University Press, 2000).

[23] *Thailand - Restrictions on Importation of and Internal Taxes on Cigarettes*, Nov. 7, 1990, GATT B.I.S.D (37th Supp.) at 200 (1990); see also World Health Org. & World Trade Org., *WTO Agreements and Public Health: A Joint Study by the WHO and the WTO Secretariat* (WTO Secretariat 2002), available online: <http://www.who.int/media/homepage/en/who_wto_e.pdf>.

health because various methods could be used to protect public health without favoring domestic production, such as bans on advertising and point-of-sale promotion. Thus, the Panel rejected the US call for the advertising ban to be lifted. The internal taxes, too, were found to be consistent with Article III:2.

Paradoxically, the opening of the domestic market to foreign producers only served to strengthen Thailand's tobacco control efforts. One of the few national institutions designed to promote tobacco control is Thailand's National Committee for the Control of Tobacco Use, which was established in 1989 and is responsible for governmental tobacco control activities. Together, Thailand's Tobacco Products Control Act and its Nonsmokers' Health Protection Act, give Thailand some of the world's most comprehensive legislative protection from involuntary exposure to tobacco smoke and tobacco marketing.[24] Moreover, an important public health precedent was set when the GATT consulted with the WHO on a trade issue involving public health.

Details of the FCTC

It was against this backdrop that the idea for an international instrument for tobacco control was initiated in May 1995 at the 48th World Health Assembly. The following year, the 49th World Health Assembly adopted resolution WHA49.17, requesting the Director-General to initiate the development of a WHO Framework Convention on Tobacco Control.

The objective of the FCTC, given in Article 2 of the Convention is to protect present and future generations from the devastating health, social, economic, and environmental consequences of tobacco consumption and exposure to tobacco smoke. The Convention places great emphasis on public education and provision of information on health consequences and addictive nature of tobacco consumption.

The preamble notes that the spread of the tobacco epidemic is a global problem with serious public health consequences and calls for a comprehensive international response to deal with the issue. It further notes that scientific evidence has established that tobacco consumption and exposure to tobacco smoke cause death, disease and disability and that cigarettes are highly engineered to create and maintain dependence. The preamble also refers to Article 12 of the International Covenant on Economic, Social and Cultural

---

[24] A.M. Halvorssen, *The Role of National Institutions in Developing and Implementing the WHO Framework Convention on Tobacco Control*, U.N. Doc. WHO/NCD/TFI/99.5, at 27.

Rights and the preamble of the WHO Constitution, both of which affirm the right of every human being to enjoy the highest attainable standard of health.

Article 1 encourages parties to adopt measures more stringent than those required under the Convention in order to better protect human health. It also encourages parties to enter into bilateral and multilateral treaties, including regional treaties provided they are compatible with the obligations under the FCTC.

The general obligations of the parties are laid down in Article 5. The parties are required to develop and implement comprehensive multisectoral national tobacco control strategies, plans and programs.[25] In order to achieve this, parties are required to establish and finance a national coordinating mechanism or focal points for tobacco control and adopt and implement effective measures, including legislative measures, to prevent and reduce tobacco consumption, nicotine addiction and exposure to tobacco smoke.[26] The parties are, however, required to carry out this obligation only in accordance with its capabilities. This reflects the hortatory language found in economic rights instruments. Under Article 5(6), parties are required, to the extent of their resources, to cooperate to raise financial resources for the effective implementation of the Convention.

Much of the Convention relies on the measures taken by the parties to implement its provisions at the national level, provision of information and cooperation among parties. Under Article 9, the Conference of Parties can propose guidelines for testing and measuring the contents and emissions of tobacco products and for their regulation. Each party is under an obligation to adopt and implement those measures only in the event they are approved by the competent national authority. Under Article 10, parties are required to adopt and implement, in accordance with national law, requiring manufacturers and importers of tobacco products to disclose information about the contents and emissions of tobacco products. Each party shall, in turn, provide such information to the public.

Article 11 deals with packaging and labeling of tobacco products. Each party shall within three years take measures to ensure that tobacco product packaging and labeling do not promote a tobacco product by false or misleading means. Each packet must carry a health warning describing the harmful effects of tobacco use and shall be approved by the competent national authority.

---

[25] FCTC, *supra* note 3, at Article 5(1).
[26] *Ibid.,* Article 5(2).

Article 12 deals with the related issue of public awareness. Parties are required to promote and strengthen public awareness of tobacco control issues, using all available communication tools. These include measures to promote public access to information on the tobacco industry, adverse health, economic and environmental consequences of tobacco production and consumption as well as training and sensitization of health workers.

Article 13 dealing with advertising, promotion and sponsorship recognizes that a comprehensive ban on advertising, promotion and sponsorship would reduce the consumption of tobacco products. Each party is required to undertake such a ban, in accordance with its constitution and constitutional principles. This includes cross-border advertising. An important constitutional obstacle that may arise is whether such a comprehensive ban would be contrary to freedom of speech and expression protected in many constitutions across the world. Many constitutions, on the other hand, contain restrictions based on public health concerns and this could be an instance where freedom of speech and expression could be restricted on the ground of public health. If challenged, the judiciary will have to weigh the restrictions with the public health impact and decide whether the restrictions were proportionate. The Convention recognizing a possible conflict with constitutional provisions calls upon those parties which are unable to undertake a comprehensive ban to apply restrictions on all tobacco advertising, promotion and sponsorship.

Article 15 deals with the illicit trade in tobacco products. Recognizing that elimination of illicit trade in tobacco products is essential for tobacco control, parties have undertaken to adopt and implement measures to ensure that all packets and packages of tobacco products are marked with the place of origin as well as its legal status. Toward the goal of eliminating illicit trade, the parties are required to monitor and collect data on cross-border trade in tobacco products, enact or strengthen legislation against illicit trade and take measures to ensure that all confiscated materials are destroyed.

The Convention also deals with the issue of sales to minors. Research suggests that most smokers start when they are teenagers and that tobacco companies target this category in their sales promotions and advertisements. Article 16 requires parties to adopt and implement measures, including legislative measures, to prohibit the sale of tobacco products to persons under the age set by national law or eighteen.

Protection of the environment has also received attention in the Convention. Article 18 provides that "In carrying out their obligations under this

Convention, the Parties agree to have due regard to the protection of the environment and the health of persons in relation to the environment in respect of tobacco cultivation and manufacture within their respective territories." Article 17 requires parties to provide economically viable alternatives for tobacco growers and individual sellers.

During the negotiating process, the issue of liability turned out to be the most contentious issue. In an attempt to deal with the issue, yet not pin down anybody for liability, the Convention calls upon parties to "consider" taking legislative action or promoting their laws to deal with criminal and civil liability, including compensation. Thus, much is left in the hands of the individual parties of the Convention. The issue of liability may be the subject of a separate protocol to be adopted later.

Sustainable Development Principles in the FCTC

The next challenge for the FCTC will be its implementation. This will involve putting in place the needed technical foundations, and translating the treaty into national laws.

A major challenge for the implementation of the FCTC may arise out of WTO challenges. On their face, none of the provisions of the FCTC seem to be inherently WTO-inconsistent; and many of the restrictions called for by some of its provisions may well be determined to be "necessary" for health protection under WTO rules. However, the relationship between WTO rules and the FCTC will depend on the manner in which its rules are applied by governments.

The US-Thai tobacco case illustrated the relevance of GATT vis-à-vis taxes, prohibitions, and human health-related exceptions to GATT rules. Other WTO agreements that may be applicable include:

- the Technical Barriers to Trade (TBT) Agreement in relation to product requirements such as packaging and labeling;
- the Agreement on Agriculture in relation to government support for tobacco production;

- the General Agreement on Trade in Services (GATS) in relation to restrictions on cigarette advertising; and
- the *Agreement on the Trade-Related Aspects of Intellectual Property Rights* (TRIPS) in relation to trademark protection and the disclosure of product information considered by producers to be confidential.

There is little doubt that FCTC measures, in so far as they may be challenged under WTO, laws must be viewed in light of sustainable development law obligations. Since 1995, the WTO's Dispute Settlement Body (DSB) has recognized an SD approach in a number of decisions.[27] In the 1998 *Shrimp-Turtle Case*, for example, the panel noted that the "first paragraph of the Preamble for the WT Agreement acknowledges that the optimal use for the world's resources must be pursued in accordance with the objective of sustainable development." In the same case, the Appellate Body stated that sustainable development "must add colour, texture and shading to our interpretation of the agreements annexed to the WTO Agreement." Additional recognition of sustainable development law principles, vis-à-vis health, has been made with regard to the right to health and the principle of equity in the context of the Doha Declaration on TRIPS and Public Health.[28]

The WTO, too, has wrestled with health-protecting measures, via the precautionary principle, in the *EC-Asbestos* case, the *Japan-Apples* case, and the *EC-Growth Hormones* case.[29] The precautionary principle would not be invoked today in order to defend tobacco control measures, per se, as these measures are clearly preventative in the face of certain science. However, a precautionary approach would have provided the necessary reversal of proof, in those times, when the GATT panel had considered arguments as to whether the foreign cigarettes were more or less harmful than domestic ones (an area of clear uncertainty in the science). A precautionary approach would have barred the US and the GATT panel from arguing that uncertain science should prevent Thailand from limiting the use of one product rather than the other, and would have placed the burden on the US to show their flavored-cigarettes were less harmful than the Thai alternatives. The use of the precautionary principle has

---

[27] For a further discussion see M. Gehring and M.C. Cordonier Segger "CISDL Legal Brief for the 'Sustainable Developments in WTO Law and 'Jurisprudence' Legal Experts Panel Event at the WTO 5th Ministerial Conference" (2003), available online: <http://www.cisdl.org/pdf/Cancun_WTO_Legal_Brief.pdf>.
[28] *Implementation of Paragraph 6 of the Doha Declaration on the TRIPS Agreement and Public Health* (1 Sept. 2003) WT/L/540, 30, available online: < http://www.wto.org/english/tratop_e/trips_e/implem_para6_e.htm>.
[29] For a further discussion see M.C. Cordonier Segger & M. Gehring, "Precaution, Health and the World Trade Organisation: Moving toward Sustainable Development" (2003) 29 *Queen's L. J.* 133.

been demonstrated[30] in more recent panels and will likely be given consideration in future WTO challenges.

Beyond the precedents set by these cases there are a number of other ISDL principles which are implicated by the FCTC.

The principle of equity and the eradication of poverty

The present generation has the obligation to refrain from depriving future generations of environmental social and economic opportunities of well-being. Tobacco and poverty are inextricably linked. Many studies have shown that in the poorest households in some low-income countries as much as 10% of total household expenditure is on tobacco. This means that these families have less money to spend on basic items such as food, education and health care. In addition to its direct health effects, tobacco leads to malnutrition, increased health care costs and premature death. It also contributes to a higher illiteracy rate, since money that could have been used for education is spent on tobacco instead.

Public Participation and Access to Information

One of ISDL's most important procedural elements, this principle calls for public participation and access to information. An established right under international human rights law, this consistent respect for fairness and due process is equally applicable to other fields including the environment (as seen in the 1998 *Aarhus Convention*) and public health.[31] In August 2000, a WHO Expert Committee concluded that tobacco industry activities against the World Health Organization would be intensified as the guiding principles and treaty obligations of the WHO FCTC gain acceptance and legitimacy worldwide. In recognition of this reality, WHO Member States unanimously adopted resolution WHA 54.18 calling on transparency in tobacco control. Understanding the tobacco industry's practices is crucial for the success of tobacco control policies. In many developing countries, marketing strategies are used that have long been banned in many developed countries. While there is not space to discuss the politics around tobacco control, there is also clear evidence that the tobacco industry has used secretive means to discredit legitimate organizations like the WHO that push for tobacco control.[32]

---

[30] *Ibid.*

[31] World Health Organization, *Committee of Experts on Tobacco Industry Documents, Tobacco Industry Strategies to Undermine Tobacco Control Activities at the World Health Organization* (2000), available online: <http://tobacco.who.int/repostiroy/stp58/who_iinquiry.pdf>.

[32] *Ibid.*

International Cooperation

In a laudable example of non-health organizations supporting the work of the WHO, the World Bank specifically requires that international agencies support the FCTC.

Inter-relationship and Integration of the Right to Health

International law supports a fundamental right to a healthy life, and indirectly supports anti-tobacco public health efforts in a number of ways.[33] The UN General Assembly recognized that "all individuals are entitled to live in an environment adequate for their health and well-being." The WHO's Constitution obliges it to minimize tobacco's unhealthy influence.[34] Some of the strongest support relates to international law and children's rights and limiting children's access to tobacco.[35] States possess a mandatory obligation to "ensure to the maximum extent possible the survival and development of the child."[36]

Looking Forward: Strengthening Institutions/Capacity Building

The passage of the FCTC was a defining moment for the global public health community and for ISDL. Questions remain, however, as to whether the WHO and individual governments will have the political and financial means to defend their public health positions when health is regarded as an object for negotiation in the same way as any of the other 160 services listed in the

---

[33] See, e.g., "Everyone has the right to life. . . ." *Universal Declaration of Human Rights,* G.A. Res. 217A, U.N. GAOR, 3d Sess., Art. 3, U.N. Doc. A/810 (1948); "States Parties. . . recognize the right of everyone to the enjoyment of the highest attainable standard of physical and mental health." *International Covenant on Economic, Social and Cultural Rights* (16 Dec. 1966) Arts. 12, 1, 993 U.N.T.S. 3, 8; "Everyone has the right to benefit from any measures enabling him to enjoy the highest possible standard of health attainable." *European Social Charter* (18 Oct. 1961) 529 U.N.T.S. 89, 92; The Right to Safe and Healthy Working Conditions; *id.* at Art. 11; "Everyone shall have the right to health, understood to mean the enjoyment of the highest level of physical, mental and social well-being. In order to ensure the exercise of the right to health, the States Parties agree to recognize health as a public good. . . ." *Additional Protocol to the American Convention on Human Rights in the Area of Economic, Social and Cultural Rights,* (14 Nov. 1988) 28 I.L.M. 156, 164, at Art. 10. "Everyone shall have the right to live in a healthy environment. . . ." *Ibid.* at Art. 11.
[34] "Health is a state of complete physical, mental and social well-being and not merely the absence of disease or infirmity. The enjoyment of the highest attainable standard of health is one of the fundamental rights of every human being. . . .". WHO Constitution, supra note 4, preamble; "The objective of the [WHO Constitution]. . . shall be the attainment by all peoples of the highest possible level of health." *Ibid.* at Art. 1.
[35] See *United Nations Convention on the Rights of the Child*, G.A. res. 44/25, annex 445 U.N. GAOR Spp. (No.49) at 167 U.N. Doc. A/44/49 (1989), Art. 24(1).
[36] *Ibid.* at Art. 6(1).

WTO's general agreement. The answer will lie in how successfully the FCTC is implemented at the country level.

Building national plans of action for tobacco control and establishing national infrastructures to implement the plans of action are key steps to implementing the FCTC. One model for implementation that has been successful in establishing domestic tobacco control laws, is the establishment of national tobacco control commissions.[37] Such institutions could be established through a legislative act or decree; their charters should be as flexible as possible. Such Commissions could act in a variety of advisory capacities and supervisory capacities by encouraging compliance with the FCTC and by monitoring domestic policies and measures. They could also play a valuable role in collecting, producing, and disseminating information materials on the FCTC and on domestic legislation to tobacco control. Broadly conceived, they could even play an investigatory role by receiving complaints from individuals and making recommendations. Such national commissions would be a useful locus for the capacity building of the legislators, jurists, health professionals and civil society organizations needed to implement the FCTC.

An ongoing concern is how to aid developing countries in implementing obligations under the treaty and how to protect those same countries from the reach of multinational tobacco companies. It is critical that the WHO collaborate in strengthening developing country institutions by assisting in the training of staff, providing advice on the domestic implementation of the FCTC, providing assistance in creating cooperative relationships with appropriate partners and managing resources. It has also been suggested that a trust fund be created to enable developing countries to participate in the FCTC.[38]

National commissions, as discussed above, would also be a useful focal point for WHO technical, financial and training assistance at the country level. They would also serve as useful decision-making points to address the two remaining substantive questions of the FCTC, namely, how liability is to be addressed, and how to harmonize obligations under the WTO and the FCTC.

Conclusions

---

[37] See Halvorssen, *supra* note 24.
[38] See A. L. Taylor & R. Roemer, *International Strategy for Tobacco Control* (WHO/PSA/96.6) (WHO: Geneva, 1996); see A. L. Taylor, "An International Regulatory Strategy for Global Tobacco Control" 21 *Yale J. Int'l Law* 257 (1996).

As discussed at the beginning of this chapter, global trade around certain products pose unique transnational threats to public health. The FCTC is an attempt to address that problem at the international level. Its success, as with all international instruments, will be dependent on the ability of FCTC advocates to mobilize, support and coordinate tobacco policy measures at country, regional and international levels, particularly for the benefit of low and middle-income countries.

24

IMPLICATIONS FOR HEALTH AND HEALTH CARE: EXPANDING THE DISCOURSE ON ETHICS AND HEALTH

Solomon R Benatar [1]

Despite spectacular achievements in science, technology and health care in the 20th Century, together with unprecedented economic growth, the beginning of the 21st Century is characterised by global instability associated with increasingly widening disparities in wealth and health. These disparities, recently described as 'a perfect crime',[2] pose strategic and moral challenges for powerful nations. Following an outline of some facts about the world and the underlying values driving progress, this chapter provides some recommendations for the paradigm shifts that hold potential to promote more sustainable progress.

An Unstable and Unsustainable World

The global economy

Globalisation is the currently popular term used to characterise the increasing interconnectedness between money, business, people and popular culture across the globe. The driving forces are neo-liberal economic policies and free market forces, which are assumed to be closely associated with the propagation of democracy and human rights. Globalisation is, however, a complex and ambiguous concept with social and ecological manifestations that reflect a long, interwoven economic and political history in which peoples, economies, cultures and political processes have been subject to increasingly pervasive transnational influences. Compression of time and space through new communication technology has sped up the process of globalisation in recent decade by uniting many across the globe. It has, however, also created new and wider divides.

---

[1] Dr. Solomon R Benatar, MBChB, FFA (SA), FRCP, FRSSAfr., Professor of Medicine, Director Bioethics Centre, University of Cape Town.
[2] J.K. Galbraith, "A Perfect Crime: Global Inequality" (2002) 131 *Daedalus* 11-25.

M.C. Cordonier Segger & C. G. Weeramantry, eds., Sustainable Justice: Reconciling Economic, Social & Environmental Law
© *2005 Koninklijke Brill NV, Printed in The Netherlands, pp.381-388.*

Positive and widely appreciated manifestations of progress associated with globalisation include advances in science and technology; increased life-expectancy; enhanced economic growth; greater freedom and prosperity; better speed and efficiency of communications and transport; and popularisation of the concept of human rights.

However, the negative aspects of globalisation need to be considered as well. In 1900 the wealthiest 20% of the world's population were 9 times richer than the poorest 20%. This ratio has grown progressively - to 30 times by 1960, 60 times by 1990 and to over 70 times by 1997.[3] It can also be argued that poverty has increased: today, almost half the world's population lives on less than US $2 per person per day and more than a billion people live on less than US $1 per day.[4] Developing country (including middle-income countries) debt grew from $0.5 trillion in 1980 to $1.9 trillion in 1994 and to $2.2 trillion in 1997.[5] Although the developing world's debt accounts for a small proportion of total world debt, it has reached substantial levels in comparison to income levels. Most of the countries that were required by the World Bank to pursue structural adjustment programs are in greater debt than ever before, and it also seems that the adverse effects of progress are being felt most severely by 80% of the world's population.[6]

The development of a complex web of material, institutional and ideological forces and the presence of powerful multinational corporations have had profound implications on the accumulation of capital and the way in which resources are controlled. In 1973, global market exchanges amounted to $15 billion daily and 70% of all money that exchanged hands on a daily basis was payment for work, while speculative financial transactions accounted for 30%. By 1998, daily global market transactions had escalated to $1.5 trillion daily of which about 5% was payment for work while speculative transactions accounted for 95%.[7]

It has recently been argued that the shift in the locus of economic power from the nation state to global corporations is also altering the balance of power in the world.[8] Boundaries between states and between foreign and domestic

---

[3] World Bank, Human Development Report 1999 *Globalization with a Human Face, Human Development Indicators* (Washington: World Bank, 1999). See also D. Rodrik, *Has Globalization Gone Too Far?* (Washington: Institute for International Economics, 1997).
[4] *Ibid.*
[5] A. R. Chowdhury, Foreign Debt and Growth in Developing Countries, available online: <http://www.wider.unu.edu/conference/conference-2001-2/parallel%20papers/4_1_Abdur.pdf>
[6] R. Labonte, T. Schrecker, D. Sanders, W. Meeus, *Fatal Indifference: the G8 and Global Health* (Ottawa: University of Cape Town Press and International Development Research Centre, 2004).
[7] W. Ellwood, *No-Nonsense Guide to Globalization* (London: Verso Press, 2003).
[8] M. Khor, "A Comment on Attempted Linkages Between Trade and Non-Trade Issues in the WTO" in J. Bhagwati and M. Hirsch, eds., *The Next Trade Negotiating Round: Examining the Agenda for Seattle* (New York: Columbia University Press, 1999) at 53. See also D. Korten, *When Corporations Rule the World* (Bloomfield: Kumarian Press, 1995).

policies seem to be becoming more blurred, affecting small states' control over their economies, and their ability to provide for their citizens. These processes have led some authors to argue that economic disparities have become so marked and their adverse effects so apparent that a very significant degree of incompatibility has arisen between neo-liberal economic policies - namely, the facilitation of globalisation -and the goals of democracy.

War, displacement of people and economic aid for development

New patterns of war and ethnic conflicts have resulted in the displacement and migration of millions of people, and the arms trade itself, (with its link to economic aid) has contributed significantly to an escalation in wars, conflicts, and torture since World War II.[9] These disruptions have forced over 25 million people to become refugees, resulting in profound effects on their lives and health. [10] Still, while global military expenditure in 1990 amounted to US $1 trillion, the annual budget of the World Health Organization (WHO) was equivalent to merely 2.5 hours of that amount.[11]

World health and health care expenditure

Health and well being are profoundly affected by complex interactions between economic, social, and political forces as well as by behavioural patterns and modern medical practices. The balance of these forces and the resulting health services that are provided vary greatly, especially between wealthy and poor countries. Life expectancy, one measure of health status, ranges from over 75 years (and rising) in wealthy countries to 40 years (and falling) in Africa. Among the poorest quintile of people in the world, 55% die of communicable diseases, as compared with 5% of the richest quintile. [12] The WHO estimated that in 1998, 11 million children and adults of working age died of six types of infectious diseases that could have been prevented for $20 per life saved. [13]

Poor countries bear over 80 percent of the global burden of disease as measured in disability adjusted life years (DALYs). [14] This burden is increasing as the epidemiological transition progresses, with added disability and suffering from non-communicable diseases. Poverty (defined as lack of economic resources, lack of education, lack of access to basic life resources such as food, water and sanitation, and lack of control over reproductive health) directly

---

[9] R. Sivard, *World Military and Social Expenditure 16th Ed*, Washington DC: World Priorities Press 1996.
[10] See Human Rights Watch, available online: < http://www.hrw.org/campaigns/refugees>.
[11] C. W. Kiefer, Militarism and world health, *Social Science and Medicine.* 1992; 31: 719-24
[12] WHO, Healthy Life Expectancy, *The World Health Report 1998* (Geneva: WHO, 1998), available online: <http://www.who.int/inf-pr-1998/en/pr98-WHA4.html>.
[13] *Ibid.*
[14] *Ibid.*

accounts for almost one third of the global burden of disease.[15] Poverty leads to poor health, which in turn aggravates poverty. Tens of millions of people, including many children, die every year of starvation - in a world with enough food to feed all.

Since the 1960s, major advances in medicine and technology have been associated with escalating expenditures on health care – but mostly in industrialised countries. In the late 1990s annual per capita expenditure on health care ranged from $4000 in the US down to less than $10 in the poorest countries in Africa.[16] It is now well established that there is a definite relationship between economic status and health and life expectancy. Both absolute and relative wealth affect health: among the developed countries, it is not the richest societies that have the best health, but rather those with the smallest income differentials between rich and poor.[17] This relationship between wealth and health underscores the need to see health and disease as intimately linked to social and economic conditions.

Half of the world's population lives in countries that cannot afford annual per capita health expenditures of more than $5-10, and many people do not have access to essential basic drugs.[18] Furthermore, even though some parasitic diseases (for example onchocerciasis, schistosomasis and lymphatic filariasis) could be controlled by mass treatment campaigns using inexpensive drugs, the infrastructure required to provide such coverage is inadequate. [19] As a result, treatment of diseases such as tuberculosis, leprosy, and HIV/AIDS, which requires a more complex infrastructure, cannot be afforded on current health care budgets in poor countries.

When comparing health services and expectations for health care around the world, it is necessary to appreciate that economic conditions, consumption patterns, and the way of life in industrialised countries may not be the best norm for the whole world. For example, the USA, with 5% of the world's population, accounts for over 20% of global energy use, and 50% of annual global expenditure on health care (over $4000 per person per year) – yet there is no universal access to health care for all US citizens.[20] Such ways of life, consumption patterns and health care practices are probably not sustainable in most countries, and even the USA.

---

[15] *Ibid.*
[16] *World Health Report 2000 Health Systems: improving performance*
[17] R. G. Wilkinson, *Unhealthy Societies: The Affliction of Inequality.* Routledge, London 1996
[18] B. Pecoul, P. Chirac, P. Trouiller, J. Pinel, "Access to Essential Drugs in Poor Countries – A Lost Battle?" (1999) *JAMA* 281 at 361-67
[19] *Ibid.*
[20] J. Iglehart, "American Health Services: Expenditure" (1999) *New England Journal of Medicine.* 340 at 70-76.

The threat of infectious diseases

Growing inequities in wealth and health and the associated urbanisation, migration, travel, ethnic conflict, displacement of people, ecological degradation, and poor conditions of life for millions of people have resulted in global instability, characterised by such new security threats as the emergence and spread of new diseases, multi-drug resistant infections, and the possibility of biological warfare.[21] The spread of infectious diseases over the past 25 years, characterised by the emergence of HIV/AIDS and the re-emergence of tuberculosis and malaria in multi-drug resistant forms provides a striking example of new threats to all. Moreover, it is clear that such pandemics cannot be dealt with through a narrow biomedical approach. A more complex systems approach is essential for sustainable development and improved global health.[22]

Ecological degradation

Population growth and the excessive consumption of earth's limited resources are having adverse ecological effects that are among our major causes of concern at the beginning of this century. During the past 100 years the world's population has increased from 1.6 billion to more than 6 billion, and the annual consumption of energy has increased 30 fold. While population growth in poor countries has been the main focus of concern for industrialised countries, consumption patterns in rich countries now pose risks of equal or greater magnitude. "Environmental capital" is being consumed more rapidly than it can be regenerated by nature and certain ecological niches are favouring the emergence of new infectious diseases. The environment has become an abused and severely compromised 'commons.' Loss of biodiversity, global warming, damage to the ozone layer, soil erosion, pollution of the air and the sea have all been allowed to escalate without sufficient attention to their implications for the future of life on our planet. Future generations will pay the price in terms of disease, impaired quality of life and reduced longevity. [23]

Dominant Values Driving the Modern World

It is widely believed that advances in scientific knowledge, free market economic growth, and the propagation of the concept of human rights will provide solutions to problems within an unstable and complex system. These

---

[21] S. R. Benatar, "The Coming Catastrophe in International Health: An Analogy with Lung Cancer" (2001) *International Journal (Canadian Institute of International Affairs) 56:* 611 -631
[22] S. R. Benatar, "The HIV/AIDS Pandemic: A Sign of Instability in a Complex Global System" (2002) *Journal of Medicine & Philosophy* 27(2):163-177.
[23] A. J. McMichael, *Planetary Overload: Global Environmental Change and the Health of the Human Species* (Cambridge: Cambridge University Press, 1993). See also T. McMichael, *Human Frontiers, Environment and Diseases: Past Patterns, Uncertain Futures* (Cambridge: Cambridge University Press, 2001).

ideas are sustained by promoting a high degree of individualism, a narrow perspective on human rights (limited to civil and political rights), and a market that drives production and consumption of private goods while devaluing public goods. In summary, the dominant concept of security is based on geo-political realism in international relations. Progressively widening disparities are threats to the self-interest of all through political terrorism, infectious diseases and other biological threats including those that accompany environmental degradation.

New Paradigms for Solutions to Global Health

The description presented above of the growing injustice leading to global instability serves as a background against which to consider what values should be promoted and how an expanded discourse on ethics could serve as a vital step towards altering the required redistribution of resources for the improvement of population health. The challenge for the 21st century is the betterment of human health and human lives worldwide. Old ways of thinking about progress and improving global health are becoming obsolete. New conceptions of sustainable development will have to be coupled to an expanded discourse on ethics that goes beyond a narrow conception of human rights, interpersonal ethics and health to include the ethics of public health and of international relations that play such important roles in determining the health of whole populations.[24]

Values that will have to be fostered to achieve such goals and improve global health and equity in the future include greater concern for the common good with a commitment to a broader perspective on human rights (inclusive of social, economic, cultural and environmental rights, and access to health care) [25] and a sense of civic responsibility reflecting solidarity with others. Individual freedoms are insufficient, and must be coupled to greater equity and solidarity for human flourishing. All nations have responsibilities that are common and differentiated in working towards the goal of global solidarity (for example developing and testing new drugs and vaccines and making these available to all in need). Security should increasingly be sought through co-operation and moral power in addition to economic and military power. Changes also need to be made to global economic policy and international trade relations in order to reduce inequity and eliminate profound poverty. Redistribution of resources, over-population and over-consumption all need to be addressed. Public participation is needed to shape the setting of health care priorities and resource allocation through processes that are accountable and reasonable.[26] Good

---

[24] S.R. Benatar, A.S. Daar & P. A. Singer, "Global Health Ethics: the Rationale for Mutual Caring" 79 (2003) *International Affairs*; 7-138.
[25] *United Nations Commission on Economic, Social and Cultural Rights*, U.N. Doc. E/C.12/2000/4 (200o).
[26] N. Daniels & J Sabin, "Accountability for Reasonableness" (1998) *Health Affairs* 17:50-64.

governance of nations, transnational corporations and health care systems should be fostered – the problems with the alternatives are illustrated by failures and successes in dealing with the HIV/AIDS pandemic. The principle of precaution should also be exercised in relation to means of advancing health (for example in relation to creating transgenic animals). Deeper insights are also needed to better understand the inter-relationship of health, well being and social justice.

An ecological approach to justice and to population health requires a shift from a predominantly anthropocentric view of the world to an eco-centric worldview that includes concern for nature and for all forms of life. A long-term perspective on life and a concern for rights that includes the well being of future generations is essential to this viewpoint. The age-old concept of stewardship of nature here replaces the idea of the subjugation of nature. Such a moral agenda could promote the human potential required to deal with threats from poverty, conflict and demographic and environmental changes. Failure to acknowledge and act on this reflects a state of moral insensitivity at the least and moral depravity at worst.

Conclusions

New infectious diseases such as HIV/AIDS, the recrudescence of tuberculosis and malaria in multi-resistant forms, the growing epidemic of non-communicable diseases, ecological degradation, escalating ethnic conflict and persistent poverty and hunger in the midst of plenty, are signs of an increasingly unstable world at the end of a period of major progress. At this time in history, when the dark side of progress becomes clear, old ways of thinking about progress and of improving health are less useful, in particular when these are narrowly defined in economic and individualistic terms. It is unlikely that relying solely on advances in scientific knowledge, free-market forces, a narrow interpretation of human rights and interpersonal ethics will provide sufficient solutions to problems within an unstable complex system. Imaginative and creative new practical approaches, associated with the wise application of scientific and social knowledge, using systems theory and supported by a broader ethics framework are required to ameliorate the adverse effects of rampant market forces. Averting the danger of setting back the clock on progress requires the amplification of the economic and military power of the G8 countries through a moral vision that is extended from 'interpersonal morality' to 'civic morality' and to an 'ethics of international relations,' with dimensions intimately linked to political, military, cultural and economic issues.[27]

---

[27] The author wishes to clarify that the views he offers are not intended to imply that the wealthy, productive and fortunate in the world should bear the whole burden of the blame for the complex series of historical developments that polarise the world. Such inequities that devalue human life can be attributed both to

corrupt leadership in developing countries and to the policies of wealthy nations in relentless pursuit of their own economic interests. See T. Pogge, *World Poverty and Human Rights* (Cambridge: Polity Press, 2002).

PART III

IMPLEMENTATION OF SUSTAINABLE DEVELOPMENT LAW

PARTICIPATION, TRANSPARENCY AND ACCESS TO JUSTICE

25

THE AARHUS CONVENTION: A NEW INSTRUMENT PROMOTING ENVIRONMENTAL DEMOCRACY

Jeremy Wates[1]

In recent decades, traditional systems of representative democracy have been increasingly supplemented by measures promoting participatory democracy. This has particularly been the case in the environmental sphere, where the interests of the public are recognized to have a particular legitimacy. Involving the public improves the quality of decision-making as well as strengthening public belief in the credibility of the decision-making process and its outcome. It is also increasingly perceived as a question of rights; the notion that the public is entitled to see its views reflected in the decisions of public authorities on an ongoing basis – rather than its role being limited to the occasional trip to the ballot box at election time – is gaining ground.

The emergence of participatory democracy is reflected in a host of national measures, of both legislative and non-legislative character. It is also reflected to a more modest extent in global and regional declarations and instruments. Perhaps the most far-reaching example of the latter is the United Nations Economic Commission for Europe (UNECE) *Convention on Access to Information, Public Participation in Decision-making and Access to Justice in Environmental Matters.*[2]

Aarhus: A New International Law on Citizens' Environmental Rights

The Convention was adopted on 25th June 1998 in the Danish city of Aarhus – hence its more common name, the Aarhus Convention - at the Fourth Ministerial Conference in the 'Environment for Europe' process. A total of 39 countries and the European Community have signed it.

The Aarhus Convention is a new kind of environmental agreement. It links environmental rights and human rights. It acknowledges that we owe an

---

[1] Jeremy Wates, M.Phil. Hons. (Cantab), Secretary to the Aarhus Convention, United Nations Economic Commission for Europe.
[2] 38 I.L.M. 517 (1998), online: UNECE <http://www.unece.org/env/pp> *[Aarhus Convention]* (entered into force 30 October 2001).

M.C. Cordonier Segger & C. G. Weeramantry, eds., Sustainable Justice: Reconciling Economic, Social & Environmental Law
© *2005 Koninklijke Brill NV, Printed in The Netherlands, pp.393-406.*

obligation to future generations. It establishes that sustainable development can be achieved only through the involvement of all stakeholders. It links government accountability and environmental protection. It goes to the heart of the relationship between people and governments. The Convention is therefore not only an environmental agreement; it is also a Convention about government accountability, transparency and responsiveness.

Tracing the Development of the Convention

The origin of the Convention can be traced back to Principle 10 of the *Rio Declaration on Environment and Development,*[3] which stresses the importance of public access to environmental information and opportunities for the public to participate in decision-making processes and to have effective access to administrative and judicial proceedings.

Within the Economic Commission for Europe (ECE) region Principle 10 was taken up and further developed, first through the preparation of a set of non-binding Guidelines on Access to Environmental Information and Public Participation in Environmental Decision-making.[4] The guidelines were endorsed by ECE Environment Ministers in October 1995 at the Third Ministerial Conference in the 'Environment for Europe' process, and are hence known as the Sofia Guidelines.

At the same time as endorsing the Guidelines, the Ministers acknowledged the need for further work in this area and agreed to consider the possibility of developing a legally binding convention. In January 1996, the Committee on Environmental Policy decided to proceed with the preparation of a draft convention and established an *ad hoc* working group for the purpose. The negotiations over the draft Convention took place between June 1996 and March 1998 in ten sessions of the Working Group.

At the Ministerial Conference in Aarhus in June 1998, thirty-five countries and the European Community signed the Convention, and in the following six-month period during which it was open for signature, four more countries signed, making a total of 40 signatories.

The Convention entered into force on October 30, 2001, ninety days after the deposit of the sixteenth instrument of ratification as laid down in the Convention itself. The first meeting of the Parties took place on October 21-23, 2002 in Lucca, Italy. By September 2004, thirty countries had become Parties to the Convention, about half of these being from Central and Eastern

---

[3] 31 I.L.M. 874 (1992).

[4] United Nations Economic Council for Europe, *Guidelines on Access to Environmental Information and Public Participation in Environmental Decision-making,* UN Doc. SOF.CONF/BD.1 (1998), online: United Nations Economic Council for Europe
<http://www.unece.org/env/documents/1995/sof/conf/bd/sof.conf.bd.1.e.pdf>.

Europe or the Commonwealth of Independent States and a similar number from the recently expanded European Union.[5] Several Western European countries, as well as the European Union itself, are actively working towards ratification.

The Role of NGOs

A unique feature of the Aarhus Convention processes has been the unprecedented level of NGO involvement. During the Convention negotiations, environmental NGOs – also known as environmental citizens' organizations or ECOs - were not only represented in the plenary sessions of the Working Group but also in virtually every drafting committee and in the small advisory group which assisted the Secretariat in the preparation of the first draft. Thus the involvement of ECOs began at an early stage and continued right throughout the process. Within each of these fora, at the discretion of the Chair, the ECO delegation was allowed to intervene on more or less the same basis as governmental delegations, and in practice availed of this opportunity intensively. Other non-governmental or quasi-non-governmental bodies, notably the Regional Environmental Center for Central and Eastern Europe, also played an active role.

The participation of ECOs unquestionably increased the relevance of the text and ensured that the officials knew many of the real concerns of the public. ECOs were in a sense recognized as the principal 'clients' of the Convention – whether regarded as the subset of the public likely to make most active use of the rights that the Convention would confer, or as the stakeholder group most likely to make use of them on behalf of the wider public. Many important elements in the text were introduced as a result of proposals by the ECO coalition, even if not always in the form initially proposed.

Several Environment Ministers and senior UN officials, as well as the Resolution of the Signatories accompanying the adoption of the Convention, acknowledged the contribution made by the ECOs to the drafting process at the Aarhus conference. The Resolution went on to recommend that NGOs should be allowed to participate not only in the activities of the Meeting of the Signatories to the Convention but also in the preparation of instruments on environmental protection in other international fora.

---

[5] Albania, Armenia, Azerbaijan, Belarus, Belgium, Bulgaria, Cyprus, Czech Republic, Denmark, Estonia, Finland, France, Former Yugoslav Republic of Macedonia, Georgia, Hungary, Italy, Kazakhstan, Kyrgyzstan, Latvia, Lithuania, Malta, Norway, Republic of Moldova, Poland, Portugal, Romania, Slovenia, Tajikistan, Turkmenistan and Ukraine.Updated information is available online:
<http://www.unece.org/env/documents/2003/inf/inf.5.e/pdf>.

The Content of the Convention

As its title suggests, the Convention contains three broad themes or 'pillars': access to information, public participation and access to justice. However, before describing these, it is worth referring to a number of important general features of the Convention.

General Features

Rights-based approach: The Convention adopts a rights-based approach. Article 1, setting out the objective of the Convention, requires Parties to guarantee rights of access to information, public participation in decision-making and access to justice in environmental matters. It also refers to the goal of protecting the right of every person of present and future generations to live in an environment adequate to health and well-being, which represents a significant step forward in international law. These rights underlie the various procedural requirements in the Convention.

A 'floor', not a 'ceiling': The Convention establishes minimum standards to be achieved but does not prevent any party from adopting measures which go further in the direction of providing access to information, public participation or access to justice.

Non-discrimination: The Convention prohibits discrimination on the basis of citizenship, nationality or domicile against persons seeking to exercise their rights under the Convention.

Definition of public authorities: The main thrust of the obligations contained in the Convention is towards public authorities, which are defined so as to cover governmental bodies from all sectors and at all levels (national, regional, local, etc), as well as bodies performing public administrative functions. Although the Convention is not primarily focussed on the private sector, privatized bodies having public responsibilities in relation to the environment, that are under the control of the aforementioned types of public authorities are also covered by the definition. Bodies acting in a judicial or legislative capacity are excluded.

Inclusion of EU institutions: The definition of 'public authority' also covers the institutions of regional economic integration organizations that become Parties to the Convention. Therefore, if the EU ratifies the Convention, the provisions of the Convention will apply to the EU institutions. The European Commission would probably feel the main impact of this, but it could also apply to the Council when it is not acting in a legislative capacity, and to the European Environment Agency.

International bodies: Apart from the special case of regional economic integration organizations such as the EU, the Convention contains a more general requirement on Parties to promote the application of its principles within the framework of international bodies and processes in matters relating to the environment. While the wording is not very specific, the inclusion of this provision shows some recognition of the need to prevent any loss of transparency and public accountability as decision-making moves onto an international level.

Non-compliance mechanism: The Meeting of the Parties to the Convention is required to establish, on a consensus basis, optional arrangements for reviewing compliance with the provisions of the Convention. Such arrangements should allow for 'appropriate public involvement'. Although the wording is not particularly strong (due mainly to opposition during the negotiations from countries which subsequently did not sign the Convention in Aarhus), this provision is given emphasis in Resolution 6, which accompanied the adoption of the Convention.

Non-ECE countries: Finally, the Convention is open to accession by non-ECE countries, subject to approval of the Meeting of the Parties.

Access to Information

The information pillar covers both the 'passive' or reactive aspect of information. This includes the obligation on public authorities to respond to public requests for information, and the 'active' aspect dealing with other obligations relating to information, such as collection, updating, public dissemination and so on.

The passive aspect is addressed in Article 4, which contains the main essential elements of a system for securing the public's right to obtain information on request from public authorities:

Presumption in favour of access: Any environmental information held by a public authority must be provided when requested by a member of the public, unless it can be shown to fall within a finite list of exempt categories.

'Any person' right: the right of access extends to any person, without the obligation to prove or even state an interest.

Broad definition of 'environmental information': the scope of information covered is quite broad, encompassing a non-exhaustive list of elements of the environment (air, water, soil etc.); factors, activities or measures affecting those

---

[6] *Ibid.*

elements; and human health and safety, conditions of life, cultural sites and built structures, to the extent that these are or may be affected by the aforementioned elements, factors, activities or measures.

Time limits: The information must be provided as soon as possible, and at the latest within one month after submission of the request. However, this period may be extended by a further month when justified by the volume and complexity of the information. The requester must be notified of any such extension and the reasons for it.

Form of information: The definition of environmental information covers information in any material form (written, visual, aural, electronic etc). There is a qualified requirement on public authorities to provide it in the form specified by the requester.

Charges: Public authorities may impose a charge for supplying information provided the charge does not exceed a 'reasonable' amount.

Exemptions: Public authorities may withhold information where disclosure would adversely affect various interests, e.g. national defence, international relations, public security, the course of justice, commercial confidentiality, intellectual property rights, personal privacy, the confidentiality of the proceedings of public authorities; or where the information requested has been supplied voluntarily or consists of internal communications or material in the course of completion. There are however some restrictions on these exemptions, e.g. the commercial confidentiality exemption may not be invoked to withhold information on emissions which is relevant to the protection of the environment.

Public interest test: To prevent abuse of the exemptions by overly-secretive public authorities, the Convention stipulates that most of the aforementioned exemptions are to be interpreted in a restrictive way, and in all cases may only be applied when the public interest served by disclosure has been taken into account.

Refusals: Refusals, and the reasons for them, are to be issued in writing where requested. A similar time limit applies as that which applies with respect to the supply of information: one month from the date of the request, with provisions for extending this by a further month when justified by the complexity of the information.

Onward referral of requests: Where a public authority does not hold the information requested, it should either direct the requester to another public authority which it believes may have the information, or transfer the request directly to that public authority and notify the requester.

The Convention also imposes active information duties on Parties. These include quite general obligations on public authorities to be in possession of up-to-date environmental information that is relevant to their functions, and to make information 'effectively accessible' to the public by providing information on the type and scope of information held and the process by which it can be obtained. It also contains several more specific provisions:

Internet access: Parties are required to 'progressively' make environmental information publicly available in electronic databases that can easily be accessed through public telecommunications networks. The Convention specifies certain categories of information (e.g. state of the environment reports, texts of legislation related to the environment) that should be made available in this form. In view of the advantages to both suppliers and those who request information to be made available in this form (e.g. reduced costs, less administrative burden, immediacy of access, possibility of linkages with related databases) and the rapid pace of technological growth, this could be an area where further elaboration of the current provision could usefully take place, either in the Convention or in its transposition at the national level.

State-of-the-environment reporting: Parties are required to produce national reports on the state of the environment at regular intervals not exceeding four years. Further elaboration under this provision could potentially lead to improved harmonisation of reporting methods across the region, thereby helping to support the EEA's reporting on the state of the pan-European environment.

Pollutant release and transfer registers (PRTRs): PRTRs have proven to be a highly effective and relatively low cost means of gathering environmental information from the private sector and putting it into the public domain, thereby exerting a downward pressure on levels of pollution. However, very few countries in the region have established PRTRs. The Convention requires Parties to take steps to progressively establish such registers. It also requires the issue to be on the agenda of the first meeting of the Parties, where further steps are to be considered, including the elaboration of an appropriate instrument, which could be annexed to the Convention (see below).

Emergency situations: Public authorities are required to immediately provide the public with all information in their possession that could enable the public to take measures to prevent or mitigate harm arising from an imminent threat to human health or the environment.

Public Participation

The Convention sets out minimum requirements for public participation in various categories of environmental decision-making.

Specific projects or activities: Article 6 of the Convention establishes certain public participation requirements for decision-making on whether to license or permit certain types of activity listed in Annex I to the Convention. This list is similar to the list of activities for which an environmental impact assessment or integrated pollution prevention and control licence is required under the relevant EU legislation. The requirements also apply, albeit in a slightly more ambivalent form, to decision-making on other activities that may have a significant effect on the environment. Activities serving national defence purposes may be exempted. Somewhat controversially, decision-making on genetically modified organisms (GMOs) was not included on the Annex I list. However, Parties are required to apply the provisions of the article to decision-making on the deliberate release of GMOs to the environment 'to the extent feasible and appropriate'. Furthermore, the issue of GMOs is given emphasis in both the preamble and the accompanying Resolution.

The public participation requirements include timely and effective notification of the public concerned; reasonable timeframes for participation, including provisions for participation at an early stage; a right for the public concerned to inspect information which is relevant to decision-making free of charge; an obligation on the decision-making body to take due account of the outcome of the public participation; and prompt public notification of the decision, with the text of the decision and the reasons and considerations on which it is based being made publicly accessible. The 'public concerned' is defined as "the public affected or likely to be affected by, or having an interest in, the environmental decision-making," and explicitly includes NGOs promoting environmental protection and meeting any requirements under national law.[7]

Programmes, plans and policies: Article 7 requires Parties to make "appropriate practical and/or other provisions for the public to participate during the preparation of plans and programmes relating to the environment." It can be argued that the term 'relating to the environment' is quite broad, covering not just plans or programmes prepared by an environment ministry, but also sectoral plans (transport, energy, tourism, etc.) where these have significant environmental implications. The Convention is less prescriptive with respect to public participation in decision-making on plans or programmes than in the case of projects or activities. However, the provisions of Article 6 relating to reasonable timeframes for participation, opportunities for early participation (while options are still open) and obligations to ensure that "due account" is taken of the outcome of the participation are to be applied in respect of such plans and programmes. Article 7 also applies, in more recommendatory form, to decision-making on policies relating to the environment.

---

[7] *Aarhus Convention, supra* note 2, at Art. 2(5).

General rules and regulations: Article 8 applies to public participation during the preparation by public authorities of executive regulations and other generally applicable legally binding rules that may have a significant effect on the environment. Although the Convention does not apply to bodies acting in a legislative capacity, this article would clearly apply to the executive stage of preparing rules and regulations even if they are later to be adopted by parliament.

Access to Justice

The third pillar of the Convention (Article 9) aims to provide access to justice in three contexts: review procedures with respect to information requests; review procedures with respect to specific (project-type) decisions which are subject to public participation requirements; and challenges to breaches of environmental law in general. Thus the inclusion of an 'access to justice' pillar not only underpins the first two pillars; it also points the way to empowering citizens and NGOs to assist in the enforcement of the law.

Access to information appeals: A person whose request for information has not been dealt with to his satisfaction must be provided with access to a review procedure before a court of law or another independent and impartial body established by law (the latter option being included to accommodate those countries which have a well-functioning office of the Ombudsperson). The Convention attempts to ensure a low threshold for such appeals by requiring that where review before a court of law is provided for (which can involve high costs), there is also access to an expeditious review procedure that is free of charge or inexpensive. Final decisions must be binding on the public authority holding the information, and the reasons must be stated in writing where information is refused.

Public participation appeals: The Convention provides for a right to seek a review in connection with decision-making on projects or activities covered by Article 6. The review may address either the substantive or the procedural legality of a decision, or both. The scope of persons entitled to pursue such an appeal is similar to, but slightly narrower than, the 'public concerned.' There exists a requirement to have a 'sufficient interest' or maintain impairment of a right (though the text also states that these requirements are to be interpreted in a manner which is consistent with 'the objective of giving the public concerned wide access to justice').

General violations of environmental law: The Convention requires Parties to provide access to administrative or judicial procedures to challenge acts and omissions by private persons and public authorities which breach laws relating to the environment. Such access is to be provided to members of the public "where they meet the criteria, if any, laid down in ... national law." In other words, the issue of standing is primarily to be determined at national level, as is the question of whether the procedures are judicial or administrative.

Other access to justice requirements: The procedures in each of the three contexts referred to above are required to be "fair, equitable, timely and not prohibitively expensive." Decisions must be given or recorded in writing, and in the case of court decisions, made publicly accessible. Assistance mechanisms to remove or reduce financial and other barriers impeding access to justice are to be considered.

Implementation and Further Development of the Convention

Although the adoption and entry into force of the Aarhus Convention were big achievements, in the long term its implementation will undoubtedly be an even greater challenge. Amending national laws to bring them into compliance with the provisions of the Convention will be a major task. Ensuring that these laws are then applied effectively will be a further challenge.

Holding these challenges in mind, many activities were undertaken following the adoption of the Convention, both to promote its effective implementation and to pave the way for its further development.

The first meeting of the signatories to the Convention took place in Chisinau, Republic of Moldova, in April 1999. The meeting adopted a work plan aimed at preparing for the first meeting of the Parties and supporting countries in their efforts to implement the Convention. Under the work plan, three task forces were established, dealing respectively with PRTRs, GMOs and the issue of a compliance mechanism for the Convention.

A second meeting of the signatories took place in Cavtat-Dubrovnik, Croatia, from July 3 to July 5, 2000, at which the activities of the three task forces were reviewed. It was proposed that an intergovernmental working group replace the PRTR task force. The recommendation consisted of charging such a body with the task of preparing a legally binding instrument on PRTRs under the auspices of the Convention, with a view to its being ready for adoption at the 5th Ministerial Conference 'Environment for Europe' (Kiev, 2003). This proposal was accepted by the Committee on Environmental Policy (CEP) during its seventh session (September 2000), and negotiations on the new instrument started early in 2001, with active participation of both industry and environmental NGOs. During its eighth session (September 2001), the CEP further decided that the instrument should take the form of a protocol to the Convention, which would also be open to accession by non-Parties and non-ECE States.

Working groups were also established on GMOs and on compliance and rules of procedure, replacing the corresponding task forces. The former is addressing the task of further developing the application of the Convention in the field of GMOs, following the prompting in the Ministerial resolution. The working group on compliance and rules of procedure is preparing draft decisions on these topics, both potentially involving innovations reflecting the spirit of the Aarhus Convention.

Two further task forces dealing with access to justice and electronic information tools were established at the second meeting of the signatories.

Other activities were undertaken to support the implementation process. An implementation guide on the Convention was prepared as a joint project amongst UN/ECE, the Regional Environmental Center for Central and Eastern Europe and the Danish Environmental Protection Agency.[8] Published in English and Russian, the guide is primarily aimed at policymakers and politicians with responsibility for transposing the Convention into their national legal systems. It seeks to promote a deeper understanding of the legal meaning of the Convention's provisions. Other information-based materials such as a bulletin have been developed. The Convention's website has been upgraded and is regularly updated with the texts of all official documents as soon as they become available.[9]

Efforts have been made to identify common problems and challenges in the implementation process and to support efforts to find practical solutions, especially in countries with economies in transition. To this end, several workshops on the Convention for both government officials and NGOs have been held: one hosted by the United Kingdom focussing on public participation at the local level (Newcastle, December 1999); two focussing on the needs of the five Central Asian countries (Turkmenistan, May 2000 and Tajikistan, June 2002); and two on those of the South Caucasus region (Georgia, December 2000 and Armenia, November 2001).

The first meeting of the Parties, which as mentioned took place in October 2002 and was held at ministerial level, made a number of fairly crucial decisions. These have set the path for the coming years by laying down the institutional architecture of the Convention as well as taking steps forward on various substantive issues:
The rules of procedure, reflecting practices developed in the negotiation of the Convention and leading up to its entry into force, include innovative provisions regarding the participation of NGOs in the Convention bodies. These include

---

[8] Stephen Stec & Susan Casey-Lefkowitz, *The Aarhus Convention: An Implementation Guide*, UN Doc. ECE/CEP/72 (2000), available online: United Nations Economic Council for Europe <http://www.unece.org/env/pp/acig.pdf>
[9] See <http://www.unece.org/env/pp/>.

an NGO presence in the Bureau of the Meeting of the Parties (in an observer capacity) and certain requirements for transparency in the processes under the Convention.

The compliance mechanism provides for consideration of communications from the public, including NGOs, about non-compliance. The compliance committee consists of eight independent experts.

The Meeting confirmed the CEP's decision to prepare a PRTR Protocol and assumed responsibility for its preparation.

Guidelines on applying the Aarhus principles in the specific field of GMOs were adopted and the Working Group on GMOs was given a mandate to continue its work, focussing on legally binding options such as an amendment to the Convention.

The Meeting gave its support to the establishment of a clearinghouse mechanism and a capacity-building service by UNECE in collaboration with UNEP. The clearinghouse was subsequently established and now serves as one of the principal repositories of information related to the themes of participatory democracy.[10]

The Meeting adopted an interim voluntary scheme of financial arrangements and agreed to discuss longer-term financial arrangements at a future meeting.

The meeting was held at the ministerial level and featured a high-level panel discussion focussed on the effective implementation of the Convention in addition to issues concerning human rights, poverty, the environment, and the outcome of the World Summit on Sustainable Development (WSSD).

The negotiations over the Protocol on PRTR came to a successful conclusion in spring 2003 and the the Protocol was adopted in Kiev, Ukraine, in May 2003 at an extraordinary meeting of the Parties held within the framework of the Fifth Ministerial 'Environment for Europe' Conference. It was signed by 36 States and the European Community.

Relevance of the Convention in a Global Context

In conclusion, the Aarhus Convention is widely accepted as the leading example of implementation of principle 10 of the 1992 *Rio Declaration on Environment and Development*. Although it is a regional instrument, its global significance is widely recognized. The United Nations Secretary-General Kofi Annan has described it as, "the most ambitious venture in environmental democracy undertaken under the auspices of the United Nations [whose] adoption was a remarkable step forward in the development of international law". Mary Robinson, former UN High Commissioner for Human Rights, has stated that the Convention is "a remarkable achievement not only in terms of

---

[10] Available online at <http://www.unece.aarhusclearinghouse.org>.

protection of the environment, but also in terms of the promotion and protection of human rights…"[11]

The global relevance of the Convention is further enhanced by the fact that it is open for accession not only by ECE Member States but also by other states members of the United Nations.

Thus the Convention may be of interest to states outside the ECE region in a number of ways: as an instrument to which such states might eventually accede, as an inspiration for developing a similar instrument in other regions, or as a model for development of national legislative frameworks. It could also serve as a valuable reference point if a decision was made, either at WSSD or subsequently, to develop a global instrument, either binding or non-binding, on procedural environmental rights.

---

[11] United Nations Economic Council for Europe, *What People Are Saying About the Aarhus Convention*, (October 2001) at 4, online: United Nations Economic Council for Europe <http://www.unece.org/env/pp/documents/compendium.pdf> .

26

PUBLIC PARTICIPATION IN AMERICAS TRADE AND ENVIRONMENT REGIMES

Marie-Claire Cordonier Segger[1] & Jorge Cabrera[2]

Public participation, supported by transparent and participatory processes, often leads to better decision-making. As reflected in the 1998 *Aarhus Convention*, openness depends on public participation supported by rights of access to information and access to justice.[3] Instruments often need to be established to facilitate the participation of diverse public and civil society voices – to move beyond passive consultations to actual engagement. Access to information depends on transparency and the active dissemination of knowledge and analysis, rather than simply data. Access to justice, often the most difficult of these three 'elements of openness', refers in part the ability of civil society to participate in dispute settlement processes, for example through a right to submit *amicus curiae* briefs, or even the medium of citizen appeals.

---

[1] Marie-Claire Cordonier Segger, MEM (Yale), BCL & LLB (McGill), BA Hons (Carl.), Director, Centre for International Sustainable Development Law (CISDL), Chair, CISDL/ILA/IDLO Partnership on International Law on Sustainable Development, Senior Manager, Americas Research Portfolio, International Institute for Sustainable Development &United Nations Environment Programme ROLAC, British Chevening Scholar & SSHRC Fellow, Exeter College, Oxford University Faculty of Law, Lecturer, International Development Law Organisation (IDLO) & Member, International Law Association (ILA) Committee on International Law on Sustainable Development. This chapter is based on research for a chapter in M.C. Cordonier Segger and M. Leichner Reynal, *Beyond the Barricades: The Americas Trade and Sustainability Agenda* (Aldershot: Ashgate, 2005), and is reproduced here with permission of the authors.
[2] Jorge Cabrera Medaglia, B.C.L & LL.M (University of Costa Rica), Lead Counsel for International Sustainable Biodiversity Law, Centre for International Sustainable Development Law (CISDL), Professor, University of Costa Rica Faculty of Law & UNED University, Tutor, WIPO Intellectual Property Law, Legal Advisor, National Biodiversity Institute (INBio) of Costa Rica, former Co-chair, UN Convention on Biological Diversity Expert Panel on ABS & Chair, CBD Sub-Working Group on IPRs. The authors would like to thank Michelle Toering, Markus Gehring, CISDL Lead Counsel for Trade, Investment and Competition, and Maria Leichner, CISDL Lead Counsel for Cross Cutting Issues, for their comments on the draft. All errors and omissions are theirs.
[3] The 1998 Aarhus Convention is one of the first binding international instruments to recognize "the right of every person of present and future generations to live in an environment adequate to his or health and well-being." United Nations Economic Commission for Europe, *Convention on Access to Information, Public Participation in Decision-making and Access to Justice in Environmental Matters*, 38 I.L.M. 517 (1998) online: UNECE <http://www.unece.org/env/pp> [*Aarhus Convention*], which has developed the principle of public participation significantly. See the chapter in this volume by Jeremy Wates. See also important case law of the European Courts, such as *Plaumann* v. *Commission* C-25/62 [1963] E.C.R. 95 at 107. See also *Spijker* v. *Commission* C-231/82 [1983] E.C.R. 2559; *Deutsche Lebensmittelwerke* v. *Commission* C-97/85 [1987] E.C.R. 2265; *Cook* v. *Commission* C-198/91 [1993] E.C.R. I-2487; *Matra* v. *Commission* C-225/92 [1993] E.C.R. I-3203; *Air France* v. *Commission* T-2/93 [1994] E.C.R. II-323; *Consorzio Gruppo di Azione Locale "Murgia Messapica"* v. *Commission* T-465/93 [1994] E.C.R. II-361.

M.C. Cordonier Segger & C. G. Weeramantry, eds., Sustainable Justice: Reconciling Economic, Social & Environmental Law
© *2005 Koninklijke Brill NV, Printed in The Netherlands, pp.407-426.*

When international processes are based on more diverse exchanges of expertise, knowledge and information, they can result in higher quality decisions, more effective domestic implementation of the law, and broader support for the measures in question. On the international level, trade and environment debates are beginning to integrate the need to facilitate greater participation by civil society and public interests. The Americas trade and sustainable development debates, as they are currently evolving, offer a good case study.[4] This chapter will address part of the sustainable development debates in the Americas, through a comparative analysis of public participation mechanisms in environmental and trade regimes.

Good governance, including through processes of democratization, empowerment and capacity-building, at all levels, are a precondition of openness in the Americas. Of course, pressures to provide information and participation mechanisms for civil society are not new or revolutionary across the Americas. Indeed, inter-American events were among the first efforts of some governments to officially include certain sectors of civil society, such as private enterprise, in multilateral conferences.[5]

However international trade debates have traditionally been kept completely closed. Governments often had to make commitments that went against the interests of a particular industry which favoured protectionist policies. Fears existed in the trade community that such protectionist special interests would gain too great a voice in processes that were expected to remain isolated and free from political pressure.

While these concerns must be recognised, a distinction can also be made between public interest organizations and civil society in general, versus private vested interests or protectionist groups. The cooperation of the former group is essential for a trade agreement to succeed in a democratic and participatory society. In this regard, the decision of Americas trade ministers in Miami to release the third draft text of the Free Trade Area of the Americas (FTAA) offers potential for greatly increased transparency and better-informed decision-making in hemispheric trade negotiations.[6]

---

[4] *International Institute for Sustainable Development, Winnipeg Principles on Trade and Sustainable Development* (Winnipeg: IISD, 1994) at 29. See also M. C. Cordonier Segger et al., *Trade Rules and Sustainability in the Americas* (Winnipeg: IISD / UNEP, 2000); M. C. Cordonier Segger et al., *Ecological Rules and Sustainability in the Americas* (Winnipeg: IISD / UNEP, 2002); and M.C. Cordonier Segger et al., *Social Rules and Sustainability in the Americas* (Winnipeg: IISD / OAS, 2004).
[5] See, e.g., S. Charnovitz, "Two Centuries of Participation: NGOs and International Conferences" (Winter 1997) 2:18 *Mich. J. Int'l L.* at 183.
[6] See *FTAA Third Draft Agreement*, FTAA Doc.TNC/w/133/Rev.2 (2003) online: <http://www.ftaa-alca.org/ftaadraft03/draft_e.asp>

Openness in Americas Trade Regimes

All countries of the Americas are members of the World Trade Organisation (WTO), and it is still seen to 'set the trend' in many areas of trade law and policy-making. This institution has changed in recent years, and is demonstrating a slow, cautious but steady movement toward higher levels of consultation with civil society and international NGOs. This movement is demonstrated by WTO Secretariat initiative to organize an annual symposium for non-governmental organizations and member states, the coordination of a calendar of parallel events to the WTO Ministerial meetings, greater emphasis on communication with the public and others through improvement of the WTO Web site. The WTO policy on their release of documents is one example of this new attitude. This policy has changed from a blanket prohibition against dissemination unless unanimously requested, to a presumption that a document will automatically be released unless a WTO member actually requests that it remain confidential. There have also been sincere efforts on the part of certain WTO member states to secure increasing transparency in national trade policy making processes through mechanisms such as the establishment of impact assessments, public consultations, advisory boards, or invitations for NGO advisors to serve on their national delegations to WTO meetings.

There have also been changes in the WTO dispute settlement procedures. Two small procedural steps towards co-operation with other regimes have generated initial hope for future openness. First, it is now recognized that in cases where scientific assessment is problematic or uncertain, including the vast majority of cases where environmental quality or public health measures are at stake, international trade lawyers may not be best placed to resolve the issues alone.[7] In the *EC – Asbestos case*, the WTO panel established an eleven-step procedure to consult with individual scientific experts.[8] This new consultation process was built step by step, and is not controversial. The Appellate Body has stated that "as long as [they] act consistently with the provisions of the DSU and the covered agreements, [they] have the authority to decide whether or not to accept and consider any information that [they] believe is pertinent and useful in an appeal."[9] Second, the WTO dispute settlement mechanism is under

---

[7] See e.g. D. Wirth, "The Role of Science in the Uruguay Round and NAFTA Trade Disciplines" (1994) 27 Cornell Int'l L.J. 818 (reprinted as monograph no. 8 in United Nations Environment Program's Environment and Trade series.)

[8] International organizations and institutions such as the World Health Organization (WHO), the International Labour Organization (ILO), the International Programme on Chemical Safety (IPCS), the International Agency for Research on Cancer (IARC) and the International Organization for Standardization (ISO) helped the WTO panel and the parties to the dispute in identifying the experts. See *European Communities – Measures Affecting Asbestos and Asbestos-Containing Products (brought by Canada)*, (2001) WTO Doc. WT/DS135/AB/R (Appellate Body Report) at paras. 5.1, 5.19. [*EC-Asbestos*], online: WTO < http://docsonline.wto.org/DDFDocuments/t/WT/DS/135ABR.doc>. The EC requested the Panel to consult a technical expert group but the Panel decided that individual experts were more appropriate.

[9] *United States – Import Prohibition of Certain Shrimp and Shrimp Products (Complaint by India, Malaysia, Pakistan, Thailand)*, (1998) WTO Doc. WT/DS58/AB/R (Appellate Body Report) at para 106-7.

increasing pressure to go much further, and agree to accept *amicus curiae*, or 'friend of the court' briefs from NGOs and others concerned with cases.[10] The most telling example of movement along this fault line occurred in the *EC – Asbestos* case, where the Appellate Body took it upon itself to issue an Additional Working Procedure accepting *amicus curiae* briefs[11] whereby "any person, whether natural or legal, other than a party or a third party to this dispute, wishing to file a written brief with the Appellate Body" was invited to apply to do so upon a specific deadline "in the interest of fairness and orderly procedure in the conduct" of the appeal.[12] This decision to establish the 'Additional Procedure' (AP) came in part because the Appellate Body had already received 13 spontaneous submissions, many from developing country industry associations, and expected to receive more in a case closely watched by public interest groups. Up to this point, unless the independent *amicus* briefs were included in the submissions of a party or a third party, they were not taken into account by the WTO dispute settlement mechanism.[13] While the Appellate Body had the authority to accept and consider *amicus* briefs where it was 'pertinent and useful' to do so,[14] non-state actors had not been offered a formal procedure to be taken into account. Written submissions from NGOs in countries as diverse as Swaziland, Sri Lanka, Korea, El Salvador, Senegal, Japan, and Colombia were received before the AP was established.[15] Unfortunately, as noted in *ICTSD Bridges*,[16] a restrictive procedure and tight deadlines limited the effectiveness of this procedural step forward. In addition, the reaction of other WTO members in spite of the prior written consent of the parties to the dispute blunted the attempt in this instance, and no *amicus* briefs were actually

---

See *United States – Imposition of Countervailing Duties on Certain Hot-Rolled Lead and Bismuth Carbon Steel Products Originating in the United Kingdom, (Complaint by UK)* (2000) WTO Doc. WT/DS138/AB/R (Appellate Body Report) at para 39.

[10] See D. Esty, "The World Trade Organisation's Legitimacy Crisis" (2002) 1 *World Trade Review* 1 at 7 – 22.

[11] *European Communities-Measures Affecting Asbestos and Asbestos- Containing Products* (2000) WTO Doc. WT/DS135/9 (Communication from the Appellate Body). See "M.C. Cordonier Segger & M. Gehring, 'Precaution, Health and the World Trade Organisation: Moving toward Sustainable Development" (2003) 29 *Queen's L. J.* 133. See also G. Marceau and P. Pedersen, "Is the WTO Open and Transparent? A Discussion of the Relationship of the WTO with Non-governmental Organisations and Civil Society's Claims for more Transparency and Public Participation" 33(1) J. World Trade 5; D. Esty, "Non-Governmental Organisations at the World Trade Organisation: Cooperation, Competition, or Exclusion" (1998) 1:1 J. Int'l Econ. L. 123.

[12] WT/DS 135/9. See *European Communities – Measures Affecting Asbestos and Asbestos-Containing Products* WT/DS135/AB/R 12 March, 2001 at paras. 54 - 57.

[13] It should be noted that, relying in part on conclusions of the Appellate Body, a North American Free Trade Agreement tribunal has recognized that there is legitimate public interest arising out of certain subject matter. The tribunal also found that its dispute settlement mechanism "could benefit from being perceived as more open or transparent; or conversely be harmed if seen as unduly secretive." See In the Matter of an Arbitration under Chapter 11 of the North American Free Trade Agreement and the UNCITRAL Arbitration Rules, *Methanex Corporation* v. *United States of America* (15 January 2001), Decision of the Tribunal on Petitions from Third Persons to Intervene as 'Amicus Curiae' at para 49 *[Methanex]*.

[14] *United States – Imposition of Countervailing Duties on Certain Hot-Rolled Lead and Bismuth Carbon Steel Products Originating in the United Kingdom*, Report of the Appellate Body adopted 7 June AB-2000-11, 8 November 2000, WT/DS138/AB/R at para 39.

[15] *EC-Asbestos, supra* note 12 at para. 53.

[16] ICTSD, "*Amicus* Brief Storm Highlights WTO's Unease with External Transparency" *Bridges Monthly Review* (Nov.-Dec. 2000) 4:9 Geneva.

given leave to be presented as a result of the AP. As such, while these measures are only a start, they can send encouraging signals at the global level.

On a sub-regional level in the Americas, non-governmental participation in trade agreements and dispute settlement is increasing. For example, in the late 1980s, the Grupo Andino has developed a method to include the private sector in its deliberations. Decision 285 of the Commission of the Cartagena Agreement allows companies, through member countries, to request that an Andean group board apply measures to either prevent or correct damage to production or exports caused by business practices that restrict free competition within the sub-region.[17] Private citizens also have access to appeal with the Andean Court of Justice, as do others.

In the NAFTA context, there is very little openness in the Trade Negotiations Commission *per se*. However, recent petitions to a tribunal established under the NAFTA Chapter 11 on an investment dispute, by the Canadian International Institute for Sustainable Development and others in the *Methanex case*, have led to openness towards the presentation of *amicus curia* briefs.[18]

In South America, the Mercosur, with political and social integration structures, provides access through an economic and social advisory council that receives information from labour, business and consumer representatives. Experts from civil society attend relevant meetings of the technical subcommittees, and present their recommendations.[19]

On a hemispheric level, considerable will exists on paper for the implementation of this principle, and mechanisms are being set in place. The Committee of Government Representatives for the Participation of Civil Society, a committee of the FTAA negotiations, permits a certain limited submissions process. However, civil society groups have requested that for better functioning, environmental and social concerns must become a specific agenda item for the committee, verifiable links must be established to the work of other FTAA negotiating committees, and all reports must be made publicly

---

[17] Commission of the Cartagena Agreement, 1991, in the World Investment Report 1997, "Transnational Corporations, Market Structure and Competition Policy" (New York and Geneva: UNCTAD, UN), at 222. See also E. Murphy, "The Andean Decisions on Foreign Investment: An International Matrix of National Law" (1990) 24, No. 3 Int'l Law, 643.

[18] A North American Free Trade Agreement arbitral tribunal has recognized that there is legitimate public interest arising out of certain subject matters. The tribunal also found that its dispute settlement mechanism could benefit from being perceived as more open or transparent; or conversely be harmed if seen as unduly secretive. See *Methanex, supra* note 13.

[19] See F. Pena, La experiencia del Mercosur, in *Participacion de la sociedad civil en los procesos de integracion : Seminario* (Montevideo : ALOP / CEFIR / CLAEH, 1998). See also Jorge Grandi and Lincoln Bizzozero, Hacia una sociedad civil del Mercosur: viejos y nuevos actors en el tejido subregional, in *Participacion de la sociedad civil en los procesos de integracion: Seminario* (Montevideo : ALOP / CEFIR / CLAEH, 1998). And see Hector Maletta, "Pobreza, Empleo e Integracion regional en el Marco macroeconomico Latinoamericano," CEFIR, Santiago de Chile, Abril de 1995, in "Aspectos de la Situación Social en los Países del MERCOSUR: Una Visión Crítica," (Documento para la Discusión) in La Situación Social en los Países del MERCOSUR (Montevideo: CEFIR, 1998).

available. The program could also include: proactive public efforts to involve public dialogue or consultation, comprehensive information disclosure and communication policies, intervener funding mechanisms for underrepresented groups, and measurable operational procedures indicating how civil-society concerns will be addressed in the context of negotiations.[20]

As such, with regard to the recent evolution of trade regimes in the Americas, three general observations can be made. First, openness is possible. Trade regimes can include provisions to encourage and support openness. Second, openness is difficult, and processes to ensure openness are still on the very cutting edge of international trade negotiations. On a continuum, measures can ranges from easier to more difficult. Provisions to ensure transparency are more straightforward in most cases, facilitated by policies to make documents available on websites, or release documents on demand. Mechanisms to ensure greater degrees of direct and indirect public participation are harder to arrange.

Considerable attention must be given to the differences between resources of one set of groups (say, northern NGOs) and another (for example, southern indigenous peoples), as well as appropriate processes to facilitate actual consultation and engagement. Finally, while provisions to ensure access to justice in trade agreements may be the most difficult to secure, they are necessary. Opening these processes requires pressure, political will and constant scrutiny, as well as keeping openness a priority when the trade-offs are needed in the endgame of a trade negotiation. Such efforts are very important. Arguably, they are necessary for a trade treaty to gain enough public acceptance to be enacted into law in most democracies today.

Openness in Americas Environmental Regimes

Environmental regimes have proved policy innovators in terms of openness, with regards to measures to secure public participation, access to information and access to justice. In particular, certain multilateral environmental accords (MEAs) have been ratified by almost all countries in the Americas, and provide interesting illustrations.

The *Basel Convention*, ratified by 21 countries in the Americas, is designed to address the problem of transboundary movement of hazardous wastes. This can directly affect communities, and as such, instruments for openness exist in the accord.[21] The 2001 *Protocol on Liability and Compensation to the Basel Convention*

---

[20] J. Audley, NWF's Communication to the Committee of Government Representatives (CGR) for the Participation of Civil Society "Open Invitation to Civil Society in FTAA Participating Countries - October 1998 (Washington, March 31, 1999).
[21] In Article 15, the Convention grants direct access with observer status to negotiating sessions and Conferences of the Parties (COP), for any national or international organization, governmental or non-governmental, with competence in the field of hazardous wastes. Article 16 also grants groups the right to

also provides examples of innovative mechanisms for openness in an environmental accord.[22] The United National Economic Commission for Latin America and the Caribbean (CEPAL) has initiated a regional process of consultations for a sub-regional accord on the transportation and disposal of hazardous wastes in Latin America and the Caribbean. The *Basel Convention* would strictly delineate the proposed regime. By establishing a regional network of centres for capacity building and technology transfer on these issues, the proposal has the potential to address one of the most serious bars to openness.

With the notable exception of the United States, most countries of the Americas have ratified the 1992 *United Nations Convention on Biological Diversity* (UN CBD). The UN CBD exists for the conservation and sustainable use of biological diversity and the fair and equitable sharing in the benefits that derive from the access to genetic resources (Article 1). It provides for the transfer of appropriate technology, access to genetic resources (in accordance with other rights) and appropriate levels of financing. The UN CBD mechanisms to facilitate public access to information are not uniquely treaty-driven, but the accord offers several examples of specific mechanisms to provide for public participation and exchange of information with the general public.[23]

In addition, in the case of the negotiations of the Working Group on Article 8 J and Related Provisions (on indigenous knowledge), different resolutions of the Conference of the Parties have called to incorporate indigenous peoples representatives in the governmental delegations. Several governments have already accomplished this step.

---

provide information to the secretariat to be transmitted to the Members. These measures are only partially successful, as lack of intervener funding means that civil society representation is generally dominated by business lobby groups, their detractors from large international NGOs and NGOs from OECD countries. In the Convention itself, access to justice, which is the third aspect, is left mainly to mechanisms provided by national authorities.

[22] The objective of promoting internal transparency is recognized in various provisions (Art. 3.6b, Art. 10.2), in particular through the obligation to inform the Secretariat of implementation measures. By publishing any non-restricted reports, the Secretariat also informs citizens. But the most interesting aspect of the Protocol is found in its provisions for access to justice. The Protocol establishes that exporting states will hold civil responsibility for damages caused by the transport or disposal of hazardous wastes. Under certain conditions, it even grants redress by holding individuals liable for damages. There is the possibility for private citizens and legal entities to seek reparation, within a ten-year prescription period, with tribunals empowered to adjudicate cases.

[23] While Article 17 mandates that the parties will facilitate the exchange of information, it does not clearly state whether this exchange is restricted to government agencies, or if it also includes the general public. There is an accountability system, outlined in Article 26, which requires periodic reports from parties to the COP, but no direct duty to ensure general public access to these reports. Article 23.5 opens space for non-governmental organizations to participate in the CBD. In addition, the secretariat plays a key role by reaching out to public and civil society actors. It ensures that in practice, the regime remains open and informative. Indeed, it has impulsed and supported the establishment of hemispheric biodiversity scientific networks and clearinghouses. In an innovation at Article 10, mechanisms of public participation are also opened to industry sectors and indigenous peoples groups, recognizing the need for close collaboration in decision making-processes. The importance of industry participation is also highlighted in Article 16, which refers to the transfer of new technologies for biodiversity conservation. Indigenous peoples involvement is seen as crucial in the implementation of *in situ* conservation mechanisms and benefit sharing, and this is noted in Article 8.

Though almost untested to date, the *2001 Cartagena Protocol on Biosafety* to the CBD provides for a new mechanism of information dissemination, directed through a Biotechnology Information Clearinghouse.[24] Should it be implemented effectively, the *Cartagena Protocol* can provide a mechanism to defuse serious public concerns through information and participation. However it does not provide such clear measures for international liability or access to justice.

Most countries in the Americas have ratified the United Nations Framework Convention on Climate Change (UN FCCC), though its *Kyoto Protocol* is still seeking further support. The UN FCCC has a series of provisions to facilitate access to information, and several public participation mechanisms.[25] The *Kyoto Protocol* does not build upon openness in the UN FCCC in the same way that other conventions have, in part because the majority of the provisions of the UN FCCC apply to activities under the *Kyoto Protocol* as well. However, the private sector, non-governmental organizations and the scientific community participated in the negotiations. In situations where many governments find themselves paralysed, inter-governmental agencies such as the World Bank, as well as regional institutions such as the EU, along with these civil society and private sectors partners, have proven their commitment by advancing the goals of the accord.

Existing inter-governmental structures could also serve as a tool for openness, providing institutional inter-American support to implement otherwise forgotten commitments. This depends mainly upon mandates from their governments. The *1996 Santa Cruz Summit Declaration* affirmed the need for full integration of civil society into the design and implementation of sustainable development policies and programs at the hemispheric and national levels.[26] Coordinated by the Environment and Sustainable Development Unit of the OAS, the Inter-American Strategy for Public Participation (ISP) was designed as an open and transparent process to implement this mandate.[27] The primary goal of the ISP is to "promote transparent, effective, and responsible public

---

[24] This system uses Internet technologies to achieve many of its goals cost-effectively. Article 23 also establishes a duty to promote public participation through education and awareness raising in the national context.

[25] At the international level, the right to access information is exercised through the obligation of the parties to present reports made public by the Conference of the Parties and the Secretary. In practice, debates can still be limited to state parties and certain international organizations with the resources to follow debates. At the national level, the FCCC also provides access to information to individuals regarding climate change and its effects, though this is more limited. Finally, in terms of access to justice in case of environmental disputes, individuals or non-governmental organizations, or even state parties, have not gained a mechanism which permits claims. As such, the FCCC addresses the principle of openness, but in a limited manner.

[26] OAS, Summit Conference on Sustainable Development, *Declaration of Santa Cruz De La Sierra and Plan of Action for the Sustainable Development of the Americas*, (1996) online: OAS <http://www.oas.org/EN/PROG/BOLIVIA/sumiteng.htm> The Declaration proclaims that the signatories "will support and encourage, as a basic requirement for sustainable development, broad participation by civil society in the decision-making process, including policies and programs, and their design, implementation and evaluation."

[27] Available online: www.oas.org/usde/isp.htm.

participation in decision-making and in the formulation, adoption and implementation of policies for sustainable development in Latin America and the Caribbean." Several aspects provide models for future hemispheric openness instruments. First, ISP has sought internal transparency by actively soliciting input from ISP project members and stakeholders.[28] Second, the strategy is pitched to address the various relevant levels. While most obligations fall at the national level,[29] at the regional level consultation processes, such as regular fora for dialogue between government and civil society, are also provided at high-level meetings convened by the OAS. Third, ISP uses case studies and concrete examples to be more accessible. It has established public participation demonstration sites in the Portland Bight, Jamaica; the Gulf of Honduras; (trans-boundary: Honduras, Belize and Guatemala); and the Bay of Ferrol in Chimbote, Peru. Fourth, ISP takes legal frameworks into account through a legal inventory and case studies. The inventory provides the first empirical assessment of participation provisions in environmental law in the Americas, while case studies offer a more complete picture of how these laws function (or fail to function) in practice. Fifth, to share data, an information network is contemplated. Indeed, a pilot regional network has been developed for disseminating information about public participation approaches in biodiversity and international waters programs. Finally, the strategy includes components on technical assistance and training, which provides for these needs in the region. Having just completed the development phase, the ISP is now launching a programme of efforts, and can be further analysed inasmuch as it achieves success in the future.

Some of the best models of innovative mechanisms for increased transparency and public participation are found in the sub-regional environmental accords (REAs) to which many countries in the Americas are accountable. Four examples in particular come to mind.

First, the NAAEC is a particularly good model for openness in a regional environmental agreement, testing various innovative mechanisms with some degree of success that has granted it some legitimacy in the eyes of civil society organizations in North America. This is based on a firm mandate. The preamble of the Agreement recognizes the importance of the civil society participation in the conservation, protection and improvement of the

---

[28] The Project Advisory Committee (PAC) has provided ongoing guidance and advice and facilitated input from government and civil society, including the private sector, labour women, indigenous populations, and other ethnic minorities.

[29] The ISP seeks to 1) promote the exchange of experiences and information between government representatives and groups in civil society for the formulation, implementation, and improvement of sustainable development policies and programs; 2) develop legal and institutional mechanisms for enabling broad participation in decisions of broad public concern; 3) facilitate access to and a flow of information among the relevant actors; 4) develop training programs to improve technical and administrative capacities so that citizens and organizations may contribute to sustainable development policies and decisions; 5) support the integration and strengthening of national sustainable development councils; and 6) develop national consultation processes to ensure that civil society may play an important role in sustainable development.

environment. Regarding the access to the information process, the agreement establishes a series of provisions related to general public access to information at all levels. According to Article 2, the parties should periodically produce reports about the state of the environment that have to be made public. In addition, administrative and legal procedures are contemplated to guarantee access. Similar provisions are in place regarding public participation. One of these mechanisms is established in Article 9, mandating the Council to hold public meetings in all its ordinary sessions and consult with non- governmental organizations, including independent experts, in decision making process. The agreement contemplates the possibility for a fact-finding record to be undertaken, even if solicited by civil society groups, in Articles 14 and 15, and grants highly controversial access to justice for investors in Chapter 11.

The Mercosur 2001 *Framework Agreement on the Environment* has two mechanisms or provisions to promote increased openness. Public participation is an objective pursued expressly, and it can be argued that specific actions on civil society participation may be agreed on in the protocols to the accord. Indeed, a close examination reveals specific preamble commitments on access to information and participation of civil society. Though the above-mentioned provisions for access to justice are present, these are provided only for the use of States.

In Chapter 1, Article 3, governments commit to the promotion of effective civil society participation in addressing environmental issues. Specific new provisions also offer certain hope. In Chapter 3, Article 6, the actors named to implement the accord include member states with the participation of appropriate national organizations *and civil society organizations;* activities include, (at Article 6 a) to increase information exchanges concerning environmental laws, regulations, procedures, policies and practice, including their social, cultural, economic and health aspects, particularly those which might affect trade or competitiveness. The transparency system contemplated sets systems in place, which, while bureaucratic in character, will depend upon the way they are operated. Institutions and much else are delegated to the future protocols and member governments. The work of the Economic and Social Council also provides mechanisms for direct participation by civil society organizations and technical experts, in particular through informal consultations held before every meeting of Technical Working Group (Sub-Grupo No. 6).

In the Central America Region, the Central American Forest Convention provides for public participation, including local communities, workers, business communities and indigenous peoples, in the planning, implementation and assessment of national forest policy enacted in compliance with the Convention.[30] The Central American Convention on Biodiversity also provides

---

[30] See the text of the Convention in the web page of the Central American Commission for Environment and Development, available online: <http//:www.ccad.ws> at Art. 5.

for public participation in biodiversity management.[31] Among its objectives, The Central American Convention for the Environment, which creates the Central American Commission for Environment and Development (CCAD), considers the promotion of decentralized, democratic and participatory environmental management [32]

Finally, the Caribbean Community is far ahead on its formal mechanisms for participation of civil society. The ratification of a *Civil Society Charter* in 1997 recognized the need for participation of a wide range of actors. This Charter is now being revisited by the CARICOM Secretariat to strengthen existing mechanisms of consultation between government and civil society. They plan to identify new mechanisms and seek a commitment to ongoing collaboration at national and regional levels. A range of issues deemed critical to the future development of the Caribbean Community is being discussed at a Caribbean Community (CARICOM) Forum. Some of the proposed issues relate to the reform of the region's education system and its relationship to employment, productivity and technology acquisition; recapturing/retaining migrating skills; instruments at the regional and national level to promote domestic savings; and focusing on the Caribbean as a "zone of peace". These would be elements in the search for a "New Model of Economic Development" for the Caribbean.[33]

At the bilateral level, there are also two new examples worthy of consideration as models for hemispheric accords.

First, public participation is an essential component of several bilateral trade agreements in the region. For instance, in the Free Trade Agreement between Canada and Costa Rica, the Environmental Cooperation Agreement (an environmental side agreement) recognizes the relevance of transparency and public participation in the development of environmental laws and policies.[34] The promotion of public participation in the process of development environmental laws is one of the side accord objectives.[35] Other provisions of the Agreement also deal with public participation and access to justice for violations of environmental laws, such as; the right of citizens to request authorities to seek potential violations of environmental laws,[36] the development of cooperation programs which may involve the public and experts,[37] the right of any citizen or non governmental organization to request information from any party on the effective implementation of environmental law in its territory and the duty to respond to the request made. This includes

---

[31] See Art. 35, among others.
[32] See Art. 2 h. See the text of the Convention, available online: <http://www. ccad.ws>

[33] Online: CARICOM <http://www.caricom.org>.
[34] See *Enviromental Cooperation Agreement between Canada and Costa Rica* (2002) La Gaceta of Costa Rica, No 127.
[35] *Canada-Chile Agreement on Environmental Cooperation* (CCAEC) (1997), Art. 1(d) online: Environment Canada<http://can-chil.gc.ca/English/Resource/Agreements/Aeccc/AECCC_1.cfm>.
[36] *Ibid.* at Art. 5.
[37] *Ibid.* at Art. 8.

the public availability of the summary of the question and the response,[38] the appointment of a focal point for the communication between any Party and the public on matters related to the implementation of the cooperation agreement,[39] the development of mechanisms to inform the public of the activities carried out under the agreement, and the involvement of the public in such activities, as appropriate.[40]

In a similar fashion, the *Free Trade Agreement between Chile and the United States,* in Chapter 19 (Environment) established an Environmental Affairs Council. According to the Agreement, the Council shall ensure a process for promoting public participation in its work and seek opportunities for the public to participate in the development and implementation of environmental activities.[41] In addition to providing receipt and consideration of public communications on matters related to the Chapter, each party shall make available to the other party and the public all the communications it receives and review in accordance with its domestic procedures[42]. Each party may also convene or consult an existing, advisory committee comprising members of its public (representatives of businesses and NGO) to offer recommendations on the implementation of the Chapter.[43] Also under the procedural matters, access to justice is provided, for violation of environmental laws.[44]

So, with regards to public participation in ecological regimes of the Americas, four general points can be made. First, openness is natural. Most environmental regimes appear to contain provisions for civil society participation, and this is not considered abnormal in the *modus operandi* of the accord negotiation or implementation. Second, openness is growing. In particular, there appears to be high public interest, recognition on the parts of governments and other actors of the value of civil society roles, and provisions for adequate participation and information. Still, these processes appear to have little provisions for access to justice, still the most challenging of the goals involved in ensuring an open system. Third, mechanisms for openness are not perfect. Public participation mechanisms in the Americas, whether at global, regional or sub-regional levels, still face the critique that they are too expensive, un-coordinated, under-resourced and chaotic. Finally, one leading question must be asked - Where is the link? It is not clear that environmental regimes have any influence on economic decisions.

---

[38] *Ibid.* at Art. 9.
[39] *Ibid.* at Art. 10.
[40] *Ibid.* at Art. 11.
[41] See *US-Chile Trade Agreement* (2003), at Art. 19.3. online: USTR <http://www.ustr.gov/new/fta/Chile/final/>.
[42] *Ibid.* at Art 19.4.1
[43] *Ibid.* at art 19.4.3
[44] *Ibid. at* art 19.8

The Need for Further Progress in the Trade and Environment Arenas

Progress for Americas Trade Regimes

In the FTAA, certain steps have been taken to ensure greater openness. First, through the creation of a civil society 'mail-box' (the Committee of Government Representatives for the Participation of Civil Society), governments have ensured a limited yet formally recognized channel for civil society recommendations to be submitted to the FTAA. Second, through the unprecedented release of the FTAA Draft Text, governments have sent a strong signal that serious expert analysis and commentary is welcome, and have provided an avenue for civil society organizations to read and consider the implications of the text during the negotiations themselves. However, upon careful study of the text, it becomes clear that in certain instances, especially the draft provisions for Investment related to transparency in dispute settlement, the FTAA does not necessarily contemplate greater levels of openness. Indeed, an early Draft of the FTAA stated instead that non-governmental participation in the FTAA dispute settlement system shall *not* be permitted. This certainly presents a mixed message.

For further progress, there is a need to strengthen openness in the FTAA. This can be done through three main recommendations. First, support is needed to develop civil society capacity to intervene both in FTAA 'mail-box' and its future manifestation as a 'consultative committee' or other instrument, and in the negotiations of the FTAA Draft Text (especially in the negotiations of text on Investment and a Dispute Settlement Mechanism). If civil society organizations were working closely with their governments and informing them of the benefits of participation, it might be less likely that the negotiations would start from such a retrogressive point. Second, there is a need to create a forum for FTAA related dialogue between civil society, business and governments, to break myths and begin to build a community of hemispheric actors. Third, there is still a need for the civil society organizations involved in the debates to keep up pressure, offer a constructive presence, and continue to address NGO priorities in other opening hemispheric, sub-regional and national spaces.

In addition to the recommendations described above, the concrete proposal of the 'sustainability impact assessment' is becoming more popular in the Americas. For many civil society and other groups in the western hemisphere, sustainable development should be the long term goal of any trade agreement. This could be recognized in the preamble of the final text of the FTAA, both as a way to diffuse opposition, and to ensure policy coherence in later legal interpretation.[45] To avoid future policy inconsistency in the FTAA, proposals can also be discussed for interpretative texts concerning potential relationships between trade, development and environment measures. For example, specific references can be included in the FTAA, to recognize an exemption for trade measures being taken pursuant to existing or new environment and development accords. [46] To help define the areas in need of such measures, sustainability reviews can be conducted *ex-ante* (prior to the conclusion of the FTAA agreement), through the use of sustainability impact assessment (SIA).

The SIA analysis can also identify useful parallel measures for trade policy, help develop proposals for liberalisation sequencing options which would mitigate or lower any negative environmental effects, and strengthen the sustainable development benefits of liberalisation.[47] Leading countries could launch processes to conduct preliminary, participatory sustainability reviews of the proposed FTAA, seeking coordinated approaches in each sub-region as appropriate. This could be done with support from the Inter-American Development Bank, the ECLAC and the Organization of American States (regional institutions which provided in-depth analysis of the region's trade structures prior to the launch of the FTAA). In particular, SIA research can focus on the specific environmental or social implications of each of the nine FTAA negotiating groups (agriculture, investment, market access, intellectual property, services and other issues). The SIA studies could compile comparative data and develop a matrix that builds upon recent work at the United Nations Environment Programme, the Organisation for Economic Cooperation and Development, various national governments, and the North American Commission for Environmental Cooperation, as well as work by NGOs and research organizations.[48] Civil society organizations could also participate as partners in all aspects of the sustainability reviews, and their ongoing or future efforts to carry out such reviews in the context of the FTAA should be supported by private foundations. In this context, governments should seek joint decisions on trade measures for environmental purposes, or methods for the mitigation of sustainability impacts of trade liberalization.

Progress for Americas Environmental Regimes

The Americas is a contiguous geographic and cultural area with common migratory species and linked ecosystems. The region could benefit from a coherent ecological cooperation agenda and increased resources or capacity

---

[45] M.C. Cordonier Segger, "Sustainable Development in the Negotiation of the FTAA" The Free Trade Area of the Americas: Issues and Visions for the Future, Interamerican Perspectives (2004) 27 *Fordham. Intl. L. J.* 1118.

[46] *Ibid.*

[47] *Ibid.*

[48] See, e.g., UNEP (2001) available online: <http://www.unep.org>, OECD (2000) available online: <http://www.oecd.org>, CEC (1996) and CEC (1999) available online: <http://www.cec.org>. See also RIDES (2003) available online: <http//www.rides.cl>.

building for the implementation of their international or domestic environmental commitments. A new, cooperative, stand-alone agreement on Americas environmental cooperation be negotiated, with a clear, coherent agenda and new, additional, effective financing measures to ensure implementation.[49]

The innovative, far-reaching 2001 *Mercosur Framework Agreement on the Environment* might provide a number of substantive starting points. The shared objective of an Americas Framework Agreement on the Environment could hold, as a goal, sustainable development and environmental protection in the western hemisphere. Such a mechanism or treaty could then provide for increased cooperation on environmental management systems and shared ecosystems, in addition to mechanisms for social participation and the protection of health. It could commit member states to cooperation on the development of instruments for environmental management including quality standards, environmental impact assessment methods, environmental monitoring and costs, environmental information systems and certification processes.

An Americas Framework Agreement on the Environment could also have provisions for the settlement of any disputes (establishing a just and effective dispute settlement process) and other general mechanisms for the implementation of the accord. An Annex to some kind of Framework Agreement on the Environment can provide a framework for the future development of protocols in key areas identified by governments. Areas for cooperation might include sustainable management of natural resources (such as protected areas, biological diversity, biosafety, wildlife management, forests, and hydrological resources); quality of life and environmental management (such as hazardous waste management, urban planning, renewable energy, improvement of soil and atmosphere/air quality); and environmental policy (such as environmental impact assessment, economic instruments, environmental information exchange, environmental awareness programs).

Additional agenda items for such a cooperation mechanism, drawn from the experiences of other sub-regional models, could also be designed. For example, the treaty might provide for cooperation in the compilation and development of methodologies for the collection of aggregated, empirical data on environmental conditions, making it available to citizens and environmental policy makers. It might also provide joint support for domestic implementation of environmental laws, by coordinating analysis, mechanisms for capacity building, policy linkage and even accountability through streamlined procedures for challenges of non-enforcement. It might also provide for the creation and strengthening of instruments for access to environmental information,

---

[49] M.C. Cordonier Segger *at al.*, *Ecological Rules and Sustainability in the Americas* (Winnipeg: IISD / UNEP, 2002).

monitoring, and capacity building, coordination of policy on new biological technologies, sciences and traditional knowledge. It might provide a space for countries in a region to join forces in efforts to address transboundary natural disasters and environmental problems, such as forest fires, air and water pollution, desertification and floods. Finally, it might also provide, where common agendas exist, regional negotiating mechanisms in multilateral environmental agreements and cooperative MEA implementation (this includes clearinghouses, experts networks, technology transfer and financing mechanisms).

In terms of administration, such a cooperative mechanism could be structured to build on existing regulatory frameworks at the national and sub-regional levels. As such, it would be able to work toward its goals through the development of administrative units within agencies, and the networking of sub-regional environmental coordination and cooperation, rather than through the creation of cumbersome new administrative structures.

In the hemispheric environmental policy arena, there has already been some limited progress in opening recent Americas negotiations to greater civil society participation. For example, during the 2001 Montreal Environment Ministerial, a signal was received by the International Institute for Sustainable Development that the Canadian government, hosts of the event, would accept comments on the documents of the conference. With 24 hours notice, a Hemispheric Working Group on Trade and Environment was able to coordinate over the Internet between civil society research institutes, through a partnership that had built over time in various hemispheric negotiations. A joint statement was quickly issued by a small consortium of experts. This went to national capitals throughout the Americas, was agreed on by the institutions, and then printed in Montreal. It was presented in a pre-meeting with the host government of the meeting, and changes were taken into account. A comparison of the Draft Environment Ministers Meeting outcomes to the recommendations of the civil society groups reveals that their input actually changed the draft agenda, leading to a modified final declaration. The process also set a series of recommendations in place for future meetings; these advisements have ensured that a future environment and health ministers meeting provides for direct participation by non-governmental organizations.

With regards to the principal topic of this chapter, what would be the elements of an optimal participation mechanism for a cooperation mechanism on the environment in the Western Hemisphere? Three specific recommendations can be made. First, in terms of participation, institutional arrangements would be necessary. There should be a provision for a joint public advisory committee, a civil society forum that reports to the Environment Ministers Meetings, and NGO accreditation to sessions. Second, in terms of transparency, concrete commitments are required, and can be facilitated by existing technologies in the

Western Hemisphere. There should be provisions for data compilation, hemispheric monitoring and reporting through linked sub-regional Web sites and publications, backed by guarantees for citizen access to this compilation of environmental information. Third, and most difficult to implement, to make the above measures meaningful, there must be provisions to ensure real, effective and optimized access to justice. These might include provisions to challenge non-enforcement of environmental laws, or appeal to sub-regional or regional courts.

Public Participation as a Linkage between New Trade and Environment Regimes

To be successful in opening trade debates in the Americas, it will be important to build a strong hemispheric civil society voice with the capacity to participate effectively in shaping trade and integration policy. Two sets of concerns exist on a hemispheric level in this respect. First, it is feared that civil society voices are of uneven strength in the FTAA process, and that increased openness might lead to unbalanced participation from some countries. When the participation of civil society exclusively reflects social and ecological concerns of the more developed partners, civil society participation might simply be used as a tool to fight so-called social / ecological dumping by less developed partners, instead of promoting their sustainable development needs. Second, while opportunities can be created by accords or mandated by governments, it is the responsibility of civil society and other groups to take them up. Often, these groups and marginalized communities lack the very capacity, analysis and resources to take advantage of spaces for dialogue. This leaves formal channels under-utilised, particularly in environmental regimes, and means disparities in regional and sub-regional representation that could hinder the development of effective processes on the hemispheric level.

Beyond these general recognitions, though, three specific recommendations can be made to further strengthen civil society participation in the Americas trade and environment debates.

In addition to civil society 'Peoples Summits,' which parallel FTAA Trade Ministerial meetings, other grassroots mechanisms are developing. These new effort offers a greater chance of obtaining the support and participation of the broader public, but more involvement is needed. For example, a civil society charter, supported by implementation mechanisms, could be developed.

Second, under auspices of leading institutions, expert networks are being created in order to foment the exchange of information, participation and cooperation between different regional actors on trade and sustainable development issues. A centre or institution could be created with a mandate to undertake capacity building, increase information analysis and flow, and provide technical support on hemispheric sustainable development issues. Policy and grant-makers would need to support the creation of such a non-advocacy mechanism that can facilitate comprehensive policy dialogues among the different interests, sub-regional perspectives and sectors.

Finally, the first step must be to open a rich and constructive dialogue. It may, for example, be possible to open a place for a broad dialogue on hemispheric trade and environment issues, with the Environment Ministers Forum of Latin America and the Caribbean as a foundation institution and technical support from other IGOs on the Americas. In partnership with the existing Hemispheric Working Group on Trade and the Environment, a Standing Conference or some kind of public advisory committee could be constituted, which would provide a place for dialogue between senior officials from governments, regional and hemispheric institutions, and the NGOs, academic institutions and private sector voices. But such dialogues must be legitimate, non-bureaucratic and inclusive. They should aim at building consensus on a focused trade and sustainability agenda that would be built upon hemispheric trade and environmental policy frameworks. Their objectives would include information sharing, networking, policy analysis and outreach. Terms of reference for such dialogues could be developed in cooperation with leading actors in the debates.

The intricacies of the new arrangement with 34 countries on very different levels of development promise interesting policy debates if the FTAA follows the dominant trend and recognizes sustainable development as one of its goals. Within the context of greater hemispheric integration, there is a new opportunity for a regional environmental cooperation mechanism to be negotiated with strong civil society participation. As negotiations enter their last phase, three overall strategies can be pursued for openness in the FTAA.

First, it is necessary to strengthen the ability of civil society to influence the creation of FTAA institutions. This will help civil society gain the capacity to analyze the sustainable development aspects of the nine FTAA negotiating group agendas, in order to take advantage of the FTAA Committee for the Participation of Civil Society and other national opportunities to participate in 'greening the FTAA'.

Second, it is necessary to strengthen hemispheric forums and institutions for environment concerns so that they have solid institutional foundations and sources of funding. Pursuing more effective sub-regional environmental cooperation mechanisms, and developing the potential for a networked Americas Framework Agreement on the Environment, or Environmental Chapter of the FTAA, can do this.

Third, civil society groups should seek to establish a forum where links between the three pillars of sustainable development (the environment, trade and human rights issues) can be addressed together.

With such an effort, greater openness in hemispheric trade and environment policy debates can help to ensure that hemispheric integration fosters, rather than frustrating sustainable development.

27

GOOD WATER GOVERNANCE THROUGH ACCESS TO INFORMATION, PUBLIC PARTICIPATION & ACCESS TO JUSTICE

Karin Krchnak[1]

In 1992, over 170 governments assembled at the Earth Summit in Rio de Janeiro and affirmed the importance of public access to information, participation, and justice in decision-making in Principle 10 of the Rio Declaration on Environment and Development. Ten years later, governments of the world reaffirmed this commitment at the World Summit on Sustainable Development (WSSD). Yet the implementation of these rights has not kept pace with the expectations generated by these international declarations. Civil society can encourage governments to establish specific commitments to increase public access to information, participation, and justice and to put their commitments into practice through independent monitoring of performance. Additionally, an active civil society can build the capacity of the public to understand their access rights and participate meaningfully in decisions that affect their lives.

The absence of information or mechanisms for participation and redress result in decisions that adversely impact, exclude, and are consequently opposed by, affected communities. Such decisions are rarely effective and are frequently illegitimate and unjust. They undermine the ability to integrate environmental concerns into development processes.

As the experience with the UN ECE Convention on Access to Information, Public Participation in Decision-making, and Access to Justice in Environmental Matters in Member States indicates, no country has fully developed policies or the organizational capacity to implement all pillars of Principle 10.[2] This is especially true in many developing countries, where

---

[1] Karin Krchnak, A.B. (Duke University), J.D.(University of Maryland School of Law), Director of The Access Initiative (TAI) and the Partnership for Principle 10 (PP10), World Resources Institute (WRI). Partnership for Principle 10, available online: <http://www.pp10.org/>.
[2] Regional Environmental Center, *Doors to Democracy: Pan-European Assessment of Current Trends and Practice in Public Participation in Environmental Matters* (Szentendre, Hungary: REG, June 1998).

M.C. Cordonier Segger & C. G. Weeramantry, eds., Sustainable Justice: Reconciling Economic, Social & Environmental Law
© *2005 Koninklijke Brill NV, Printed in The Netherlands, pp.427-446.*

transparency and inclusion have a shorter history and often face stronger resistance by special interests inside and outside governments. One example is Indonesia, where NGOs, some government agencies as well as a number of groups in Parliament have been promoting a Freedom of Information Act, while other interest groups in the government and Parliament have opposed its adoption and have been keeping the draft in Parliamentary Commissions for years. A strong national constituency, armed with credible and reliable information about the overall status of Principle 10, can overcome such resistance and move implementation forward, through either adoption of relevant policies and legislation or capacity development.

The only way to identify critical gaps is to produce the necessary information on the status of the whole system, both in terms of policy development and organizational capacity, through assessments using a common framework of indicators. The results of the assessments, however, will not lead to policy or organizational change at a national level without a broad national constituency, and at the international level without a global constituency, and mechanisms for cooperation, assistance and accountability.

Importance of Access Issues in the Water Sector

Over the past decade, many developing countries have begun to rethink how their utility sectors are organized, including whether or not to open the sectors to market competition and foreign investment. The water sector is one such utility, with significant social and economic importance. With an estimate that close to one-half of the world's population will live under conditions of water stress or scarcity by 2025, conflicts and potential human rights abuse over water are expected to increase dramatically. Already, conflict over privatization of water has led to violent protest in several countries. And in the first round of national assessments undertaken by The Access Initiative, access to information about water quality emerged as a key area for improvement in most countries.

Increasing access to water can have substantial impact on education, health, and economic livelihoods. Increasing access to water can also increase access to other basic needs such as food. With such a wide range of potential impacts from the water sector, it is critical to expand decision-making to include constituencies for the poor and for the environment.

The water policies that countries adopt determine whether private investment will result in projects and technologies that improve water efficiency and expand water services to the rural and urban poor. For this reason it is critical to develop mechanisms that citizens and public interest groups in developing countries can use to keep governments accountable for the decisions they make about sectors that deliver basic human services, and which have significant impact on the local and global environment.

A more open and transparent process for involvement in water decision-making processes would better identify appropriate goals for effective water management and conservation. Civil society engagement would serve as a vehicle to integrate social and environmental goals in approaches to water management, and as an instrument of accountability. It will help ensure involvement and ownership of decisions by local populations and address the needs of the poor, the people whose opinions and ideas are most often muted in development decisions. The poor generally give government institutions low grades in terms of their fairness, accountability, and responsiveness.

This process would give countries a practical tool to use in working toward achieving Millennium Development Goal 7 *Ensure Environmental Sustainability*, Target 10 to reduce the proportion of people without sustainable access to safe drinking water and basic sanitation. Broad access to information about water management allows people to find out whether they can use the water available to them for drinking, swimming, irrigating their crops, or fishing. With that knowledge, people can make informed choices and protect themselves from harm.

Information about water may also mobilize public opinion and urge polluters and governments to reduce pollution and to improve water quality. Initial TAI research found that the public rarely has easy access to useful information about the quality of drinking and surface water. As a result, individuals and communities cannot protect themselves from contaminated water or monitor the improvement of its quality.

Assessing & Improving information Disclosure, Transparency & Accountability

The Access Initiative (TAI) is a global coalition of civil society groups dedicated to promoting the implementation of Principle 10 and closing the gaps between international commitments to information and participation and national laws and practices.[3] TAI helps civil society organizations generate national-level assessments and monitor government performance through the use of an indicator toolkit developed by TAI partners. The interactive CD-ROM toolkit, *Assessing Access to Information, Participation and Justice for the Environment: A Guide (Version 1.1)*, helps non-governmental organizations (NGOs) and governments identify ways that their countries can improve public access to information, participation and justice. National assessments of law and practice for access

---

[3] The Access Initiative (TAI) is led by a core team comprised of the World Resources Institute (USA) (which also serves as the Secretariat), the Environmental Management and Law Association (Hungary), the Thailand Environment Institute (Thailand), Corporación Participa (Chile), and Advocates Coalition for Development and the Environment (Uganda). For more information, visit www.accessinitiative.org.

have been conducted in nine pilot-test countries with launches occurring in at least 20 more countries in 2004-2005.

In creating the Partnership for Principle 10 (PP10), civil society organizations joined with governments, regional and global organizations to translate the results of The Access Initiative assessments into improved policy and practice. With WRI as the Secretariat, the Partnership for Principle 10 builds on The Access Initiative, but is a distinct entity. While TAI is a civil society coalition focused on independent assessments of the access principles at the national level, PP10 works with a wide range of stakeholders including governments, international organizations, UN agencies, and civil society, to review policy recommendations and translate the results of the assessments into law and practice. For more information, visit www.pp10.org.

In addition to adding countries to TAI and through this process of bringing additional partners into PP10, WRI is starting to adapt the indicators to other areas, such as the energy and water sectors. The TAI methodology sets the baseline for good governance in terms of access to information, public participation, and justice in the environmental sector. However, to help countries and all stakeholders within countries achieve sustainable development, it is important that the methodology be adapted to a specific sector like water. It will help governments and civil society organizations to assess government performance, thereby offering a practical tool through which to monitor progress toward achieving the Millennium Development Goal #7, Target 10, as well as the Rio and Johannesburg commitments. It will also offer a method for dialogue with industry on how to improve environmental performance, transparency and accountability. Further, by adapting the methodology to the water sector, governments and civil society will be better able to assess obstacles to achieving sustainable development.

The Access Initiative (TAI) Tool-kit

The toolkit of indicators, produced on a CD-ROM called *Access to Information, Participation, and Justice: A Guide, Version 1.1*, measures both law and practice. Practice is assessed through case studies that national NGO coalitions select. The methodology specifically measures the following:

- Comprehensiveness and quality of the general legal framework for access to information, participation, and justice.
- Degree of available access to selected types of information about the environment.
- Degree of public participation in decision-making processes in selected sectors by actors in the development process at various levels.
- The accessibility of justice, both redress and remedy.

- Comprehensiveness and quality of capacity building efforts to encourage informed and meaningful public participation.

Table 1 lists the categories of indicators that teams may use to assess access to information and public participation in the water sector. As noted above, WRI is working to adapt the methodology to the water sector. For a detailed list of the indicators please see Attachment A.

Initial TAI Results

As Table 2 shows, the TAI pilot teams[4] assessed 8 cases of access to information from systems to monitor water quality. All national teams found the water quality monitoring systems they assessed had operated for more than three years. All monitoring systems except those in India, where reports were available but inconsistent, have provided regular reports at least over this period. Some of the monitoring systems have operated for decades. For example, RandWater in South Africa started operating in 1927.

In terms of the breadth of parameters monitored, monitoring systems are categorized as either comprehensive or basic. National teams in five countries (Hungary, India, Mexico, South Africa, and the United States) found that the systems chosen monitor a comprehensive set of physical, bacterial, chemical, and viral parameters in water. Systems in two countries (Thailand and Uganda) monitor a more basic set.

The quality of the system for providing water quality information also depends on how the monitoring networks are coordinated. Monitoring systems can cover a single urban area, as in Mexico or Indonesia; entire countries, as in Hungary, India, Chile, and Thailand; or large regions within a country, such as the State of California in the United States.

In Thailand, the monitoring of drinking water from the tap, by contrast, is divided among several bodies—the Metropolitan Waterworks, Provincial Waterworks Authorities, and the private Universal Utilities company. The monitoring of bottled water comes under another body—the Food and Drug Administration. While the Thai air monitoring networks are relatively coordinated, numerous agencies and organizations are monitoring and collecting information about drinking water quality.

---

[4] In 2001-2003, The Access Initiative (TAI) conducted pilot assessments in nine countries to test its methodology and identify needs for improved access. The results described here are taken from the assessments available online: <http://www.accessinitiative.org>, see also I. Petkova *et al.*, *Closing the Gap: Information, Participation, and Justice in Decision-making for the Environment* (Washington: World Resources Institute, 2002).

In Hungary (please see Box 1 for a more detailed case study), different aspects of drinking and surface water monitoring, however, are managed by different agencies, and neither the system nor the data are coordinated or integrated. The lesson to be drawn from both the Thai and the Hungarian examples is straightforward: unified and integrated systems provide a more coherent picture of water quality and present less of a challenge in obtaining information.

The Thai team also found that, while it could obtain some analytical data on the quality of tap water from water authorities, the country's Food and Drug Administration (FDA) provides no analytical monitoring on contaminants in bottled water. The FDA only notes the conclusion of its analysis: whether the quality of the drinking water of the selected brand is "safe." This policy means that consumers cannot check for the presence of specific contaminants. This lack of detail can be particularly relevant to vulnerable populations such as children, pregnant women, and older people.

Information technologies facilitate public access to information. Websites increasingly provide an opportunity for the public to learn more about water quality monitoring issues. In Hungary, the National Health Action Program website provides widespread coverage of environmental and health issues. In California, a website for the Environmental Justice Coalition for Water encourages citizens to become involved in monitoring the water quality in their communities.

Two countries provide examples of how water data can be disseminated. In South Africa, RandWater uses a website to provide users with updates on water issues. A map highlights in red areas where water should not be used for drinking without treatment and where contact should be avoided because of microbiological health effects, for example. In the United States, water suppliers disseminate annual reports to customers about their drinking water.

Detailed information on drinking and surface water quality, on the other hand, is difficult to obtain in all but two of the pilot countries: the United States and South Africa. Under the 1996 amendments to the Safe Drinking Water Act, the United States requires water suppliers to provide customers with annual reports. These reports are usually mailed with bills; many are also posted on the Internet. Teams in five countries (Hungary, India, Mexico, Thailand, and Uganda) found no active dissemination of data on drinking water quality for the public on the Internet or in the press. In Mexico and Uganda, teams could not obtain the data at all; in India, data could be obtained only through a personal contact.

In short, there are considerable differences in the performance of government agencies in providing information to the public about drinking or surface water quality. Collectively, performance in providing water quality information scores weak. This should be contrasted to assessment of information disclosure and public participation with regard to air quality which the assessment teams found to be strong.

Since the nine pilot tests, civil society coalitions in approximately 20 countries have started or are planning to do so in conducting an assessment using the TAI methodology. Two case studies are included below from Ukraine and Estonia to highlight the limited access to information and public participation in the water sector. More thorough assessments of the water sector in countries around the globe are planned once the methodology is adapted.

Case Study - Hungary

A Water Emergency

The Hungarian team[5] used the cyanide pollution of the River Tisza as the case study in assessing access to information and public participation in Hungary. The disaster occured at 10:00 p.m. on 30 January 2000 near Baia Mare in Romania when a strongly poisonous, high concentration cyanide compound used during the preparation of ore entered into the Lápos, side river of the Szamos from the non-ferrous metal mine of the Australian-Romanian joint venture Aurul SA. The dam of the slime storage-segregation lake of the new environmentally friendly water circulating technology slipped, then broke through as a result of the pressure of ice accumulated. The leaking water and slime fell over the protection dam of the trap pool for almost two days. Interventions to reduce the pollution were unsuccessful. The pollution proceeded from the stream to the Szamos, then from there to the river Tisza, reaching the Hungarian border on 1 February. The cyanide pollution devastated the full section of the Tisza in Hungary until a dead river and a mass of dead fish remained.

A month later in the middle of March again several dams burst at Baia Borsa, Romania, as a result of which different heavy metals (e.g., copper, lead, and zinc) entered the rivers. This pollution series was the most serious environmental disaster that ever occurred in Hungary. The "bed washing" effect of the following all-time high flood wave fortunately diminished significantly the extent of the damages.

The team selected the case study because the pollution affected the sphere of authority of all the public administration bodies, with all of them playing a role in carrying out assessing and mitigating the damage, informing the public. The Government Commissioner's Office coordinated all of this.

---

[5] The TAI-Hungary assessment was led by the Environmental Management Law Association which provided this case study.

Informing the Public

The regional water management directorates were informed of the emergency first, a half day before the "cyanide wave" reached Hungary. The Romanian authorities sent the first measuring results in the afternoon of 31 January to the Upper-Tisza-Region Environmental Inspectorate. The first sign arriving from the Romanian part came characteristically on informal channels: both the disaster relief and the water management consulted each other first confidentially, by telephone. A "higher level" official notification arrived only days later. It was extremely difficult to determine who was informed and how about the emergency.

The disaster relief organs immediately took the necessary measures in order to inform the population and to prevent accidents. With the help of local mayors, the local civil defense offices informed the public by loudspeaker about the necessary precautionary measures and about the water-withdrawal, well-using and fishing prohibitions that entered into force. The next day these same warnings were communicated through the press. The effectiveness of information dissemination is indicated by the fact that no one came into contact and fell ill from the contaminated water.

About the extent of the pollution and its consequences, the water management and the environmental authorities disseminated information to the public. The Upper-Tisza-Region Water Management Directorate communicated the daily water-quality measuring results. The director of the Upper-Tisza-Region Environmental Inspectorate decided to publish all the information while at the same time he reserved the right to make statements for himself alone, thus securing the control of authenticity of outgoing information.

A number of agencies took action. For example, the county health officers measured the quality of drinking water while the Fish-breeding Research Institute examined the survival of individual fish species. However, they played less of a role in informing the public. Non-governmental organizations established their own information dissemination system.

A coordinating discussion took place on 2 February at the National Disaster Relief Chief Directorate with the participation of the competent experts of the Ministry for Environment, the National Water Management Chief Directorate, the National Health Officer's Service and the National Disaster Relief Chief Directorate about the situation and the necessary measures. According to the unanimous judgment of the public administration experts interviewed by the assessment team, the authorities reacted quickly and professionally, while at the local level they found the cooperation among the partner institutions working on the same field appropriate as well. This was confirmed also by the non-governmental organizations. Coordination problems appeared rather at the higher public administrative level. In particular, the Minister of Environment tried to reduce the seriousness of the situation in the first days.

In addition, the public and non-governmental organizations felt that information was confused and unsatisfactory in the first days. One could not assess exactly of what type and what magnitude of pollution existed; governmental statements appeared to contradict the pictures showing masses of dead fish. The Ministry of Environment's website had data on the situation but at some point, for unknown reasons, the information was removed from the site.

On 15 February, the government appointed a Tisza Government Commissioner to strengthen coordination among the responsible departments. However, from the beginning, the new office could not carry out its task as it did not have clear authority or financial means. In terms of territorial institutes, it was not clear who was responsible for reporting; at the inspectorate, for example, they were informed that the Ministry reports to the government commissioner's office, but in spite of this the office expected them to give reports. At the same time, the new institute was always open and helpful to non-governmental organizations.

In contrast to the quick and adequate measures of public dissemination of the disaster, there was little information after the disaster and the lifting of the restrictions. This was partly caused again by the unclear state of the spheres of authority, but by this time also the interest of the press was diminished.

The assessment of the consequences and the longer term effects was controlled by the Ministry for Environment. The Ministry ordered studies directly from VITUKI (Water Management Scientific Research Institute), and partly supported those carried out by non-governmental organizations and research institutes. However, the materials once prepared remained the Ministry's intellectual property and the research results were not published. Even the government commissioner's office could obtain the study of the VITUKI only with great difficulties. It was not published despite repeated requests by non-governmental organizations. Through their own channels, the environmentalists tried to spread the results, information that they had obtained only by means of personal contacts.

The main task of the Tisza Government Commissioner's Office was to prepare an international convention about similar cases with a sphere of authority covering the whole catchment area. Neither they nor other institutes made a comprehensive retrospective evaluation about the measures of the "acute" period. Evaluations of the case were carried out by a number of departmental authorities. However, none of these materials were assembled into a consistent system. In addition, no common action plan was prepared for the future.

Information and information dissemination problems arose in terms of the long term management of water. It was never made clear when the disaster was over and what further precautionary measures the local population might need to observe. The Ministry for Environment kept the studies analyzing the long term ecological effects from the public referring to its intellectual property right. Heated protest by non-governmental organizations arose as a result of the situation.

Case Study - Ukraine

Water-Related Emergencies

The TAI-Ukraine team[6] selected a case involving pollution of groundwater in five settlements of the Pervomaysk district of the Mykolayiv oblast caused by a number of extremely toxic chemical agents (the so called "Accident in Boleslavchik"). The emergency took place in 2000. The case was selected because it is rather typical for Ukraine, resulted from military activities, and generated significant media interest.

The following research questions (indicators) were used to assess access to information for *environmental emergencies*:

- Existence of agencies, officials that are responsible for distribution among public of information about influence of environmental emergencies on environment and health of people.
- Assessing quality of information that is given in reports to representatives of public about results of investigating consequences of environmental emergencies.
- Availability of information about environmental emergency in Internet.
- Availability of information about results obtained from investigation of reasons and consequences of environmental emergency in Internet.
- Possibilities for mass media to obtain information *at the moment* of environmental emergency.
- Possibilities to obtain information from media representatives *after* environmental emergency.
- Quality of information that is available for the public at the moment of environmental emergency.

Among all above indicators, the highest score was given to the presence of information about environmental emergencies on the Internet. This type of

---

[6] The TAI-Ukraine assessment was led by Eco-Pravo Kyiv which provided this case study.

information is freely located on web-site of the Ministry on Emergencies of Ukraine. However, the public had no access to on-line information about the impact of this environmental emergency on people's health and environment, especially about its effect on quality of drinking water.[7]

Water Monitoring in Kyiv

The Ukraine team examined water monitoring in Kyiv since it is a large industrial city, and water monitoring in Yevpatoriya as a small city with a recreation infrastructure. Quality of and access to information about *water monitoring* was assessed on the basis of the following indicators:

- Presence of agencies and state officials that are responsible for gathering and distributing information about quality of drinking water.
- The number and variety of parameters that has been used for drinking water monitoring.
- Putting information on drinking water quality monitoring in Internet.
- Possibilities for public to get free access to reports on quality of drinking water.

Results showed that the indicator related to water monitoring received the highest index. On the other hand, the middle index was shown by the indicator related to placing monitoring data in Internet. Regarding possibilities for public to get free access to reports on quality of air and drinking water, the value of this indicator could be considered to be rather high. There are two main methods that the public has for obtaining information from reports on the state of air and drinking water: (1) a written request addressed to the Central Geophysical Observatory under the Ministry of Environmental Protection of Ukraine; and (2) a request to the State Department of Environmental Resources of Kyiv city and AR Crimea correspondently.

Public Participation

It was rather difficult for the team to find empirical material related to public participation for the chemical sector. The team focused on the role of the public in the development of the National Environment Health Action Plan (NEHAP) and the Law of Ukraine "On drinking water and water supply system" of January 10, 2002. Assessment of public participation in decision-making related to implementation of policy, strategy, plans, programs and legislation was made on the basis of the following indicators:

---

[7] This conclusion is also confirmed by participants of meetings made by population of five settlements suffered from man-caused pollution. They turned to the authority with requests to create independent international commission in order to discover reasons of diseases, and spoke out about the need to listen every day to reports on the state of ecology in the affected region.

- Period of time that is required for preliminary acquaintance with draft decisions.

- Quality of information that might stimulate (support) public participation in fulfillment of decisions (volume of information, reliability, efficiency as a showing of correspondence to the nowadays conditions).

- Availability and accessibility of documents related to decisions that were made for implementing policy, strategy, program and legislation (in places of public access: libraries, web-sites etc.).

- Level of external (outer) consultations regarding parameters and contents of decisions.

- Spread of consultations at the stage of developing draft decisions.

- Timeliness of information distributed among public about results of conducted consultations at the stage of development and implementation of corresponding decisions.

The team found that there no public participation in developing the above documents for the chemical sector. However, all of the documents were available and accessible for public.

Case Study – California, United States

Drinking Water Monitoring

The TAI-US team[8] examined drinking water monitoring in California. The California Department of Health Services' Division of Drinking Water and Environmental Management is responsible for enforcement of the federal and state Safe Drinking Water Acts (SDWA) and has regulatory oversight of public water systems throughout the state (the state is authorized to manage the federal program). This involves regulatory oversight of about 8,700 public water systems delivering drinking water to most state residents. Oversight of small water systems (less than 200 service connections) has been delegated to 35 county health departments. Private wells and small community systems—common among migrant agricultural communities and smaller, generally lower-income rural communities—are not monitored as consistently as large public systems. Lack of direct state oversight of these small water systems raises concerns about environmental justice and public health equity.

---

[8] TAI-US was carried out by the Clean Water Action/Clean Water Fund (CWA/CWF), the Silicon Valley Toxics Coalition, and the Ohio Citizen Action Education Fund. The case study is taken from the TAI-US report, TAI-US, *At the Frontlines of Democracy: Strengthening the Public Voice in State Decisions that Affect the Environment* (Washington: The Access Initiative, June 2004).

California must follow federal drinking water guidelines, and Consumer Confidence Reports (CCRs) are required by the SDWA. These reports must clearly convey concerns about drinking water safety to consumers—including water quality and the detection of contaminants. A Clean Water Action and Clean Water Fund analysis of California water utilities in 2001 found that 10 percent of CCRs had prominent unqualified safety statements about drinking water that failed to acknowledge deficiencies, to provide specific warnings for vulnerable populations, or to provide more general cautions to the public.[9] Over 20 percent included inappropriate safety language within the CCRs, and nearly one third of the CCRs had misleading statements about concentration measurements (minimizing the health impacts associated with small concentrations of contaminants).

CCRs must also include specific warnings relating to drinking water quality relevant to vulnerable populations such as infants, pregnant women, and aged or immune-impaired persons. CWA reviewed these warnings in 249 California utility CCRs, and found that only 49 percent of the CCRs provided complete and prominent warnings. Of the remaining 51 percent, twelve utilities excluded, downplayed, or provided incomplete warnings, while the others "buried" the information in their reports.[10] Specific information on sources of contamination required in CCRs was also lacking, and EPA was slow to complete Source Water Assessments—a responsibility it still retains despite state delegation—identifying likely sources of contaminants. As of the end of 2003, EPA had completed assessments for 16,029 California drinking water sources, which supply 7,504 public water systems out of 8,600 located throughout the state.[11]

The team found that there is comprehensive, regular drinking water monitoring. Monitoring results are broadly distributed and readily accessible via mandated Consumer Confidence Reports (CCR) and supplementary notification upon detection of a violation. However, data on water treatment chemical byproducts and emerging contaminants are lacking or more difficult to obtain. Specific information on sources of contamination (as required by CCR mandate) is lacking. Within 3 years from the time of state program approval by U.S. EPA, Source Water Assessments identifying likely sources of contaminants must be completed for public water systems in all states. Small water systems receive less government oversight and less consistent monitoring. Health and safety information is often misleading or missing. California's Department of Health Services has not yet provided a complete and integrated drinking water quality database online.

---

[9] Clean Water Action/ Clean Water Fund and CALPIRG Charitable Trust, *Measuring Up II: An Evaluation of Water Quality Information Provided to Drinking Water Consumers in California* (Los Angeles: CWA/CALPIRG, 2001).
[10] *Ibid.*
[11] California Department of Health Services, Drinking Water Source Assessment and Protection (DWSAP) Program, January 6, 2004 update: www.dhs.cahwnet.gov/ps/ddwem/dwsap/DWSAPindex.htm.

Public Participation in Setting Water Policy

Water policy in the American West has historically reflected the concerns of urban and rural water districts, state and federal resource agencies, and corporate agribusiness and other industries. Recently, environmental interests have become increasingly represented in the debate and the policy-making process. But water debates still frequently fail to include other sectors that face persistent water-related problems, such as farm workers, low-income urban residents, rural communities, and subsistence fishers (often marginalized from other policy debates as well). Because water quality and water delivery challenges often affect low-income communities and communities of color, failure to address persistent problems raises environmental justice concerns.

Despite state and federal measures seeking to address water-related concerns of these communities, California resource agencies have yet to develop adequate procedures and programs to bring their voices sufficiently into the debate over water services and water-related environmental and health impacts. But since 1999, a nongovernmental organization, the California-based Environmental Justice Coalition for Water (www.ejwatercoalition.org) has elevated issues on water and environmental justice for low-income communities to the regional and state levels. By bringing new voices to the debate, the Coalition of over 50 community and policy groups from around the state has sought to ensure that traditionally marginalized groups become represented in the debate over water policy development, management, and planning, as well as on-the-ground projects.

The team initially focused on a joint state and federal effort, known as the CALFED Bay-Delta Program, to address water supply, water quality, and ecological needs for two-thirds of the state's watersheds. During development of the CALFED programmatic environmental impact statement (EIS) and environmental impact report (EIR), the state provided the team with planning documents, maps, and draft "Records of Decision" along with detailed technical appendices.[12] They also held a series of meetings with Coalition members between 1999 and 2000 at the request of the coalition. Armed with this information, and the opportunity to interact with CALFED, the Coalition successfully raised environmental justice concerns to help guide implementation of the program. The final programmatic EIS/EIR and Record of Decision commit CALFED programs and its partners to develop a comprehensive environmental justice implementation plan.

---

[12] Specific information on the impacts of these policies on low-income communities of color was lacking, with the exception of limited information on the potential impacts on farm worker communities.

Two team members were appointed to serve on the CALFED Bay-Delta Advisory Committee (predecessor to the California Bay-Delta Public Advisory Committee), which unanimously endorsed inclusion of environmental justice principles and commitments to substantively address environmental justice in CALFED's Framework for Action. Subsequently, the Bay-Delta Public Advisory Committee established an Environmental Justice Subcommittee to ensure these program commitments are monitored and, ultimately, implemented. While the process still faces challenges, it has been an important step forward in the institutionalization of environmental justice concerns in state environmental policy.

Despite this progress, problems still emerged. In July 2003, state and federal water officials met secretly in Napa, California, to hammer out the elements of an agreement on implementation of the CALFED Record of Decision. The result of these meetings, known as the "Napa Agreement," would increase water supplies by enhancing water contractors' operational flexibility and determine how the additional water would be allocated. The result would be as much as one million acre/feet of water per year being sent south of the Delta and Sacramento-San Joaquin basin to southern California. Environmental and Environmental Justice Coalition advocates cried foul, and U.S. Congressman George Miller (D-CA) wrote a strong letter inquiring into the legal authority under which the meeting was held and the "Napa Agreement" had been reached. Subsequently, legislation was introduced in the California legislature to block "a plan crafted behind closed doors by state and federal water officials."[13] The term "Napa Agreement" was dropped by the agencies involved; however, elements of the agreement were presented to the Program's Public Advisory Committee in late 2003, and NGOs considered this a major violation of the spirit of CALFED.

Moreover, the CALFED process has given little attention to engaging affected communities for whom English is not a native language. Although multiple public registers for CALFED exist, including on the state website and at public libraries, these are generally available only in English. Despite the fact that many affected persons are native Spanish speakers and have limited or no ability to read or work in English, only limited Spanish language "outreach materials" on the program (basic summary brochures lacking meaningful detail) were made available.[14] CALFED's Bay Delta Program office (renamed the California Bay Delta Authority in 2003) held one workshop jointly with the Environmental Justice Coalition for Water in which Spanish language

---

[13] SB 2 was introduced by State Senator Michael J. Macado (D-Linden). The quote is taken from the Senate Majority Caucus article, "Senator Machado Introduces Bill to Prohibit Additional Water Pumping from Delta Waters," http://democrats.sen.ca.gov/servlet/gov.ca.senate.democrats.pub.news.View?ID=211.

[14] Of the 19,295,124 adults (18 years and over) in California, 21.4 percent reported Spanish as their language. Of these Spanish speakers 1,533,581, or 37.2 percent, reported that they speak English "not well" or "not at all." That's equal to 7.9 percent of California's total adult population for 1990. *See* Census of Population and Housing, 1990 Summary Tape File 3 [California]; http://countingcalifornia.cdlib.org/title/stf3.html.

interpretation was provided (Redding, California, Nov 8, 2001); however, this *followed* adoption of the Record of Decision.[15]

Case Study - Estonia

Drinking Water Monitoring

The Estonia team[16] assessed access to drinking water monitoring data in a small town in South-East Estonia, where drinking water problems are known to exist and these problems represent the case of the whole region (Please see Attachment B for the scores generated in the team's assessment of this case). The town is also representative in the terms of administrative capacity.

If compared to air monitoring data, dissemination of drinking water data is not very developed. One of the reasons is perhaps that air monitoring belongs to the jurisdiction of the Ministry of the Environment (where several trainings and projects have been carried out to implement the Aarhus convention), but drinking water falls under the control of the Ministry of Social Affairs.

There is a strong legal mandate for drinking water monitoring, but there is a problem with making this data public. However, the Ministry of Social Affairs has initiated a project for disseminating drinking water monitoring data to the public via the Internet.

Enterprise Level Information

The Estonia team assessed five enterprises from two sectors: energy and mining (2 enterprises); and, forestry and agriculture (3 enterprises). In the case of forestry enterprises, the team looked at the felling data compliance primarily, As these enterprises do not use much water, the two forestry enterprises were not considered relevant for the water sector. However, data from the three other enterprises provided information on access issues in the water sector.

In general, enterprises report quite detailed information on water pollution, as they are required to obtain a permit to emit pollutants. In addition, pollution charges are calculated on the basis of these compliance reports. These reports are submitted to the regional units of the Ministry of the Environment, which forward the data to the Information Centre of the Ministry of the Environment.

---

[15] The CALFED Programmatic Record of Decision was adopted on August 28, 2000. For the full text and appendices, see http://calwater.ca.gov/Archives/GeneralArchive/RecordOfDecision2000.shtml.
[16] The TAI-Estonia assessment was led by Stockholm Environmental Institute-Tallinn which provided this case study.

However, if trying to obtain this data, one meets several obstacles. The Information Centre of the Ministry of Environment does not issue single enterprise's pollution data, as they are afraid that enterprises might interprate this as violation of business confidentiality, although the act of ratification the Aarhus convention says these data should be public. Thus, the Information Centre forwards the information request to the specific enterprise the request concerns and the dissemination of data depends on the willingness of the enterprise. The larger enterprises of Estonia have understood the necessity of communicating information to the public and they also make their pollution data public in form of voluntary environmental reports, for example. The team did not encounter problems in obtaining data from the energy sector enterprises, which are large and have good public relations departments. But there is a problem of getting pollution information from small enterprises, which have significant impact on environment (particularly in the case of a pork farm evaluated by the team).

Case Selections Evaluating Quality And Accessibility Of Water Quality Information			
Country	Case Selection	Quality[i]	Accessibility
Hungary[ii]	Information from four networks: - KoFe – the Environment Inspectorate has 12 regional institutes that monitor surface water quality - ANTSZ – County Health Officers Service Network has 19 institutes and supervises drinking water quality - VIZIG – Water Management Directorate - RIV – regional emission analyzing stations cover entire country	Intermediate	Weak
India	Information from the rivers network (MINARS) as well as Ministry of Environment and Forests, Central Pollution Control Board and 11 state Pollution Control Boards. Assessed drinking water supply in municipalities of Gwalior, Chiplun, Chandigarh	Intermediate	Weak
Indonesia[iii]	Information from the Jakarta Clean River Program monitoring the Ciliwung River, a primary source of water for Jakarta.	Weak	Weak
Mexico[iv]	Information from the Lerma-Cutzamala Monitoring System, the principal water supply for Mexico City.	Strong	Weak
South Africa	Information from RandWater, a national supplier of drinking water.	Intermediate	Intermediate
Thailand	Bottled water information from the Food and Drug Administration. Tap water information from: - Metropolitan Waterworks Authority (MWA) - Provincial Waterworks Authority (PWA) - Universal Utilities, a private water supply company in Chachengsoa province	Weak	Weak
Uganda	- Information from a system monitoring the wastewater discharged into the Rukoki River (A source of water for local communities and their livestock) by the Kasese Cobalt Company Ltd., which extracts cobalt from pyrite about 400 km from Kampala. - Information from a drinking water monitoring system in Kampala.	Weak	Weak
United States: California	Information from the California Department of Health Services, Division of Drinking Water and Environmental Management, which oversees 8,700 public water systems; 35 county health departments cover smaller systems.	Intermediate	Strong

Categories of Access to Information and Public Participation Indicators

Access to Information

Information about environmental emergencies.
Questions addressed timeliness of public notice; breadth, quality, and content of information distributed; and investigation and monitoring aimed at preventing future incidents.

Information about water quality.
Questions addressed comprehensiveness of monitoring, as well as distribution and accessibility of monitoring data.

Information about environmental performance of industrial facilities.
Questions addressed legal mandates for reporting, including compliance reporting; standardization, periodicity, and specificity of reporting; availability of exemptions for confidential information; release and transfer data management; and dissemination.

Categories of Access to Decision-making Processes

Policy-Making Decisions

Participation in the formulation of Sector or Regional Policies, Plans, and Programs

Questions addressed timelines and scope of public notice; breadth of consultation in drafting and formulation; lead-time for public comments on proposals; feedback and transparency in communication of final decisions; and accessibility of performance monitoring and review procedures.

Project-Related Decisions

Participation in Concessions, Facility Siting, and Environmental Permitting
- *Questions addressed* accessibility of rules governing award procedures; timeliness and scope of notice of intent to award concession or permit; degree of consultation or input in selection/award criteria; transparency of award process and final decision on award; accessibility of performance monitoring and review procedures; and accessibility of close-out or remediation plan.

---

[i] Monitoring systems score weak on quality when they collect information for only a few parameters characterizing the quality of water.
[ii] Obtained data from almost all 12 inspectorates and from 7 of 19 public health offices in four weeks. Seven of the 19 offices responded on drinking water.

iii Indonesia submitted a single value for both air and water quality information.
iv Mexico disseminates drinking water information at the state level but not by individual water supply.

(ii)

FINANCING SUSTAINABLE DEVELOPMENT

28

SUSTAINABLE DEVELOPMENT AND THE GLOBAL ROLE OF INTERNATIONAL FINANCIAL INSTITUTES

Ko-Yung Tung[1]

Law and development are two sides of the same coin. The global community has increasingly recognized the relationship between the rule of law and the economic well-being of a country. Without a strong rule of law, economic growth will not be equitable; and it will not be sustainable in economic, social, environmental, or other respects. This chapter will first discuss the relationship between the rule of law and equitable, sustainable economic development, drawing upon the World Bank's perspective and experience. Examples will be given of the World Bank's efforts to support systemic law and justice reforms to reduce poverty with lasting results. The chapter will then present the various international environmental legal regimes in the evolution of sustainable development. Next, the chapter will illustrate how the World Bank's innovative policies and varied activities, contribute to the promotion of sustainable development.

Promoting the Rule of Law as a Vital Component of Development

The rule of law as a condition of equitable, lasting development

A prerequisite to sustainable development and the alleviation of poverty is an increased support for legal and judicial reform as well as good governance.[2] Recent studies have demonstrated the positive link between a strong rule of law

---

[1] Ko-Yung Tung, A.B. Physics magna cum laude, J.D., (Harvard), Fellow, University of Tokyo Faculty of Law, Of counsel, O'Melveny & Myers LLP, former Vice President and General Counsel, The World Bank and Secretary-General, International Centre for the Settlement of Investment Disputes.This chapter is based on the keynote paper presented by Dr. Tung to Sustainable Justice 2002: Implementing International Sustainable Development Law, a Conference co-hosted by the CISDL, the World Bank and the United Nations Environment Programme, and sponsored by the government of Canada, June 14-16, 2002, in Montreal, Canada.

[2] See U.N. *General Assembly Declaration on the Right to Development*, GA Res.41/128, Annex, 41 U.N. GAOR Supp. No. 53 U.N. Doc. A/41/153 (1986) at 186. See also A. Khalfan & M.. C. Cordonier Segger, "International Human Rights Obligations and Levels of Financing for Development," CISDL Legal Brief written for the United Nations International Conference on Financing for Development (Monterrey: March, 2002), with updated version as chapter in this volume.

M.C. Cordonier Segger & C. G. Weeramantry, eds., Sustainable Justice: Reconciling Economic, Social & Environmental Law
© *2005 Koninklijke Brill NV, Printed in The Netherlands, pp.449-468.*

and economic development.[3]   As nations improve their legal and judicial systems, human development was shown to advance to the next level.[4] Conversely, weak legal and judicial systems were found to undermine the fight against poverty.[5]   They divert investment to markets with more predictable rules-based environments; they deprive important sectors of the use of productive assets; they mute the voice of citizens in the decision-making processes; they leave vulnerable individuals and groups unprotected from violence and other forms of abuse that exacerbate economic inequalities; and they allow the spread of environmental degradation, corruption, money laundering and other problems that further weaken communities and economies.[6]

Recent historical events provide concrete examples showing that the rule of law is a vital mechanism for sustainable economic growth.[7]   The Asian financial crises of the 1990s, for example, demonstrated that a viable legal and regulatory structure, including sound economic laws and regulations, is essential to sustain and increase efficiency and attract long-term foreign investment.[8]   In addition, the experiences of the transitional economies of Eastern Europe have proved that adopting a market economy alone will not ensure prosperity in the long run.[9]   For transition economies, perhaps even more than for others, sustainable growth requires predictability[10] and transparency, as well as sound economic laws and regulations.[11]   There is thus a strong case for governments and international financial institutions to support systemic legal and judicial reform as part of their agenda to move towards sustainable development and what Nobel Laureate Amartya Sen has called 'the freedom of individuals'.[12]

An appreciation of the many dimensions of poverty is essential to fully understand the link between the rule of law and the alleviation of poverty. Poverty is not just a lack of economic resources. It is also a lack of freedom. This encompasses not only the lack of economic security, but also physical, environmental and social security. Poor people do not have access to the

---

[3] See D. Kaufman, A. Kraay & P. Zoido-Lobaton, "Governance Matters," Working Paper No. 2196, World Bank Policy Research Department (Washington: The World Bank, 1999).
[4] See Amartya Sen, *Development as Freedom* (Alfred A. Knopf, 1999).
[5] Ko-Yung Tung, (Lecture presented to the Yale Law School in New Haven, Connecticut, April 29, 2002).
[6] *Ibid.*
[7] James D. Wolfensohn, (Lecture presented to the Annual Bank Conference on Development Economics, in Paris, June, 1999), online: World Bank <http://www.worldbank.org/html/extdr/extme/jdwsp062199.htm>; See also Legal Vice Presidency: *Legal and Judicial Sector Assessment Manual*, (The World Bank: Washington, 2002).
[8] *Ibid.*
[9] See Ibrahim F.I. Shihata, *The World Bank in a Changing World*, Vol. III (The Hague: London Martinus Nijhoff, 2000) at Part One, Ch. 6. [Shihata]
[10] For a discussion on the importance of predictability in development, see *Ibid.* Shihata describes the conditions for human progress as including "physical security, a minimum measure of stability and predictability, fair competition on a level playing field and a social safety net to protect the poor and vulnerable," and the rule of law as "a prerequisite for the attainment and preservation of these conditions").
[11] See also *supra* note 7.
[12] See *supra* note 4.

freedoms and choices that the wealthy take for granted.[13] The poor often lack access to food, clean water, shelter, education and health. They are particularly vulnerable to disease, dislocation, and natural disasters. Finally, they are often powerless to influence key decision-makers on policies that directly influence their lives.[14] Poverty represents a general lack of opportunity, including the opportunity to get an education, to be healthy, or even to work. It is also the lack of rights that people know that they have and that they could enforce. Because poverty is a lack of freedom in these many ways, development, as Amartya Sen notes, "is best seen as enhancement of freedom in a very broad sense."[15]

The World Bank has long recognized these many facets of poverty. The Bank's 2000/2001 World Development Report on *Attacking Poverty* proposed to tackle poverty by promoting opportunity, facilitating empowerment, and enhancing security.[16] The 2002 World Development Report, *Building Institutions for Markets*, went a step further, and added the process of institution-building to the dialogue of development.[17] A critical part of this process is building institutions that safeguard the rule of law and good governance. And one of the most effective ways to attack poverty in all its dimensions at an institutional level is the development of a sound legal framework and of practical mechanisms through which systems of law and justice can be implemented to serve all peoples- not just the powerful- to enhance individual and community freedom and to ensure equality.[18] As World Bank President James D. Wolfensohn declared at a global conference on law and justice in St. Petersburg, Russia, in July 2001, "an effective legal and judicial system is not a luxury, but a key component of a well functioning state and an essential ingredient in long-term development."[19] As he also observed:

> "[T]he quality of the legal norms in a society and the manner in which they are administered have clear and direct impacts on the extent to which citizens have a voice in the government decisions that affect their lives, the extent to which there are official safety nets and mechanisms that help them cope with economic and natural shocks, and the ways open to them to overcome disadvantages and to grasp opportunities."[20]

---

[13] *Ibid.*

[14] See Deepa Narayan, *et al., Voices of the Poor: Can anyone hear us?*, (New York: Oxford University Press for the World Bank, 1999).

[15] *Supra* note 4.

[16] Ross Larson, Bruce and Meta de Coquereaumont, principal eds. *World Development Report 2000/2001: Attacking Poverty.* (Washington, D.C.: World Bank, 2001).

[17] See *World Development Report, Building Institutions for Markets,* (Washington, D.C.: World Bank, 2002).

[18] See James D. Wolfensohn, (Opening Remarks at the Conference on Empowerment, Security & Opportunity through Law and Justice in St. Petersburg, Russia, July 9, 2001), online: World Bank < http://www.worldbank.org/html/extdr/extme/jdwsp070901.htm>.

[19] *Ibid.*

[20] *Ibid.*

Similarly, the author's predecessor, late Ibrahim F.I. Shihata, former Senior Vice President and General Counsel of the World Bank, remarked on many occasions that a sound legal framework is a prerequisite for the guarantee of sustainable and equitable development.[21] The majority of commentators would agree with Shihata that, "In all countries, law, which is often used to maintain the status quo, has had a quintessential role in guiding and legitimizing the development process."[22] To analyze how law can be used to achieve sustainable development in the long run, one must consider the components that constitute a "rule of law."

As a starting point, one may consider the rule of law in terms of process. Shihata, for example, described the rule of law as a structure built on three pillars:[23] The first pillar is a system of "objective rules," which are known in advance by all the stakeholders and effectively enforced;[24] the second pillar is a system of "appropriate processes," under which rules are made, enforced and changed when necessary;[25] and finally, the third pillar is the need for "well-functioning public institutions," which are not only staffed by trained individuals, but are also transparent and accountable to the people who are bound by the rules and regulations, and which function without arbitrariness or corruption.[26] To summarize, the rule of law is a system which has (i) legally binding rules, (ii) appropriate processes for the application of these rules, and (iii) well-functioning institutions to apply, enforce and – as necessary – modify these rules. [27] The system should guarantee basic rights, enhance predictability of strong judicial processes, and protect citizens and organizations from an arbitrary use of state authority and lawlessness.[28]

It bears emphasis that the judiciary plays a particularly crucial role in a system that is based on the rule of law.[29] As Shihata noted, "law is not merely the collection of written laws and regulations. It also includes not only the manner in which these rules are implemented by government agencies, but also how

---

[21] See *supra* note 9; see also Ibrahim F.I. Shihata, "Good Governance and the Rule of Law of Law in Economic Development," Preface in Ann Seidman, Robert B. Seidman &Thomas W. Walde, eds., *Making Development Work: Legislative Reform for Institutional Transformation and Good Governance.* (Kluwer Law International, 1999);
Ibrahim F.I. Shihata, "Legal Framework for Development and the Rule of Law of the World Bank in Legal Technical Assistance" in Ibrahim F.I. Shihata, ed., *The World Bank in a Changing World,* Vol. II (USA: World Bank, 1995) [Legal Framework]; ; Ibrahim F.I. Shihata, *Complementary Reform- Essays on Legal, Judicial and Other Institutional Supported by the World Bank,* (The Stationery Office Books, 1997).
[22] *Ibid.* Legal Framework.
[23] *Ibid.*
[24] *Ibid.*
[25] *Ibid.*
[26] *Ibid.*
[27] See S. Schlemmer-Schulte, "The World Bank's Promotion of the Rule of Law in Developing Countries" in S. Schlemmer-Schulte & K. Tung, eds., *Liber Amicorum Ibrahim F.I. Shihata: International Finance and Development Law* (Kluwer Law International, 2001).
[28] *Ibid.*
[29] Legal Framework, *supra* note 21.

they are applied and interpreted by judges and arbitrators."[30]   Therefore, a sound, independent judiciary is crucial to a properly-functioning state under the rule of law. Going beyond just process, the concept of a rule of law must also be understood in substantive terms, whereby it should embody the substantive norms of justice and equity.[31]

Promoting the Rule of Law: A View from the World Bank

Establishing the rule of law, as defined above, is not a finite process, but "requires continuous legal reform" in all aspects of the legal framework (including all the rules, processes and institutions of the legal framework).[32]   In this ongoing process, the World Bank, with its declared vision of "a world free of poverty," has taken a key role with its partners to assist its member countries in strengthening the rule of law as a means of fostering equitable economic growth and sustainable poverty reduction.

The Comprehensive Development Framework (CDF) developed by the World Bank recognizes legal and judicial institutions as key pillars in the fight against poverty.[33]   The CDF is a process designed to bridge the gap between macroeconomic policies and the social and structural foundations essential to each country's long-term sustainable and equitable growth. The CDF is not a blueprint to be applied to all countries in a uniform manner. In the short run, the CDF envisages mechanisms to bring people together and build consensus, to forge stronger partnerships that allow for strategic selectivity, to reduce wasteful competition, and to emphasize the achievement of concrete results. In the long run, the CDF aims to improve development effectiveness and help countries reach their central goals of poverty reduction.[34]   As Amartya Sen has observed, the CDF rejects the "compartmentalized view of the process of development."[35]   Instead, the CDF presents a comprehensive approach, applied through a lens of "causal interdependence," which recognizes that "legal development is constitutively involved in the development process."[36]   This integral element of legal development under the CDF, in Sen's view, "is not just about what the law is and what the judicial system formally accepts and asserts." Rather, this element of legal development "must, constitutively, take note of the enhancement of people's capability – their freedom – to exercise

---

[30] *Ibid.*
[31] See R. Dworkin, *A Matter of Principle* (Cambridge: Harvard University Press, 1985); M. Stephenson, *The Rule of Law as a Goal of Development Policy* (The World Bank Group, 2004), online: World Bank <http://www1.worldbank.org/publicsector/legal/ruleoflaw2.htm>.
[32] See J. D. Wolfensohn (Keynote address presented to the Annual Bank Conference on Development Economics, June 21, 1999). Available online: World Bank <http://www.worldbank.org/html/extdr/extme/jdwsp062199.htm>.
[33] See A. Sen, "What is the Role of Legal and Judicial Reform in the Development Process?" (Keynote address presented to Comprehensive Legal and Judicial Development, June 5, 2000). Available online: World Bank <http://www4.worldbank.org/legal/ljr_2k/ljrconference_agenda.html>.
[34] *Supra* note 4 at 126-127.
[35] *Ibid.*
[36] *Ibid.*

the rights and entitlements that we associate with legal progress."[37]   Sen thus emphasizes that legal and judicial reforms are important not only for legal development itself - even if as a component of the CDF approach- but also for the development of economics and other fields of human endeavor.

The World Bank's assistance to its member countries under the CDF accordingly covers a broad spectrum of activities in the legal and judicial sectors. The key elements of Bank-financed legal and judicial reform projects include assisting members in supporting judicial independence, providing judicial and legal training and capacity building, strengthening good governance practices (including anti-corruption legislation), increasing access to justice for the poor and other disadvantaged groups, improving legal education and outreach across society, and developing alternative dispute resolution mechanisms.   There are currently more than three hundred Bank-funded projects in legal and judicial reform.[38] Some of the Bank-financed projects in this area include: supporting delivery of legal services to poor women in Ecuador, Jordan and Sri Lanka;[39] assisting Georgia and Russia with creative legal and judicial reform programs that include a media component for public outreach in order to increase public access to law and justice;[40]assisting countries such as Indonesia, Lithuania, Philippines, Sri Lanka, Tunisia and Uganda to improve financial and private sector capacity through new banking legislation and institutional strengthening;[41] and administering comprehensive judicial and legal sector assessments in countries such as the Federal Republic of Yugoslavia, Mongolia, Romania and Vietnam.[42]

---

[37] *Ibid.*

[38] See Legal and Judicial Reform Group, "Initiatives in Legal and Judicial Reform," (World Bank: Legal Vice Presidency, May 2002), online: <http://www4.worldbank.org/legal/leglr/publications_ljr.html>.

[39] See Legal Vice Presidency, "Initiatives in Legal and Judicial Reform," (World Bank: Legal Vice Presidency, 2003) at 38, online: World Bank <http://www4.worldbank.org/legal/publications/LJR-Initiatives-2003.pdf>, World Bank: Ecuador: Judicial Reform Project, Loan No. 4066-EC approved April 13, 1995, for US$10.7 million (equivalent); The World Bank Group, *Japan Social Development Fund Grant Proposal,* online: World Bank <http://www.worldbank.org/rmc/jsdf/Jordan%20Legal%20Aid%20Services.pdf>,   Jordan: Legal Aid for Poor Women (JSDF Grant) US $ 191,000 (equivalent). Legal Vice Presidency, "Initiatives in Legal and Judicial Reform" (World Bank: Legal Vice Presidency, 2003) at 49, online: World Bank <http://www4.worldbank.org/legal/publications/LJR-Initiatives-2003.pdf>, Sri Lanka: Legal and Judicial Reform Project, Credit No. 3384-LK approved June 20, 2000 for US$18.2 million (equivalent).

[40] See Legal Vice Presidency, "Initiatives in Legal and Judicial Reform," (World Bank: Legal Vice Presidency, 2003)   at   28,   online: World   Bank   <http://www4.worldbank.org/legal/publications/LJR-Initiatives-2003.pdf>, Georgia: Judicial Reform Program, Credit No. 3263-GE approved June 29, 1999, for US$13.4 million (equivalent); *Ibid.* at 46, Russian Federation: Legal Reform Project, Loan No. 4036-RU approved June 13, 1996, for US$58.0 million (equivalent).

[41] See World Bank: Indonesia: Banking Reform Assistance Project, Project ID. P055755 approved December 4, 2002; Lithuania: Enterprise & Financial Sector Assistance Project, Project ID. P008536 approved April 13, 1995; Philippines: Banking System Reform Loan Project, Project ID. P056524 approved December 3, 1998; Sri Lanka: Sri Lanka Central Banking Strengthening Project, Project ID. P071131 approved June 19, 2001; Tunisia: National Rural Finance Project, Project ID. P005720 approved May23,1995; Uganda: Financial Market Assistance Project, Project ID. P044213 approved May 27, 1999.

[42] See World Bank: Federal Republic of Yugoslavia: Private Sector Development Technical Assistance Grant Project, Project ID. P074145 approved by June 29, 2001; The World Bank Group, "Mongolia- Legal and Judicial   Reform   Project,"   online: World   Bank   <http://www-wds.worldbank.org/servlet/WDS_IBank_Servlet?pcont=details&eid=000094946_01121708452144>, Mongolia: Legal and Judicial Reform Project, Project ID. P074001 approved December 21, 2001, The World Bank Group, "Romania:

In each case, the Bank seeks to ensure that each legal and judicial reform project responds to the specific needs and priorities of the country concerned. The direct importation of concepts or mechanisms from other legal systems may not be appropriate. Coordination and participation of all the stakeholders in the reform process, as well as an understanding that legal and judicial reform is a long-term process, are critical in ensuring a successful project. Finally, the Bank explicitly recognizes that law and justice activities within each country must be evaluated within the comprehensive approach to the reform process, as outlined under the CDF, and in the light of the general objective of sustainable development.

Promoting Environmentally and Socially Sustainable Development

The Evolving Agenda for Sustainable Development

The global community can foster sustainability for future generations by supporting the concept of environmentally and socially sustainable development and the evolution of international sustainable development law. There is thus a need for continued discourse to determine how sustainable development may evolve as another aspect of the larger sustainable development agenda. The 1987 Report of the World Commission on Environment and Development, *Our Common Future*, memorably summarized the concept of sustainable development as "development that meets the needs of the present without compromising the ability of future generations to meet their own needs."[43] As Professor Phillipe Sands has noted, sustainable development was then an idea whose time had come, but no one knew what to do with it.[44] The concept was enthusiastically embraced by the Brundtland Commission in 1987, and then endorsed by various international organizations and conferences.

It was at the 1992 UN Conference on Environment and Development held in Rio de Janeiro, Brazil, that governments began to endorse sustainable

---

Private and Public Sector Institution Building" Project, online: World Bank <http://web.worldbank.org/WBSITE/EXTERNAL/NEWS/0,,contentMDK:20067844~menuPK:34471~ pagePK:40651~piPK:40653~theSitePK:4607,00.html>, Romania: Private and Public Sector Institution Building Loan Project, Project ID. P069679 approved September 12, 2002; See World Bank Group, "Viet Nam: Power Development Project:" online: World Bank <http://www-wds.worldbank.org/servlet/WDS_IBank_Servlet?pcont=details&eid=000009265_3961029221429>, Vietnam: Power Development Project, Project ID. P042236 approved February 31, 1999.
[43] World Commission on Environment and Development, *Our Common Future* (Oxford: Oxford University Press, 1987) The Commission's recommendations led to the Earth Summit - the United Nations Conference on Environment and Development (UNCED) in Rio de Janeiro in 1992; See also, A. Boyle & D. Freestone, *Introduction to International Law and Sustainable Development: Past Achievements and Future Challenges* (Oxford: Oxford University Press, 1999) at 13. [Boyle & Freestone]
[44] P. Sands, "International law in the Field of Sustainable Development" (1994) 65 *Brit. Y.B. Int'l L.* 303 at 317.

development as a global policy. The 1992 *Rio Declaration on Environment and Development* presented the first consensus in the international community on some of the core principles of environmental protection and sustainable development.[45] Principle 4, for example, endorses the integration of environmental protection in the development agenda.[46]

The Rio Principles also identify various elements as the basis of sustainable development law, including the sustainable utilization of natural resources, and the notion of inter-generational equity. They also represent a delicate balancing of interests between the needs of developed and developing countries in this field.[47] Principle 27 of the Rio Declaration called specifically for further developments in the field of international law for the purpose of sustainable development.

Importantly from a legal perspective, therefore, the 1992 Earth Summit in Rio recognized that any effort to support sustainable development must include legal instruments and mechanisms as a basis for action. The necessity for a global response to legal matters resulted in Chapter 39 of Agenda 21 which was adopted by more than 178 governments at the Rio Summit to "[the] further development of international law on sustainable development, giving special attention to the delicate balance between environmental and developmental concerns."[48] Agenda 21 declares that the overall objective of the review and development of international environmental law "should be to evaluate and to promote the efficacy of that law and to promote the integration of environment and development policies through effective international agreements or instruments taking into account both universal principles and the particular and differentiated needs and concerns of all countries."[49]

Agenda 21 also recognizes the unique needs of developing countries in the strengthening and capacity building of their legal institutions in the field of environmental law, as well as the need specifically to "promote and support the effective participation of all countries concerned, in particular developing countries, in the negotiation, implementation, review and governance of international agreements or instruments, including appropriate provision of technical and financial assistance and other available mechanisms for this purpose."[50]

---

[45] See Boyle & Freestone, *supra* note 43.
[46] United Nations Conference on Environment and Development, *Rio Declaration on Environment and Development*, 1992, UN Doc. A/CONF.151/5/Rev. 1, 31 I.L.M. 874. [Rio Declaration].
[47] *Ibid.*, at principle 4 ,which states: "In order to achieve sustainable development, environmental protection shall constitute an integral part of the development process and cannot be considered in isolation from it."
[48] United Nations Conference on Environment and Development, *Agenda 21*, 1992, U.N. Doc. A/CONF.151/PC/100/Add. 1, at para. 39.1(a) [*Agenda 21*].
[49] *Ibid.*
[50] *Ibid.*

According to the editors of *International Law and Sustainable Development*, the Rio Instruments' most "potentially revolutionary aspect… is that it makes a state's management of its own domestic environment and resources a matter of international concern for the first time in a systematic way."[51] An example of the application of this new approach is found in the United Nations Environment Program (UNEP) study of 1995, which identifies the need to mainstream environmental law into other areas of development law and policy, in response to a request from the Commission on Sustainable Development, of concepts pertaining to international law and sustainable development.

Sustainable development has affected international case law as well. Author Rosalyn Higgins, for example, cites the decision of the International Court of Justice in the *Case Concerning the Gabčikovo-Nagymaros Dam*, in which the Court referred for the first time to the need to reconcile economic development with protection of the environment and expressed that as "the concept of sustainable development."[52]

In an attempt to guide the mainstreaming of environmental and social sustainability concerns into international standards, the International Law Association's Committee on the Legal Aspects of Sustainable Development laid out a set of "Principles of International Law for Sustainable Development," which were adopted as the New Delhi Declaration of Principles of International Law Relating to Sustainable Development ("New Delhi Declaration").[53] These principles are: the duty of states to ensure sustainable use of natural resources to which they have sovereign rights; the principle of equity and the eradication of poverty for the well-being of future generations; the principle of common but differentiated obligations in terms of the common accountability of states for the protection of the environment, but taking into account the different capabilities and responsibilities of each state; the principle of the precautionary approach to human health, natural resources and the environment under the assumption that natural eco-systems are "vulnerable rather than disposable"; the principle of public participation and access to information and justice, including a citizen's appeal process to address concerns that are not headed by leaders; the principle of good governance; and the principle of integration and interrelationship, in particular in relation to human rights and social, economic and environmental objectives.

---

[51] See Boyle & Freestone, *supra* note 43.

[52] Rio Declaration, *supra* note 46 at chapter 5, which states: "All States and all people shall cooperate in the essential task of eradicating poverty as an indispensable requirement for sustainable development, in order to decrease the disparities in standards of living and better meet the needs of the majority of the people of the world."

[53] International Law Association, *New Delhi Declaration of Principles of International Law Relating to Sustainable Development*, Resolution 3/2002, 70th Conference of the International Law Association (April 2002). [*New Delhi Principles*].

The New Delhi Declaration notes that there exists a great need for an international law standpoint on issues of social, economic, financial and environment activities and objectives. It recognizes a further need to improve international law in the area of sustainable development, with an emphasis on both developmental and environmental considerations, in order to acquire a more balanced and comprehensive international law on sustainable development, as called for in Principle 27 of the Rio Declaration and Chapter 39 of *Agenda 21,* as well as in the various resolutions on legal aspects of sustainable development of the International Law Association. Since Rio, various international conventions have been established to address most serious environmental concerns facing the world at present. These include the Basel Convention on the Control of Transboundary Movements of Hazardous Wastes and Their Disposal (in force 1992), the Convention on Biological Diversity (1992) and the U.N. Convention to Combat Desertification (1994). The World Bank's involvement on the Convention on Biological Diversity through the Global Environment Facility, and UN Framework Convention on Climate Change are discussed below.

Sustainable Development Law: A View of World Bank Strategy and Policies

Over the last twenty years, the World Bank has made great strides in its endorsement of sustainable development pathways. The ways in which the Bank aims to help its member countries address environmental challenges to development were recently outlined in its Environmental Strategy Paper entitled *Making Sustainable Commitments*, published July 12, 2002.[54] The strategy identifies three main objectives: (1) improving the quality of life, (2) improving the quality of growth, and (3) improving the quality of global commons.[55]

The first objective, that of improving the quality of life, is targeted to (i) reduce environmental health risks by reducing people's exposure to environmental hazards; (ii) enhance the livelihood of the poor by helping them secure access to resources and sustainable use thereof; and (iii) reduce people's vulnerability to environmental risks such as natural disasters and climate change by providing information and access to information.[56]

The second objective, that of improving the quality of growth, includes the promotion of better policy, regulatory, and institutional frameworks, including the strengthening of safeguard systems and practices in member countries as well as within the Bank itself.[57] With regard to its internal practice, for example, the World Bank seeks to ensure that environmental goals are incorporated into

---

[54] World Bank, "Making Sustainable Commitments: An Environment Strategy for the World Bank," (Washington D.C.: World Bank, 2001).
[55] *Ibid.*
[56] *Ibid.*
[57] *Ibid.*

all aspects of Bank operations, rather than limited to the attention of a specialized group of environmental experts.[58]

The World Bank aims to meet the third objective, that of improving the quality of global commons, through a poverty-focused environmental agenda by channeling funds to poorer countries to meet environmental goals through mechanisms such as the Global Environment Facility and the Montreal Protocol.[59] To further the work, Bank staff are presenting and disseminating information on the Bank's environmental and social safeguard policies among client country stakeholders to help raise awareness and develop the policy discussion. The Bank has developed a policy framework to ensure that all its investment projects not only do not harm the environment, but also have beneficial effects in sustainable development.

The World Bank now has ten environmental, social, and international law policies called the "Safeguard Policies." These policies cover Environmental Assessment,[60] Natural Habitats,[61] Forestry,[62] Pest Management,[63] Involuntary Resettlement,[64] Indigenous Peoples,[65] Cultural Property,[66] Safety of Dams,[67] International Waterways,[68] and Projects in Disputed Areas.[69] The Bank's policy on Disclosure of Information is increasingly being grouped with the preceding ten Safeguard Policies.[70] The Bank's Safeguard Policies are obligatory (binding on staff), not merely hortatory (good practice).[71] They apply to all components of Bank-financed projects. All elements of any project receiving Bank financing therefore must comply with these policies, even if the Bank is not the sole or major financier of that project. In addition, the impact of the Safeguard Policies has been broadened by many borrowing countries' incorporation of parts of these policies into national law. The private sector is also increasingly looking to the Bank's Safeguard Policies as a model for its own purposes. Thus, the Bank's Safeguard Policies are providing important benchmarks of good practices whose influence reaches beyond Bank-financed projects.

---

[58] *Ibid.*
[59] *Ibid.*
[60] Environmental Assessment — OP 4.01, January 1999
[61] Natural Habitats — OP 4.04, September 1995
[62] Forestry — OP 4.36, September 1993
[63] Pest Management — OP 4.09, December 1998
[64] Involuntary Resettlement — OP 4.12, December 2001
[65] Indigenous Peoples — OP 4.20, September 1991
[66] Cultural Property — OPN 11.03, September 1986; Draft 4.11
[67] Safety of Dams — OP 4.37, September 1996
[68] International Waterways — OP 7.50, October 1994
[69] Projects in Disputed Areas — OP 7.60, November 1994
[70] Disclosure of Information — BP 17.50, October 1997. In addition to the Safeguard Policies, the World Bank also has Operational Policies in the areas of Operational Strategies, Fiduciary Requirements, Project Analysis and Review Requirements and Internal Processing Documents; See World Bank Operational Policy Reform: Progress Report (CODE 98-13 March, 1998).
[71] See D. Freestone, "Environmental and Social Safeguard Policies of the World Bank and the Evolving Role of the Inspection Panel" in I. Kanami, A. Kiss & D. Shelton, eds. *Economic Globalization and Compliance with International Environmental Agreements* (The Hague: Kluwer Law International, 2002).

The World Bank's Safeguard Policy on Environmental Assessment ("EA") is a prime example of the innovation and impact of the Bank's Safeguard Policies. The EA policy was first published in 1984, as the first environmental policy of the Bank and the first EA requirement of any international financial institution. Notably, this policy explicitly refers to international law in its express prohibition against Bank financing for projects that would contravene the borrowing country's obligations under international environmental law.[72]   In 1992, the Bank's version of the EA requirement was codified as Principle 17 of the Rio Declaration on Environmental Impact Assessments.   The Principle states that the "Environmental Impact Assessment, as a national instrument, shall be undertaken for proposed activities that are likely to have a significant adverse impact on the environment and are subject to a decision of a competent national authority."[73]   The World Bank's EA policy has also been used as a model by other international financial institutions and by national governments.[74]   A recent study of Sub-Saharan Africa, for example, showed that environmental impact assessment legislation partly modeled after the Bank's requirements, and including consultation and disclosure requirements, has now been adopted by twenty-four countries.[75]

Compliance with the Bank's Safeguard Policies and other operational policies is supported by an investigative mechanism, the Inspection Panel.   The Board of Executive Directors of the World Bank approved a Resolution establishing the Inspection Panel in 1993.   The Panel, which exists as an independent entity within the Bank, is comprised of three members appointed by and responsible to the Board who hold office for five-year terms.[76]   The Panel's mandate is to investigate "failure of the Bank to follow its operational policies and procedures with respect to the design, appraisal and/or implementation of a project" where such failure "has had or threatens to have a material adverse effect."[77]   The initial request for inspection may be brought to the Inspection Panel only by project-affected parties (or their representatives) in the territory of the borrowing country or by an Executive Director of the Bank.   The Bank was the first international financial institution to establish such an accountability mechanism to promote compliance with environmental and social safeguards and related operational policies. [78]   Since its establishment in 1993, the Panel

---

[72] See OP 4.01, para. 3, on Environmental Assessment.

[73] Rio Declaration, *supra* note 46 at principle 17.

[74] M. Gehring, *Sustainability Through Process for World Trade Law* (Center for International Sustainable Development Law (CISDL) Legal Brief prepared for the Third Preparatory Committee for World Summit Sustainable Development, New York, 25 March – 5 April 2002. See also M. Gehring and M.C. Cordonier Segger, Sustainable Developments in World Trade Law (The Hague: Kluwer Law International, 2005).

[75] M. A. Bekhechi & J. Mercier, *The Legal and Regulatory Framework for Environmental Impact Assessments: A Study of Selected Countries in Sub-Saharan Africa* (Washington, D.C.: World Bank, 2002).

[76] Resolution No. IBRD 93-10; Resolution No. IDA 93-6; reproduced in I. F. Shihata, The World Bank Inspection Panel: In Practice (New York: Oxford University Press, 2000) at 271.

[77] *Ibid.*.at para. 12 of the Resolution No. IBRD 93-10; Resolution No. IDA 93-6.

[78] D. Freestone, "International Financial Institutions and the Marine Environment: A view from the World Bank" in M. Nordquist, J. N. Moore & S. Mahmoudi, eds. *The Stockholm Declaration and Law of Marine*

has received 26 requests, of which it has registered all but three. To date, the Bank's Executive Directors have authorized seven full inspections.[79]

Sustainable Development: World Bank Activities in the Context of the WSSD

The World Bank's portfolio since 1988 includes about $15 billion in lending for environmental projects (i.e., projects with primary or major environmental objectives). In FY 2000 alone, over forty environmental projects were funded with $1.6 billion from the World Bank and equivalent co-financing. These amounts represent funds that developing countries and countries with economies in transition are borrowing, as loans or credits, for environmental improvement projects. This extensive lending program is supported by the approximately 250 environmental and social experts on the World Bank's staff. The Bank also collaborates with a wide range of partners in the realm of sustainable development. These partners include not only the Bank's member countries, but also other international organizations, private sector partners, and civil society.

The following examples of Bank policies and activities illustrate various ways in which the Bank seeks to further these objectives.

First, the World Bank participates in the Global Environment Facility (GEF). The GEF is the designated "financial mechanism" of two international treaties-the Convention on Biological Diversity and the United Nations Convention on Climate Change (UNFCC). GEF collaborates with other international agreements and treaties such as the Montreal Protocol and the Vienna Convention on Ozone Layer Depleting Substance. It is thus a significant effort to forge global cooperation and to implement global environmental protection.[80] The World Bank serves as Trustee, as well as an Implementing Agency (with UNDP and UNEP), of the GEF. Established in 1991, the GEF operates as a "mechanism for international co-operation for the purposes of providing new and additional grant and concessional financing to meet the

---

Environment: (The Hague: Kluwer Law International, 2003) 119. (Since then, the Inter-American Development Bank and the Asian Development Bank have established similar inspection functions, and the International Finance Corporation has established a Compliance Adviser/Ombudsman's office).

[78] Nepal/Arun III Proposed Hydroelectric Project and Restructuring of IDA Credit; India/NTPC Power Generation Project; China/Western Poverty Reduction Project; Kenya/Lake Victoria Environmental Management Project; Ecuador/ Mining Development and Environmental Control Technical Assistance Project; Chad Petroleum Development Project, Management of the Petroleum Economy Project, Petroleum Sector Management Capacity-Building Project; India Coal Sector Environmental and Social Mitigation Project and Coal Sector Rehabilitation Project.

[80] S. A. Silard, "The Global Environment Facility: A New Development in International Law and Organization." 28 *Geo.Wash. Int'l L.Rev.* 607.

agreed incremental costs of measures to achieve global environmental benefits in the following focal areas: (a) Climate Change; (b) Biological Diversity; (c) International Waters; and (d) Ozone Layer Depletion."[81] Since the Earth Summit in Rio, the World Bank has mobilized more than US$4 billion dollars for GEF to help finance over 1000 projects to enhance global environmental benefits in 160 countries.[82] Total financing for these projects is more than US$16 billion.[83]

In May 2001, the GEF Council agreed to add two new focal areas to the mandate of GEF: New Land Degradation and Persistent Organic Pollutants. In addition, at the seventh session of the Conference of the Parties (COP7) to the UN Framework on Climate Change in Morocco in November 2001, the COP agreed to establish three new funds that would be under the administration of the GEF.[84] These funds primarily deal with technology transfer and mitigation in the sectors of energy, industry and transportation.[85]

Second, the World Bank is host to the Prototype Carbon Fund (PCF). To provide assistance in the implementation of the UNFCC and the Kyoto Protocol, the Bank established the Prototype Carbon Fund ("PCF") a multi-donor trust fund by a World Bank Resolution on July 20, 1999.[86] By 2001, the size of the PCF had reached US$145 million with contributions from both governments and private donors.[87] These contributions are used to purchase greenhouse gas emission reductions which are designed to be in compliance with the evolving regulatory framework of the Kyoto Protocol project-based mechanisms, namely Joint Implementation (JI) and the Clean Development Mechanism (CDM).[88] Alleviating the crippling effects of climate change on poorer countries will require private as well as public investment. Efficient market-based mechanisms are crucial to lowering the costs of climate change mitigation and to channeling private capital to cleaner technologies and more

---

[81] GEF Instrument, para. 2. Note that para. 3 reads: "The agreed incremental costs of activities concerning land degradation, primarily desertification and deforestation as they relate to the four focal areas shall be eligible for funding."

[82] *Supra* note 54.

[83] *Ibid.*

[84] *Ibid.*

[85] *Ibid.*

[86] Resolution 99-1 authorizing the establishment of PCF, approved by the Executive Directors of the International Bank for Reconstruction and Development (IBRD).

[87] Governments include: Canada, Finland, Japan, the Netherlands, Norway and Sweden. Private Investors include: Japanese electric power companies of Tokyo, Chubu, Chugoku, Kyushu, Shikoku, and Tohoku; the trading houses Mitsubishi and Mitsui; BP Amoco from the United Kingdom; Deutsche Bank and RWE from Germany; Electrabel from Belgium; Gaz de France from France; and Norsk Hydro and Statoil from Norway, Fortum of Finland and Rabobank (through Gilde Strategic Situations BV) from the Netherlands.

[88] *Kyoto Protocol to the UN Framework Convention on Climate Change*, UN Doc. FCCC/CP/1997/7/Add.2 (1997) at art. 3.1.Under the United Nations Framework Convention on Climate Change (UNFCCC), the Kyoto Protocol contains legally binding commitments to limit or reduce emissions. Under the Protocol, industrialized countries must reduce their emissions by at least 5% below 1990 levels in the period between 2008-2012.

socially and environmentally sustainable development.[89] By the end of 2001, the PCF team had reviewed 130 Project Idea Notes from a range of countries as diverse as Chile, Czech Republic, Latvia, and Uganda. Out of these project ideas, 25 projects have been identified for further development and 19 were eventually approved. The PCF has demonstrated how the flexible mechanisms created by the Kyoto Protocol can work in practice with an innovative partnership among donors, private investors, and governments.[90]

In 2001, the PCF also launched a capacity-building program in partnership with the World Bank Institute (WBI). To date, there have been training workshops in Chile, Honduras, Hungary, and Uganda, aiming to build the capacity of host countries to better understand the emerging carbon market and to design and implement JI and CDM projects effectively.[91]

Third, the World Bank has supported the 1987 Montreal Protocol on Substances that Deplete the Ozone Layer,[92] one of the most comprehensive and successful international environmental agreements to date. After ratification by 29 countries and the EC, representing approximately 82 percent of world consumption of ozone-depleting substances, the Montreal Protocol came into force on January 1, 1989. In 1990, the Parties to the Montreal Protocol established the Multilateral Fund to Implement the Montreal Protocol to provide financial and technical assistance, including the transfer of technology, to developing countries. Article 10 of the London Amendments to the Montreal Protocol details the institutional arrangements in relation to the Multilateral Fund. It is administered by a Secretariat and an Executive Committee, which develops and monitors the implementation of specific operational policies, guidelines and administrative arrangements, including the disbursement of resources, for achieving the objectives of the Multilateral Fund and the Protocol.

In 1991, as the GEF was being established, the World Bank agreed with the United Nations Development Programme (UNDP) and UNEP to assist in implementing what was then the interim Multilateral Fund. In June 1991, the Bank entered into a bilateral Ozone Project Agreement with the Protocol's Executive Committee to manage investment projects with resources that would be transferred from the Multilateral Fund to a newly established Ozone Projects Trust Fund (OTF) (established by the same Resolution of the Board as that which established the GEF).[93] Together with the UNDP, UNEP, and

---

[89] The World Bank Group: Trust Funds Division, *Prototype Carbon Fund TFO23446 Report and Financial Statements* June 30, 2001 (Washington: World Bank, 2001).

[90] See Prototype Carbon Fund, online: PCF < http://prototypecarbonfund.org>.

[91] *Supra* note 54.

[92] For a discussion of the innovative legal methods the Convention and the Protocol has used to keep pace with developments of scientific understanding in this field seeDavid Freestone, "The Road From Rio: International Environmental Law After the Earth Summit" (1994) 6 *J. Envtl. L.* 193.

[93] For commentary, see P. Sand, "Trusts for the Earth; New Financial Mechanisms for International Environmental Protection" in David Freestone & Surya Subedi, eds. *Contemporary Issues in International Law: A*

UNIDO, the World Bank now acts as the implementing agency for operations. The World Bank's Montreal portfolio has over 450 investments in projects with an environmental focus.[94]

Fourth, the World Bank supports the Global Mechanism of the Convention to Combat Desertification. The Convention to Combat Desertification came into force in 1996, and although the World Bank is not a signatory to the Convention to Combat Desertification (CCD) it supports the Convention through many of its programs. In July 2000, the World Bank approved the sum of US $ 2.5 million to the Global Mechanism of the CCD. The objective of this grant was to encourage participation of civil society and the private sector in combating the issue of desertification. In addition, the Bank has been actively promoting various regional efforts to address these issues especially in Sub-Saharan Africa. For example under the Africa Land and Water Initiative, the Bank is coordinating the Integrated Land and Water Management Action Program and activities on the Soil Fertility Initiative for Africa.[95]

Fifth, the World Bank hosts a Critical Ecosystems Partnership Fund. In 2000 the World Bank and the GEF agreed with Conservation International ("CI") to finance a Critical Ecosystems Partnership Fund ("CEPF"). The CEPF is hosted by CI, which now has collaboration and financing from the John D. and Catherine T. MacArthur Foundation and the Government of Japan. The CEPF is designed on the premise that there are a number of critical "hotspots" in the world, which combine high levels of biodiversity with high levels of threat.[96] A strategy designed to preserve global biodiversity should, the CEPF argues, focus attention on these areas as a matter of first priority. These areas often cross national boundaries and are identified by ecosystem type. The CEPF also seeks to ensure that civil society is engaged in conservation efforts in the hotspots.

The CEPF provides funding mainly to NGOs as well as community and grassroots organizations in order to strengthen biodiversity conservation efforts. It seeks to engage all the stakeholders within a "biodiversity hotspot," of which there are currently 25. Although these hotspots include only 1.44 percent of the land surface of the planet, they represent 44 percent of all the plants on Earth.[97] According to conservative data, at least 65 percent of all vascular plants and over 70 percent of the world's birds, mammals, reptiles and amphibians occur within these hotspots.[98] These hotspots are: Tropical Andes,

---

Collection of the Josephine Onoh Memorial Lectures (161-184. The Bank has a specific Operational Policy (OP/BP 10.21) on *Investment Operations Financed by the Multilateral Fund for the implementation of the Montreal Protocol* (November 1993).

[94] *Supra* note 54.

[95] The World Bank, *The World Bank and Agenda 21* (Washington, D.C.: World Bank, 2002).

[96] See Critical Ecosystems Partnership Fund, available online: <http://www.cepf.net/xp/cepf/>.

[97] See generally J. Brunnée & E. Hey, eds., *Yearbook of International Environmental Law*, vol. 11 (Oxford: Oxford University Press, 2000).

[98] *Ibid.*

Sundaland, Mediterranean Basin, Madagascar and Indian Ocean Islands, Indo-Burma, Caribbean, Atlantic Forest Region, Philippines, Cape Floristic Province, Mesoamerica, Brazilian Cerrado, Southwest Australia, Mountains of South Central China, Polynesia/Micronesia, New Caledonia, Choco-Darien/Western Ecuador, Guinean Forests of Western Africa, Western Ghats and Sri Lanka, California Floristic Province, Succulent Karoo, New Zealand, Central Chile, Caucuses, Wallacea, Eastern Arc Mountains and Coastal Forests of Tanzania and Kenya.[99] Current CEPF projects include approved ecosystem profiles for the Atlantic Forest, the Cape Floristic region, Choco-Manabi Corridor (Choco-Darien W. Ecuador) the Philippines, Southern Mesoamerica and Sumatra (Sunderland).

Sixth, a comprehensive WWF/ World Bank Partnership has been established for Forests and Biodiversity. At the Rio+5 Summit in 1997 the World Bank made a commitment to provide support for sustainable forestry goals – namely, support to harness the potential of forests to reduce poverty by integrating forests into the agenda of sustainable development. The Bank has recognized the key role of governance in sustainable forestry, particularly in countries where it works to enhance law enforcement and curb the money-laundering that results from illegal logging.[100] The Bank has also formed partnerships to help maintain forest system biodiversity.

The Bank's Forestry Alliance with the World Wildlife Fund (WWF) is an example of the Bank's efforts to establish sustainable forestry management practices through partnerships with governments, donors and civil society. The WWF/World Bank Forestry Alliance aims to increase global areas of real protected forests in order to reduce "paper parks" and enhance the use of sustainable forestry.[101] The alliance is built on three concepts: (i) harnessing the potential of forests to reduce poverty; (ii) integrating forests into sustainable economic development; and (iii) protecting global forest values. The WWF/World Bank Forestry Alliance has recognized that this strategy must use a multi-tiered and multi-sectoral approach to effectively achieve sustainability and poverty alleviation.

Seventh, the World Bank has assisted by funding environmental projects called the Environmental Management Projects (EMP) which enhance environmental policymaking capacity and procedure in client countries, develop environmental legislation and regulations consistent with principles of sustainable development as defined in international conventions, and strengthen environmental institutions to ensure the implementation and enforcement of domestic laws. For example, the Mexican EMP helped to disperse

---

[99] See CEFP website for a map detailing these hotspots at www.cepf.net.
[100] The World Bank, *Making Sustainable Commitments: An Environment Strategy for the World Bank* (Washington, D.C.: World Bank, 2001).
[101] *Ibid.*

environmental management functions from federal to state and municipal levels, and to convert the federal agency into a higher level policy coordination and quality assurance body.[102] Another was the Benin EMP where the Bank was able to strengthen Benin's Council on Sustainable Development that presides over the implementation and compliance of international environmental conventions. In the Madagascar EMP, the project objectives included conservation and management of Madagascar's biodiversity, promotion of the sustainable development and management of the country's natural resources, improvement of the populations living condition and development of country's human resources and institutional capacity.

The Bank has further assisted countries in designing and implementing environmental projects which have specific regional objectives and promote conservation activities at this level. That included projects ranging from regional seas, lakes, and forest ecosystems. The Ship-Generated Waste Management Project for the Caribbean Countries provided finances to develop and adopt cost recovery legislation including fees on cruise ship passengers and a legislation based on the ratification and effective implementation and enforcement of the International Convention for the Prevention of Pollution from Ships.

Eighth, the World Bank engages in significant sustainable development related capacity building activities. The Bank's natural resource management portfolio is continuously changing from the traditional natural resources management projects to projects that influence institutions and regulatory frameworks that govern the use of natural resources. These projects include strengthening of environmental institutions, environmental support programs, and institutional capacity building for protected areas. The Bank provided help to client countries to develop capacity to undertake environmental assistance of projects, to audit environmental management of existing facilities and to improve capacity to develop and enforce environmental legislation.

Ninth, the World Bank supports National Environmental Action Plans (NEAP). The Bank has assisted many countries to develop NEAP and programs to aid them in defining their environmental priorities and seeking funding from donor agencies. The Bank provided for more than thirty countries such as Cote d'Ivoire, Zambia, Burkina Faso, Algeria, Senegal Cameroon and Chad. The Bank has provided countries with environmental studies and profiles in order to reinforce its environmental policy and dialogue with its member countries including Algeria, Argentina, Brazil, Chile, India, Morocco and Sierra Leon.

---

[102] *Supra* note 95.

Tenth, significant initiatives have been implemented to develop national capacity to conduct environmental impact assessments of development projects and policies, leading to substantial improvements in the implementation of environmental impact assessment (EIA) within countries in Africa, the Middle East, North Africa, and Asia. For example, African EIA Capacity Building Initiative achieved the establishment of regulatory frameworks for EIA in many countries and strengthened regional institutions such as the African Institute for Environmental Assessment (SAIEA).

Conclusion: Opportunities and Challenges for Partnerships

The World Bank has become a key player in assisting countries to implement international conventions and treaties that have resulted since the concept of sustainable development was first embraced by the international community at the 1992 Earth Summit in Rio. The Bank has set benchmarks in the areas of environmental assessment and other safeguard policies, which other international organizations, governments, and private enterprise are now using as examples in their commitment to sustainable development. By increasing its environmental portfolio, the World Bank has also reaffirmed its commitment to environmental protection and sustainable development. Finally, by including a wide array of legal and judicial reform activities in its portfolio, the World Bank is also showing its commitment to furthering good governance and the rule of law, which are necessary prerequisites to equitable and lasting development.

The challenge for the World Bank is to continue strengthening its support for sustainable development through its law and justice portfolio, its environmental portfolio, and its partnerships with the various stakeholders in the process of sustainable development. In all its work, the World Bank seeks the leadership, guidance, and commitment of its member countries in order to effectively promote sustainable development goals and meet the needs of each country, without compromising the ability of future generations to live on this planet.

29

A RIGHTS-BASED APPROACH TO ANALYSING INTERNATIONAL FINANCIAL INSTITUTIONS

*Jorge Daniel Taillant**

This chapter reflects on the human rights implications of the general policy and programs of the principal International Financial Institutions (IFIs) - the World Bank (the Bank)[1] and the International Monetary Fund (the Fund).[2] It focuses particularly on the policy implications of charter mandates of the IFIs, and general program of work, project preparation and development strategies. The chapter articulates practical ways in which the IFIs can constructively incorporate rights-based policies in their lending and assistance programs.

The Establishment of the World Bank and IMF

The Bank and its sister institutions, comprising the World Bank Group, were created with a very specific purpose in mind: to assist in the reconstruction of post-World War II Europe.[3] The Fund's founding purpose was unequivocally targeted to attaining financial stability in the international economic arena, and was largely concerned more with trade balances, exchange rate stability and balance of payments. The Fund was not meant, originally, to focus on reversing underdevelopment. At the time, particularly at the mid-century birth of Bretton Woods, underdevelopment was not the primary concern of the industrialized world; rebuilding *itself* was. Its focus on transition from wartime to peacetime, and the importance assigned to investment, balance of payments, and

---

* Jorge Daniel Taillant, B.A. (U. Cal., Berkeley), M.A. (Georgetown), Executive Director of the Center for Human Rights and Environment (CEDHA), Argentina. This chapter is based on a paper prepared for the 2002 Conference co-hosted by the Centre for International Sustainable Development Law, the United Nations Environment Programme, the World Bank and the International Law Association, Sustainable Justice 2002: Implementing International Sustainable Development Law held in Montreal, Canada from June 13-15, 2002.
[1] Hereinafter "the Bank".
[2] Hereinafter "the Fund or the IMF".
[3] See generally the World Bank Articles of Agreement, online: The World Bank Group <http://web.worldbank.org/WBSITE/EXTERNAL/EXTABOUTUS/0,,contentMDK:20040600~menuP K:34625~pagePK:34542~piPK:36600~theSitePK:29708,00.html>; and the IMF Articles of Agreement (entered into force 27 December 1945), online: The International Monetary Fund <http://www.imf.org/external/pubs/ft/aa/index.htm>.

M.C. Cordonier Segger & C. G. Weeramantry, eds., Sustainable Justice: Reconciling Economic, Social & Environmental Law
© *2005 Koninklijke Brill NV, Printed in The Netherlands, pp.469-478.*

guarantees, is a clear reflection of the reasons behind the creation of the Bretton Woods system.

Since this time, these two institutions, despite their non-development focused mandates, have become two of the most important development institutions in the world. Today they are faced with a very different and interdependent international economy than there existed at their onset, as well as a new set of unavoidable development-related and very urgent issuesfor the health of the world economy requiring international attention and address.[4]

Today, the Bank has been assigned a much broader mandate, and the Bank itself recognizes its "primary focus to be helping the poorest people and the poorest countries."[5] Its "Articles of Agreement", ironically however, makes absolutely no mention of poverty.

While the charters of the Bank and Fund do not make reference to the international developmental issues which are of most concern today, we must not too hastily place these international economic institutions outside of the international context in which they have developed and evolved over time. Further, we must also consider that the Bretton Woods agreements which established the Bank and later the Fund were adopted in communal spirit with, and more or less at the same historical moment as, world leaders gathered to create the United Nations and adopt the Universal Declaration of Human Rights (UDHR). In this respect, the creation of these institutions paved the way for a more cohesive, collaborative and harmonic international development arena. And in this respect, the Bank and Fund must not divorce themselves with the natural progress of the international economic and development dynamics which they help shape.

At the time of the creation of these institutions, it was clear that global leaders considered the Bank and the Fund to be critical institutions upon which to build modern society, which itself was envisioned to be constructed upon the pillars of a new "united" system. The UDHR, in this spirit, attempts to capture every actor in this society under its umbrella. According to the Preamble of the UDHR:

> "Every individual and every organ of society, keeping this Declaration constantly in mind, shall strive by teaching and education to promote respect for these rights and freedoms and by progressive measures, national and international, to secure their universal and effective recognition and observance, both among the

---

[4] See generally A. Sen, *Development as Freedom* (Oxford: Oxford University Press, 1999).
[5] "IMF/World Bank PRSP Comprehensive Review" (3 June 2002), online: Poverty Reduction Strategies and PRSPs Home <http://www.worldbank.org/poverty/strategies/review/index.htm>.

peoples of Member States themselves and among the peoples of territories under their jurisdiction."[6]

As such, it is clear that the IFIs fall under this umbrella.

Reflections on Rights Based Significance of Articles and IFI Agendas:

It is important to consider the significance and relevance that human rights may have (or should have) for IFIs, and whether IFIs should be conducting their programmatic work grounded on a "rights based" framework, or at least to "respect these rights and secure their universal and effective recognition and observance."[7]

The IMF has approached this issue with cautious resistance. It has steadfastly held on to its mandate, which is clearly financial in scope, mainly diverting responsibilities for social development to its sister organization, the Bank, who ironically by its own mandate is just as out of place as the IMF on the issue of development. However, in a context of increasing public scrutiny of its structural adjustment loans and conditionalities, which have a significant impact on policy decisions, the IMF begun to assume *some* responsibility for its subscriptions. It has begun to take hesitant initial steps towards recognizing and addressing its impact on social factors.

The Bank has, meanwhile, and in contrast to the IMF, been more forthcoming in taking on a role as a "development organization" for poor countries, taking several bold development steps beyond its charter mandate. It has developed programs on poverty alleviation, the rule of law, environmental protection, and other issues relevant to both economic and social development, as well as infrastructure development in the world's most needy societies. The Bank has even begun to address rights issues - indigenous peoples' rights, gender equality, and access to education, and also explicitly embraced economic, cultural and social rights. It has emphasized the importance of good governance, the rule of law, independence of the judiciary, freedom of expression, freedom of association, and freedom of the press. In its 1998 report, the Bank states: "The World Bank believes that creating the conditions for the attainment of human rights is a central and irreducible goal of development."[8] It further points out that "without the protection of human and property rights, and a comprehensive framework of laws, no equitable development is possible."[9]

---

[6] *Universal Declaration of Human Rights*, GA Res. 217 (III), UNGAOR, 3d Sess., Supp. No. 13, UN Doc. A/810 (1948), preamble.
[7] *Ibid.*
[8] The International Bank for Reconstruction and Development/The World Bank, *Development and Human Rights: The Role of the World Bank* (Washington; 1998), online: The World Bank <http://www.worldbank.org/html/extdr/rights/>.
[9] *Ibid.*

Despite these developments, both institutions have strongly resisted assuming any responsibility for the assurance or guarantee of human rights. The standard argument centers on their unwillingness to place conditionality on countries for *not* complying with human rights obligations under the treaties they have signed. In other words, they do not wish to become human rights policemen. Obviously, countries like China are vehemently opposed to international development institutions discussing their human rights record. Clearly, their fear is the potentially adverse impact on their international trade, due to the risk of suffering trade sanctions for poor human rights records. Human rights, in this respect, is seen by many non-western or underdeveloped nations as merely another weapon wielded by the west (namely the USA and Europe) to hinder free trade and economic progress. This is also the view of many western underdeveloped countries like Argentina and Brazil, which refuse to speak of human rights in forums such as the WTO and other regional trade organizations, claiming that this is just another way for the US and Europe to gain an upper hand in competition, or to protect market access.

The rights-based development discussion has also turned towards debating whether IFIs should or should not police human rights, suggesting that given that international human rights grant individuals entitlements, subsequently, others (namely states) have obligations to ensure such entitlements. Framing the discussion in these terms has unfortunately led to widespread resistance to the rights based debate on the part of the IFIs, and has raised the risk that these institutions will reject the rights-based approach altogether for fear of having to assume policing duties. The debate need not have gone down this path.

Responsibility of IFIs (beyond Articles of Agreement)

The IFIs, however resistant they may be to address human rights, cannot divorce themselves from ever-growing international pressures to bring development issues towards the attainment of basic human dignity, which in essence has much to do with the a human rights-based approach to development. While international political debate was focused on civil and political rights during the cold war years, the end of that era, and the steady disappearance of dictatorial regimes have turned international attention to the realization of economic, cultural and social (ESC) rights. The International Covenant on Economic, Social and Cultural Rights, which came into force in 1976, outlines the basic human rights deriving from the inherent dignity of the human person. These include the right to self-determination, fair remuneration, social security, food, education, health, culture, and an adequate standard of living. Since their adoption however, these rights have been largely overlooked, mainly due to the lack of political will. Civil and political rights were first on the agenda, as western democratic societies placed these rights far and above rights focusing on basic human dignity. Further, the realization of ESC rights in a largely unequal global society suggested that attaining such rights for all would be no easy task. Yet, the fall of communism and the reduction in the number of dictatorships, as well as the unequal distribution of wealth, the alarming increase in global poverty, and concerns over global health have allowed ESC rights to surface to the forefront of the development agenda.

IFIs have also recognized that striving for universal education and access to health for example are in fact reasonable, worthwhile targets and certainly within the scope of their work programs, even if their articles of agreement do not specifically mandate such program activity and policy design. Indeed, James Wolfenson -who has steered the Bank in directions yet unexplored- has collaborated with UN Agencies such as the High Commission for Human Rights, and suggested that a rights based approach for development is not far off on the agenda.

Still, IFIs generally stand cautiously behind their Articles of Agreements, arguing that their role as development organizations is limited to what is outlined in these mandates, and that to step beyond these limits would be unwise. Some critics feel that the concept of non-intervention in political affairs is held up highly by IFIs and used conveniently when it best suits the IFIs to do so, while it is totally ignored when it serves the immediate interests of force-feeding IFI policy onto governments. In this respect, there is at least a moral obligation on institutions like the Fund and the Bank to be consistent with their own actions, and accept that they have, in practice, a much broader scope and impact than their charters would suggest.

Poverty Reduction Strategies

The Bank and Fund's concerted latest attempt to address global poverty is summed up in an instrument and process that began in 1999, and which is called Poverty Reduction Strategy Papers (or PRSPs). A PRSP is essentially an outline of a country strategy, or program, aimed at reducing poverty in the poorest country members[10] of the Bank and the IMF. A key characteristic of the PRSP is that it is supposed to be a country-owned process. The Bank has over the last several years made an attempt to gain more country participation in the development of its lending portfolio; and, while the extent to which the Bank staff actually drafts entire project proposals may vary between countries, Bank-heavy ownership and design of projects is fairly standard, especially in the poorest of countries where need for development financing is urgent, and the skills, human resources and funding to carry out complex consultations are extremely limited. The PRSP attempts to reverse this tendency.

---

[10] Referred to as IDA countries at the Bank

The PRSP follows a loosely defined process grounded on four core elements that all PRSPs should provide: a) a description of the country's participatory process in the PRSP; b) a poverty diagnosis; c) the establishment of targets, indicators, and monitoring systems; and d) definition of priority public actions. Preliminary results since the launching of the PRSP process two years ago, and according to Bank reviews of the process, have demonstrated several tangible results.[11] These include a growing sense of ownership of government's poverty reduction strategies, as well as some civil society commitment to the process; a more open dialogue with civil society has been attained where PRSPs have been tried; a sense that poverty-related issues have taken on a more prominent place on the development agenda; a donor community that has embraced the PRSP process; a recognition of the need for realism in setting goals and targets, and managing expectations; identification of the need to improve prioritization of policies and programs; recognition of the importance of a transparent process; and prioritization of the aim of long-term poverty reduction.

The Bank strongly stresses the participatory nature of the PRSP process. Effective participation is key to the value and legitimacy of the instrument. The PRSP does not make any attempt to embrace human rights or even use rights-based language in the description of the underlying goals of the exercise. In fact, the target and nature of the PRSP is largely left to the government to determine through, in principle, a participatory process.

The PRSP process is geared to focus on poverty, which is obviously of great concern in the rights-based approach debate. Yet poverty is not discussed from a rights-based perspective. One of the central concerns, from the Bank's perspective, is to gain participatory input from civil society in the formulation of the strategy. However, the Bank has agreed – and with considerable civil society support for the decision- *not* to prescribe how this process is to be encouraged or designed. It is left to each government to determine how participation should take place. The only element that the Bank requests from the government is an explanation as to how participation was carried out in the preparation of the PRSP.

Some issues surface from the Bank's own review of the PRSP process, and from civil society comments on the process. Firstly, the PRSP process is, despite efforts to make this a country-driven process, a Bank-owned initiative: it is designed and launched from within the Bank for countries to carry out. Inasmuch as the participating countries are concerned, it is yet one more procedure that they must comply with in order to be considered for further financing of programs. The Bank itself has concluded that the "incentives

---

[11] International Development Association & IMF, *Review of the Poverty Reduction Strategy Paper (PRSP) Approach: Early Experience with Interim PRSPs and Full PRSPs* (April 2002) at 5, online: The World Bank <http://www.worldbank.org/poverty/strategies/review/earlyexp.pdf>.

provided by the approach have induced governments […] to prepare their strategies too quickly, unduly compromising the quality of the strategies in terms of both technical content and broad-based country ownership."[12] Numerous civil society organizations have complained that their input has been generally ignored by their government.

Secondly, the participatory nature and effectiveness of the process is, by the Bank's own assessment, widely varied. It is also difficult to compare processes in the over 50 cases of PRSPs submitted to the Bank since there is no standard procedure or guidelines as to how participation is to be carried out. The participating country decides how to carry out participation, in what manner and to what degree. Civil society groups have also complained that participation is only on the table for select policies and sectors, and that relatively *no* participation existed in the formulation of broader macro-economic policy.

Thirdly, the Bank's assessment shows that the Ministry of Finance is generally the direct counterpart and interested party in the development of the Bank's programs: "Sectoral ministries are less fully involved than core ministries, such as the Ministry of Finance or the Ministry of Planning."[13]

Fourthly, an important concern related to the PRSP process is the link between policy and outcomes. This issue is key to the present discussion, since rights-based outcomes are central to linking policy and programs to human rights. The best we can hope for in terms of a rights-based approach to IFI programming is that such programs have a clear and positive impact on the attainment of basic levels of human dignity, measuring for improvement in basic human rights indicators, including quality of life, access to education and basic health services.

On a more positive note, the PRSP process has succeeded, in the view of many civil society groups, to bring critical development issues (which are also rights-based issues) such as access to education and health to the forefront of the development debate. Civil and political rights have also appeared on the agenda of several of the experimental PRSPs to date, in addition to concerns over governance and corruption issues.[14]

---

[12]*Ibid.*

[13] *Ibid.*

[14] At least in one case (Bolivia) the strong emphasis on participation actually influenced civil society to work towards implementing national laws on participation.

Considerations for Implementing a Rights-Based Approach to PRSPs

The PRSP is one instrument of the Bank and the Fund that can serve to bring human rights concerns to the IFI agenda. Such an approximation is, however, at present, only indirect since the PRSP in unlikely to make any reference to the objective of attaining human rights. Poverty reduction, by nature, centers on critical human rights issues, such as improving access to education and basic health services which are central to the PRSP process. In this respect we can see basic human rights issues being addressed, at least implicitly, by the PRSP process. The focus on, and the efforts to strengthen participatory mechanisms is certainly a rights-based issue, albeit a procedural right.

There are, however, some areas in which PRSPs, and more generally the Bank and the Fund, can and should seek to take bold steps towards establishing a development framework explicitly committed to realizing universal human rights. Certain examples are discussed below.

First the IFIs can and should play a role in setting targets and establishing indicators. Targets are key to understanding how policies and programs impact on real life situations. Indicators help evaluate the progress that is made towards a specific target. The establishment of targets and development of indicators should be inspired by universal human rights. This would not in anyway classify the Bank or the Fund as human rights policemen, but rather it would help orient IFI projects towards addressing basic human rights concerns.

Second, the IFIs can support and stimulate more research on the relationship between policies and outcomes with respect to their impact on human rights. Third, the Bank and other IFIs, generally, should seek greater input and collaboration from other UN Agencies, such as the Office of the High Commission for Human Rights, the International Labor Organization and the World Health Organization. Collaboration technical assistance and capacity building between agencies would help introduce critical human rights issues into the development agenda of the IFIs.

Fourth, at present, the Bank relies on the judgment of its staff to determine what the targets should be, without always being able to ensure proper expertise or understanding of basic rights issues. Bank staff should receive training on human rights and on the implications of Bank policies on the attainment (or not) of universal human rights.

Finally, with regards to public participation, more effort is needed to ensure real and effective participation. This is true at the national level as well as at the international level, where civil society input in the design and preparatory phase (ex-ante) of IFI projects is more valuable than the present process of ex-post review of projects. IFIs should make it part of the evaluation process to consult with civil society groups on each of their supervisory missions.

Conclusions

The United Nations recently initiated a discussion on the incorporation of human rights into the work of all agencies of the UN. A paper was commissioned to study the relationship between human rights and poverty reduction, and specifically the PRSP process.[15] The paper calls upon developed countries to take into account international human rights obligations in relation to international assistance; take measures to ensure coherent and consistent application of these obligations across their international policy-making processes; support human rights-related development projects and help developing states to fulfill their core obligations; ensure that commercial activities for which the state has direct responsibility conform to international human rights standards; and take reasonable measures to ensure that the overseas operations of companies headquartered in their jurisdiction are respectful of the international human rights obligations of both home and host states. We are seeing a general trend in the development arena towards human rights streamlining, compliance and promotion. The IFI agenda has already begun this debate and will undoubtedly, have to move in this direction.

This chapter highlights the shared responsibility and feasibility of IFIs in the human rights arena. IFIs should not be thought of as policemen of human rights treaties, but rather as promoters of the realization of universal human rights, a task which they are more than prepared to undertake. What is left is merely political commitment to take this bold step.

---

[15] P. Hunt, M. Nowak & S. Osmani, *Draft Guidelines: A Human Rights Approach to Poverty Reduction Strategies* (Geneva: OHCHR, 2002). For review in 2003. See also P. Hunt, "Relations between the UN Committee on Economic, Social and Cultural Rights and International Financial Institutions", in W. van Genugten *et al*, *World Bank, IMF and Human Rights* (Nijmegen: Wolf Legal Publisher, 2003); B. Lyon, "A Post-Colonial Agenda for the United Nations Committee on Economic, Social and Cultural Rights, (2002) 10 *American University Journal of Gender, Social Policy and Law* 535. And see Poverty and the International Covenant on Economic, Social and Cultural Rights (Statement adopted on 4 May 2001) Committee on Economic, Social and Cultural Rights, E/2002/22-E/C.12/2001/17), ANNEX VII. And see L. Gibbons, "UNICEF's Rights-Based Approach and PRSPs: Experiences, Synergies and Tensions" Paper presented to UNICEF, World Vision & World Bank Conference, Democratising Development: Deepening Social Accountability through PRSPs (25 September 2002).

30

PROMOTING SUSTAINABLE LIVELIHOODS AND CONFLICT PREVENTION THROUGH LEGAL AND JUDICIAL REFORM

Ashfaq Khalfan[1]

This chapter examines, from a sustainable livelihoods approach, the links that exist between weak legal and judicial arrangements, conflict and security, and the lack of public confidence in the state. In light of the implications of these links, this chapter identifies preliminary research needs and provides initial policy recommendations for development agencies.

These inter-twined issues are important to address, as a means to prevent the likely occurrence of conflict or social breakdown in fragile states, to ensure that post-conflict states establish measures that can build public confidence in the state, and to generate 'buy-in' from diverse communities so as to ensure a sustainable transition from conflict.

Legal and judicial reform work is becoming prominent and necessary in development work globally. However, overseas development agencies often have few policy guidelines on these issues. They usually preferred to invest on a project by project basis, whenever it appeared that national expertise had a good fit with a certain developing country's legal and judicial contexts. However, it becomes appropriate, as legal and judicial reform is increasingly recognised as a key determinant for the success and sustainability of development efforts, to shift from a project-by-project approach to a more comprehensive strategy guided by policy.

[1] Ashfaq Khalfan, B.A (Hons.), B.C.L., LL.B. (McGill), Director, Centre for International Sustainable Development Law (CISDL), Programme Director, Water Rights, Center on Housing Rights and Evictions (COHRE). This chapter is based on legal research that was conducted for the Canadian International Development Agency, on related topics. The author would like to thank Naresh Singh and Mark Berman, CIDA, Sumudu Atapattu and Debbie Locker, CISDL, and Thea Herman, former Head of International Cooperation of the Canadian Department of Justice, for their intellectual contributions.

Background: Legal and judicial systems, the sustainable livelihoods approach and links to conflict prevention

Legal and judicial systems

The term 'legal and judicial system' as defined in this chapter refers to the regime of institutions which address legal claims, such as courts and their judicial system, human rights commissions, ombudsman institutions, and unofficial dispute settlement systems (community institutions). It is not used to describe institutions primarily related to the executive or legislative system.

 In 2001, the Organization for Economic Cooperation and Development's (OECD) Development Assistance Committee Guidelines on Helping Prevent Violent Conflict (referred to as The DAC Guidelines) stated: "A predictable and reliable legal system is an essential factor for democratization, governance and human rights. The absence of a fair justice system can trigger frustrations which impede peace-building and conflict prevention. A justice system perceived as unpredictable, inaccessible and arbitrary can trigger resistance within society, as well as confrontation and repression by the state".[2] This policy guidance is reflected in the outcomes of the 2002 Johannesburg Declaration of the World Summit for Sustainable Development (WSSD), which states "Good governance within each country and at the international level is essential for sustainable development. At the domestic level, sound environmental, social and economic policies, democratic institutions responsive to the needs of the people, the rule of law, anti-corruption measures, gender equality and an enabling environment for investment are the basis for sustainable development."[3]

The DAC Guidelines[4] indicate that the failures of a legal and judicial system can cause conflict. Arguably, they do not adequately acknowledge the distinct role played by such systems – which includes the resolution of particular forms of conflict, where political systems could be unsuccessful. Strong courts that are autonomous, seen as legitimate and which are willing to address distributional issues can make a difference. One example is the Supreme Court of India, which has passed judgement on contentious disputes over water rights between Indian states, or the Belgian Constitutional Court – which can address complaints of minority rights violations referred to it by a group of parliamentarians from any particular ethnic group (known as the 'alarm bell'

---

[2] Development Assistance Committee, *DAC Guidelines on Conflict, Peace and Development Co-operation* (Paris: Organisation for Economic Cooperation and Development, 1997) at 117. See also *ibid.* at 57 (All references are to the 2001 supplemented version of the Guidelines) [*DAC Guidelines*].
[3] *Report of the World Summit on Sustainable Development Johannesburg,* UN Doc. A/CONF.199/20 (2002) 4 [*Johannesburg Declaration*].
[4] *DAC Guidelines, supra* note 2.

procedure).[5] The legal and judicial system represents one of the primary means in which politically and or economically dis-empowered groups can seek redress and restitution of their rights.

Requirements of the legal and judicial system

A 1997 CIDA study carried out by Stephen Toope elaborated elements of the role of the legal and judicial system. In summary, these include articulation, formulation and drafting of rules; application and interpretation of rules; the provision of legal representation and advice and the promotion of public access.[6] Characteristics, or 'factors' in an effective judicial and legal system, it was found, can include: accountability – a system subject to external evaluation and criticism; anti-corruption; efficacy; equality under the law; equality of access; internal value preferences - openness and transparency, fairness, consistence, predictability; legitimacy (indigenous support); non-retroactivity of rules; stability but flexibility; and timeliness and understandable and reasonable parameters for the legal system."[7]

A number of other required factors can be added to the above, particularly in the context of conflict prevention. First, much can be gained by taking pro-active steps to ensure access to justice for communities living in poverty, internally displaced people and minority communities. This requires the legal and judicial system to address systemic issues rather than to rely solely on the complaints of those able to access the official system. Examples of such action by judicial mechanisms include the establishment of commissions of inquiry by courts subsequent to a judgment on an individual case (India), and development of legal aid systems for criminal and civil issues.

Second, much can be done through the establishment of non-judicial mechanisms for redress. A growing number of countries are establishing institutions such as human rights commissions which accept (or even solicit) complaints at no cost, have a strong investigative capacity and are able to monitor human rights violations and other complaints on a continuous basis.[8] These institutions are a primary means to ensure access to justice, and can extend the reach of the legal and judicial system.[9]

---

[5] A similar system exists in South Tyrol, Italy. The decision of the Canadian Supreme Court in the *Reference re Secession of Quebec* [1998] 2 S.C.R. 217 has developed international fame as an example of a court decision that has addressed disputes between various levels of government in a manner that received broad acceptance.

[6] Stephen J. Toope, "Programming in Legal and Judicial Reform: An Analytical Framework for CIDA Engagement" (Ottawa: CIDA, 1997). Toope provides further discussion of these issues in "Legal and Judicial Reform through Development Assistance: Some Lessons" (2003) 48 *McGill L. J.* 3.

[7] *Ibid.*

[8] 'Other' complaints can include complaints of inefficiency or arbitrariness on the part of government officials – actions that may not constitute a 'human rights' violation. It is normally Ombudsman institutions that address such complaints.

[9] These types of institutions are recommended in the *DAC Guidelines, supra* note 2 at 52 (the potential benefit of such institutions was indicated when the Constitutional Court of South Africa asked the country's national human rights commission to monitor the implementation of its decision on housing rights). See also *The*

Third, the overall transparency and accountability of the judicial system is crucial. The judicial system, the primary guardian over the legislature and executive, requires its own checks and balances. These can be promoted by addressing issues of appointment of members, and the establishment of judicial services commissions, as well as through technical matters such as adequate training, and the development of reporting systems.

Fourth, it is useful to have an effective civil society presence in (or alongside) legal and judicial systems. Civil society can catalyze and support the legal and judicial system. It can act as a watchdog and monitor the implementation of government commitments, or signal non-compliance by other actors. Civil society groups use a variety of tools in order to carry out these actions, ranging from public interest litigation to research and advocacy, to social mobilization.

Fifth, attention must be paid to the enforceability of decisions. Particular issues relate to the control of legal and judicial systems over military and security forces. As noted by the DAC Guidelines, efforts to strengthen the rule of law and respect for human rights should include requiring institutions to formulate and interpret the law as much as those who implement and enforce it.[10] This requirement should lead to the careful consideration of the contentious issue of utilising development assistance for security sector reform.[11]

The above characteristics indicate, first, the utility of the legal and judicial system in resolving social conflicts and, second, that there are significant degrees of qualitative prerequisites in order for these systems to play their role. Countries in which such institutions do not exist, are ineffective, or subordinate to the government, will find inter-group conflicts pressed onto the political plane, potentially overloading such institutions. As such, it is necessary to carry out legal and judicial reform in a manner that recognises the particular contribution of such institutions to the prevention and resolution of conflict, and therefore utilise a conflict lense in implementing such changes.

Sustainable Livelihoods

As noted by the United Nations Secretary General, good governance is possibly the most important factor in eradicating poverty and promoting development.[12] Sustainable livelihoods are both a goal of development, and an approach to it. Many states have recently accepted the need for sustainable livelihoods and the

---

Government of the Republic of South Africa and Others v Grootboom and Others, 2000 (11) BCLR 1160 (CC), further discussed in the case study on South Africa.

[10] *DAC Guidelines*, supra note 2 at 115.

[11] *DAC Guidelines*, supra note 2 at 40 (the *DAC Guidelines* implicitly lament the fact that ODA eligibility does not yet extend to civilian oversight of defence and military issues and sectors).

[12] Quoted in UNDP, *Human Development Report 2002* (Oxford: UNDP, Oxford University Press, 2002) at 51.

insights of its approach (or elements of it).[13] A sustainable livelihoods approach to governance requires a specific focus on the poorest and most marginalised communities.

The sustainable livelihoods approach is characteristic of a broad shift in the manner in which poverty eradication is being approached by decision-makers. Although development thinking on poverty has historically focused primarily on income poverty, there is growing consensus on broader conceptions of poverty. These include aspects such as "lack of productive resources sufficient to ensure sustainable livelihoods ... unsafe environments, and social discrimination and exclusion... a lack of participation in decision-making and in civil, social and cultural life."[14] The sustainable livelihoods approach moves the focus of poverty eradication strategies away from the 'needs' of the poor and towards their energies, talents, knowledge and adaptive strategies. It is less concerned with 'jobs' and instead draws attention to the 'livelihoods' of the poor, often in the context of severe environmental degradation.[15]

From the viewpoint of governance, the sustainable livelihoods approach is not intended to leave the poor to fend for themselves. Indeed, the poor have a human right to seek state policies and assistance, and that this right consists of more than not to be marginalized; it consists in the opportunity to pursue a livelihood.[16] External interventions are appropriate if they build on the social, human and natural capital of the poor, so as to render them more sustainable and more productive. A critical aspect of sustainable livelihoods is the

---

[13] 2002 Johannesburg Plan of Implementation, in Report of the World Summit on Sustainable Development, Johannesburg, South Africa, August 26 to Sept 4, 2002, A/CONF.199/L.1. In Chapter II on Poverty Eradication, at para 10 governments agree to "strengthen the contribution of industrial development to poverty eradication and sustainable natural resource management." This includes actions at all levels to: "c) Promote the development of micro, small and medium-sized enterprises, including by means of training, education and skills enhancement, with a special focus on agro-industry as a provider of livelihoods for rural communities; d) Provide financial and technological support, as appropriate, to rural communities of developing countries to enable them to benefit from safe and sustainable livelihood opportunities in small-scale mining ventures;" and "f) Provide support for natural resource management for creative sustainable livelihoods for the poor." In addition, at para. 40, governments recommend to "i) Adopt policies and implement laws that guarantee well defined and enforceable land and water use rights and promote the legal security of tenure, recognizing the existence of difference national laws and/or systems of land access and tenure, and provide technical and financial assistance to developing countries as well as countries with economies in transition that are undertaking land tenure reform in order to enhance sustainable livelihoods." And at para. 42, governments agree to d) implement programmes to promote diversification and traditional mountain economies, sustainable livelihoods and small-scale production systems, including specific training programmes and better access to national and international markets, communications and transport planning, taking into account the particular sensitivity of mountains."

[14] World Summit for Social Development (1995) UN World Summit for Social Development, U.N. Doc. A/CONF.166/9 (1995), at para. 9, (Programme of Action, Chapter II (Eradication of Poverty). Poverty has been more recently defined by the UN Committee on Economic, Social and Cultural Rights as "[A] human condition characterized by sustained or chronic deprivation of the resources, capabilities, choices, security and power necessary for the enjoyment of an adequate standard of living and other civil, cultural, economic, political and social rights." *Poverty and the International Covenant on Economic, Social and Cultural Rights,* UN ESCOR, 2001, UN Doc. E/C.12/2001/10 at para. 8.

[15] Kristin Helmore & Naresh Singh, *Sustainable Livelihoods: Building on the Wealth of the Poor* (Bloomfield: Kumarian, 2001) at 1-4.

[16] *Ibid.* at 85.

participation and empowerment of the poor.[17]   In turn, this requires states and international agencies to transfer power to communities, in order for them to generate self-reliant economies and community moneys, to collectively participate in the management of their natural resources and to create inclusionary local governance (through mechanisms such as participatory budgeting).[18]

There are also macro-level requirements of good governance. These include: fiscal prudence, pro-poor policies and participatory formulation of policies and services to support sustainable livelihoods (examples include: health, education, infrastructure, applied technological research and extension services, credit and grants for income-generation, and grants for risk-reduction projects).[19]

Given the focus of the sustainable livelihoods approach to poverty and environmental issues, it is normally not addressed in the same context as legal and judicial reform or conflict prevention. Yet there are clear and recursive linkages between these sectors. The sustainable livelihoods approach re-focuses debates on community governance and the extent to which the state (and international donors) can take a facilitative but empowering role. State inputs and regulations required to ensure sustainable livelihoods should be provided for and regulated by the legal and judicial system. This is significant, as the poor are in a weaker position to claim their rights to such state facilitation and assistance, and to protect themselves against incursions on their livelihoods.

Efforts in legal and judicial reform are moving in this direction. They have grappled with issues such as how to expand access to justice, what is the role of alternate dispute resolution systems and how these mesh with traditional dispute resolution mechanisms. They also address concerns with how to ensure compliance with international standards and the question of how to integrate indigenous peoples governance systems without rendering these static.[20]

Conflict prevention efforts need to be taken into account within the sustainable livelihoods approach. The recursive relationship makes it necessary to view efforts at poverty eradication from a 'conflict lens.' For example, the Three Thousand houses project in Eastern Sri Lanka, allocated social housing in equal number between the three major communities in the area (Tamil, Muslim, and Sinhalese, who were of roughly equal population), rather than on a the basis of greatest need.[21] This decision was made because of acute inter-communal sensitivities in the area. Although this measure was controversial, it was

---

[17] *Ibid* at 9.
[18] Society for International Development (SID), *Building New Coalitions around the Sustainable Livelihoods Approach: A SID-UNDP International Workshop* (Rome: SID, 2000) at 5.
[19] Helmore & Singh, *supra* note 15 at 54-55, 67-68.
[20] These are listed in the *DAC Guidelines*, *supra* note 2 at 118 and 120-121. See also International Council on Human Rights Policy, *Local Perspectives: Foreign Aid to the Justice Sector* (Geneva: ICHRP, 2003) at 60.
[21] *DAC Guidelines*, *supra* note 2 at 31.

necessary and indicates the results of integrating a conflict lens into development.

Highlights of a Case Study on South African Legal and Judicial Reform

In the post-apartheid years, the social fabric of South Africa has been unravelled by abject poverty, AIDS/HIV pandemic and high crime rates. Compounding this state of affairs is the existence of weak legal, judicial and institutional arrangements that led to low public confidence in the State.

A number of donor interventions have been prominent in the South African legal and judicial system. One of the most prominent actions has been support for the South African Truth and Reconciliation Commission, which played a prominent role in resolving post-conflict issues. Donors have also provided support for building a Network of Independent Monitors, crisis intervention facilities and paralegal assistance. Such programmes have been buttressed by mediation activities, training courses and public awareness campaigns to reduce violence and help those affected by violence.[22]

This case study focused on a particular kind of assistance that has addressed a number of concerns considered in the main paper, namely the using the legal and judicial institutions to pro-actively foster conflict prevention and support for sustainable livelihoods.

The 1996 South African Constitution was developed with significant external support –in the form of expert and technical advice- and that, in addition to the extensive participation of the population in the formulation of the Constitution. The Constitution is notable for its inclusion of socio- economic rights provisions, designed to address social and economic imbalances created under apartheid. The Constitution is also notable for setting out a significant level of decentralisation.[23]

Constitutional litigation in South Africa has effectively addressed significant issues of resource disparities. For example, the *Grootboom* decision of the Constitutional Court recognised and implemented the right of homeless persons to emergency assistance from the state.[24] The decision required the state to re-direct a portion of its housing welfare spending to the most urgent cases of need. The decision has been implemented by the government, and indeed, a portion of the budget of the national housing authority is set aside for emergency assistance – known as the 'Grootboom' allocation.[25] In 2003, in the

---

[22] OECD, *Peacebuilding Fund Approved Projects* (1997-1999) (Paris: OECD, 2000).

[23] For an analysis of the political claims of the constitution see K. Klare, "Legal Culture and Transformative Constitutionalism" (1998) 14 *S.A. J.H. R.* 146.

[24] *The Government of the Republic of South Africa and Others v Grootboom and Others*, 2000(11) BCLR 1160 (CC).

[25] Presentation by Geoff Budlender of the Legal Resources Centre (South Africa), who helped litigate the case. November 2002: Canadian Department of Foreign Affairs Seminar on Economic, Social and Cultural

Richtersveld case,[26] the Constitutional Court ruled in favour of the recognition of indigenous land title, a decision which clearly holds promise if juxtaposed to events in Zimbabwe. Indeed, land control is an issue that could spark off conflict in South Africa. The involvement of the Constitutional Court, an institution that has significant legitimacy, an ability to address resource issues such as land and which is racially inclusive[27] could play a positive role in addressing the land question.

Constitutional litigation in South Africa has been carried out by legal non-governmental organisations (NGOs), such as the Legal Resources Centre and the Community Law Centre, which derive considerable financial support from external funders. In addition, they have benefited from technical support from peers in developed states, for example through the Legal Assistance Programme carried out by the Canadian Bar Association with financial support from CIDA. The aim of this project was to strengthen the capacity of the Legal Resources Centre to undertake constitutional litigation and related legal development and research, and to provide support to a regional network of public interest advocacy groups in the Southern African region. The Legal Resources Centre raised a number of issues before the Court, including *Grootboom* above.[28]

The Legal Resources Centre's Constitutional Litigation Unit also provided significant policy advice to the South African government on legislation covering mining, health and safety and environmental protection. An evaluation of this project concludes that the Legal Resources Centre played an important role in ensuring that the government's accountability to the Constitution was real and that it has also contributed significantly 'to the growth of a culture that gives meaning to the term "the supremacy of the Constitution."'[29]

Litigation alone has not always been sufficient to achieve the substantive changes in law required by the most marginalised groups. In the case of access to anti-retroviral drugs, where there was significant resistance from the state, a grassroots campaign was required in order to spur government action. The Treatment Action Campaign began as an organ of civil society responding to the HIV-AIDS pandemic in South Africa. In September 1999, the TAC pressed for the acceleration of government programmes for the prevention of mother-to-child transmission of HIV. The Minister of Health responded that this could

---

Rights. See also interview with Budlender in M. Langford, *Litigating Economic, Social and Cultural Rights: Achievements, Challenges and Strategies* (Geneva: Centre on Housing Rights and Evictions, 2003), online: COHRE <www.cohre.org>.

[26] *Alexhor Ltd. V. Richtersveld Community and others*, (2003) CCT 19/03.

[27] The current court covers a shade of ethnic and political backgrounds, with the result that decision would not be seen to be foregone. It comprises four black justices, four white justices (two of whom, however, are former members of the ANC) and one judge of Asian origin.

[28] C. Plaskett, *Impact Assessment: Canada-South Africa Constitutional Litigation and Legal Development Project, Canadian Bar Association, Legal Resources Centre*, (Ottawa: Canadian Bar Association, 2002) at 15.

[29] *Ibid* at 29.

not be done because of government concerns about, among other things, the safety and efficacy of the drug Nevirapine. TAC mounted a public pressure campaign. The Government made a conciliatory gesture by making the drug available in only two provinces, but public sector doctors could not prescribe the drug (even though government made it available and the manufacturer provided it free of charge throughout the country).

TAC then launched an application ordering the government to give expectant mothers the drug to prevent transmission at birth of HIV. In the *Treatment Action Campaign* case, the High Court ruled in favour of the compulsory provision of the drugs. The Constitutional Court upheld this judgement – in part by pointing to the measures that the government has instituted on a pilot basis in response to civil society pressure.[30] Even then, the victory of the TAC at the High and Constitutional courts was not complete, in that the government still was reluctant to make the drug available. Further litigation and the threat of contempt of court procedures against the Minister of Health were necessary to promote further compliance.[31] It has therefore been argued that the TAC case reveals the inherent limitations of litigation. Success depends upon a strategy, which combines political and legal action. Without the vibrant organization which launched the litigation, it is doubtful that economic, social and cultural rights legislation can be successful.[32] Efforts by civil society to propagate and explain the rights proved necessary in order for marginalised groups to claim their rights – it has been quipped that 'Treatment literally should follow *Treatment Action*.'[33]

Although South African constitutional jurisprudence is young, it is nevertheless possible to state that the investment in constitutional reform and litigation are yielding concrete benefits promoting more sustainable livelihoods and preventing conflicts which otherwise might have spilled over to the political realm, threatening the stability of the state. Support for such programmes should be bolstered with assistance to institutions with a mandate for popular engagement and education.

Issues, Impacts and Policy Recommendations

This section addresses a number of issues regarding the role that legal and judicial institutions can – and should - play in preventing conflict and promoting sustainable livelihoods. It suggests policies that could guide or influence international development programmes.

---

[30] *Minister of Health and Others v Treatment Action Campaign and Others* 2002 (10) BCLR 1033 (CC).
[31] Mark Heywood, "Contempt or Compliance: The TAC case after the Constitutional Court Judgement" in (2003) ESC Rights Review.
[32] See interviews with Mark Heywood and other South African activists in Langford, *Litigating Economic, Social and Cultural Rights, supra* note 25.
[33] This point was made by a Namibian NGO activist at a CIDA Seminar on AIDS and Human Rights, August 2002, Ottawa.

Addressing ethnic and political divisions in legal and judicial reform

Legal and judicial institutions may not render fair decisions or may remain under-utilised due to ethnic divisions. They may also not admit consideration of grievances underlying conflict, either due to restricted mandates or a legal culture that eschews politically charged issues or those that relate to resource allocations. For example, most courts and human rights institutions are unwilling to address social and economic rights grievances, or macro-economic grievances, which may underlie poverty or conflict. Where a source of conflict results stems from the social exclusion of a particular group (e.g. Masai in Kenya) or state efforts to improve the position of a previously disadvantaged group (e.g. Sindhis in Pakistan), most courts or other institutions are unable or unwilling to address such concerns, preferring to leave this issue to the legislature.

The situation described above undermines a potential conflict resolution mechanism and can be a source of grievance. The DAC Guidelines recognise that the combination of majoritarian political institutions and "winner take all" elections can harm prospects of peaceful transitions – particularly if inadequate preparation has occurred. Similar concerns relate to legal and judicial institutions.[34] A primary example is Sri Lanka where substantial state and donor agency efforts have been devoted to strengthening institutions such as the judiciary and the Sri Lankan Human Rights Commission. The bulk of the complaints and cases lodged at these institutions do not come from excluded and marginalized sectors, such as women and ethnic minorities. One explanation for this characteristic is a number of court decisions that have been widely critiqued as being ethnically biased.[35] Alternatively, such groups have appeared to focus on the political process as a means to achieve redress.[36]

This question raises challenges for legal and judicial reform projects. The simplest solution is to carry out training of legal and judicial officials. However, there is a limit to what can be achieved with workshops. A number of further solutions may be identified.

First, support civil society organizations that can be expected to drive the legal and judicial institutions concerned. Civil society groups and coalitions can

---

[34] *DAC Guidelines, supra* note 2 at 56.
[35] The most famous case in this regard was the *In Re The Thirteenth Amendment to the Constitution and the Provincial Councils Bill* [1987] 2 SLR 312 at 382, 364-6, which assessed the need for a popular referendum for the enactment of that amendment to the Constitution, the decisions of four of the nine Supreme Court judges were from a biased, Sinhalese perspective. Justice Wanasundera, whose reasons were supported by three other judges, stated that the Sinhala-Only official language policy had been a major plank in the manifestos of the "leading Sinhala political parties in the country." Justice Wanasundera argued Buddhist relics in the North-Eastern Province would be at the mercy of a Tamil-controlled Provincial Council.
[36] See for a background analysis Ashfaq Khalfan "Constitutional Reform in Sri Lanka and the Protection of Regional and National Minorities" (2001) 165 *Law and Society Trust Review* 1.

activate the institutions and provide pressure for them to address distributional issues, particularly where they include groups with legal capacity as well as pressure groups and social movements. The South African case study indicates examples of an effective institution driven by civil society groups such as the Treatment Action Campaign and Legal Resources Centre.

Second, engage in, and support careful design of legal and judicial institutions, taking into account the need to represent a variety of ethnic and political interests.

Reforms may be required in the design of institutions, through the creation of new institutions or by adapting the mandate and scope of existing institutions. An increasing tendency in efforts to build confidence in the state has included constitutional reform, with public participation and public civil education. Examples include South Africa, Uganda and Kenya. Constitutional reform is of considerable value as it can set out the manner in which property rights, social welfare spending and political representation is structured. Constitutional reform has been promoted in particular as a component of conflict prevention interventions, as indicated by the promulgation of constitutional-type documents in Bosnia-Herzegovina, Northern Ireland and Macedonia as a means to end conflict.

Donor efforts have focused upon ensuring judicial independence, adequate conditions and infrastructure. However, such measures may not be sufficient in situations in which the judiciary is under-representative or under-performing in addressing conflict situations sufficiently. A key challenge – one unresolved even in many developed countries – is the appointment of the judiciary in a manner that ensures adequate representation of key political and ethnic interests in the country. For example, in the South African case study, the South African Judicial Services Commission was established to select the judiciary. The Commission comprises a variety of stakeholders, political parties (including opposition parties), the Bar Association, and other groups.

Third, recognise the limits of legal and judicial institutions in certain contexts and consider alternative means. One option could be to support the development of power-sharing institutions. These may be appropriate in certain contexts if they operate in a manner consistent with non-discrimination and minority rights. Examples include Northern Ireland after 1998, and the first post-apartheid government in South Africa.[37] However, such systems should complement, rather than displace, legal and judicial institutions. Indeed, legal and judicial reforms can develop in parallel to a power-sharing agreement, each form of institution constituting a guarantee for the other. The Good Friday

---

[37] See A. Lijphart, "The Puzzle of Indian Democracy: A Consociational Interpretation" (1996) 90:2 American Political Science Review 258 at 258; A. Reynolds, "A Constitutional Pied Piper: The Northern Irish Good Friday Agreement" (1999-2000) 114: 4 *Political Science Quarterly* 613 at 621.

Agreement in Northern Ireland, which included a power-sharing executive and legislature, also included strong Equality and Human Rights Commissions.[38] A second option is to consider resort to international institutions or arbitration. For example, an international appeal court set up with five Senior Commonwealth judges from Australia, New Zealand and Britain sat in judgement on legality of the Fijian government established after the failure of the coup in Fiji of 2000. The Court ordered new elections, which were held.[39] The DAC Guidelines recognise that regional mechanisms can play such a role in regard to human rights violations.[40] In fact, international mechanisms could play a conflict resolution role in a great variety of situations in addition to those relating to human rights.

It is essential to carefully tailor such arrangements to the context. Horowitz notes: "The search for arrangements to reduce conflict must be premised on the general requirement of a close fit between, on the one hand, constraints and opportunities that derive from the dynamics of the conflict, and, on the other hand, prescriptions to abate the conflict. *A priori* prescriptions will not do."[41] Therefore, such power-sharing mechanisms should consider: the extent to which political parties and factions are shaped on ethnic lines, the permanence of ethnic divisions, the number of ethnic formations,[42] their relative sizes, and traditions of accommodation between various elite leaders.

Approaches to addressing the needs of the poorest in legal and judicial reform

A sustainable livelihoods approach, as discussed in s. 2.3, requires that the legal and judicial system ensure effective governance at the grassroots; including effective mechanisms to settle private disputes, regulation of the actions of State officials, effective implementation of legislation and policy and guarantees that the basic needs of all are provided by the State in a equitable and non-discriminatory manner to the maximum extent permitted by a State's available resources. Comprehensive reform of the legal and judicial system may certainly be to the benefit of the poorest, as it can be expected that law matters more for the poor than the rich, as the latter often have alternative means to protect their interests. However, such a connection is hard to prove, and it is often the case that legal and judicial systems are less accessible to the poorest.[43] Therefore, it is

---

[38] C. McCrudden, "Mainstreaming Equality in the Governance of Northern Ireland" (1999) 22 Fordham Int'l L.J. 1696 at 1755; P. Mageean & M. O'Brien, "From the Margins to the Mainstream: Human Rights and the Good Friday Agreement" (1999) 22 Fordham Int'l L.J. 1499 at 1520-1529.

[39] BBC Online, "Court outlaws Fiji military government," 1 March, 2001. <<http://www.bbc.co.uk>>. The new elected government is composed entirely of ethnic Fijians, in violation of executive power-sharing specified in the Constitution. An appeal to the courts is pending.

[40] *DAC Guidelines, supra* note 2 at 47.

[41] D. Horowitz, *Ethnic Groups in Conflict* (Berkeley: University of California, 1985) at 576.

[42] Exclusion tends to occur over longer periods of time, where there is only a small number of ethnic formations, and is less likely when there are many ethnic formations, allowing the configuration of shifting coalitions.

[43] Toope [2003], above note 6 at 7.

necessary for development agencies to promote a form of legal and judicial reform that is closely targeted to the objectives of poverty eradication.

Legal and judicial reform therefore has to deal with the 'reach' of a system as well as its content. For example, in addressing the situation of squatters who otherwise lack access to land, courts normally address these purely as property disputes, in which legal title is the trump card. Kenyan courts have consistently upheld forced evictions of squatter communities by those with legal title, and have never been utilized as a means to address ethnically-defined disputes between various squatter communities over access to land or rent charges. When they continue unaddressed, or worse, the injustice is buttressed and enforced by legal and judicial institutions, the ability to gain sustainable livelihoods is severely compromised. Such disputes have led to low-level violent conflict in Kenya's informal settlements.[44]

There are examples of courts having played a role in providing justice to those facing poverty. The primary example is the Supreme Court of India, which over the last few decades has passed judgements requiring government bodies to cease discrimination in education against marginalized castes, to ensure appropriate treatment of the mentally disabled and to require hospitals to refrain from withholding emergency medical treatment.[45]

Several policy options can be identified for further development. First, development cooperation can support the establishment of courts or commissions to address resource management and distribution issues, as part of legal and judicial reform. It is not inevitable that disputes over financial resources can only be addressed by parliamentary bodies. India's Finance Commission, composed of five experts, decides on the distribution of resources between states on the basis of principles such as progressive reduction of inequalities between states. South Africa's court system has addressed issues of distribution of resources by addressing issues such as land title of indigenous groups (the Richtersveld case), provision of state assistance to displaced communities (the Grootboom case) and state provision of urgently needed health care (Treatment Action Campaign).[46] In some circumstances, the main reform need is to provide infrastructural support and capacity development to pre-existing commissions whose efficacy is limited by the lack of sufficient State funding.

Second, development cooperation can promote access to information and decision-making and access to justice. Legal and judicial reform in this respect

---

[44] Mwambi Mwasaru, "Human Rights in the Struggle against Poverty: A Case for an Alternative Paradigm, (Mombasa: Ilishe Trust, 2003, forthcoming).
[45] *Paschim Banga Khet Mazdoor Samity and Others* v. *State of Bengal and Another,* (1996) A.I.R. at 2426 (SCC), *Vikram Deo Singh Tomar* v. *State of Bihar,* (1988) Supp. SCC 734 at 736.
[46] These are discussed in the case study on South Africa above.

includes reform of institutions as well as the development of capabilities to *access* such institutions. Corruption and lack of transparency in legal and judicial institutions is a primary challenge. However, even in 'clean' systems, however, there is a need to ensure that the poor are not systematically excluded. Greater access can be fostered by supporting community legal clinic and paralegals or by developing administrative tribunals with simplified procedures that can dispense justice efficaciously.

Community-level justice and dispute resolution systems offer significant promise. Their legitimacy and cultural acceptability, particularly among non-elite communities, enhances their ability to address the needs of the poor. Traditional institutions may have been integrated or linked to the lowest level of the State's governance apparatus. It has therefore been argued that to ensure that justice is accessible to all of the population, there is a need for dynamic legal pluralism. This requires engagement with the different forms of order that exist within communities. At the same time, such institutions may be undemocratic or dominated by men or members of privileged ethnic or social groups. Thus, there may be a need for reform of such institutions, or the establishment of oversight mechanisms.

Public legal education schemes and community clinics that address the most primary concerns of a community can improve the ability of marginalized groups – such as women in family law disputes, tenants and workers – to negotiate for a better livelihood. There is a critique that many public education programmes are too general and do not take account of weak literacy skills of the population.[47] Care needs to taken to ensure that outreach programmes are not too general, and rely on the spoken word (e.g. radio), vernacular languages and, in all cases, in plain language. These programmes should be developed with the participation of constituencies.

In addition to preventing or resolving conflict, civil society organisations can play other important roles. Legal advocacy groups can represent the interests of marginalized communities. The South African case study indicates examples of judicial institutions acting on the basis of competent and innovative cases brought by civil society groups such as the Treatment Action Campaign and Legal Resources Centre. It should be noted that it is entirely appropriate to support advocacy groups that engage in public advocacy as a complement to their engagement with legal and judicial institutions – as noted in the South Africa case study, public pressure coupled with the authority of a court judgement put pressure on the South African government to publicly provide retroviral medicines to prevent mother to child transmission of HIV. Legal aid clinics can address the individual concerns of members of marginalized groups

---

[47] Toope [2003] above note 6 at 44.

and provide legal information in an accessible manner targeted to the needs of such communities.

Third, support constitutional reform and legislative development. Reforms may be required in the design of institutions, through creation of new institutions or by adapting the mandate and scope of existing institutions (such as by permitting an institution to investigate and adjudge on distributional issues by rendering economic and social rights justiciable). There is a legitimate concern that simply writing good laws and Constitutions that are not implemented constitutes a waste of resources, and generates cynicism. Such may be the case where unrealistic and purely aspirational legislation is created. Nevertheless, the content of the law, and the means by which it is interpreted can constitute as much a barrier to justice than cumbersome or expensive procedures.[48] For example, although squatter communities in Kenya gained the support of legal advocacy groups and were able at times to access the judicial system and receive a fair hearing, the *content* of Kenyan laws on land use constituted the barrier to any change. Legislative change can make a difference, particularly if designed in a consultative process involving implementers and beneficiaries.

There continue to exist a number of critical areas in which there are few applicable international norms (or those that exist are vague or under-inclusive), or where international norms do not address governance issues such as the rule of law. Examples include minority rights, indigenous peoples' rights, religion and human rights. While standards exist in relation to minority rights, there are a wide variety of potential and valid options for power-sharing and a number of voting options.[49] In addition, a human rights approach does not provide all the answers to grievances related to discrepancies between resource distribution and ethnicity. If institutions adopt a human rights focus that addresses systemic discrimination, they will tend to support claims for redistribution and affirmative action policies. Institutions that adopt an individualist approach will tend to undermine such efforts. The conflict between these two visions of rights lie at the heart of conflicts in Sri Lanka and Rwanda – where a politically dominant majority sought redistribution of wealth from an economically advanced minority. Similar potential conflicts exist in countries such as Malaysia and Indonesia.

Policy Research Needs for the Involvement of Development Agencies in Legal and Judicial Reform

This chapter has provided a few thoughts to guide a legal and judicial reform initiatives. It now lists a number of research needs in this area. First, there

---

[48] Toope [2003], *supra* note 6 at 21.
[49] See for an overview: Y. Ghai, *Public Participation and Minorities* (London: Minority Rights Group, 2001), available online: < www.mrg.org>.

should be more comprehensive assessment of development agency involvement in institutional reform, the results of improved institutional development, access to justice, identification of potential 'gaps' in programming, leading to recommendations.

Second, it will be important to consider how legal and judicial institutions, particularly those supported by international donors, can ensure increased access for minorities and socially excluded groups. What are the means by which social exclusion is programmed into reform efforts? What are the alternatives in cases where such institutions are non-responsive?

Third, there is more work to be done to evaluate and learn the results of innovative approaches to enhance poverty issues and conflict prevention in institutional reform. How can donors address substance in programming to improve the rule of law? How can it be structured to ensure local participation? How can such work be tied to universal norms?

Fourth, it would be useful to consider the best means to foster increased linkages between legal and judicial reform, poverty reduction and environmental protection (including a sustainable livelihoods approach) and conflict prevention. What is the link between these agendas, and security sector reform? Scholarship in this area may also evaluate whether and where donor programmes in each of these areas are overly segmented, and propose solutions. It should consider best practices from a number of interventions, and how scarce resources could be maximised.

Fifth, more research is needed to define and understand the optimal role of civil society institutions in diverse legal and judicial reform efforts. Much can be gained by a comparative study of the best practices in terms of donor support for these institutions.

Such future scholarship would make an important contribution to the task of ensuring the sustainability, efficacy and legitimacy of legal and judicial reform in developing countries, and of international development cooperation more broadly.

Entry Points for Development Support for Legal and Judicial Reform

This section will consider entry points for development agencies to promote legal and judicial reform of a type that prevents conflict and promotes sustainable livelihoods governance. It considers procedural elements as well as substantive initiatives in planning interventions as a means to strengthen the governance of legal and judicial reform.

It is not suggested that this list of entry points should necessarily constitute the full extent of development agency intervention. There will always be a role for technical assistance, capacity building and institutional development for the legal and judicial system on its own merits. Rather, this list is intended to suggest priorities for intervention, which would guide decisions on which aspects of the legal and judicial system should be dealt with first.

Integrate conflict prevention and poverty eradication/ sustainable livelihoods as targeted objectives for legal and judicial reform

Development agencies working on legal and judicial reform in a particular country can support the development of national objectives as a guiding framework for legal and judicial reform. These should apply international and national goals such as conflict prevention and poverty reduction. Such objectives should be defined in a specific and implementable manner, rather than being simply rhetorical.

This approach would improve on the objectives of most current legal and judicial reform efforts by development agencies. Some institutions, such as the World Bank, focus on establishing legal frameworks in order to facilitate investment and a stable economic environment.[50] The majority of multilateral agencies and development agencies, and the OECD's Development Assistance Committee, have objectives that have more social and political content such as 'promoting the rule of law,' 'promoting human rights and democratisation' or 'improving access to justice,' followed by a list of projects that ameliorate or refurbish the legal and judicial system.[51]

Such objectives are not incorrect given that a well-functioning legal system is fundamental to all aspects of a country's development. However, these objectives may be under-inclusive by neglecting the full potential contribution of the legal system to poverty eradication and conflict prevention. In addition, given a significant array of competing demands for limited resources, a more targeted set of objectives would focus legal and judicial reform on the most critical demands of poverty eradication and conflict prevention. As discussed, such programmes would address critical issues such as the appointment of the

---

[50] World Bank, Legal Department, *The World Bank and Legal Technical Assistance: Initial Lessons*, Policy Research Working Paper No. 1414 (Washington: World Bank, 1995) at 7-8. For example, the World Bank *Legal and Judicial Reform Assessment Manual* (Washington: World Bank, 2002) available online: <www.worldbank.org>, assesses the legal and judicial reform system in isolation from levels and forms of poverty or potential or existing conflict. The indicators it proposes are not disaggregated on gender, regional or ethnic lines, not does it address levels of access by impoverished groups.
[51] For example, OECD, Development Assistance Committee, *Final Report of the Ad Hoc Working Group on Participatory Development and Good Governance: Part 1* (Paris: OECD, 1997) at 10, online: OECD <http://www.oecd.org>.

judiciary, the ability to address social and economic rights claims and creation of new institutions to address the claims of the marginalized.[52]

Invest in coherent national strategies and integrated needs assessments

Legal and judicial reform programmes implemented with donor support should be coherent in preventing and addressing conflict situations, and addressing the needs of the poorest. In addition, the sum of donor supported programmes must make sense in the context of existing institutions, and the social, political and economic context. However, coordination among donors has not been the norm. Cambodia, for example, is notorious for the bitter feuding occurred among donor agencies over whether the country should adopt a common or civil law system.[53] A number of bilateral donors are reluctant to engage in cost-sharing schemes as this would not assist in their objective of raising their profiles.[54]

In a scenario in which there is a plethora of donors acting in the legal and judicial reform sector, there is a need for a single development agency to take responsibility for organising consultations among national authorities, key national stakeholders, other donor agencies and multilateral institutions, with a view to developing a comprehensive national strategy on legal and judicial reform and an evaluation of current reform programmes.[55] National representation at consultations should not be limited to justice ministries, but should also include representation of social services, rural development and environment ministries. A comprehensive strategy must consider the role to be played by non-judicial mechanisms and the role to be played by institutions outside the legal and judicial sector in supporting these initiatives.

A further role for development agencies in this context is to support an independent needs analysis for effective legal and judicial reform policy. Development of a coherent strategy is expensive, but would enhance the overall quality of legal and judicial reform in a particular country. Legal and judicial reform carried out with a conflict lens (and indeed a human rights and gender lens) would have to be contextual and anticipate the grievances that the institution would be expected to address. This raises a challenge for donor agencies by increasingly requiring them to focus on substantive political issues rather than on procedural institutional development. Such intervention could arguably contradict the increasingly accepted principle of national ownership of

---

[52] To avoid a 'straw-man' critique, the OECD definition does refer to the need for equality of treatment, whatever one's social status. However, this concept needs to be pushed a little further in the direction of targeting the access to justice needs of the poorest.

[53] *Local Perspectives: Foreign Aid to the Justice Sector, supra* note 20 at 71.

[54] Toope [2003], *supra* note 6 at 40.

[55] Such an agenda item would virtually guarantee the attendance of the primary donors in a country.

development programmes, as stated in the Monterrey Consensus on Financing for Development.[56]

Heavy intervention, without prior joint legal research and cooperation among experts from donor and recipient countries, would at best, lead to a use of resources that is not directly targeted to primary development goals, and at worst, cause development efforts to negate each other. Linked to the above point is the need for development agencies to develop their own in-country expertise.[57]

Identify and support 'watchdog organisations' for the legal and judicial system

As noted, development agencies can rely on civil society organisations as a key element of an overall reform strategy. Financial assistance can be provided to legal advocacy groups that are representing the interests of marginalized groups where there is a reasonable prospect that such institutions could lead to an equitable solution, or would help generate pressures that could lead to meaningful

In addition, a development agency could also support linkages among civil society organisations cross-nationally, including through financial support for pre-existing networks. A development agency may utilise civil society expertise within its own country, as was the case for the Canadian Bar Association's Legal Assistance Network which worked in South Africa. In many situations, however, development agencies would be better served by supporting collaboration and strategy sharing between civil society organisations in similarly situated developing countries.

Support constitutional reform and legislative development

As noted above, effective legal and judicial reform requires institutional reform that addresses major political concerns related to the distribution of power and resources in a society. Development agencies should support the difficult and resource-intensive process of reform in these areas. This may be done by offering technical assistance, or offering to finance the reform process. In the absence of state cooperation, or where a development agency is acting alone, assistance could be provided to civil society organisations with the capacity to foster a national dialogue on this issue in order to influence national decision-making in this area.

---

[56] See, in particular, *Monterrey Consensus on Financing for Development* UN Doc. A/Conf. 198/11, 22 March 2002 at para 43.
[57] Toope [2003], above note 6 at 28.

Many previous reform efforts have faltered where there have been entrenched interests in the legal and judicial systems opposed to change, or where open procedural mechanisms have not been established. Simply adapting the law may make no difference to marginalized communities. This is particularly so in cases in which there is a lack of judicial independence, widespread corruption and a lack of simplified and inexpensive procedural mechanisms to access such systems.

As discussed below, legitimacy and national ownership is important. For this reason, many reform efforts focus on improving the procedures and efficiency of legal and judicial systems. However, the demands of conflict prevention and addressing the needs of the poorest requires that the substantive laws applicable be addressed. Donor involvement and negotiations with local beneficiaries can be structured on international norms and policy guidance – which would partly constrain the choices available. A study of beneficiary views towards human rights assistance to the justice sector has noted that beneficiaries generally consider that international standards provide a common frame of reference for negotiations and can reduce the perception that the donor is promoting particular foreign policy goals.[58] For example, sustainable development related legal and judicial reform can be carried out with clear reference to guidance provided in the outcomes of the recent 2002 WSSD. A new programme has been led by UNEP and a council of appellate court judges to provide judicial education in the area of environment and sustainable development law. Substance is decided at the multilateral level, informed by the identification of needs by the judges themselves, and Canadian research institutions are cooperating to provide training materials and instructors.[59]

As noted above, international commitments on certain issues, such as affirmative action, may be non-existent or heavily contested. In such circumstances, a development agency should rely on international commitments related to process – such as the need for widespread consultation and inclusion of minority and excluded groups in decision-making.[60] In areas where norms have not been internationally agreed, the role of donor agencies can emphasise a facilitative approach, for example, by providing expertise and sharing best practices. An example was the support for engagement of international lawyers in the development of the South African Constitution. Interventions of this nature could foster horizontal linkages between experts in the field from developing countries and practitioners in the developing country.

---

[58] *Local Perspectives: Foreign Aid to the Justice Sector, supra* note 20 at 85-86.
[59] See *Report of the Global Judges Symposium on Sustainable Development and the Rule of Law* (Nairobi: UNEP, 2002), available online: <www.unep.org>.
[60] See footnotes 7 and 8 above.

There may also be circumstances where a donor has very little to offer in terms of technical expertise, but may yet play a catalytic role. For example, the Canadian Federal Department of Justice has convened seminars for judicial and state officials in Afghanistan on addressing human rights in Islamic Sharia law, in which expertise was provided by lawyers from other Muslim countries.[61]

Finally, donor agencies must be aware of circumstances where reform of legal and judicial institutions alone will not be sufficient, and where reform of the political sphere is instead required, as discussed above. An awareness of such circumstances would allow development agencies to provide detailed early warning to relevant departments in donor governments and international institutions that there is a need for diplomatic intervention. In addition, it would facilitate the development of a conflict prevention or resolution 'package' in which an appropriately designed legal and judicial system will invariably play an important part.

Develop the capacity of decision-makers to address non-traditional legal issues

In certain circumstances, reform is required in 'institutional cultures' rather than institutions in order for legal and judicial institutions to address issues of resource disputes between communities, or the claims of marginalized communities to land and other resources. In all scenarios where legal institutions appear to be in a position to take on a significant role, there is a significant need to develop tools for decision-making, including on issues such as litigation of social and economic rights and resolution of inter-group conflicts, at the state and community level.

Therefore, a new area for development agency intervention is to create linkages between similarly situated decision-makers to work on discrete issues, primarily at regional levels. Development agencies should not rely solely on expertise within their own state, but may wish to draw upon resources from developing countries that have exhibited successes in these areas.

It is necessary to avoid undue optimism about the role that can be played by an underdeveloped or discredited legal and judicial system. The most active judiciaries in developing countries, such as those in India, South Africa and Argentina, are in countries that have sophisticated legal systems and legal traditions that developed over a significant number of years. Where legal and judicial institutions do not have the capacity and tradition of playing an important policy role, such capabilities cannot simply be created in the traditional project cycle.

---

[61] Interview with Thea Herman, Director, International Cooperation Department, Canadian Department of Justice, September 15, 2003.

In addition, judicial training, a common form of external intervention, is not often useful unless it is coordinated with broader reform initiatives. Indeed, it may deflect pressures for more substantial reform.[62] Therefore, development agencies will often have to take a long-term approach, such as supporting sustained training by law faculties and institutions that provide continuing legal education, such as Bar Associations. In circumstances where the judiciary is resistant to change, or adopts a conservative view of the judicial function, donor agencies can recommend and provide support for the creation of new institutions, such as human rights commissions, or expansion of their mandate to include social and economic rights. Such initiatives can create a platform for committed reformers to promote changes in national policies. National human rights commissions, such as in Uganda and Rwanda, have shown themselves to be loci for change, yet often remain under-funded, or are restricted in their mandate.

Develop institutions and programmes that reach the poor

As noted above, it will almost always be necessary to create new subsidiary institutions, or to improve the capacity of marginalized communities to access justice systems. A contextual analysis, and a consideration of the likely impacts, is required before providing support for traditional community based institutions. However, it would generally be inappropriate for development agencies to lobby against the introduction of traditional or religious legal systems, even where negative effects may be expected. Where national governments have decided upon the introduction of such systems, donor intervention could be in the form of support for legislation and training to ensure that international human rights standards are applied by traditional institutions. Support may also be provided for oversight institutions, including appeal systems, over traditional mechanisms. Finally, financial and technical assistance may be provided to civil society groups representing key vulnerable constituencies.[63]

Development agencies can provide assistance to non-judicial institutions, such as human rights commissions or Public Defender Offices that have investigative as well as adjudicative functions. Where possible, development agencies should support programmes by such institutions that aim to identify situations of systemic discrimination and to generate authoritative recommendations for State action. Public legal education by such institutions, or by civil society groups also has promise. However, donors should require, as a condition of support, that the providers of such services explicitly include

---

[62] Toope [2003], *supra* note 6 at 43.
[63] These recommendations may also apply to countries where there is strong pressure for the introduction of courts applying Islamic Shari'a law. Intervention of this nature is less likely to meet the charge of cultural imperialism. Such courts currently exist in many Muslim countries, with their mandate limited to personal law matters such as family law and inheritance.

constituencies in the design of their programmes, and that their proposals reflect a sound analysis of the primary challenges affecting the proposed constituency, as well as a detailed communications plan targeted to the linguistic and literacy profile of the constituency.

From the perspective of a development agencies that have to be strategic in their interventions, there may be many gains from focusing on the 'access' issue. First, it is normally cheaper, as it does not involve large 'bricks and mortar' costs, which are normally left to larger donors.[64] Second, the outcomes are more closely linked to the traditional objectives of development. Such projects may not lead to increased 'profile' in capital cities of recipient countries, however, intervention of this sort is much more likely to lead to success stories. If communicated effectively, such 'stories' can sustain domestic support for development assistance in the donor country.

---

[64] Interview with Thea Herman, *supra* note 61.

(iii)

COMPLIANCE AND DISPUTE SETTLEMENT

31

THE ROLE OF THE INTERNATIONAL COURT OF ENVIRONMENTAL ARBITRATION AND CONCILIATION

Xabier Ezeizabarrena[1]

Environmental rights are a key aspect of the rule of law.

During the second half of the 20th century, increasing development has been observed, either under international or domestic laws, of certain universal ethical, moral and political rules: human rights.

The development of human rights law is demonstrated by the establishment of, for instance, the European Court of Human Rights[2] (ECHR) and its jurisprudence, as well as the provision, in many national constitutions, of systems for an effective judicial protection of these rights. The adoption of a human rights framework to address environmental problems can assist countries and other claimants to discover certain common legal premises, within the framework offered by international sustainable development law.

In theory, these conceptions are well developed. However, in terms of practical implementation and enforcement, many challenges still remain. In particular, subject to a few exceptions, national courts have not yet sufficiently recognised the existence of the required customary or principles of international environmental law necessary for individuals, non-governmental organizations (NGOs) and municipalities to derive claims from the violation of environmental rights.

---

[1] Xabier Ezeizabarrena, M.Sc. (University of Basque Country), Lawyer, Member of the Bar of San Sebastian (Spain) and Staff Lawyer of the International Court of Environmental Arbitration and Conciliation (ICEAC), Assistant Professor, University of the Basque Country Faculty of Law (Administrative and Environmental Law), Member, International Bar Association, Visiting Fellow 2003/04, European Studies Centre, St. Antony´s College, Oxford, Councillor of San Sebastian City Council. This paper is an adapted version of the study published by the Secretary General and the Secretary General Assistant of the ICEAC, Dr. E. Rehbinder & Dr. D. Loperena, "Legal Protection of Environmental Rights: The Role and Experience of the ICEAC" (2001) *Environmental Policy and Law* 6:31.
2 The European Court of Human Rights was established by the *Convention for the Protection of Human Rights and Fundamental Freedoms* (4 November 1950) 213 UNTS 221, Eur. T.S.5, E.C.H.R., available online: <http://www.echr.coe.int>.

M.C. Cordonier Segger & C. G. Weeramantry, eds., Sustainable Justice: Reconciling Economic, Social & Environmental Law
© *2005 Koninklijke Brill NV, Printed in The Netherlands, pp.505-512.*

Judicial Protection of Environmental Rights

Existing mechanisms

The current lack of judicial protection of environmental rights by recourse to national courts is not compensated through the availability of international judicial review. There are various international dispute settlement mechanisms which address environmental issues in specific contexts, such as the International Tribunal for the Law of the Sea, the Court of Justice of the European Community (CJEC) and the above-mentioned ECHR. In addition, there exists an environmental chamber of the International Court of Justice (ICJ), though it has not often been accessed by governments for a variety of reasons. Furthermore, decisions of the World Trade Organization's (WTO) dispute settlement bodies may also affect environmental matters. The Permanent Court of Arbitration (PCA) is also actively working in this field during the last years.

Need for international arbitration and conciliation

One of the main tasks of institutionalised arbitration and conciliation of environmental disputes is to protect the rights of peoples to an adequate environment by granting individuals and non-governmental organisations access to justice. Arbitration could also develop a substantive right to a healthy environment based on existing international human rights, principles previously mentioned, as well as statutory law applicable under the relevant conflicts rules. This would comprise prevention, restitution and compensation of environmental harm. The deficit analysis presented above clearly shows that individuals and NGOs are not adequately protected in international environmental disputes. Their role must be strengthened in order to achieve sustainable development.

The Role of the International Court of Environmental Arbitration and Conciliation

Origin of the court

Expressing concern about the absence of adequate control on compliance by states with international environmental law, Dr. Demetrio Loperena proposed the creation of an International Court of Environmental Arbitration and Conciliation (ICEAC) at the International Congress on Environmental Law held in Cuernavaca, (Mexico) in 1993. Highly welcomed by the participants of the Congress, the proposal sparked a series of discussions among academic experts on the subject, resulting in a call to supporters to convene in Mexico City from the 21st to the 23rd of November, 1994. They agreed to constitute the International Court of Environmental Arbitration and Conciliation as a civil association under Mexican law. During the constitutive session, the Secretary General and the Assistant Secretary General were appointed,[3] the provisional statutes were approved, and a list of experts on environmental law were chosen to become members of the Court. Although this decision was made in the form of a closed list, it remained open to other legal cultures. It was initially formed by professors of 26 different nationalities.[4]

The statutes of the International Court were set forth during three plenary sessions held by the Court. The first of them was held in San Sebastian (Spain) on 19 and 20 July 1995, the second in Mexico and Cancun between 27 November and 4 December 1995, and the last in Nea Epidauros (Greece) on 12 and 13 September 1996.

Meanwhile, thanks to the funding support of the Basque Government and the University of the Basque Country, the administrative office of the Court was set up in San Sebastian, Spain for processing the Court cases. Thus the institution began its operation, which it continues to this day.

Modes of operation

Access to the Court is not limited; parties may be natural or legal persons, public or private, national or international. In particular, the procedure is open to individuals or NGOs who challenge the conformity of administrative decisions taken by states and their subdivisions with applicable law.

In all types of procedures for the resolution of controversies, the Court applies: international treaties of environmental protection; general principles of international environmental law; relevant national law, in accordance with generally accepted rules of private international law and other pertinent rules for conflicts of law; and any other principles, rules or standards which the Court deems relevant, including equity.

---

[3] Dr. Ramón Ojeda and Dr. Demetrio Loperena respectively.
[4] Michael Bothe, Germany. Raúl Brañes †, Mexico. Luis Caeiro Pitta. Portugal. Jorge Caillaux, Peru. Guillermo Cano †, Argentina. Vassili Costopoulos, Greece. Ricardo Cronembold, Bolivia. Deirdre Exell Pirro, Australia. Maryse Grandbois, Canada. Freddy Luis Heinrich Balcázar, Bolivia. Alexander Kiss, France. Oleg Kolbasov †, Russia. Paulo Affonso Leme Machado, Brazil. Demetrio Loperena Rota, Spain. Zdenek Madar, Zcheck Republic. Mateo Magariños †, Uruguay. Susan Mandiberg, USA. Ramón Martín Mateo, Spain. Ramón Ojeda Mestre, Mexico. Miguel Patiño Posse, Colombia. Eduardo Pigretti, Argentina. Zygmunt Plater, USA. Amedeo Postiglione,. Italy. Michel Prieur, France. Rita Raum-Degrève, Luxembourg. Eckard Rehbinder, Germany. Mary Sancy, Belgium. Dinah Shelton, USA. Rafael Valenzuela, Chile. Andrew Waite, United Kingdom. Luis Ricardo Zeledón, Costa Rica. Akio Morishima, Japan. Boraoui Soukeina, Tunisia. Charles Okidi Odidi, Kenya.

The activities of the Court comprise mainly three important procedures: arbitration, conciliation and consultative opinions

The Court may issue consultative opinions in relation to any legal environmental matter of international concern at the request of any kind of entity whether public or private, national or international. The full texts of consultative opinions are available on application to the Secretariat, unless a party applying for an opinion requests otherwise.

The nature of consultative opinions may be divided into three broad categories. First, they may be preventive in nature, in order to ascertain whether a proposed project is compatible with environmental law. They may be confirmatory, to corroborate that an action has been carried out in compliance with environmental law. Lastly, they may be denunciatory in order to enquire whether an action by an individual complies with environmental law; if it is not then the information is made available to the international community.

This chapter argues that there is a need for international arbitration and conciliation on environmental matters. However, the relative success of the Court does not mean that every single petition reaches the final procedural phase. Often, the petitioners abandon their cases. Apart from this, cases have presented two common features to date. First, all public institutions named as defendants have rejected the petitions for conciliation. This is presumably because the defendants enjoy the domestic privilege of compulsory enforcement of administrative acts in their own countries. As a result, they see no reason to take a risk that may paralyse their actions or require action where none has been taken, or is seen to be cost-effective. Secondly, in most cases, the petitioners are citizens or conservationists who lack the economic resources to afford an ordinary procedure of the Court[5].

A Summary of Recent Cases (1994-2001)[6]

Itoiz Case (Spain) (EAS 1/95)

Petition of the ITOIZ Association at the end of 1995 before the ICEAC to request mediation work relating to a dam project in the Pyrenees. This case is now pending before the ECHR and showed at domestic level the lacks of the rule of Law towards the environment within the Spanish context.

---

[5] Therefore in 1998 the General Secretariat established a system of free justice for those petitioners without financial resources (provided that the Court is able to assume the administrative expenses).
[6] The full texts of the Consultative Opinions are available at the website of the Court, available online: <http://iceac.sarenet.es>.

Cerro Largo Case (Uruguay) (EAS OC 1/96)

On the 1st December 1995 the Plenary of the Court admitted the petition for a Consultative Opinion presented by the municipality of the Department of Cerro Largo (Uruguay), with regard to air pollution from a heating plant in a Brazilian town, close to the border of Uruguay.

Zaga Vaca Case (Mexico) (EAS OC 2/96)

Petition of Mr. David Zaga Vaca before the ICEAC for a Consultative Opinion on different grounds with regard to the procedure of separation, packaging, storage, pick up, transportation, treatment and final disposal of hospital wastes, chemical products and general waste, regardless of their risk and registration before the mark and patents authority of Mexico through the Department of Industrial and Intellectual Property.

Barajas Airport Enlargement Case (Spain) (EAS C 1/96)

Petition for conciliation requested in September, 1996 by 14 municipalities of Madrid affected by the enlargement of Barajas airport. The subject of the dispute was the plan by of AENA (Airworthiness Spanish Authority) to build a third runway to allow the airport to increase its operating capacity. In this context, the economic interest of the domestic administrations involved overcame to any environmental interest whatsoever.

Hidalgo Case (Mexico) (EAS C 1/97)

Petition for conciliation before the ICEAC in the matter of the Hidalgo Bridge. The dispute concerns the construction of a motorway connection and a new international bridge between Ciudad Hidalgo and Tecun Uman, (Guatemala) in the north of Ciudad Hidalgo. According to the Town Development Planning of the Centre Town of Ciudad Hidalgo, Suchiate municipality, Chiapas (Mexico), the bridge will be built just three kilometres upstream from the current bridge. It was a clear example of transboundary problems for the efficient enforcement of international environmental law.

Sierra Blanca Case (USA) (EAS OC 6/98)

In July 1998, the Human Rights Commission of the National Political Council of the Mexican Revolutionary Party (PRI) petitioned the ICEAC to issue a Consultative Opinion on the location of a low-level radioactive waste disposal site in Sierra Blanca (Texas, USA).

Sonora Case (Mexico) (EAS OC 7/98)

In August 1998, the General Secretariat of the Court received a petition from Mr. Domingo Gutierrez Mendivil, on behalf of the Sonora Academy of Human Rights (Mexico) for a Consultative Opinion on the transportation and spill of polluted wastes in a particular area close to the U.S.-Mexico border.

Haritzalde Matter (Spain / Basque Government) (MERIDIAN FROG)

The European Office of the Court received a petition from the President of the Haritzalde Ecologist Association, Mr. Xabier Rubio Pilarte, requesting a conciliation procedure for a dispute concerning the meridian frog. The parties to the dispute include: the Association, the Guipuzcoa provincial government and the Basque government. The frog is listed as a "strictly protected fauna species" by the Convention on the Conservation of European Wildlife and Natural Habitats.[7] The Basque Catalogue of Endangered Wild Fauna and Flora, considers it the most endangered amphibian in the Basque Country.[8]

In cases where a request for reconciliation fails, the petition also requests that the Court issue a Consultative Opinion, the grounds and basis of which could be used by a domestic judge to halt works that endanger the species. The work of the ICEAC gave a remarkable legal ground to ease the environmental considerations of the domestic court to assume precautionary measures and enforce EU and international law.

Consultative Opinion (EAS OC 7/99)

In November 1999, "Ecologistas en Acción" requested that the ICEAC initiate a Consultative Opinion procedure in order to study the possible incompatibility of the *Agreement on Trade-Related Aspects of Intellectual Property Rights*[9] of the WTO with certain aspects of intellectual property rights. Of particular concern was article 27.3 (b) of the *Convention on Biological Diversity*[10], particularly article 27.3(b). This case gives a legal answer to a common international problem that is extended worldwide and whose different approaches do not seem to be properly faced by domestic courts.

Non Selective Fisheries Matter (EAS OC 9/00)

During March 1999, the Court received a petition for a Consultative Opinion from the Hondarribia Fishermen's Guild (Spain) and the French-Spanish Association ITSAS GEROA (Sant Jean de Luz). It was regarding the problem

---

[7] *Convention on the Conservation of European Wildlife and Natural Habitat,* 1979, CETS No.: 104 [also known as the Bern Convention].
[8] *Protection of the Meridian Frog,* (2000) Consultative Opinion, H.M.C. Zdenek Madar, EAS CC 9/2000 at I.2.
[9] *Agreement on Trade-Related Aspects of Intellectual Property Rights,* 15 April 1994, *Marrakesh Agreement Establishing the World Trade Organization,* Annex 1C, The Legal Texts: The Results of the Uruguay Round of Multilateral Trade Negotiations 320 (1999), 1869 U.N.T.S. 299, 33 I.L.M. 1197 (1994).
[10] 5 June 1992, 31 I.L.M. 818, 837.

of drift-nets and pelagic trawlers in the European Community and their lawfulness in light of Community and international law. It is an excellent example of the linkages of the three fields of sustainable development. The economic, the social and the environmental pillars are all present in this context, and the case demonstrated the potential for the interpretation of law within the principles of sustainability.

More detailed information on pending cases will only be available once the cases have been concluded and subject to agreement of the parties.[11]

Conclusion

The experience of the *International Court of Environmental Arbitration and Conciliation* shows that from the point of view of concerned individuals and NGOs, there is a need for an international alternative dispute settlement mechanism to deal with environmental conflicts. Of course, given their relationship with individuals and NGOs, states and their subdivisions are reluctant to submit themselves to such adjudication. Still, it can be observed that the international law of the environment has taken several steps forward to strengthen the participation and access to justice of non-state actors. There is still a long way to go before the access of these actors to international adjudication is granted full recognition. In light of its flexible procedure for issuing consultative opinions, its independence and broad scope of legitimacy, the International Court of Environmental Arbitration and Conciliation (ICEAC) clearly offers one helpful international forum for the international independent resolution of environmental disputes. In addition, with regards to human rights and economic development questions, there is potential for further development, as the ICEAC has demonstrated itself ready and willing to assume new roles, and consider environmental and other human rights within the context of an emerging and integrated field of sustainable development law.

In terms of transparency, public participation and access to justice, through interdependent case-by-case mediation and arbitration, many states are increasingly willing to demonstrate flexibility with regards to traditional perspectives on the concept of sovereignty. There is space for individuals and other actors to activate such dispute resolution and arbitration procedures, wherever a State has submitted itself to the jurisdiction of the ICEAC. The present challenge will be to undertake such submissions, and to activate the mechanisms that exist for dispute resolution. The ICEAC can provide a useful mechanism for the development and real enforcement of the integrated principles and rules of sustainable development, both through direct protection

---

[11] All the information about the Court, Statutes, Members and the texts of the resolved cases is available at http://iceac.sarenet.es

of individuals, and through increased respect for the collective rights of legal persons.

32

ENFORCING SUSTAINABLE DEVELOPMENT THROUGH THE INTER-AMERICAN HUMAN RIGHTS SYSTEM

Romina Picolotti[1] & Marie-Claire Cordonier Segger[2]

Sustainable development has three main dimensions: social, environmental and economic. One important area of linkage between social development and environmental protection, in international law, involves the protection of the human rights of sustainable development advocates. International human rights commissions and courts can provide an effective set of legal mechanisms to protect the rights of advocates who question harmful or un-sustainable development activities, for example, destructive and degrading timber exploitation, mining, large-scale dams or gas pipelines.

The international community has recognized the importance of the protection of human rights, including the right to a clean and healthy environment and other rights related to sustainable development, as found in the Inter-American Human Rights system, as well as in national and international law.[3] For many years, the Organization of American States ('OAS') and the Inter-American Commission on Human Rights ('IACHR', or 'the Commission') have expressly and repeatedly recognized the important role played by human rights defenders

---

[1] Romina Picolotti, BCL (Córdoba), LL.M (American University), is President and Founder of the Center for Human Rights and Environment. This chapter is primarily based on two *amicus curia* briefs presented by CEDHA, CIEL and other colleagues, to the Inter-American Human Rights Commission and the Court. CEDHA is a non-profit organization founded in 1999 to defend victims of human rights violations caused by environmental degradation. The authors express sincere thanks to Daniel Taillant, Executive Director of CEDHA and CISDL Honorary Fellow, and to Anna Granova, CISDL Research Fellow, for their reviews and excellent substantive contributions to this chapter.

[2] Marie-Claire Cordonier Segger, MEM (Yale), BCL & LLB (McGill), BA Hons (Carl.), Director, Centre for International Sustainable Development Law (CISDL), Chair, CISDL/ILA/IDLO Partnership on International Law on Sustainable Development, Senior Manager, Americas Research Portfolio, International Institute for Sustainable Development & United Nations Environment Programme ROLAC, British Chevening Scholar & SSHRC Fellow, Exeter College, Oxford University Faculty of Law, Lecturer, International Development Law Organisation (IDLO) & Member, International Law Association (ILA) Committee on International Law on Sustainable Development.

[3] Judge Weeramantry of the International Court of Justice reflects this view: "The protection of the environment is ... a vital part of contemporary human rights doctrine, for it is a *sine qua non* for numerous human rights such as the right to health and the right to life itself. It is scarcely necessary to elaborate on this, as damage to the environment can impair and undermine all the human rights spoken of in the Universal Declaration and other human rights instruments." *Case Concerning the Gabčíkovo-Nagymaros Project* (Hungary/Slovakia) [1997] I.C.J. Rep. 7; *(Separate Opinion of Judge C. G. Weeramantry)* reprinted 37 I.L.M. 162 at 4.

M.C. Cordonier Segger & C. G. Weeramantry, eds., Sustainable Justice: Reconciling Economic, Social & Environmental Law
© *2005 Koninklijke Brill NV, Printed in The Netherlands, pp.513-546.*

in civil society. Sustainable development conflicts, which compete in their seriousness with human rights violations, are increasingly coming to world's attention, often in the context of disputes involving indigenous peoples and the territory they inhabit.

Both the OAS and the IACHR have expressed growing concern over the violations of human rights of these people, including the right to property and the right to freedom of expression. Indigenous and other grassroot sustainable development activists often engage into public debates on behalf of powerless and disenfranchised people against destructive large-scale initiatives, which severely impact their local potential for sustainable development. However, all too often the rights of these poor people to ownership and control of their land are violated. Furthermore, consequently to the above-mentioned activities, the human rights of the very activists themselves may be violated.

This pattern was brought to the Commission's attention in three recent cases regarding the violations of the human rights of indigenous peoples and local environmental groups involved in conflicts over large-scale development activities threatened their land. The first precedent-setting case was that of *Lhaka Honhat*,[4] which, due to limited space available, is only dealt with briefly in this chapter. The two recent cases, the pending case of *Montiel & Cabrera* (involving the human rights of grassroots anti-logging advocates in Guerrero, Mexico) and the *Awas Tingni* case[5] (dealing with human rights of indigenous anti-logging advocates from Nicaragua) are discussed in this chapter as case studies.

All these cases concern both the collective rights of indigenous communities to property, as well as the rights of individual activists. There is a troubling and important dimension to the violation of the human rights of the individual indigenous or grassroots activist for sustainable development. Not only are his or her rights to express opinions, to associate with like-minded individuals, to seek judicial redress, and to participate in government decision-making violated, but the rights of those communities they represent are also violated. The Commission has expressed concern about the 'chilling effect' of the violations of the human rights of journalists and human rights defenders, inasmuch as they affects the society at large. When indigenous and local leaders have their individual rights violated, the intent and effect of these violations is to violate collective rights by also silencing and intimidating others in their communities. The institutions of the Inter-American Human Rights system, especially its Commission and its Court, have responded to such violations, which yielded important results for the sustainable development of the Americas.

---

[4] *Association of Lhaka Honhat Aboriginal Communities v. The State of Argentina* Case No. 12094.
[5] *Awas Tingni Mayagna (Sumo) Indigenous Community v. The Republic of Nicaragua* Case No. 23/01.

Global Commitment to the Protection of the Human Rights of Sustainable Development Advocates

The underlying sustainable development issue which leads to the violation of the human rights of the advocate almost invariably concerns the degradation of land and resources used or owned by indigenous and/or poor and politically powerless indigenous peoples.

In order to delineate a State's responsibilities to guarantee the human rights of sustainable development advocates, it is necessary now to review the body of international law which collectively requires governments to protect human rights defenders, including sustainable development advocates, and allows them to exercise their rights to freedom of expression concerning environmental, social and economic matters, freedom of participation in public affairs concerning such matters, freedom of petition concerning such matters, and freedom of association concerning such matters.

The Declaration on the Right and Responsibility of Individuals, Groups, and Organs of Society to Promote and Protect Universally Recognized Human Rights and Fundamental Freedoms

The right to defend human rights is protected by a variety of international standards and principles. On December 9, 1998, on the eve of the fiftieth anniversary of the Universal Declaration of Human Rights, the United Nations General Assembly adopted the *Declaration on the Right and Responsibility of Individuals, Groups and Organs of Society to Promote and Protect Universally Recognized Human Rights and Fundamental Freedoms.*[6] The Declaration has become commonly known as the '*Declaration on Human Rights Defenders.*' It sets out the rights of human rights defenders, identifying specific freedoms and activities which are fundamental to their work, including the right to know, seek, and receive information about human rights and fundamental freedoms, the right to participate in peaceful activities against violations of human rights, the right to criticize and protest governments' failures to enforce human rights standards, and the right to make proposals for improvement. By referring to the right to act collectively, the Declaration pays special attention to freedom of association and the right to act in collaboration with others for the protection of human rights. The Declaration requires that states address these rights and freedoms to ensure human rights defenders may carry out their work freely, without interference or fear of threats, retaliation or discrimination.

The *Declaration on Human Rights Defenders* is a set of principles, based on legal standards enshrined in international human rights law adopted by every member of the United Nations ('the UN') through their participation in the UN

---

[6] U.N.Doc.A/RES/53/144, March 8, 1999.

General Assembly. To encourage implementation of the Declaration, the 1999 session of the UN Commission on Human Rights called on all states to provide and give effect to the Declaration and to report on their efforts. The Commission urged all the UN human rights bodies and mechanisms to look at specific types of human rights violations wherever they occur and to take the provisions of the Declaration into account in their work. The IACHR has discussed the Declaration with approval.[7]

The right to a healthy environment is gaining recognition in the international system. The ICESCR includes a right to a clean environment. The term 'healthy environment' was also incorporated in the 1988 *Additional Protocol to the American Convention on Human Rights*. The Hague Declaration of 1989 was one of the most important international statements before the United Nations Conference on Environment and Sustainable Development (UNCED) that connected environmental degradation to human rights issues. It declared that environmental harm threatens "the right to live in dignity in a viable global environment."[8] Interest in and support for recognizing a right to healthy environment has continued to develop momentum since the UNCED. A major development was publication of the 1994 *Final Report on Human Rights and the Environment, of the Commission on Human Rights Sub-commission on Prevention of Discrimination and Protection of Minorities*, more generally known as the 'Ksentini 1994 Report,' which discussed the legal foundations of a right to a satisfactory environment. A right to a healthy environment is also included in the United Nations Environment Programme's 1993 Proposal for a Basic Law on Environmental Protection and the Promotion of Sustainable Development. It includes within its 'Governing Principles' the "....right of present and future generations to enjoy a healthy environment and decent quality of life..."[9] The Draft Principles on Human Rights and the Environment (which is attached to the 1994 Ksentini Report states that "[a]ll persons have the right to a safe and healthy working environment."[10] It is also noteworthy that a right to environment has been included in many national constitutions around the world.

In early 1999, the human rights organization Amnesty International and the American environmental organization Sierra Club announced a joint campaign to highlight attacks on environmental defenders. In a subsequent report entitled 'Environmentalists Under Fire: Ten Urgent Cases of Human Rights Abuses', the two groups underscored the severity of the human rights abuses of

---

[7] *Infra* at part IV.C.

[8] http://www.earthaction.org/en/archive/97-05-envinst/haguedecl.html accessed on September, 14 2004.

[9] Proposal for a Basic Law on Environmental Protection and the Promotion of Sustainable Development) (1993) available online <http://www.unep.org/DPDL/law/Publications_multimedia/index.asp>, (Last accessed September 14, 2004).

[10] Available online: <http://www.cedha.org.ar/docs/doc90-part1-eng.htm> and <http://www.cedha.org.ar/docs/doc90-part2-eng.htm>.

environmental defenders.[11] The Center for Human Rights and Environment (CEDHA) and the Centre for International Environmental Law (CIEL) have compiled a summary of cases from around the world in which environmental advocates have had their fundamental rights abused, demonstrating a trend of intimidation for those who advocate environmental rights, and sustainable development.

This pattern was noted by the Special Rapporteur in her review of cases brought to the Human Rights Committee and to the Inter-American Commission on Human Rights by or on behalf of indigenous peoples. The Special Rapporteur noted that: "the human rights violations at issue almost always arise as a consequence of land rights violations and environmental degradation and indeed are inseparable from these factors."[12] It seems likely that the Declaration can be implemented to protect advocates of sustainable development, including human rights activists, but also local and indigenous communities questioning large-scale economic development projects and environmental defenders.

The Special Representative on Human Rights Defenders

In addition, the UN Secretary-General appointed a Special Representative on Human Rights Defenders with a mandate to monitor, document and intervene on behalf of human rights defenders under threat. Pursuant to the Commission's Resolution 2000/61 dated April 26, 2000, Ms. Hina Jilani, the Special Representative of the Secretary-General on Human Rights Defenders, in her first annual report, specifically included references to those striving for indigenous peoples rights and a clean environment among the group of human rights defenders requiring protection. She stated: "In my view the term 'human rights defenders' is not restricted only to those seeking protection and promotion of civil and political rights. The Declaration... recognizes those striving for the promotion, protection and realization of social, economic and cultural rights as human rights defenders. Therefore, those defending the right to a healthy environment, or promoting the rights of indigenous peoples would, by no means, fall outside the ambit of any definition of a human rights defender."[13]

Expert Assessment of the need for Protection of Environmental Human Rights Defenders

Even more recently, a United Nations joint expert seminar on the connections between human rights and the environment included in its study the

---

[11] "Environmentalists Under Fire: Ten Urgent Cases of Human Rights Abuses" (January, 2000) Introduction to the 2nd edition at 3.
[12] UNHRC, "Human Rights and the Environment: Final Report prepared by Mrs. Fatma Ksentini, Special Rapporteur" E/CN.4/Sub.2/1994/9, July 6, 1994 at para.88.
[13] U.N. Doc.E/CN.4/2001/94, at Cuba letter.

importance of protecting both 'traditional' human rights advocates and environmental advocates.[14]   The seminar centered on an expert assessment made two days prior to the seminar that concluded that the "normative links between the fields of human rights and the environment need to be reinforced" and that there is a need to "ensure that persons promoting the protection of human rights and the environment are not penalized, persecuted or harassed for their activities."[15] The experts further "noted with concern that in certain jurisdictions individuals and groups associated with the protection and promotion of human rights and the environment are being prevented from carrying out their legitimate activities."[16]

Defending Sustainable Development Advocates in the Inter-American Human Rights System

OAS General Assembly Resolutions and Country Reports

As early as 1990, the OAS General Assembly spoke of the importance of protecting human rights defenders and organizations, resolving: "To reiterate the recommendation made in previous years to governments of member states that they provide the guarantees and facilities needed to non-governmental human rights organizations so that they may continue their efforts to promote and defend human rights, and that they respect the freedom and integrity of the members of those organizations."[17]

The governments of the Americas have given particular recognition to the importance of human rights defenders. In recent years, continued attention to this issue has become something of an annual trend.

For example, in June 1999, in a resolution entitled "Human Rights Defenders in the Americas," adopted by the General Assembly of the OAS,[18] governments stated their intention to implement the Declaration on Human Rights Defenders passed by the United Nations. In particular, they agreed to recognize and support the "important work [carried out by human rights defenders] and their valuable contribution to the promotion, observance, and protection of fundamental rights" in the Americas.   The resolution calls on state members to provide "Human Rights Defenders with the necessary guarantees and facilities to continue freely carrying out their work of promoting

---

[14] The seminar took place in Geneva on January 16, 2002 as a collaboration of the Office of the High Commissioner for Human Rights and the United Nations Environment Programme. It was organized at the invitation of the United Nations Commission on Human Rights, pursuant to Sub-Commission on Human Rights Decision 2001/111. E/CN.4/SUB.2/DEC/2001/111. The seminar's report will be on the agenda at the Commission on Human Rights 58th Session.

[15] Final text (January 16, 2002), Meeting of Experts on Human Rights and the Environment, January 14-15, 2002, Conclusions at para. 18, available online: <http://www.unhchr.ch/environment/conclusions.html>.

[16] *Id.* at para. 13.

[17] AG/RES. 1044, June 8, 1990, operative paragraph 4.

[18] AG/RES. 1671 (XXIX-O/99).

and protecting human rights," as well as to adopt "the necessary steps to guarantee their life, liberty, and integrity."[19]

In June 2000, the OAS General Assembly adopted another resolution regarding human rights defenders, reiterating its support for their valuable work and urging, "member states to intensify their efforts to adopt the necessary measures... to guarantee the life, personal well-being, and freedom of expression of human rights defenders, in keeping with internationally accepted principles and standards."[20]

In June, 2001, an OAS General Assembly resolution "urge[d] member states to step up their efforts to adopt the necessary measures, in keeping with their domestic law and with internationally accepted principles and standards, to guarantee the life, personal safety, and freedom of expression of human rights defenders."[21] In the Executive Secretary's view, "when defenders of human rights themselves become victims, democratic society as a whole is under attack."[22]

And on June 4, 2002, the OAS General Assembly "condemn[ed] actions that directly or indirectly prevent or hamper the work of human rights defenders in the Americas;" urged member states to "step up their efforts to...safeguard the lives, personal safety, and freedom of expression of human rights defenders;" invited member states to "publicize and enforce the instruments of the inter-American system and the decisions of its bodies on this matter" including the UN Declaration on Human Rights Defenders; invited the Inter-American Commission on Human Rights to "continue to pay due attention to the situation of human rights defenders in the Americas and to consider, *inter alia*, preparing a comprehensive study on the matter and to give due consideration to this situation at the level it may judge appropriate and continue the dialogue and cooperation with the United Nations, in particular with the office of the Special Representative of the UN Secretary-General to Report on the Situation of Human Rights Defenders, through the Inter-American Commission on Human Rights and the Permanent Council."[23]

---

[19] *Id.*

[20] AG/RES.1711 (XXX-O/00).

[21] AG/RES. 1818 (XXXI-O/01).

[22] Press Release No. 27/01, Oct. 22, 2001.

[23] AG/RES. 1842 (XXXII-O/02); On March 19, 2002, several weeks before the OAS GA, an Experts Seminar on Human Rights and the Environment met and a) reviewed and assessed the existing linkages between human rights and environment as is manifest in the hemisphere and at a global level; b) assessed the effects of environmental degradation on the full enjoyment of human rights in the Americas; c) drafted recommendations to the OAS on how to move beyond Resolution 1819. For more information on the seminar sponsored by the Center for International Environmental Law (CIEL), available online: <http://ciel.org/Announce/cedha_seminar_details.html> and the Center for Human Rights and Environment (CEDHA), available *online:* <http://www.cedha.org.ar/hr-env-meeting-au.htm>.

Recognition of a Right to a Healthy Environment in the Inter-American System

Most countries of the Americas have signed the "Protocol of San Salvador" to the *American Convention on Human Rights*, which gives express recognition to the right to a healthy environment at Article 11, which states: "Everyone shall have the right to live in a healthy environment and have access to basic public services." It also states that: "[t]he States Parties shall promote the protection, preservation, and improvement of the environment."[24] As will be discussed, the interpretive virtue of Article 29 of the American Convention, a strong argument may be made suggesting for existence of an obligation on the part of the countries that are subject to the jurisdiction of the IACHR to enforce this right. This express recognition of the right to a healthy environment in the Inter-American system reflects the general trend in human rights and environmental law to recognize the right to a healthy environment.[25] In fact, the constitutions of eighteen Central and South American nations recognize the importance of a healthy environment.[26] For example, in 1998, a key paragraph was added to Article 4 of the Mexican Constitution, which now contains the words "all persons have the right to an environment appropriate for their development and well-being."[27] Despite stylistic variations, each articulation of the right to a healthy environment contains the same identifiable core: the right to an environment that supports physical and spiritual well-being, for sustainable development.

---

[24] O.A.S. Additional Protocol to the American Convention on Human Rights in the Areas of Economic, Social and Cultural Rights, "Protocol of San Salvador," 28 ILM 156, 161 (1988).

[25] The right to a healthy environment has been included in many national constitutions and statutory schemes around the world, and has been recognized in a growing number of national judicial decisions. *See* Annex III to the 1994 Ksentini Report, *supra* note 10. The Ksentini Report itself supports the right to a healthy environment. *Id.* (discussing the legal foundations of a right to a "satisfactory" environment); Article 24 of the African Charter on Human and Peoples Rights, 21 I.L.M. 58 (1982) (providing that "[a]ll peoples shall have the right to a general satisfactory environment favorable to their development."); Article 28 of the draft United Nations Declaration on the Rights of Indigenous Peoples, U.N. Doc. E/CN.4/Sub.2/1994/2/Add. 1 (recognizing the right of indigenous peoples to "protection of the total environment... of their lands...as well as to assistance for this purpose from States and through international cooperation"); Article XIII(1) of the Draft of the Inter-American Declaration on the Rights of Indigenous Peoples, approved by the Inter-American Commission on Human Rights, O.A.S. Doc. OEA/Ser/L/V/II.90, Doc. 9 rev. 1, September 18, 1995 (recognizing "the right to a safe and healthy environment, which is an essential condition for the enjoyment of the right to life and collective well-being."); Title I, Article 2, para. 9, Proposal for a Basic Law on Environmental Protection and the Promotion of Sustainable Development, Document Series on Environmental Law No. 1, UNEP Regional Office for Latin America and the Caribbean, Mexico, D.F., 1st. Ed., 1993 (providing within its Governing Principles the "right of present and future generations to enjoy a healthy environment and decent quality of life....").

[26] Bolivia de 1967 (artículo 137), Brasil de 1988 (artículo 225), Chile de 1980 (artículo 19), Colombia de 1991 (artículos 8,49, 79,80,86 y 88), Costa Rica (artículos 46 y 50) (Reforma Constitucional 7607 de 29 de mayo de 1996; Reforma Constitucional 7412 de 3 de junio de 1994), Cuba de 1992 (artículos 11 y 27), El Salvador de 1983 (artículo 69), Ecuador de 1983 (artículo 19), Guatemala de 1985 (artículo 97), Guyana de 1980 (artículos 25 y 36), Haití de 1987 (artículos 253 y 258), Honduras de 1982 (artículo 145), México de 1917 (artículo 4, para. 5), Reformada en 1998, Nicaragua de 1987 (artículos 60 y 102), Panamá de 1980 (artículo 110), Paraguay de 1967 (artículo 132), Perú de 1993 (artículo 2 inc. 22), and Uruguay de 1997 (artículo 47).

[27] G.H Flanz *et al* ed *Constitutions of the World* Vol 12 (2004) Issued April 2004; available online: http://info4.juridicas.unam.mx/ijure/fed/9/5.htm?s= accessed on September 14, 2004.

The Relevance of Recent Developments in International Law to Decisions in the Inter-American Human Rights System

In permitting the human rights of 'campesinos' and indigenous peoples who question unsustainable development projects, such as timber operations, mining or large scale construction projects or dams, Article 29 of the American Convention may encourage the Commission to take into account contemporary development of international law, by preventing the Commission from ignoring relevant international instruments.[28] On this matter, the Inter-American Court of Human Rights has stated: "A certain tendency to integrate the regional and universal systems for the protection of human rights can be perceived in the Convention. . . . Special mention should be made in this connection of Article 29, which contains rules governing the interpretation of the Convention, and which clearly indicates an intention not to restrict the protection of human rights to determinations that depend on the source of the obligations."[29]

Judge Rodolfo E. Piza Escalante of the Inter-American Court of Human Rights has described this integrative role of Article 29 as ". . . the need to interpret and integrate each standard of the Convention by utilizing the adjacent, underlying or overlying principles in other international instruments, in the country's own internal regulations and in the trends in effect in the matter of human rights, all of which are to some degree included in the Convention itself by virtue of the aforementioned Article 29...."[30]

In the Advisory Opinion No. 5, the Inter-American Court has explained this reasoning.[31] As a criterion to resolve potential conflicts between two or more human rights provisions, the *pro homine* criterion was held to apply. This means

---

[28] *American Convention on Human Rights,* Nov. 22, 1969, OAS Treaty Ser. No. 36, 1144 U.N.T.S. 123 (entered into force July 18, 1978) [*hereinafter American Convention*]. Art. 29 provides that: "No provision of the Convention may be interpreted as: a) permitting any State Party, group, or person to suppress the enjoyment or exercise of the rights and freedoms recognized in this Convention or to restrict them to a greater extent than is provided for herein; b. restricting the enjoyment or exercise of any right or freedom recognized by virtue of the laws of any State Party or by virtue of another convention to which one of the said states is a party; c. precluding other rights or guarantees that are inherent in the human personality or derived from representative democracy as a form of government; or d. excluding or limiting the effect that the American Declaration of the Rights and Duties of Man and other international acts of the same nature have."
[29] IACHR, "Other Treaties" Subject to the Consultative Jurisdiction of the Court (Art. 64 of the American Convention on Human Rights), Advisory Opinion OC-1/82 of September 24, 1982, Inter-Am.Ct.H.R. (Ser. A) No.1 (1982), para. 41, footnotes omitted.
[30] IACHR, Proposed Amendments to the Naturalization Provisions of the Constitution of Costa Rica, Advisory Opinion OC-4/84 of January 19, 1984 (Ser. A), No. 4 (1984), at para. 2, 3, and 6.
[31] 51: "We think rather that with respect to the interpretation of treaties, the criterion can be established that the rules of a treaty or a convention must be interpreted in relation with the provisions that appear in other treaties that cover the same subject. It can also be contended that the provisions of a regional treaty must be interpreted in the light of the concepts and provisions of instruments of a universal character. .... 52. The foregoing conclusion clearly follows from the language of Article 29 which sets out the relevant rules for the interpretation of the Convention. Subparagraph (b) of Article 29 indicates that no provision of the Convention may be interpreted as restricting the enjoyment or exercise of any right or freedom recognized by virtue of the laws of any State Party or by virtue of another convention to which one of the said states is a party. Hence, if in the same situation both the American Convention and another international treaty are applicable, the rule most favorable to the individual must prevail. ...."

that a right is interpreted in a manner that is most comprehensive and most favorable to the individual, while the provision that establishes restrictions must be applied in the narrowest manner. Article 29 serves at the same time as both a criterion to resolve potential conflict between international human rights provisions, and as the rule for interpretation of the rights contained in the American Convention.

Since the adoption of the American Convention, specific rights in international human rights law pertaining to human rights defenders – and environmental defenders in particular – have been developed. All of these rights have been furthered at the international level through development of various legal principles. Article 29 of the American Convention specifically requires the adoption of the trends in effect in international law concerning the violation of these rights.

The Case of the *Mayagna (Sumo) Awas Tingni Community* v. *Nicaragua.*

The Awas Tingni Community is a Mayagna or Sumo indigenous community of the Atlantic (or Caribbean) Coast of Nicaragua ('the Community'), consisting of approximately 630 persons.[32]

The main village of the Community is on the Wawa River, in the Municipality of Waspan, in the North Atlantic Autonomous Region (RAAN). The Community is organized and functions under a traditional leadership structure based on custom and recognised by the Nicaraguan constitution.[33] The lands occupied and used by the Community, apart from providing a means of sustenance for the Community's members, are crucial to its existence, continuity, and culture.

On March 13, 1996, the State of Nicaragua, through the Ministry of the Environment and Natural Resources (MARENA), awarded a 30-year concession to Sol del Caribe, S.A. (SOLCARSA) for exploitation of tropical forest within the territory claimed and owned by the indigenous communities.

In early September 1995, the Community filed for *Amparo* (protection of a constitutional right) with the Courts of Nicaragua in an attempt to stop the concession. The Supreme Court of Nicaragua found the State responsible for failing to fulfill its obligations under national and international law to take the steps necessary to protect the use and enjoyment by indigenous communities of

---

[32] This description of the facts is based directly upon the IACHR, "Complaint of the Inter-American Commission on Human Rights, Submitted to the Inter-American Court of Human Rights in the Case of the Awas Tingni Mayagna (Sumo) Indigenous Community Against the Republic of Nicaragua" (2002) 18 *Arizona J. Int.& Comp. L.* 19:1.

[33] Articles 89 and 180 of the *Nicaraguan Constitution*, and by article 11(4) of the *Statute of Autonomy of Nicaragua's Atlantic Coastal Region*, Law No. 28 of 1987.

their ancestral lands, and it is responsible for actively violating the rights of the Community to its land. The actions and omissions, all attributable to the State, were found to have caused substantial injury to the Community, whose material and spiritual survival depends on the protection of its rights.

With demarcation being a problem, on March 21, 1996 the Community requested the Plenary Session of the Regional Council, assistance in demarcating their ancestral lands and stopping further progress in awarding the concession without the consent of the communities.

Even though the Nicaraguan Supreme Court itself considered the concession granted by the State to be illegal, the State did not comply with the Court's order, thus enabling SOLCARSA to continue violating property rights of the Community for more than a year. On May 7, 1998, the State of Nicaragua accepted its international responsibility for the actions and omissions that had violated the rights of the indigenous Community. However, it did not undertake measures to fully remedy those violations.

Faced with a flagrant violation of their rights, the petitioners requested that the Commission act as a mediator in a process of dialogue between the State of Nicaragua and the Community, for the purpose of developing and agreeing on measures to protect the Community's rights to its land.

The case addressed several extremely significant issues for the protection of indigenous peoples rights, including their collective rights to property. They were: (a) the need for special legal protection for indigenous peoples; and (b) recognition of the collective rights of indigenous peoples.

Need for Special Legal Protection for Indigenous Peoples

The indigenous nature of the Awas Tingni case required that the Inter-American Court implement special protection since without it, the essential preconditions for the enjoyment of other rights do not exist and the purpose of the American Convention would not be served. [34]

The term 'special protection' contains within it the principle of non-discrimination, the *rationale* being the principle of 'juridical equality.' This is understood to be a measure of justice that provides for reasonably equal treatment to everyone in the same circumstances. Applying the principle of 'juridical equality' requires that factual inequalities be recognized in order for law to address them and achieve justice. In other words, the special

---

[34] Article 31 (1) of the Vienna Convention on the Law of Treaties provides that: "[A] treaty shall be interpreted in good faith in accordance with the ordinary meaning to be given to the terms of the treaty in their context and in the light of its object and purpose." 23 May 1969, 1155 UNTS 331; available online: <http://www.un.org/law/ilc/texts/treaties.htm> (Last accessed September 14, 2004).

circumstances faced by indigenous peoples throughout the Americas and worldwide require special legal treatment in order to render justice. [35]

Even though the best way of achieving special protection is by the development and application of specific law, Article 29 of the American Convention can already support special legal protection for the indigenous peoples of Awas Tingni. In order to do this, the American Convention should be interpreted to integrate Nicaragua's international obligations under the American Convention with other international instruments freely entered into by Nicaragua; and take into account the contemporary development of concepts that encompass indigenous values such as the concept of collective rights.

Recognition of the Collective Rights of Indigenous Peoples

Collective rights are thought of as rights that cannot be exercised but in-groups or rights where right holders are collective agents. Their collective characteristic is what constitutes their value. Therefore the deprivation of its collectiveness will imply the emptiness of the content of the right, and subsequently, its non-existence. The first 'category' of collective rights is rights that can only be exercised in a group, as is the case with the right to freedom of expression. An individual in isolation cannot realize his or her right to freedom of expression; rather an individual must be able to share ideas with others to fully enjoy this right. The second 'category' are rights in which the rights holders are collective agents. The right in this category, for example, the right to culture and the right to community-based property, can only be enjoyed if the group as a whole realizes the right.

Collective rights, such as the right to land and other natural resources, cultural integrity, environmental security, and control over their own development, can be found with every known indigenous community rights system, as was the case of the Awas Tingni community. The case was important with regards to the collective characteristic of the right to property and its implications concerning: the right to life, the right to a healthy environment, the right to culture and the right to participate in government.

---

[35] The IACHR has consistently advocated for special protection of indigenous peoples in reports as well as in its resolutions. The Commission, for example, adopted a resolution (IACHR 1972, 90-1) stating that "for historical reasons and because of moral and humanitarian principles, special protection for indigenous populations constitutes a sacred commitment of the states.

i. The collective perspective on the right to property under Article 21 of the American Convention

The indigenous right to property is a community-based right that derives from long-term relationships between indigenous peoples and the natural resources that sustain them.[36]

In the case of Awas Tingni, the Mayagna Sumo community clearly had a system of communal property in which the land belongs collectively to the community. The collective right of the Mayagna Sumo peoples, to own on a community basis the rights to land they have traditionally occupied, is expressly recognized in Articles 5 and 89 of the Nicaraguan Constitution. Article 5 of the Nicaragua Constitution reads: "The State recognizes the existence of indigenous peoples, who enjoy the rights, obligations and guarantees recognized in the Constitution, especially those that maintain and develop their identity and culture...so as to maintain the communal forms, enjoyment, use and benefit of their lands, all in conformity with the law..."[37] In addition, Article 89 of the Nicaragua Constitution reads: "...The State recognizes the communal forms of property of the Atlantic Coast Communities' lands; it also recognizes the enjoyment, use and benefit of the waters and forests of their communal lands..."[38] The definition of communal land is provided by article 36 of the Autonomy Statute of Nicaraguan Atlantic Coast Autonomous Region, which states, in Article 36: "Communal property is the land, water and forest that have traditionally pertained to the [indigenous] communities of the Atlantic Coast."[39] As such, Nicaragua's internal laws in this case expand the concept of right to property express in Article 21 of the American Convention. Article 29 of the American Convention in this case required that the Inter-American integrated Nicaragua's domestic legislation in the interpretation of Article 21. The Court recognized the collective right to property of the indigenous peoples of Awas Tingni.

ii. The collective perspective on the right to life under Article 4 of the American Convention

Understanding the contextual complexities of indigenous peoples and their relationships to their land and other natural resources is essential for promoting

---

[36] See the report of the U.N. Special Rapporteur on Human Rights of Indigenous Peoples E/CN.4/Sub.2/1999/18 (June 3, 1999) which states "...In summary, each of these examples underscores a number of elements that are unique to indigenous peoples: (1) a profound relationship between indigenous peoples and their lands, territories and resources exists; (2) that this relationship has various social, cultural, spiritual, economic, and political dimensions and responsibilities; (3) that the collective dimension of this relationship is significant; and (4) that the inter-generational aspect of such a relationship is also crucial to indigenous peoples identity, survival and cultural viability."

[37] G.H Flanz *et al* ed *Constitutions of the World* Vol 13 (1998) Issued August 1998; available online: http://info4.juridicas.unam.mx/ijure/fed/9/5.htm?s (last accessed September 14, 2004).

[38] G.H Flanz *et al* ed *Constitutions of the World* Vol 13 (1998) Issued August 1998; available online: http://info4.juridicas.unam.mx/ijure/fed/9/5.htm?s (last accessed September 14, 2004).

[39] Act No. 28 of 1987.

their legal interests and well being. This requires an appreciation of the collective relationship between life and land. The basis of all substantive legal rights is the right to life. Safeguarding this fundamental right is an essential condition for enjoying the entire range of civil and political rights. Displacement from ancestral domains and damage to the local environment invariably harms the cultural integrity and well being of indigenous peoples, and often leads to physical harm and the loss of life. Analysis of Awas Tingni community-based property right pursuant to Article 21 required consideration of the right to life under Article 4. In the case of *Bernard Ominayak & The Lubicon Lake Band* v. *Canada*, the applicants alleged that the government of the province of Alberta had deprived the Lake Lubicon Indians of their means of subsistence and their right to self-determination by selling oil and gas concessions on their lands. The HR Committee found historical inequities and certain more recent developments, including oil and gas exploration, to be threatening the way of life of the Lake Lubicon Band and were thus violating minority rights, contrary to Article 27 of the ICCPR.[40]

The threat to the right to life in its collective and individual dimension of the Mayagna Sumo peoples was also real and concrete. This threat would remain permanent, like Damocles' sword, if the State failed to take positive, adequate and effective measures to protect indigenous territories and rights. As incursions into indigenous territories increase, the symbiotic tie between culture, land and life for the Awas Tingni community becomes more and more self-evident. Consequently a violation of the community-based property rights of Awas Tingni necessary implied a violation of the right to life consecrated in Article 4 of the American Convention.

The right to life entails negative as well as positive obligations. Thus the right to life implies the negative obligation not to practice any act that will result in the arbitrary deprivation of human life and the positive obligations to take all appropriate measures to protect and preserve human life. The European Commission of Human Rights recognizes that Article 2 of the *European Convention of Human Rights* imposed on states the positive obligation *de prendre des mesures adéquate pour protéger la vie*. Further, the Human Rights Committee stated regarding Article 6 of the UN *Covenant on Civil and Political Rights* that states are required "to take positive measures to ensure the right to life, including steps to reduce the infant mortality rate, prevent industrial accidents, and protect the environment."[41] From this perspective, the right to a healthy environment appears as a corollary to the right to life.

As mentioned above, in the realm of international law, the right to a healthy environment is found in several environmental agreements as well as in human rights instruments. The distinctive nature of indigenous peoples' relationship to

---

[40] G.A. res. 2200A (XXI), 21 U.N. GAOR Supp. (No. 16) at 52, U.N. Doc. A/6316 (1966), 999 U.N.T.S. 171
[41] G.A. res. 2200A (XXI), 21 U.N. GAOR Supp. (No. 16) at 52, U.N. Doc. A/6316 (1966), 999 U.N.T.S. 171

the environment within their ancestral domains is captured in the proposed *American Declaration on the Rights of Indigenous Peoples*, which in its preamble, recognizes "the respect for the environment accorded by the cultures of indigenous peoples of the Americas." [42]

In the same vein, the draft *United Nations Declaration on the Rights of Indigenous Peoples*, provides (in Article 25) that indigenous peoples have the right to maintain and strengthen their distinctive spiritual and material relationship with the lands territories, waters and coastal seas and other resources which they have traditionally owned or otherwise occupied or used, and to uphold their responsibilities to future generations in this regard.[43] As the president of the Inter-American Court has noted, "The right to a healthy environment has individual and a collective dimensions - being at a time an 'individual' and a 'collective' right - in so far as its subjects or beneficiaries are concerned. Its 'social' dimension becomes manifest in so far as its implementation is concerned (given the complexity of the legal relations involved). And it clearly appears in its 'collective' dimension in so far as object of protection is concerned (a *bien commun*, the human environment)."[44]

In sum, the right to life, which has a corollary the right to a healthy environment, imposed the positive obligation to Nicaragua, in this case, to take adequate measures to protect the environment of the Awas Tingni community. The degradation of forest and the depletion of bio-diversity, by timber companies with the acquiescence of the Nicaraguan state, is in direct conflict with the international legal obligations of the state.

The recognition by the Inter-American Court of the obligation of the Nicaraguan state to protect the environment of the Awas Tingni community and its correlative right to a healthy environment, would have the potential the minimal legal guaranties for the enjoyment of their basic human rights, assuring the applicability or juridical equality.

iv. The collective perspective and the right to participate in government under Article 23 of the American Convention

Article 23 of the American Convention articulates the right to participate in government. More recent international instruments, including ones focused

---

[42] Available online: http://www.cidh.org/Indigenous.htm. It explicitly acknowledges "the special relationship" between indigenous peoples and the environment, lands, resources and territories on which they live. The preamble also recognizes "that in many indigenous cultures, traditional collective systems for control and use of land and territory and resources, including bodies of water and coastal areas, are a necessary condition for their survival, social organization, development and their individual and collective well-being ..."

[43] Available online: <http://www.unhchr.ch/indigenous/main.html> (last accessed Sept 14, 2004).

[44] International Human Rights Law Group (IHRLG) and Center for International Environmental Law (CIEL), *Amici Curiae Awas Tingni Mayagna (Sumo) Indigenous Community v. The Republic of Nicaragua,* available online: <http://www.cedha.org.ar/docs/curiae1.htm>.

more on sustainable development issues, such as Agenda 21, the Desertification Convention and the Beijing Declaration, make clear that participatory partnerships involving both state and non-state actors, including indigenous communities such as the Awas Tingni, are developing rapidly as a means for facilitating more equitable access and sustainable use of natural resources. One of the first major international documents to make public participation a central developmental objective, including the achievement of equitable socio-economic development, was the 1986 United Nations General Assembly 'Declaration on the Right to Development.' Its preamble states, *inter alia*: "Recognizing that development is a comprehensive economic, social, cultural and political process, which aims at the constant improvement of the well-being of the entire population and of all individuals on the basis of their active, free and meaningful participation in development and in the fair distribution of benefits arising therefrom...."[45]

Though not a legally binding document, the role of public participation as a necessary means for achieving sustainable development was clearly identified in 1987 in *Our Common Future*. In the context of the 1992 UNCED, 'effective participation' was identified as a *sine qua non* for achieving sustainable development.[46] It refers particularly to the significance of participation in promoting sustainable development by specific groups of the public, including indigenous peoples and NGOs.[47]

In light of the application of Article 29 of the American Convention to this case, the right to participate in government- consecrated in Article 23 - should be integrated with the evolution of international law in this matter. As such the Awas Tingni community has a right to participate in decisions concerning the exploitation of their natural resources. The Government of Nicaragua did not respect with right when it granted a timber concession for part of the indigenous territory of Awas Tingni. In light of the failure to comply with international laws on participation, there was an urgent need to ensure that the Government of Nicaragua is officially informed of where the indigenous territory of the Awas Tingni is located and to recognize the community-based property rights of the Awas Tingni. No other remedy could have ensured that the mistakes of the recent past will not be perpetrated anew.

The basic human rights of indigenous peoples in the Americas have long been neglected. This case presented an unprecedented opportunity for the Inter-

---

[45] Article 1 of the Declaration, which defines the "right to development," recognizes universal public participation as essential for the expression of the right. It asserts that: "The right to development is an inalienable human right by virtue of which every human person and all peoples are entitled to participate in, contribute to, and enjoy social, cultural and political development, in which all human rights and fundamental freedoms can be fully realized." Available online: http://www.unhchr.ch/html/menu3/b/74.htm.

[46] World Commission on Environment and Development, *Our Common Future* (Oxford: Oxford University Press, 1987).

[47] *Ibid.*

American Court to establish an important legal precedent by which the human rights of indigenous peoples can be recognized and protected.

The Decision of the Inter-American Court Establishing the Collective Rights of Indigenous Peoples

On August 31, 2001, the Inter-American Court of Human Rights, the highest human rights tribunal in the western hemisphere, issued its judgment in the *Case of the Mayagna (Sumo) Awas Tingni Community v. Nicaragua*. Affirming that indigenous peoples have rights to the lands and resources they traditionally have used and occupied, the decision was a milestone in a prolonged legal dispute between the Awas Tingni community and the state of Nicaragua.[48] The *Awas Tingni* decision was also the first case in which an international tribunal with legally-binding authority has ruled in favor of indigenous peoples' collective rights, thus setting a precedent of enormous importance for the Americas and elsewhere.

In its decision, the Inter-American Court concluded that Nicaragua had violated the rights of the Mayangna community of Awas Tingni by granting a logging concession within the community's traditional territory without its consent and by ignoring the consistent complaints and requests of Awas Tingni urging demarcation of the territory. The Court found that the right to property, as affirmed in the Inter-American Convention on Human Rights, protects the traditional land tenure of indigenous peoples.

As a remedy for the violation of the community's human rights, the Court ordered Nicaragua to demarcate and title the community's traditional lands within a period of fifteen months, as well as to reform its laws and administrative procedures to effectively guarantee the land rights of all indigenous peoples in the country. After the decision was issued, the government declared publicly its intent to implement the decision. Despite the government's promise and the community's willingness to move forward, additional lobbying of the government, and further advocacy within the inter-American human rights system was needed to advance the implementation process.[49]

---

[48] S. James Anaya & Claudio Grossman "The Case of Awas Tingni v. Nicaragua: A New Step in the International Law of Indigenous Peoples" 19 *Ariz. J. Int'l & Comp.* Law 1 (2002); also available at: www.law.arizona.edu/Journals/AJICL/AJICL2002/vol191/introduction-final.pdf.

[49] E. Melba McLean Cornelio, "El caso Awas Tingni v. Nicaragua: Hacia el reconocimiento de los derechos de propiedad comunal indígena en la Costa Atlántica" (Presentation, University of the Autonomous Regions of the Caribbean Coast of Nicaragua (URACCAN) in Managua, Nicaragua, Sept. 8 - 10, 2004), available online: <www.law.arizona.edu/depts/iplp/advocacy_clinical/awas_tingni/documents/melbaarticulo.pdf>.

Implementing the Order of the Inter-American Court

Unfortunately, due to the lack of an effective response on the part of the Nicaragua to the Awas Tingni community's continuous demands for protection of its traditional lands against illegal logging activities and the ongoing invasion of communal lands led the implementation team to resort once again to the Inter-American Court. Setting yet another international precedent, the Court issued a resolution on provisional measures, in which it ordered Nicaragua to urgently take specific action to protect the community's rights and interests in its traditional lands.

A new phase of the implementation process was opened in January 2003 with the adoption of the new indigenous land demarcation law by the Nicaraguan National Assembly. This law defines a set of rules and procedures for the demarcation of indigenous communal lands in the Atlantic Coast. Relevant Nicaraguan officials have declared that Awas Tingni will be the first community to get its land titled under the new law. In 2004 the first phase of the demarcation and titling process was completed with a diagnostic study and set of maps documenting the community's demographics and traditional land tenure - a first step under the new law towards achieving a title over these lands.

From the outset, the community, its advisors, and the organizations that gave their support were aware that a legal victory before the Inter-American Court would constitute only the first step toward achieving full recognition and protection of indigenous peoples' communal land rights in Nicaragua.[50] However, in this case, the Inter-American Court had a unique opportunity to begin to address indigenous peoples' human and environmental rights, recognizing the special relationship indigenous peoples have with their land and resources, and in so doing protecting and promoting the basic human rights of indigenous peoples in an adequate and effective manner. It rose to the occasion. The final decision, if adequately implemented, holds potential to equitably balance the interests at stake and promote the well-being of Nicaragua and all of its citizens, especially those who had long endured discrimination and injustice.

---

[50] S. James Anaya, "The Awas Tingni Petition to the International Commission on Human Rights: Indigenous Lands, Loggers, and Government Neglect in Nicaragua" (1996) 9 *St. Thomas L. Rev.* 157. See also S. James Anaya & S. Todd Crider, "Indigenous Peoples, the Environment, and Commercial Forestry in Developing Countries: The Case of Awas Tingni, Nicaragua" (1996) 18 *Hum. Rts. Q.* 345.

The Case of *Teodoro Cabrera García and Rodolfo Montiel Flores* v. *Mexico*

A second case concerning sustainable development advocates has entered the Inter-American Human Rights system. The forest resources of the state of Guerrero are among the most important natural resources in Mexico. Several years ago, local farmers from the mountainous Costa Grande region of Guerrero state began to notice that their local rivers had become mere threads of water, the rivers' fish and crayfish were dying, and agricultural harvests were increasingly inadequate. The farmers believed that these problems were due to massive logging operations that had started in 1995, when the former Governor of Guerrero had given Boise Cascade, a U.S.-based transnational lumber company, exclusive rights to the region's rich forest resources. For decades, Guerrero's peasants had lived on *ejidos* (communal farms), and Article 27 of the Mexican Constitution guaranteed their collective rights to these inalienable lands. However, Article 27 was amended to allow *ejidos* to be privatized, and the North American Free Trade Agreement permitted timber companies to buy from local forestry *ejidos*. Mills were increasing production in order to compete, and would often run two lumber shipments – though they only paid for one – by illegally transporting lumber at night. Neither Mexican nor foreign companies reforested the land as required by law. In 1997 and 1998, farmers formed the Organization of Peasant Environmentalists from the Mountains of Petatlán and Coyuca de Catalán (OCESP) to protect the Costa Grande's natural resources. Among the most active members and organizers of the organisation were two local campesinos, Rodolfo Montiel Flores and Teodoro Cabrera Garcia. August 1997, marked the first of many times soldiers came to Rodolfo Montiel's home, threatening him and his family.

Through peaceful protests and legal channels, Montiel and Cabrera and their fellow OCESP members promoted environmental awareness and the reforesting of exploited lands, and challenged excessive logging. They filed complaints before various local, state, and federal governmental officials, denouncing environmental destruction and illegal logging practices. They repeatedly requested financial and material assistance in reforestation and sustainable development efforts from the state congress, the Secretary of the Environment (SEMARNAT), and even the army stationed in Petatlán. Their complaints and appeals were met with silence.

In February 1998, more than one hundred farmers gathered to block the roads to prevent the transport of lumber. Several such actions were staged in following months. The actions and other mobilizations carried out by OCESP had mixed results. In the first half of 1998, logging of the forests in the area was briefly suspended, and Boise Cascade withdrew, citing "difficult business conditions," owed in part to OCESP's anti-logging campaign. Boise Cascade's withdrawal did not halt logging, however. Other Mexican and transnational companies continued to exploit the forests at a rapid rate without any attempt to reforest the land. The Banco Nuevo *ejido*, near Montiel's home in Mameyal ejido, was successful in driving the Union away from its forest. The Union struck back by sending hired men to burn Banco Nuevo's forests. Mameyal was also burned in revenge for the actions OCESP was carrying out. Even more significant was the increasing presence of the Mexican Army in the region. According to witnesses, a strong wave of repression ensued for members of the OCESP, through arbitrary detention, torture, murders, and forced disappearance.

The attempts to suppress OCESP's efforts to halt the damaging consequences of logging culminated in the events of May 2, 1999.[51] On that day, approximately forty military officers from the 40th Infantry Battalion of the Mexican Army entered the community of Pizotla, in the municipality of Ajuchitlán del Progreso, Guerrero. As the soldiers arrived, they fired against a group of people who were gathered near the outside of Teodoro Cabrera's house. Among the people present were Rodolfo Montiel, Teodoro Cabrera and Salomé Sánchez Ortiz. Prior to the attack and the gunshots, the military officers had addressed the three, and Salomé Sánchez, Teodoro Cabrera and Rodolfo Montiel, ran away. One of the shots hit Salomé Sánchez, killing him.

Rodolfo Montiel and Teodoro Cabrera were found and detained without an arrest warrant. That night, they were transferred to the mountains, where they were interrogated and subjected to further violence. Rodolfo Montiel was interrogated while being subjected to acts of torture and cruel treatment.[52] During the torture, he was questioned about his activities with the Organización de Campesinos Ecologistas de la Sierra de Petatlán (OCESP) and was pressured to confess that he was part of an armed group, which he consistently denied, as he is not. Similarly, Teodoro Cabrera was taken to the mountainside, where he was interrogated and subjected to different forms of torture. The victims were not given any opportunity to exercise their right to adequate defense counsel, either when the Army held them in incommunicado detention, or when they were at the Public Ministry. Based on the self-incriminating statements they signed under torture, Rodolfo Montiel was presented as a probable suspect in the crimes of sowing marijuana and carrying firearms, and Teodoro Cabrera was accused of carrying firearms. They were formally detained and processed, first by the First Instance Criminal Court of Mina under criminal case 13/99 (even though the body is not competent to

---

[51] The following facts concerning the violations of Montiel and Cabrera's human rights are derived from the petition filed with this Commission on their behalf on October 25, 2001.

[52] According to testimony, one officer pulled him by the jaw, holding his head back, while the other lay across his shoulders; soldiers beat him in the stomach using their knees and kicks; soldiers pulled him by the testicles repeatedly, causing him intense pain to the point where he lost consciousness; soldiers administered electric shocks to his right thigh after wetting him; and soldiers threatened him with death and told him that they knew how to reach his family.

take on the case, as it deals with alleged federal crimes), and subsequently by the Fifth District Court of the 21st Circuit under case file 61/99.

On August 26, 1999, following the questioning of the military personnel who had participated in the illegal and incommunicado detention, torture, and extraction of self-incriminatory statements under coercion, the victims' defense team asked the presiding judge to denounce the events before the Public Ministry so that investigations could be initiated. In response, the Fifth District Judge ordered the Federal Public Prosecutions Office to open the initial investigation (Averiguación Previa) into the alleged participation of military officers Artemio Nazario Carballo, Calixto Rodríguez Salmerón, José C. Calderón Flabiano and others in the crime of torture. An initial investigation began as ordered, then the Prosecutions abdicated responsibility to the Military Attorney General of Justice on the basis that the officers allegedly responsible for the crime were military officers in active service.[53]

The victims' defence team filed a complaint with the National Human Rights Commission (CNDH). On July 14, 2000, the CNDH issued recommendation 8/2000, addressed to the national defence ministry, but omitted to state its position over the unconstitutionality of the jurisdiction of the Military Attorney-General for the torture investigation. On August 28, 2000, the Fifth District Judge of the 21st Circuit Court, based in Iguala, Guerrero, sentenced Rodolfo Montiel to six years and eight months of imprisonment, and Teodoro Cabrera to ten years of imprisonment. The sentence was based on the confession extracted from the victims under torture, incommunicado detention, and without access to a lawyer. Appeals followed. On May 9, 2001, the Amparo Appeals Court ordered that the medical examination relating to the torture suffered by the victims be admitted as evidence. The defense offered as proof before the First Unitary Circuit Court, in the "re-run" of the hearing, a medical report issued by forensic experts Morris Tidball and Christian Thramsen. However, on July 16, 2001, the Unitary Court once again confirmed the guilty sentence against the victims.

On October 19, 2001, Digna Ochoa, formerly a member of Montiel and Cabrera's defense team, was assassinated. Five days later, on October 24, 2001, the victims' defense counsel presented the Amparo, challenging the sentence. And on November 8, 2001, Mexican President Vicente Fox freed Rodolfo Montiel and Teodoro Cabrera.

---

[53] The initial investigation was transferred to the Military Public Ministry of the 35th Military Zone in Chilpancingo, Guerrero towards the end of November 1999. The military investigator resolved and shelved the investigation on June 13, 2000, concluding that there was no evidence to support the torture charge. Up until this time, the case file consisted of the three statements of officers Artemio Nazario Carballo, Calixto Rodríguez Salmerón, and José C. Calderón Flabiano, who ratified the information previously given and denied that they had practiced torture. The investigator failed to carry out basic tasks, such as taking statements from the victims and from witnesses who saw the military operatives, and undertaking medical examinations of the victims.

The State of Mexico, through members of the Army and other agents, had effected reprisal on the two campesino ecologists for the 'crime' that they had committed: of having an environmental conscience, participating in and steering an independent organization of campesinos from the region, and defending the forests and those who depended on it against ignorance, abuse, and the appropriation of its natural resources. On December 6, 2000, the federal Attorney General for the Protection of the Environment (PROFEPA) acknowledged the grave damage caused to the ecosystem of the Sierra de Petatlán and cancelled seven of the main logging permits that had earlier been granted, among them El Mameyal, Montiel's native community and the origin of his environmental struggle. [54]

Fortunately, the crucial work performed by Rodolfo Montiel and Teodoro Cabrera has been widely recognised by important organizations that work in defense of the environment and human rights, including Amnesty International and the Sierra Club. This recognition culminated in Mr. Montiel's receiving (while incarcerated) the prestigious Goldman Environmental Prize[55], the Sierra Club's "Chico Mendes prize"[56], the "Don Sergio Méndez Arceo" human rights prize[57] and the "Roque Dalton prize."[58]

Addressing Violations of the Rights of Sustainable Development Advocates in the Inter-American Human Rights System

The entirely lawful activities of many of those who speak out against unsustainable development nonetheless lead soldiers to arrest them, torture them, hold them incommunicado, and deprive them of due process in their trials. In essence, these defenders of sustainable development usually do three things, for which the State will deprive them of their human rights:

---

[54] The deforestation that was denounced by environmental organizations has been investigated. According to a study by the National Commission for Knowledge and Use of Biodiversity (CONABIO), which answers to the federal executive, in just eight years, from 1992 to 2000, forty percent of the forest (86,000 hectares) of the Sierra de Petatlán y Coyuca de Catalán, was lost. But this did not take place before another member of OCESP suffered a similar fate: on March 13, 2000, gunmen in Coyuca de Catalán abducted Maximino Marcial Jaimes, an OCESP member from Pizotla.
[55] The *Goldman Environmental Prize* was created to honor people for their efforts to defend ecosystems and is given to representatives of the six global regions. Environmental organizations consider it the Nobel Prize of the environmental world.
[56] The *Chico Mendes* prize is given in recognition to the person or non-governmental organization outside of the United States that has demonstrated extraordinary valor in its efforts to protect the environment.
[57] The *Don Sergio Méndez Arceo* national human rights prize is given to acknowledge, stimulate, and support organizations, groups and persons who have stood out for their bravery in defending and promoting a culture of respect for human rights in Mexico. It is given in honour of Don Sergio Méndez Arceo VII Bishop of Cuernavaca, Morelos, who was recognized for his work in defense of the human rights of underprivileged people.
[58] The *Roque Dalton Medal* has been awarded since 1985 by the Council of Cooperation with Culture and Science in El Salvador, to praise and stimulate different contributions towards peace, independence, sovereignty, self-determination, solidarity, conservation and promotion of a Latin American culture and in particular a Salvadorean culture.

- they speak out against unsustainable projects, activities and policies, and organize meetings and actions in local communities to discuss these projects, a lawful exercise of their right to freedom of expression guaranteed under Article 13 of the American Convention;

- through organisations, they often communicate their concerns to their governments, and petition the government on numerous occasions to halt unsustainable activities, a lawful exercise of their right to participate in government guaranteed under Article 23 of the American Convention, and of their right to petition the government under Article XXIV of the American Declaration of the Rights and Duties of Man; and

- they serve as organizers of, and are active members of, groups and coalitions that seek to halt unsustainable projects and often, to develop and promote alternatives, a lawful exercise of their right to association guaranteed under Article 16 of the American Convention and Article XXII of the American Declaration .

The Inter-American Human Rights Commission has noted the particular relevance of these articles to the situation of human rights defenders: "Several other articles of the Convention may have particular relevance for human rights workers. Among others, Article 13 of the Convention, providing for the right to freedom of thought and expression, plays an important role in the analysis of attacks against human rights workers. Article 15, establishing the right of assembly, and Article 16, establishing the right to freedom of association, also provide protections relevant to human rights workers. The new Declaration on Human Rights Defenders approved by the United Nations Commission on Human Rights also establishes certain principles which provide guidance in analyzing the rights of human rights defenders. This instrument provides that, '[e]veryone has the right, individually and in association with others, to promote and to strive for the protection and realization of human rights and fundamental freedoms at the national and international levels.' For the purpose of promoting and protecting human rights, all persons have the right to meet and assemble peacefully and to form, join and participate in non-governmental organizations or to communicate with such organizations. The Draft Declaration also provides that all persons have the right to make complaints regarding the policies and actions of individual officials or governmental bodies regarding human rights violations." [59] (Citations omitted.)

Moreover, in performing all of the actions above, those who question unsustainable development projects are also exercising their right to advocate for a healthy environment, a right that is itself guaranteed under Article 11 to the San Salvador Protocol.[60] Twice in the past two years, the OAS General Assembly has taken note of the link between human rights and the

---

[59] 1999 Colombia Report, chapter VII at paras 3 and 4.
[60] San Salvador Protocol, *supra* note 23.

environment, and of how protection of the one may well enhance protection of the other.[61]

The largely procedural individual human rights, when exercised in the context of advocating for a healthy environment, have come to be commonly known as 'environmental due process' rights.

One international legal scholar explains: "The Universal Declaration of Human Rights recognizes that environmental due process rights are as important to the full realization of human rights as substantive protections. Denial of these fundamental rights of freedom of association, of opinion and of expression, and of the right to take part in government, endangers the protection of substantive human rights. The Universal Declaration of Human Rights codifies these procedural rights in Article 8 (effective remedy); Article 19 (freedom of opinion and expression); Article 20 (freedom of association); Article 21 (right to take part in government); and Article 26 (right to education). Articles 2(3), 19, 21, 22, and 25 of the International Covenant on Civil and Political Rights set forth these same procedural guarantees as fundamental human rights. Similarly, Part III of the Draft Declaration [of Principles on Human Rights and the Environment] sets out the procedural aspects of human rights necessary for the full realization of environmental rights. These rights are enabling rights; they make it possible for people to contribute actively to the protection of their environment."

The scholar continues "Likewise, the absence of respect for these rights not only increases the likelihood of environmental degradation, but also increases the chances that such damage will be irreversible... Only when procedural rights are honored is collective action in support of environmental protection possible... The environmental dimension of these procedural human rights constitutes the foundation of environmental protection because without these procedural protections, no protection of substantive environmental rights is possible."[62]

In order to exercise these or any other substantive human rights, an individual must be afforded the whole panoply of rights guaranteed by the American Convention. The U.N. Declaration on Human Rights Defenders has specifically recognized and protected this corollary right, at Article 2: "Each State has a prime responsibility and duty to protect, promote and implement all human rights and fundamental freedoms, *inter alia*, by adopting such steps as may be necessary to create all conditions necessary in the social, economic, political and other fields, as well as the legal guarantees required to ensure that

---

[61] AG/RES. 1819 (XXXI-O/01) and AG/RES. 1896 (XXXII-O/02).
[62] Ziemer, "Application in Tibet of the Principles on Human Rights and the Environment," 14 *Harv. Hum. Rts. J.* 233 (Spring 2001) at 263-65.

all persons under its jurisdiction, individually and in association with others, are able to enjoy all those rights and freedoms in practice."[63]

The American Convention provides to the same effect in Article 1.1 when it obligates the States Parties to "undertake to respect the rights and freedoms recognized herein and to ensure to all persons …the free and full exercise of those rights and freedoms…," and in Article 2, when it further obligates the States Parties to "adopt…such legislative or other measures as may be necessary to give effect to those rights or freedoms [referred to in Article 1]." When they violated the rights of those who question unsustainable development, states violate both of these articles. States violate Article 1.1 by failing to respect and protect the rights and freedoms guaranteed by the American Convention. In addition, States can be in violation of Article 2 because they are already on notice as to the need to adopt additional measures to give effect to human rights and freedoms, yet often, have failed to take the recommended measures.

i. Violation of the right of freedom of expression under Article 13 of the American Convention

Under Article 13 of the American Convention "Everyone has the right to freedom of thought and expression. This right includes freedom to seek, receive, and impart information and ideas of all kinds, regardless of frontiers, either orally, in writing, in print, in the form of art, or through any other medium of one's choice." Because of the important role that human rights defenders can play as leading advocates for environmental protection and sustainable development, they can be singled out by a State for suppression of their human rights. Such violations were particularly insidious because they represented an attempt to suppress not only the freedom of expression of the individuals in that moment in a public debate, but that of others who expressed similar views or who might consider expressing similar views. The IACHR has identified a number of aspects of the right to freedom of expression, three of which are of particular relevance. First, the Special Rapporteur for Freedom of Expression has commented on the critical role that the right of freedom of expression plays in a democratic society, particularly in regard to political expression, at Principle 1: "Freedom of expression in all its forms and manifestations is a fundamental and inalienable right of all individuals. Additionally, it is an indispensable requirement for the very existence of a democratic society… Freedom of expression, therefore, is not just the right of individuals, but of society as a whole."[64]

---

[63] U.N.Doc.A/RES/53/144, March 8, 1999.
[64] Special Rapporteur's Report (2000), Declaration of Principles of Freedom of Expression, Principle 1 and para. 7.]

The second important aspect of the right to freedom of expression is that it is a collective right, or as stated above, it is "not just the right of individuals, but of society as a whole." The Special Rapporteur's earlier report gave additional details on the collective nature of this right: "Article 13 indicates that freedom of thought and expression 'includes freedom to seek, receive, and impart information and ideas of all kinds... This language... implies a collective right to receive any information whatsoever and to have access to the thoughts expressed by others."[65]

Most specifically, the IACHR has identified the "chilling effect" on all of society when an individual's right to freedom of expression is violated: "...This type of persecution is worrying not only insofar as it places individuals at serious risk, but also as it has a broader effect of sowing fear and 'chilling' the freedom of expression and action of such groups."[66] While the right to freedom of expression is certainly broad enough to protect the activities of those expressing their views in opposition to destructive practices and in support of their right to enjoy their livelihoods and the right to healthy environment, human rights Rapporteurs have expressly noted the need to protect speech relating to environmental issues: "All persons have the right to hold and express opinions and to disseminate ideas and information regarding the environment."[67]

ii. Violation of the right to participate in government, under Article 23 of the American Convention, and under Article XXIV of the American Declaration.

Often, as did Montreal and Cabrera, advocates will file numerous complaints with the government in an attempt to halt destructive, unsustainable practices. In these ways, such advocates and their organizations exercise their guaranteed rights to participate directly in public affairs and to petition their government. Under Article 23 of the American Convention, "Every citizen shall enjoy the following rights and opportunities... to take part in the conduct of public affairs, directly or through freely chosen representatives." Under Article XXIV of the American Declaration of the Rights and Duties of Man: "Every person has the right to submit respectful petitions to any competent authority, for reasons of either general or private interest, and the right to obtain a prompt decision thereon." Both of these rights are violated by states when actions are taken in retaliation for the involvement of advocates for sustainable development.

This has been recognized by the IACHR. For example, the IACHR's 1997 "Report on Ecuador" found that the right of participation was violated when

---

[65] Special Rapporteur's Report (1998), ch. II *as part of* 1998 IACHR Annual Report.]
[66] 2001 Guatemala Country Report, OEA/Ser.L/V/II.111, doc. 21, April 6, 2001.]
[67] Special Rapporteur on Human Rights and the Environment, "Draft Declaration Principles on Human Rights and the Environment" (1994), at para. 16.

oil development on the lands of the Huaorani people was undertaken without allowing their participation in decision-making concerning the project: "The quest to guard against environmental conditions which threaten human health requires that individuals have access to information, participation in relevant decision-making processes, and judicial recourse... Public participation is linked to Article 23 of the American Convention, which provides that every citizen shall enjoy the right 'to take part in the conduct of public affairs, directly or through freely chosen representatives,' as well as to the right to receive and impart information.... The Commission encourages the State to enhance its efforts to promote the inclusion of all social sectors in the decision-making processes which affect them."[68]

In her final report, the UN Rapporteur for Human Rights and the Environment described the critical nature of public participation in both environmental and human rights decision-making processes, at 219: "The right of popular participation in its various forms ranks high in importance for promoting and protecting human rights and the environment. The basic right to popular participation is provided for in article 21 of the Universal Declaration of Human Rights and a number of international instruments... Although many people are prevented from participating in decisions, there is a growing national and international trend, including at the international funding institutions, to allow the participation of individuals and groups in all stages of activities involving the environment."[69]

Recent international treaties related to both protection of the environment, and sustainable development, uniformly mandate that affected persons be included in the planning process.[70] In terms of 'soft law', the historic 1992 *Rio Declaration* recognizes a right to participation, at Principle 10: "Environmental issues are best handled with the participation of all concerned citizens, at the relevant level. At the national level, each individual shall have appropriate access to information concerning the environment that is held by public authorities, including...the opportunity to participate in decision-making processes."[71] Paragraph 18 of the 1994 "Draft Declaration of Principles on Human Rights and the Environment" similarly provides: "All persons have the right to active, free, and meaningful participation in planning and decision-making activities and processes that may have an impact on the environment and development..."[72] Chapter 8 of Agenda 21, a comprehensive and detailed blueprint for the future implementation of sustainable development, is largely

---

[68] "Report on the Situation of Human Rights in Ecuador," OAS Country Report (1997), Chapters VIII and IX.
[69] E/CN.4/Sub.2/1994/9, July 6, 1994.
[70] *See* Shelton, "Human Rights and Environmental Issues in Multilateral Treaties Adopted between 1991 and 2001," Background Paper No. 1, Joint UNEP-OHCHR Expert Seminar on Human Rights and the Environment, January 14-16, 2002 (Geneva).
[71] Rio Declaration on Environment and Development (U.N. Conference on Environment and Development, Rio de Janeiro, June 13, 1992, U.N. Doc. A/CONF. 151/26), at Principle 10.
[72] *Supra* note 72.

devoted to ways to ensure participation by affected individuals in development projects.[73] The Beijing Declaration,[74] Articles 2(6) and 3(8) of the 1991 ECE Convention on Environmental Impact Assessment[75]; the 1992 Convention on Biological Diversity[76]; the 1993 Council of Europe Convention on Damage Resulting from Activities Dangerous to the Environment[77]; the 1994 Desertification Convention United Nations Convention to Combat Desertification in those Countries Experiencing Serious Drought and/or Desertification, particularly in Africa,[78]; and the Convention on Access to Information, Public Participation in Decision-Making and Access to Justice in Environmental Matters (UNECE Convention)[79], all reflect the same goals of facilitating participation in the decision-making process by affected persons. The provisions in Articles 2, 5 and 8 of Declaration on Human Rights Defenders,[80] the most recent international human rights instrument specifically dealing with human rights defenders similarly protects the right to participate in public affairs and to petition the government.

In light of the application of Article 29 of the American Convention to this case, the right to participate in public affairs (already consecrated in Articles 13 and 23 of the Convention) and the right to petition (similarly guaranteed by Article XXIV of the American Declaration) should be taken into account as part of the evolution of international human rights and environmental law in this matter.

iii. Violation of the right to freedom of association under Article 16 of the American Convention and Under Article XXII of the American Declaration.

States can violate an individuals lawful exercise of their right to freedom of association by punishing them for organizing and being among the most active members of an organization established to address sustainable development issues, including conflicts surrounding socio-economic development projects that do not take environmental problems into account. The right to freedom of association is guaranteed under Article 16 of the American Convention which states, in subsection 1, that "Everyone has the right to associate freely for ideological, religious, political, economic, labor, social, cultural, sports, or other purposes…" The IACHR has held that "when individual members [of an association] are forced to abandon their activities, they also suffer violations of their right to freedom of association."[81] States' reprisals against sustainable

---

[73] U.N. Conference on Environment and Development, Rio de Janeiro, June 13, 1992 at Principle 10, U.N. Doc. A/Conf. 151/26.
[74] A/Conf.177/L.5/Add.15, 14 September 1995.
[75] 30 I.L.M. 802 (1991)
[76] 31 I.L.M. 818 (1992) at Article 14
[77] 150 European Treaty Series (1993)
[78] UN G.A.D. A/AC.241/15/Rev.7, 33 I.L.M. 1328 (1994) at Article 5
[79] UN Doc. ECE/CEP/43 (April 21, 1998)
[80] *Supra* note 7.
[81] Colombia Country Report (1999), Chapter VII, para. 73.

development advocates, as well as reprisals against other members of their organisations, are designed to force their members to abandon their individual and organizational activities to question and debate unsustainable development projects. However, the right to freedom of association is protected under and defined to a greater extent by other international law instruments, pursuant to Article 29 of the American Convention, and is protected generally as an accepted norm of customary international law.[82] Indeed, recently, the right to freedom of association has been enumerated in the context of environmental issues in paragraph 19 of the 1994 "Draft Declaration of Principles on Human Rights and the Environment", which states "All persons have the right to associate freely and peacefully with others for purposes of protecting the environment or the rights of persons affected by environmental harm."[83]

The Appropriate Remedies under Article 63.1 of the American Convention

The Inter-American Court of Human Rights has defined the scope of the Commission's duty under Article 63.1 of the American Convention to remedy violations of rights or freedoms protected by the Convention: "The remedy for the damage caused by the infraction of an international obligation requires, when possible, full restitution (*restitutio in integrum*), which consists in the re-establishment of the prior situation. If this is not possible, the international tribunal can order the adoption of measures that ensure the infringed rights, remedy the consequences that the infractions produced, as well as establish the payment of compensation for the damages caused."[84]

Sustainable development advocates can suffer permanent damage to their health resulting from acts of torture, as well as having been arbitrarily accused and imprisoned. Both they and their families are often uprooted. It is not possible to return things to their previous state. Because of the impossibility of a *restitutio in integrum,* and observing the criteria established by the Court, a remedy can consist of the adoption of measures that ensure the infringed rights, remedying the consequences produced by the infractions, and the establishment of compensation to be paid to the injured party for the damages caused. Each will be briefly addressed in turn in this final section.

---

[82] Article 20 of the Universal Declaration of Human Rights of 1948; Article 22 of the ICCPR; Article 11 of the *European Convention for the Protection of Human Rights and Fundamental Freedoms;* Article 11 of the African Charter on Human and Peoples' Rights.

[83] Special Rapporteur on Human Rights and the Environment, *supra* note 72.

[84] "Barrios Altos" Case (*Chumbipuma Aguirre et. al. v. Peru*), Reparations (Art.63.1 American Convention on Human Rights), Sentence of November 30 of 2001; *Cfr Cesti Hurtado Case,* para. 33; *"Niños de la Calle" Case (Vinagran Morales et. al), Reparations,* para. 60; and *"Panel Blanca" Case (Paniagua Morales et. al.). Reparations,* para. 76.

i. The adoption of measures that ensure the infringed rights are respected.

Pursuant to Article 1.1 of the American Convention, a State is obligated to adopt administrative, legislative, and judicial measures to ensure the free and full exercise of rights protected by the Convention. As a corollary to this obligation, the State has the obligation to investigate and sanction those responsible for the violation of the human rights of individuals seeking to halt unsustainable development, and the duty to prevent future violations.

First, with regards to the duty to investigate and sanction those responsible, the first part of the remedy in this case should be the prompt, effective, and impartial investigation of complaints relating to the violation of the human rights of such advocates, and the sanction of all material instigators, actors, accomplices and obstructors of the facts. As has been found by the Court, at "…the investigation of the facts and sanctioning of those responsible…is the obligation of the State …[and is] an obligation that must be discharged seriously and not as a mere formality."[85] The remedy with respect to the investigation and sanctioning of those responsible can consist of requiring a State that is found to be violating these rights to adopt the following measures. First, withdrawal of Military Justice from judicial proceedings for the investigation and sanctioning of those responsible for the torture infringed upon advocates, so that the case be submitted to a common court. Second, the sanctioning of those responsible should include punitive damages. It is worth highlighting that, in addition to being a sanction, punitive damages play a very important preventive role based on their highly persuasive character. This is why the remedy, according to the Inter-American Court, should necessarily consider this type of damage award, which fuses a sanction and preventive duties into one legal mechanism. Third, ensure that torture and other human rights violations are assessed and sanctioned as such by competent jurisdictional bodies, in accordance with the international definition of human rights violations. Fourth, ensure that necessary measures are taken to immediately execute apprehension orders against judicial police officers, which have not been fulfilled in the course of the criminal process, including the preventive suspension of security officers that have taken part in the arrest or detention of sustainable development advocates, while the claims for the violation of their human rights are definitively resolved. Fifth, investigation and judgment of the conduct of intervening judges, in relation to the responsibilities that, by action or omission, they bear.

Second, with regards to the duty to prevent further human rights violations, this is often closely related to the impunity enjoyed by individuals, including soldiers, who violate the human rights of advocates. Lack of action on the part

---

[85] Inter-American Court of Human Rights, "*Panel Blanca*" *Case; ibid. Paniagua Morales et. al. v. Guatemala Case*; Reparations (Art.63.1 American Convention on Human Rights), Sentence of May 25, 2001; *Suarez Rosero Case, Reparations, ibid.* para. 79; and *El Amparo Case, Reparations,* para. 61*ca.*

of a State can be argued to imply a tacit consent for these violations to continue. As the Inter-American Court of Human Rights has stated, ".... the State that leaves human rights violations unpunished, violates its duty to ensure free and full exercise of the rights of the people within its jurisdiction...."[86] It has also held that "...by impunity one must understand the failure on the whole to investigate, prosecute, capture, try, and condemn those responsible for violations of human rights protected by the American Convention ...The State has the obligation to use all the legal means at its disposal to combat that situation, since impunity fosters chronic repetition of human rights violations, and total defenselessness of victims and their relatives".[87]

Therefore, the remedy in such a context should also include the adoption of measures necessary to prevent the repetition of violations of human rights consecrated in the American Convention. An essential step in preventing human rights abuses and combating impunity is to offer all the guaranties necessary for human rights advocates (including environmental activists) to perform their important function without any abusive interference from authorities. If there is a National Commission on Human Rights, as well as other human rights and environmental institutions, these Commissions must have the support of the government in order to effectively monitor human rights violations and advocate on behalf the victims. A State, if found in violation, must adopt measures necessary to fulfill the recommendations of the National Commission on Human Rights. In particular, the State should modify its domestic, legislative, and administrative instruments in order to firmly and definitively eradicate torture from the criminal justice system. And to achieve all of these goals, such a State should limit the value attached to extra-judicial confessions, if there is a 'principle of immediacy', its erroneous interpretation may need to be modified in their law, and the civil jurisdiction of the military justice system should also be reduced.

ii. Remedying the consequences produced by the infractions.

Because extra-judicial confessions obtained by means of torture served as the sole evidence of the fabricated crimes "committed" by sustainable development advocates, the legal process against sustainable development advocates are absolutely and irrefutably null and void. It is essential that the true facts be revealed and acquittals ordered.

---

[86] *Cfr. Bamaca Velasquez Case*, para. 129; *Blake Case, Reparations*, para. 121 and Third Resolutive Point; *Suarez Rosero Case, Reparations, ibid.* para. 107 and Sixth Resolutive Point.
[87] Inter-American Court of Human Rights, "*Panel Blanca*" *Case, ibid., Paniagua Morales and others v. Guatemala Case, ibid.*, Reparations (Art.63.1 American Convention on Human Rights); Sentence of May 25, 2001.

'Campesinos' and indigenous peoples that witness the desertification of their lands, riverside dwellers that have their rivers polluted, and coastal dwellers suffering exhausted fishing resources and degraded water resources, can expect only misery and forced exile. Sustainable development advocates, such as 'campesinos' and indigenous peoples, know this very well. For this reason, they continue to strive to defend their cultural and environmental identity, despite serious risks to their lives. Alternatively, their lives, culture, rights, and future can be gradually wiped out. The illegal arrest and treatment of advocates constitutes not only an obstacle to their personal commitment to the defense of the environment, but also a severe impact on their organizations. By means of torture, illegal apprehension of sustainable development leaders, and the unpunished assassination of its members, a state of terror is generated among other campesino or indigenous advocates that participate in environmental or human rights organizations. A State found in violation of this can be called upon to assume its corresponding responsibility and remedy the damages caused to the individuals and their organisation. For example, it could be required to grant technical and financial support to the organization; provide its members the guaranties necessary for them to perform their functions; study the extent of the damages suffered by the communities and mediate the means to halt environmental degradation produced by intensive exploitation of natural resources; investigate which human rights are infringed by the degradation that results from excessive exploitation of natural resources; and mediate the means necessary to legally protect the natural resources on which the survival of the communities depends.

iii. The establishment of compensation to be paid to the injured party for the damages caused.

On the subject of appropriate compensation to injured parties, the Inter-American Court has stated: "Concerning material damage (*supra* 10.1, 10.3 and 10.6), from the time the Court has submitted its first sentence as regards remedies, it has recognized that the violations of the rights protected create for the victim a right to remedy the consequences produced by the breach which includes the payment of an indemnity as compensation for material and moral damages."[88] Material damage includes within its scope emerging damages and loss of profits. In this case, the victims and their relatives must be fairly compensated for the damages suffered. The situation brings about serious damages to these individuals, to their relatives, and to their organisations; damages that must be considered in order to establish fair compensation.

Finally, the moral damage suffered must also be remedied. Sustainable development advocates are often subject to humiliation, inhuman and degrading treatment, and torture; they can see their partners and colleagues

---

[88] Case *Gustavo Adolfo Cesti Hurtado v. Peru*; Interpretation of the remedy sentence; (Art.63.1, American Convention on Human Rights); Sentence of November 27, 2001.

assassinated, bear the disgrace of being unlawfully arrested, and remained deprived of their freedom for an extensive period.

Conclusions

Many well-known international human rights advocacy organizations such as Amnesty International and Human Rights Watch, as well as the Center for Human Rights and Environment (CEDHA) in Argentina, have been working for decades toward social justice. An important component is the need to protect the human rights of human rights advocates themselves. Indeed, in partnership with governments and international organizations, they have achieved some considerable success in the international arena.

The context of violations of the human rights of sustainable development advocates is most often public debates and disputes over land and the degradation or unsustainable use of natural resources. The violation of the rights of these 'sustainable development advocates' has two principal ramifications. First, it means that the abuses of individual human rights of such advocates are occurring as an additional consequence of the violation of other human rights – typically the rights to life, property, culture, health, and a healthy environment – of the affected peoples they represent. Second, it means that the abuses of human rights of sustainable development advocates will, in turn, result in additional violations of the affected people's rights. This occurs by virtue of the "chilling effect" that these individual violations have on the larger group, deterring the group from exercising its own rights to challenge the initial human rights violations that have been visited upon them. It is a vicious circle that must be broken.

PART IV

FUTURE DIRECTIONS FOR SUSTAINABLE DEVELOPMENT LAW

33

THE NEW DELHI DECLARATION OF PRINCIPLES OF INTERNATIONAL LAW RELATING TO SUSTAINABLE DEVELOPMENT[1]

Commentary by Nico Schrijver[2]

Prof. Nico Schrijver is Chair of the ILA Committee on International Law on Sustainable Development, and was Rapporteur of the ILA Committee on the Legal Aspects of Sustainable Development which, through ten years of intense international scholarly review and debate, developed the 2002 New Delhi Declaration of Principles of International Law Relating to Sustainable Development. This brief commentary shares certain of his thoughts on the concept of sustainable development, and the process of developing the ILA New Delhi Declaration of Principles.[3]

The concept of 'sustainable development' has attracted considerable attention in recent years and has become of pivotal importance in scientific and political discourse. Increasingly, it has also gained importance in the practice of states and of relevant international organizations concerned with environmental conservation and development.

Following its introduction into international politics by the *World Commission on Environment and Development* in 1987, the concept of sustainable development

---

[1] See "ILA New Delhi Declaration of Principles of International Law Relating to Sustainable Development" in Kluwer Academic Publishers *International Environmental Agreements: Politics, Law and Economics* 2, 2 2002, 209-216, available online: http://www.kluweronline.com/issn/1567-9764/current. For a comprehensive discussion of principles and practices related to sustainable development and international law, see the recent N. Schrijver & F. Weiss (eds.), *International Law and Sustainable Development: Principles and Practice* (Leiden: Martinus Nijhoff Publishers, 2004) at 699.
[2] Prof. Nico Schrijver, Ph.D. (Groningen), Professor Public International Law, Free University of Amsterdam, Chair of the International Law Association (ILA) Committee on Int'l Law on Sustainable Development, former Rapporteur, the ILA Committee on Legal Aspects of Sustainable Development, Chairperson, Academic Council on the United Nations.
[3] See N. Schrijver and F. Weiss, *"Editorial"* in Kluwer Academic Publishers *International Environmental Agreements: Politics, Law and Economics* 2, 2 2002, 105 - 108, available online: <http://www.kluweronline.com/issn/1567-9764/current>. This chapter is based on editorial comments made by Professors Schrijver and Weiss, providing a commentary to the Principles in order to offer an insight into the views of the international experts who participated in the elaboration of the ILA Principles that are reproduced herein, with permission of the authors. All errors are responsibility of the editors.

M.C. Cordonier Segger & C. G. Weeramantry, eds., Sustainable Justice: Reconciling Economic, Social & Environmental Law
© *2005 Koninklijke Brill NV, Printed in The Netherlands, pp.549-560.*

rapidly acquired a prominent place on the international political agenda.[4] The documents resulting from the 1992 *United Nations Conference on Environment and Development*, held at Rio de Janeiro in 1992, were focused on sustainable development as their ultimate objective.

Since then and within a remarkably short period of time, sustainable development has been securely endorsed, and has been recognized in a number of instruments of international law. Thus, various environmental treaties incorporate sustainable development, for example the *UN Framework Convention on Climate Change* (1992), the *UN Convention on Biological Diversity* (1992), the *UN Convention to Combat Desertification and Drought* (1994) and the *International Tropical Timber Agreement* (1994). Sustainable development also features in the *Straddling Stocks Convention* (1995) as well as in the preamble to the 1994 *Agreement on the Establishment of the World Trade Organisation* (WTO) according to which Members should, in their trade and economic relations, allow for the 'optimal use of the world's resources in accordance with the objective of sustainable development'. In the Doha Declaration of the Fourth Ministerial Conference of 14 November 2001, Ministers confirmed their commitment to the objective of sustainable development. They stated: "We are convinced that the aims of upholding and safeguarding an open and non-discriminatory multilateral trading system, and acting for the protection of the environment and the promotion of sustainable development can and must be mutually supportive."[5]

Reference may also be made to the clear policy response by the European Union and by the European Community to the call for 'sustainable development' as formulated at the UN Conference on Environment and Development. Indeed, both the *Treaty on European Union and the European Community Treaty*, as amended by the 1997 *Treaty of Amsterdam*, have given the objective of sustainable development a prominent place. Thus, the Treaty includes objectives such as 'economic and social progress and a high level of employment and to achieve balanced and sustainable development' (Art. 2). Furthermore, Article 6 of the revised *EC Treaty* stipulates the integration of environmental protection requirements in all Community policies and activities "with a view to promoting sustainable development." Sustainable development is also an over-arching objective in the various development co-operation treaties of the EU, such as the *Cotonou Agreement* (2001).

Sustainable development or related concepts also feature in a number of international judicial decisions of the 1990s, for example those of the International Court of Justice in the *Nuclear Tests Case* (New Zealand v. France, 1995), in its Advisory Opinion to the UN General Assembly on *The Legality of the Threat or Use of Nuclear Weapons* (1996) and in the *Gabcikovo-Nagymaros case* (Hungary/Slovakia, 1997) concerning a dam project in the river Danube.

---

[4] *Ibid.*
[5] *Ibid.*

Reference must also be made to the recognition by the WTO Appellate Body of the objective of sustainable development, most notably in the *United States-Import Prohibition of Certain Shrimp and Shrimp Products Case* (1998), commonly known as the *Shrimp-Turtles case*. Many of these decisions and treaties are analysed in this volume, and other recent scholarly work.[6]

It follows that sustainable development has become an established objective of the international community, arguably one vested with some degree of normative rather than merely exhortatory status in international law.[7]

However, the fact of its broad acceptance and use does not affirm that its scope and contents are clear. As such it may be ranged alongside the economic paradigm of 'comparative advantage' which has come to be regarded and accepted as the '*Grundnorm*' of trade, or for that matter with the political promise of greater benefits from 'trade not aid', a slogan which brought many developing countries into the GATT/WTO. However, though its lack of precision must be recognised, various dimensions of the concept of sustainable development may be distinguished, covering a number of domains. As has been stated elsewhere, these include "sustainable use of natural resources; sound economic development, both of developing and industrialized countries; integration of developmental and environmental concerns; inter- and intra-generational equity; a temporal dimension; and respect for human rights and public participation." [8]

All these elements are aptly reflected in the description of sustainable development as formulated in the *New Delhi Declaration of Principles of International Law Relating to Sustainable Development*, adopted by the International Law Association in April 2002. The New Delhi Declaration is not, of course, an international legal treaty, or even a non-binding 'soft law' declaration between States. Rather, it is the result of ten years of joint scholarship and investigation, the International Law Association (ILA) Committee on Legal Aspects of Sustainable Development, under the chairmanship of Dr. Kamal Hossain, former Minister of Foreign Affairs of Bangladesh. These scholars came to a joint resolution on seven indivisible principles of international law related to sustainable development, though these were not intended as an exhaustive list.

The New Delhi Declaration recognises that the objective of sustainable development involves a comprehensive and integrated approach to economic, social and political processes, which aims at the sustainable use of natural resources of the Earth and the protection of the environment on which nature and human life as well as social and economic development depend and which

---

[6] See, e.g., N. Schrijver & F. Weiss, eds., *International Law and Sustainable Development: Principles and Practices* (Leiden: Martinus Nijhoff, 2004).
[7] *Supra* note 3.
[8] *Supra* note 3.

seeks to realize the right of all human beings to an adequate living standard on the basis of their active, free and meaningful participation in development and in the fair distribution of benefits resulting therefrom, with due regard to the needs and interests of future generations.[9]

The 2002 *Johannesburg World Summit on Sustainable Development*, where the New Delhi Declaration was presented, provided an important opportunity for addressing the role of international law in the pursuance of sustainable development. However, for now, one may conclude soberly that although the chief elements of a future global regime of governance for sustainable development might currently be in place (including consensus on problems, objectives, principles, institutional underpinning and on the crucial role of civil society in all its diversity), much remains to be accomplished.

Moving forward from the Johannesburg Summit, one might chance the tentative prediction that the unflagging commitment to sustainable development as demonstrated by key players of any future global partnership for a regime of governance for sustainable development (governments, IGOs, NGOs, enterprises, segments of civil society) since 1992 will, over time, crystallize into a more sophisticated normative prescription of international law. It would be reasonable to expect that all the efforts already made, through standard setting, studies, conferences, consultation papers and guidelines, would in the end contribute to the shaping and enhancement of international law in this area of global concern.[10]

As this volume turns to a consideration of future directions, it can be observed that the 2002 New Delhi Principles of International Law Related to Sustainable Development, as the product of nearly ten years of shared academic work, provide a first crucial and definitive tool for scholars, courts, national and international policy-makers and legal professionals, in relation to guiding principles of international law on sustainable development.

The Principles in the 2002 *New Delhi Declaration of the ILA* provide a first blueprint for the emerging field of sustainable development law and policy,[11] and are worth reproducing in full below.

---

[9] *Supra* note 3.
[10] *Supra* note 3.
[11] See M. C. Cordonier Segger and A. Khalfan, *Sustainable Development Law: Principles, Practices and Prospects* (Oxford: Oxford University Press, 2004).

Resolution 3/2002

SUSTAINABLE DEVELOPMENT

NEW DELHI DECLARATION OF PRINCIPLES OF INTERNATIONAL LAW RELATING TO SUSTAINABLE DEVELOPMENT[12]

The 70th Conference of the International Law Association, held in New Delhi, India, 2-6 April 2002,

HAVING CONSIDERED the five consecutive reports (1994-2002) of the Committee on Legal Aspects of Sustainable Development and its efforts to identify existing and emerging principles of international law in the field of sustainable development,

HAVING BEEN INFORMED about the Committee's research seminar on *International Law and Sustainable Development. Principle and Practice*, held in Amsterdam with close cooperation from the Amsterdam Institute for International Development of the Free University, Amsterdam and the University of Amsterdam, 29 November-1 December 2001,

TAKING NOTE of the books resulting from research seminars under the auspices of the Committee on *The Right to Development in International Law* (1992), *Sustainable Development and Good Governance* (1995), *International Economic Law with a Human Face* (1998) and *International Law and Sustainable Development: Principle and Practice* (2002),

WELCOMING the initiative 'Sustainable Justice 2002: Implementing International Sustainable Development Law' of the Centre for International Sustainable Development Law, Montréal,

ADOPTS the New Delhi ILA Declaration on Principles of International Law relating to Sustainable Development, as annexed to this resolution,

REQUESTS the Secretary-General to forward the Report of the Committee and this Declaration to the UN Commission on Sustainable Development, the UN Secretary-General and his Special Representative on Sustainable Development, UNCTAD, UNEP, the WTO, the World Bank and other

---

[12] See "ILA New Delhi Declaration of Principles of International Law Relating to Sustainable Development" in Kluwer Academic Publishers *International Environmental Agreements: Politics, Law and Economics* 2, 2 2002, 209-216, available online: http://www.kluweronline.com/issn/1567-9764/current. See also N. Schrijver & F. Weiss, eds., *International Law and Sustainable Development: Principles and Practice* (Leiden: Martinus Nijhoff Publishers, 2004) at 699.

relevant intergovernmental and non-governmental organizations for their consideration, including organizations at the regional level.

NEW DELHI DECLARATION OF PRINCIPLES OF INTERNATIONAL LAW RELATING TO SUSTAINABLE DEVELOPMENT

The 70th Conference of the International Law Association, held in New Delhi, India, 2-6 April 2002,

NOTING that sustainable development is now widely accepted as a global objective and that the concept has been amply recognized in various international and national legal instruments, including treaty law and jurisprudence at international and national levels,

EMPHASIZING that sustainable development is a matter of common concern both to developing and industrialized countries and that, as such, it should be integrated into all relevant fields of policy in order to realize the goals of environmental protection, development and respect for human rights, emphasizing the critical relevance of the gender dimension in all these areas and recognizing the need to ensure practical and effective implementation,

TAKING THE VIEW that there is a need for a comprehensive international law perspective on integration of social, economic, financial and environmental objectives and activities and that enhanced attention should be paid to the interests and needs of developing countries, particularly least developed countries, and those adversely affected by environmental, social and developmental considerations,

RECALLING that in its Report on *Our Common Future* (1987), the World Commission on Environment and Development identified the objective of sustainable development as being '…to ensure that it meets the needs of the present without compromising the ability of future generations to meet their own needs',

CONCERNED about growing economic and social inequalities between and within States as well as about the ability of many developing countries, particularly least developed countries, to participate in the global economy,

RECOGNIZING the need to further develop international law in the field of sustainable development, with a view to according due weight to both the developmental and environmental concerns, in order to achieve a balanced and comprehensive international law on sustainable development, as called for in Principle 27 of the Rio Declaration and Chapter 39 of Agenda 21 of the UN Conference on Environment and Development as well as in the various resolutions on legal aspects of sustainable development of the International Law Association,

AFFIRMING that consideration should be given to the interaction of States, intergovernmental organizations, peoples and individuals, industrial concerns and other non-governmental organizations as participants in multilateral development co-operation,

AWARE of the concern expressed by the UN General Assembly during its 19th Special Session in 1997 to review progress achieved since the 1992 UN Conference on Environment and Development that 'the overall trends for sustainable development are worse today than they were in 1992'; and of the General Assembly's call 'to continue the progressive development and, as and where appropriate, codification of international law related to sustainable development',

RECOGNIZING that the forthcoming World Summit on Sustainable Development, convened by the United Nations General Assembly in Johannesburg, South Africa, 26 August-4 September 2002, provides an important opportunity for addressing the role of international law in the pursuance of sustainable development,

REAFFIRMING the ILA's Seoul Declaration on Progressive Development of Principles of Public International Law Relating to a New International Economic Order, as adopted by the 62nd Conference of the International Law Association held in Seoul in 1986,

TAKING INTO ACCOUNT the United Nations General Assembly Declaration on the Right to Development of 1986,

TAKING FURTHER INTO ACCOUNT the Rio Declaration on Environment and Development and related documents ensuing from the 1992 UN Conference on Environment and Development, as well as the final documents resulting from the series of world conferences on social progress for development (Copenhagen, 1993), human rights (Vienna, 1993), population and development (Cairo, 1994), small islands states and sustainable development (Barbados, 1994), women and development (Beijing, 1995), least-developed countries (Brussels, 2001) and financing for development (Monterrey, 2002), respectively,

EXPRESSES the view that the objective of sustainable development involves a comprehensive and integrated approach to economic, social and political processes, which aims at the sustainable use of natural resources of the Earth and the protection of the environment on which nature and human life as well as social and economic development depend and which seeks to realize the right of all human beings to an adequate living standard on the basis of their active, free and meaningful participation in development and in the fair distribution of benefits resulting therefrom, with due regard to the needs and interests of future generations,

IS OF THE OPINION that the realization of the international bill of human rights, comprising economic, social and cultural rights, civil and political rights and peoples' rights, is central to the pursuance of sustainable development,

CONSIDERS that the application and, where relevant, consolidation and further development of the following principles of international law relevant to the activities of all actors involved would be instrumental in pursuing the objective of sustainable development in an effective way:

NEW DELHI DECLARATION OF PRINCIPLES OF INTERNATIONAL LAW RELATING TO SUSTAINABLE DEVELOPMENT

1. The duty of States to ensure sustainable use of natural resources

It is a well-established principle that, in accordance with international law, all States have the sovereign right to manage their own natural resources pursuant to their own environmental and developmental policies, and the responsibility to ensure that activities within their jurisdiction or control do not cause significant damage to the environment of other States or of areas beyond the limits of national jurisdiction.

States are under a duty to manage natural resources, including natural resources solely within their own territory or jurisdiction, in a rational, sustainable and safe way so as to contribute to the development of their peoples, with particular regard for the rights of indigenous peoples, and to the conservation and sustainable use of natural resources and the protection of the environment, including ecosystems. States must take into account the needs of future generations in determining the rate of use of natural resources. All relevant actors (including States, industrial concerns and other components of civil society) are under a duty to avoid wasteful use of natural resources and promote waste minimization policies.

The protection, preservation and enhancement of the natural environment, particularly the proper management of climate system, biological diversity and fauna and flora of the Earth, are the common concern of humankind. The resources of outer space and celestial bodies and of the sea-bed, ocean floor and subsoil thereof beyond the limits of national jurisdiction are the common heritage of humankind.

2. The principle of equity and the eradication of poverty

The principle of equity is central to the attainment of sustainable development. It refers to both inter-generational equity (the rights of future generations to enjoy a fair level of the common patrimony) and intra-generational equity (the rights of all peoples within the current generation of fair access to the current generation's entitlement to the Earth's natural resources).

The present generation has a right to use and enjoy the resources of the Earth but is under an obligation to take into account the long-term impact of its activities and to sustain the resource base and the global environment for the benefit of future generations of humankind. 'Benefit' in this context is to be understood in its broadest meaning as including, inter alia, economic, environmental, social and intrinsic benefit.

The right to development must be implemented so as to meet developmental and environmental needs of present and future generations in a sustainable and equitable manner. This includes the duty to co-operate for the eradication of poverty in accordance with Chapter IX on International Economic and Social Co-operation of the Charter of the United Nations and the Rio Declaration on Environment and Development as well as the duty to co-operate for global sustainable development and the attainment of equity in the development opportunities of developed and developing countries.

Whilst it is the primary responsibility of the State to aim for conditions of equity within its own population and to ensure, as a minimum, the eradication of poverty, all States which are in a position to do so have a further responsibility, as recognised by the Charter of the United Nations and the Millennium Declaration of the United Nations, to assist States in achieving this objective.

3. The principle of common but differentiated responsibilities

States and other relevant actors have common but differentiated responsibilities. All States are under a duty to co-operate in the achievement of global sustainable development and the protection of the environment. International organizations, corporations (including in particular transnational corporations), non-governmental organizations and civil society should co-operate in and contribute to this global partnership. Industrial concerns have also responsibilities pursuant to the polluter pays principle.

Differentiation of responsibilities, whilst principally based on the contribution that a State has made to the emergence of environmental problems, must also take into account the economic and developmental situation of the State, in accordance with paragraph 3.3.

The special needs and interests of developing countries and of countries with economies in transition, with particular regard to least developed countries and those affected adversely by environmental, social and developmental considerations, should be recognized.

Developed countries bear a special burden of responsibility in reducing and eliminating unsustainable patterns of production and consumption and in contributing to capacity-building in developing countries, inter alia by providing financial assistance and access to environmentally sound technology. In particular, developed countries should play a leading role and assume primary responsibility in matters of relevance to sustainable development.

4. The principle of the precautionary approach to human health, natural resources and ecosystems

A precautionary approach is central to sustainable development in that it commits States, international organizations and the civil society, particularly the scientific and business communities, to avoid human activity which may cause significant harm to human health, natural resources or ecosystems, including in the face of scientific uncertainty.

Sustainable development requires that a precautionary approach with regard to human health, environmental protection and sustainable utilization of natural resources should include accountability for harm caused (including, where appropriate, State responsibility), planning based on clear criteria and well-defined goals, consideration of all possible means in an environmental impact assessment to achieve an objective (including, in certain instances, not proceeding with an envisaged activity) and, in respect of activities which may cause serious long-term or irreversible harm, establishing an appropriate burden of proof on the person or persons carrying out (or intending to carry out) the activity.

Decision-making processes should endorse a precautionary approach to risk management and in particular should proceed to the adoption of appropriate precautionary measures even when the absence of risk seems scientifically assured.

Precautionary measures should be based on up-to-date and independent scientific judgment and be transparent. They should not result in economic protectionism. Transparent structures should be established which involve all interested parties, including non-state actors, in the consultation process.

Appropriate review by a judicial body or administrative action should be available.

5. The principle of public participation and access to information and justice

Public participation is essential to sustainable development and good governance in that it is a condition of responsive, transparent and accountable governments as well a condition for the active engagement of equally responsive, transparent and accountable civil society organizations, including industrial concerns and trade unions. The vital role of women in sustainable development should be recognised.

Public participation in the context of sustainable development requires effective protection of the human right to hold and express opinions and to seek, receive and impart ideas. It also requires a right of access to appropriate, comprehensible and timely information held by governments and commerce on economic and social policies regarding the sustainable use of natural resources and the protection of the environment, without imposing undue financial burdens upon the applicants and with due consideration for privacy and adequate protection of business confidentiality.

The empowerment of peoples in the context of sustainable development requires access to effective judicial or administrative procedures in the State where the measure has been taken to challenge such measure and to claim compensation. States should ensure that where transboundary harm has been, or is likely to be, caused, individuals and peoples affected have non-discriminatory access to the same judicial and administrative procedures as would individuals and peoples of the State from which the harm is caused if such harm occurred in that State.

6. The principle of good governance

The principle of good governance is essential to the progressive development and codification of international law relating to sustainable development. It commits States and international organizations:
(a) to adopt democratic and transparent decision-making procedures and financial accountability;
(b) to take effective measures to combat official or other corruption;
(c) to respect due process in their procedures and to observe the rule of law and human rights; and
(d) to implement a public procurement approach according to the WTO Code on Public Procurement.

Civil society and non-governmental organizations have a right to good governance by States and international organizations. Non-state actors should be subject to internal democratic governance and to effective accountability.

Good governance requires full respect for the principles of the 1992 Rio Declaration on Environment and Development as well as the full participation of women in all levels of decision-making. Good governance also calls for corporate social responsibility and socially responsible investments as conditions for the existence of a global market aimed at a fair distribution of wealth among and within communities.

7. The principle of integration and interrelationship, in particular in relation to human rights and social, economic and environmental objectives

The principle of integration reflects the interdependence of social, economic, financial, environmental and human rights aspects of principles and rules of international law relating to sustainable development as well as of the needs of current and future generations of humankind.

All levels of governance – global, regional, national, sub-national and local – and all sectors of society should implement the integration principle, which is essential to the achievement of sustainable development.

States should strive to resolve apparent conflicts between competing economic, financial, social and environmental considerations, whether through existing institutions or through the establishment of appropriate new ones.

In their interpretation and application, the above principles are interrelated and each of them should be construed in the context of the other principles of this Declaration. Nothing in this Declaration shall be construed as prejudicing in any manner the provisions of the Charter of the United Nations and the rights of peoples under that Charter.

34

GOVERNING AND RECONCILING ECONOMIC, SOCIAL AND ENVIRONMENTAL REGIMES

Marie-Claire Cordonier Segger[1]

The World Summit on Sustainable Development (WSSD) in Johannesburg attracted 45,000 people from over 180 countries. Sustainable development is clearly a world priority. But it appears that sustainable is still hard to implement in a straightforward way.

This is not surprising. Sustainable development is a global goal rather than just one project or regulation. From formulation to implementation and monitoring, in law and in policy, three interrelated international spheres of action – economic, environmental and social – are shaped by the sustainable development objective. This conceptual challenge has a very practical result. Systems of governance and international cooperation for sustainable development are incredibly complex, and not very coherent. For sustainable development to be realised, there must be better accommodation, reconciliation and (in some instances) integration between economic development, social development and environmental protection.

This chapter contains a short summary of existing sustainable development governance structures, based on the JPOI, highlighting several specific aspects of the institutional arrangements for sustainable development that are relevant to international law. It then briefly discusses the dispute settlement forums where international sustainable development related disputes are currently resolved. It closes by proposing elements of a 'principled' legal test that international or domestic law-makers and judges might use when seeking to

[1] Marie-Claire Cordonier Segger, MEM (Yale), BCL & LLB (McGill), Director of the Centre for International Sustainable Development Law (CISDL), Chair, CISDL/ILA/IDLO Partnership on International Law on Sustainable Development, Senior Manager of Americas Research Portfolio for the International Institute for Sustainable Development and the United Nations Environment Programme ROLAC, British Chevening Scholar & SSHRC Fellow, Exeter College, Oxford University Faculty of Law. This chapter is a based on legal research for M.C. Cordonier Segger & A. Khalfan, *Sustainable Development Law: Principles, Practices & Prospects* (Oxford: Oxford University Press, 2004), with permission of the authors. The author is grateful to Foreign Affairs Canada, the British Chevening Awards, and the Social Sciences and Humanities Research Council of Canada, for their generous support for this research.

M.C. Cordonier Segger & C. G. Weeramantry, eds., Sustainable Justice: Reconciling Economic, Social & Environmental Law
© 2005 Koninklijke Brill NV, Printed in The Netherlands, pp.561-592.

reconcile social, economic and environmental policies and laws in the interest of sustainable development.

It examines the international regimes that currently govern accommodation, reconciliation and integration between the three substantive 'pillars' of sustainable development, considering how they could intersect in international policy and law. Two aspects are these regimes are particularly relevant.

First, if possible, it is best to avoid substantive international policy conflicts by ensuring coordination and coherence between the initiatives of international organisations with overlapping mandates. As such, the chapter examines the current international institutional architecture of sustainable development, to see how existing policy-making systems can accommodate, reconcile and integrate international social, economic and environmental objectives related to sustainable development. Second, when international disputes do arise, it is important that accommodation, reconciliation and integration can take place in a peaceful way. It is the proposal of this author that when this is done among parties who share a commitment to sustainable development, not only must the stakeholders or parties come to a just resolution, but also, the relevant aspects of all three fields of substantive law and policy should be at least accommodated, if not reconciled or integrated. Hence, the chapter briefly examines different international courts and tribunals in which economic, environmental and social priorities have recently come to a head, and considers this jurisprudence.

Further legal research is imperative to permit a comprehensive analysis of the legal aspects of accommodation between overlapping or conflicting social, economic and environmental interests, priorities and legal rights or obligations, reconciliation of such priorities, and finally, the integration of these, from the perspective of sustainable development law. This chapter will only discuss two particular aspects of sustainable development governance, presenting a very broad overview as a basis to propose certain elements of a legal test of 'sustainable development' in policy and in a judicial forum, and to inspire further legal research.

Sustainable Development Governance and the Results of the 2002 WSSD

Global systems of sustainable development governance, after the 2002 World Summit for Sustainable Development, have arguably been clarified.[2] The Johannesburg Plan of Implementation (JPOI) attempted, in Chapter XI on the 'institutional framework for sustainable development', to encourage greater

---

[2] The WSSD was mandated by the UN GA, see "Ten-year Review of Progress Achieved in the Implementation of the Outcome of the United Nations Conference on Environment and Development" UNGA Res A/RES/55/199 20 Dec 2000.

coherence.[3] In the WSSD negotiations, government officials, experts and NGOs struggled to review existing, rather inchoate international governance structures within and outside the United Nations, gaining a detailed understanding of their interrelations. Several key proposals to improve sustainable development governance were debated and accepted.[4] While the final text of the JPOI did not make as much progress as many may have hoped,[5] much of the existing sustainable development governance system was clarified, and certain important steps were taken.

The 2002 JPOI sheds some light on the current global institutional[6] architecture for sustainable development.

A careful analysis of the JPOI suggests that international institutions whose mandates relate to sustainable development, led by the United Nations itself, are linked by a nascent, rudimentary governance system, inasmuch as they are responsible for the implementation of the 1992 Agenda 21[7] and the 2002 WSSD outcomes. These institutions identify and address emerging sustainable development governance challenges. They also have roles in implementing other internationally agreed development goals, such as the objective of the 2000 *United Nations Millennium Declaration*, the 2002 *Monterrey Consensus on Financing for Development*,[8] and the relevant outcomes of other major UN conferences and international agreements.[9]

According to the JPOI, there is a need for all of these actors to strengthen commitments to sustainable development, and integrate the economic, social and environmental dimensions of sustainable development in a balanced

---

[3] See the Johannesburg Plan of Implementation, Report of the World Summit on Sustainable Development, Johannesburg (South Africa) (4 Sept. 2002) UN Doc. A/CONF.199/20:
<http://www.un.org/esa/sustdev/documents/WSSD_POI_PD/English/POIToc.htm>
[4] See "Sustainable Development Governance" (Paper prepared by the World Summit for Sustainable Development Governance Working Group Vice-Chairs Ositadinma Anaedu and Lars-Goran Engfeldt). Available online: <www.johannesburgsummit.org/html/documents/prepcom3docs/governance30.3.rev1.doc>.
[5] UN University, *Sustainable Development Governance: The Question of Reform: Key Issues and Proposals.* (Tokyo: United Nations University Institute for Advanced Studies, 2002).
[6] In this book, an institution is defined as '*a network of organisations and other actors that are working towards a common mandate, supported by a common organisational structure.*' This definition encompasses the goals and rules, those devising them, and the coordination mechanisms and structures that are used to achieve the goals within the rules. See UNDP, *Capacity Development for Governance for Sustainable Human Development* (New York: UNDP, 1996). See also M. Lovei, and P. Pillai, *Assessing Environmental Policy, Regulatory and Institutional Capacity: A World Bank Policy Note* (Washington, D.C.: World Bank, 2003).
[7] *Agenda 21*, Report of the UNCED, I (1992) UN Doc. A/CONF.151/26/Rev.1, (1992) 31 I.L.M. 874. [Hereinafter *Agenda 21*]. References to Agenda 21, in the JPOI, also include the 1992 *Rio Declaration on Environment and Development, Report of the United Nations Conference on Environment and Development*, U.N. Doc. A/CONF.151/6/Rev.1, (1992), 31 I.L.M. 874 (1992) and the 1997 *Programme for the Further Implementation of Agenda 21* GA Res. A/RES/S-19/2, UN GAOR, 19th Sess., UN Doc. A/Res/S-19/2 (1997).
[8] Further information on the International Conference on Financing for Development, held in Monterrey, Mexico from 18-22 March, 2002, can be found at the ECOSOC website, online: <http://www.un.org/esa/ffd>.
[9] Further information on the international series of conferences from 2002 can be found at the ECOSOC website, online: <http://www.un.org/esa>.

manner. There is also a need to enhance implementation of Agenda 21,[10] to strengthen coherence, coordination and monitoring; to better promote the rule of law and strengthen governmental institutions. The JPOI highlights several priorities for governance. These include the need to increase effectiveness and efficiency;[11] to enhance participation and effective involvement of civil society and other relevant stakeholders;[12] to strengthen capacities for sustainable development at all levels;[13] and to strengthen international cooperation.

To meet these wide-ranging objectives, the JPOI defines an international sustainable development governance system. It sets out an international framework that is meant to enhance and link the work of different institutions dealing with economic, social and environmental issues. This global framework for sustainable development governance is complex and multi-tiered. It can be described as an inter-linked system of institutions, and the international, regional and national regimes in which they operate. This regime is shaped on three principal levels:
- international (including the United Nations General Assembly, the United Nations Economic and Social Council (ECOSOC), and the United Nations Commission for Sustainable Development (UNCSD),[14] but also other agencies and international organisations),
- regional (including the UN Regional Commissions and other regional and sub-regional bodies, including the regional development banks) and
- national (which includes local authorities).[15]

Economic, social and environmental pillars of sustainable development governance:

Integration was recognised as an essential element of global sustainable development governance. Many institutions have been established, on several levels, to implement mandates from all three pillars of sustainable development. The JPOI recognizes the need to strengthen and better integrate the social, economic and environmental dimensions of sustainable development into policies and programmes at all these levels. As such, sustainable development governance is not simply about international environmental governance -

---

[10] This includes the mobilization of financial and technological resources as well as capacity-building programmes, particularly for developing countries.

[11] This can be done, in part, by limiting overlap and duplication of activities of international organizations, both within and outside the United Nations system, based on their mandates and comparative advantages.

[12] As well as promoting transparency and broad public participation, to further implement Agenda 21, *supra* note 7.

[13] Including the local level, in particular those of developing countries.

[14] Further information on the United Nations Commission on Sustainable Development and its relationship to other international organisations can be found at the UN CSD website, online: <http://www.un.org/esa/sustdev/csd.htm>.

[15] Further information on the United Nations Commission on Sustainable Development and its relationship to other international organisations can be found at the UN CSD website, online: <http://www.un.org/esa/sustdev/csd.htm>. Further information on the broader United Nations system of agencies, and their relationship to other international organisations, can be found at the UN website, online: <http://www.un.org>.

indeed, those discussions were carried out outside the WSSD.[16] Rather, in the new sustainable development governance system, it was recognised that all three fields of sustainable development law and policy – economic, social and environmental – needed to be strengthened. And where there is overlap or intersection between the fields, including for cross-cutting or emerging issues, several forums have been charged to facilitate more coordinated and coherent implementation activities.[17]

First, the JPOI identifies a clear need for further collaboration between the WTO and the United Nations Conference on Trade and Development (UNCTAD), the International Labour Organisation (ILO), the United Nations Development Programme (UNDP), the UNEP and other relevant organisations and agencies. The exact nature of these links, as well as calls for trade and financing institutions to take sustainable development goals more seriously, were highly controversial points in negotiations leading up to the WSSD. In the international economic area, debates centred on the need to further enhance the contribution of trade and finance institutions to sustainable development. There were strong claims, especially from developing countries, to go beyond the provisions of the Monterrey Consensus for more concrete commitments on financing for sustainable development.

The JPOI calls for trade and financial agencies to enhance the integration of sustainable development goals into their activities and take full account of national programmes to achieve sustainable development. It also calls on countries to take concrete action to implement the *Monterrey Consensus* at all levels. It further indicates the need to ensure a 'dynamic and enabling international economic environment' and the importance of promoting global economic governance through 'addressing the international finance, trade, technology and investment patterns that have an impact on the development prospects' of developing countries.[18] As such, in the international economic pillar, three priorities emerge. There is a need to re-focus trade and financial policies toward sustainable development, to deliver on commitments made in Monterrey on financing for development, and to deal with international finance, trade, technology and investment patterns that have impacts on (or block) development prospects.

---

[16] See UNEP/GCSS.VII/6, Annex I. The United Nations Environment Programme Governing Council, the Global Ministers of Environment Forum, and the international environmental governance (IEG) process are discussed earlier in this book, at Part I – The Foundations.

[17] This is particularly important for developing countries with newly designed national development strategies (including those for economic growth, or poverty reduction). These countries are often facing simultaneous pressures from international agencies, different treaty commitments and global markets.

[18] In this respect, the JPOI recommends that the international community ensure support for structural and macroeconomic reform, a comprehensive solution to the external debt problem and increasing market access for developing countries. It also observes that efforts to reform the international financial architecture need to be sustained with greater transparency and the effective participation of developing countries in decision-making processes. Finally, it is stated that a universal, rules-based, open, non-discriminatory and equitable multilateral trading system, as well as meaningful trade liberalization, can substantially stimulate development worldwide, benefiting countries at all stages of development.

The JPOI also recognises that the social dimension of sustainable development needs to be strengthened. It recognises the need to promote the full integration of sustainable development objectives into programmes and policies of bodies that have a primary focus on social issues. It also emphasizes the need to strengthen follow-up to the outcomes of the World Summit for Social Development and its five-year review, and take into account their reports. In the negotiations, it was important to several developing countries that the social agenda be recognised as broader than simply labour rights, and that the work of the ILO[19] was placed in the broader context of social development. The consensus, in the end, to refer to 'bodies that have a primary focus on social issues' proved to bridge this gap.

International environmental governance is carried out through the implementation of the outcomes of UNEP's Governing Council Seventh Special Session, Decision I: International Environment Governance (IEG).[20] This decision was the result of a ministerial-level intergovernmental process, established by the UNEP governing council, addressing issues and options for strengthening international environmental governance.[21] In the negotiations for the JPOI, some actors sought to re-open the IEG process. As environmental governance is only one part of sustainable development governance (and as the IEG decision had been the result of very difficult negotiations), this idea was rejected. The IEG process clarified and streamlined the global system of environmental governance, helped to stabilise UNEP financing arrangements through a modified system of assessed contributions, recognised the Environmental Management Group within the UN system, helped to 'group' MEAs along programmatic lines, and re-focused attention on the UNEP Governing Council / UNEP Global Forum of Environment Ministers as the hub of a global network of environmental institutions. As did the IEG, the JPOI left one controversial point for resolution in the United Nations General Assembly. Specifically, it invited the 'General Assembly... to consider the important but complex issue of establishing universal membership for the Governing Council/Global Ministerial Environment Forum' (GMEF). Universal membership in the GMEF may be the first step toward the establishment of a global environmental organisation or mechanism.

The role of the international community in sustainable development governance

On the international level, according to the JPOI, a cooperative system is centred on the role of the broader international community and three specific

---

[19] Further information on the International Labour Organisation can be found at the ILO website, online: <http://www.ilo.org>.

[20] Further information on the United Nations Environment Programme, and the international environmental governance negotiations, can be found at the UNEP website, online: <http://www.unep.org/IEG>.

[21] See also M.C. Cordonier Segger, A. Khalfan, M. Gehring, *International Environmental Governance for Sustainable Development: A Legal Brief* (Montreal: CISDL, 2001) available online: <http://www.cisdl.org>.

international institutions: the United Nations General Assembly (UNGA), the United Nations Economic and Social Council (ECOSOC), and the United Nations Commission for Sustainable Development (UNCSD), and linked to other international organisations.

Collaboration, according to the JPOI, must be encouraged within and between the UN system, the International Financial Institutions, the Global Environment Facility and the World Trade Organisation (WTO). To do this, a rather complex grouping of institutions, including the United Nations Chief Executive Board (CEB), the UN Development Group and the Environment Management Group (EMG) and other inter-agency coordinating bodies, are directed to coordinate.[22] This cooperation does not is not meant to take place through additional meetings- rather, it is to be mainly operational, in partnership with others at all levels.

In three slightly new points, the JPOI also mentions the need for timely completion of negotiations on a comprehensive *United Nations Convention against Corruption*,[23] recommends that the international community promote corporate responsibility and accountability,[24] and encourages multi-stakeholder dialogue. There was a trade-off between an explicit recognition of the U.N. and international law, very much desired by the EU, many developing countries and others, and global support for an Anti-Corruption Convention, very much desired by the USA. Interestingly, in the end, it appears that both groups achieved their goal. The JPOI emphasizes that "a vibrant and effective United Nations system is fundamental to the promotion of international cooperation for sustainable development and to a global economic system that works for all." It notes the importance of a firm commitment to "the ideals of the United Nations, the principles of international law and those enshrined in the Charter of the United Nations" (a clear recognition that the principles of international law have evolved beyond those specifically mentioned in the Charter). It also commits to strengthening the United Nations system and other multilateral institutions and promoting the improvement of their operations.

The role of the UN General Assembly, ECOSOC and the CSD:

The General Assembly of the United Nations (UN GA) was recommended to adopt sustainable development as a key element of the overarching framework for UN activities, particularly for achieving the internationally agreed development goals, including those contained in the *Millennium Declaration*. It is also to give overall political direction to the implementation of Agenda 21 and

---

[22] Further information on the United Nations system of agencies, and their relationship to other international organisations, can be found at the UN CSD website, online: <http://www.un.org/esa/sustdev/csd.htm>.
[23] Including the question of repatriation of funds illicitly acquired to countries of origin and promoting stronger cooperation to eliminate money laundering.
[24] For further proposals on how this could be done, see M.C. Cordonier Segger, "Sustainability and Corporate Accountability Regimes: Implementing the Johannesburg Summit Agenda" (2003) 12:3 *R.E.C.I.E.L.*

its review. This sets a global mandate in place, so that all other UN Agencies will support sustainable development objectives.

But on the international level, the UN GA's Economic and Social Council (ECOSOC) [25] and its Commission on Sustainable Development (UN CSD)[26] will play key roles.

First, the JPOI grants a stronger role to the UN ECOSOC, especially in matters of coordination. ECOSOC is mandated to increase its role in overseeing system-wide coordination and the balanced integration of economic, social and environmental aspects of United Nations policies and programmes aimed at promoting sustainable development. It is to organize periodic consideration of sustainable development themes in regard to the implementation of Agenda 21, including the means of implementation. It is to make full use of its high-level, coordination, operational activities and its general meetings to take into account all relevant aspects of the work of the United Nations on sustainable development.[27] It is also to promote greater coordination, complementarity, effectiveness and efficiency of activities of its functional commissions (such as the Commission on Sustainable Development, the Commission on Social Development, and others) and other subsidiary bodies; and ensure that there is a close link between the role of the Council in the follow-up to the Summit and its role in the follow-up to the Monterrey Consensus.[28] It is requested to intensify its efforts for gender mainstreaming.[29]

Second, the JPOI also recognizes the UN CSD, as a Commission of the ECOSOC, will continue to be the high-level forum within the UN system for consideration of issues related to integration of the three dimensions of sustainable development. The UN CSD is only one agency among many involved in sustainable development law and policy,[30] but - as the focus for the

---

[25] Explicit provisions regarding the United Nations Economic and Social Council (ECOSOC), and the General Assembly Resolutions 48/162 and 50/227, reaffirmed ECOSOC as the central mechanism for coordination of the UN system in this aspect, and its specialised agencies and supervision of subsidiary bodies, in particular its functional commissions (such as UN CSD). See *Charter of the United Nations,* 26 June 1945, Can. T.S. 1945 No. 7. See also *Agenda 21, supra* note 11. Further information on the United Nations Economic and Social Council can be found at the UN ECOSOC website, online: <http://www.un.org/esa/coordination/ecosoc>.

[26] The role, functions and mandate of the United Nations Commission on Sustainable Development (UN CSD) were set out in *Agenda 21, supra* note 11, and adopted in General Assembly Resolution 47/191. Further information can be found at the UN CSD website, online: <http://www.un.org/esa/sustdev/csd.htm>.

[27] In this context, the Council is directed to encourage the active participation of major groups in its high-level segment and the work of its relevant functional commissions, in accordance with the respective rules of procedure.

[28] To that end, the Council is asked to explore ways to develop arrangements relating to its meetings with the Bretton Woods Institutions and the World Trade Organization, as set out in the Monterrey Consensus.

[29] The JPOI also streamlined a little - the Committee on Energy and Natural Resources for Development was terminated, and its work transferred to the UN CSD.

[30] According to the JPOI, the UN CSD continues to be the high-level commission on sustainable development within the United Nations system. It serves as a forum for consideration of issues related to integration of the three dimensions of sustainable development. The JPOI recognizes that although the role, functions and mandate of the Commission set out in Agenda 21, *supra* note 7, and adopted in the UN

UN System on these issues – it remains an important one. It is directed to place more emphasis on actions that enable implementation at all levels, including promoting and facilitating partnerships involving Governments, international organizations and relevant stakeholders for the implementation of Agenda 21. Implementation means more work for policy bodies, but a different kind of work.

To understand how this changes sustainable development governance, a little history is needed. The role, functions and mandate of the UN CSD were set out in Agenda 21 and adopted in General Assembly Resolution 47/191.[31] In the 1992 Earth Summit preparatory process, a follow up mechanism was needed for the United Nations to track progress toward sustainable development. In the end, it was agreed that a new functioning Commission would be set up, under the auspices of the United Nations ECOSOC.[32] At Chapter 38, Agenda 21 states that "...to ensure the effective follow-up of the Conference, as well as to enhance international cooperation and rationalization the intergovernmental decision making capacity for the integration of environment and development issues and to examine the progress of the implementation of Agenda 21 at the national, regional and international levels, a high level Commission on Sustainable Development should be established in accordance with Article 68 of the Charter of the UN."[33]

After the Earth Summit in 1992, the UN General Assembly agreed that the ECOSOC would establish a high level Commission as a functional council body, and elect representatives of 53 states to serve for up to three-year terms. As such, the UN CSD is made up of 53 members, a third of which are up for election each year.[34] One of the interesting aspects of elections to the UN CSD is that these have been actively pursued by countries, unlike many other UN Commissions. Between 1992 and 2002, the UN CSD met once a year for two or three weeks, as a functional ECOSOC Commission with a full time secretariat based in New York, and it was given a clear identity within the UN system. The Secretariat is located within the Department for Social and Economic Affairs (DESA). DESA also has secretariats for the Commissions on Population, Status of Women and Social Development, offering a good opportunity for collaboration. Relevant intergovernmental organizations and specialized agencies (UNEP, WHO, UNDP and others, including financial institutions) designated representatives to advise and assist the Commission, serving as focal points between sessions. The 1992 Earth Summit had also seen

---

General Assembly Resolution 47/191 continue to be relevant, the UN CSD needs to be strengthened and other relevant institutions and organizations taken into account.
[31] Further information on the United Nations Commission on Sustainable Development can be found at the UN CSD website, online: <http://www.un.org/esa/sustdev/csd.htm>.
[32] *Supra* note 29.
[33] *Agenda 21, supra* note 11 at Chapter 38. See also the *Charter of the United Nations, supra* note 29, at Art. 68.
[34] The allocation of seats is 13 from Africa, 11 from Asia, 6 from Eastern Europe, 10 from Latin America and the Caribbean and 13 from Western Europe and North America.

an unprecedented involvement of stakeholders in the preparatory process and the Summit itself. Agenda 21 contains nine chapters dealing with the role of Major Groups.[35] In its first ten years of work, the UN CSD established innovative formal and informal procedures which gave major groups extremely high involvement in their work, and excellent access to deliberations.

The UN CSD's mandate was originally fairly broad.[36] The UN CSD did not negotiate treaties. If an issue required a stronger legal framework, initial discussions took place at CSD, but were then designated to an appropriate body to negotiate legally binding actions. In the years between 1992 and 2002, several critiques were raised by developing countries and others.[37] However, the CSD also developed a track record of certain achievements for international sustainable development policy, as a 'soft law' forum.[38] In international law on sustainable development, such soft law instruments[39] are common. Mainly, the UN CSD provided space for dialogue, coordination and eventual cooperation which leads to international instruments. The involvement of major groups at the CSD has increased each year, with formal and informal procedures being developed.[40]

---

[35] The Major Groups in Agenda 21 are Youth, Women, Farmers, NGOs, Local Government, Business, Academics, Indigenous People, and Trade Unions. See *Agenda 21*, *supra* note 7, at ch. 24 – 32.

[36] See UNGA Resolution 1993/207. UN CSD was to monitor progress on the implementation of *Agenda 21* and activities related to the integration of environmental and developmental goals by governments, NGOs, and other UN bodies; to monitor progress towards the target of 0.7% GNP from developed countries for Overseas Development Aid; to review the adequacy of financing and the transfer of technologies as outlined in *Agenda 21*; to receive and analyse relevant information from competent NGOs in the context of *Agenda 21* implementation; to enhance dialogue with NGOs, the independent sector, and other entities outside the UN system, within the UN framework; and to provide recommendations to the General Assembly through the Economic and Social Council (ECOSOC).

[37] They had expected the UN CSD to provide an effective body to monitor progress towards the target of 0.7% GNP, ensuring adequate financing and the transfer of sustainable-development related technologies, but this was not perceived to have happened. The UN CSD looked at finance and technology transfer themes in isolation from issues that might have enabled an effective argument for new funds. In addition, while occasionally development, transport, energy or agriculture Ministers would attend if their sector was being discussed, UN CSD was rarely attended by Ministers with budgets to deliver additional financing for sustainable development. Other critiques were also raised.

[38] According to F. Dodds, these have included recommendations to codify Prior Informed Consent procedures (1994); the establishment of an Inter Governmental Panel on Forests (1995) and an International Forum on Forests (1997); supporting the Washington Global Plan of Action on protecting the marine environment from land-based activities (1996), agreeing to the replenishment of Global Environmental Facility (GEF) (1997); setting a firm date of 2002 for governments to produce their National Sustainable Development Strategies (1997); establishing a new process in the General Assembly to discuss oceans (1999); agreeing that new consumer guidelines would include sustainable development (1999); and developing an International Work Programme on Sustainable Tourism (1999). See F. Dodds, "Reforming the International Institutions" in *Earth Summit 2002: A New Deal*, F. Dodds, ed., (London: EarthScan, 2002), online: <http://www.earthsummit2002.org/es/issues/Governance/governance.htm#Sustainable%20Governance>.

[39] The 1972 *Stockholm Declaration,* the 1992 *Rio Declaration* and the 2002 *Johannesburg Declaration* are all non-binding instruments, as are the 1992 *Forest Principles* adopted at UNCED. While not binding in the traditional sense, many statements of principles, guidelines, and codes of practices are influential international instruments. For example, the 2002 *Bonn Guidelines on Access to Genetic Resources and Fair and Equitable Sharing of their Benefits*, the 1990 FAO *Guidelines on the Operation of Prior Informed Consent.*

[40] These included access and speaking privileges in formal and informal meetings (1993); questions during national presentations (1994); Dialogue Sessions (1997); interventions in Heads of State meeting of the UN General Assembly Special Session (1997); and inclusion of outcomes in Ministerial discussion and official UN CSD Intersessional records (1999). The involvement of civil society organisations and Major Groups in the

The new mandate of the UN CSD will focus on reviewing and monitoring the progress in implementation of Agenda 21, and fostering coherence of implementation, initiatives and partnerships. The UN CSD will still develop recommendations, but negotiations will be limited to every two years, and the number of themes addressed in each session will be constrained. As such, the UN CSD has been limited to a few clarified and strengthened functions.

It will review and evaluate progress, address new challenges and opportunities, and promote further implementation of sustainable development. It will focus on the cross-sectoral aspects of specific issues, provide a forum for policy integration.[41] In relation to its role in facilitating implementation, the UN CSD is directed to emphasize various aspects. It will review progress and promote the further implementation of Agenda 21, identifying constraints on implementation and making recommendations to overcome those constraints. It will also serve as a focal point for the discussion of partnerships that promote sustainable development, including sharing lessons learned, progress made and best practices. In addition, it will review issues related to financial assistance and transfer of technology for sustainable development, as well as capacity-building. This was a significant point for developing countries – many felt that members of UN CSD had not lived up to their UNCED commitments on development assistance. It will provide a forum for analysis and exchange of experience on measures that assist sustainable development planning, decision-making and the implementation of sustainable development strategies. Finally, it will take into account significant legal developments in the field of sustainable development, with due regard to the role of relevant intergovernmental bodies in promoting the implementation of Agenda 21 relating to international legal instruments and mechanisms.[42]

WSSD process has been unprecedented, with concrete steps being taken to ensure participation at each level. See F. Dodds, *supra* note 38. The 1992 Earth Summit had also seen an unprecedented involvement of stakeholders in the preparatory process and the Summit itself. *Agenda 21* contains nine chapters dealing with the role of major groups. The Major Groups in *Agenda 21* are Youth, Women, Farmers, NGOs, Local Government, Business, Academics, Indigenous People, and Trade Unions. See *Agenda 21*, *supra* note 7, at Ch. 24.

[41] Including through interaction among Ministers dealing with the various dimensions and sectors of sustainable development through the high-level segments.

[42] For a proposal on sustainable development governance, the role and future mechanisms for the UN CSD to facilitate implementation and take into account significant legal developments in the field of sustainable development, see M. C. Cordonier Segger, "Significant developments in sustainable development law and governance: A proposal" (2004) 28:1 *U. N. Natural Resources Forum* 61–74.

The CSD's new work program is mandated to reflect these developments.[43] At its eleventh session, the Commission on Sustainable Development decided that its multi-year programme of work beyond 2003 would be organized on the basis of seven two-year cycles, with each cycle focusing on selected thematic clusters of issues. In 2004 – 2005, the CSD will address Water, Sanitation and Human Settlements. In 2006 – 2007, it will address Energy for Sustainable Development, Industrial Development, Air Pollution / Atmosphere and Climate Change. In 2008 – 2009, it will address Agriculture, Rural Development, Land, Drought, Desertification and Africa. In 2010 – 2011, it will address Transport, Chemicals, Waste Management and Mining, and a Ten Year Framework of Programmes on Sustainable Consumption and Production Patterns. In 2012 – 2013, it will address Forests, Biodiversity, Biotechnology, Tourism and Mountains. And in 2014-2015, it will address Oceans and Seas, Marine Resources and Small Island Developing States.

In each of these areas, it will take into account significant legal developments in the field of sustainable development. In each cycle, the thematic clusters of issues will be addressed in an integrated manner with regard to the economic, social and environmental dimensions of sustainable development. The Commission further agreed that means of implementation should be addressed in every cycle and for every relevant issue, action and commitment. Linkages to other cross-cutting issues are also to be addressed in every cycle.[44] Finally, the CSD is also mandated to share best practices and lessons learned in sustainable development, using contemporary methods of data collection and dissemination, especially information technologies.

The role of other international institutions

In terms of the role of other international institutions, the new sustainable development governance framework stresses the need for international institutions both within and outside the UN system to enhance their contribution to sustainable development.[45] The Secretary-General of the United

---

[43] The work program was directed to continue to provide for more direct and substantive involvement of international organisations as well as major groups in its work; give greater consideration to the scientific contributions to sustainable development; further the contribution of educators to sustainable development including, where appropriate, in the activities of the UN CSD; and promote best practices and lessons learned in sustainable development, as well as use of contemporary methods of data collection and dissemination, including broader use of information technologies. In regard to the practical modalities and work program of UN CSD, specific decisions were made later, in the UN CSD 11 Meeting, when the Commission's thematic work program was elaborated.

[44] These include: Poverty eradication, Changing unsustainable patterns of consumption and production, Protecting and managing the natural resource base of economic and social development, Sustainable development in a globalizing world, Health and sustainable development, Sustainable development of SIDS, Sustainable development for Africa, Other regional initiatives, Means of implementation, Institutional framework for sustainable development, Gender equality, and Education.

[45] These include international financial institutions (IFIs), the World Trade Organisation (WTO) and the Global Environment Facility (GEF), and the JPOI directs them to enhance, within their mandates, their cooperative efforts to promote effective and collective support to the implementation of Agenda 21 at all levels. This is to be done with enhanced collaboration, not only on Agenda 21 but also for the outcomes of

Nations is encouraged to use the Chief Executives Board for Coordination to further promote system-wide inter-agency cooperation and coordination on sustainable development, to take appropriate measures to facilitate exchange of information, and to keep ECOSOC and CSD informed of different actions being taken to implement Agenda 21. A report by the Secretary-General on the "Follow-up to Johannesburg and the Future Role of the CSD"[46] shed some clarity on this constellation of actors, and outlined new roles for various different aspects of the system.[47] Myriad other roles were also recognized in the JPOI, and it refers directly to the contributions of different UN Agencies to sustainable development.[48] The need to streamline and open the international sustainable development governance system was also recognised.[49]

Other international aspects of the new sustainable development governance agenda should also be highlighted. The JPOI agreed to strengthen UNDP capacity building programmes for sustainable development. It committed to strengthen cooperation among UNEP and other UN bodies and specialized agencies, the Bretton Woods Institutions and the WTO, within their mandates. The UNEP, UN-Habitat, UNDP and UNCTAD were also requested to strengthen their contribution to sustainable development programmes and the implementation of Agenda 21 at all levels, particularly in the area of promoting capacity building. Finally, in a welcome step, governments established that the 1994 *United Nations Convention to Combat Desertification and Drought*, like other Rio Conventions, will have a dedicated, specific and permanent financial mechanism. To follow up from this decision, land degradation was indeed recognised as a GEF focal area, through the decisions of the GEF Second Assembly in October 2002.

---

the World Summit on Sustainable Development, relevant sustainable development aspects of the Millennium Declaration; the Monterrey Consensus; and the outcomes of the Fourth WTO Ministerial Meeting (Doha).

[46] 18 February 2003 E/CN.17/2003/2.

[47] It purports a shift in focus from reporting and supporting normative discussions to implementation with a greater emphasis on specific thematic areas and goals/objectives; support for the follow-up mechanisms by other UN Conferences held during the last decade; promotion of stronger linkages between global intergovernmental deliberations and implementation measures at a country level; institution of more flexible, action-oriented, innovative and inclusive approaches with UN Agencies and non-UN actors; and promotion of overall integration of the three components of sustainable development. The report also points to the need for strengthening the UN CSD and expanding its resources so as to enable it to fulfill its original mandate of a coordinating body within the UN system and its new post-Johannesburg mandate for implementation of the WEHAB agreements.

[48] The JPOI stresses that UNDP has capacity building programmes for sustainable development. It commits to strengthen cooperation among UNEP and other UN bodies and specialized agencies, the Bretton Woods Institutions and the WTO, within their mandates. The UNEP, UN-Habitat, UNDP and UNCTAD are also expected to strengthen their contribution to sustainable development programmes and the implementation of Agenda 21 at all levels, particularly in the area of promoting capacity building. Johannesburg Plan of Implementation, *supra* note 7.

[49] Governments also agreed to streamline the international sustainable development meeting calendar in favour of more time spent on practical matters related to implementation. They will encourage partnership initiatives for implementation by all relevant actors.

Sustainable development governance at the regional (and sub-regional) levels

According to the JPOI, regional sustainable development governance must also be strengthened. The United Nations Regional Commissions, as well as other regional and sub-regional institutions and bodies, are given a special role in the implementation of Agenda 21 and the outcomes of the World Summit on Sustainable Development.[50] Their role, in particular, is to facilitate and promote a balanced integration of the economic, social and environmental dimensions of sustainable development into the work of regional, sub-regional and other bodies. They will facilitate exchange of experiences related to best practices, case studies and partnerships. They will also assist in the mobilization of technical and financial assistance, as well as facilitate the provision of adequate financing for sustainable development programmes and projects, including those related to poverty eradication. They will also continue to promote multi-stakeholder participation and encourage partnerships to support implementation of Agenda 21 at the regional and sub-regional levels. Finally, the JPOI specifically recognises the need to support the sustainable development programmes of certain groups.[51]

Sustainable development governance at the national, sub-national and local levels.

Sustainable development governance also has a very important national dimension. According to the JPOI, countries will promote coherent and coordinated approaches to institutional frameworks for sustainable development, strengthening domestic authorities and mechanisms necessary for policy-making, coordination and implementation and enforcement of laws. Countries also committed to take immediate steps to make progress in the formulation and elaboration of national strategies for sustainable development, and to begin implementing these strategies by 2005.[52] In WSSD negotiations, this concrete target was viewed as a significant step forward by most countries.[53] Each country has the primary responsibility for its own sustainable development, reiterated the JPOI, they should promote sustainable development at the national level by, *inter alia*, enacting and enforcing clear and

---

[50] This includes improving intraregional coordination and cooperation on sustainable development the regional commissions, United Nations Funds, programmes and agencies, regional development banks and other regional and sub-regional institutions and bodies. It also includes support for development, enhancement and implementation of agreed regional sustainable development strategies and action plans, reflecting national and regional priorities.

[51] For example, the New Partnership for Africa's Development (NEPAD) and the inter-regional aspects of the globally agreed Barbados Programme of Action for the Sustainable Development of Small Island Developing States.

[52] To this end, as appropriate, strategies should be supported through international cooperation, taking into account the special needs of developing countries, in particular the least developed countries. Such strategies, which, where applicable, could be formulated as poverty reduction strategies that integrate economic, social and environmental aspects of sustainable development, should be pursued in accordance with each country's national priorities.

[53] The delegation of Norway was aware that such a statement could also weaken earlier Agenda 21 commitments, and worked to strengthen these and other commitments.

effective laws. Countries were encouraged to strengthen governmental institutions, including by providing necessary infrastructure, by promoting transparency and accountability, and fair administrative and judicial institutions.

In addition, all countries should also promote public participation, including through measures that provide access to information regarding legislation, regulations, activities, policies and programmes,[54] according to the JPOI. Governments called for support for developing country (and economy in transitions) efforts to enhance national and local institutional arrangements for sustainable development,[55] highlighting the need to enhance the role and capacity of local authorities, and to link with the 1996 *United Nations Conference on Human Settlements (UN Habitat II) Agenda*.

As such, the implementation of international law on sustainable development has been directly strengthened in three ways. First, the UN CSD has a new mandate to take into account significant legal developments in the field of sustainable development. Second, international organizations from each 'pillar' of sustainable development are mandated to focus on coherence, coordination and cooperation in their policies and operations, and many international institutional mechanisms are set in place or strengthened to encourage this. Third, national governments are specifically charged to enact clear and effective domestic laws, to promote fair administrative and judicial institutions, and to provide access to information on legislation and regulations.

Participation of major groups

Governments and inter-governmental agencies will not be alone in their efforts. The JPOI recognized the need for governments to enhance partnerships between governmental and non-governmental actors, including all major groups, as well as volunteer groups, on programmes and activities for the achievement of sustainable development at all levels. It appears that Stephen Toope and others were correct in observing that international law and policy is being broadened to include actors other than States as norm-generating actors.[56] Non-state actors now help to develop, implement and comply with norms. An important factor has been the emergence of international and regional organisations within which government officials and experts, as well as

---

[54] It commits to foster full public participation in sustainable development policy formulation and implementation, and to ensure that women can participate fully and equally in policy formulation and decision-making. It also mentions sustainable development councils and/or coordination structures, and multi-stakeholder participation.

[55] This could include promoting cross-sectoral approaches in the formulation of strategies and plans for sustainable development, such as, where applicable, poverty reduction strategies, aid coordination, encouraging participatory approaches and enhancing policy analysis, management capacity and implementation capacity, including mainstreaming a gender perspective in all those activities.

[56] See J. Brunée and S.J. Toope "International Law and Constructivism: Elements of an Interactional Theory of International Law" (2000) 39(1) *Col. J. Trans'l. Law* 19 at 48. The writers refer to lawmaking as a mutually generative activity, and the dual function of States as both makers and observers of international law.

non-governmental individual and group actors, interact and consider alternative policy options to address emerging problems.[57] These emerging international regimes consist of networks, partnerships between States and these non-state actors (including inter-governmental organisations, civil society and private sector associations). The JPOI also acknowledged the need to further consider the relationship between environment and human rights, including the right to development (with full and transparent participation of Member States of the United Nations and observer States). And it commits to promote and support youth participation in programmes and activities relating to sustainable development.[58]

International Settlement of Sustainable Development Related Disputes

Several important international disputes related to sustainable development have arisen in recent years. Only an extremely small percentage of sustainable development related disputes actually arise between two or more states, and are subject to the jurisdiction of an international court or tribunal. An even smaller percentage are of such importance, for the countries involved, as to be brought to an expensive and lengthy international court or tribunal proceeding. Indeed, it is almost surprising that in recent years, so many such disputes have filtered up into formal international dispute settlement processes.

It is important for the international order that accommodation, reconciliation and integration of sustainable development issues can take place in a peaceful way.[59] Not only must the stakeholders and parties to the dispute find a just resolution, but also, for sustainable development, the substantive social, economic and environmental priorities should be reconciled, in order to ensure that the resulting actions contribute to development that can last in the interests of both present and future generations.

Proliferation of international mechanisms for cooperation appears to be a key characteristic of globalisation. In recent years, many learned scholars have analysed the growing complexity of the international system of courts and tribunals.[60] Due to the limits of space, this section will simply survey a few

---

[57] On the role of international organisations as sites of interaction and arenas for coalition building at the international level, see H. Breitmeier, "International Organizations and the Creation of Environmental Regimes" in O. Young, ed., *Global Governance: Drawing Insights From the Environmental Experience* (Cambridge: MIT Press, 1997) at 87-114.

[58] For example, supporting local youth councils or their equivalent, and encouraging their establishment where they do not exist.

[59] See, in general, J. Collier & V. Lowe, *The Settlement of International Disputes: Institutions and Procedures* (Oxford: Oxford University Press, 1999). And see L. Caflisch, *The Peaceful Settlement of Disputes Between States: Universal and European Perspectives* (Leiden: Martinus Nijhoff, 1998). See also P.G. Carrozza, "Subsidiarity as a Structural Principle of International Human Rights Law" (2003) 97 *American Journal of International Law* 38.

[60] See, in particular, the Project on International Courts and Tribunals, available online: <http://www.pict-pcti.org/>. The descriptions of courts and tribunals in this section are based primarily on the excellent comparative materials of the PICT. See also C. Romano, "The Proliferation of International Tribunals: Pieces of the Puzzle" (1999) 31:4 *N.Y.U. J. Int'l. L.& Pol.* 709. And see J. I. Charney, "The Impact on the

different international courts and tribunals in which economic, environmental and social priorities have recently come to a head, highlighting the places in an international governance system where such disputes can be addressed by an adjudicatory body.

i. Sustainable Development in the International Court of Justice

The World Court, or the International Court of Justice (ICJ) and its predecessor, the Permanent Court of International Justice (PCIJ), remains the only judicial forum before which States can bring virtually any legal dispute, whether it arises out of the alleged violation of an international agreement or out of customary international law. The ICJ is one of the six principal organs of the United Nations. It is the principal judicial organ of the cardinal international organization the only one with universal scope and membership. The ICJ's function is twofold: to settle in accordance with international law the legal disputes submitted to it by States, and to give advisory opinions on legal questions submitted by duly authorized international organs and agencies.

All members of the UN are parties to the Court's Statute, which is an integral part of the UN Charter, though the Court is competent to hear a case only if the States concerned have accepted its jurisdiction (hence the criticism of impracticability). Such jurisdiction can be accorded through an ad hoc agreement to submit the dispute to the Court, the jurisdictional clause of a treaty, or the reciprocal effect of optional declarations. The Court also has advisory jurisdiction, as UN organs and UN specialized agencies can request opinions of the Court, and in principle these opinions are consultative in character, not binding as such on the requesting bodies. Certain instruments or regulations can, however, stipulate in advance that the advisory opinion shall be binding. The ICJ may also exercise appellate jurisdiction, for example, as the court of appeal of the International Labour Organisation (ILO) Administrative Tribunal.

Several advisory opinions and contentious cases have recently arisen in the World Court which required the reconciliation of competing social, economic and environmental priorities, and legal claims. While the limits of space do not permit an analysis here, three leading cases bear specific mention. First, the Advisory Opinion on the *Legality of the Threat or Use of Nuclear Weapons*[61] touched upon the social and environmental consequences and impacts of the use of

---

International Legal System of the Growth of International Courts and Tribunals" (1999) 31:4 *N.Y.U. J. Int'l. L.& Pol.* 697. See also, as cited by C. Romano, C. Tomuschat, "International Courts and Tribunals with Regionally Restricted and/or Specialized Jurisdiction" in *Judicial Settlement of International Disputes: International Court of Justice, Other Courts and Tribunals, Arbitration and Conciliation: An International Symposium* (Max-Planck Institut fur Auslandisches Ffentliches Recht und Volkerrecht, 1987) at 285-416; G. Guillaume, "The Future of International Judicial Institutions" (1995) 44 *Int'l & Comp. L.Q.* 848. See also T. Buergenthal, "Proliferation of International Courts and Tribunals: Is it Good or Bad" (2001) 14 *Leiden Journal of International Law* 267-275.
[61] [July 8 1996] I.C.J. Rep. 226.

nuclear weapons, with leading judges expressing particular concern for effect upon future generations. Second, the *Case Concerning the Gabčikovo-Nagymaros Project*[62] and its much commented extraordinary Separate Opinion of Judge C. G. Weeramantry[63], specifically noted the need for reconciliation between environment and development with respect to an international dam project, in which the Vice-President of the Court raised various points related to the status of sustainable development in international law. Third, the Advisory Opinion on the *Legal Consequences of the Construction of a Wall in the Occupied Palestinian Territory,*[64] which addressed the legal consequences arising from the construction of the wall being built by Israel, the occupying Power, in the Occupied Palestinian Territory, including in and around East Jerusalem, and specifically commented upon the rights to work, to health, to education and to an adequate standard of living of those impeded by the wall. Several other cases and advisory opinions have also addressed these issues, and would merit further study from the perspective of sustainable development law.[65]

ii. Sustainable Development in the World Trade Organisation Dispute Settlement Mechanism

The World Trade Organization (WTO) deals with the promotion and regulation of international trade at a global level, in order to help trade flow as freely as possible, to achieve further liberalization gradually through negotiation, and to provide an impartial means of settling disputes. As has been discussed elsewhere in this volume, it was established in 1994 to replace the less structured system of the 1948 *General Agreement on Tariffs and Trade* (GATT). The 1994 *Agreement Establishing the WTO* introduced an Annex on dispute settlement, the *Understanding on Rules and Procedures Governing the Settlement of Disputes* (DSU), which created a Dispute Settlement Body (DSB) and a Standing Appellate Body (AB). The DSB is a political body comprising representatives of all WTO members, which administers the WTO dispute settlement system.[66]

---

[62] (Hungary v Slovakia), [1997] I.C.J. Rep. 7.

[63] *Case Concerning the Gabčikovo-Nagymaros Project* (Hungary v.Slovakia), (Separate Opinion of Judge C. G. Weeramantry), [1997] I.C.J. Rep 7.

[64] [July 9 2004] I.C.J. List 131 (Advisory Opinion).

[65] See, for example, the *Case Concerning Nuclear Tests (New Zealand and Australia v. France)*, [1974] I.C.J. Rep. 457; the *Case Concerning Military and Paramilitary Activities in and Against Nicaragua* (Nicaragua / U.S.A.) [June 27, 1986] I.C.J. Rep. 14 (Judgment on Merits); the *Case Concerning Elettronica Sicula S.p.A.* (ELSI) (United States v. Italy), [1989] I.C.J. Rep. 15; the *Case Concerning Certain Phosphate Lands in Nauru (Nauru v. Austl.)* [June 26, 1992] I.C.J. 240 (Preliminary Objections); the *Case Concerning Maritime Delimitation in the Area between Greenland and Jan Mayen* (Denmark v. Norway), [1993] I.C.J. Rep. 38; and the *Case Concerning Kasikili / Sedudu Island (Botswana/Namibia)* [December 13 1999] I.C.J. Rep. 14. There are also several which have not yet been decided by the court.

[66] The DSB supervises the process of consultation between disputing members; establishes panels to settle disputes, adopts or rejects panel or AB recommendations; maintains surveillance of implementation of rulings and recommendations, and eventually authorizes retaliatory measures in cases of non-implementation of recommendations. See J. H. Jackson, "Fragmentation or Unification Among International Institutions: The World Trade Organization" (1999) 31 *N.Y.U. J. Int'l. L & Pol.* 823.

If a dispute arises between members of the WTO over their respective obligations, a consultation process is the first step. If these fail, other dispute settlement procedures (e.g., mediation, good offices, etc.) are available. If these also fail, the complaining party may request the DSB to establish an *ad hoc* Panel. Panels conduct hearings on the dispute, issue a report on the merits of the case, and the recommendations become binding after their adoption by the DSB. Adoption by the DSB is automatic unless all WTO members agree to reject it, and an additional procedure is needed for enforcement. The Panel report may be appealed, but only on legal grounds before the AB, a permanent body composed by seven individuals. The appeal is heard before a three-person division of the AB, who may uphold, modify or reverse the findings of the panel. The report of the AB is then to be adopted by the DSB and has binding force unless it is unanimously rejected.

Several important decision of the WTO Panel and Appellate body have addressed competing social, economic and environmental claims, particularly in the area of overlap between trade and the environment, generating a tremendous body of scholarly debate and literature.[67] While the limits of space do not permit an analysis here, certain leading cases, also summarized elsewhere in this volume, bear specific mention.[68]

First, the *US-Gasoline*[69] (1996) was a GATT challenge to US measures that addressed urban motor vehicle pollution, in which the AB found that these standards were arbitrary discrimination and a disguised restriction on international trade. Second, the *EC-Hormones*[70] (1998) involved an SPS challenge to EC measures banning imports of hormone-treated beef without being sufficiently based on risk assessment, debating (but not resolving) the status of the precautionary principle in international law.

Third, the *US-Shrimp*[71] (1998) involved a GATT challenge to US measures banning shrimp caught using methods that threatened endangered species of sea turtles from import. The Panel and AB found that the measures treated similarly placed countries differently, lacked flexibility and due process, and did not involve serious multilateral negotiations for sea turtle protection, and thereby constituted arbitrary and unjustifiable discrimination under Article XX.

---

[67] See M. Stillwell, in this volume. See also F. Francione, *Environment, Human Rights and International Trade* (Oxford: Hart, 2001); and see D. Esty, *Greening the GATT: Trade, Environment and the Future* (Washington: Institute for International Economics, 1994), for an overview. For a review of recent cases, from a civil society perspective, see S. Porter & H. Mann, *State of Trade and Environment Law* (Winnipeg: IISD, 2003).
[68] See M. Stillwell, in this volume. And see M. Gehring & M. C. Cordonier Segger, eds., *Sustainable Developments in World Trade Law* (The Hague: Kluwer Law International, 2005). The following summary of cases is based on such analysis.
[69] *United States – Standards for Reformulated and Conventional Gasoline*, AB-1996-1, WT/DS2/AB/R (1997). (Appellate Body Report).
[70] *EC Measures Concerning Meat and Meat Products (Hormones)*, AB-1997-4, WT/DS26/AB/R, WT/DS48/AB/R (1998). (Appellate Body Report).
[71] *United States – Import Prohibition of Certain Shrimp and Shrimp Products*, AB-1998-4, WT/DS58/AB/R (1998). (Appellate Body Report).

In a later case, *US-Shrimp 21.5*[72] (2001), there was an unsuccessful challenge to US measures to implement the first decision in *US-Shrimp,* as these were found to be justified under Article XX, subject to certain requirements, including that the US continue to seek a negotiated solution to protect sea turtles.

In a fourth case, *Australia-Salmon*[73] (1998), an SPS challenge of an Australian import ban on uncooked salmon (to protect against invasive species), the link with sufficient risk assessment was again found to be a concern, and the measures were held to constitute arbitrary or unjustifiable distinctions. In *Japan-Varietals*[74] (1999), the SPS Agreement was also used to find that Japanese measures banning imports of certain fruit crops to address the risk of invasive species were maintained without sufficient scientific evidence and raised concerns about objective risk assessment, and were not (as provisional measures) reviewed within a reasonable period. In a fifth case, *EC-Asbestos*[75] (2001), there was an unsuccessful challenge under the TBT Agreement and the GATT to a French ban on imports of white chrysotile asbestos fibers and products containing them. The AB found that based on the differences between the products, asbestos and its substitutes could not be considered 'like-products' under the GATT, and that the French measure was justified as a necessary measure for the protection of human life or health.[76]

iii. Sustainable Development in the International Tribunal on the Law of the Sea (ITLOS)

Established in 1982 by the United Nations Convention on the Law of the Sea (UNCLOS), the International Tribunal for the Law of the Sea (ITLOS) became operational in 1996 when the UNCLOS entered into force. The ITLOS is one of four possible means available to the parties of UNCLOS to settle disputes, others include International Court of Justice, arbitration under Annex VII of the Convention, and special arbitration under Annex VIII. With several exceptions, the ITLOS does not, in principle, have jurisdiction over a dispute unless both parties have agreed to it, by way of ad hoc declaration, special agreement or previous optional declaration. It functions in a way similar to the ICJ. However, unlike the ICJ (and more similar to the European Court of Justice), the ITLOS is endowed with a permanent special chamber with

---

[72] *United States – Import Prohibition of Certain Shrimp and Shrimp Products, Recourse to Article 21.5 by Malaysia,* AB-2001-4, WT/DS58/AB/RW (2001). (Appellate Body Report).
[73] *Australia – Measures Affecting Importation of Salmon,* AB-1998-5, WT/DS18/AB/R (1998). (Appellate Body Report).
[74] *Japan – Measures Affecting Agricultural Products,* AB-1998-8, WT/DS76/AB/R (1999). (Appellate Body Report).
[75] *European Communities – Measures Affecting Asbestos and Asbestos-Containing Products,* AB-2000-11, WT/DS135/AB/R (2001). (Appellate Body Report).
[76] For further analysis from a sustainable development perspective, see, e.g., M. Gehring and M.C. Cordonier Segger, "The WTO Asbestos Cases and Precaution: Sustainable Development Implications of the WTO Asbestos Dispute" (2003) 15 *Oxford J. Env. L.* 289. See also M.C. Cordonier Segger & M. Gehring, "Precaution, Health and the World Trade Organisation: Moving toward Sustainable Development" (2003) 29 *Queen's L. J.* 133.

compulsory jurisdiction over a particular category of dispute. The 11-member Seabed Disputes Chamber (SBDC) hears disputes concerning activities in the seabed, ocean floor and subsoil beyond the limits of national jurisdiction (the area managed by the International Seabed Authority, which was established pursuant to the UNCLOS). Locus standi before the SBDC is different from the one before the full Tribunal. States and the International Seabed Authority have standing before the Chamber, as do companies and individuals of States parties.

This feature distinguishes the ITLOS from other international judicial bodies with universal membership and scope, like the ICJ and the World Trade Organization dispute settlement system, where non-state entities are not allowed to bring claims (to a certain extent this applies also to the International Criminal Court). Unlike most international judicial bodies, which decide cases virtually solely on the basis of international law, the SBDC can reach outside those limits. The SBDC can apply the UNCLOS; principles of international law; the rules, regulations and procedures of the International Sea-bed Authority; as well as terms of contracts concerning activities in matters relating to them.

Many of the cases addressed by the ITLOS in recent years relate to balancing or reconciliation of competing social, economic and environmental priorities. While the limits of space do not permit an analysis here, three leading cases bear specific mention.

First, the provisional measures determination in the *Southern Bluefin Tuna (New Zealand and Australia v. Japan)*[77], addressed the need for limits for the sustainable use of tuna fisheries stocks, though the final decision in this case found no jurisdiction. The separate opinion of a leading tribunal member is particularly enlightening with regard to the meaning and status of the precautionary principle in international law. Second, the *MOX Plant Case (Ireland v. United Kingdom) Provisional Measures*[78] addresses concerns about potential environmental and other consequences of the construction of a downwind nuclear plant. This issue continues to be debated in the European context. Finally, in the initial proceedings of the *Case concerning the Conservation and Sustainable Exploitation of Swordfish Stocks in the South-Eastern Pacific Ocean*[79] a concern for the sustainable use of natural resources, in this case, swordfish stocks, launched two

---

[77] *Provisional Measures* (1999), Case 3 and 4, (International Tribunal of the Law of the Sea), online: ITLOS <http://www.itlos.org/start2_en.html>.

[78] (2001), Case 10 (International Tribunal of the Law of the Sea), online: ITLOS <http://www.itlos.org/start2_en.html>

[79] *(Chile/European Community)* (2001), Case 7 – Order 2001/1, (International Tribunal of the Law of the Sea), online: ITLOS <http://www.itlos.org/start2_en.html>. See also *Case concerning the Conservation and Sustainable Exploitation of Swordfish Stocks in the South-Eastern Pacific Ocean (Chile/European Community)* (2003), Case 7 – Order 2003/2, (International Tribunal of the Law of the Sea), online: ITLOS <http://www.itlos.org/start2_en.html>.

international cases which provide a fascinating illustration of the need to better reconcile international social, economic and environmental legal regimes.[80]

Several other cases and advisory opinions have also addressed these issues, and would merit further study from the perspective of sustainable development law.[81]

iv. Sustainable Development in Investment Arbitrations

The International Centre for Settlement of Investment Disputes (ICSID) was established in 1965 by the Convention on the Settlement of Investment Disputes between States and Nationals of Other States (which has been ratified to date by 136 states), to facilitate the settlement of disputes arising between states and foreign private investors by way of arbitration and conciliation. The Additional Facility for the Administration of Conciliation, Arbitration and Fact-Finding Procedures (Additional Facility), which enables use of ICSID arbitration and conciliation facilities by states not parties to the ICSID Convention (or nationals of such states), extends its reach and provides a fact-finding capacity. ICSID, as part of the World Bank Group, is a permanent administrative structure supporting and facilitating ad hoc dispute settlement procedures, maintaining a list of potential arbitrators and conciliators for parties to choose from; and providing registry and secretariat services.

Commitments to 'ICSID arbitration' are often found in investment contracts between governments of member countries and investors from other member countries.[82] More than 20 investment laws and over 1000 bilateral investment

---

[80] At first, the *EC - Chile Swordfish Dispute* appeared as two cases, according to M. Gehring. "The first was initiated before the WTO against provisions in Chilean Fisheries Law that prohibited port entry of EU vessels carrying swordfish. According to the European Communities, this restriction violated GATT Article V on the freedom of transit and GATT Article XI, which prohibits quantitative restrictions. The other case was filed by Chile in a special Chamber of the International Tribunal of the Law of the Seas (ITLOS) in Hamburg. Chile alleged that the EC's swordfish fishing practices violated UN Convention on the Law of the Sea (UNCLOS) Articles 116 to 119 on the conservation of living recourses in the high seas, as well as UNCLOS Article 64 on the failure to co-operate with the coastal state in case of highly migratory species." However, he notes, the "underlying issue in these international charges was identical. Large trawlers from countries of the European Union fished swordfish right outside Chile's Exclusive Economic Zone." Legal limits were needed on fish size, for conservation of the stocks, and by-catch consisted of sharks, turtles and other endangered marine species. Chile adopted conservation measures aimed at protecting not just of the species but also of traditional fishing methods. But European vessels, using non-sustainable practices, still wanted to unload their fish in Chilean ports for transhipment to the United States. After the Chileans filed the case in ITLOS, negotiations began. The ITLOS special Chamber suspended proceedings, and the process for the constitution of a WTO panel on *Chile Measures affecting the transit and importation of swordfish* was also suspended. Both were put on hold after Chile and the EC reached an 'arrangement' on 25 January 2001. See M. Gehring, "Sustainable Development Angles to the Swordfish Dispute" (2001) *Bridges J. ICTSD* 5:7 at 13 – 15.
[81] *Case concerning Land Reclamation by Singapore in and around the Straits of Johor (Malaysia v. Singapore), Provisional Measures* (2003), Case 12 – Order of 8 October 2003, (International Tribunal of the Law of the Sea), online: <http://www.itlos.org/start2_en.html>.
[82] Recourse to conciliation and arbitration under the ICSID Convention is, in principle, voluntary. However, once the parties have consented, including through treaties, they are bound to carry out their undertaking. All contracting states, whether or not parties to the dispute, are required to recognize awards rendered pursuant to the ICSID Convention as binding and enforce them. Such awards are not subject to appeal or other

treaties also contain advance consent by governments to submit investment disputes to ICSID arbitration, which has led to in increasing number of cases using ICSID procedures. To date, more than 70 cases have been submitted to ICSID (mostly for arbitration), involving over 34 different governments. Foreign private investors are normally plaintiff against a state, often a developing country. Many address claims over such events as civil strife, alleged expropriation or denials of justice, and actions of the state political subdivisions (e.g., regions or federated states). There is neither space nor scope, in this chapter, to analyse the many ICSID claims which involve competing social, economic and environmental priorities and laws. However, it is important to note that these arbitrations, particularly when an investor raises a claim against a state in a confidential setting concerning non-transparency, discrimination or expropriation subject to compensation for a state's social or environmental measures, can directly address underlying issues of sustainable development. Often, the threat of an expensive claim being brought to an arbitral tribunal can assist an investor in convincing a state not to enact such laws.

v. Sustainable Development in the Regional Courts and Tribunals

Investment arbitration is part of the provisions of the North American Free Trade Agreement and several new bi-lateral trade treaties modeled upon in, which also contain various international trade dispute resolution mechanisms, and parallel environmental and social 'factual-reporting', 'complaints' and 'clearing-house' mechanisms.[83]

In addition to the International Criminal Court, consideration of which is beyond the scope of the present chapter, there are many regional human rights tribunals that are increasingly being called upon to address human rights obligations of great relevance to sustainable development, particularly in the realm of social, economic and cultural rights, and the collective rights of indigenous peoples, as well as the more typically analysed right to a clean and healthy environment. These courts and tribunals include the Inter-American Court of Human Rights, addressed elsewhere in this volume, the European Court of Human Rights, also discussed in this volume, and the African Court of Human Rights.

Similarly, other regional courts and tribunals, such as the Andean Court of Justice, the European Court of Justice, and the new Caribbean Court of Justice, a discussion of which would (and does) fill many volumes of analysis, can

---

remedy, except those agreed in the Convention, such as the remedy of annulment. See ICSID, available online: <www.worldbank.org/icsid/>.
[83] M.C. Cordonier Segger & M. Leichner Reynal, *Beyond the Barricades: An Americas Trade and Sustainability Agenda* (Aldershot: Ashgate, 2004). J. Kirton, and V. Maclaren, eds., Linking Trade, Environment, and Social Cohesion: NAFTA Experiences, Global Challenges (Aldershot: Ashgate, 2002). See also, more generally, A. Kiss, D. Shelton & K. Ishibashi *Economic Globalization and Compliance with International Environmental Agreements* (New York: Kluwer Law International, 2003).

become forums for the resolution of claims which require the accommodation, reconciliation and integration of social, economic and environmental regimes.

Elements of a 'Principled' Juridical Test to Reconcile Social, Economic and Environmental Priorities, Policies and Laws

Though important efforts have been undertaken in the United Nations and in the World Summit for Sustainable Development to encourage coherence and coordination, the international institutional architecture for sustainable development remains diffuse and fragmented. A proliferating number of international courts and tribunals are being called upon to address increasing numbers of disputes related to sustainable development, as their jurisdictions are extended, and as they continue to develop bodies of decisions that are either binding or provide persuasive authority. Are there elements of a 'legal test' for sustainable development that could be developed,[84] to assist in the accommodation, reconciliation or integration of competing social, economic and environmental claims?

While it is beyond the scope of this preliminary discussion to provide a comprehensive answer to this question, given the global importance of the topic and the great diversity of potential conflicts, it is hoped that such an answer can be developed. As a conclusion to this chapter, two questions will be raised and discussed, and a proposal will be made, to encourage future legal research. First, the question of a legal definition for sustainable development will be briefly canvassed. Second, the nature of sustainable development, in international law, will also be discussed. Third, certain elements will be proposed that a judge or jurist might take into account, when seeking to reconcile competing social, economic and environmental claims.

i. A juridical definition of sustainable development?

After two decades of scholarly debates and practical experience, there is remains the need to clearly define sustainable development, in the law. Significantly, neither the 'soft law' 1992 *Agenda 21*, nor the 2002 *Johannesburg Plan of Implementation* provide an agreed definition of sustainable development.[85] However, as mentioned elsewhere, it is likely that initially, the very vagueness of this concept is one of the reasons that it has been so broadly adopted, as a

---

[84] The author would like to thank Hon. Mr. Justice Georg Ress, European Court of Human Rights, Professor Nico Schrijver, Free University of Amsterdam, Dr. Duncan French, Sheffield University and Dr. Ximena Fuentes, Chile, for their guidance and substantive intellectual contributions to this conversation, particularly at the International Law Association 2004 in Berlin and following meetings in Santiago of Chile.

[85] It is noteworthy that it was possible to hold a 'World Summit on Sustainable Development', with the participation of over one hundred heads of state and more than 25,000 delegates, without such a definition having being clearly set out.

treaty objective and a policy goal.[86]   As for other universal concepts, such as self-determination, justice or democracy, many definitions are possible.

Certain international guidance has been provided. *Our Common Future,* the 1987 *Brundtland Report,* sought for parallel problems of global environmental degradation and global lack of social and economic development to be addressed together.[87] In the *Brundtland Report,* sustainable development was defined as "development that meets the needs of the present without compromising the ability of future generations to meet their own needs."[88] The 2002 *Johannesburg Declaration,* at para. 5, specifically commits to "assume a collective responsibility to advance and strengthen the interdependent and mutually reinforcing pillars of sustainable development - economic development, social development and environmental protection - at the local, national, regional and global levels."

Such definitions might be useful in policy circles, and indeed, have been widely adopted in international declarations and domestic policy statements. However, they are not particularly helpful to determine the parameters of an international treaty commitment to 'sustainable development' or the precise normative content of sustainable development in international law. As has been noted by Vaughan Lowe, how can one determine the needs of present generations? Are these needs also rights or entitlements? And how can one predict what will be the exact needs of generations to come?[89] In addition to jurists, many economists, ecologists, as well as other scientists and development scholars have devoted much effort to developing the necessary indicators and instruments to answer these questions. But for deeper exploration of the meaning of sustainable development, it is necessary to turn to a different, more precise but also more treacherous part of the global debates: international law.

One definition of sustainable development, in international law, has recently been agreed in one regional treaty between developing countries, the 2002 *Convention for Cooperation in the Protection and Sustainable Development of the Marine and Coastal Environment of the Northeast Pacific.* In Art. 3(1)(a), the parties adopted a definition which states that sustainable development means:

> "[Sustainable development is:] the process of progressive change in the quality of life of human beings, which places them as the centre and

---

[86] B. Simma, "Foreword" in N. Schrijver & F. Weiss, eds., *International Law and Sustainable Development* (Leiden: Martinus Nijhoff, 2004). See also M.C. Cordonier Segger & A. Khalfan, *Sustainable Development Law: Principles, Practices and Prospects* (Oxford: Oxford University Press, 2004).

[87] World Commission on Environment and Development, *Our Common Future* (Oxford: Oxford University Press, 1987).

[88] *Ibid.* ("The members of the World Commission on Environment and Development came from 21 very different nations. [...] We are unanimous in our conviction that the security, well-being, and very survival of the planet depend on such changes, now.").

[89] V. Lowe, "Sustainable Development and Unsustainable Arguments" in A. Boyle and D. Freestone, eds., *International Law and Sustainable Development: Past Achievements and Future Challenges* (Oxford: Oxford University Press, 1999) at 27.

primary subjects of development, by means of economic growth with social equity and transformation of production methods and consumption patterns, sustained by the ecological balance and life support systems of the region. This process implies respect for regional, national and local ethnic and cultural diversity, and full public participation, peaceful coexistence in harmony with nature, without prejudice to and ensuring the quality of life of future generations."[90]

The original treaty language is Spanish, and a straightforward translation cannot do justice to the central concepts of the agreed definition. With relation to 'development', it focuses on a human-scale, human-centred process of progressive change in quality of life for human beings. With relation to 'sustainability', it calls for economic growth which respects social equity, carried out through the transformation of production methods and consumption patterns, in such a way that there is respect for the ecological balance and life support systems of the region. (In this context, the 'region' refers to Central America and the regional sea in question). It also provides for other elements: respect for diversity, public participation, peaceful coexistence with nature, and inter-generational equity.

How to distil such a poetic, all-encompassing definition into an English-language formulation that can be used each day, with a plain and ordinary meaning, by jurists and others, without tautological repetitions? The following may serve to continue the discussion:

Sustainable development is the procedural and substantive requirement to accommodate, reconcile or integrate economic growth, social justice (including human rights) and environmental protection, for participatory improvement in our collective quality of life which can benefit present and future generations.

Such a definition is in harmony with the definition proposed in the 2002 *Northeast Pacific Treaty*. It emphasizes the three 'pillars' highlighted in the Johannesburg Declaration. It considers the need to "reconcile economic development with protection of the environment..." which the I.C.J. has found "is aptly expressed in the concept of sustainable development", [91] in its most relevant majority decision on this issue to date, and also the need for "integration"[92] highlighted by the WTO Appellate Body in its most relevant decision. It contains an element of human-centred development to meet human needs in the statement 'our collective quality of life', the element of public participation, an element of potentiality in the word 'can', and an element of the

---

[90] The 2002 *Convention for Cooperation in the Protection and Sustainable Development of the Marine and Coastal Environment of the Northeast Pacific* 18 February 2002, City of Antigua, Guatemala. (Translation provided by author). Available online: http://www.cep.unep.org/services/nepregseas/Convention_English_NEP.doc
[91] *Case Concerning the Gabčikovo-Nagymaros Project (Hungary/Slovakia)* (1997), I.C.J. Rep. 7 at 140.
[92] *United States – Import Prohibition of Certain Shrimp and Shrimp Products,* AB-1998-4, WT/DS58/AB/R (1998). (Appellate Body Report).

need for development to last over the long term in an equitable way, in the reference to the need to benefit both present and future generations.

ii. What is the status of sustainable development in international law?

A commitment to sustainable development appears, often as an objective or preambular reference, in almost all international treaties related to environmental, social and economic issues since the 1992 Rio de Janeiro Earth Summit. Indeed, over 300 treaties are specifically referenced in the 2002 *Johannesburg Plan of Implementation* from the World Summit on Sustainable Development. As observed by Judge Weeramantry in his Separate Opinion in the *Case Concerning the Gabcikovo-Nagymaros Dam*,[93] there is "wide and general acceptance by the global community" of sustainable development. Sustainable development has also been innovatively applied by judges in domestic courts around the world.[94] However, it is also important to consider the normative status of sustainable development in international law. Is sustainable development a binding principle of international customary law? Is it simply a broad policy goal, without specific meaning? Or is it something else?

It is not clear that 'sustainable development' can be accurately characterized as a principle of customary international environmental law.[95] There are two reasons that this is problematic.

First, the goal of international environmental law is, broadly, 'protection of the international environment.' But this is not the goal of sustainable development, a concept that focuses principally on improving the quality of life of human beings in a way that can last. Sustainable development law is complementary to environmental law. It has an important environmental component, in that it recognizes that to be sustainable, development cannot exceed the limits of the environment. But it is not primarily focused on the protection of environmental integrity, or on the preservation of nature for its intrinsic worth.

---

[93] (Hungary/Slovakia) [1997] I.C.J. Rep. 7.

[94] National cases applying the concept of sustainable development include: *Vellore Citizens Welfare Forum* v. *Union of India* (1996, Supreme Court of India) and *Bulankulame* v. *Secretary, Ministry of Industrial Development and Others* (the Eppawela Case) (2000, Supreme Court of Sri Lanka). In *Rajendra Parajuli and Others* v. *Shree Distillery Pvt. Ltd. & Others*, the Supreme Court of Nepal (Writ No. 3259, 1996) stated that sustainable development means "every industry has an obligation to run its development activities without creating environmental deterioration. The environment should not be viewed narrowly. It is imperative for any industry to be cautious towards the environment while it is in operation." In this instance, the Court ordered the company to comply with a prior agreement to keep the environment free of pollution in the affected area.

[95] Customary international law as a recognised source of international law, from the *Statute of the International Court of Justice*, 26 June 1945, T.S. No. 933, 59 Stat. 1055, 3 Bevans 1179., as discussed in *North Sea Continental Shelf Cases (Federal Republic of Germany v. Denmark; Federal Republic of Germany v. Netherlands)*, [1969] I.C.J. Rep. 3. International environmental law as comprehensively documented and summarized in P. Sands, *Principles of International Environmental Law*, 2nd ed. (Cambridge: Cambridge University Press, 2003), in A. Kiss & D. Shelton, *International Environmental Law* (New York: Transnational Publishers, 2000) and in D. Hunter, D. Zaelke, & J. Salzman, *International Environmental Law and Policy* (New York: Foundation Press, 2002). It is notable that Hunter, Zaelke & Salzman also call to question, in their second edition, the characterization of sustainable development as a customary norm of international environmental law.

Second, it is unlikely that sustainable development has the 'fundamentally normative character' required to be a principle in itself. As noted by David Freestone and Alan Boyle, there does not appear, as yet, to be a customary international legal principle that requires States to 'develop sustainably.'[96] As Vaughan Lowe has observed, in his interpretation of Judge C. G. Weeramantry's visionary Separate Opinion in the *Gabcikovo-Nagymaros case*, sustainable development is more likely to have an interstitial normative character, in international law.[97] Indeed, sustainable development may serve as a different type of norm in its own right,[98] one that facilitates and requires a balance between conflicting legal norms relating to environmental protection, social development and economic growth. Sustainable development, when applied in treaty negotiation or dispute settlement, can hence be considered a "meta-principle, acting upon other legal rules and principles – a legal concept exercising a kind of interstitial normativity, pushing and pulling the boundaries of true primary norms when they threaten to overlap or conflict with each other."[99] This characterisation is in accordance with the majority decision of the World Court on this issue.[100]

---

[96] A. Boyle and D. Freestone, *International Law and Sustainable Development: Past Achievements and Future Challenges* (Oxford: Oxford University Press, 1999).

[97] V. Lowe, "Sustainable Development and Unsustainable Arguments" in A. Boyle and D. Freestone, eds., *International Law and Sustainable Development: Past Achievements and Future Challenges* (Oxford: Oxford University Press, 1999) at 30.

[98] V. Lowe, "The Politics of Law-Making: Are the Method and Character of Norm Creation Changing?" in M. Byers, ed. *The Role of Law in International Politics: Essays in International Relations and International Law* (Oxford: Oxford University Press, 2000) at 214-215.

[99] V. Lowe, "Sustainable Development and Unsustainable Arguments" in A. Boyle and D. Freestone, eds., *International Law and Sustainable Development: Past Achievements and Future Challenges* (Oxford: Oxford University Press, 1999) at 31.

[100] At para 140, in the *Case Concerning the Gabčíkovo-Nagymaros Project (Hungary/Slovakia)* (1997), I.C.J. Rep. 7, the majority stated that "It is clear that the Project's impact upon, and its implications for, the environment are of necessity a key issue. The numerous scientific reports which have been presented to the Court by the Parties — even if their conclusions are often contradictory — provide abundant evidence that this impact and these implications are considerable. In order to evaluate the environmental risks, current standards must be taken into consideration. This is not only allowed by the wording of Articles 15 and 19, but even prescribed, to the extent that these articles impose a continuing — and thus necessarily evolving — obligation on the parties to maintain the quality of the water of the Danube and to protect nature. The Court is mindful that, in the field of environmental protection, vigilance and prevention are required on account of the often irreversible character of damage to the environment and of the limitations inherent in the very mechanism of reparation of this type of damage. Throughout the ages, mankind has, for economic and other reasons, constantly interfered with nature. In the past, this was often done without consideration of the effects upon the environment. Owing to new scientific insights and to a growing awareness of the risks for mankind — for present and future generations — of pursuit of such interventions at an unconsidered and unabated pace, new norms and standards have been developed, set forth in a great number of instruments during the last two decades. Such new norms have to be taken into consideration, and such new standards given proper weight, not only when States contemplate new activities but also when continuing with activities begun in the past. This need to reconcile economic development with protection of the environment is aptly expressed in the concept of sustainable development. For the purposes of the present case, this means that the Parties together should look afresh at the effects on the environment of the operation of the Gabčíkovo power plant. In particular they must find a satisfactory solution for the volume of water to be released into the old bed of the Danube and into the side-arms on both sides of the river." Due to the specific facts of this case, only procedural requirements were imposed by the use of the concept.

While there is doubt that a legally binding 'principle of sustainable development' exists at present, a growing body of 'international law in the field of sustainable development' or 'sustainable development law' can be identified, analysed and implemented.[101] "Even if there is no legal obligation to develop sustainably, there may nevertheless be, through incremental development, law 'in the field of sustainable development'."[102]

The recognition of sustainable development as a field of law is supported by many references made by governments in agreed consensus statements. In the 1992 *Rio Declaration*, governments committed to the "further development of international law on sustainable development, giving special attention to the delicate balance between environmental and developmental concerns."[103] Governments also recognized the "need to clarify and strengthen the relationship between existing international instruments or agreements in the field of environment and relevant social and economic agreements or instruments, taking into account the special needs of the developing countries…"[104] *Agenda 21* emphasizes the need to ensure that developing countries can participate in "treaty making in the field of international law on sustainable development."[105] The 1997 *Plan of Further Implementation of Agenda 21*,

---

[101] Sustainable development law is further defined in M.C. Cordonier Segger & A. Khalfan, *Sustainable Development Law: Principles, Practices and Prospects* (Oxford: Oxford University Press, 2004). On the process of development of international law in this manner, see J. Brunnée & S.J. Toope "International Law and Constructivism: Elements of an Interactional Theory of International Law" (2000) 39(1) *Col. J. Trans'l. Law* 19. See also M. Byers, ed., *The Role of Law in International Politics: Essays in International Relations and International Law* (Oxford, OUP, 2000).

[102] P. Sands, 'International Law in the Field of Sustainable Development' (1994) 65 *B. Y. Int'l. L.* 303.

[103] *Rio Declaration on Environment and Development*, Report of the United Nations Conference on Environment and Development, U.N. Doc. A/CONF.151/6/Rev.1, (1992), 31 I.L.M. 874 (1992), especially at Principle 27 on international law and *Agenda 21*, Report of the UNCED, I (1992) UN Doc. A/CONF.151/26/Rev.1, (1992) 31 I.L.M. 874, especially at Chapter 39, on international law.

[104] *Ibid.*

[105] At Chapter 39, entitled International Legal Mechanisms and Instruments, at para 39.1, a basis for action is identified. It states that… "the following vital aspects of the universal, multilateral and bilateral treaty-making process should be taken into account: (a) The further development of international law on sustainable development, giving special attention to the delicate balance between environmental and developmental concerns; (b) The need to clarify and strengthen the relationship between existing international instruments or agreements in the field of environment and relevant social and economic agreements or instruments, taking into account the special needs of developing countries; (c) At the global level, the essential importance of the participation in and the contribution of all countries, including the developing countries, to treaty making in the field of international law on sustainable development. … (e) Future projects for the progressive development and codification of international law on sustainable development should take into account the ongoing work of the International Law Commission; (f) Any negotiations for the progressive development and codification of international law concerning sustainable development should, in general, be conducted on a universal basis, taking into account special circumstances in the various regions." Agenda 21 continues, at 39.10, stating that "In the area of avoidance and settlement of disputes, States should further study and consider methods to broaden and make more effective the range of techniques available at present, taking into account, among others, relevant experience under existing international agreements, instruments or institutions and, where appropriate, their implementing mechanisms such as modalities for dispute avoidance and settlement. This may include mechanisms and procedures for the exchange of data and information, notification and consultation regarding situations that might lead to disputes with other States in the field of sustainable development and for effective peaceful means of dispute settlement in accordance with the Charter of the United Nations, including, where appropriate, recourse to the International Court of Justice, and their inclusion in treaties relating to sustainable development."

similarly, states that "it is necessary to continue the progressive development and, as and when appropriate, codification of international law related to sustainable development."[106]And the 2002 *Johannesburg Plan of Implementation* requests the United Nations Commission on Sustainable Development to track, and take into account, "significant legal developments in the field of sustainable development, with due regard to the role of relevant intergovernmental bodies in promoting the implementation of Agenda 21 relating to international legal instruments and mechanisms."[107]

It is beyond the scope of this chapter to discuss the emerging principles, international instruments or disputes which are part of this area of law.[108] Such topics are covered elsewhere in this volume.[109] But it is important to note that recognition of sustainable development law is not just a change in semantics. It is a conceptual shift, one that facilitates and may even require legal scholarship and judicial analysis that can balance between three intersecting systems of international law: international economic, human rights and environmental law.

iii. Elements of a legal test for sustainable development?

For the purposes of this analysis, sustainable development can be defined as 'the procedural and substantive requirement to accommodate, reconcile or integrate economic growth, human rights and environmental protection, for participatory, equitable improvement in our collective quality of life that can last over the long term.' In international law, sustainable development is conceived as an objective of many international treaties, and as an interstitial norm, one which can assist judges and decision-makers to balance between other, competing norms, such as the imperative to realise a human right, the duty to protect the environment, or a treaty commitment to free trade rules. As such, the substantive aspect of this 'interstitial norm' is the requirement that all three sets of priorities be reflected in the substantive outcomes of a given dispute or conflict.

---

[106] In particular, at para 109, it states that "Taking into account the provisions of chapter 39, particularly paragraph 39.1, of Agenda 21, it is necessary to continue the progressive development and, as and when appropriate, codification of international law related to sustainable development. Relevant bodies in which such tasks are being undertaken should cooperate and coordinate in this regard." See G. A. res. S-19/2. U.N. GAOR, 19th Special Sess. (1997). A/RES/S-19/2.

[107] *Plan of Implementation*, Report of the World Summit on Sustainable Development, A/CONF.199/20 Johannesburg, South Africa, August 26-September 4, 2002 at para 148.

[108] See the "ILA New Delhi Declaration of Principles of International Law Relating to Sustainable Development", reproduced in this volume. And see N. Schrijver and F. Weiss, eds., *International Law and Sustainable Development* (Leiden: Martinus Nijhoff, 2004) at 699.

[109] See, e.g., M. C. Cordonier Segger and A. Khalfan, *Sustainable Development Law: Principles, Practices and Prospects* (Oxford: Oxford University Press, 2004). See also M.C. Cordonier Segger, "Significant Developments in Sustainable Development Law and Governance: A Proposal" (2004) *U.N. Natural Resources Forum* 28:1. And see FAO, *International Law and Sustainable Development Since Rio* (Rome: FAO, 2002). See also M.C. Cordonier Segger, A. Khalfan, M. Gehring & M. Toering, "Prospects for Principles of International Sustainable Development Law after Johannesburg: Common but Differentiated Responsibilities, Precaution and Participation" (2003) 12:3 *R.E.C.I.E.L.* 54.

What would be the juridical test for such an objective? How could judicial reasoning determine that a particular decision, or course of action, will contribute to sustainable development? Three particular elements might be proposed, in this regard, for a 'principled approach.'

First, the jurist would need to clearly define the interests at stake, both in terms of the relevant legal rights and duties of the parties, and also the general social, economic and environmental interests of the broader community (in accordance with the principle of good governance). If the dispute has extensive implications for domestic or international levels, these present and future public interest might need to be taken into consideration, with special attention to the needs of the most vulnerable (in accordance with the principle of equity, which includes both inter-generational and intra-generational equity, based on fraternity). This definition of interests will be specific to each case, but could be done clearly at the outset of reasoning.

Second, the jurist would need to seek ways to accommodate between, or reconcile, the competing interests. Three particular principles of sustainable development law would be particularly relevant here. First, the jurist might inquire as to whether there is a particular renewable resource or common concern at stake, such as a particular fishery or forest, upon which societies, economies and ecosystems depend (the duty to ensure sustainable use of natural resources). Related to this, it may also be necessary to determine whether all parties have complied with their duty to notify each other of the proposed uses, to consult with environment and development decision-makers in each country, and to negotiate solutions in good faith. Second, the jurist might inquire as to whether a science-based, objective, sustainability impact assessment has determined a certain threshold of exploitation beyond which the resource cannot be sustained, and where the science is uncertain, to determine whether precautionary measures been contemplated, so that the lack of certain science is not used as a basis for postponing measures to mitigate or compensate for serious or irreversible damage (the principle of the precautionary approach to human health, natural resources and ecosystems). Third, public participation, including through consultation of all stakeholders, is essential in determining whether a society and economy depend on sustainable use of a resource. As such, the jurist might inquire as to whether appropriate levels of consultation and participation have been undertaken (the principle of public participation, access to information and justice).

Third and finally, often, sustainable development conflicts are not very straightforward, and do not simply involve shared management of one natural resource. As such, two other fundamental principles might come into play to assist in a process of accommodation and reconciliation, at the moment of double-checking a solution proposed by the application of the other principles and the earlier two steps. First, the jurist would need to consider whether the resolution imposes burdens on countries or actors that have traditionally suffered from disadvantages, and have not benefited from past unsustainable practices. If it does, exceptions might need to be created for these countries or parties (in accordance with the principle of common but differentiated responsibilities), or the resolution re-considered. Second, the jurist might need to specifically turn their mind toward the inter-relations and interdependence of the social, economic and environmental aspects of the dispute. Essentially, the jurist would seek to ensure that neither the economic, nor the environmental, nor the social priorities had been completely ignored. While there are few clear bright lines, and no hard and fast rule, as each factual situation is different, it would not 'sustainable' to allow one or the other dimension of sustainable development to be excluded (the principle of integration).

The ultimate test of this reasoning would be, of course, whether the resolution leads to an improvement in the collective quality of life that can last over the long term.

Such a principled approach, which is both substantive and procedural, might assist jurists, including treaty negotiators, judiciaries and arbitrators, in using the interstitial concept of sustainable development to accommodate and reconcile competing social, economic and environmental interests.

35

A FUTURE AGENDA ON IMPLEMENTATION OF SUSTAINABLE DEVELOPMENT LAW: THE INTERNATIONAL JURISTS MANDATE

At an international conference "Sustainable Justice 2002: Implementing International Sustainable Development Law" on June 14, 2002, in Montreal, Canada, international jurists gathered to discuss and agree a mandate for the implementation of sustainable development law on the global level.[1]

This Mandate was presented to the delegates of the 2002 World Summit on Sustainable Development by representatives from the Centre for International Sustainable Development Law (Marie-Claire Cordonier Segger and Ashfaq Khalfan, Directors), the International Law Association Committee on the Legal Aspects of Sustainable Development (Nicholas Schrijver, Committee Rapporteur), and the International Development Law Organisation (Pia Rodriguez, Programme Director), at the occasion of the launch of a new research and capacity building partnership for international law on sustainable development, on August 29, 2002.[2]

The text of the Mandate, which had been signed by over 2002 distinguished jurists, international law professors and scholars, legal professionals and judges, is reproduced below in its entirety, in order to guide the work of the next decade of sustainable development lawyers.

---

[1] See Centre for International Sustainable Development Law (CISDL), World Bank, United Nations Environment Programme and International Law Association of Canada, *Sustainable Justice 2002: Implementing International Sustainable Development Law Report* (Montreal: CISDL / World Bank / UNEP / ILA, 2002), available online: < http://www.cisdl.org/conference_report/>.
[2] See Centre for International Sustainable Development Law (CISDL), International Law Association Committee on the International Law on Sustainable Development (ILA) and International Development Law Organisation (IDLO), Johannesburg Legal Experts Event, available online: <http://www.cisdl.org/press008.html>. See also United Nations Commission on Sustainable Development, Outline of International Law for Sustainable Development Partnership, available online: <http://www.un.org/esa/sustdev/partnerships/law/intlawsustdev.PDF>.

M.C. Cordonier Segger & C. G. Weeramantry, eds., Sustainable Justice: Reconciling Economic, Social & Environmental Law
© *2005 Koninklijke Brill NV, Printed in The Netherlands, pp.593-598.*

The International Jurists Mandate for the Implementation of International Sustainable Development Law

We, justices, legislators, government officials, legal scholars, professionals and representatives of civil society organisations assembled 13-15 June 2002 in Montreal at the International Conference "Sustainable Justice 2002: Implementing International Sustainable Development Law";

Acknowledging the serious social, economic and environmental challenges facing the peoples of the world;

Concerned with the continuing failure to implement universal human rights, the deterioration of the global environment, and the increase in the number of people living in absolute poverty;

Recognising that governance for sustainable development is not yet fully coherent, and that international courts, institutions, legal scholars and professionals need practical legal principles and tools to navigate overlapping and sometimes conflicting international human rights, economic and environmental legal obligations;

Recalling foundational and continuing work of other fora and international agencies[3];

Reaffirming Chapter 39 of the 1992 *Agenda 21*, which recognises the need to continue progressive development and codification of international law related to sustainable development, and urges cooperation and coordination in this regard; and which also recognises the need to improve the effectiveness of legal institutions, mechanisms and procedures; and to address actual or potential conflicts between environmental and social/economic agreements or instruments;

Reaffirming Section 3 of the 1997 *Programme for the Further Implementation of Agenda 21*, which recognises that economic development, social development and environmental protection are interdependent and mutually reinforcing

---

[3] Including the Brundtland Experts Group on Environmental Law (1987), the Rio Declaration of Principles on Environment and Development (1992) and the final documents of other UN Conferences, the Agenda for Development by the UN Secretary-General (1995); the Report of the Expert Group Meeting on Identification of Principles of International Law for Sustainable Development, UN Secretariat (1995), the revised IUCN Draft Covenant on Environment and Development (2000), the UNEP Montevideo Programmes on International Environmental Law Aiming at Sustainable Development II (1997) and III (2000), the Limoges Declaration adopted by the World Meeting of Environmental Law Associations (1990), the Johannesburg Declaration (2002), the Johannesburg Plan of Implementation (2002), and other efforts.

components of sustainable development; and that equity, justice, and social and environmental considerations must guide economic growth;

Recognising the need, in 2002, for a concerted and strengthened agenda to advance the understanding, development and implementation of international sustainable development law at the intersection of environment, economic and social regimes, on mutually agreed terms and with the full participation of those affected;

Supporting the leading efforts of the International Law Association's Committee on the Legal Aspects of Sustainable Development, in the context of their debates on the relevant general principles of international law such as the rule of law in international relations, including international economic relations; the duty to cooperate for global development and protection of the environment; the principle of observance of human rights; and the principle of integration in particular;

Supporting in particular the 2002 *New Delhi International Law Association Declaration on Principles of International Law relating to Sustainable Development*, from the 70th Conference of the International Law Association, which calls for the application, consolidation and further development of the following principles of international law in the field of sustainable development;
- The duty of States to ensure sustainable use of natural resources;
- The principle of equity and the eradication of poverty;
- The principle of common but differentiated responsibilities;
- The principle of the precautionary approach to human health, natural resources and ecosystems;
- The principle of public participation and access to information and justice;
- The principle of good governance;
- The principle of integration and interrelationship, in particular in relation to human rights and social, economic and environmental objectives.

Announce the Emergence of a New Global Partnership for the Implementation of International Sustainable Development Law

We call upon all partners to advance the understanding, development and implementation of international sustainable development law, through:

Interdisciplinary Partnerships: Build and strengthen interdisciplinary partnerships for international sustainable development law; and encourage key international economic, social and environmental institutions to collaborate, in cooperation with sustainable development bodies, to address priority sectors and issues.

Innovative Legal Instruments: Support the analysis, development and implementation of innovative, integrated international sustainable development law instruments, including treaties, dispute settlement mechanisms and decisions, national and international frameworks, and new forms of contract law, to promote coherence in areas where international economic, environmental or human rights legal obligations can overlap or conflict.

Legal Research and Knowledge Networks: Develop further legal research and knowledge network programmes related to international sustainable development law through courts, legal and professional associations, academic institutions, and civil society.

Subsidiary Legal Regimes: Develop and strengthen international law related to sustainable development on the global, regional, sub-regional, bi-lateral or local levels closest to those most affected.

Transparency, Accountability and Civil Society Participation: Ensure transparency and civil society involvement in international economic, environmental and human rights law, and particularly in the areas of integration or overlap.

Legal Capacity Building, Expertise and Technical Assistance: Develop and strengthen capacity building programmes, networks of expertise and coordinated technical assistance, for more effective negotiation, implementation, enforcement, monitoring and governance of international sustainable development law, with particular attention to the needs and abilities of developing country legal communities.

Sustainable Development Dispute Settlement: Ensure transparency, access to relevant environmental, social or economic expertise, and civil society participation in deliberations of tribunals, courts and panels in disputes related to sustainable development.

Reporting, Compliance and Enforcement: Design innovative cooperative mechanisms to ensure more effective compliance with international sustainable development law, and strengthen monitoring, implementation and enforcement systems.

Legal Measures to Finance Sustainable Development: Ensure that the conditions exist to fulfil legal obligations in economic, environmental and human rights law relating to financing and international assistance, leverage mutually agreed sustainable development support from socially responsible corporations, and increase investment in sustainable technologies, projects and systems.

International Sustainable Development Law in 2002: Launch a new research and implementation agenda for international sustainable development law in 2002 by building an integrated social, environmental and economic legal partnership to implement the WSSD outcomes, strengthening political and institutional support, and engaging all relevant actors in the implementation of international sustainable development law.

Best Practices in International Sustainable Development Law and Policy

We further call upon States, intergovernmental organisations, legal associations, academics, courts and legal professionals, to test, share and where appropriate further develop integrated sustainable development law and policy instruments, including:

- Community implementation and integrated regional sustainable development law (as shown by the *UN Desertification Convention*);
- Use of civil, political, economic, social and cultural human rights mechanisms for poverty eradication and environmental protection (as indicated by the Committee on Economic, Social and Cultural Rights in General Comment No.14 (Right to Health), its *Statement on Poverty* and the text of the *International Covenant on Economic, Social and Cultural Rights* itself);
- International consultation and complaints procedures for citizen and civil society groups, which result in investigation, monitoring and factual reports, even potential financial penalties, in alleged instances of non-compliance with social, economic or environmental law (as established by the 1994 *North American Agreement on Environmental Cooperation,* and the 1994 *North American Labour Cooperation Agreement*);
- Sustainable development impact assessment techniques, including integrated analysis of economic, social or environmental policies, programmes and projects (as carried out by the European Union for proposed global trade liberalization negotiations);
- Domestic legal mechanisms to ensure corporate social and environmental accountability, including enforcement of foreign direct liability and civil responsibility claims, mandatory environmental and social reporting and new duties for corporate director to take account of environmental and social matters in decision-making;
- Domestic legal mechanisms to ensure government accountability for environment and sustainable development, including enforcement of government agencies to establish sustainable development strategies, and implement these strategies (as practised by Canada through Commissioners for environment and sustainable development);
- International alternative dispute resolution for environment and sustainable development (such as the *International Court of Environmental Arbitration and Conciliation*);

- Provisions in national laws that directly incorporate sustainable development, encouraging the mainstreaming of sustainable development practice in judicial decision-making by the highest courts;
- Advanced informed consent and prior informed consent regimes (as established by the 2002 *Cartagena Protocol on Biosafety* of the 1992 *United Nations Convention on Biological Diversity* and other instruments);
- Explicit endorsements of sustainable development in international jurisprudence (such as in the *Gabcikovo-Nagymaros case* of the *International Court of Justice*).
- An increasing emphasis on the practical implementation of sustainable development (for example, the development of the *United Nations Framework Convention on Climate Change* frameworks on capacity-building, and the *Prototype Carbon Fund* of the World Bank and partners);
- Benefit-sharing provisions for sustainable natural resource use contracts (through the implementation of the *Bonn Guidelines*, and the negotiation of an international regime in the 1992 *United Nations Convention on Biological Diversity* Ad Hoc Working Group on Access and Benefit-Sharing);
- Increasing explicit institutional consideration of environmental and social factors in the operation of international economic institutions (such as the WB's newly updated *Safeguard Policies*);
- Debt sustainability analysis mechanisms linked to poverty eradication and environmental protection (as recommended in the 2002 *Monterrey Consensus* document of the 2002 *United Nations Conference on Financing for Development*);
- Mechanisms to ensure appropriate harmonisation of standards (as established in the UN Economic Commission for Europe's 1999 *Water and Health Protocol* to ensure drinking water supply in adequate quantity and quality, prevention and control of water borne diseases);
- Mutually agreed trade and liability measures for environmental and social purposes with private sector involvement and responsibility (as provided by the 2002 *Rotterdam Convention on Persistent Organic Pollutants* to ensure environmentally sound trade in hazardous chemicals and pesticides, or the 2000 *Protocol on Liability and Compensation of the Basel Convention*);
- Global multilateral guidelines aimed at generating public rights of access to information, public participation in decision-making and access to justice, to be prepared with the participation of civil society and drawing upon existing experience, including regional initiative designed to implement Principle 10 of the Rio Declaration, such as the *Aarhus Convention on Access to Information;*
- Inspection panel mechanisms for communities to be heard concerning projects which might affect their needs and interests (as practiced though the World Bank *Inspection Panel* mechanism);
- Provisions to facilitate the submission of *amicus curiae* briefs by interested groups in economic dispute settlement procedures (as attempted by the World Trade Organisation Appellate Body in the *EU-Asbestos* dispute).

RECOMMENDED RESOURCES

E. Agius, ed., *Future Generations and International Law* (London: Earthscan Publications, 1998).

P. Alston, "Conjuring up New Human Rights: A Proposal for Quality Control" (1984) 78 *A.J.I.L.* 607.

P. Alston, "Making Space for New Human Rights: The Case of the Right to Development" (1988) *Harv. Hum. Rts. Y.B.* 3.

P. Alston and G. Quinn, "The Nature and Scope of States Parties' Obligations under the International Covenant on Economic, Social and Cultural Rights" (1987) 9 *Hum. Rts. Q.* 156.

P. Alston, "The Fortieth Anniversary of the Universal Declaration" in J. Berting *et al.*, eds. *Human Rights in a Pluralist World, Individuals and Collectivities* (1990).

P. Alston, ed., *Peoples' Rights* (Oxford: Oxford University, 2001).

C. F. Amerasinghe, *Principles of the Institutional Law of International Organizations* 2nd Ed. (Cambridge: Cambridge University Press, 2004).

O. Anaedu and L. Engfeldt, "Sustainable Development Governance" Paper prepared by the World Summit for Sustainable Development Governance Working Group Vice-Chairs Ositadinma Anaedu and Lars-Goran Engfeldt, (New York: WSSD, 2002).

S. Arrowsmith, *Government Procurement in the WTO* (The Hague: Kluwer Law International, 2002).

A. A. Asouzu, *International Commercial Arbitration and African States: Practice, Participation and Institutional Development* (Cambridge: Cambridge University Press, 2001).

S. Atapattu, "Sustainable Development: Myth or Reality? A Survey of Sustainable Development under International Law and Sri Lankan Law," (2001) 14 *Geo. Int'l Envtl. L. Rev.* 265.

J. E. Austin & C. E. Bruch, *The Environmental Consequences of War: Legal, Economic, and Scientific Perspectives* (Cambridge: Cambridge University Press, 2001).

xliii

M. Austen & T. Richards, *Basic Legal Documents on International Animal Welfare and Wildlife Conservation* (The Hague: Kluwer Law International, 2000).

I. Ayres and J. Braithwaite, *Responsive Regulation: Transcending the Deregulation Debate* (Oxford: Oxford University Press, 1992).

S. Baker, M. Kousis, D. Richardson & S. Young, eds., *The Politics of Sustainable Development* (London: Routledge, 1997).

K. Banks, "Civil Society and the North American Agreement on Labor Cooperation" in J. Kirton and V. Maclaren, eds., *Linking Trade, Environment and Social Cohesion: NAFTA Experiences, Global Challenges* (Aldershot: Ashgate, 2002).

K. Bastmeijer, *The Antarctic Environmental Protocol and its Domestic Legal Implementation* (The Hague: Kluwer Law International, 2003).

U. Baxi, "The Development of the Right to Development" in J. Symonides, ed., *Human Rights: New Dimensions and Challenges* (Ashgate: Ashgate, 1998).

C. Bellmann, G. Dutfield & R. Meléndez-Ortiz, *Trading in Knowledge: Development Perspectives on TRIPS, Trade and Sustainability* (London: Earthscan / ICTSD, 2003).

E. Benvenisti, "Domestic Politics and International Resources" in M. Byers, ed., *The Role of Law in International Politics: Essays in International Relations and International Law* (Oxford: Oxford University Press, 2000).

J.M. Bergerat, "Tripping over Patents: Aids, Access to Treatment and the Manufacturing of Scarcity" (2002) 17 *Conn. J. Int'l L.* 157.

G. A. Bermann, "Taking Subsidiarity Seriously: Federalism in the European Community and the United States" (1994) 94 *Colum. L. Rev.* 331.

D. Brack, "Multilateral Environmental Agreements: An Overview" in H. Ward & D. Brack, eds., *Trade, Investment and the Environment* (London: Royal Institute of International Affairs and Earthscan, 2000).

D. Bradlow, "A Test Case for the World Bank" (1996) 11 *Am. U. J. Int'l L. & Pol'y* 247.

H. Breitmeier, "International Organisations and the Creation of Environmental Regimes" in O. Young, ed., *Global Governance: Drawing Insights from the Environmental Experience* (Cambridge: MIT Press, 1997) at 87-114.

M. Bowman & A. Boyle, *Environmental Damage in International and Comparative Law - Problems of Definition and Valuation* (Oxford: Oxford University Press, 2002).

M. Bowman & C. Redgwell, *International Law and the Conservation of Biological Diversity* (The Hague: Kluwer Law International, 1995).

A. Boyle & M. Anderson, eds., *Human Rights Approaches to Environmental Protection* (Oxford: Clarendon Press, 1996).

A. Boyle & D. Freestone, eds., *International Law and Sustainable Development: Past Achievements and Future Challenges* (Oxford: Oxford University Press 1999).

D. Bradlow, "Social Justice and Development: Critical Issues Facing the Bretton Woods System: The World Bank, the IMF, and Human Rights" (1996) 6 *Transnat'l. L. & Contemp. Probs.* 47

J.L. Brierly, *Law of Nations*, 6th ed. (Oxford: Clarendon Press, 1963).

C. Brower & J. Brueschke, *The Iran-United States Claims Tribunal* (The Hague: Kluwer Law International, 1998).

D. R. Brown, "Transboundary Environmental Impacts in a European Context" (1997) 3 *Eur. Env't* 80.

E. Brown Weiss, "Environmentally Sustainable Competitiveness: A Comment" (1993) 102 *Yale L.J.* 2123

E. Brown Weiss, *In Fairness to Future Generations: International Law, Common Patrimony, and intergenerational Equity* (New York: Transnational, 1989).

E. Brown Weiss, "International Environmental Law: Contemporary Issues and the Emergence of a New World Order" (1993) 81 *Geo. L.J.* 675.

E. Brown Weiss, "The Emerging Structure of International Environmental Law" in N. J. Vig & R. S. Axelrod, eds., *The Global Environment: Institutions, Law, and Policy* (Washington: Congressional Quarterly, 1999) at 98.

E. Brown Weiss, P.C Szasz & D.B. Magraw, *International Environmental Law: Basic Instruments and Reference* (New York: Transnational, 1992).

I. Brownlie, *Principles of Public International Law* (Oxford: Oxford University Press, 1998).

J. Brunnée & S.J. Toope "International Law and Constructivism: Elements of an Interactional Theory of International Law" (2000) 39 (1) *Colum. J. Transnat'l L.* 19.

J. Brunée & S. J. Toope, "Environmental Security and Freshwater Resources: Ecosystem Regime Building" (1997) *A.J.I.L.* 26 at 40.

W. Burns, "The International Convention to Combat Desertification: Drawing a Line in the Sand?" (1994) 16 *Mich. J. Int'l L.* 831.

L. K. Caldwell, *International Environmental Policy* (Durham: Duke University Press, 1996).

L. K. Caldwell, "Beyond Environmental Diplomacy" in J. E. Carroll, ed., *International Environmental Diplomacy* (Cambridge: Cambridge University Press, 1988) at 16.

J. Cameron, "International Law and the Precautionary Principle" in T. O' Riordan, J. Cameron & A. Jordan, eds., *Reinterpreting the Precautionary Principle* (London: Cameron May, 2001).

J. Cameron & J. Abouchar, "The Status of the Precautionary Principle in International Law" in D. Freestone & E. Hey, eds., *The Precautionary Principle and International Law: The Challenge of Implementation* (The Hague: Kluwer Law International, 1996).

J. Cameron & J. Abouchar, "The Precautionary Principle: A Fundamental Principle of Law and Policy for the Protection of the Global Environment" (1991) 14 *B.C. Int'l & Comp. L. Rev.* 1.

J. Cameron, P. Demaret & D. Geradin, eds., *Trade & The Environment: The Search For Balance* (London: Cameron May, 1994).

P. D. Cameron & D. Zillman, *Kyoto: From Principles to Practice* (The Hague: Kluwer Law International, 2001).

L. Campiglio, L. Pineschi & D. Siniscalco Treves, eds., *The Environment After Rio: International Law and Economics* (Boston: Graham & Trotman, 1994).

A.A. Cancado Trindade, ed., *Human Rights, Sustainable Development and the Environment* (San José, Costa Rica: Instituto Interamericano de Derechos Humanos, 1992).

M. Cappelletti, M. Seccombe & J. Weiler, eds., *Integration through Law* (New York: W. de Gruyter, 1986).

A. Cassese, *International Law* (Oxford: Oxford University Press, 2001).

J.G. Castel, A.L.C. de Mestral and W.C. Graham, *The Canadian Law and Practice of International Trade* (Toronto: Montgomery, 1991).

Center for International Sustainable Development Law, Legal Brief: *International Environmental Governance for Sustainable Development* (December 2001), online: <http://www.cisdl.org>.

Centre for International Sustainable Development Law, Legal Brief: *Sustainable Competition Law* (10 September 2003) online: <http://www.cisdl.org>.

W. B. Chambers, ed., *Inter-linkages: The Kyoto Protocol and the International Trade and Investment Regimes* (Tokyo: United Nations University Press, 2001).

S. Charnovitz, "Regional Trade Agreements and the Environment" (1995) 37:5 *Environment* 95.

W. Choi, *'Like Products' in International Trade Law - Towards a Consistent GATT/WTO Jurisprudence* (Oxford: Oxford University Press, 2003).

R. Churchill and V. Lowe, *The Law of the Sea* (Oxford: Oxford University Press, 1999).

W. C. Clark, "A Transition towards Sustainability" (2001) 27 Ecology L.Q. 1021.

B. Clark, "Environmental Impact Assessment (EIA): Scope and Objectives" in *Perspectives on Environmental Impact Assessment* (Dordrecht: D. Reidel Publishing Co, 1984).

A. M. H. Clayton & N. J. Radcliffe, *Sustainability: A Systems Approach*, (London: Earthscan, 1996).

M. Colchester, *Salvaging Nature Indigenous Peoples, Protected Areas and Biodiversity Conservation* World Rainforest Movement and World Wildlife Fund Discussion Paper 55 (Geneva: United Nations Research Institute for Social Development, 1994).

H. Collins, "The Voice of the Community in Private Law Discourse" (1997) 3 *Eur. L.J.* 407.

M.C. Cordonier Segger, "Significant Developments in Sustainable Development Law and Governance: A Proposal" (2004) *United Nations Natural Resources Forum* 28:1.

M.C. Cordonier Segger "Sustainability and Corporate Accountability Regimes: Implementing the Johannesburg Summit Agenda" (2003) *R.E.C.I.E.L.* 12:3.

M.C. Cordonier Segger & A. Khalfan, *Sustainable Development Law: Principles, Practices and Prospects* (Oxford: Oxford University Press, 2004).

M.C. Cordonier Segger et al., *Social Rules and Sustainability in the Americas* (Winnipeg: IISD / OAS, 2004).

M.C. Cordonier Segger et al., *Ecological Rules and Sustainability in the Americas* (Winnipeg: IISD / UNEP, 2002).

M.C. Cordonier Segger et al., *Trade Rules and Sustainability in the Americas* (Winnipeg: IISD, 1999).

M.C. Cordonier Segger et al., "Prospects for Principles of International Sustainable Development Law after WSSD: Common but Differentiated Responsibilities, Precaution and Participation" (2003) 12:3 *R.E.C.I.E.L.*

M.C. Cordonier Segger *et al.*, "A New Mechanism for Hemispheric Cooperation on Environmental Sustainability and Trade" (2002) 27:2 *Columbia Journal of Environmental Law* 613.

M.C. Cordonier Segger, "Sustainable Development in the Negotiation of the FTAA - The Free Trade Area of the Americas: Issues and Visions for the Future, Interamerican Perspectives" (2004) 27 *Fordham. Intl. L. J.* 1118.

M.C. Cordonier Segger & N. Borregaard, "Sustainability and Hemispheric Integration: A Review of Existing Approaches" in C. Deere & D. Esty, eds., *Greening the Americas*, (Boston: MIT Press, 2002).

M.C. Cordonier Segger & M. Leichner Reynal, eds., *Beyond the Barricades: The Americas Trade and Sustainability Agenda* (Aldershot: Ashgate, 2005).

M.C. Cordonier Segger & M. Gehring, 'Precaution, Health and the World Trade Organisation: Moving toward Sustainable Development' (2003) 29 *Queen's L. J.* 133.

H. D. Cooper, "The International Treaty on Plant Genetic Resources for Food and Agriculture" (2002) 11 *R.E.C.I.E.L.* 1.

J. Crawford, ed., *Rights of Peoples* (Oxford: Oxford University Press, 1992).

J. Crawford, *The International Law Commission's Articles on State Responsibility – Introduction, Texts and Commentaries* (Cambridge: Cambridge University Press, 2002).

M. Craven, *The International Covenant on Economic, Social and Cultural Rights: A Perspective on its Development* (Oxford: Clarendon, 1995).

Crucible Group II, *Seeding Solutions, Volume 1. Policy Options for genetic resources, People, Plants, and Patents Revisited* (IDRC and IPGRI, 2000).

A. D' Amato & S. K. Chopra, "Whales: Their Emerging Right to Life" (1991) 85 *Am. J. Int'l. L. 1.*

K. Danish, "International Environmental Law and the "Bottom-Up" Approach: A Review of the Desertification Convention" (1995) 3 *Ind. J. Global Leg. Stud.* 133.

William J. Davey, "The WTO Dispute Settlement System" (2000) 3:1 *J. Int'l Econ. L.* 15.

M. Decleris. *The Law of Sustainable Development: General Principles, A Report for the European Commission* (Brussels: European Commission, 2000).

C. Deere, *Net Gains: International Trade, Sustainable Development and Fisheries* (Washington: IUCN - World Conservation, 1999).

K. de Feyter, *World Development Law: Sharing Resources for Development* (Antwerp: Intersentia, 2001).

C. de Fontaubert, *Achieving Sustainable Fisheries: Implementing the New International Regime* (Gland: IUCN, 2003).

P.J.I.M. de Waart, "Securing Access to Safe Drinking Water through Trade and International Migration", in E. Brans et al., eds., *The Scarcity of Water: Emerging Legal and Policy Responses* (The Hague: Kluwer Law International, 1997) at 116-17.

J. C. Dernbach, "Sustainable Development as a Framework for National Governance" (1998) 49 *Case W. Res.* 1.

E. Dewailly, A. Nantel, J.P. Weber & F. Meyer, "High Levels of PCBs in Breast Milk of Inuit Women from Arctic Québec" (1989) *Bull. Environ. Contam. Toxicol.* 43.

D. Devuys, "Sustainability Assessment: the Application of a Methodological Framework" (1999) 1:4 *Journal of Environmental Assessment Policy and Management* 459.

E. Dinerstein et al., *A Conservation Assessment of the Terrestrial Ecoregions of Latin America and the Caribbean* (Washington: WWF & World Bank, 1995).

J. M. Djossou, *L'Afrique, le GATT et l'OMC: Entre territoires douaniers et régions commerciales*, (Sainte-Foy: Presses de l'Université Laval, 2000).

F. Dodds, ed., *Earth Summit 2002: A New Deal* (London: EarthScan, 2002).

C. Dommen & P. Cullet, *Droit International de L'Environment, Textes de base et reference* (The Hague: Kluwer Law International, 2001).

M. Drumble, "Poverty, Wealth and Obligation in International Environmental Law" (2002) 76 *Tul. L. Rev.* 843.

P. Duncanson Cameron, *Competition in Energy Markets: Law and Regulation in the European Union* (Oxford: Oxford University Press, 2002).

P. Dupuy, "Soft Law and the International Law of the Environment" (1991) 12 *Mich. J. Int'l L.* 420

W. Durbin, *A Comparison of the Environmental Provisions of the NAFTA, the Canada-Chile Trade Agreement and the Mexican-European Community Trade Agreement* (New Haven: Yale Centre for Environmental Law and Policy, 2000).

G. Dutfield, *Intellectual Property Rights, Trade and Biodiversity* (London: Earthscan, 2000).

R. H. Edwards & S. N. Lester, "Towards a More Comprehensive World Trade Organisation Agreement on Trade Related Investment Measures" (1997) 33 *Stan. J. Int'l L.* 169.

M. A. Echols, *Food Safety and the WTO: The Interplay of Culture, Science and Technology* (The Hague: Kluwer Law International, 2001).

A. Eide, C. Krause & A. Rosas eds., *Economic, Social and Cultural Rights,* 2nd rev. ed. (Norwell: Kluwer Academic Publishers, 2001).

J. A. Ekpere, "TRIPs, Biodiversity and Traditional Knowledge: OAU Model Law on Community Rights and Access to Genetic Resources" (2003) 7:5 *Bridges Journal* 11.

1

D. Esty, *Greening the GATT: Trade, Environment and the Future* (Washington: Institute for International Economics, 1994).

D. C. Esty & D. Geradin, "Market Access, Competitiveness, and Harmonization: Environmental Protection in Regional Trade Agreements" (1997) 21 *Harv. Envtl. L. Rev.* 265.

T.F.M. Etty & H. Somsen, *Yearbook of European Environmental Law* 4 (Oxford: Oxford University Press, 2004)

European Commission, *Communication from the European Commission on the Precautionary Principle* COM 1 (2000), WTO doc. WT/CTE/W/147G/TBT/W/137 (27 June 2000).

D. P. Fidler, *International Law and Infectious Diseases* (Oxford: Clarendon Press, 1999).

D. P. Fidler, "The Future of the World Health Organisation: What Role for International Law" (1998) 31 *Vand. J. Transnat'l, L.* 1079.

D. Fidler, "Trade and Health: The global Spread of Disease and International Trade" (1997) 40 *Germ. Y. B. Int'l L.* 30.

D. Fidler, "Return of the Fourth Horseman: Emerging Infectious Diseases and International Law" (1997) 81 *Minn. L. Rev.* 771.

D. Fidler, "International Law and Global Public Health" 48 *U. Kan. L. Rev.* 1.

D. Fidler, "A Globalized Theory of Public Health Law", 30 *J. L. Med. & Ethics* 150.

F. Francione, *Environment, Human Rights and International Trade* (Oxford: Hart, 2001).

D. Freestone and E. Hey, eds., *The Precautionary Principle and International Law. The Challenge of Implementation* (New York: Kluwer International, 1996).

L. Frischtak, *Antinomies of Development: Governance Capacity and Adjustment Responses* (World Bank, 1993).

C. Ford, "Judicial discretion in international jurisprudence: Article 38(1)(C) and "general principles of law" 5 *Duke J. of Comp. & Int'l Law* 35-86 (1994).

E. Fox, "Anti-trust and Regulatory Federalism: Races Up, Down and Sideways" (2000) 75 *N.Y.U.L. Rev.* 1781.

E. Fox, "Competition Law" in A. Lowenfeld, International Economic Law (Oxford: Oxford University Press, 2002) at 340 -383.

J. Fox & L. Brown, *The Struggle for Accountability: The World Bank, NGOs, and Grassroots Movements* (Cambridge, MA: MIT Press, 1998).

T. M. Franck, *Fairness in International Law and Institutions* (Oxford: Oxford University Press, 1995).

D. French, "Developing States and International Environmental Law: The Importance of Differentiated Responsibilities" (2000) 49 *International & Comparative Law Quarterly* 35.

P. Gallagher, *Guide to the WTO and Developing Countries* (The Hague: Kluwer Law International, 2000).

F. V. Garcia-Amador, "The Proposed New International Economic Order: A New Approach to the Law Governing Nationalization and Compensation" (1980) 12 *Lawyer of the Americas* 1

D. B. Gatmaytan, "Half a Landmark Case: Reflections on Oposa v. Factoran" (1994) 6 *Philippine Natural Resources Law Journal* 30.

A. I. Gavil, *et al., Antitrust Law in Perspective: Cases, Concepts and Problems in Competition Policy* (St. Paul: Thomson West, 2002) 38.

P. Grady & K. Macmillan, *Seattle and Beyond: The WTO Millennium Round* (Ottawa: Global Economics Ltd and International Trade Policy Consultants Inc., 1999)

K. R. Gray, "International Environmental Impact Assessment" (2000) 11 *Colo. J. Int'l Envtl. L. & Pol'y* 83.

M. Gehring and M.C. Cordonier Segger, "The WTO Asbestos Cases and Precaution: Sustainable Development Implications of the WTO Asbestos Dispute" (2003) 15 *Oxford J Envtl L* 289.

M. Gehring and M.C. Cordonier Segger, eds., *Sustainable Developments in World Trade Law* (The Hague: Kluwer Law International, 2005).

K. Gent, "Deutsches Stromeinspeisungsgesetz und Europäisches Wettbewerbsrecht" (1999) *Energiewirtschaftliche Tagesfragen - Zeitschrift für die Elektrizitäts- und Gasversorgung* 854-858.

D. Gerber, *Law and Competition in Twentieth-Century Europe - Protecting Prometheus* (Oxford: Oxford University Press, 2001).

D. Gervais, *The TRIPS Agreement: Drafting History and Analysis* (London: Sweet & Maxwell, 1998).

M. Ghezuhly *et al.*, "International Health Law" (1998) 32 *Int'l Law* 539.

C. Giagnocavo & H. Goldstein, "Law Reform or World Reform: The Problem of Environmental Rights" 35 *McGill L. J.* 345.

K. Ginther, E. Denters & P.J.I.M. de Waart eds., *Sustainable Development and Good Governance* (The Hague: Kluwer Law International, 1995).

E. Gitli and C. Murillo, in C. Deere & D. Esty, eds., *Greening the Americas*, (Boston: MIT Press, 2002).

M. Goransson, "Liability for Damage to the Marine Environment" in A. Boyle and D. Freestone, eds., *International Law and Sustainable Development: Past Achievements and Future Challenges* (Oxford: Oxford University Press, 1999).

D. G. Goyder, *EC Competition Law* 4th ed. (Oxford: Oxford University Press, 2003).

K. R. Gray, "International Environmental Impact Assessment" (2000) 11 *Colo. J. Int'l Envtl. L. & Pol'y* 83.

D. A. Grossman, "Warming Up To a Not-So-Radical Idea: Tort-Based Climate Change Litigation" (2003) 28 Colum. J. Envtl. L. 1.

L. Guruswamy and B. Hendricks, *International Environmental Law* (St. Paul, Minn.: West, 1997).

A. Guzman, "Why LDCs Sign Treaties that Hurt Them: Explaining the Popularity of Bilateral Investment Treaties" (1998) 38 *Va. J. Int'l Law* 639.

G. Handl & R. E. Lutz, *Transferring Hazardous Technologies and Substances* (The Hague: Kluwer Law International, 1990).

G. Handl, *Multilateral Development Banking: Environmental Principles and Concepts Reflecting General International Law and Public Policy* (The Hague: Kluwer Law International, 2001)

X. Hanqin, *Transboundary Damage in International Law* (Cambridge: Cambridge University Press, 2003).

D. Harris and S. Livingstone, eds. *The Inter-American System of Human Rights* (Oxford: Clarendon, 1998)

G. Hartkopf and E. Bohne, *Umweltpolitik, vol. 1: Grundlagen, Analysen, und Perspektiven* (Opladen: Westdeutscher Verlag, 1983).

R. Heathcote, *The Arid Lands: Their Use and Abuse* (Tokyo, United Nations University, 1983).

D. Held, *Models of Democracy* (Stanford: Stanford University Press, 1987).

K. Helmore & N. Singh, *Sustainable Livelihoods: Building on the Wealth of the Poor* (Bloomfield: Kumarian Press, 2001).

G. Hermes, *Staatliche Infrastrukturverantwortung : rechtliche Grundstrukturen netzgebundener Transport- und Übertragungssysteme zwischen Daseinsvorsorge und Wettbewerbsregulierung am Beispiel der leitungsgebundenen Energieversorgung in Europa* (Tuebingen: Mohr Siebeck, 1998).

J.A. Hernandez, "How the Feds are Pushing Nuclear Waste on Reservations" (1994) *Cultural Survival Quarterly* 40.

G. Herrmann, "The Role of UNCITRAL" in I. Fletcher, L. Mistellis & M. Cremona *eds., Foundations and Perspectives of International Trade Law* (London: Sweet & Maxwell, 2001) 28-36.

R. L. Herz, "Litigating Environmental Abuses Under the Alien Tort Claims Act: A Practical Assessment" (2000) 40 *Va. J. Int'l L.* 545.

J. E. Hickey, Jr., & V. R. Walker, "Refining the Precautionary Principle in International Environmental Law" (1995) 14 *Va. Envtl. L.J.* 423.

R. K. Hitchcock, "International Human Rights, the Environment, and Indigenous Peoples" (1994) 5 *Colo. J. Int'l Envtl. L. & Pol'y* 1.

J. Holder, *Environmental Assessment - Legal Regulation of Decision Making* (Oxford: Oxford University Press, 2003).

J. Holmberg, *Defending the Future: A Guide to Sustainable Development* (London: Earthscan, 1988).

H. Hofbauer, G. Lara & B. Martinez, *Health Care: A Question of Human Rights, Not Charity* (Mexico City: FUNDAR, 2002).

S. Horton, "Peru and ANCOM: A Study in the Disintegration of a Common Market." (1982) 1 *Texas International Law Journal* 17.

D. Hunter, J. Salzman and D. Zaelke, *International Environmental Law and Policy,* 2nd ed. (New York: Foundation Press, 2003).

D. Hunter, J. Sommer and S. Vaughan, *Concepts and Principles of International Law* (Nairobi: UNEP, 1998).

G. Hyden & M. Bratton, eds., *Governance and Politics in Africa* (Boulder: Lynne Rienner Publishers, 1993).

IBRD, *International Bank for Reconstruction and Development Operational Policy* 4.01 (Washington: IBRD, 1999)

IBRD, *The Convention on the Settlement of Investment Disputes: Documents Concerning the Origin and Formulation of the Convention* (Washington: IBRD, 1970).

ICTSD, "Comercio y medio ambiente en los acuerdos regionales" (1999) 2:1 *Puentes Entre el Comercio y el Desarollo Sostenible* (Quito: ICTSD/FFLA, 1999).

E. V. Iglesias, *El nuevo rostro de la integracion regional en America Latina y el Caribe* (Washington: Inter-American Development Bank, 1997)

Inter American Development Bank, *Integration and Trade in the Americas* (Washington: IDB, 1996).

International Council on Human Rights Policy, *Duties sans Frontieres: Human Rights and Global Social Justice* (Geneva: ICHRP, 2003).

International Institute for Sustainable Development (IISD), *Impoverishment and Sustainable Development* (Winnipeg: IISD, 1996).

International Law Commission (ILC), D*raft Articles on the Non-Navigational Uses of International Watercourses,* U.N. Doc. A/46/10 (1991); U.N. Doc. A/CN.4/L492 & Add. 1 (1994).

International Monetary Fund, *Code of Good Practices on Fiscal Transparency - Declaration of Principles* (1998) April 16, 1998, 37 I.L.M. 942.

International Union for Conservation of Nature and Natural Resources, *An Explanatory Guide to the Cartagena Protocol on Biosafety* (Cambridge, UK: International Union for Conservation of Nature and Natural Resources and FIELD, 2003)

Iran-United States Claims Tribunal Reports (Cambridge: Grotius, 1981 – 1993).

John H. Jackson, *The Jurisprudence of GATT and the WTO* (Cambridge: Cambridge University Press 2000).

J. Jackson, *The World Trading System: Law and Policy of International Economic Relations,* 2nd ed (Boston: MIT Press, 1997).

H.K. Jacobson and E. Brown-Weiss, "Strengthening Compliance with International Environmental Accords: Preliminary Observations from a Collaborative Project" (1995) 1 *Global Governance* 119.

H. K. Jacobson, *Networks of Interdependence: International Organisations and the Global Political System*, 2d ed. (New York: Knopf, 1984).

W. Jaeger, *Regulierter Wettbewerb in der Energiewirtschaft* (Baden-Baden: Nomos, 2002).

M. Janis, R. Kay and A. Bradley, *European Human Rights Law: Texts and Materials* (Oxford: Oxford University Press, 2000)

R. Jennings, "What Is International Law and How Do We Tell It When We See It?" (1981) 37 *A.S.D.I.* 59.

A.L. Jernow, "*Ad Hoc* and Extra-conventional Means for Human Rights Monitoring" in P.C. Szasz, ed., *Administrative and Expert Monitoring of International Treaties* (New York: Transnational, 1999).

P. Jha & F.J. Chaloupka, eds., *Tobacco Control in Developing Countries* (Oxford: Oxford University Press, 2000).

P. Kahn, "Contrats d'Etat et Nationalisation – Les Apports de la Sentence Arbitrale du 24 Mars, 1982" 109 *J. Droit Int'l* 844 (1982).

B. Kingsbury, "The Concept of Compliance as a Function of Competing Conceptions of International Law" (1998) 19 *Mich. J. Int'l Law* 345

A. Kirchner, *International Marine Environmental Law: Institutions, Implementation and Innovations* (The Hague: Kluwer Law International, 2003).

C. Kirkpatrick, *The Impact of the Uruguay Round on Least Developed Countries' External Trade: Strengthening the Capacity of LDCs to Participate Effectively in the World Trade Organisation and to Integrate into the Trading System* (Manchester: Manchester University Press, 1998).

J. Kirton, and V. Maclaren, eds., *Linking Trade, Environment, and Social Cohesion: NAFTA Experiences, Global Challenges* (Aldershot: Ashgate, 2002).

A. Kiss, D. Shelton & K.Ishibashi, *Economic Globalization and Compliance with International Environmental Agreements* (The Hague: Kluwer Law International, 2003).

A. Kiss, "The Implications of Global Change for the International Legal System" in E. Brown Weiss, ed., *Environmental Change and International Law* (Tokyo: United Nations University Press, 1992) 319-325.

A. Kiss & D. Shelton, *International Environmental Law,* 2nd ed. (New York: Transnational Publishers, 1994).

A. Kiss & D. Shelton, *Judicial Handbook on Environmental Law (Draft)* (Nairobi: UNEP, 2004).

N. Klein, *Dispute Settlement in the UN Convention on the Law of the Sea* (Cambridge: Cambridge University Press, 2004).

T. Klindt, *Die Umweltzeichen "Blauer Engel" und "Europäische Blume" zwischen produktbezogenem Umweltschutz und Wettbewerbsrecht* (1998) *Betriebsberater* 545.

H. H. Koh, "Why do Nations Obey International Law?"(1997) 106 *Yale L.J.* 2599.

P. Konz, C. Bellmann, L. Assuncao & R. Melendez-Otiz, *Trade, Environment, and Sustainable Development Views from Sub-Saharan Africa and Latin America: A Reader* (Geneva: UNU/IAS & ICTSD, 2000).

M. Koskenniemi, "Breach of Treaty or Non-Compliance? Reflections on the Enforcement of the Montreal Protocol" (1992) 3 *Y.B. Int'l. Env'tl. L.* 123

A. Kothari, "Beyond the Biodiversity Convention: A View from India" in V. Sanchez and C. Juma, eds., *Biodiplomacy: Genetic Resources and International Relations* (Nairobi: ACTS, 1994) 67.

F. V. Kratochwil, *Rules, Norms and Decisions. on the Conditions of Practical and Legal Reasoning in International Relations and Domestic Affairs* (Cambridge: Cambridge University Press, 1989) 201.

F. Kratochwil, and J.G. Ruggie, "International Organisation: a State of the Art on an Art of the State" (1986), 40(4) *Int'l. Org.* 753 at 768.

K. Kummer, *International Management of Hazardous Wastes - The Basel Convention and Related Legal Rules* (Oxford: Oxford University Press, 1995).

J. Kurtz, "A General Investment Agreement in the WTO?: Lessons from Chapter 11 NAFTA and the OECD Multilateral Agreement on Investment" (2002) 23 *Journal of International Economic Law* 713-789.

W.M. Lafferty & J. Meadowcroft, *Implementing Sustainable Development - Strategies and Initiatives in High Consumption Societies* (Oxford: Oxford University Press, 2000).

B. Lal Das, *The WTO Agreements: Deficiencies, Imbalances and Required Changes* (London: Zed Books, 1998).

W. Lang, ed., *Sustainable Development and International Law* (London: Graham & Trotman/Martinus Nijhoff, 1995).

M. Langford, A. Khalfan, C. Fairstein, and H. Jones, *Legal Resources for the Right to Water: International and National Standards* (Geneva: COHRE, 2004).

H. Lauterpacht, *The Development of International Law by the International Court* (London: Stevens, 1958).

J.W. Le Deuc, "World Health Organization Strategy for Emerging Infectious Diseases" (1996) 275 *J.A.M.A.* 318.

S. Lederberg, R.E. Shope, S.C. Oak, eds., *Emerging Infectious Diseases: Microbial Threats to Health in the United States* (Washington D.C.: Institute of Medicine, National Academy Press, 1992).

A. Lindroos, *The Right to Development* (Helsinki: The Erik Castren Institute of International Law and Human Rights Research Reports, 1999).

A. L'Hirondel & D. Yach, "Develop and Strengthen Public Health Law" (1998) 51 *World Health Stat. Q.* 79.

M. Lovei & P. Pillai, *Assessing Environmental Policy, Regulatory and Institutional Capacity: A World Bank Policy Note* (Washington: World Bank, 2003).

V. Lowe, "Sustainable Development and Unsustainable Arguments" in A. Boyle and D. Freestone, eds., *International Law and Sustainable Development: Past Achievements and Future Challenges* (Oxford: Oxford University Press, 1999).

V. Lowe, "The Politics of Law-Making: Are the Method and Character of Norm Creation Changing?" in M. Byers, ed. *The Role of Law in International Politics: Essays in International Relations and International Law* (Oxford: Oxford University Press, 2000).

A. Lowenfeld, *International Economic Law* (Oxford: Oxford University Press, 2002).

S. Lyster, *International Wildlife Law: An Analysis of International Treaties concerned with the Conservation of Wildlife* (Cambridge: Cambridge University Press, 1985).

R. Mackenzie et al., *An Explanatory Guide to the Cartagena Protocol on Biosafety* (Cambridge: IUCN, 2003).

G.F. Maggio, "Inter/intra-Generational Equity: Current Applications under International Law for Promoting the Sustainable Development of Natural Resources" (1997) 4 *Buff. Envt'l. L.J.* 161.

G.F. Maggio & O. J. Lynch, *Human Rights, Environment, and Economic Development: Existing and Emerging Standards in International Law and Global Society* (World Resources Institute, 1996).

K. E. Mahoney & P. Mahoney, eds., *Human Rights in the Twenty-first Century: A Global Challenge* (The Hague: Kluwer Academic Publishers, 1993).

H. Mann & K. von Moltke, *NAFTA's Chapter 11 and the Environment - Addressing the Impacts of the Investor-State Process on the Environment* (Winnipeg: International Institute for Sustainable Development, 1999).

G. Marceau, *Anti-Dumping and Anti-Trust Issues in Free-Trade Areas* (Oxford: Clarendon Press, 1994).

E. Marden, "The Neem Tree Patent: International Conflict over the Commodification of Life" (1999) 22 *Boston Col. Int'l & Comp. L Rev.* 2:279.

S. Marks, "Emerging Human Rights: A New Generation for the 1980s?" (1980-1) 33 *Rutgers L. Rev.* 435.

J. Mathis, *Regional Trade Agreements in the GATT/WTO Article XXIV and the Internal Trade Agreement* (The Hague: T.M.C. Asser Press, 2002).

M. Matsushita, T. J. Schoenbaum & P. C. Mavroidis, *The World Trade Organization - Law, Practice, and Policy* (Oxford: Oxford University Press, 2004).

M. Matsushita, "International Cooperation in the Enforcement of Competition Policy" (2002) *Washington University Global Studies Law Review Vol.* 1:463.

S. McCaffrey, *The Law of International Watercourses - Non-Navigational Uses* (Oxford: Oxford University Press, 2003).

P. McAuslan, "Good Governance and Aid in Africa" (1996) 40 *J. Afr. L.* 168 at 168-82.

C. McCrudden, "International Economic Law and Human Rights: A Framework for Discussion of the Legality of 'Selective Purchasing' Laws under the WTO Government Procurement Agreement" (1999) 2:1 *J. Int'l Econ. L.* 3.

C. McCrudden, "Labour Rights Revisited: International Investment Agreements and the Social Clause Debate" in M. Irish, ed., *The Auto Pact: Investment, Labour and the WTO* (New York: Aspen, 2003).

D. McGoldrick, "Sustainable Development and Human Rights: An Integrated Conception" (1996) 45 *Int'l & Comp. LQ.* 796.

H. McGoldrick, "Sustainable Development: The Challenge to International Law" (1994) *R.E.C.I.E.L.* 3.

D. H. Meadows et al., *Beyond the Limits* (New York: Universe Books, 1972).

R. Meléndez-Ortiz & C. Bellmann, *Commerce international et développement durable: Voix africaines et plurielles* ICTSD (Paris: Editions Charles Léopld Mayer, 2002).

L. Mills & I. Serageldin, *Governance and the External Factor* (Washington: World Bank, 1992).

C. Milner and O. Morrisey, "Measuring Trade Liberalization in Africa" in M. McGillvray and O. Morrisey, eds., *Evaluating Economic Liberalization. Case-Studies in Economic Development* 4 (New York: St. Martin's Press, 1999 / London: Macmillan Press, 1999)

B. Moldan & S. Billharz, *Sustainability Indicators: Report of the Project on Indicators of Sustainable Development* (Chichester: John Wiley, SCOPE 58, 1997).

W. J. Mommsen, *The Age of Bureaucracy: Perspectives on the Political Sociology of Max Weber* (Oxford: Oxford University Press, 1974).

M. Moore, *Doha and Beyond: The Future of the Multilateral Trading System* (Cambridge: Cambridge University Press, 2004).

D. Morrow, "Poverty Reduction Strategy Papers and Sustainable Development" (Workshop on Poverty and Sustainable Development, Ottawa, January 2001).

C. S. Morton, *Progress Toward Free Trade in the Western Hemisphere Since 1994* (La Jolla: Institute of the Americas, 1998).

B. Müller, *Equity in Climate Change: the Great Divide* (Oxford: OISE, 2002).

D. A. Munro & M. W. Holdgate, eds., *Caring for the Earth: A Strategy for Sustainable Living* (Geneva: IUCN, 1991).

S. Murphy, "The ELSI Case: An Investment Dispute at the International Court of Justice" (1991) 16 *Yale J. Int'l L.* 391.

E. Neumayer, "Multilateral Agreement on Investment: Lessons for the WTO from the Failed OECD Negotiations" (1999) 46 *Wirtschaftspolitische Blätter* 618-628.

E.C. Nieuwenhuys & M.M.T.A. Brus, *Multi-lateral Regulation of Investment* (The Hague: Kluwer Law International, 2001).

A. Nikiforuk, *The Nasty Game: The Failure of Environmental Assessment in Canada* (Canada: Sierra Club, 1997).

A. Nollkaemper, "The Precautionary Principle in International Environmental Law: What's New Under the Sun?" (1991) 22 *Marine Pollution Bulletin* 3.

S. Nooteboom & K. Wieringa, "Comparing strategic environmental assessment and integrated environmental assessment" (1999) *Journal of Environmental Assessment Policy and Management* Vol. 1 No. 4 441.

H. Nordström & S. Vaughan, *Trade and Environment, WTO Special Study 4* (Geneva: WTO, 1999).

M. Nordquist & J. Norton Moore, *Current Marine Environmental Issues and the International Tribunal for the Law of the Sea* (Leiden: Martinus Nijhoff, 2001).

North American Commission for Environmental Cooperation, *Assessing Environmental Effects of the North American Free Trade Agreement (NAFTA): An Analytic Framework (Phase II)* and *Issue Studies* (Montreal: NACEC, 1999).

OAS, *Acuerdos de comercio e integracion en las Americas – Un compendio analitico* (Washington: OAS, 1997).

OAS, *Human Rights: How to Present a Petition in the Inter-American System* (Washington: OAS, 2000).

S. Oberthür & H. E. Ott, eds., "Developing Country Participation (Articles 10, 11)" in *The Kyoto Protocol: International Climate Policy for the 21st Century* (Berlin: Springer Verlag, 1999).

OECD Secretariat, "Timing and Public Participation Issues in Undertaking Environmental Assessments of Trade Liberalisation agreements", (paper presented at Workshop on *Methodologies for Environmental Assessment of Trade Liberalization Agreements*, Paris: OECD, October 1999).

OECD, *Freight and the Environment: Effects of Trade Liberalisation and Transport Sector Reforms* (Paris: OECD, 1997).

OECD, *Policies to Enhance Sustainable Development* (Paris: OECD, May 2001).

P. N. Okowa, "Procedural Obligations in International Environmental Agreements" (1996) *Brit. Y.B. of Int'l L.* 275.

P. N. Okawa, *State Responsibility for Transboundary Air Pollution in International Law* (Oxford: Oxford University Press, 2000).

T. A. O'Keefe, "An Analysis of the Mercosur Economic Integration Project from a Legal Perspective" (1994) 28:2 *The International Lawyer* 28, 439.

J. Oloka-Onyango, "Human Rights and Sustainable Development in Contemporary Africa: A New Dawn, or Retreating Horizons?" (2000) 6 *Buff. Hum. Rts. L. Rev.* 39.

M. K. Omalu, *NAFTA and the Energy Charter: Treaty Compliance with, Implementation and Effectiveness of International Investment Agreements* (The Hague: Kluwer Law International, 1999).

T. O'Riordan, A. Jordan and J. Cameron, eds., *Reinterpreting the Precautionary Principle* (London: Cameron May, 2001).

T. Padoa-Schioppa, *Regulating Finance - Balancing Freedom and Risk* (Oxford: Oxford University Press, 2004).

R.A. Painter, "Human Rights Monitoring: Universal and Regional Treaty Bodies" in P.C. Szasz, ed., *Administrative and Expert Monitoring of International Treaties* (New York: Transnational, 1999).

M. Pallemaerts, "The Future of Environmental Regulation: International Environmental Law in the Age of Sustainable Development: A Critical Assessment of the UNCED Process" (1996) 15 *Journal of Law & Com.* 623

D. Palmeter & P. C. Mavroidis, "The WTO Legal System: Sources of Law" (1998) 92 *A.J.I.L.* 398.

D. Palmeter & P.C. Mavroidis, *Dispute Settlement in the World Trade Organization: Practice and Procedure* 2nd Ed. (Cambridge: Cambridge University Press, 2004).

C. Parry, *The Sources and Evidences of International Law* (Manchester: Manchester University Press, 1965).

J.C.N. Paul, "The United Nations Family: Challenges of Law and Development: The United Nations and the Creation of an International Law of Development" (1995) 36 *Harv. Int'l L.J.* 307.

S. Patandin, P.C. Dagnelie, P. Mulder, E. Op de Coul, J.E. Van der Veen, N. Weisglas-Kuperus & P.J.J Sauer "Dietary exposure to polychlorinated biphenyls and dioxins from infancy to adulthood: A comparison between breast-feeding, toddler, and long-term exposure." (1999) 107 *Environ.Health Perspect.* 45.

D. W. Pearce & G. D. Atkinson, "Capital Theory and Measurement of Sustainable Development: An Indicator of "Weak" Sustainability" (1993) 8 *Ecological Economics* 103-8.

F. Perrez, "The Relationship between Permanent Sovereignty and the Obligation Not to Cause Transboundary Environmental Damage" (1996) 26 *Environmental Law* 1187.

F. Perrez, "The World Summit on sustainable Development: Environment, Precaution and Trade – A Potential for Success and/or Failure" (2003) 12:3 *R.E.C.I.E.L.*

F. Perrez, *Cooperative Sovereignty: From Independence to Interdependence in International Environmental Law* (The Hague: Kluwer Law International, 2000).

E.U. Petersmann, "From the Hobbesian International Law of Coexistence to Modern Integration Law: The WTO Dispute Settlement" (1998) 1:2 *J. Int'l Econ. L.* 175.

B. J. Plotkin, "Mission Possible: The future of the International Health Regulations" (1996) 10 *Temp. Int'l & Comp. L. J.* 503.

G. Posser, *Grundfragen des Abfallrechts : Abgrenzung von Produkt/Abfall und Verwertung/Beseitigung (München : Beck,* 2001).

S. Prakash, "Towards a Synergy Between Intellectual Property Rights and Biodiversity" (1999) *Journal of World Intellectual Property* 2:5.

R. Pritchard, *Economic Development, Foreign Investment and the Law* (The Hague: Kluwer Law International, 1996).

D. Quist & I. Chapela, "Transgenic DNA Introgressed into Traditional Maize Landraces in Oazaca, Mexico" (2001) 414 *Nature* 541.

Rat von Sachverständigen für Umweltfragen, *Umweltprobleme der Nordsee* (Stuttgart: Kiepenheuer & Witsch, 1980).

J. Razzaque, *Public Interest Environmental Litigation in India, Pakistan and Bangladesh* (The Hague: Kluwer Law International, 2004).

J. Rein, "International Governance through Trade Agreements: Patent Protection for Essential Medicines" (2001) 21 *N.W. J. Int'l L. & Business* 379.

A. C. Reynaud, *Labour Standards and the Integration Process in the Americas* (Geneva: ILO, 2001).

B. Rich, *Mortgaging the Earth: The World Bank, Environmental Impoverishment, and the Crisis of Development* (Boston: Beacon Press, 1994).

B. J. Richardson, *Environmental Regulation through Financial Organisations, Comparative Perspectives on the Industrialised Nations* (The Hague: Kluwer Law International, 2002).

M. Rodriguez-Mendoza, "The Andean Group's Integration Strategy" in *Integrating the Hemisphere – Perspectives from Latin America and the Caribbean* (Bogota: Inter-American Dialogue, 1997).

N. Roht-Arriaza, "Shifting the Point of Regulation: The International Organisation for Standardization and Global Lawmaking on Trade and the Environment" (1995) 22 *Ecology L.Q.* 479.

G. Roth & C. Wittich, eds., *Max Weber, Economy and Society: An Outline of Interpretive Sociology* (Berkeley: University of California Press, 1968).

I. Roth, *Umweltbezogene Unternehmenskommunikation im deutschen und europäischen Wettbewerbsrecht* (Frankfurt: P. Lang, 2000).

A. R. Rosencranz, R. Campbell & D. A. O'Neil, "Rio Plus Five: Environmental Protection and Free Trade in Latin America" (1997) *Georgetown International Environmental Law Review* 9.

L. Ruessmann, "Putting the precautionary principle in its place: Parameters for the proper application of a precautionary approach and the implications for developing countries in light of the Doha WTO ministerial" (2002) 17 *Am. U. Int'l L. Rev.* 905.

N. de Sadeleer, *Environmental Principles - From Political Slogans to Legal Rules* (Oxford: Oxford University Press, 2002).

M. Salazar Xirinchas, *Towards Free Trade in the Americas* (Washington: OAS / Brookings Institute, 2002).

G. Sampson, *Trade, Environment and the WTO: The Post-Seattle Agenda*, Overseas Development Council Policy Essay No. 27 (Washington: ODC, 2001).

P. Sands, *Principles of International Environmental Law: Frameworks, Standards and Implementation* 1rst ed. (Manchester: Manchester University Press, 1996).

P. Sands, *Principles of International Environmental Law* 2nd ed. (Cambridge: Cambridge University Press, 2003).

P. Sands, "International Law in the Field of Sustainable Development" (1994) 65 *Br. Yrbk. of I.L.* 303.

P. Sands, "European Community Environmental Law: The Evolution of a Regional Regime of International Environmental Protection" (1991) 100 *Yale L.J.* 2511.

D. A. Sarokin & J. Schulkin, "Environmental Justice: Co-evolution of Environmental Concerns and Social Justice (1994) 14 *The Environmentalist* 121.

O. Schachter, *Sharing the World's Resources* (Bangalore: Allied, 1977).

T. Schoenbaum, "International Trade and Protection of the Environment: The Continuing Search for Reconciliation" (1997) 91:2 *American Journal of International Law* 281.

N. Schrijver, *Permanent Sovereignty over Natural Resources: Balancing Rights and Duties* (Cambridge: Cambridge Univ. Press 1997).

N. Schrijver and F. Weiss "Editorial" 2 *International Environmental Agreements: Politics, Law and Economics* 2 2002, 105 – 108.

C. H. Schreuer, *The ICSID Convention: A Commentary* (Cambridge: Cambridge University Press, 2001).

R. A. Sedjo, "Ecosystem Management: An Unchartered Path for Public forests" (1995) 10 *Resources for the Future* 1.

I. Seidl-Hohenveldern, *International Economic Law,* 3rd Ed. (The Hague: Kluwer Law International, 1999).

A. Seidman *et al.*, "Building Sound National Frameworks for Development and Social Change" (1999) 4 *C.E.P.M.L. & P. J.* 1.

S. K. Sell, "TRIPS and the Access to Medicines Campaign" (2002) 20 *Wis. Int'l L.J.* 481.

S. Shaw & R. Schwartz "Trade and Environment in the WTO - State of Play" (2002) 36 *J.W.T.* 129.

I. F. I. Shihata, "The World Bank and the Environment: A Legal Perspective" (1992) 16 *Maryland Journal of International Law and* Trade 1.

I. F. I. Shihata, "The World Bank and the Environment: Legal Instruments for Achieving Environmental Objectives" in I. F. I. Shihata, *The World Bank in a Changing World, Vol. II* (Leiden: Martinus Nijhoff Publishers, 1995).

D.A. Silien, "Human Rights Monitoring: Procedures and Decision-Making of Standing United Nations Organs" in P.C. Szasz, ed., *Administrative and Expert Monitoring of International Treaties* (New York: Transnational, 1999) 83.

N. Singh & R. Strickland, eds., *From Legacy to Vision: Sustainability, Poverty and Policy Adjustment* (Winnipeg: International Institute for Sustainable Development, 1996).

A.-M. Slaughter, "Governing Through Government Networks" in M. Byers, ed., *The Role of Law in International Politics: Essays in International Relations and International Law* (Oxford: Oxford University Press, 2000).

L. B. Sohn, "The Stockholm Declaration on the Human Environment" (1973) *Harv. Int'l L.J.* 423

M. Sornarajah, *The International Law on Foreign Investment* 2nd Ed. (Cambridge: Cambridge University Press, 2004).

R. N. Stavins, ed., *Economics of the Environment,* 4th ed. (New York: W.W. Norton & Company, 2000).

H. Steiner and P. Alston, *International Human Rights in Context: Law, Politics, Morals,* 2nd edn. (Oxford: Oxford University Press, 2000).

P. L. Stenzel, "Can NAFTA's Environmental Provisions Promote Sustainable Development?" (1995) 59 *Alb.L. Rev.* 43

J. Stiglitz, *Globalization and its Discontents* (London: Penguin Books, 2002).

O. Stokke, *Governing High Seas Fisheries - The Interplay of Global and Regional Regimes* (Oxford: Oxford University Press, 2001).

C. D. Stone, *Should Trees Have Standing? Legal Rights for Natural Objects* (Los Altos, California: William Kaufmann, Inc., 1974).

A.O. Sykes, "Trips, Pharmaceuticals, Developing Countries, and the Doha 'Solution' " (2002) 3 *Chi. J. Int'l L.* 47.

P. C. Szasz, "Introduction" in P.C. Szasz, ed., *Administrative and Expert Monitoring of International Treaties* (New York: Transnational, 1999).

C. Tan. "Tackling the Commodity Price Crisis Should be WSSD's Priority" (Malaysia: Third World Network, 2002) online: < http://www.twnside.org.sg/title/jb14.htm>

A. L. Taylor, "Making the World Health Organization Work: A Legal Framework for Universal Access to the conditions for Health", (1992) 18 *Am. J. L. & Med.* 301.

A. L. Taylor, *An International Regulatory Strategy for Global Tobacco Control,* (1996) 21 *Yale J. Int'l Law* 257.

A.L. Taylor & D.W. Bettcher, "WHO Framework Convention on Tobacco Control: A Global "Good" For Public Health" (2000) 78:7 *Bulletin World Health Organization* 920-9.

J. C. Thomas, "Investor-State arbitration under NAFTA Chapter 11" 37 (1999) *The Canadian Yearbook of International Law* 99-137.

S. Thomas-Nuruddin, "Protection of the Ozone Layer: the Vienna Convention and the Montreal Protocol", in P.C. Szasz, ed., *Administrative and Expert Monitoring of International Treaties* (New York: Transnational, 1999) 113.

U.P. Thomas, "The CBD, the WTO, and the FAO: The Emergence of Phytogenetic Governance" in P.G. LePrestre, ed., *Governing Global Biodiversity: The Evolution and Implementation of the Convention on Biological Diversity* (Aldershot: Ashgate, 2002) 177.

M. Thornton., "Since the Breakup: Developments and Divergences in ANCOM's and Chile's Foreign Investment Codes." (1983) 1 *Hastings International and Comparative Law Review* 7.

A. Timoshenko, *Environmental Negotiator Handbook* (The Hague: Kluwer Law International, 2003).

A. Tolentino, "Good Governance Through Popular Participation in Sustainable Development" in K. Ginther, E. Denters & P.J.I.M. de Waart eds., *Sustainable Development and Good Governance* (The Hague: Kluwer Law International, 1995).

K. Tomasevksi, *Responding to Human Rights Violations 1946-1999* (The Hague: Martinus Nijhoff, 2000).

S. J. Toope, "Emerging Patterns of Governance" in M. Byers, ed., *The Role of Law in International Politics: Essays in International Relations and International Law* (Oxford: Oxford University Press, 2000) 91.

M. J. Trebilcock, "What Makes Poor Countries Poor? The Role of Institutional Capital in Economic Development" in E. Buscaglia, W. Ratliff & R. Cooter, eds., *The Law and Economics of Development* (London: JAI Press Inc., 1997) 15.

P. Trepte, *Regulating Procurement - Understanding the Ends and Means of Public Procurement Regulation* (Oxford: Oxford University Press, 2004).

T. Treves, "The Settlement of Disputes According to the Straddling Stocks Agreement of 1995" in *International Law and Sustainable Development: Past Achievements and Future Challenges*, A. Boyle and D. Freestone, eds. (Oxford: Oxford University Press, 1999).

J.P. Townsend, *Price, Tax and Smoking in Europe* (Copenhagen: World Health Organization, 1998).

A. Trouwborst, *Evolution and Status of the Precautionary Principle in International Law* (Kluwer Law International: The Hague, 2002).

T. C. Trzyna, ed., *A Sustainable World: Defining and Measuring Sustainable Development* (Sacramento: California Institute of Public Affairs, 1995).

D. Tussie & P. I. Vasquez, "The FTAA, MERCOSUR and the Environment" (1997) 9:3 *International Environmental Affairs: A Journal for Research and Policy*.

M. Ul-Haq, *Reflections on Human Development* (Oxford: Oxford University Press, 1995).

United Nations Commission on Human Rights, *Joint Report by the Independent Expert on Structural Adjustment Programmes and the Special Rapporteur on Foreign Debt,* UN ESCOR, 2000, UN Doc. E/CN.4/2000/51.

United Nations Conference on Trade and Development and General Agreement on Tariffs and Trade Secretariat, *An Analysis of the Proposed Uruguay Round Agreement with Particular Emphasis on Aspects of Interest to Developing Countries* (Geneva: UNCTAD/GATT Secretariat, 1993), MTN.TNC/W/122.

United Nations Conference on Trade and Development, *Newly Emerging Environmental Policies with a Possible Trade Impact: A Preliminary Discussion – Report by the UNCTAD Secretariat* (New York: United Nations, 1995).

United Nations Conference on Trade and Development, *Trade and the Environment: Issues of Key Interest to the Least Developed Countries* (New York: United Nations, 1997).

United Nations Development Programme, *Capacity Development for Governance for Sustainable Human Development* (New York: UNDP, 1996).

United Nations Development Programme, *Human Development Report 2000* (Oxford: Oxford University Press, 2000).

United Nations Environment Programme, *Final Report of the Expert Group Workshop on International Environmental Law Aiming at Sustainable Development,* UNEP/IEL/WS/3/2, (1996).

United Nations Environment Programme, *International Environmental Governance SS.VII/1, Report of the Governing Council on the Work of its Seventh Special Session/Global Ministerial Environment Forum* (13-15 February 2002) UNEP/GCSS.VII/6, Annex I.

United Nations Environment Programme, *Goals and Principles of Environmental Impact Assessment* (Nairobi: UNEP, 1987).

United Nations Environment Programme (UNEP) and International Institute for Sustainable Development (IISD), *Environment and Trade: A Handbook* (Winnipeg: IISD / UNEP, 2000).

United Nations Environmental Programme, *Environmental Impact Assessment; Issues, Trends and Practice* (Geneva: UNEP, 1996).

United Nations ESCOR, Commission on Human Rights, Sub-commission on Prevention of Discrimination of Minorities, *Review of Further Developments in Fields with which the Sub-Commission has been concerned, Human Rights and the Environment*: Final Report prepared by Mrs. Fatma Zohra Ksentini, Special Rapporteur, U.N. Doc. E/CN. 4/Sub.2/1994/9 (1994).

United Nations High Commissioner for Human Rights and the United Nations Environmental Programme, *Meeting of Experts on Human Rights and the Environment, 14-15 January, 2002: Conclusions,* online: OHCHR, www.unhchr.ch/environment/conclusions.

United Nations Secretary-General, *Follow-up to Johannesburg and the Future Role of the CSD* 18 February 2003 E/CN.17/2003/2.

United Nations University, *Sustainable Development Governance: The Question of Reform: Key Issues and Proposals.* (Tokyo: United Nations University Institute for Advanced Studies, 2002).

United States Centers for Disease Control and Prevention, *Addressing Emerging Infectious Disease Threats: A Prevention Strategy for the United States* (1994).

P. Uvin & I. Biagiotti, "Global Governance and the 'New' Political Conditionality" (1996) 2 *Global Governance: A Review of Multilaterism and International Organisations* 377.

G. Van Calster, "Green Procurement and the WTO – Shades of Grey" 11 (3) *R.E.C.I.E.L.* 3.

J.L. Varela, "Regional Trends in International Law and Domestic Environmental Law: the Inter-American Hemisphere" in S.J. Rubin and D.C. Alexander, eds., *NAFTA and the Environment* (The Hague: Kluwer Law International, 1996).

D. Vignes, "Protection of the Antarctic Marine Fauna and Flora: The Canberra Convention and the Commission Set Up by It" in F. Francioni & T. Scovazzi, eds., *International Law for Antarctica* (The Hague: Kluwer Law International, 1996).

R. B. von Mehren & P. Nicholas Kourides, "International Arbitrations between States and Foreign Private Parties: The Libyan Nationalization Cases" (1981) 75 *Am. J. Int'l L.* 476.

K. von Moltke, "International Commission and Implementation of Law" in J.E. Carroll, ed., *International Environmental Diplomacy* (Cambridge: Cambridge University Press, 1988) at 90.

K. von Moltke, *International Environmental Management, Trade Regimes and Sustainability* (Winnipeg: International Institute for Sustainable Development, 1996).

K. von Moltke, *The Organisation of the Impossible* (Winnipeg: International Institute for Sustainable Development, 2001).

K. von Moltke, *An International Investment Regime? Implications for Sustainable Development* (Winnipeg: International Institute for Sustainable Development, 2000).

K. von Moltke, "The *Vorsorgeprinzip* in West German Policy," Appendix 3, Royal Commission on the Environment, Twelfth Report (Berlin: RCE, 1988).

D. Vogel, *Trading Up: Consumer And Environmental Regulations In A Global Economy* (Cambridge: Harvard University Press, 1995)

H. Walkowiaz, "AIDS in National and International Law" (Proceedings of the Ninety-Sixth Annual Meeting of the American Society of International Law, March 16, 2002) (2002) 96 *Am. Soc'y Int'l L. Proc.* 320.

P. S. Watson, J. E. Flynn & C. Conwell, *Completing the World Trading System, Proposals for a Millennium Round* (The Hague: Kluwer Law International, 1999).

J. H. H. Weiler, *The EU, the WTO and the NAFTA - Towards a Common Law of International Trade* (Oxford: Oxford University Press, 2000).

A. Weale, G. Pridham, M. Cini, D. Konstadakopulos, M. Porter & B. Flynn, *Environmental Governance in Europe - An Ever Closer Ecological Union?* (Oxford: Oxford University Press, 2000)

R. A. Westin, *Environmental Tax Initiative & International Trade Treaties* (The Hague: Kluwer Law International, 1997).

D. A. Wirth, "The Rio Declaration on Environment and Development: Two Steps forward and One Back, or Vice Versa?" (1995) 29 *Ga. L. Rev.* 599.

A. Weale, "Ecological Modernisation and the Integration of European Environmental Policy" in J. D. Liefferink et al.., eds., *European Integration and Environmental Policy* (Cambridge: Cambridge University Press, 1993).

C. Weeramantry, "Right to Development" (1985) *Indian J.I.L.* 482.

B. Weintraub, "Science, International Environmental Regulation, and the Precautionary Principle: Setting Standards and Defining Terms" (1992) 1 *N.Y.U. Envtl. L.J.* 173.

R. Wesseling, *The Modernisation of EC Antitrust Law* (Oxford: Hart, Studies in European law and Integration, 2000).

World Bank, *A Framework for the Design and Implementation of Competition Law and Policy* (Paris: World Bank & OECD, 1999).

World Bank, *Development in Practice Series: Curbing the Epidemic; Governments and the Economics of Tobacco Control* (Washington: World Bank, 1999).

World Bank, *The State in a Changing World* (Washington: World Bank, 1997).

World Bank, *Governance: The World Bank's Experience* (Washington: World Bank, 1994).

World Bank, *World Bank Operational Manual on Poverty Reduction*, OD 4.15 (December 1991) (Washington: World Bank, 1991).

World Bank, *World Development Report 2000/01* (Oxford: Oxford University Press, 2001).

World Bank, *Sub-Saharan Africa: From Crisis to Sustainable Growth* (Washington: World Bank, 1989).

World Bank, *Social Indicators of Development* (Washington: World Bank, 1995).

World Bank, *World Development Indicators*, CD-ROM (Washington: The International Bank for Reconstruction and Development/The World Bank, 1999).

World Bank, *World Development Report: Knowledge for Development* (Oxford: Oxford University Press, 1999).

World Bank, *The World Bank Inspection Panel, Resolution 93-10,* online: World Bank http://www.worldbank.org/html/ins- panel/operatingprocedures.html.

World Commission on Environment and Development, *Our Common Future* (Oxford: Oxford University Press, 1987).

World Health Organization, *World Heath Report 1999: Making a Difference* (Geneva: World Health Organisation, 1999) 78.

World Health Organization, "Revision of the International Regulations: Progress Report" (January, 1999) 74 *Weekly Epidemiology Rec.*

World Health Organization, "Economics of Tobacco Control" (Aug. 20, 1999) WHO Doc. A/FCTC/WG1/2.

World Health Organization, (July, 1998) 78 *Weekly Epidemiology Rec.*

World Health Organization, "International Health Regulations" (July 25, 1969) *International Health Regulations,* 3d ann. ed., 91983.

World Health Organization and World Trade Organization, *WTO Agreements and Public Health: A Joint Study by the WHO and the WTO Secretariat* (WTO/WHO, 2002).

World Resources Institute, *Global Biodiversity Strategy* (Washington: WRI, 1992).

World Trade Organisation Working Group on the Interaction between Trade and Competition Policy, *Overview of Members' National Competition Legislation - Note by The Secretariat,* WT/WGTCP/W/128/Rev.2, 4 July 2001.

World Trade Organisation Secretariat, *Trade, Development and the Environment* (The Hague: Kluwer Law International, 2000).

F. Yamin & J. Depledge, *The International Climate Change Regime: A Guide to Rules, Institutions and Procedures* (Cambridge: Cambridge University Press, 2004).

F. Yamin, "Biodiversity, Ethics and International Law" (1995) 71:3 *International Affairs* 529.

K. Ziegler, Völkerrechtsgeschichte (München: C.H. Beck Verlag, 1994).

D. M. Zillman, A. Lucas & G. Pring, *Human Rights in Natural Resource Development* (Oxford: Oxford University Press, 2002).

RECOMMENDED WEBSITES

Bank Information Centre < http://www.bicusa.org>

Centre on Housing Rights and Evictions – Right to Water Programme, <http://www.cohre.org/water>

Centre for Human Rights and Environment (CEDHA) < http://www.cedha.org>

Center for International Environmental Law < http://www.ciel.org>

Centre for International Sustainable Development Law, online: < http://www.cisdl.org>

Desertification Convention < http://www.unccd.int>

Drylands Development Centre's Global Drylands Imperative <www.undp.org/dpa/frontpagearchive/2002/february/25feb02/>.

EarthJustice < http://www.earthjustice.org>

EarthRights International < http://www.earthrights.org>

ECOSOC <http://www.un.org/esa>.

Ethical Globalization Initiative <http://www.eginitiative.org/index.html>.

ESCR-Net < http://www.escr-net.org>

European Committee on Social Rights <http://www.coe.int/T/E/Human_Rights/Esc/>

Foundation for International Environmental Law and Development <http://www.field.org>

General Direction Trade of the European Commission, DG Trade online <http://trade-info.cec.eu.int/europa/index_en.php>.

Genetic Resources Action International <http://www.grain.org>

Global Policy Forum <http://www.globalpolicy.org>

Human Rights Watch <http://www.hrw.org>

International Centre for the Settlement of Investment Disputes (ICSID) < http://www.worldbank.org/icsid/>.

Inter-American Commission on Human Rights <http://www.cidh.oas.org/DefaultE.htm>

International Centre for Trade and Sustainable Development (ICTSD) < http://www.ictsd.org>.

International Development Law Organisation < http://www.idlo.int>

International Institute for Environment and Development (IIED) <http://www.iied.org/wssd/index.html>.

International Institute for Sustainable Development (IISD) <http://www.iisd.org>

International Labour Organisation <http://www.ilo.org>.

International Trade Center < http://www.itc.org>

Johannesburg Summit < http://www.johannesburgsummit.org>

Organisation of Economic Cooperation and Development < http://www.oecd.org>

Overseas Development Institute Rural Policy and the Environment Group <http://www.odi.org.uk/RPEG/NR.html>

Partnership for Principle 10 (PP10) <www.pp10.org>

Programme of Action of the World Summit for Social Development 1995, <http://www.visionoffice.com/socdev/wssdpa-2.htm>

United Nations <http://www.un.org>.

United Nations Commission on International Trade Law <http://www.uncitral.org> and ICC <http://www.iccwbo.org>.

United Nations Commission on Sustainable Development <http://www.un.org/esa/sustdev/csd.htm>

United Nations Economic and Social Council
<http://www.un.org/esa/coordination/ecosoc>

United Nations Environment Programme < http://www.unep.org>

United Nations High Commissioner for Human Rights <www.unhchr.ch>

World Bank < http://www.worldbank.org>

World Resources Institute < http://www.wri.org>

World Trade Organisation < http://www.wto.org>

OTHER MATERIALS

ILA Resolution 3/2002: *New Delhi Declaration of Principles of International Law Relating to Sustainable Development*, in ILA, Report of the Seventieth Conference, New Delhi (London: ILA, 2002).

Intergovernmental Panel on Climate Change, Third Assessment Report, Working Group I, *Climate Change 2001:The Scientific Basis,* online: <http://www.ipcc.ch>.

Intergovernmental Panel on Climate Change, Third Assessment Report, Working Group II, *Climate Change 2001: Impacts, Adaptation and Vulnerability,* 13-16 February 2001, online: <http://www.ipcc.ch>.

Intergovernmental Panel on Climate Change, Third Assessment Report, Working Group III, *Climate Change 2001: Mitigation,* online: <htttp://www.ipcc.ch>.

Report by the Secretary-General on the Follow-up to Johannesburg and the Future Role of the CSD, 18 February 2003, E/CN.17/2003/2.

Report of the High-Level Panel on Financing for Development to the Secretary General, 26 June 2001, U.N. Doc. A/55/1000.

Report of the World Summit on Sustainable Development, Johannesburg, South Africa, August 26 to Sept 4 2002, A/CONF.199/20.

Report of the Expert Seminar on Human Rights and Extreme Poverty, UN Commission on Human Rights, 57th Sess., UN Doc. E/CN.4/2001/54/Add.1 (2001).

Report of the Secretary-General on Combating Poverty, UN Commission on Sustainable Development acting as the preparatory committee for the World Summit on Sustainable Development, Organizational Sess., UN Doc. E/CN.17/2001/PC/5 (2001).

Statement of the UN Committee on Economic, Social and Cultural Rights to the Third Ministerial Conference of the World Trade Organisation (Seattle, 30 November to 3 December, 1999). UN. Doc. E.C.12/1999/9.

United Nations Committee on Economic, Social and Cultural Rights, *Poverty and the International Covenant on Economic, Social and Cultural Rights,* UN ESCOR, 2001, UN Doc. E/C.12/2001/10.

Committee on Economic, Social and Cultural Rights, *General Comment No.2: International Technical Assistance Measures,* UN ESCOR, 1990, UN Doc. E/1990/23.

United Nations Committee on Economic, Social and Cultural Rights, *General Comment No. 3, The Nature of States Parties' Obligations,* UN ESCOR, 1990, UN Doc. E /1991/23.

United Nations Committee on Economic, Social and Cultural Rights, *General Comment No. 4: The Right to Adequate Shelter,* E/1992/23-E/C.12/1991/4 Annex III.

United Nations Committee on Economic, Social and Cultural Rights, *General Comment No. 12: The Right to Adequate Food,* UN ESCOR, 1999, UN Doc. E/C.12/1999/5.

Committee on Economic, Social and Cultural Rights, *General Comment No.14: The Right to the Highest Attainable Standard of Health,* UN ESCOR, 2000, UN Doc. E/C.12/2000/4.

United Nations Committee on Economic, Social and Cultural Rights, General Comment No. 15 (2002) on "The Right to Water," E/C.12/2002/11, 26 November 2002.

United Nations Human Rights Committee, *General Comment No. 6,* UN GAOR, 1982, Supp. No. 40, UN Doc. A/37/40.

World Intellectual Property Rights Organisation, Intergovernmental Committee on Intellectual Property and Genetic Resources, Traditional Knowledge and Folklore, 5th sess., Doc. WIPO/GRTKF/IC/5/12 (2003).

The Centre for International Sustainable Development Law thanks the World
Bank Legal Vice-Presidency, the United Nations Environment Programme
and the International Law Association, co-hosts of
Sustainable Justice 2002: Implementing International Sustainable Development Law
Montreal, Canada, 13-15 June 2002.

This anthology is published under the auspices of the Partnership on
International Law for Sustainable Development that was launched at the 2002
World Summit on Sustainable Development by the CISDL, the International
Development Law Organisation and the International Law Association.

The partners gratefully acknowledge the financial support of the Government
of Canada, the Policy Research Initiative, the International Development
Research Centre (IDRC) of Canada, the Government of Québec, and
McCarthy Tetrault LLP.

ACKNOWLEDGEMENTS

The editors, Marie-Claire Cordonier Segger, Director of the Centre for International Sustainable Development Law (CISDL), and H.E. Judge Christopher Gregory Weeramantry, former Vice-President of the International Court of Justice, owe particular thanks and acknowledgement to many individuals and institutions for their assistance with this volume.

The editors convey sincere gratitude to the members of the CISDL, most of whom contributed chapters to this book, and also to a roster of distinguished international advisors, who provided intellectual guidance, review and support throughout the development of the conference and this resulting book. These include James Cameron, Baker & McKenzie, James Crawford, Daniel Bethlehem and Nick Sinclair-Brown, Lauterpacht Research Centre for International Law at Cambridge University, Francois Crepeau, University of Montreal, Kamal Hossain, International Law Association, Omar El-Arini, Montreal Protocol Multilateral Fund, Daniel Esty, Yale University, David Freestone, World Bank, Charles D. Gonthier, Supreme Court of Canada, Bakary Kante, Halifa O. Drammeh and Brennan van Dyke, United Nations Environment Programme, Vaughan Lowe, All Soul's College at Oxford University, Simon Potter, Canadian Bar Association, Pia Rodriguez, International Development Law Organisation, David Runnalls, Mark Halle and Konrad von Moltke, International Institute for Sustainable Development, Nico Schrijver, Free University of Amsterdam, Stephen Toope, Pierre Elliot Trudeau Foundation, Gérald R. Tremblay, McCarthy Tétrault LLP, Hamdullah Zedan & Dan Ogolla, United Nations Convention on Biological Diversity, and many others. Special thanks are also owed to Nicholas Kasirer, Armand de Mestral, Richard Janda, Robert Godin, Myron Frankman, Peter Brown, Wajeeh Elali, Adelle Blackett and Jaye Ellis at McGill University, among many others there.

The editors deeply thank Jessica Adley, Sarita R. Keirouz, Karin Baqi and Sidney Thompson of McGill Law Faculty and Chris Pettit of the WICPER, for their dedication, determination, creativity and excellent research assistance, as well as Rene Steiner at SteinerGraphics for his kind contributions to layout and design. The editors also thank Annebeth Rosenboom at Martinus Nijhoff Press for her capable assistance in publishing.

Sustainable Justice 2002: The Conference

This anthology gathers the contributions of distinguished national and international judges, legal professionals and scholars to a conference, *Sustainable Justice 2002: Implementing International Sustainable Development Law* which was co-hosted by the Centre for International Sustainable Development Law (CISDL), the United Nations Environment Programme, the World Bank and the International Law Association Committee on the Legal Aspects of Sustainable Development, in Montreal, Canada in June 2002.

The editors gratefully acknowledge the financial and in-kind support of the Government of Canada through Foreign Affairs Canada and International Trade Canada (Hon. Pierre Pettigrew, Hon. Bill Graham & Richard Ballhorn), Environment Canada through the 2002 World Summit for Sustainable Development Secretariat (Hon. David Anderson), Justice Canada (Hon. Irwin Cotler, Ruth Barr & Marc Dubois), and the Canadian International Development Agency (Brian Emmet, Paul Samson & Naresh Singh).

The editors also thank, for their kind support, the International Development Research Centre of Canada (Gisele Morin-Labatut), the Policy Research Initiative of the Privy Council of Canada (Pearl Eliadis), and the government of Quebec (Jacques DuFour & Benjamin Teitelbaum).

And the editors thank, for their generous contributions, the leading law firms of McCarthy Tétrault LLP, (Canada), and Edward Nathan and Freidland (Pty) Ltc. (South Africa), as well as the IUCN (World Conservation Union), the Canadian Bar Association, the International Law Association and the Quebec Bar (Marc Sauvé). Thanks to Ontario Power Generation (Helen Howes), and Noranda Inc. (Helene Gagnon & David Rodier) for their sponsorship.

Finally, the editors convey their gratitude to the many distinguished keynote speakers, expert panellists and participants of Sustainable Justice 2002, held in Montreal from 13-16 June 2002, for their contributions which shaped the International Jurists Mandate for the Implementation of International Law and profoundly shaped the content of this volume.

In addition to those who contributed to this volume, these speakers included distinguished international experts such as Secretary General Nitin Desai, World Summit for Sustainable Development; Hon. Cheryl Gillwald, Deputy Minister of Justice for South Africa; Dr. Kamal Hossain, International Law Association Committee on Legal Aspects of Sustainable Development; Hon. Kezimbira Miyingo, Minister of State for the Environment for Uganda; Dr. Lal Kurukulasuriya, United Nations Environment Programme; Mr. David Runnalls,

International Development Research Centre; Dr. Naresh Singh, Canadian International Development Agency; and Ambassador Vicente Vallenilla, Mission of Venezuela to the United Nations; among many others.

ABOUT THE CISDL

It is the mission of the Centre for International Sustainable Development Law (CISDL) to promote sustainable societies and the protection of ecosystems by advancing the understanding, development and implementation of international sustainable development law. The CISDL is an independent legal research centre which collaborates with the McGill Law Faculty in engaging students and interested faculty members in sustainable development law research and scholarly initiatives. The CISDL also has a close partnership with the Oxford University Faculty of Law, and the Université de Montreal Faculty of Law, and works with Yale University, the University of Costa Rica, the University of Nairobi, and a network of developing country faculties of law. It is guided in its work by its Board of Governors, and a distinguished roster of leading experts in international environmental, economic and social law, representing developing and developed countries, from intergovernmental and nongovernmental organizations, academic institutions and private practice.

The CISDL, after co-hosting with the United Nations Environment Programme (UNEP), the World Bank and the International Law Association, the *Sustainable Justice 2002: Implementing International Sustainable Development Law* Conference in Montreal, June 2002, presented the results at the 2002 UNEP *Global Judges Symposium on Sustainable Development and the Role of Law*, the 2002 *Enviro-Law Conference* in Durban, South Africa, and to the 2002 *World Summit for Sustainable Development* (WSSD) in Johannesburg, South Africa. With the International Development Law Organization and the International Law Association, also the UNEP and the World Bank, the CISDL chairs a Partnership, under the auspices of the United Nations, to analyze and implement the WSSD outcomes with regard to International Law for Sustainable Development. The partners report annually to the United Nations Commission on Sustainable Development.

For further information, please see www.cisdl.org.